Lecture Notes in Computer Science   15900

Founding Editors

Gerhard Goos
Juris Hartmanis

Advanced Research in Computing and Software Science
Subline of Lecture Notes in Computer Science

More information about this series at https://link.springer.com/bookseries/558

Wolfgang E. Nagel · Diana Goehringer ·
Pedro C. Diniz
Editors

Euro-Par 2025: Parallel Processing

31st European Conference on Parallel and Distributed Processing
Dresden, Germany, August 25–29, 2025
Proceedings, Part I

 Springer

Editors
Wolfgang E. Nagel
Technische Universität Dresden
Dresden, Germany

Diana Goehringer (ID)
Technische Universität Dresden
Dresden, Germany

Pedro C. Diniz (ID)
University of Porto
Porto, Portugal

ISSN 0302-9743   ISSN 1611-3349 (electronic)
Lecture Notes in Computer Science
ISBN 978-3-031-99853-9   ISBN 978-3-031-99854-6 (eBook)
https://doi.org/10.1007/978-3-031-99854-6

Preface

This book is one of the three volumes comprising the proceedings of the 31st International Conference on Parallel and Distributed Computing (Euro-Par 2025), which took place in Dresden, Germany, from 25 to 29 August 2025. Euro-Par 2025 was jointly organized by the Center for Information Services and High Performance Computing (ZIH) and the Faculty of Computer Science at Technische Universität Dresden.

Euro-Par is the prime European conference covering all aspects of parallel and distributed processing, ranging from theory to practice, from small to the largest parallel and distributed systems and infrastructures, from fundamental computational problems to applications, from architecture, compiler, language and interface design and implementation, to tools, support infrastructures, as well as application performance aspects.

Euro-Par participants include researchers from academic institutions, government laboratories, and industrial organizations. Euro-Par aims to be the primary choice of such professionals for presenting new results in their specific areas. Euro-Par provides an excellent forum for focused technical discussion, as well as interaction with a large, broad, and diverse audience. In addition, Euro-Par provides a platform for a number of technical workshops aimed at smaller and emerging communities.

Previous conference editions were held in Stockholm, Lyon, Passau, Southampton, Toulouse, Munich, Manchester, Paderborn, Klagenfurt, Pisa, Lisbon, Dresden, Rennes, Las Palmas, Delft, Ischia, Bordeaux, Rhodes, Aachen, Porto, Vienna, Grenoble, Santiago de Compostela, Turin, Göttingen, Warsaw, Lisbon, Glasgow, Limassol, and Madrid.

This year's Euro-Par 2025 accepted papers were organized in the following 6 tracks:

- Programming, Compilers and Performance
- Scheduling, Resource Management, Cloud, Edge Computing and Workflows
- Architectures and Accelerators
- Data Analytics, AI and Computational Science
- Theory and Algorithms
- Multidisciplinary, Domain-Specific and Applied Parallel and Distributed Computing

A total of 264 full papers were submitted by authors from 41 different countries representing all populated continents. The selection process was very competitive with each submission having an average number of 3.77 double-blind reviews. No paper had fewer than 3 reviews and several papers had 5 reviews. After intensive online discussions between the reviewers, each track proposed sets of papers for acceptance, further discussion, or rejection. The papers from all tracks were reviewed and discussed in an online selection meeting in April 2025. As a result, 78 papers were selected to be presented at the conference and published in these proceedings, resulting in a 29.5% acceptance rate.

In addition, the following 6 accepted papers were invited to be presented in a plenary session and compete for the Euro-Par 2025 *Best Paper* award:

- A. Delval, P. de Oliveira Castro, W. Jalby, E. Renault, "Noise Injection for Performance Bottleneck Analysis".
- L.-C. Canon, A. Dugois, I. Jecker, P.-C. Héam, "Approximation Bounds for SLACK on Identical Parallel Machines".
- J. Xue, T. Xiong, L. Chao, R. Xue, "SimPoint+: More Stable, Accurate and Efficient Program Analysis".
- X. Wang, S. Miao, Z. Zhu, P. Qu, Y. Zhang, "AlphaSparseTensor: Discovering Faster Sparse Matrix Multiplication Algorithms on GPUs for LLM Inference".
- J. Spaan, K.-H. Chen, D. A. Bader, A.-L. Varbanescu, "Wedge-Parallel Triangle Counting for GPUs".
- A. Sahu, A. S. P. V. M. Aditya, G. Ramakrishna, M. S. Nikhil, K. Kothapalli, D. S. Banerjee, "External GPU Biconnected Components".

To enhance the reproducibility of research publications in Euro-Par, the conference encourages authors to submit artifacts, such as source code, data sets, and reproducibility instructions. Following the notification of acceptance, the authors were encouraged to submit artifacts for evaluation. A total of 28 artifacts were submitted in support of accepted papers and evaluated by the Artifact Evaluation Committee (AEC) coordinated by Massimo Torquati and Olaf Krzikalla, who successfully reproduced results for 16 artifacts. These papers are marked in the proceedings by a special stamp and the artifacts are available online in the Zenodo repository.

In addition to the technical program, we had the pleasure of hosting three distinguished *Keynote* talks by:

- Florina Ciorba, University of Basel, Switzerland.
- Martin Schulz, Technical University of Munich, Germany.
- Domenico Talia, University of Calabria, Italy.

Euro-Par 2025 began with two days of workshops coordinated by Jeronimo Castrillón and Demetris Zeinalipour, which was followed by three full conference days dedicated to the main sessions. A poster and demo session, a PhD symposium organized by Michael Färber and Leonel Sousa, and a special session for female scientists were held alongside the main conference. Ahmed Kamaleldin and Lester Kalms were responsible for managing the poster and demo session. The invited session for female scientists was organized by Ayesha Afzal and Marta Garcia-Gasulla. A selection of the papers presented at the workshops are published in separate Springer LNCS volumes. Contributions presented at the PhD symposium, the poster session, and the invited session for female scientists are also published in the same volume.

We would like to thank all the Authors, Chairs, Program Committee Members, and Reviewers who contributed to the success of Euro-Par 2025. We would also like to thank all our industrial and institutional sponsors for their support. Our gratitude goes out to the Euro-Par Steering Committee and the organizers of Euro-Par 2024 for their invaluable support throughout the preparation of this year's event. Finally, we would like to thank Diana Häsener, Jacqueline Papperitz, and the local organizing team at the Center for Information Services and High Performance Computing (ZIH) and the Faculty of Computer Science at Technische Universität Dresden, whose dedication and hard work made this event possible. It was a great pleasure and honor to host Euro-Par 2025 at Technische Universität Dresden. We hope that all participants enjoyed the event.

August 2025   Wolfgang E. Nagel
                                                                      Diana Goehringer
                                                                        Pedro C. Diniz

Organization

General Chair

Wolfgang E. Nagel   TU Dresden, Germany

Program Committee Chair

Diana Goehringer   TU Dresden, Germany

Workshop Chairs

Jerónimo Castrillón   TU Dresden, Germany
Demetris Zeinalipour   University of Cyprus, Cyprus

Proceedings Chair

Pedro C. Diniz   Universidade do Porto, Portugal

PhD Symposium Chairs

Michael Färber   TU Dresden, Germany
Leonel Sousa   Universidade de Lisboa, Portugal

Posters and Demos Chairs

Ahmed Kamaleldin   TU Dresden, Germany
Lester Kalms   TU Dresden, Germany

Women in HPC Chairs

Marta Garcia-Gasulla	Barcelona Supercomputing Center, Spain
Ayesha Afzal	University of Erlangen-Nürnberg, Germany

Local Organization Chair

Diana Häsener	TU Dresden, Germany

Web Chairs

Jacqueline Papperitz	TU Dresden, Germany
Ahmed Kamaleldin	TU Dresden, Germany

Steering Committee

Fernando Silva (SC Chair)	University of Porto, Portugal
Dora Blanco Heras (Vice-chair)	University of Santiago de Compostela, Spain
Christos Kaklamanis	Computer Technology Institute and Press "Diophantus", Greece
Demetris Zeinalipour	University of Cyprus, Cyprus
Ewa Deelman	University of Southern California, USA
Felix Wolf	Technical University of Darmstadt, Germany
George Papadopoulos	University of Cyprus, Cyprus
Henk Sips	Delft University of Technology, The Netherlands
Ivona Brandić	Technical University of Wien, Austria
Jesus Carretero	University Carlos III of Madrid, Spain
Krzysztof Rzadca	University of Warsaw, Poland
Leonel Sousa	University of Lisbon, Portugal
Maciej Malawski	AGH University of Science and Technology, Poland
Marco Aldinucci	University of Turin, Italy
Massimo Torquati	University of Pisa, Italy
Phil Trinder	University of Glasgow, UK
Ramin Yahyapour	GWDG, Göttingen, Germany
Rosa M. Badia	Barcelona Supercomputing Center, Spain
Tomàs Margalef	Autonomous University of Barcelona, Spain
Wolfgang E. Nagel	TU Dresden, Germany

Honorary Members

Christian Lengauer	University of Passau, Germany
Luc Bougé	ENS Rennes, France
Ron Perrott	University of Oxford, UK
Karl Dieter Reinartz	University of Erlangen-Nürnberg, Germany

Scientific Organization

Track 1: Programming, Compilers and Performance

Chairs

Ana-Lucia Varbanescu	University of Amsterdam, The Netherlands
João M. P. Cardoso	Universidade do Porto, Portugal

Program Committee

Lucas Mello Schnorr	Universidade Federal de Rio Grande do Sul, Brazil
Walter Binder	University of Lugano, Italy
Peter Thoman	University of Innsbruck, Austria
Johannes Doerfert	Lawrence Livermore National Laboratory, USA
Cristina Silvano	Politecnico di Milano, Italy
Georg Hager	Erlangen Regional Computing Center, Germany
Carlo Bertolli	AMD, Inc., USA
Guoliang Jin	North Carolina State University, USA
Bruno Bodin	Yale-NUS College, Singapore
Ivy Peng	KTH Royal Institute of Technology, Sweden
Tobias Kenter	University of Paderborn, Germany
Nick Brown	University of Edinburgh, UK
Veronica Vergara Larrea	Oak Ridge National Laboratory, USA
Sotirios Xydis	National Technical University of Athens, Greece
Ivan Ivanov	Tokyo Institute of Technology, Japan
Orlando Moreira	Snap, Inc., The Netherlands
R. Govindarajan	Indian Institute of Science, India
Artur Podobas	KTH Royal Institute of Technology, Sweden
Stéphane Genaud	Icube - University of Strasbourg, France
Stefano Markidis	KTH Royal Institute of Technology, Sweden
Siegfried Benkner	University of Vienna, Austria
Miwako Tsuji	RIKEN, Japan

Bernhard Egger	Seoul National University, South Korea
Hans Vandierendonck	Queen's University Belfast, UK
Jean-Baptiste Besnard	Data Direct Networks, USA
Tom Deakin	University of Bristol, UK
Paul Carpenter	Barcelona Supercomputing Center, Spain
Serena Curzel	Politecnico di Milano, Italy
Giuseppe Tagliavini	University of Bologna, Italy
Seyong Lee	Oak Ridge National Laboratory, USA
Pedro Valero-Lara	Oak Ridge National Laboratory, USA
Diego R. Llanos	University of Valladolid, Spain

Track 2: Scheduling, Resource Management, Cloud, Edge Computing and Workflows

Chairs

Sascha Hunold	TU Wien, Austria
Daniel Cordeiro	Universidade de São Paulo, Brazil

Program Committee

Anirban Mandal	Renaissance Computing Institute, USA
Dante Sánchez-Gallegos	Universidad Carlos III de Madrid, Spain
Radu Prodan	University of Klagenfurt, Austria
Luciana Arantes	Sorbonne University, France
Luiz F. Bittencourt	University of Campinas, Brazil
Valeria Cardellini	University of Roma "Tor Vergata", Italy
Loris Marchal	Centre National de la Recherche Scientifique, France
Jacopo Soldani	University of Pisa, Italy
Marco Lapegna	University of Naples Federico II, Italy
Joanna Berlińska	Adam Mickiewicz University, Poland
Francesc Lordan	Barcelona Supercomputing Center, Spain
Guillaume Pallez	Inria, France
Anne Benoit	École normale supérieure de Lyon, France
Maciej Malawski	AGH University of Science and Technology, Poland
Nectarios Koziris	National Technical University of Athens, Greece
Nikela Papadopoulou	University of Glasgow, UK
Jason Riedy	Advanced Micro Devices, Inc., USA
Minming Li	City University of Hong Kong, China
Oliver Sinnen	University of Auckland, New Zealand
Pierre-Francois Dutot	Université Grenoble Alpes, France

Silvio Rizzi	Argonne National Laboratory, USA
Javid Taheri	Karlstad University, Sweden
Alok Tripathy	UC Berkeley, USA
Massimo Villari	University of Messina, Italy
Veronika Rehn-Sonigo	FEMTO-ST, France
Alfredo Goldman	University of São Paulo, Brazil
Carla Osthoff Barros	National Laboratory for Scientific Computing LNCC, USA
Muhammad Ajmal Azad	Birmingham City University, UK
Anthony Danalis	University of Tennessee, USA
Carlos Guerrero	Universitat de les Illes Balears, Spain
Krzysztof Rzadca	University of Warsaw, Poland
Vladimir Vlassov	KTH Royal Institute of Technology, Sweden
Katzalin Olcoz	Universidad Complutense de Madrid, Spain
Maxime Gonthier	University of Chicago, USA
Fanny Pascual	Sorbonne Université, France
Anderson Andrei da Silva	Hewlett Packard Labs, USA
Marios Dikaiakos	University of Cyprus, Cyprus
Carlos A. Varela	Rensselaer Polytechnic Institute, USA
Atakan Aral	University of Vienna, Austria
Francisco Brasileiro	Universidade Federal de Campina Grande, Brazil
Ramin Yahyapour	University of Göttingen, Germany
Rodrigo N. Calheiros	Western Sydney University, Australia
Ciprian Dobre	University Politehnica of Bucharest, Romania

Track 3: Architectures and Accelerators

Chairs

Kentaro Sano	RIKEN, Japan
Holger Fröning	Heidelberg University, Germany

Program Committee

Xing Cai	Simula Research Laboratory, Norway
Teresa Cervero	Barcelona Supercomputing Center, Spain
Manuel F. Dolz	Universitat Jaume I, Spain
Jorge G. Barbosa	University of Porto, Portugal
Hatem Ltaief	King Abdullah University of Science and Technology, Saudi Arabia
Carlos Reaño	Universitat de València, Spain
Ryohei Kobayashi	Institute of Science Tokyo, Japan
Julio Sahuquillo	Universitat Politècnica de València, Spain

Vladimir Getov   University of Westminster, UK
Pedro Javier Garcia   Universidad de Castilla-La Mancha, Spain
Tanja Harbaum   Karlsruhe Institute of Technology, Germany
Jesus Escudero-Sahuquillo   University of Castilla-La Mancha, Spain
Antonio J. Peña   Barcelona Supercomputing Center, Spain
Marcus Paradies   LMU Munich, Germany
Dirk Pleiter   University of Groningen, The Netherlands
Kazem Shekofteh   Heidelberg University, Germany
Esteban Mocskos   University of Buenos Aires, Argentina
Rohit Prasad   CEA, France
George Michelogiannakis   Lawrence Berkeley National Laboratory, USA
Yoshiki Yamaguchi   University of Tsukuba, Japan
Boma Anantasatya Adhi   Universitas Indonesia, Indonesia
Christian Plessl   Paderborn University, Germany
Christoph Kessler   Linköping University, Sweden
Antonino Tumeo   Pacific Northwest National Laboratory, USA
Davide Bertozzi   University of Manchester, UK
Keita Teranishi   Oak Ridge National Laboratory, USA
Samuel Thibault   Université Bordeaux 1, France
Tomohiro Ueno   RIKEN, Japan
Toshihiro Hanawa   University of Tokyo, Japan
Jason Bakos   University of South Carolina, USA
Mattias O'Nils   Mid Sweden University, Sweden
Giovanni Agosta   Politecnico di Milano, Italy
Shinji Sumimoto   University of Tokyo, Japan
Dhabaleswar Panda   Ohio State University, USA
Heiner Litz   Stanford University, USA
Ryusuke Egawa   Tokyo Denki University, Japan
Kazuhiko Komatsu   Tohoku University, Japan
Li Zhang   TU Darmstadt, Germany
Benjamin Klenk   NVIDIA Inc., USA
Francesca Palumbo   University of Cagliari, Italy
Christian Terboven   RWTH Aachen University, Germany
Alex Delis   University of Athens, Greece
Oscar Plata   University of Málaga, Spain

Track 4: Data Analytics, AI and Computational Science

Chairs

Erhard Rahm   Leipzig University, Germany
Jeyan Thiyagalingam   Rutherford Appleton Laboratory, UK

Program Committee

Shadi Ibrahim	Inria, Rennes Bretagne Atlantique Research Center, France
Rizos Sakellariou	University of Manchester, UK
Massimo Torquati	University of Pisa, Italy
Jorji Nonaka	RIKEN, Japan
Hao Dai	Shenzhen Institutes of Advanced Technology, China
Rafael Tolosana-Calasanz	Universidad de Zaragoza, Spain
Yang Wang	Shenzhen Institutes of Advanced Technology, China
Michael Kuhn	Otto von Guericke University Magdeburg, Germany
Achim Basermann	German Aerospace Center, Germany
Ashiq Anjum	University of Leicester, UK
Ramon Nou	Universitat Politécnica de Catalunya, Spain
Jože M. Rožanec	Jožef Stefan Institute, Slovenia
Dana Petcu	West University of Timisoara, Romania
Douglas Thain	University of Notre Dame, USA
Dalibor Klusacek	CESNET, Czech Republic
Hideyuki Kawashima	Keio University, Japan
José M. Cecilia	Universitat Politècnica de València, Spain
Manolis Marazakis	Institute of Computer Science, FORTH, Greece
Feiyi Wang	Oak Ridge National Laboratory, USA
Rafael Ferreira da Silva	Oak Ridge National Laboratory, USA
Matthias Boehm	TU Berlin, Germany
Alexandru Costan	Inria, France
Youngjae Kim	Sogang University, South Korea
M. Mustafa Rafique	Rochester Institute of Technology, USA
Ligang He	University of Warwick, UK
Osamu Tatebe	University of Tsukuba, Japan
Odej Kao	TU Berlin, Germany
Josef Spillner	Zurich University of Applied Sciences, Switzerland
Sukhpal Singh Gill	Queen Mary University of London, UK
Reza Farahani	University of Klagenfurt, Austria

Track 5: Theory and Algorithms

Chairs

Francesco Silvestri	University of Padova, Italy
Erik Saule	University of North Carolina Charlotte, USA

Program Committee

Othon Michail	University of Liverpool, UK
Pierre Fraigniaud	Université Paris Cité and CNRS, France
Jee Choi	Georgia Institute of Technology, USA
Samuel McCauley	Williams College, USA
Rezaul Chowdhury	State University of New York at Stony Brook, USA
Achour Mostéfaoui	Université Nantes, France
Manuel Penschuck	Goethe University Frankfurt, Germany
Vaishali Surianarayanan	University of California, Santa Barbara, USA
Lionel Eyraud-Dubois	Inria Bordeaux Sud-Ouest, France
Lata Narayanan	Concordia University, Canada
Helen Xu	Georgia Tech, USA
Yusuke Nagasaka	Fujitsu Limited, Japan
Albert-Jan Yzelman	Huawei Technologies France, France
Shikha Singh	Williams College, USA
Quanquan Liu	Northwestern University, USA
Fabien Dufoulon	Lancaster University, UK
Sanjukta Bhowmick	University of North Texas, USA
Flavio Vella	University of Trento, Italy
Kirk Pruhs	University of Pittsburgh, USA
Cynthia Phillips	Sandia National Laboratories, USA

Track 6: Multidisciplinary, Domain-Specific and Applied Parallel and Distributed Computing

Chairs

Alba C. Melo	University of Brasília, Brazil
Gihan Mudalige	University of Warwick, UK

Program Committee

Stefka Fidanova	Institute of Information and Communication Technologies, Bulgaria
Yiannis Papadopoulos	Advanced Micro Devices, Inc., USA
Dragi Kimovski	University of Klagenfurt, Austria
Tobias Flynn	Imperial College London, UK
Alvaro Coutinho	Universidade Federal do Rio de Janeiro, Brazil
Pasqua D'Ambra	Institute of Applied Mathematics-CNR, Italy
Maria Fazio	University of Messina, Italy
Davor Davidovic	Rudjer Bošković Institute, Croatia
Juan F. R. Herrera	University of Edinburgh, UK

Artifact Evaluation

Chairs

Massimo Torquati	University of Pisa, Italy
Olaf Krzikalla	German Aerospace Center, Germany

Artifact Evaluation Committee

Valerio Besozzi	Università di Pisa, Italy
Johannes Wendler	German Aerospace Center, Germany
Javier Garcia Blas	Universidad Carlos III de Madrid, Spain
Julian Braun	German Aerospace Center, Germany
Jasmin Mohnke	German Aerospace Center, Germany
Maximilian Höchel	German Aerospace Center, Germany
Marco Edoardo Santimaria	University of Turin, Italy
Nicolò Tonci	University of Pisa, Italy
Gabriele Mencagli	University of Pisa, Italy
Giulio Malenza	University of Turin, Italy
Dominik Vietinghoff	German Aerospace Center, Germany

Contents – Part I

Contents – Part II

Data analytics, AI, and Computational Science

Contents – Part III

Programming, Compilers
and Performance

Noise Injection for Performance Bottleneck Analysis

Aurélien Delval[1,2(✉)] ⓘ, Pablo de Oliveira Castro[2] ⓘ, William Jalby[2] ⓘ,
and Etienne Renault[1] ⓘ

[1] SiPearl, Maisons-Laffitte, France
{aurelien.delval,etienne.renault}@sipearl.com
[2] Université Paris-Saclay, UVSQ, LI-PaRAD, Guyancourt, France
{aurelien.delval,pablo.oliveira,william.jalby}@uvsq.fr

Abstract. Bottleneck evaluation plays a crucial part in performance tuning of HPC applications, as it directly influences the search for optimizations and the selection of the best hardware for a given code. In this paper, we introduce a new model-agnostic, instruction-accurate framework for bottleneck analysis based on *performance noise* injection. This method provides a precise analysis that complements existing techniques, particularly in quantifying unused resource slack. Specifically, we classify programs based on whether they are limited by computation, data access bandwidth, or latency by injecting additional noise instructions that target specific bottleneck sources. Our approach is built on the LLVM compiler toolchain, ensuring easy portability across different architectures and microarchitectures which constitutes an improvement over many state-of-the-art tools. We validate our framework on a range of hardware benchmarks and kernels, including a detailed study of a sparse-matrix–vector product (SPMXV) kernel, where we successfully detect distinct performance regimes. These insights further inform hardware selection, as demonstrated by our comparative evaluation between HBM and DDR memory systems.

Keywords: noise injection · performance analysis · bottleneck detection · compilation · LLVM

1 Introduction

Modern High-Performance Computing (HPC) systems are increasingly adopting heterogeneous architectures to meet the growing demands for computational performance and energy efficiency. This heterogeneity occurs at several levels: processing units level (CPUs, GPUs, FPGAs, and other accelerators), memory level (HBM, DDR, CXL, NVLink, and others), microarchitectures (e.g. on AArch64: Cortex-M, Cortex-A, Neoverse-N1, Neoverse-V1, Neoverse-V2) and SIMD extension level. All those combinations offer a wide range of optimization options for both the programmer and the compiler, the goal being to achieve full

© The Author(s), under exclusive license to Springer Nature Switzerland AG 2026
W. E. Nagel et al. (Eds.): Euro-Par 2025, LNCS 15900, pp. 3–23, 2026.
https://doi.org/10.1007/978-3-031-99854-6_1

and balanced use of hardware resources (computing elements, memory bandwidth, and I/O).

However, in practice, this balance is rarely achieved, as one resource often becomes a bottleneck, hence the need for tools to detect them. Once an imbalance is identified, various well-known optimizations can address the specific performance issues. For compute-bound codes, improvements can come from vectorization or replacing costly operations like divisions and square roots. For data-access-bound codes, optimizing data access patterns is a common approach. Similarly, for I/O-bound codes, performance gains can be achieved by optimizing access patterns or scheduling synchronization points more efficiently. While some general optimizations can provide quick performance boosts, the most effective strategies typically depend on the specific characteristics of the code and the underlying hardware. Therefore, detecting bottlenecks is essential for guiding performance optimization and selecting the most suitable hardware system for a given workload, including considerations such as microarchitecture and memory types.

To identify application bottlenecks, existing research primarily relies on abstractions and approximations. Static approaches like the roofline model and its derivatives [10] analyze FLOPS and arithmetic intensity to estimate the potential for improving compute or bandwidth-bound codes, but often neglect cache or latency effects. Simulation or emulation-based methods [4] are either complex to configure or oversimplify hardware details (NUMA effects, memory controller latency). These methods are useful for testing different hardware configurations and predicting how an application might behave with more cores or memory, or even on future hardware. However, they have two major drawbacks: (1) they require extensive computation time and dedicated hardware, and (2) abstracting certain hardware details can lead to misinterpretation of bottlenecks. To overcome these limitations, alternative approaches not relying on abstract performance models have been developed, such as performance-event sampling techniques, or decremental analysis that remove parts of the binary to identify bottlenecks [3]. Yet, to interpret measured data, these still rely on some level of abstractions or assumptions. Thus, they may fail to accurately capture performance bottlenecks in the same way as purely static methods.

To better identify imbalances in resource usage, this paper introduces a novel approach based on *noise injection*. The key idea is to insert assembly instructions (or *noise*) into performance-critical sections of the code to stress various bottlenecks. Thanks to the strong Out-of-Order (OoO) capabilities of modern hardware, injecting noise into a constrained resource will significantly impact performance, whereas doing so in an underutilized resource will have little effect. In Sect. 2, we define the *absorption* metric which quantifies how much noise can be injected into a code without slowdown. This metric is used to quantify the usage of each bottleneck source. Unlike existing techniques, this method does not rely on heavy abstractions nor strong assumptions about hardware behavior. As a result, 1) we can precisely determine the root causes of bottlenecks, with an accuracy on the order of a single cycle; 2) the method does not require a detailed performance model and can be easily ported to new architectures. Our approach is designed to be both modular and flexible. First, different types of noise can be defined to stress various resources such as the Floating Point Unit (FPU) or the Load Store Unit (LSU), as detailed in Sect. 2. Additionally, our method is fully integrated into the LLVM compiler infrastructure. Section 4 demonstrates our method using hardware characterization benchmarks that target memory bandwidth, latency, and compute performance. These benchmarks also serve as a basis for comparing different systems in terms of microarchitectures and memory types by evaluating their resilience to noise and revealing unexpected architectural behaviors. Finally, Sect. 6 presents a case study on a sparse matrix-vector product kernel, showing how our tool detects transitions between bottleneck phenomena that remain hidden with other benchmarking tools (reviewed in Sect. 5.1).

2 Description of the Noise Injection Methodology

2.1 Preliminary Definitions

Let $\mathcal{I}$ be an Instruction Set Architecture (ISA). We use $\Sigma_{\mathcal{I}}^*$ to denote the set of finite sequences that we can build over $\mathcal{I}$, that is to say, the set of all possible assembly programs. A language $\mathcal{L}_{\mathcal{I}}$ is a subset of programs. In this paper, we define the *noise* language, $\mathcal{N}_{\mathcal{I}}$ which can be seen as a generator of assembly patterns. For the sake of simplicity, let us denote it by $\mathcal{N}$. The language $\mathcal{N}$ is built as the union of multiple sub-languages called *noise modes*. Several noise modes can be considered: `fp_add64`, consisting in FP64 scalar add instructions; `l1_ld64` consisting of scalar loads hitting the L1 cache, and `memory_ld64` falling in memory; `int64_add` consisting in integer scalar add instructions. Figure 1 depicts those noise modes in AArch64 ISA. The left-hand side (a) represents `fp_add64` noise (i.e. `fadds`) while the right-hand side (b) represents `memory_ld64` noise (i.e. `ldrs`).

More complex noise modes are possible, with larger noise patterns or by combining multiple existing patterns. However, for all ISA and noise modes considered in this paper, the resulting languages are simple since they use alphabets of size one. For any such noise mode $\mathcal{N}_M \in \mathcal{N}$, let $\Sigma_{\mathcal{N}_M} = \{n_{\mathcal{M}}\}$ be its alphabet, with $n_{\mathcal{M}}$ its corresponding *noise pattern* (which we denote n for simplicity). Thus the assembly snippets generated by $\mathcal{N}_M$ are $\mathcal{N}_M^* = \{n^k, \forall k \in \mathbb{N}\}$, where n^k is the word obtained after concatenating k patterns n (for $k = 0$, we obtain ϵ the empty string). We call k the *noise quantity* of n^k.

2.2 Resources and Saturation Phases

The term *hardware resources* in the context of CPUs refers to the fundamental components that enable processors, memory, and peripheral devices to interact effectively. In this paper, we mostly focus on the internal resources of the CPU (e.g. Arithmetic and Logic Unit, Vector Processing Units) and memory

```
1  fadd d31, d31, d31
2  fadd d30, d30, d30
3  fadd d29, d29, d29
4  fadd d28, d28, d28
5  ...
```

(a) `fp_add64` noise

```
1  # Overhead
2  adrp x..., 4 <funcname+0x...>
3  ldr x..., [x...]
4  # Payload
5  ldr w28, [x...]
6  ldr w27, [x...]
7  [...]
8  ...
```

(c) `11_1d64` noise. In gray are highlighted the "overhead" instructions not part of the useful noise payload (see Section 2.3).

Fig. 1. Definition of basic AArch64 patterns, `fp_add64` and `11_1d64`, which are useful to quantify compute and data-access bottlenecks.

(e.g. Cache Hierarchy, Memory Management Unit). Depending on the microarchitecture, one can observe variations in terms of performance. Noise injection helps analyze performance bottlenecks by highlighting architectural variations. For example, on AArch64, the BF16 Dot Product (`bfdot`) has a latency of 4 on Neoverse V1 and 5 on Neoverse V2, while the FP16 reduction (`faddv`) latency decreases from 13 on Neoverse V1 to 8 on Neoverse V2.

By introducing increasing amounts of noise in these resources, both the original and noisy instructions begin to interact with each other. This interaction leads to performance degradation, eventually reaching a point where noise becomes dominant and fully saturates its target resource. To assess the availability of different CPU resources, we define *absorption* as the number of additional instructions a code can handle before experiencing performance degradation. Naturally, this absorption capacity depends heavily on the target machine and the nature of the injected noise. In practice, up to three distinct phases may be observed, though the first two do not always appear.

First, an *absorption phase*, during which performance is not affected at all by the noise. Injected instructions are filling cycles that were previously stalling, either because of bubbles in the pipeline or high latencies of some memory operations. Then, a *transient phase*, where performance starts degrading. In the general case, the behavior of performance can become unpredictable and unstable, as it will be very dependent on the OoO implementation of the tested machine [24]. Finally, a *saturation phase*, where injected noise becomes completely dominating compared to the original case. The system has reached its asymptotic behavior as

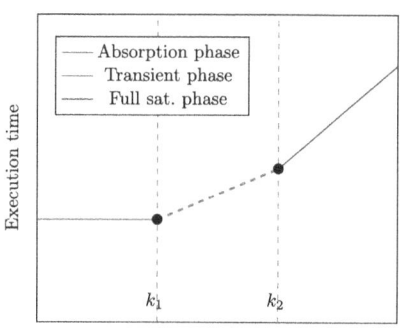

Fig. 2. Idealized model of codes' behavior when subject to increasing noise.

run time starts increasing linearly, or at least in a consistent way. Figure 2 shows an idealized representation of how a code responds to noise, highlighting the three phases just described. During the absorption phase, performance remains unchanged, appearing as a flat section in the plot. After k_1 patterns, performance starts suffering from injected noise. After k_2 patterns, the code is fully saturated and the system reaches asymptotic behavior (more details in Sect. 4). To characterize the usage of a given resource, the *absorption* metric is used. This corresponds to the value of k_1 in our model[1]. The main idea between this metric is that a *lower value* indicates a *saturated resource*, whereas a *higher value* indicates an *unsaturated resource*.

2.3 Payload and Overhead

One aspect requiring special attention is the side effects introduced by our noise, as it is important to ensure that it does not affect the semantics of the original code. Given $\mathcal{L}_c$ the language of the snippet of code and $\mathcal{N}_M$ the chosen noise mode. Without loss of generality, we consider here $\mathcal{L}_c$ to be a finite language. When injecting any quantity k of noise into $\mathcal{L}_c$, we obtain $\mathcal{L}_R = \mathcal{L}_c \cup \mathcal{N}_M$ s.t any $s_r \in \mathcal{L}_R = s_1.n^k.s_2$ with "." the sequence concatenation symbol and $(s_1.\epsilon.s_2) = (s_1.s_2) \in \mathcal{L}_c$. Trivially for $k = 0$, the property holds since $n^k = \epsilon$ and $(s_1.s_2) \in \mathcal{L}_c$. For arithmetic noise, one can consider a machine with an infinite number of registers (without loss of generality since the compilers can perform *spilling* to conform to the limited number of registers of actual machines). Therefore the set of registers used per n^k, denoted $\mathcal{R}_n$ can differ from the set of registers used by both s_1 and s_2 (denoted by $\mathcal{R}_s$). As a consequence, the evaluation of s_r restricted to registers $\mathcal{R}_s$ will result in $s_1.s_2$. Since $\mathcal{R}_n$ cannot impact other registers, the original semantics are not affected. In such a situation, similarly to what is done with partial order reduction in model-checking, one can build one representative execution, ignoring some others, with the same semantics. Notice that this scheme of proof also holds for other noise modes: one just has to ensure that there are no conflicts between the noise semantics and the code semantics.

In practice, there may be cases where register spilling can not be avoided. However, this will only happen when introducing a read-after-write (RAW) dependency, as opposed to a write-after-write (WAW) dependency. The phenomenon can also be mitigated by limiting the number of registers cycled by the noise pattern, as long as it is sufficient to not induce stalls between the noise instructions themselves. It is also possible to detect when spilling does happen by statically analyzing the generated assembly code. All in all, while register spilling is a constraint to be aware of, it can be limited and detected by the techniques mentioned above, and its likeliness depends on a wide range of criteria, such as the register pressure of the original code (already a potential performance issue by itself), the target microarchitecture, or the noise mode. Some noise modes might also have an inherent *overhead* to set up the relevant noise instructions. This observation can be generalized by splitting injected instructions into two sets: *payload* instructions -corresponding to the useful noise instructions to

---

[1] When measuring experimental data, it is possible to automatize the computation of absorption by fitting the obtained series to this model.

inject- and *overhead* (whether they are spill instructions or inherent to the noise mode). The size of both sets of instructions can be computed by statically analyzing the code produced by the compiler. This permits evaluation of the *quality* of the injection, ensuring that noise did not produce unexpected and significant side effects that may bias analysis. Note that when possible (e.g. when using previously untouched callee saved registers), the compiler can hoist overhead instructions out of the target loop, making its impact as small as possible.

2.4   Renormalization of Absorption by Code Size

Another important factor to consider is the impact of the noise quantity relative to the number of instructions in the original loop. Larger code sizes may indeed provide more opportunities for the OoO execution engine to utilize a noise instruction to fill a stall. This is particularly important when comparing different versions of the same code. The most obvious example of this is loop unrolling. This brings us to the definition of two methods for measuring absorption. $s_r = s_1.n^k.s_2$ is the assembly program obtained after injection of k patterns of any noise mode $\mathcal{N}_M$. When only considering loop nests, l_r can be defined as the substring of s_r corresponding to the target loop body. Because n^k is itself a substring of l_r, it is possible to write $l_r = l_1.n^k.l_2$. The *relative payload* size is defined as

$$\widehat{P}(k) = \frac{k}{|l_1.l_2|} \tag{1}$$

where $|l_1.l_2|$ denotes the size of $l_1.l_2$. Now, let $Abs_{\mathcal{N}}^{raw}(l_r)$ the absorption of loop l_r for noise mode $\mathcal{N}_M$, expressed in number of raw noise patterns (that is the *absolute* or *raw* absorption). The *relative absorption* is defined as

$$Abs_{\mathcal{N}}^{rel}(l_r) = \widehat{P}(Abs_{\mathcal{N}}^{raw}(l_r)) \tag{2}$$

Intuitively, this corresponds to the number of patterns that can be injected per instruction of the original loop body before reaching saturation. Depending on the context, it may be more suitable to use either the absolute or relative definition of the absorption metric, the relative definition being particularly adapted to the study of loop mutations that greatly affect code size (such as unrolling or interleaving).

3   Implementation of a Compiler-Level Injection Framework

Different approaches can be used to implement a framework for code modifications—specifically, for instruction injection. The first approach, binary patching, modifies compiler-generated binaries directly. Although successfully employed by tools such as MAQAO and MADRAS [25], binary patching is challenging to port to new architectures; for example, MADRAS does not yet support

AArch64. The second approach, dynamic code manipulation, is implemented by tools like Intel PIN [15], DynamoRIO [5], and Valgrind [20]. While these tools are mature, they incur a run time overhead that is undesirable when precise performance measurements are required.

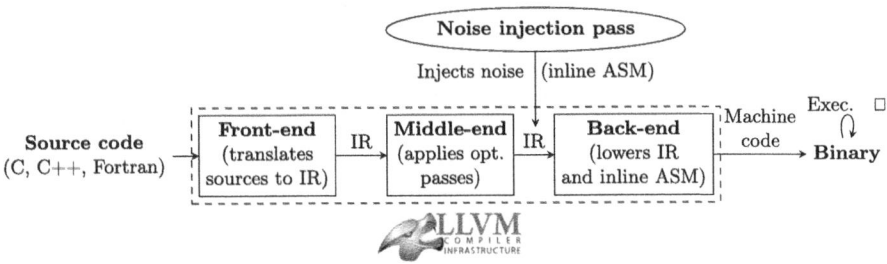

Fig. 3. Pipeline of LLVM-based noise injection. Noise is injected after all middle-end optimizations.

3.1   Overview of the Tool

As a consequence, a compiler-level injection approach was chosen, building on the LLVM [14] infrastructure. Although this confines the tool to a single toolchain, LLVM's growing adoption in the HPC landscape and its support for distributing plugins as standalone middle-end passes make this limitation acceptable. Figure 3 illustrates our LLVM-based injection workflow, which primarily consists of a plugin pass extending the compiler middle end. Our approach requires that the injected noise be both fine-grained and semantics-preserving, while also being robust against compiler optimizations. To meet these requirements, noise is injected via inline assembly at the LLVM Intermediate Representation (IR) level. This allows writing the noise directly in assembly and specifying used registers as clobbered, ensuring that live and callee-saved registers are properly saved and restored. Using the `volatile` qualifier guarantees that the noise is not optimized away by the compiler. Additionally, interferences with other optimization passes are avoided by performing the injection at the last optimization pass in the middle end. Since LLVM IR is target agnostic, the method is easily portable to other architectures, with the main effort being the development of noise pattern generators for each target ISA.

In addition, and to simplify the process for end-users, a high-level *noise controller* tool that automates the noise injection pass on target applications was developed. This tool relieves users from the tedious task of manually invoking the noise injection pass and manages experiments by automatically varying noise quantities and modes. Users can specify target loop nests either by using a custom loop pragma —integrated into the LLVM frontends to easily test different noise modes— or through a configuration file, which allows the use of the noise injection plugin without modifying the LLVM frontend. Although noise is typically injected into the innermost loop for maximum sensitivity, our mechanism also permits selecting any loop level for both injected noise and timing probes.

To reduce experimentation time, the tool employs several strategies. First, to be able to noise and monitor multiple hot regions simultaneously, it is important to be able to time them individually. This is done by placing timing probes (calling a custom runtime library) around each loop or loop nest individually. Additionally, a clustering algorithm groups executions into performance classes, assuming similar run times indicate shared characteristics [21]; each class is then analyzed independently. Also, an online saturation detection method monitors run times and deviations, halting injection when noise effects become significant. To minimize rebuild times, the tool selectively updates source files containing target regions, avoiding full rebuilds and saving time in large applications.

Supporting OpenMP and MPI parallelism requires special care. Our runtime library and `memory_ld64` noise mode require careful handling: the former uses a hashmap for timing samples, which could be problematic with concurrent threads, while the latter loads from a dedicated buffer in a chaotic pattern to minimize cache hits and prefetching. Both issues are resolved using Thread Local Storage (TLS), assigning threads/processes their own hashmaps or load buffers. When possible, timing probes are placed around OpenMP parallel regions to ensure the main thread submits hashmap entries. Future work includes selectively noising threads or processes to induce desynchronization [9].

3.2   Methodology for Characterizing an Application

Studying an application through the noise injection method first requires knowing which hot loops are interesting to target. This information can be obtained using a profiler. With no prior information about those loops' bottlenecks, running the application with one or a few different noise quantities is usually a time saver. This will give an idea of the sensitivity of the code to the noise. Codes that are very sensitive to noise and can only absorb a few instructions -if any- are usually those that exhibit bottlenecks at the CPU core level. This is typically the case with compute-bound codes. On the other side of the spectrum, codes that can absorb very large quantities of noise (such as a few dozen instructions) are those that have some data access bottlenecks at the cache or memory levels, whether this is due to bandwidth or latency. Our experiments, on both mini-applications and real ones -and on various architectures-, show that values around 20 or 30 FP or L1 instructions are a good starting point, as this typically roughly corresponds to the tipping point between the two categories. Once the general sensitivities of the noise regions have been established, one can start running the code through increasing noise quantities following the process described in the previous section. For loops that appear robust to noise, it is usually preferable to use a step of 5 or even 10 instructions between successive noise payloads. The obtained absorption value should give indications about the general behavior of each target loop for further studies.

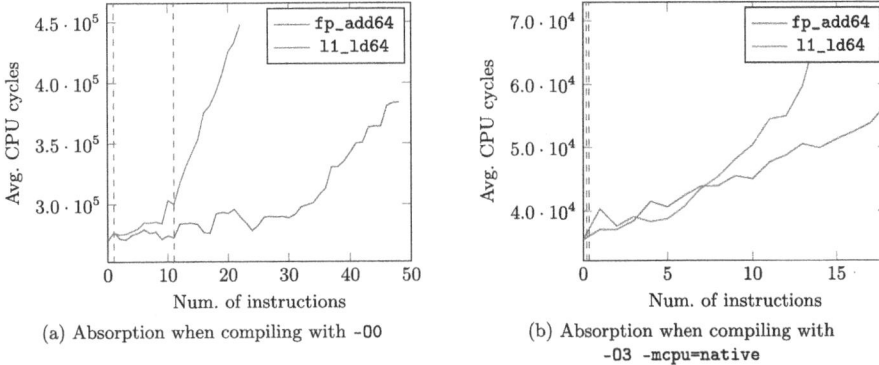

(a) Absorption when compiling with -O0

(b) Absorption when compiling with -O3 -mcpu=native

Fig. 4. Absorption of a matrix product example with different compiler flags. Figure (a) absorbs 11 instructions, whereas in Figure (b), a single noise instruction increases running time demonstrating that the compiler optimizations effectively eliminate the performance bottleneck.

4 Validation on Reference Benchmarks

4.1 Introductory Example: Dense Matrix Product

Figure 4(a) demonstrates the noise injection pass on a simple matrix product example, running on an Amazon Graviton 3, and compiled with clang -O0. The amount of noise is increased progressively to observe its impact. Under fp_add64 noise, the code appears quite robust, being completely unaffected by up to 11 instructions. Under 11_ld64 noise, however, performance degrades instantly. This clearly indicates that the code is data-access-bound. This is because the code was purposefully built in -O0: in LLVM, this does not include the mem2reg optimization pass, which promotes memory accesses to register accesses. As a consequence, the resulting assembly code is clogged with unnecessary load and store instructions that saturate the LSU while leaving the FPU mostly unused. Figure 4(b) presents the same experiment with -O3 -mcpu=native, exploiting hardware resources much more efficiently.

4.2 Validation Using Hardware Characterization Benchmarks

We validate our noise injection methodology using established hardware characterization benchmarks: STREAM[2] for memory bandwidth, lat mem rd from LMBench[3] for memory latency, and Coral HACCmk[4] for compute-bound operations. This approach serves two purposes: it confirms our tool's ability to detect and quantify specific hardware bottlenecks, and it provides practical insights for application developers through cross-architecture comparisons using the absorption metric.

---

[2] https://www.cs.virginia.edu/stream/ref.html.

[3] https://lmbench.sourceforge.net/.

[4] https://asc.llnl.gov/coral-benchmarks#haccmk.

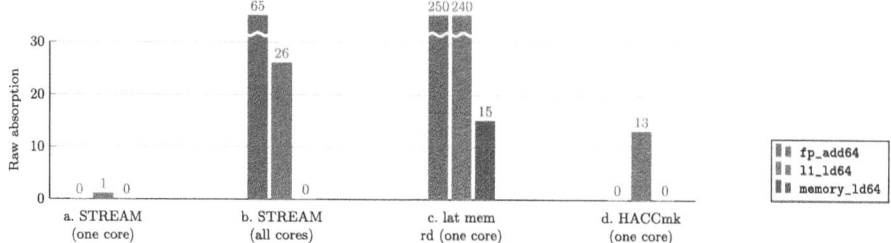

Fig. 5. Raw absorptions for the three hardware characterization benchmarks on Amazon Graviton 3.

Validation on Graviton 3. Figure 5 shows results from all three benchmarks executed on an Amazon Graviton 3 system, with one scalar element loaded per iteration in both STREAM and lat mem rd.

– For the **STREAM** benchmark, the sequential run (a.) results in low absorption values that reflect core-level limitations. In contrast, the parallel execution (b.) stresses the full memory bandwidth of the socket, causing loads to stall longer and enabling the absorption of many more noise instructions. Notably, while large quantities of `fp_add64` and `11_1d64` noise are absorbed, `memory_1d64` noise is not. To ensure that the absence of absorption in `memory_1d64` noise is due to bandwidth saturation rather than an imbalance between injected noise and loop body size, we repeated the experiment after unrolling the code (see Table 1). These stable results confirm that the lack of absorption in `memory_1d64` noise is a consequence of bandwidth saturation.
– The **lat mem rd** benchmark reinforces these findings while highlighting an important distinction: unlike STREAM, it absorbs substantial `memory_1d64` noise. This difference occurs because lat mem rd stalls first from dependencies between consecutive loads rather than bandwidth constraints. The ability to absorb up to 15 `memory_1d64` instructions differentiates latency-bound from bandwidth-bound operations.
– The compute-bound **HACCmk** benchmark exhibits absorption only in `11_1d64`, with no measurable absorption in `fp_add64`. This aligns with expectations that it saturates compute resources.

In summary, these results demonstrate that the noise injection methodology effectively captures all three types of bottlenecks—memory bandwidth, memory latency, and compute. By providing a nuanced, instruction-level absorption metric, this approach offers insights that go far beyond direct performance measures alone, thereby enabling more precise and targeted performance optimizations.

Comparison of AArch64 and x86 Systems. While Fig. 5 shows noise absorption on a specific (Graviton3) system, Table 1 provides a wider analysis by comparing performance and absorption metrics across three AArch64 systems -

Ampere Altra (Neoverse N1), Amazon Graviton 3 (Neoverse V1), Nvidia Grace (Neoverse V2) - and two x86 systems - Sapphire Rapids with and without HBM.

- For **STREAM** (bandwidth-bound benchmark), absorption inversely correlates with performance. Systems with more load stalls and lower performance exhibit higher absorption, confirming that stalled cycles have potential for being exploited. This is especially true for the x86 Sapphire Rapids machine where the only difference is the memory type. For this machine, we observe slightly more FP absorption with DDR, consistent with its lower performance. Variations can also be observed across AArch64 microarchitecture generations. The transition from N1 to V1 introduces a more advanced out-of-order execution engine (the pipeline core size increasing from 8 to 15), leading to better performance and increased absorption. A further evolution from V1 to V2 brings a slight performance improvement, which in turn reduces the amount of possible absorption. From a perspective of fine analysis of microarchitectural changes, our approach therefore exhibits interesting metrics.
- For **lat_mem_rd** (latency-bound benchmark), similar trends can be observed: absorption inversely correlates with performance. As we move across AArch64 microarchitecture generations, the amount of noise that can be injected increases. This reflects the growing complexity of newer chips, featuring larger network-on-chip (NoC) designs and more advanced memory systems (DDR4 vs. DDR5) with higher latency. On Sapphire Rapids, absorption capacity plateaus, highlighting the well-known NoC saturation [17] issue in this architecture. While this may limit its usefulness for characterization, exploring access patterns could provide insights into a broader range of real-world applications.
- In the compute-bound **HACCmk** benchmark, we observe microarchitectural differences. Graviton 3 (V1) and Nvidia Grace (V2) behave similarly, absorbing significant `fp_add64` noise with minimal `l1_ld64` absorption. In contrast, Ampere Altra (N1) shows no measurable absorption, suggesting either more balanced resource usage or a frontend/dispatch bottleneck. The same goes for Sapphire Rapids, where the compiler was able to vectorize the code, thus enabling further optimizations. This highlights how microarchitectural implementations can produce markedly different behaviors across or even within the same instruction set architectures.

Our absorption metric thus provides fine-grained insights into hardware resource usage beyond what traditional performance metrics reveal, offering a valuable tool for system selection and optimization. In particular, unicore measurements can be extremely misleading in driving optimization search: our experiments show that small code changes will often have an impact on unicore performance (as demonstrated by the low absorption values), but will often be overshadowed by much stronger data-access effects when scaling to multicore. This will be shown again in Fig. 7 on the SPMXV kernel example.

Table 1. Raw absorptions on different systems. All benchmarks were compiled with LLVM 18.1.8. (*) Code for this benchmark/noise combination was unrolled to better highlight resources saturation.

Machine:	Ampere Altra	Graviton 3	Grace	Sapphire Rapids	
Microarchitecture:	**Neoverse**	**Neoverse**	**Neoverse**	**Golden Cove**	
	N1	**V1**	**V2**		
Cores count:	80	64	72	40	
Base Core frequency (GHz):	3.0	2.6	3.2	2.2	
Socket count:	2	1	2	2	
Memory Type:	DDR	DDR	DDR	DDR	HBM
STREAM (max core count)					
Performance (GB/s):	168 GB/s	262 GB/s	381 GB/s	211 GB/s	541 GB/s
FP/L1/mem* abs.	47/27/0	65/26/0	21/16/0	80/80/0	24/21/0
lat_mem_rd (1 core)					
Performance (ns):	87.7 ns	118 ns	153 ns	92 ns	122 ns
FP/L1/mem abs. ≈	90/20/2	250/240/15	300/300/16	270/180/18	270/180/18
HACCmk (1 core)					
Performance (s):	6.02 s	9.85 s	3.65 s	4.25 s	
FP/L1/mem abs.	0/0/0	0/13/0	0/9/0	0/0/0	

5 Comparison with Other State-of-the-Art Characterization Tools

5.1 Existing Methods for Detecting Performance Bottlenecks

The key idea developed in this paper is to propose a framework to insert assembly instructions into performance-critical sections. As a consequence, we can characterize, with a cycle level precision, how much hardware resources are saturated. In the literature, other methods for performance and bottleneck analysis exist but have limitations. Table 2 summarizes the strengths and weakness of these approaches which fall into three categories: dynamic, static, or modification. Each technique is evaluated w.r.t. portability (criteria 1), hardware specificity (criteria 2), robustness (criteria 3), low-side effects (criteria 4), interpretability (criteria 5), and execution cost (criteria 6). A closer look shows that our approach meets most of the criteria compared to existing work. Indeed: the LLVM-based implementation ensures easy portability (1); the method is purely based on measuring execution time and does not make any abstraction through performance models (2); it applies to the vast majority of codes without specific restrictions, with support for OpenMP and MPI parallelism (3); overhead on top of noise payloads is reduced to the minimum and rarely necessary (4); the absorption metric is measured in instructions, which gives an intuitive evaluation of available resources (5). However, despite efforts to reduce the cost of this process, it does require re-building and re-running the target application multiple times, which can be a long process depending on the use case (6). The following subsections further detail other methods and tools and evaluate them with regard to the six criteria.

Dynamic Analysis. A common approach to hardware performance monitoring is using standard tools like Linux's `perf` to access Hardware Performance Monitoring Units (PMU). These counters provide insights for cache hits, cache misses, stalls, IPC, and more. However, these counters are often poorly documented (depending on the microarchitecture) and trigger security problems[5]. Even if some effort has been made to create unified interfaces (such as PAPI [19]) or analysis methods (Intel Top-Down [27]), this issue persists. More fundamentally, interpreting hardware event data can be challenging [18] even for advanced users, making it difficult to diagnose performance issues (criteria 5). Lastly, the roofline model and its derivatives measure a code's FLOPS, combined with an evaluation of arithmetic intensity. Comparing these to the peak performance of the machine provides a quick way to estimate if a code is bound by the memory bandwidth or by the peak compute performance of the machine. However, this family of models neglects architectural aspects that are also bottleneck sources, such as memory latency, cache hierarchies, different NUMA nodes, ...

Table 2. Comparison of bottleneck analysis methods. "✓": the method meets the criteria; "✗": the method does not meet the criteria; "∿": the method meets the criteria to some extent. *(*) Decremental analysis is evaluated on the basis of DECAN's implementation.*

Method	Category	Portable	HW specific	Robust	Low side-effects	Interpretable	Fast
PMU	Dynamic	∿	✓	✓	✓	✗	∿
Roofline model	Dynamic	✓	✗	✗	N/A	✗	∿
Code analyzers	Static	✗	∿	✗	N/A	✓	✓
Decremental analysis*(*)*	Modification	✗	✓	∿	✗	✓	∿
[this paper] Noise Injection	Modification	✓	✓	✓	✓	✓	✗

Static Analysis. An alternative approach is to simulate the performance of assembly code snippets. One such approach is the ECM model [12], which provides performance estimation by combining both an in-core and a data transfer model. However, it does make some assumptions by neglecting cache and latency effects, making it similar to the roofline model. Other tools such as LLVM-MCA[6], uiCA [1] and MAQAO CQA [7] perform in-depth code analysis at the core level. CQA, in particular, is extended by UFS [22], which simulates execution on an

---

[5] It requires adjusting the `perf_event_paranoid` kernel setting on Linux systems and can give insights about applications that run in parallel in dockerized/virtual machine contexts.

[6] https://llvm.org/docs/CommandGuide/llvm-mca.html.

idealized out-of-order (OoO) machine. Sniper generalizes this approach to multicore scenarios [6] and Gus [23] allows the modification of microarchitectural constants to artificially tune available resources. Such static models offer the advantage of being fast and collecting critical metrics like port occupancy and stalls. However, they have several limitations. First, they make strong assumptions about memory accesses (limited by bandwidth or hitting L1 cache), which can lead to severely biased results when latency becomes the limiting factor or when the actual L1 hit rate is low (criteria 3). Second, porting these models to new architectures is challenging, as it requires fine-tuning with numerous microarchitecture-dependent constants, potentially taking weeks of expert work (criteria 1). In contrast, our approach only requires basic knowledge about the target instruction set to port the existing noise modes (although defining more advanced noise modes could require finer knowledge). Finally, static models struggle to accurately capture complex phenomena like instruction reordering and branch prediction, making them less reliable substitutes for real performance measurements (criteria 2).

It is also worth mentioning that various machine learning techniques have been applied to the problem of performance prediction [26].

Modification-Based Approaches. This category comprises methods that modify the target program to infer performance characteristics from the modified version, such as the noise injection method presented in this paper. In particular, it is quite similar to differential analysis, a method implemented by MAQAO's DECAN module [13]. DECAN generates different variants of an original binary, each corresponding to a potential bottleneck source for which instructions have been removed. By comparing the performances of the original and modified program versions, it is possible to infer which resource was the main bottleneck in the original code. Noise injection performs similar modifications to deduce performance bottlenecks. However, it adopts an *incremental* approach, while DECAN is *decremental*. While both can be complementary, removing instructions from the original code can have several harmful side effects (criteria 4). The most obvious one is that this completely breaks the code's semantics. DECAN solves this by keeping a copy of the original loop body and executing both versions at each iteration, so as to preserve the original control flow and overall behavior. More problematic, deleting instructions will have unpredictable side effects on the remaining ones. First, this may remove inter-instruction dependencies. Second, those deletions will free the tested bottleneck resource and all shared ones (reordering buffers, reservation stations), allowing the remaining instructions to "spread" on all available resources more easily. Finally, the implementation of differential analysis made by DECAN relies on MAQAO's MADRAS module for static binary patching [25], making it hardly portable (criteria 1). The beginning of Sect. 3 goes into further detail on the topic of code modification.

Discussion. Some tools also use the idea of noise injection to evaluate programs' resilience, albeit in a different way and goal. The HPAS [2] and GREMLINS [16] tools allow users to generate a variety of external system noises, whether that is by consuming CPU time, creating cache or memory contention. The goal is to

Table 3. Comparison of DECAN and noise injection for FP/LS bottleneck analysis. In DECAN, a lower metric indicates a saturated resource, while in noise injection a lower absorption value signals a bottleneck.

Scenario	DECAN (Decremental)	Noise Injection (Incremental)
1) Compute-bound	LS variant runs significantly faster than FP variant (LS saturation is low, FP saturation is high)	FP absorption is low, while LS absorption is high
2) Data-bound	FP variant runs significantly faster than LS variant (FP saturation is low, LS saturation is high)	LS absorption is low, while FP absorption is high
3) Full Overlap	Both FP and LS variants run close to the original reference (both saturations are high)	Both FP and LS absorptions are very low
4) Limited Overlap	Both FP and LS variants run significantly faster than the reference (both saturations are low)	Ambiguous absorption levels (moderate) indicating strong interdependencies

evaluate programs' resilience to OS noise. Tools like REFINE [11] use a similar approach to ours by injecting "internal" noise at the compiler level. However, they focus on evaluating resilience to soft errors, such as bitflips.

5.2   Comparison with MAQAO DECAN

The previous section highlights some similitude with MAQAO DECAN [3,13]. On the one hand, DECAN uses a subtractive approach (it removes instructions). On the other, our approach is additive (it adds instructions). This section aims to clarify the main differences. First, it should be noted that both approaches have close strategies to stress hardware resources: floating-point arithmetic can be stressed by any fp_[...] noise, while DECAN has a FP variant for that (keeping only FP instructions). Similarly, load/store is stressed through ll_ld64 or memory_ld64 noises, while DECAN has a LS variant. Despite these similarities, our approach is more fine-grained since one can inject any type and quantity of noise, whereas DECAN deletes all instructions of some given types. DECAN defines its *saturation* metric as

$$Sat(\text{VAR}) = \frac{T(\text{VAR})}{T(\text{REF})} \tag{3}$$

with $T(\text{VAR})$ and $T(\text{REF})$ designating the execution times of the modified and reference codes respectively. Therefore in DECAN, a lower metric (i.e., a variant running faster than the reference) signals that the removed resource was saturated, whereas in our method a lower absorption value indicates that only a few injected instructions are needed to degrade performance, thereby identifying a bottleneck.

Table 3 summarizes the expected behavior of DECAN versus our noise injection method with regard to their respective metrics. The limited overlap scenario of case 4) can not be fully understood by DECAN only, as it can arise as a consequence of two situations: either there are heavy dependencies between the FP and LS instructions flows, or the code has a shared microarchitectural bottleneck at the frontend level that disappears after removing instructions. Noise injection on the other hand is capable of distinguishing them. Because of our incremental approach, we do not alter the original pressure on dispatch ports, allowing us to distinguish both cases.

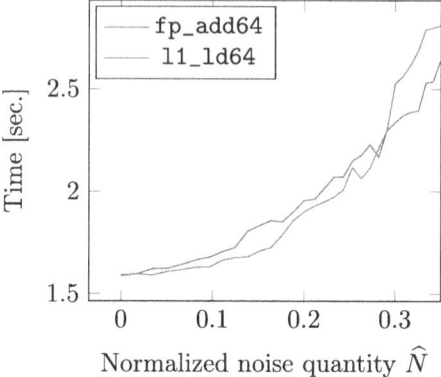

Fig. 6. `livermore_livermore:lloops.c_1351` kernel with FP arithmetic and L1 noise. It exhibits little to no absorption with similar behaviors between noise modes, hinting at a frontend bottleneck.

Experimental Comparison. This section illustrates the above discussion on an example picked from the LORE loop repository [8]. Because DECAN is available only on x86 (cf. the "Portability" criteria, mentioned in the previous section), this experiment was run on an Intel Xeon Gold 6254 CPU. Figure 6 demonstrates how combining our noise injection with DECAN's differential analysis enables fine-grained performance investigations. The function `livermore_livermore:lloops.c_1351` comprises two major dependency channels of FP computations using identical input values, resulting in a relatively high arithmetic intensity of 0.22 FP operations per loaded byte, as reported by CQA. At first glance, one might expect this code to be compute-bound. This expectation is supported by DECAN, which yields $Sat_{FP} = 0.81$ and $Sat_{LS} = 0.12$, suggesting an FP bottleneck. However, the absorption values tell a different story: as shown in the figure, both Abs^{rel}_{FP} and Abs^{rel}_{LS} approach zero with similar trends, a condition that might indicate full utilization and overlapping of the two resources (full saturation, case 3). DECAN, however, has already ruled out this full saturation scenario, implying instead a frontend bottleneck. Furthermore, MAQAO's CQA and UFS static code analyzers corroborate this interpretation by reporting the front end as a bottleneck —estimating an overhead of 0.75 cycles per iteration— although its subtractive approach caused DECAN to overlook it. Integrating differential analysis with noise injection uncovered a second critical bottleneck in the code. This case is particularly challenging because the overlapping bottleneck sources would have been missed by DECAN alone, potentially guiding programmers toward suboptimal optimizations.

6   Use Case: Analysis of the SPMXV Kernel

SPMXV[7], a reference benchmark for the European Processor Initiative (EPI), is a sparse matrix-vector multiplication algorithm using Compressed Sparse Row (CSR) storage. This section analyzes the SPMXV kernel on an Amazon Graviton 3 system in light of our methodology. Our goal is twofold: predict the efficiency of future memory systems (DDR versus HBM) and understand how varying the swapping probability q affects the dominant performance bottlenecks.

The SPMXV kernel accesses matrix elements in a regular, stride-1 fashion, but the vector elements are accessed indirectly based on the matrix's column indices. By tuning the swapping probability q, which randomly swaps non-zero elements within a row, we systematically increase the irregularity of these indirect accesses. This parameter is crucial since it reshapes the memory access pattern at the kernel's critical multiplication step. Figure 7 shows the performance and absorption levels for varying core numbers c and swap probabilities q. To cover a range of workloads, we consider two different matrices. **Matrix (a):** A small 134k × 134k matrix (44 MB) where, at $q = 0$, the entire dataset fits within the L2 and L3 caches. Here, the kernel exhibits excellent scaling with negligible absorption, indicating that performance is primarily limited by core-level

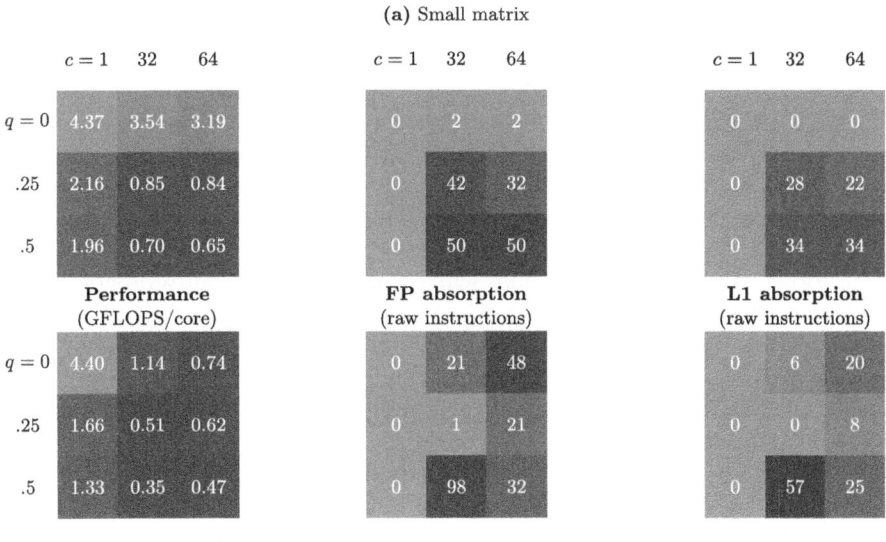

(a) Small matrix

(b) Large matrix

Fig. 7. Graviton 3 performance (measured in GFLOPS/core) and absorption (FP and L1) of SMPXV on small and large matrices, using varying numbers of cores c and swap probabilities q. In matrix (b), it seems counter-intuitive to see both absorptions drop specifically for $q = 0.25$. However, this corresponds to the tipping point between the dominance of bandwidth and latency effects.

---

[7] https://git-ce.rwth-aachen.de/hpc-public/epi-spmxv.

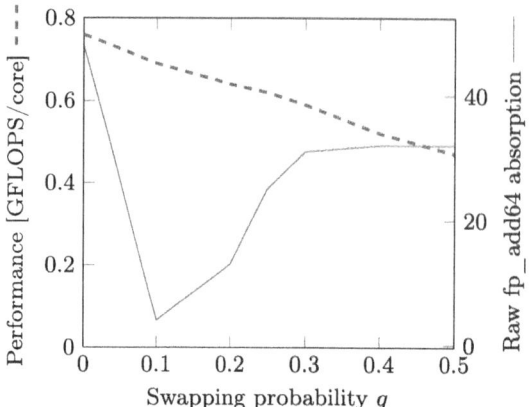

Fig. 8. Evolution of performance and absorption on large matrix (b) in function of swapping probability q (G3, 64 cores). While performance only decreases, absorption drops and increases again, indicating a transition between two different regimes (presumably bandwidth, then latency boundness).

Table 4. Performances of SPMXV on large matrix (b) running on Sapphire Rapids. HBM performance collapse when q increases, confirming that with higher values of q the benchmark becomes latency-bound.

Performances (GFLOPS/core)	DDR	HBM
$q = 0$	0.239	0.238
$q = 0.25$	0.233	0.066
$q = 0.5$	0.201	0.058

effects rather than by memory bandwidth. As q increases, performance degrades and the absorption metric rises, signaling a shift toward latency limitations. **Matrix (b):** A large 1346k × 1346k matrix (480 MB) that, even at $q = 0$, shows signs of a memory bandwidth bottleneck with nearly linear access patterns. As q increases, performance declines further; however, the absorption metric first drops and then increases again. This non-monotonic behavior reveals a transition from a bandwidth-bound regime to one dominated by latency effects, a nuance missed by traditional performance measures (Table 4). Figure 8 shows how FP absorption captures the two regimes while performance measures do not.

To further confirm our regime-transition hypothesis, we ran the large matrix on a Sapphire Rapids Intel Xeon Max 9460 system with both DDR and HBM memory. While performance at $q = 0$ was similar for both memory types, higher q values resulted in a dramatic collapse in performance on HBM. This supports our analysis: instead of fetching small amounts of data frequently, HBM retrieves large bursts of data at once, which has a severe penalty when random memory accesses become prevalent. Notably, conventional tools fall short in this analysis. DECAN, for example, struggles because it duplicates the innermost loop (which typically iterates only a few times) leading to unstable timing measurements. Static models (e.g. MAQAO CQA/UFS) do not apply here, as the kernel is dominated by cache and memory effects. Hardware counters yield multiple, often confusing metrics that obscure the underlying bottleneck. In contrast, our noise injection approach provides a single, intuitive absorption metric that was able to pinpoint the transition between bottleneck regimes. Noise injection captures the subtle interplay between bandwidth and latency limitations in the SPMXV kernel. This capability to detect hidden performance regimes underscores the value of our tool in scenarios where traditional methods are either inapplicable or overly complex to interpret and provide actionable insights to select between different memory families.

7   Conclusion and Future Work

Contributions. In this paper, we introduce a model-agnostic, instruction-accurate noise injection framework for bottleneck analysis. Our approach inserts carefully selected assembly instructions into performance-critical loops to probe specific hardware resources, namely the floating-point unit, L1 cache, and memory, to quantify the available noise through an absorption metric. By controlling the injected noise, we determine the precise point at which performance begins to degrade, allowing us to classify regions as compute-, bandwidth-, or latency-bound. We validate our framework on a suite of hardware benchmarks, demonstrating its effectiveness for comparing different systems and its advantages over methods that rely on oversimplified assumptions. By doing so, we notably show that fine-grained unicore optimizations are often overshadowed by the bandwidth or latency of memory accesses that appear in more representative multicore scenarios. Moreover, our application to the SPMXV benchmark shows that the absorption metric reliably captures transitions between bandwidth and latency limitations and offers practical insights for selecting between HBM or DDR memory.

Future Work. Future efforts will focus on the continuation of the presented experiments, as well as methodological refinements and tool enhancements. Notably, experiments on lat mem rd and SPMXV suggest that it is not easy to characterize how latency stalls can be exploited, and different access patterns seem to create complex behaviors that should be further explored. On the implementation side, we plan to streamline the user workflow by automating the identification of hot loops. This can be done by instrumenting all loop nests at the IR level so that users would no longer need to separately profile the target code. Methodologically, our framework permits the definition of additional noise modes; future studies will explore more complex and combined patterns and extend noise injection to target other resources, such as intermediate cache levels or I/O subsystems. Finally, selectively injecting noise into specific threads or processes during parallel communications may provide deeper insights into applications' resilience to desynchronization at both the thread and node levels. Source code of the LLVM injection plugin and information to reproduce this paper's experiments can be found on the following GitHub repository: https://www.github.com/sipearl/eris

Disclosure of Interests. The authors have no competing interests to declare that are relevant to the content of this article.

References

1. Abel, A., Reineke, J.: uiCA: accurate throughput prediction of basic blocks on recent Intel microarchitectures. In: ICS '22: 2022 International Conference on Supercomputing (2022). https://dl.acm.org/doi/pdf/10.1145/3524059.3532396
2. Ates, E., Zhang, Y., Aksar, B., Brandt, J., et al.: HPAS: An HPC performance anomaly suite for reproducing performance variations. In: Proc. of the 48th International Conference on Parallel Processing (2019). https://doi.org/10.1145/3337821.3337907
3. Bendifallah, Z.: Generalization of the Decremental Performance Analysis to Differential Analysis. Université de Versailles-Saint Quentin en Yvelines (Sep, Theses (2015)
4. Binkert, N., Beckmann, B., Black, G.: Reinhardt, other: the gem5 simulator. SIGARCH Comput. Archit. News (2011). https://doi.org/10.1145/2024716.2024718
5. Bruening, D., Amarasinghe, S.: Efficient, transparent, and comprehensive runtime code manipulation. Ph.D. Thesis, Massachusetts Institute of Technology (2004)
6. Carlson, T.E., Heirman, W., Eeckhout, L.: Sniper: exploring the level of abstraction for scalable and accurate parallel multi-core simulation. In: Proc. of 2011 International Conference for High Performance Computing, Networking, Storage and Analysis (2011). https://doi.org/10.1145/2063384.2063454
7. Charif-Rubial, A.S., Oseret, E., Noudohouenou, J., Jalby, W., et al.: CQA: a code quality analyzer tool at binary level. In: 2014 21st International Conference on High Performance Computing (HiPC) (2014). https://doi.org/10.1109/HiPC.2014.7116904
8. Chen, Z., Gong, Z., Szaday, J.J., Wong, D.C., et al.: Lore: A loop repository for the evaluation of compilers. In: 2017 IEEE International Symposium on Workload Characterization (2017). https://doi.org/10.1109/IISWC.2017.8167779
9. Fiedor, J., Vojnar, T.: Noise-based testing and analysis of multi-threaded C/C++ programs on the binary level (2012). https://doi.org/10.1145/2338967.2336813
10. Gavoille, C.: A Performance Projection Approach for Design-space Exploration on Arm HPC Environment. Université de Bordeaux, Theses (2024)
11. Georgakoudis, G., Laguna, I., Nikolopoulos, D.S., Schulz, M.: Refine: realistic fault injection via compiler-based instrumentation for accuracy, portability and speed. In: Proc. of the International Conference for High Performance Computing, Networking, Storage and Analysis (2017). https://doi.org/10.1145/3126908.3126972
12. Hofmann, J., Eitzinger, J., Fey, D.: Execution-cache-memory performance model: Introduction and validation (2017)
13. Koliaï, S., Bendifallah, Z., Tribalat, M., Valensi, C., et al.: Quantifying performance bottleneck cost through differential analysis. In: Proc. of the 27th International ACM Conference on International Conference on Supercomputing (2013). https://doi.org/10.1145/2464996.2465440
14. Lattner, C., Adve, V.: LLVM: a compilation framework for lifelong program analysis and transformation. In: International Symposium on Code Generation and Optimization, 2004. CGO 2004. (2004). https://doi.org/10.1109/CGO.2004.1281665
15. Luk, C.K., Cohn, R., Muth, R., Patil, H., et al.: Pin: building customized program analysis tools with dynamic instrumentation. In: Proc. of the 2005 ACM SIGPLAN Conference on Programming Language Design and Implementation (2005). https://doi.org/10.1145/1065010.1065034

16. Maiterth, M.: Scalability under a power bound using the gremlins framework. Tech. Rep. (2015). https://doi.org/10.2172/1183550

17. McCalpin, J.D.: Bandwidth limits in the intel Xeon max (sapphire rapids with HBM) processors. In: High Performance Computing: ISC High Performance 2023 International Workshops (2023). https://doi.org/10.1007/978-3-031-40843-4_30

18. Moseley, T., Vachharajani, N., Jalby, W.: Hardware performance monitoring for the rest of Us: a Position and Survey. In: 8th Network and Parallel Computing (2011).https://doi.org/10.1007/978-3-642-24403-2_23

19. Mucci, P.J., Browne, S., Deane, C., Ho, G.: PAPI: a portable interface to hardware performance counters (1999)

20. Nethercote, N., Seward, J.: Valgrind: a framework for heavyweight dynamic binary instrumentation. In: Proc. of the 28th ACM SIGPLAN Conference on Programming Language Design and Implementation (2007). https://doi.org/10.1145/1250734.1250746

21. de Oliveira Castro, P., Kashnikov, Y., Akel, C., Popov, M., et al.: Fine-grained benchmark subsetting for system selection. CGO '14 (2018). https://doi.org/10.1145/2544137.2544144

22. Palomares, V., Wong, D.C., Kuck, D.J., Jalby, W.: Evaluating out-of-order engine limitations using uop flow simulation. In: Proc. of the 9th International Workshop on Parallel Tools for High Performance Computing, September 2015 (2016)

23. Pompougnac, H., Dutilleul, A., Guillon, C., Derumigny, N., Rastello, F.: Performance bottlenecks detection through microarchitectural sensitivity (2024)

24. Tomasulo, R.M.: An efficient algorithm for exploiting multiple arithmetic units. IBM J. Res. Dev. (1967). https://doi.org/10.1147/rd.111.0025

25. Valensi, C.: A generic approach to the definition of low-level components for multi-architecture binary analysis. Ph.D. Thesis, Versailles-St Quentin En Yvelines (2014)

26. Wu, N., Xie, Y.: A survey of machine learning for computer architecture and systems. ACM Comput. Surv. (2022). https://doi.org/10.1145/3494523

27. Yasin, A.: A top-down method for performance analysis and counters architecture. In: 2014 IEEE International Symposium on Performance Analysis of Systems and Software (ISPASS) (2014). https://doi.org/10.1109/ISPASS.2014.6844459

Scalable Code Generation for RTL Simulation of Deep Learning Accelerators With MLIR

Jie Tong, Wan-Luan Lee, Umit Yusuf Ogras, and Tsung-Wei Huang[✉]

University of Wisconsin–Madison, Madison, WI, USA
{jtong36,wanluan.lee,uogras,tsung-wei.huang}@wisc.edu

Abstract. As deep learning accelerators scale in complexity, efficient Register Transfer Level (RTL) simulation becomes crucial for reducing the long runtime of hardware design and verification. However, existing RTL simulators struggle with high compilation overhead and slow simulation performance, particularly for large deep learning accelerator designs, where components are heavily reused and hierarchically structured. This inefficiency arises because existing simulators repeatedly regenerate and recompile redundant code, failing to leverage the structural parallelism inherent in deep learning accelerators. To address this challenge, we propose ScaleRTL, a scalable and unified code generation flow that automatically produces optimized parallel RTL simulation code for deep learning accelerators. Built on the MLIR infrastructure, ScaleRTL identifies repetitive design patterns, reduces code size and compilation time, and generates efficient simulation executables that exploit both CPU and GPU parallelism. Compared to state-of-the-art RTL simulators, ScaleRTL achieves a compilation speedup of three to five orders of magnitude and up to $15\times$ and $300\times$ simulation speedup on CPU and GPU, respectively.

Keywords: RTL simulation · MLIR · GPU code generation

1 Introduction

ASIC accelerators play a critical role in boosting the performance of deep learning backbone applications, such as GEMM, DNNs, and transformers in the modern AI industry [2]. To validate the functionality of a hardware design before physical implementation, *Register Transfer Level* (RTL) simulation plays a key role in regression testing, debugging, and design space exploration. However, with the rapidly increasing size and complexity of deep learning accelerators, RTL simulation has become significantly more time-consuming. For instance, recent research has reported that RTL simulation can take several hours to days to achieve coverage closure for validating a deep learning accelerator [10]. Thus, accelerating RTL simulation is critical for managing increasing design complexity and meeting short time-to-market demands in the accelerator market.

W. E. Nagel et al. (Eds.): Euro-Par 2025, LNCS 15900, pp. 24–37, 2026.
https://doi.org/10.1007/978-3-031-99854-6_2

To mitigate the runtime challenge of RTL simulation, researchers have proposed various parallel RTL simulation algorithms. For example, Verilator [12], a widely used open-source RTL simulator, transpiles Hardware Description Language (HDL) into C++ based on RTL abstract syntax trees (ASTs) and uses disjoint-set-based partitioning to enable multithreading. RepCut [15] converts RTL source code to FIRRTL [5] and introduces a replication-aided partitioning algorithm to reduce synchronization overhead in parallel simulation. Khronos [17] and BatchSim [13] parse RTL designs using MLIR and generate evaluation functions through LLVM IR. RTLflow [10], built atop Verilator, transpiles RTL code into CUDA for GPU execution but requires thousands of input stimuli to outperform CPU-based simulation. Despite improved performance, innovations of parallel RTL simulators have evolved largely in *isolation*, and many shareable components have been largely ignored. Consequently, designing new RTL simulation algorithms is extremely time-consuming and error-prone due to numerous software fragmentations, duplicated engineering efforts, and re-innovations of code optimizations.

On the other hand, prior research on parallel RTL simulation has primarily focused on generic RTL designs, such as digital circuits written in SystemVerilog or High-Level-Synthesis (HLS) languages. For a given RTL source, existing simulators flatten the entire design into an *RTL graph* [12], where nodes represent logic elements containing a set of instructions, and edges represent data dependency between nodes. Then, these simulators partition the RTL graph into dependent subgraphs for parallelism and generate evaluation functions. An *evaluation function* simulates the graph for a cycle by consuming inputs and propagating them through the graph. However, these approaches do not exploit structural information. Even when partitions consist of homogeneous logic elements, they still regenerate the same evaluation code for those elements. As shown in Fig. 1(a) and (b), when a systolic array contains explicitly duplicated processing elements (PEs), existing RTL simulators continue to regenerate evaluation functions for structurally identical partitions. This results in inefficiencies, as these simulators repeatedly generate and recompile redundant code instead of leveraging the structural parallelism inherent in deep learning accelerators. Prior works such as Verilator [12] and Dedup [16] offer limited support for deduplication in RTL simulation code generation. Verilator [12] focuses on small SystemVerilog statements and does not handle full structural components, while Dedup [16] targets multi-core SoC-style designs that emphasize heterogeneity and connectivity, rather than scalability of deep learning accelerators.

To tackle these challenges, we introduce *ScaleRTL*, a scalable code generation flow that automatically generates optimized parallel RTL simulators for deep learning accelerators. Figure 1(c) illustrates the ScaleRTL flow. Unlike prior works, ScaleRTL introduces a structural-parallelism-aware partitioning method that identifies structurally parallel components in a deep learning accelerator design and generates evaluation functions for these components. As a result, the generated and compiled evaluation functions can be reused during simulation, avoiding redundant code generation that traditional compilers and simulators

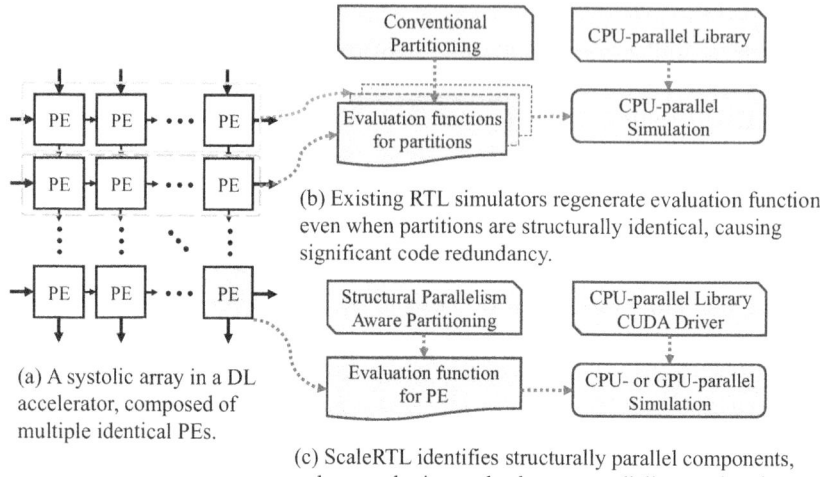

(a) A systolic array in a DL accelerator, composed of multiple identical PEs.

(b) Existing RTL simulators regenerate evaluation functions even when partitions are structurally identical, causing significant code redundancy.

(c) ScaleRTL identifies structurally parallel components, reduces code size, and enhances parallelism exploration.

Fig. 1. Comparison of existing RTL simulation approaches and ScaleRTL.

fail to eliminate. To unify the code generation flow for both CPU- and GPU-parallel simulation, ScaleRTL builds atop the *multi-level intermediate representation* (MLIR) project [7], which supports versatile and customizable dialects and IR transformations. For CPU-parallel simulation, ScaleRTL emits evaluation functions in LLVM IR, compiles them into object files, and links them with a simulation wrapper containing the CPU-parallel library. For GPU-parallel simulation, ScaleRTL emits evaluation functions in PTX format, loads the kernel using the CUDA driver, and executes it using CUDA Graph to reduce repetitive launch overhead. We summarize our technical contributions as follows:

- We introduce a scalable code generation flow that exploits structurally parallel components and eliminates redundant code in deep learning accelerator RTL simulation.
- We develop a unified code generation flow that automatically generates CPU- and GPU-parallel RTL simulators using MLIR, which enables simulation across different architectures.
- We integrate CUDA Graph to reduce kernel launch overhead, further accelerating GPU-parallel RTL simulation.

We evaluate ScaleRTL on a set of deep learning accelerator RTL designs. Compared to state-of-the-art RTL simulators, ScaleRTL achieves a compilation speedup of three to five orders of magnitude and up to 15× and 300× simulation speedup on CPU and GPU, respectively. To the best of our knowledge, ScaleRTL is one of the earliest research efforts to explore the application of MLIR and GPUs in deep learning accelerator RTL simulation. We open-sourced[1] ScaleRTL to support hardware design and EDA-inspired compiler research.

---

[1] https://github.com/TongJieGitHub/ScaleRTL.

2 Background and Motivation

2.1 RTL Simulation and Development Challenge

RTL design source code is typically written in hardware description languages (HDLs) like SystemVerilog or Chisel. To enable simulation, these designs are translated into C++ or LLVM IR, wrapped in a simulation framework, and compiled into an executable. Full-cycle simulators, such as Verilator [12], Khronos [17], and BatchSim [13], are widely used to capture cycle-accurate outputs and exploit parallelism. In these simulators, the RTL design is transformed into a directed graph, known as the *RTL graph*, where nodes represent logic elements and edges denote data dependencies. Simulating each cycle corresponds to evaluating this graph, where input values propagate through logic elements to produce outputs. This evaluation process is repeated thousands to millions of times to validate the design's functionality [10].

The typical approach to building an RTL simulator involves representing the RTL graph in an intermediate representation, applying optimizations, and generating efficient simulation code. For example, RTLflow [10] leverages an AST-based IR to capture high-level RTL information, partitions the IR into macro tasks, and schedules them across threads for parallel execution. Similar strategies have been adopted by existing simulators [3,4,9,12,13,15,17]. However, innovations in simulation IRs and parallel algorithms have evolved in isolation, leading to software fragmentation, duplicated engineering efforts, and redundant code optimization. This lack of modularity makes developing new RTL simulation algorithms highly time-consuming and error-prone.

2.2 MLIR

MLIR [7] is a novel infrastructure designed to simplify the building of new compiler components atop the LLVM project. Specifically, MLIR provides a rich set of composable abstractions, including operations, types, attributes, and regions, that empower developers to represent programs at multiple levels of abstraction. Developers can also define custom dialects and transformation methods to achieve unified code optimizations across diverse sources. To preserve designers' intent and capture high-level information, we build ScaleRTL on top of the popular FIRRTL [5] and CIRCT IRs, which directly models the RTL source. The primary benefit of using MLIR is its capability to offer deeper insights at the IR level compared to the source code, allowing for greater opportunities to exploit data parallelism.

3 ScaleRTL

Figure 2 illustrates the proposed ScaleRTL framework. At a high level, ScaleRTL compiles RTL source code (FIRRTL) into RTL simulation executables for both CPU and GPU targets. It is built atop MLIR [7] and CIRCT IR, which provide off-the-shelf dialects and compilation passes for general-purpose compilation and hardware modeling. ScaleRTL consists of three main components: Structural parallelism analysis and partitioning, CPU-parallel code generation, and GPU-parallel code generation. Additionally, we integrate CUDA Graph [8] to further enhance the performance of GPU-based simulation.

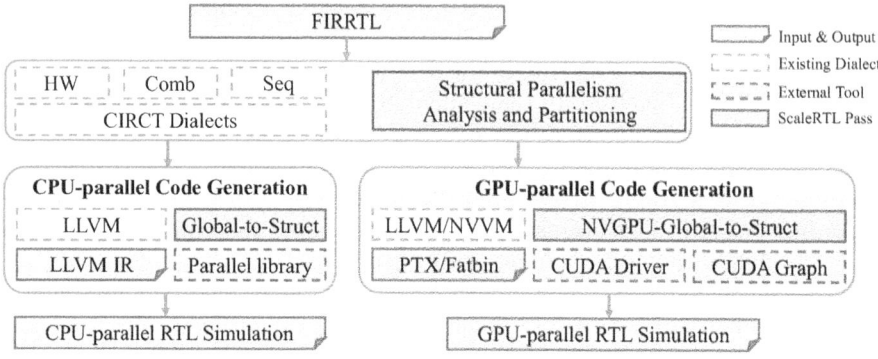

Fig. 2. Overview of ScaleRTL.

3.1   Structural Parallelism Analysis and Partitioning

The first step in RTL simulation code generation is to use CIRCT tools to convert the FIRRTL source design into CIRCT dialects, such as Comb, Seq, and HW. Listing 1 provides an example of a GEMM design written in the HW dialect.

```
module {
  hw.module @GEMM(%arg0: i32, %arg1: i32, ...) -> i32 {
    ...
    %PE.io_data_2_out_bits, ... = hw.instance "PE" @PE(
        clock: %clock: i1, reset: %reset: i1, ...) -> (
        io_data_2_out_bits: i16, ...)
    %PE_1.io_data_2_out_bits, ... = hw.instance "PE_1"
        @PE(clock: %clock: i1, reset: %reset: i1, ...) ->
        (io_data_2_out_bits: i16, ...)
    ...
  }
}
```

Listing 1. Example RTL Design in HW Dialect.

Unlike generic RTL designs, GEMM exhibits a highly homogeneous layout, where most components, such as PEs and interconnects, are repetitively instantiated. Additionally, from a hardware perspective, these subsequent lines of code are semantically parallel. Thus, we can leverage structural parallelism in deep learning accelerator designs to construct a highly parallel simulator. A key step in this process is to analyze the code, identify and count repetitive components, and extract and partition them from the original top-level design. To achieve this, we design a pass in MLIR that performs these analyses. This pass examines hardware module hierarchies in MLIR by computing direct and flattened instance counts within a `hw::InstanceGraph`. It identifies the top-level module using a heuristic, computes direct instance counts, and recursively derives flattened counts–estimating the occurrence of each module in a fully flattened design. The pass then returns these counts as a mapping. With this analysis, we can partition the original design into multiple instances and extract repetitive instances as separate modules.

3.2 CPU-Parallel Simulation Code Generation

After analyzing repetitive components and decomposing the deep learning RTL design into separate modules, we apply a set of IR transformations. This process converts the design from the HW dialect to the LLVM dialect, enabling efficient simulation of each module. An example of this MLIR-based transformation is shown in Listing 2.

```
1   module attributes {llvm.data_layout = ""} {
2     ...
3     llvm.mlir.global internal @shiftreg()  : i1
4     llvm.mlir.global linkonce_odr @clock()  : i1
5     llvm.mlir.global linkonce_odr @reset()  : i1
6     ...
7     llvm.func @PE() {
8       ...
9       %25 = llvm.mlir.addressof @shiftreg : !llvm.ptr<i1>
10      %25 = llvm.mlir.addressof @reset : !llvm.ptr<i1>
11      %26 = llvm.load %25 : !llvm.ptr<i1>
12      ...
13      llvm.store %7121, %10412 : !llvm.ptr<i16>
14      llvm.return
15    }
16  }
```

Listing 2. Example RTL evaluation code in LLVM Dialect.

In the LLVM dialect, signals and internal states are allocated as global variables in the data segment. When lowered to LLVM IR and further to an object file, the evaluation function `@PE` is bound to these global variables. For deep learning accelerators with thousands of PEs, this approach leads to compiling identical code thousands of times, resulting in a large executable with severe code redundancy. To address this, we propose a new simulation paradigm that decouples data from the evaluation function. Instead of binding to global variables, we define a struct that holds all signals and states in a header file and pass a pointer to this struct as an argument to the evaluation function. We refer to this as the `Global-to-Struct` pass.

Listing 3 provides an example where the evaluation function takes a struct pointer as an argument, with the struct defined in a header file. To correctly determine memory locations within the struct, we record the byte offsets of all data during the code generation phase. This ensures that the evaluation function can accurately access the converted addresses without error. By separating data from the function, we compile the evaluation function only once, while allocating multiple instances of the struct at runtime. This allows multiple instances of the function to be launched concurrently, reducing data hazards and synchronization overhead. With the function and header file prepared, we use a CPU-parallel library (OpenMP) to perform parallel simulation for each cycle.

```
1  // LLVM Dialect
2  module attributes {llvm.data_layout = ""} {
3    llvm.func @PE(%arg0: !llvm.ptr<i8>) {
4      %0 = llvm.mlir.constant(0 : i64) : i64
5      %1 = llvm.getelementptr %arg0[%0] : (!llvm.ptr<i8>,
           i64) -> !llvm.ptr<i8>
6      %2 = llvm.bitcast %1 : !llvm.ptr<i8> to !llvm.ptr<i16
           >
7      ...
8      llvm.return
9    }
10 }
11 // C++ header file
12 typedef struct EvalContext {
13   // Field 0 - Original global: @mem_ext - Byte offset: 0
14   char mem_ext[8];
15   ...
16 } EvalContext;
17 void PE(EvalContext* ctx);
```

Listing 3. Example RTL evaluation code in LLVM dialect with a struct pointer as an argument, and the corresponding struct defined in a C++ header file.

3.3 GPU-Parallel Simulation Code Generation

Figure 3 illustrates the GPU code generation process in ScaleRTL. Unlike prior work [14], which uses the GPU dialect to generate GPU-based simulation code, we found that relying solely on the provided GPU dialect limits control over kernel management and optimization from the host side. To address this challenge, we design a host-side CUDA code generator that automatically invokes CUDA driver APIs to load modules, manage memory, and launch kernels. On the device side, similar to CPU-parallel code generation, we generate the evaluation function in the LLVM dialect. Since GPU supports launching thousands of threads that execute the same kernel function in a SIMT fashion, we first allocate a chunk of device memory for structs. For each thread, it is essential to compute the correct address and offset to locate the corresponding struct that the thread will evaluate. To achieve this, we precompute and map each data address during code generation by calculating the base address of the struct and the offset of a given data field. Listing 4 shows an example evaluation kernel using the NVVM dialect, where thread and block IDs are retrieved and used to compute global memory addresses. Once the LLVM and NVVM dialects are generated, we use the LLVM static compiler llc to lower the code to PTX. To reduce the overhead of just-in-time (JIT) compilation, where PTX is offloaded to the GPU and compiled to SASS for the first execution, we use the PTX assembler ptxas to compile PTX into architecture-specific binaries and package them as a fatbin. This approach improves GPU performance while maintaining compatibility across different GPU architectures.

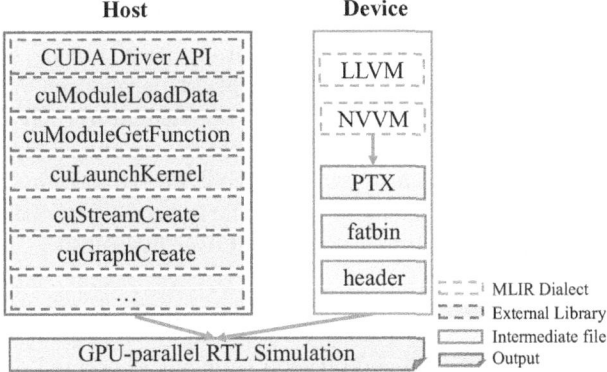

Fig. 3. GPU code generation flow in ScaleRTL.

```
 1  module attributes {llvm.data_layout = ""} {
 2    llvm.func @PE(%arg0: !llvm.ptr<i8>) {
 3        %0 = nvvm.read.ptx.sreg.tid.x : i32
 4        %1 = nvvm.read.ptx.sreg.ctaid.x : i32
 5        %2 = nvvm.read.ptx.sreg.ntid.x : i32
 6        ...
 7        %10 = llvm.getelementptr %arg0[%9] : (!llvm.ptr<i8
             >, i64) -> !llvm.ptr<i8>
 8        ...
 9        llvm.return
10    }
11  }
```

Listing 4. Example GPU-based RTL evaluation code in LLVM and NVVM Dielact.

RTL simulation typically runs for thousands of cycles. If we use stream-based execution, repetitive kernel launches will accumulate significant overhead. To mitigate this issue, we leverage CUDA Graph [8] to merge successive kernel calls into a single simulation task graph to reduce kernel launch overhead and improve GPU-based simulation performance.

4   Experimental Results

We evaluate the performance of ScaleRTL on four deep learning accelerator RTL designs: Conv2D [6], GEMM [6], Gemmini [2], and SIGMA [11]. Experiments are conducted on a 64-bit Linux machine with an Intel i5-13500 CPU and an NVIDIA RTX A4000 GPU. CPU code generation utilizes LLVM 17's `clang` and `llc` compilers, while GPU code generation employs CUDA Toolkit 12.6, targeting compute capability 8.6. All code is compiled with the `-O2` optimization flag. In the following sections, we refer to ScaleRTL with CPU code generation as *ScaleRTL$_C$* and ScaleRTL with GPU code generation as *ScaleRTL$_G$*. We consider Verilator [12], Khronos [17], and BatchSim [13] as baseline CPU-based simulators. Verilator and BatchSim are configured with 4 threads, while Khronos runs in single-threaded mode as it doesn't support parallelism. All simulations use a single input stimulus; therefore, we do not include the GPU-based RTL simulator RTLflow [10], as it is designed for batch-stimulus scenarios, which is a different scope of work. We also exclude ESSENT [1] and its successors [15, 16], as they encounter out-of-memory errors during code generation. To ensure consistency, all simulation results are averaged over five runs.

4.1   Code Generation and Compilation Results

Table 1 presents the end-to-end compilation time and generated executable size for Conv2D, GEMM, Gemmini, and SIGMA across different RTL simulators. The end-to-end compilation time includes the transformation from RTL source code to simulation code (C++ or LLVM IR) and the subsequent compilation and linking process to generate the final binary. For baseline simulators (Verilator, Khronos, and BatchSim), their inability to detect repetitive components leads to significant redundant code generation and compilation overhead. As the number of PEs increases, both compilation time and executable size grow proportionally. Even worse, compiling designs with thousands of PEs can take several hours to days, which could significantly hamper the turnaround time of hardware designs. In contrast, ScaleRTL$_C$ and ScaleRTL$_G$ complete compilation in just a few seconds, achieving up to 70,000× compilation speedup compared to the baselines. This improvement comes from ScaleRTL's ability to detect repetitive components in deep learning accelerator designs, generating evaluation functions only for PEs and other critical units, and invoking them with the corresponding data structures at runtime.

    To demonstrate the scalability of ScaleRTL's compilation time, Fig. 4 shows the compilation time of Gemmini and SIGMA on different RTL simulators as the number of PEs increases. The results clearly indicate that ScaleRTL achieves sublinear overhead growth, even as the design size increases exponentially. This trend highlights ScaleRTL's efficiency and scalability in handling deep learning accelerator RTL simulations, even for large-scale designs.

Table 1. Comparison of compilation time (T) and generated executable size for Conv2D, GEMM, Gemmini, and SIGMA among different RTL simulators.

Design	#PEs	Verilator		Khronos		BatshSim		ScaleRTL$_C$		ScaleRTL$_G$	
		T(s)	Size(MB)	T(s)	Size(MB)	T(s)	Size(MB)	T(s)	Size(MB)	T(s)	Size(MB)
Conv2D	2^7	9	0.4	6	0.2	3	0.6	2	0.08	4	1.1
	2^9	13	1.1	103	0.8	20	2.4	2	0.08	4	1.1
	2^{11}	39	3.8	2633	3.5	302	9.6	2	0.08	4	1.1
	2^{13}	163	15	41428	14	7796	39	2	0.08	4	1.1
GEMM	2^7	25	0.3	2	0.1	3	0.4	1	0.05	4	1.1
	2^9	48	0.9	27	0.5	11	2	1	0.05	4	1.1
	2^{11}	224	3.1	1135	2.3	139	7.7	1	0.05	4	1.1
	2^{13}	2053	12	72477	9	2751	31	1	0.05	4	1.1
Gemmini	2^5	83	2.3	118	0.7	38	0.8	25	0.3	4	1.2
	2^7	380	8.5	1897	3	592	3.3	33	0.3	5	1.2
	2^9	1621	34	26183	12	9439	13	33	0.3	5	1.2
	2^{11}	17893	132	357498	47	92673	52	32	0.3	5	1.2
SIGMA	2^5	41	0.7	7	0.2	9	0.3	3	0.1	8	1.4
	2^7	94	2.3	99	0.9	59	1.3	3	0.1	10	1.4
	2^9	443	8.7	1552	3.9	1053	5	3	0.1	10	1.4
	2^{11}	4920	35	22248	16	10969	20	4	0.1	11	1.4

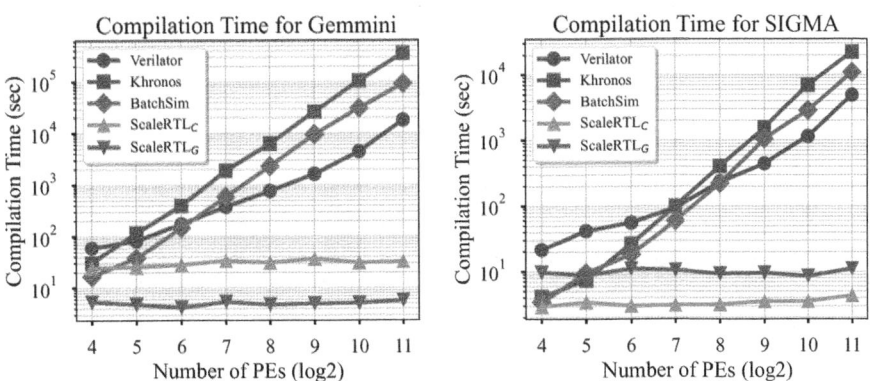

Fig. 4. Compilation time of Gemmini and SIGMA accelerators among different RTL simulators as the number of PEs increases exponentially.

4.2   Overall Simulation Performance Comparison

Figure 5 shows the simulation speedup of Conv2D, GEMM, Gemmini, and SIGMA on different RTL simulators, over the baseline Verilator. For small-scale designs, ScaleRTL$_C$ and ScaleRTL$_G$ do not outperform other simulators, as the baseline simulators can fit the RTL design within the cache and apply optimizations for higher efficiency. However, for mid-scale to large-scale designs,

ScaleRTL$_C$ and ScaleRTL$_G$ exhibit increasing speedup as the design size grows. This is because ScaleRTL$_C$ evaluates components by passing pointers to structs, improving data locality and reducing synchronization overhead. Additionally, ScaleRTL$_G$ employs a block of threads to evaluate identical components, which

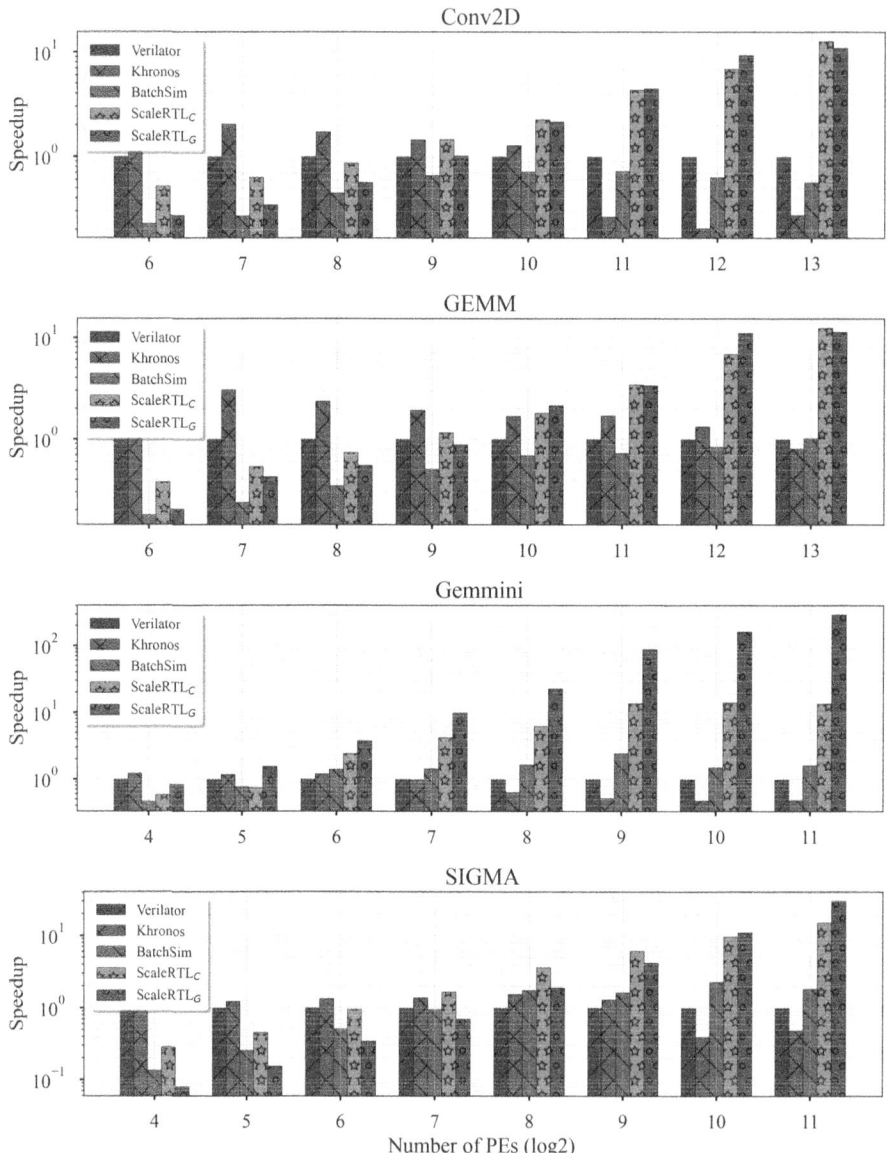

Fig. 5. Overall simulation speedup of Conv2D, GEMM, Gemmini, and SIGMA on different RTL simulators as the number of PEs increases exponentially. Speedup is measured relative to the baseline Verilator.

exploits highly parallel SIMT execution on the GPU. Consequently, ScaleRTL$_C$ achieves a 12×–15× speedup, and ScaleRTL$_G$ achieves an 11×–300× speedup at the largest design sizes.

4.3   CPU and GPU Simulation Runtime Analysis

Figure 6 shows the simulation time of Gemmini and SIGMA on different RTL simulators as the number of PEs increases exponentially. All CPU-based simulators, including ScaleRTL$_C$, exhibit linear or superlinear simulation growth because CPU threads are limited, and the total executed instructions scale proportionally with the design size. In contrast, ScaleRTL$_G$ exhibits sublinear growth. For instance, the simulation time for Gemmini remains around 0.1 s, even as the size increases from 2^4 to 2^{11}. This is because GPU consists of multiple streaming multiprocessors (SMs), each capable of managing thousands of threads. As a result, GPU-based simulation benefits from latency hiding through context switching and achieves higher concurrency. This underscores ScaleRTL's efficiency and scalability in deep learning accelerator RTL simulation, especially for large-scale designs.

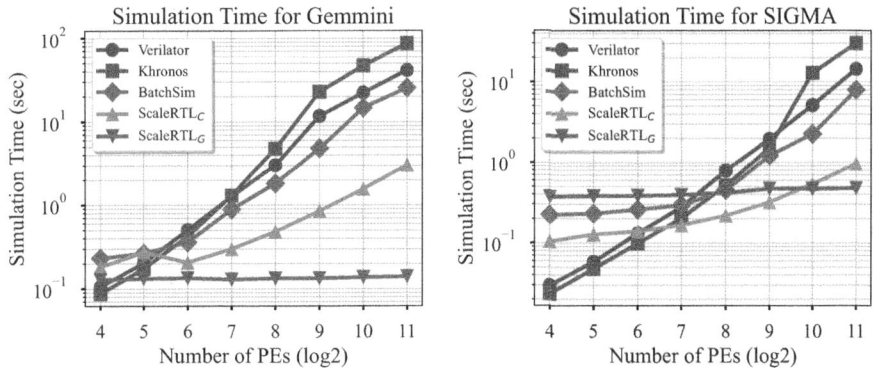

Fig. 6. Simulation time of Gemmini and SIGMA accelerators on different RTL simulators as the number of PEs increases exponentially.

4.4   Performance Result of CUDA Graph

Figure 7 compares the performance of CUDA Stream-based and CUDA Graph-based execution. Since GPU-based simulation involves consecutive kernel calls, connecting these kernels into a graph is crucial to reducing kernel launch overhead. Figure 7a and 7b illustrate simulation time over increasing cycles for both GPU-based approaches on the large Gemmini and SIGMA designs.

CUDA Graph-based simulation consistently outperforms stream-based simulation across all evaluated scenarios. For instance, in the Gemmini design, CUDA Graph-based simulation reduces execution time by a consistent 60 milliseconds compared to stream-based execution.

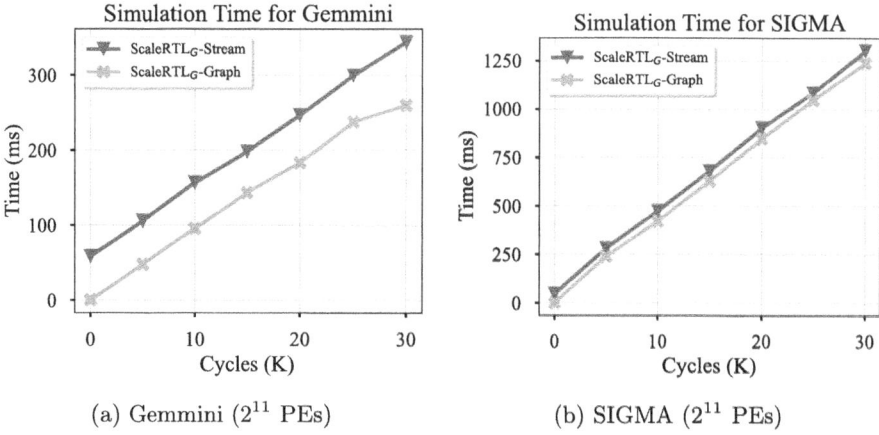

(a) Gemmini (2^{11} PEs)   (b) SIGMA (2^{11} PEs)

Fig. 7. Simulation results comparing CUDA Stream-based and CUDA Graph-based execution.

5   Conclusion

This paper presents *ScaleRTL*, a scalable and unified code generation flow that automatically produces optimized parallel RTL simulations for deep learning accelerators. Built atop the MLIR infrastructure, ScaleRTL identifies repetitive design patterns, reduces code size, accelerates compilation, and generates efficient parallel simulation executables for both CPU and GPU targets. Compared to state-of-the-art RTL simulators, ScaleRTL achieves a compilation speedup of three to five orders of magnitude and up to 15× and 300× simulation speedup on CPU and GPU, respectively. Future work includes integrating ScaleRTL with MLIR and CIRCT to support the compiler community in exploring RTL simulation research.

Acknowledgments. This project is supported by NSF grants 2235276, 2349144, 2349143, 2349582, and 2349141.

Disclosure of Interests. The authors have no competing interests to declare that are relevant to the content of this article.

References

1. Beamer, S., Donofrio, D.: Efficiently exploiting low activity factors to accelerate RTL simulation. In: 2020 57th ACM/IEEE DAC, pp. 1–6. IEEE (2020)
2. Genc, H., et al.: Gemmini: enabling systematic deep-learning architecture evaluation via full-stack integration. In: DAC 2021, pp. 769–774. IEEE (2021)
3. Huang, T.W., Lin, D.L., Lin, C.X., Lin, Y.: TaskFlow: a lightweight parallel and heterogeneous task graph computing system. IEEE Trans. Parallel Distr. Syst. **33**(6) (TPDS) (2022)
4. Huang, T.W., Wong, M.: OpenTimer: a high-performance timing analysis tool. In: IEEE/ACM International Conference on Computer-Aided Design (ICCAD) (2015)
5. Izraelevitz, A., et al.: Reusability is FIRRTL ground: hardware construction languages, compiler frameworks, and transformations. In: 2017 IEEE/ACM International Conference on Computer-Aided Design (ICCAD), pp. 209–216. IEEE (2017)
6. Jia, L., Luo, Z., Lu, L., Liang, Y.: TensorLib: a spatial accelerator generation framework for tensor algebra. In: 2021 58th ACM/IEEE Design Automation Conference (DAC), pp. 865–870. IEEE (2021)
7. Lattner, C., et al.: MLIR: scaling compiler infrastructure for domain specific computation. In: CGO 2021, pp. 2–14. IEEE (2021)
8. Lin, D.L., Huang, T.W.: Efficient GPU computation using task graph parallelism. In: European Conference on Parallel and Distributed Computing (Euro-Par) (2021)
9. Lin, D.L., Huang, T.W., Miguel, J.S., Ogras, U.: TaroRTL: accelerating RTL simulation using coroutine-based heterogeneous task graph scheduling. In: Euro-Par 2024 (2024)
10. Lin, D.L., Ren, H., Zhang, Y., Khailany, B., Huang, T.W.: From RTL to CUDA: a GPU acceleration flow for RTL simulation with batch stimulus. In: ACM International Conference on Parallel Processing (ICPP) (2022)
11. Qin, E., et al.: SIGMA: a sparse and irregular GEMM accelerator with flexible interconnects for DNN training. In: 2020 IEEE International Symposium on High Performance Computer Architecture (HPCA), pp. 58–70. IEEE (2020)
12. Snyder, W.: Verilator: open simulation goes multithreaded. In: ORConf (2018)
13. Tong, J., Chang, L., Ogras, U.Y., Huang, T.W.: BatchSim: parallel RTL simulation using inter-cycle batching and task graph parallelism. In: 2024 IEEE Computer Society Annual Symposium on VLSI (ISVLSI), pp. 789–793. IEEE (2024)
14. Trevisan Jost, T., Thangamani, A., Colin, R., Loechner, V., Genaud, S., Bramas, B.: GPU code generation of cardiac electrophysiology simulation with MLIR. In: European Conference on Parallel Processing, pp. 549–563. Springer (2023)
15. Wang, H., Beamer, S.: RepCut: superlinear parallel RTL simulation with replication-aided partitioning. In: Proceedings of the 28th ACM International Conference on ASPLOS, vol. 3, pp. 572–585 (2023)
16. Wang, H., Nijssen, T., Beamer, S.: Don't repeat yourself! coarse-grained circuit deduplication to accelerate RTL simulation. In: Proceedings of the 29th ACM International Conference on Architectural Support for Programming Languages and Operating Systems, vol. 4, pp. 79–93 (2024)
17. Zhou, K., Liang, Y., Lin, Y., Wang, R., Huang, R.: Khronos: fusing memory access for improved hardware RTL simulation. In: Proceedings of the 56th Annual IEEE/ACM International Symposium on Microarchitecture, pp. 180–193 (2023)

Scheduling Task and Data Parallelism in Array Languages with Work Assisting

Ivo Gabe de Wolff$^{(\boxtimes)}$, David van Balen ,
and Gabriele K. Keller

Utrecht University, Utrecht, Netherlands
i.g.dewolff@uu.nl

Abstract. High level languages for parallelism need to be performant on a wide range of workloads: they may be data-parallel and/or task-parallel, as well as regular or irregular. Scheduling, which is implemented via an interaction between the runtime system and the generated code, has a significant impact on the performance and scalability of these languages. In this paper, we demonstrate the integration of Work Assisting, our dynamic scheduler combining task-parallel and data-parallel schedulers, in combinator-based parallel array languages. These languages require fusion for high performance, and often feature scans to support irregular computations. Chained scans, the fastest parallel scans in our experiments, require a data-parallel scheduler as provided by Work Assisting. We show how code can be generated with support for fusion and chained scans, which can also fuse better than classic three-phase scans. We present the integration of Work Assisting into an actual compiler and runtime system of a such a language, Accelerate, and evaluate its performance in this context for a range of applications.

Keywords: Functional array languages · Scheduling · Code generation

1 Introduction

Functional parallel array languages, such as APL [16], DaCe [31], Futhark [15], SaC [14], Lift [26] and Accelerate [20], aim at providing the programmer with a convenient programming model, which provides portability over a range of architectures, while still achieving performance which is as close to hand-optimized, architecture specific implementations as possible [28]. However, in contrast to customized, highly specialized solutions, the compilers and runtimes of these high-level languages cannot assume much about a program. They therefore have to employ strategies which work well on a large range of programs, which is especially the case for scheduling: the system should distribute the parallel workload efficiently, whether the program contains task and/or data parallelism, as well as whether it is regular or irregular. In parallel languages, scheduling is implemented via an interaction between the runtime system and the generated code.

In the context of code generation, compilers for array based functional languages have to solve two concrete problems: they have to fuse array traversals,

© The Author(s), under exclusive license to Springer Nature Switzerland AG 2026
W. E. Nagel et al. (Eds.): Euro-Par 2025, LNCS 15900, pp. 38–52, 2026.
https://doi.org/10.1007/978-3-031-99854-6_3

often expressed in the high-level language via higher-order operations, such as maps, scan, folds and permutations, to generate the optimal number of loops. Furthermore, efficient code has to be generated for the different communication patterns, even when they are fused with other patterns. Among these, scans, also known as generalised prefix sums, are the most challenging. As scans are used extensively when expressing irregular parallel algorithms in array languages, an efficient parallel implementation for scans is particularily important.

Given the importance of scheduling, it is not surprising that a wide range of strategies have been proposed, and the choice of the strategy influences which parallel algorithms can be expressed in the language. Work stealing [7] or variants of it are commonly used in parallel languages and libraries, for instance in OneTBB [24], Halide [23] and Manticore [13]. It is a task-parallel scheduling strategy, but it can also be used for data parallel applications by splitting a data-parallel computation in multiple tasks [27]. However, some data-parallel algorithms require a dedicated data-parallel scheduler; for instance, chained scans [11,12,21] require that blocks of an array are distributed or claimed in a specific order. Another reason why explicit data-parallel schedulers might be chosen is that they potentially have smaller overhead than task-parallel schedulers for purely data-parallel computations. For this reason, some languages and libraries, including SaC [14] and early versions of OpenMP [1], have thus chosen to use a data-parallel scheduler, and those cannot exploit task parallelism. Work Assisting [9] is a scheduler for mixed data and task parallelism: it uses a task-parallel scheduler for task parallelism, and a data-parallel scheduler within a data-parallel subcomputation.

In earlier work [9], we have introduced the Work Assisting scheduler and evaluated its performance in stand-alone benchmarks. Since then, we implemented Work Assisting in the compiler of Accelerate to futher investigate the integration of Work Assisting with code generation, fusion, and other optimizations in a compiler, and to perform benchmarks on larger programs. We report on these findings in this paper; we discuss how suitable Work Assisting is as scheduling strategy for a parallel array language, and how it interacts with code generation with fusion. We compare the performance of Accelerate with Work Assisting to that of Futhark [15], a performant stand-alone parallel language with a very similar programming model, as well as hand-optimized, base-line implementations. The implementation we present in this paper is able to:

- handle task and data parallelism,
- support parallel chained scans [11,12,21],
- support aggresive fusion [29], and
- perform no dynamic allocations for scheduling (except for the task queue).

We discuss how these together help to achieve the desired high performance for data parallel array languages.

The remainder of this paper is structured as follows. After laying a background on parallel array languages in Sect. 2, we introduce the Work Assisting runtime in Sect. 3. We elaborate on code generation for the data-parallel subcomputations, which we call *kernels* following GPU terminology, in Sect. 4. We present benchmarks in Sect. 5.

2   Preliminaries

There are several kinds of parallelism in functional array programming. Each of these require special handling and are supported to various degrees in the different languages. First, we have the array operations which operate in parallel over the values of the array. We call the parallelism within an array operation *data parallelism*. These operations may be simple maps of sequential operations over one-dimensional or multi-dimensional arrays, or operations that require some additional communication like folds, scans or permutations. Compilers typically require that array operations are not started from within other array operations, either by language design or a compiler pass [4].

Due to the absence of side-effects, purely functional languages in general expose another potential source of parallelism: computations which have no data dependency can be evaluated in parallel, without affecting the result. We call the parallelism between array operations *task parallelism*. This implicit task parallelism can be exploited by the compiler to reduce the overhead of data-parallel operations like scans that do not scale linearly, or keep processors busy when the explicit data parallelism available is not sufficient. Since Accelerate is embedded in Haskell, task parallelism in Accelerate may also occur when a Haskell program runs multiple Accelerate programs.

Since only the outer level of the program may contain task parallelism, acting as a wrapper around data-parallel computations, we can compile the task-parallel and data-parallel parts of the program separately. We will call the compiled data-parallel computations *kernels*, as our model is similar to the GPU model.

2.1   Fusion

Fusion, a program transformation which combines several traversals of a data structure, is an important optimization to reduce the memory footprint and execution time of a program. This is especially important for functional array languages, as they advocate constructing a program using small building blocks like parallel maps, folds and scans. Unfortunately, in the parallel context, the problem is more difficult, since the parallel structure needs to be maintained. We can split fusion into two subproblems: deciding what operations should be fused, and generating code for a fused set of operations. Accelerate uses an Integer Linear Programming formulation for the former [29]. In this paper we only focus on the latter and present how we generate code for a list of operations that are fused together. There are two relevant consequences of Accelerate's fusion system for this paper. Firstly, operations may be *vertically fused*, in which case the corresponding array is not manifest in memory. Instead, a produced value is stored in a scalar variable and is directly consumed by another array operation. Secondly, it is not practical to design specialized skeletons or templates for some of the combinators, as Accelerate previously did [8]. Instead, we need a single template that we can instantiate to express any combination of array operations.

2.2 Chained Scans

Scans, generalized prefix sums, are an important parallel primitive for many, especially irregular, applications. At each index, they compute the combined value of all prior values. We found that chained scans [12,21], whereas originally designed for GPUs, are also the fastest scans on multi-core CPUs [11]. These scans operate with a single traversal over the data, in contrast to the more commonly used reduce-then-scan. We explain the working of chained scans together with the code we generate for them in Sect. 4.2.

Scans are commonly used for compaction or filtering, which can be implemented using a scan followed by a scatter (permute), as shown in Listing 1. Using chained scans and a sufficiently flexible fusion system, a filter can be implemented using a single traversal over the input [21]. To enable this, we must allocate an array with the size of the input for the output, and shrink it to the correct size later, as we do not know the output size in advance.

3   Work Assisting Runtime

The core idea behind our Work Assisting scheduler [9] is to primarily use the task-parallel scheduler. Only when the system runs out of tasks, threads try to *assist* in a kernel (a data-parallel computation) of another thread. These kernels can be found via a shared array called *activities*, where threads share the kernel they are currently working on. This array has one slot per thread. Scheduling within a kernel happens with a dynamic data-parallel scheduler. In the current implementation of Accelerate, we use self scheduling [17] with atomic fetch-and-add: when a thread needs to claim new work within a data-parallel kernel, it does so by atomically incrementing a shared counter for that kernel.

Most important types and definitions of the runtime can be found in Listing 2.

We introduced Work Assisting in [9]. However, the Accelerate implementation which we describe and evaluate here differs in a few minor ways: In the original description, a task can be a data-parallel task, while a task in the Accelerate

---

Listing 1. Simplified definition of filter, which can be fused into a single kernel except for the shrink at the end.

```
function filter(predicate, input)
    ps ← map(\x → if predicate x then 1 else 0, input)
    (destination, output_size) ← scanl'((+), 0, ps)
    ws ← zipWith3(\x p d → if p then Just (d, x) else Nothing, input, ps, destination)
    output ← Uninitialized array with the same size as input
    scatter(output, ws)
    return shrink(output, output_size)
```

implementation *returns* a data-parallel computation, which we call a *kernel*. We handle *EmptySignal* outside of the work function in the runtime, to simplify code generation. Furthermore, we do not store *work_size* explicitly; instead it is computed in the work function and only available within that function. The finish function is not explicitly stored; it is now handled by calling the work function with a magic value and by storing a continuation task in the kernel. We changed *work_index* and *work_size* to 64-bit integers.

3.1   Program as a Coroutine

Array languages have a clear separation between the data-parallel parts of the program (kernels) and the control flow between them. The outer level of a program consists of the control flow and administrative work, and may contain task parallelism. To support task parallelism in this outer level, we compile this into a coroutine [22], a function that can be suspended during its execution. We suspend the coroutine when we launch a kernel and the execution of the coroutine is resumed after the kernel is finished. It is also suspended when we need to synchronize with another part of the program, e.g. when we need to join the execution after a fork.

Our implementation is similar to the stackless coroutines in for instance Rust [19]. The variables of the coroutine are stored in an object on the heap which we call a Program (Listing 2). This object also contains a pointer to the function of the program (the *program function*) and a reference count.

When suspending the function, the system marks where (at which state or location in the program) the function should resume. Whereas this is typically stored in the object, Program in our case, we store it outside of that object, in a task. A task is then a pointer to a program and a location in that program. This allows the coroutine to be in multiple states concurrently. This allows us to implement *fork* without allocations: a fork is implemented by scheduling a task of the same program, at a different location. The coroutine is compiled into the program function and takes the Program and the location in the program as arguments.

Listing 2. Core Types for the Runtime System

```
struct Workers
    int thread_count;
    TaskScheduler* task_scheduler;
    KernelLaunch* activities;
struct Program
    int reference_count;
    ProgramFunction run;
    data;     // Variables of the program

struct Task
    Program* program;
    int location;
function schedule(Workers*, Task)
function schedule_after(Workers*,
    Task, Signal, SignalWaiter)
function signal_resolve(Workers*,
    Signal)

type ProgramFunction
    (Workers*, int thread_index, Program*, int location) → KernelLaunch*
```

Synchronization within a program is implemented using a Signal, which is similar to a future or promise in other languages. Tasks may wait on a signal, until another task resolves the signal. A signal can be resolved once and does not contain an actual value. Waiting tasks are stored in a concurrent linked list of SignalWaiter objects. These objects are preallocated in the program for each point in the program where it waits on a signal.

3.2   Kernels

When a program needs to execute a data-parallel computation, it returns an object describing the launch of that kernel. The program object contains a pre-allocated kernel launch object for each kernel in the program, and we can thus start a kernel without memory allocations.

The kernel launch object contains a fixed form header, and the input and output arrays of this kernel and their sizes. If the operations in the kernel require it, we can also allocate additional memory called *kernel memory* in that object, for instance for communication between threads for a scan.

In the header, we store a *kernel function*, the function that all threads working on this kernel should call. As its arguments, this function gets a pointer to the kernel launch object and an index *first_index*, denoting the index of the tile we should first work on. The header also contains the task which could be executed after the kernel.

The work within a kernel is split in tiles. Argument *first_index* is the index of the tile that this thread should work on first. The Work Assisting runtime has already claimed this tile. Later tiles are claimed by the work function itself via atomic fetch-and-add. The function is also called with two magic values. It is called with *first_index* $= -1$ before the parallel work of this kernel starts, where it may initialize kernel memory. Finally, it is called with *first_index* $= -2$ after the parallel work of the kernel, for instance to write the result of a fold to the output array when all threads have finished.

4   Code Generation for Data Parallelism

Now that we have seen the runtime system and the method of generating code for the task-parallel part of the program, we can focus on the data-parallel kernels in the program. The work of a kernel is scheduled via tiles: the workload is split into tiles, which are claimed one by one via atomic fetch-and-add. Whereas some data-parallel combinators are more naturally implemented by splitting the load in a fixed number of tiles, and some in fixed size tiles, we always use fixed size tiles for uniformity. This way we can compile all the combinators into one generic form. This is needed for fusion, as any combinator can be fused with any other combinator.

Fixed size tiles are required for chained scans [12], as they expect that the data of a tile fits in the cache. The structure of our generated code is mainly dictated by our support for chained scans. We first present this general form, and then explain how the array combinators can be compiled into this form.

4.1 Generic Format for Code Generation

We present the generic structure into which we can compile any array operation in Listing 3. The highlighted lines are the places where operation specific code can be inserted. We first explain this generic structure, and then show how how concrete operations emit code at what parts of this structure in Sect. 4.2.

Listing 3. Template for a kernel, with tile size 2048.

When compiling an array combinator, code may be placed at the highlighted positions.

```
struct Arg
    KernelFunction* work_function; Program* program; int program_location;
    int active_threads; int work_index;
    A: Declare kernel memory
function kernel(Arg* arg, int first_index)
    tile_count ← (arg→n + 2047)/2048
    if first_index = −1 then
        B: Initialize kernel memory
        return tile_count > 1
    else if first_index = −2 then
        C: Finalize kernel
        return
    previous_idx ← −1; sequential ← true; tile_idx ← first_index
    D: Thread initialization
    while tile_idx < tile_count do
        if tile_idx ≠ previous_idx + 1 then sequential ← false
        start ← tile_idx * 2048; end ← min(start + 2048, arg→n)
        if sequential then
            E': Before tile loop
            for i in start...end do    // Tile loop
                F': Body of tile loop
            G': After tile loop
        else
            E: Before tile loop
            for i in start...end do    // Tile loop
                F: Body of tile loop
            G: After tile loop
            for i in start...end do    // Tile loop
                H: Body of next tile loop
        previous_idx ← tile_idx
        tile_idx ← atomic_fetch_add(&arg→work_index, 1)
    I: Thread finalization
```

A kernel is compiled into a function and an accompanying object that contains the data (references to the input and output of the kernel and their sizes) and administrative information for the kernel. Array combinators may also reserve space in this object (label **A**). We call this *kernel memory*, which may be used for communication between the threads working on this kernel.

Before and after the parallel work of a kernel, the kernel function is called to initialize the launch (with $first\_index = -1$) and finalize the kernel ($first\_index = -2$). Array combinators can emit initialization and finalization code respectively at label **B** and **C**. A fold for instance uses this to set the reduced value to zero at **B** and write the final result to the output at **C**. After initialization, a thread returns whether the kernel may be executed in parallel. If the input is small, the kernel function will decide to not run the work in parallel.

To perform the parallel work, multiple threads will call the work function. Array combinators may place code to initialize a thread at label **D**. Afterwards a thread will repeatedly handle a tile. It first works on tile $first\_index$, claimed by the Work Assisting runtime, and later claims tiles using atomic fetch-and-add. Within that while loop, we traverse the data in that tile in a *tile loop*. We can place code before (**E**), within (**F**) and after the tile loop (**G**). We allow combinators to insert specialized code for sequential execution (**E'**, **F'** and **G'**). As long as a thread is the only thread to work on a kernel, it will operate in a sequential mode, and as soon as another thread also works on this kernel, it will switch to the parallel mode. Only scans generate different code, as they require two tile loops in the parallel mode. We thus allow combinators to also generate code in a later tile loop (**H**). Finally, combinators may emit code to finalize a thread (**I**). For a commutative fold, we use this to let a thread contribute its locally reduced value to the global value.

All operations in a kernel are compiled to this format, and are placed together in one kernel. If an operation declares that it needs a second tile loop (by generating code at label **H**), later operations will also be placed in that tile loop. If a kernel contains multiple of those operations, it will thus have more than two tile loops. If a kernel only has a single tile loop in the parallel mode, the single-threaded mode is discarded, as it would already not have single-threaded overhead.

4.2   Generating Code in the Generic Format

To illustrate that the array combinators in Accelerate can be compiled to this format, we demonstrate this translation for several combinators. First, embarrassingly parallel combinators like map and generate only need to generate code at labels **F** and **F'**.

Scans Scans are the most complicated combinators. We show the generated code corresponding with $(ys, z) = $ scanl' $(+)$ 0 xs in Listing 4, which is an exclusive left-to-right scan where the prefix values of xs are stored in ys, and the total reduced value in z. Scans require synchronization between the threads, for which they need two variables in kernel memory, defined at label **A** and initialized at label **B**. Variable *scan_index* denotes the index of the tile that should next be incorporated in the prefix value in *scan_prefix*.

If we ignore the special sequential mode for sequential execution, the scan requires two tile loops to handle a tile of the input. In the first tile loop, it reduces the values in the tile to an aggregate (**E** and **F**). It then waits for its turn to update the *scan_prefix* (**G**). With the found prefix value, it then performs a scan over this tile in another tile loop (**H**). This chained scan thus needs to block between the two tile loops, but in return it gets better memory performance as the values of *xs* of this tile are likely to still be in cache in the second tile loop. The chained scan may be changed to a chained scan *with decoupled look-back* [21], to reduce the impact of the synchronization at label **G**. We are also considering to implement that in Accelerate.

To assure that the parallel chained scan executed on a single core performs as fast a sequential scan, we add a special sequential mode [11]. This is important when the program also contains task parallelism, as it then might be sufficient to only exploit task parallelism. Variable *sequential* tracks whether this was the only thread working on the scan. The sequential mode operates with one tile loop, where it can directly execute the scan (labels **E'**, **F'** and **G'**).

Fold Folds, or reductions, can be compiled in two ways. Since it is common that the operator of a fold is commutative, we have a specialized implementation of folds for commutative folds. Note that it is always required that the operator is associative for parallel execution, but commutativity is not required.

Listing 4. Code Generation for Exclusive Scan, $(ys, z) = \text{scanl'} (\oplus) 0 \; xs$

A int *scan_prefix*; int *scan_index*;
B $arg{\rightarrow}scan\_prefix \leftarrow 0$
  $arg{\rightarrow}scan\_index \leftarrow 0$
C $*(arg{\rightarrow}z) \leftarrow arg{\rightarrow}scan\_prefix$
E' $prefix \leftarrow arg{\rightarrow}scan\_prefix$
F' $arg{\rightarrow}ys[i] \leftarrow prefix$
  $prefix \leftarrow prefix \oplus arg{\rightarrow}xs[i]$
G' $arg{\rightarrow}scan\_prefix \leftarrow prefix$
  $arg{\rightarrow}index \leftarrow tile\_idx + 1$

E $aggregate \leftarrow 0$
F $aggregate \leftarrow aggregate \oplus arg{\rightarrow}xs[i]$
G while $arg{\rightarrow}scan\_index \neq tile\_idx$ do
  | // Wait
  $prefix \leftarrow arg{\rightarrow}scan\_prefix$
  $arg{\rightarrow}scan\_prefix \leftarrow prefix \oplus aggregate$
  $arg{\rightarrow}scan\_index \leftarrow tile\_idx + 1$
H $arg{\rightarrow}ys[i] \leftarrow prefix$
  $prefix \leftarrow prefix \oplus arg{\rightarrow}xs[i]$

Listing 5. Code Generation for Commutative Fold, $y = \text{fold} (\oplus) 0 \; xs$

A int *fold_lock*;
  int *fold_accumulator*;
B $arg{\rightarrow}fold\_lock \leftarrow 0$
  $arg{\rightarrow}fold\_accumulator \leftarrow 0$
I while atomic_swap($\& arg{\rightarrow}fold\_lock, 1) \neq 0$ do
  | // Wait
  $arg{\rightarrow}fold\_accumulator \leftarrow arg{\rightarrow}fold\_accumulator \oplus local$
  $arg{\rightarrow}fold\_lock \leftarrow 0$

C $*(arg{\rightarrow}y) \leftarrow arg{\rightarrow}fold\_accumulator$
D $local \leftarrow 0$
F $local \leftarrow local \oplus arg{\rightarrow}xs[i]$
F' $local \leftarrow local \oplus arg{\rightarrow}xs[i]$

If the operator of a fold is not (known to be) commutative, we generate code via the same pattern as the code of parallel scans. This *chained fold* has more overhead than two-step folds due to the additional synchronizations, but it does allow us to generate code in the generic format. When we implement scans with a decoupled look-back [21], we also expect to lower the overhead of folds as well.

The generated code of a commutative fold is shown in Listing 5. Since the operator is commutative, we may compute a local result per thread and at the end of the work for this thread, incorporate that local result in the global result (**I**). This happens once per thread instead of once per tile. The global value is stored in kernel memory, together with a lock (**A**).

4.3   Fused Away Arrays

By fusion, some arrays do not have to be fully manifest in memory. Instead, we introduce local variables for these arrays that either contain a single value or one value per element of a tile, depending on whether the array is used in multiple tile loops. We introduce this at **D** using *alloca*, to allocate them on the stack. LLVM may change this stack allocation to a variable stored in a register.

5   Benchmarks

To investigate the performance of Accelerate with the new Work Assisting scheduler and support for chained scans, we performed benchmarks on various applications taken from CFAL, Comparing Functional Parallel Array Languages [28]. We compare the performance of Accelerate with a reference implementation not in an array language, and Futhark, a stand-alone functional parallel array language. We ran the benchmarks on a machine with an AMD 2950X processor (16 cores, 32 threads) with 32GB of RAM on Ubuntu 22.04.

5.1   N-Body and MultiGrid

We first briefly discuss two benchmarks of CFAL, before we discuss a detailed case study on the Quickhull benchmark. *N-body* is a naive implementation of n-body simulation and *MultiGrid* (MG) computes a solution to a differential equation. The latter was taken from the NAS benchmarks [3]. The implementations are available online[1] and we present the results in Table 1.

The n-body benchmarks show that the Work Assisting scheduler scales well in Accelerate. All languages scale well in the medium and large input, but Futhark and the OpenMP implementation scale worse on the small input. Scheduling is more difficult here, as there is less data parallelism available. Accelerate scales better than the other implementations here.

The OpenMP reference implementation of MG in Fortran is highly specialized, and these specializations are not directly possible in high level array

---

[1] https://github.com/ivogabe/CFAL-bench-new-accelerate or [10].

languages. Their compilers cannot apply the same optimizations automatically, which gives them a large disadvantage in this application. As for the topic of this paper, both Futhark and Accelerate scale well to 32 threads. However on class C, Accelerate performs worse, both single-threaded and on 32 threads.

Table 1. N-body and MultiGrid benchmarks

N-body	Small		Medium		Large	
Input size	10^3		10^4		10^5	
Steps	10^5		10^3		10^1	
Threads	1	32	1	32	1	32
OpenMP	190 s	23.5 s	232 s	13.7 s	193 s	13.6 s
Futhark	157 s	26.0 s	158 s	12.1 s	167 s	12.0 s
Accelerate	162 s	14.6 s	162 s	11.6 s	162 s	11.4 s
MG	Class A		Class B		Class C	
Input size	$256{\times}256{\times}256$		$256{\times}256{\times}256$		$512{\times}512{\times}512$	
Steps	4		20		20	
Threads	1	32	1	32	1	32
OpenMP	0.66 s	0.46 s	2.92 s	2.26 s	21.3 s	17.4 s
Futhark	3.65 s	0.68 s	15.5 s	3.00 s	127 s	24.3 s
Accelerate	3.68 s	0.67 s	17.0 s	3.11 s	168 s	51.2 s

5.2 Quickhull

Quickhull is an algorithm to compute the hull of a set of points, in our case two dimensional points. Its structure is similar to quicksort, as it recurses twice on smaller sets. However, depending on the shape of the input, these two sets might together be significantly smaller than the input and the recursion depth thus depends on the shape of the input. Hence we measure the performance on three different input shapes: rectangle, circle and quadratic. For these inputs, the points were sampled from a rectangle or circle, or near a quadratic curve.

This application has nested parallelism, as the two parallel recursive calls may perform more parallel work. There are various ways to implement this in a parallel array language. Flattening [6] converts nested parallelism into flat parallelism.To further investigate the performance of Accelerate with its new scheduler and chained scans, we have implemented an entirely flattened implementation (**Flat**), and various implementations that do use task parallelism and are partially flattened. **Split** is flattened after an initial split, and implementations **Rec 2** and **Rec 5** use task-parallel recursion for the first two or five levels, and are flattened afterwards. All implementations make heavy use of scans.

We report the execution times of these in Table 2, together with two reference implementation: one in ParlayLib [5], that uses task parallelism instead of flattening, and the implementation in Futhark from the CFAL project, which is entirely flattened. The code is available online[2]. Our implementations are faster than Futhark, both single-threaded and on 32 threads. Futhermore, they scale more than Futhark. They do not scale as well as the reference implementation in ParlayLib. However, that implementation is not in an array language and manually reuses memory. Due to the functional nature of Accelerate, we do not want to concern the user with memory management. Instead, we should let the compiler optimize the program with for instance in-place updates.

Table 2. Benchmarks of various implementations of Quickhull. Lower is better.

	Rectangle		Circle		Quadratic	
Input size	25 M		25 M		25 M	
Output size	48		1057		358 K	
Recursion depth	7		11		21	
Threads	1	32	1	32	1	32
Reference implementations						
ParlayLib	2.18 s	0.096 s	2.13 s	0.14 s	12.2 s	1.58 s
Futhark	1.89 s	0.56 s	1.64 s	0.54 s	10.9 s	3.38 s
Accelerate						
Flat	1.06 s	0.26 s	1.00 s	0.30 s	8.36 s	2.29 s
Split	0.80 s	0.25 s	0.96 s	0.29 s	8.05 s	2.29 s
Rec 2	0.75 s	0.19 s	1.00 s	0.23 s	8.23 s	2.17 s
Rec 5	0.79 s	0.19 s	0.94 s	0.22 s	8.03 s	1.96 s

6   Related Work

Runtimes for parallel languages and frameworks are often build around work stealing [7], as we discussed in the introduction. Work stealing stores task in a queue per thread. This reduces contention on a queue, and improves cache coherency by primarily letting threads take tasks from their own queue. Only if that queue is empty, it will try to *steal* tasks from other threads. Work stealing may be used as the task-parallel scheduler in Work Assisting.

Other schedulers for mixed data and task parallelism do exist [25,30], but they are less flexible: these schedulers fix the number of threads for a kernel at its start, in contrast to our scheduler.

---

[2] https://github.com/ivogabe/quickhull-benchmarks or [10].

To implement data parallelism via task parallelism, the data parallel workload needs to be split in tasks. The granularity of the parallel work influences the scheduling overhead [18,24]. When implementing data parallelism via task parallelism, tasks should not be split into too many tasks, as that gives scheduling overhead, whereas too few tasks may result in work imbalance between the cores, especially for irregular computations. Lazy Binary Splitting [27] only splits work further depending on whether the local task queue is empty, and Heartbeat scheduling [2] only shares new tasks at fixed intervals, to prevent scheduling too many tasks. For data parallel schedulers like self scheduling [17], granularity must also be controlled. Smaller tile sizes might however be possible since claiming a tile requires only a single atomic increment and no allocations.

7   Conclusion

In this work we show the suitability of Work Assisting for parallel array languages. By employing both a task- and a data-parallel scheduler, we can efficiently exploit both forms of parallelism in array programs. We elaborated on the integration between the runtime and the generated code, via coroutines for the task-parallel part of the program, and the template for code generation of data-parallel kernels. We support parallel chained scans, and can fuse them more than other fusion systems. Using our implementation of Work Assisting in Accelerate, we evaluated the performance in various benchmarks. Our implementation is often competitive with or faster than baseline implementations.

Artifact Availability. The artifact is available in the Zenodo repository [10].

Disclosure of Interests. We have no relevant competing interests to declare.

References

1. OpenMP Application Programming Interface, version 5.2. Tech. rep. (2021). https://www.openmp.org/specifications/
2. Acar, U.A., Charguéraud, A., Guatto, A., Rainey, M., Sieczkowski, F.: Heartbeat scheduling: provable efficiency for nested parallelism. In: Proceedings of the 39th ACM SIGPLAN Conference on Programming Language Design and Implementation, pp. 769–782 (2018)
3. Bailey, D., et al.: The NAS parallel benchmarks 2.0. Tech. rep., Technical Report NAS-95-020, NASA Ames Research Center (1995)
4. Blelloch, G.E.: NESL: a nested data parallel language. Carnegie Mellon Univ. (1992)
5. Blelloch, G.E., Anderson, D., Dhulipala, L.: ParlayLib-a toolkit for parallel algorithms on shared-memory multicore machines. In: Proceedings of the 32nd ACM Symposium on Parallelism in Algorithms and Architectures, pp. 507–509 (2020)
6. Blelloch, G.E., Sabot, G.W.: Compiling collection-oriented languages onto massively parallel computers. J. Parallel Distrib. Comput. **8**(2) (1990)
7. Blumofe, R.D., Leiserson, C.E.: Scheduling multithreaded computations by work stealing. J. ACM (JACM) **46**(5), 720–748 (1999)

8. Chakravarty, M.M.T., Keller, G., Lee, S., McDonell, T.L., Grover, V.: Accelerating Haskell array codes with multicore GPUs. In: DAMP '11: The 6th workshop on Declarative Aspects of Multicore Programming. ACM (2011)
9. De Wolff, I.G., Keller, G.: Work assisting: linking task-parallel work stealing with data-parallel self scheduling. In: The 10th ACM SIGPLAN International Workshop on Libraries, Languages and Compilers for Array Programming, pp. 13–24 (2024)
10. De Wolff, I.G., Van Balen, D., Keller, G.: Artifact for the paper: scheduling task and data parallelism in array languages with work assisting (2025). https://doi.org/10.5281/zenodo.15602901
11. De Wolff, I.G., Van Balen, D.P., Keller, G.K., McDonell, T.L.: Zero-overhead parallel scans for multi-core CPUs. In: Proceedings of the 15th International Workshop on Programming Models and Applications for Multicores and Manycores (2024)
12. Dotsenko, Y., Govindaraju, N.K., Sloan, P.P., Boyd, C., Manferdelli, J.: Fast scan algorithms on graphics processors. In: Proceedings of the 22nd annual international conference on Supercomputing, pp. 205–213 (2008)
13. Fluet, M., Rainey, M., Reppy, J., Shaw, A., Xiao, Y.: Manticore: a heterogeneous parallel language. In: Proceedings of the 2007 workshop on Declarative aspects of multicore programming, pp. 37–44 (2007)
14. Grelck, C., Hinckfuß, K., Scholz, S.B.: With-loop fusion for data locality and parallelism. In: Butterfield, A., Grelck, C., Huch, F. (eds.) Implementation and Application of Functional Languages, pp. 178–195. Springer, Berlin Heidelberg, Berlin, Heidelberg (2006)
15. Henriksen, T., Serup, N.G., Elsman, M., Henglein, F., Oancea, C.E.: Futhark: purely functional GPU-programming with nested parallelism and in-place array updates. In: Proceedings of the 38th ACM SIGPLAN Conference on Programming Language Design and Implementation, pp. 556–571 (2017)
16. Hui, R.K., Kromberg, M.J.: APL since 1978. Proc. ACM on Program. Lang. 4(HOPL), 1–108 (2020)
17. Kruskal, C.P., Weiss, A.: Allocating independent subtasks on parallel processors. IEEE Trans. Softw. Eng. 10, 1001–1016 (1985)
18. Loidl, H.W., Hammond, K.: On the granularity of divide-and-conquer parallelism. In: Proceedings of the 1995 Glasgow Workshop on Functional Programming (1995)
19. Matsakis, N.D., Klock, F.S.: The Rust language. ACM SIGAda Ada Letters (2014)
20. McDonell, T.L., Chakravarty, M.M., Keller, G., Lippmeier, B.: Optimising purely functional GPU programs. ACM SIGPLAN Not. 48(9), 49–60 (2013)
21. Merrill, D., Garland, M.: Single-pass parallel prefix scan with decoupled look-back. NVIDIA, Tech. Rep. NVR-2016-002 (2016)
22. Moura, A.L.D., Ierusalimschy, R.: Revisiting coroutines. ACM Trans. Program. Lang. Syst. (TOPLAS) 31(2), 1–31 (2009)
23. Ragan-Kelley, J., et al.: Halide: decoupling algorithms from schedules for high-performance image processing. Commun. ACM 61(1), 106–115 (2017)
24. Robison, A., Voss, M., Kukanov, A.: Optimization via reflection on work stealing in TBB. In: 2008 IEEE International Symposium on Parallel and Distributed Processing, pp. 1–8. IEEE (2008)
25. Sbirlea, A., Agrawal, K., Sarkar, V.: Elastic tasks: Unifying task parallelism and SPMD parallelism with an adaptive runtime. In: European Conference on Parallel Processing, pp. 491–503. Springer (2015)
26. Steuwer, M., Remmelg, T., Dubach, C.: Lift: a functional data-parallel IR for high-performance GPU code generation. In: 2017 IEEE/ACM International Symposium on Code Generation and Optimization (CGO), pp. 74–85. IEEE (2017)

27. Tzannes, A., Caragea, G.C., Barua, R., Vishkin, U.: Lazy binary-splitting: a run-time adaptive work-stealing scheduler. ACM SIGPLAN Not. **45**(5), 179–190 (2010)
28. Van Balen, D., et al.: Comparing parallel functional array languages: programming and performance. arXiv preprint arXiv:2505.08906 (2025)
29. Van Balen, D., Keller, G., De Wolff, I.G., McDonell, T.L.: Fusing gathers with integer linear programming. In: Proceedings of the 1st ACM SIGPLAN International Workshop on Functional Programming for Productivity and Performance, pp. 10–23 (2024)
30. Wimmer, M., Träff, J.L.: Work-stealing for mixed-mode parallelism by deterministic team-building. In: Proceedings of the twenty-third annual ACM symposium on Parallelism in algorithms and architectures, pp. 105–116 (2011)
31. Ziogas, A.N., et al.: Productivity, portability, performance: data-centric python. In: Proceedings of the International Conference for High Performance Computing, Networking, Storage and Analysis, pp. 1–13 (2021)

THAPI: Tracing Heterogeneous APIs

Solomon Bekele[1]($\boxtimes$), Aurelio Vivas[2], Thomas Applencourt[1],
Servesh Muralidharan[1], Bryce Allen[1], Kazutomo Yoshii[1], Swann Perarnau[1],
and Brice Videau[1]

[1] Argonne National Laboratory,Illinois, USA
{sbekele,tapplencou,servesh,ballen,kazutomo,swann,bvideau}@anl.gov
[2] University De Los Andes, Bogotá, Colombia
aa.vivas@uniandes.edu.co

Abstract. As we reach exascale, production High Performance Computing (HPC) systems are increasing in complexity. These systems now comprise multiple heterogeneous computing components (CPUs and GPUs) utilized through diverse, often vendor-specific programming models. As application developers and programming models experts develop higher-level, portable programming models for these systems, debugging and performance optimization requires understanding how multiple programming models stacked on top of each other interact with one another. This paper discusses THAPI (Tracing Heterogeneous APIs), a portable, *programming model-centric* tracing framework: by capturing comprehensive API call details across layers of the HPC software stack, THAPI enables fine-grained understanding and analysis of how applications interact with programming models and heterogeneous hardware. Leveraging state of the art tracing framework like the Linux Trace Toolkit Next Generation (LTTng) and tracing much more than other tracing toolkits, focused on function names and timestamps, this approach enables us to diagnose performance bottlenecks across the software stack, optimize application behavior, and debug programming model implementation issues.

Keywords: High-Performance Computing (HPC) · Programming Models · Tracing and Monitoring · Debugging

1 Introduction

The pursuit of exascale computing and the broader evolution of high-performance computing has led to massive computational capabilities. With high performance and energy efficiency in mind, these systems are being designed with a mixture of CPUs, GPUs, FPGAs, and other accelerators sourced from different manufacturers such as Intel, NVIDIA, AMD and others. As of November 2024, nine of the top ten fastest systems in the TOP500 list are heterogeneous [22]. The heterogeneity at the hardware level pushes the diversity in the programming environments, expanding the spectrum of programming models available for high-performance computing applications. These programming models layer upon one another, resulting in a tightly integrated system that adds to its intricacy. Portable

© The Author(s), under exclusive license to Springer Nature Switzerland AG 2026
W. E. Nagel et al. (Eds.): Euro-Par 2025, LNCS 15900, pp. 54–70, 2026.
https://doi.org/10.1007/978-3-031-99854-6_4

models like Kokkos [23] target Intel, NVIDIA, and AMD GPUs using SYCL [19], CUDA [17], and HIP [5] backends, respectively. There are portable implementations of programming models that extend support to architectures they were not originally designed for. For example, HIP is designed for AMD GPUs, and now there are experimental implementations, such as HIPLZ [24] and HIPCL [6], which extend its compatibility to Intel GPUs by leveraging Level-Zero and OpenCL, respectively. This growing complexity in programming environments makes the task of introspecting and analyzing the interactions among programming models – and their relationship with applications – more challenging.

1.1 Background and Motivation

To analyze performance, debug errors, and resolve performance issues, it is important to understand the performance of applications across different programming models. This includes identifying potential sources of inefficiencies that may arise from layering of APIs, runtime translations and architectural differences.

Vendors offer tools specific to their products, such as Intel's vTune [3], Nvidia's Nsight [18], AMD's ROCprof [4]. Although they work well in their respective environments, they do not have the capability to work with portable applications on a variety of platforms and programming models.

Performance analysis tools, with cross-platform support help fill this gap. Tools like TAU [20], HPCToolkit [21], and Score-P [14] are third-party tools that provide performance profiling and tracing capabilities for HPC systems. These tools gather performance information through instrumentation and sampling, and provide insight through their analysis and visualization tools. While these tools offer robust performance analysis features, they capture only limited information about lower-level programming model context, which is essential for runtime developers and system programmers. Their primary focus is the timing of API calls rather than the complete call context.

```
THAPI: 21:41:26.240059291 - x4204c0s1b0n0 - vpid: 124765, vtid: 124765
    - lttng_ust_ze:zeCommandListAppendMemoryCopy_entry: {hCommandL
    ist: 0x000000000508aea8, dstptr: 0xff007ffffff90000, srcptr:
    x00007fffedceab98, size: 472, hSignalEvent: 0x0000000005165898,
    numWaitEvents: 0, phWaitEvents: 0x0000000000000000, phWaitEvent
    s_vals: [ ] } }

TAU: {''event-type'': ''entry'', ''name'': ''zeCommandListAppendMemoryCopy'',
    ''time'': ''4710005.000000'', ''node-id'': ''0'', ''thread-id'': ''2'' }
```

For instance, the plain text above illustrates the trace event content for the entry of Level-Zero API call `zeCommandListAppendMemCopy` as captured by both THAPI and TAU during the execution of the 505.lbm_t benchmark from SPEChpc 2021. This example highlights the difference in the level of detail recorded by the two tools. TAU captures minimal information in regard to the call, focusing on its metadata (name, timestamp, node-id, thread-id). Whereas THAPI records detailed API call information, including arguments such as source and destination pointers, transfer size, command list handle, and metadata (e.g., timestamp, node ID, process ID, thread ID, and name). For instance, from these details, we can deduce that the operation is data transfer from host to device, as indicated by the memory addresses: the source pointer starts with 0x00, indicating host memory, while the destination pointer begins with 0xff, implying device memory. We also know the size of the transfer and more. These low-level details are essential for reconstructing the execution flow, ensure reproducibility, and detecting errors and unexpected behavior. We will demonstrate later how such detailed information can be valuable.

In this paper, we propose THAPI, a *programming model-centric*, tracing framework for heterogeneous HPC systems. THAPI supports the aforementioned variety of platforms—diverse hardware, heterogeneity, programming models and workloads—and helps programmers and system designers to understand applications' performance, debug errors, identify performance bottlenecks, and find potential opportunities for optimization. THAPI captures as much context as possible while maintaining minimal overhead.

As we mentioned earlier, tools like TAU [20], Score-P [14] and HPCToolkit [21] provide a wide range of functionalities, THAPI, however, complements these tools with the following contributions:

- For Runtime Developers and Performance Engineers: THAPI provides a portable tracing framework that captures the low-level programming model context that is essential to understand runtime behavior of applications. It collects all API calls along with their arguments (values behind input and output pointers) facilitating the introspection of the interaction between layered programming models (e.g. HIP on top of Level-Zero backend for HIPLZ). Additionally, it profiles GPU execution, offering a comprehensive view of heterogeneous runtime behavior.
- For Tools Developers: THAPI demonstrates automatic generation of tracepoints and analysis tools plugins from the programming model headers simplifying the instrumentation process and the maintenance of the tool.
- For Application Developers: Complementary analysis plugin tools generated automatically from the programming models that can produce portable summary and timeline visualization.
- Sampling service that captures rich execution context by reading GPU performance counters.

THAPI supports a wide range of heterogeneous programming models, including CUDA, OpenCL, HIP, Level-Zero as well as hybrid parallel programming models such as MPI and OpenMP. Its modular code architecture allows for seamless additions of future programming models and facilitates continuous enhancements.

The rest of the paper is organized as follows: Sect. 2 delves into prior works centered on performance analysis and debugging within HPC. Section 3 discusses the details of our tracing framework. Section 4 presents various test cases demonstrating the effectiveness of the tool. In Sect. 5, we showcase the assessment results of our proposed framework, and Sect. 6 wraps up the paper with a conclusion.

2   Related Work

Historically, performance analysis tools have focused on CPUs and are more advanced for them. However, the emergence of heterogeneous systems has driven the development of tools targeting these architectures. There is a body of work on performance tools for heterogeneous systems. Vendors like NVIDIA, Intel, and AMD offer several tools that provide monitoring capabilities targeting their GPUs, CPUs, or both. NVIDIA's Nsight Compute and System [18], AMD's ROCprof [4] and OmniTrace [1], and Intel's VTune [3] and Profiling Tools Interfaces for GPU (PTI-GPU) [12] provide a tracing and profiling frameworks targeting their respective GPUs. While these tools provide mechanisms to trace and profile GPU-accelerated applications, their capabilities are mainly confined to programming models designed for their respective hardware platforms, limiting portability.

Several open-source tools have been developed or extended to support heterogeneous system architectures. Established tools such as TAU [20], HPCToolkit [21], and Score-P [14] have been in the HPC space for a long time. TAU is a portable profiling and tracing toolkit for performance measurement and analysis. In recent years, it has been extended to support heterogeneous systems, enabling it to monitor GPU activities through vendor-provided interfaces like CUTPI, ROCm, and Level-Zero. It supports both instrumentation- and sampling-based performance data gathering and utilizes analysis tools to generate aggregate profiles and event traces in a timeline. Similarly, HPCToolkit [21] is a performance measurement and analysis tool for heterogeneous systems. It collects call path profiles and execution traces for performance analysis and gathers hardware counter data using `perf` events. Tools such as Score-P [14] and Caliper [7] also support both profiling and sampling-based performance analysis. However, THAPI stands out with unique and complementary capabilities, demonstrated by the richness of the information it collects, its use of automatic tracepoint generation, and its comprehensive support for major heterogeneous programming models. Notably, LTTng-hsa [16] and LTTng-clust [8] are the most comparable tools, both built on top of LTTng. However, they focus on specific subsets of programming models – LTTng-clust targets the OpenCL environment, while LTTng-hsa is limited to the ROCr runtime.

3   THAPI

Tracing is a well-known performance analysis technique that captures the sequence of runtime events and their timing during program execution. Events are collected using tracepoints placed through instrumentation at required points in the code statically or dynamically. THAPI is a heterogeneous API tracing and profiling tool that collects host and device runtime behavior. It utilizes the Linux Trace Toolkit Next Generation (LTTng) [9] for event tracing and offers complementary analysis tools, built on the Babeltrace2 library, to analyze traces and provide actionable insights. THAPI also incorporates Perfetto [11] to enable timeline visualization. In this section, we first introduce LTTng, the tracing framework integrated into THAPI's development. We then provide a high-level overview of THAPI, followed by a detailed discussion of the methodology used to generate tracepoints and analysis tools within the framework.

3.1 LTTng

LTTng is an open-source, state-of-the-art tracing infrastructure for Linux systems. It supports kernel-space and userspace tracing via LTTng-modules and LTTng-UST, respectively. It is a well maintained and established infrastructure used in leading data-centers. It utilizes lockless, per-CPU ring buffers for both the kernel and userspace tracing, avoiding inter-core communication and achieving low overhead and high throughput. If the application produces more events than can be consumed by the disk, LTTng drops these events rather than blocking the execution.

LTTng's traces use the Common Trace Format (CTF), a standardized binary format optimized for performance. The traces can be parsed with the Babeltrace2 tools into a human-readable text format. With tracepoint overhead on the order of nanoseconds [10] and the capability of its relay daemons to stream over the network, LTTng stands as an ideal solution for large-scale deployment. We chose LTTng for THAPI because of its efficiency, performance-focused design, compatibility with various Linux systems, and availability of trace processing and analysis tools, making it well-suited for our requirements.

3.2 Overview

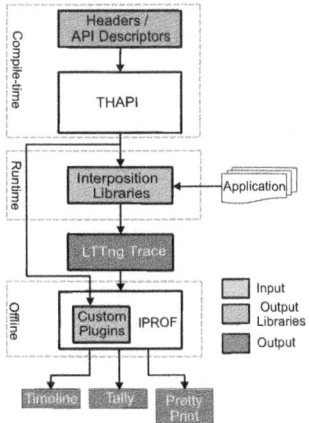

Fig. 1. THAPI's workflow for analysis of HPC applications

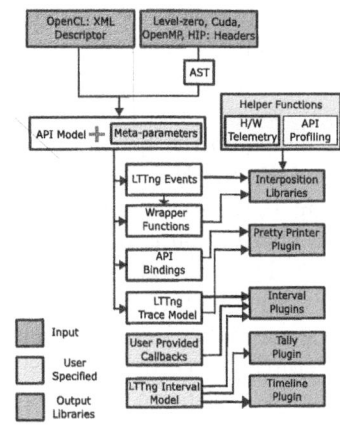

Fig. 2. Internal architecture of THAPI

As shown in Fig. 1, THAPI can be viewed as a tool comprising two logically distinct components: one for trace collection and another for trace analysis. The trace collection component performs programming model-centric tracing through an interception library. It traces all API entry and exit points (OpenCL, CUDA, Level-Zero, HIP, MPI) or tracing callbacks (OMPT), preserving low-level details, arguments, and results at each point. The trace model is automatically generated – derived from headers or API XML descriptions (in the case of OpenCL) – as illustrated in Fig. 1. Trace parsing utilizes the Babeltrace2 library (IPROF) and custom plugin tools automatically generated from the API model, producing various trace views, including Pretty Print (text), Tally (summary), and Timeline (visualization).

Tracing presents significant challenges, especially when we save everything in relation to the API calls. These challenges include runtime overhead, managing large data volumes, and balancing granularity with performance impact. THAPI addresses these issues through two main strategies. First, it employs selective event tracing, enabling the activation or deactivation of specific events [9]. It also offers the ability to selectively trace specific groups of ranks in a large-scale setting. Second, it performs offline analysis of the collected traces effectively reducing runtime overhead.

3.3 Automatic Tracepoint Generation

Tracepoints are hooks inserted into a code to enable tracing of specific events. As the complexity and diversity of programming models and APIs continue to grow, manual management of tracepoints becomes difficult. To tackle the challenges posed by the growing number of tracepoints, the THAPI tracing framework relies on the automatic generation of tracepoints. We use a systematic approach that harnesses automation and structured data extraction to ensure that all relevant events are traced comprehensively. Figure 2 illustrates the complete process of automatic tracepoint and analysis plugin tools generation. In this section, we focus specifically on the interception library and the rich tracepoint generation process. The process begins by parsing the API headers or description, depending on the specific programming model utilized. For CUDA, Level-Zero, OpenMP, and HIP, headers are parsed to capture details about the APIs. For OpenCL, the structured data is accessed directly from the XML API description. This information is parsed in to intermediary YAML file, that we call the API model. From the API model we can directly generate the interception library and tracepoints. However, this approach only gives access to the arguments on the stack and lacks detailed information (e.g., input or output memory content, structures passed by reference, etc.). Moreover, GPU timing information is not accessible, as shown in Scenario 1, Fig. 3. For example, whether a pointer is in or out, and the value behind the pointer argument cannot be inferred directly from the headers alone, necessitating the inclusion of this expert knowledge as supplementary metadata.

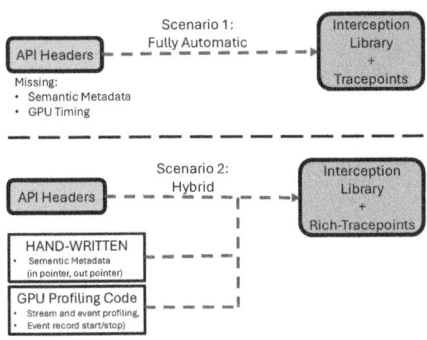

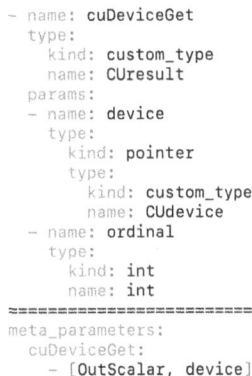

Fig. 3. Comparison of Fully Automatic and Hybrid tracing approaches

Fig. 4. API Model of cuDeviceGet parsed from the Cuda headers and its user-provided meta-parameter

In Scenario 2, the API model is enriched by user provided semantic metadata (in/out pointer) and GPU Profiling Code to capture GPU timings (Cuda record entry/record exit, before submission, Level-Zero profiling/get the info during wait ...) and generates the interception library and tracepoints. THAPI utilizes this approach where the API model combined with user-provided Meta-Parameters, transforming into rich LTTng Events, and Wrapper Functions, which provide a seamless integration point for tracing within the application code, thereby providing a streamlined methodology to create comprehensive, user-customized model for event tracing as shown in Fig. 2. The Helper Functions implement the GPU profiling code that captures GPU timings, find kernel details and monitor device telemetry. The LTTng Trace Model, derived from the API model is essential for the generation of the Babeltrace2 based plugin tools: Pretty print plugin and Interval plugins. Interval plugins enable detailed timing analysis based on the start and end times of events. Figures 4, 5, and 6 illustrate the translation of API Model to Trace Model and LTTng events for the cuDeviceGet API call. This structured, multi-phase procedure ensures accurate and efficient translation of API descriptions into actionable tracepoints.

In summary, THAPI relies on automation to generate tracepoints automatically due to the difficulty of manual management. This automated approach ensures thorough and consistent tracing across different programming models and APIs. It also makes THAPI easy to maintain, as it only requires updating the meta-parameters for the few added functions when one of the supported programming models is updated. In theory, other tools also can re-use our LTTng tracepoints for their own applications or tools.

```
- :name: lttng_ust_cuda:cuDeviceGet_entry
  :payload:
  - :name: device
    :cast_type: CUdevice *
    :class: unsigned
    :class_properties:
      :field_value_range: 64
      :preferred_display_base: 16
  - :name: ordinal
    :cast_type: int
    :class: signed
    :class_properties:
      :field_value_range: 32
- :name: lttng_ust_cuda:cuDeviceGet_exit
  :payload:
  - :name: cuResult
    :cast_type: CUresult
    :class: signed
    :class_properties:
      :field_value_range: 32
    :be_class: CUDA::CUResult
  - :name: device_val
    :cast_type: CUdevice
    :class: unsigned
    :class_properties:
      :field_value_range: 32
```

Fig. 5. LTTng trace model for cuDeviceGet

```
TRACEPOINT_EVENT(
  lttng_ust_cuda,
  cuDeviceGet_entry,
  TP_ARGS(
    CUdevice *, device,
    int, ordinal
  ),
  TP_FIELDS(
    ctf_integer_hex(uintptr_t,
        device, (uintptr_t)(device))
    ctf_integer(int, ordinal, ordinal)
  )
)

TRACEPOINT_EVENT(
  lttng_ust_cuda,
  cuDeviceGet_exit,
  TP_ARGS(
    CUdevice *, device,
    int, ordinal,
    CUresult, cuResult
  ),
  TP_FIELDS(
    ctf_integer(int32_t,
        cuResult, cuResult)
    ctf_integer(CUdevice,
    device_val, (device ? *device : 0))
  )
)
```

Fig. 6.   Tracepoint   for cuDeviceGet

3.4 Babeltrace2 Analysis Tools

The LTTng trace, once gathered, undergoes parsing and analysis using the Babeltrace2 library-based plugins tailor-made to produce specialized outputs. Babeltrace2 [2] is a reference parser implementation for CTF, offering a modular plugin model infrastructure that allows users to create custom plugins. We generated several plugins, incorporating source, filter, and sink components, to analyze the trace data efficiently. As we discussed in the last section, in order to overcome the time-consuming, complicated, and prone to errors nature of manually building plugins, we automated the plugin generation process.

To achieve this, we developed a mechanism called `Metababel`, which attaches user-defined callbacks to trace events (generated automatically from the LTTng trace model). Therefore, all the plugins (implemented in C/C++) are collections of callbacks that are executed when events occur.

`Metababel` abstracts Babeltrace2 details, such as reading CTF files, unpacking fields, and generating downstream messages, simplifying post-processing scripts. This simplification streamlines post-processing scripts, allowing users to leverage its functionality without needing to understand the intricacies of Babeltrace2. In the future, `Metababel` can expand to support reading OTF traces or enhance CTF reading performance by incorporating a custom reader to bypass Babeltrace2.

We provide these complementary plugins for generating outputs such as Pretty Print (readable text), Tally (summarized data), and Timeline (visualization), enabling diverse and comprehensive perspectives on traced data. This approach supports detailed analysis while offering flexibility in output generation to suit the specific needs and contexts of various use cases and investigations. Additionally, users can develop and use custom plugin tools to analyze the LTTng traces according to their unique requirements. Figure 7 illustrates the overall trace collection and analysis process. Tracing begins by launching the application using the `iprof` launcher (`./iprof [options] -- ./application`). `iprof` allows filtering events, choosing tracing modes, turning on or off features such as hardware telemetry, and specifying parsing and analysis types for the collected traces according to the user's needs. Once the LTTng traces are collected, the Babeltrace2 library uses the CTF reader and Muxer plugins to read and serialize messages by timestamp, and the custom plugins then generate the desired views of the trace.

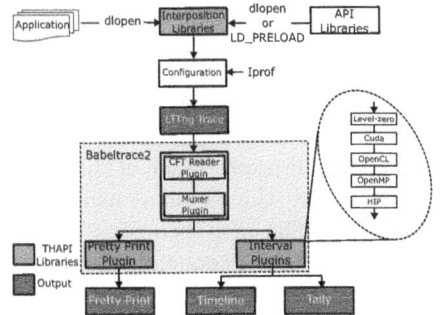

Fig. 7. Babeltrace2-based trace analysis tools

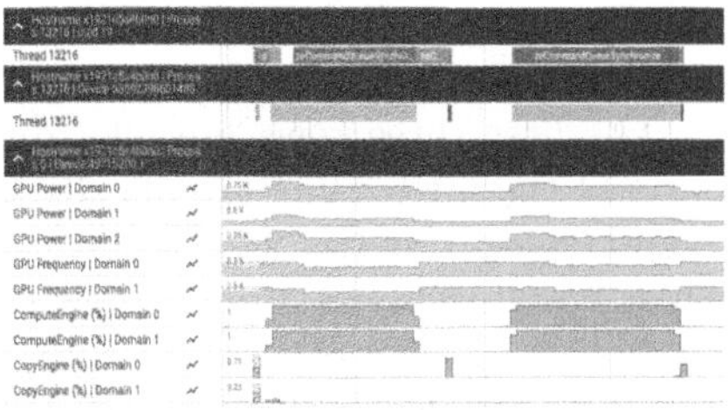

Fig. 8. Timeline collected from convolution1D benchmark run on Aurora

3.5   Device Sampling with THAPI

Sampling device telemetry, in conjunction with API traces, provides a more holistic view of system performance and behavior. The meticulous collection of these metrics is crucial for conducting in depth analyses on performance-to-power ratio, thermal management, and hardware-software co-optimization. In this section, we showcase the device telemetry daemon infrastructure, implemented via the Level-Zero APIs, in a concise manner. The Level-Zero Application Programming Interface (API) offers direct-to-metal interfaces for offloading to accelerator devices and is designed to be compatible across various compute device architectures, including GPUs, FPGAs, and other accelerator architectures. Our framework leverages Level-Zero Core and Sysman (System Management) APIs. The Core APIs are employed to initialize Level-Zero and discover drivers and available devices. Subsequently, the Sysman APIs are utilized to sample the energy, operating frequency, memory stats, fabric stats, and device utilization.

The device sampling framework is implemented as a daemon program that can be optionally enabled with THAPI using the `-sample` option. When activated, it begins sampling device counters at a user-defined sampling interval, with a default period of 50ms. The collected metrics are then streamed into the LTTng trace for analysis.

3.6 Timeline

Timeline visualization is important for identifying performance bottlenecks and enabling optimization. To visualize the traces, we utilized Perfetto [11] – a trace collection and visualization framework by Google. Since Perfetto requires data in Protocol Buffers (protobuf) format, we implemented a mechanism to convert the trace data accordingly. The timeline is structured with multiple rows illustrating the gathered API traces and corresponding device samplings. Each compute node utilizes the topmost rows to represent the host and device API calls respectively. As can be seen from Fig. 8, the first row depicts the host process and the second row shows the device. For each GPU within a node, as illustrated in Fig. 8, there are multiple rows representing the device telemetry.

The first three rows are allocated to showcase power traces from different parts of the GPU chip, specifically labeled as `Power|Domain 0`, `Power|Domain 1`, and `Power|Domain 2`. The first indicates the overall power usage of the GPU, while `Power|Domain 1` and `Power|Domain 2` display the power consumption attributed to each of the two tiles in PVC GPUs. The next two rows display the operational frequencies of each tile, denoted as `GPU Frequency|Domain 0` and `GPU Frequency|Domain 1`. Following these, two rows represent the compute engine utilization for tile 0 and tile 1, respectively. The final two rows depict the utilization of the copy engines in the first and second tiles. Depending on the user's sampling configuration, the content of the timeline may vary.

3.7 On-node Processing

Users have the option to save only the aggregate of the trace, which is lightweight and typically in the range of kilobytes, depending on storage availability and usage requirements. These aggregates can be replayed to generate tally profiles and are the default setting for multi-node experiments. In such scenarios, each local master sends its aggregate to the global master, where the summaries are combined into a composite profile. Traces are temporarily stored in local scratchpad memory to generate these aggregates. For detailed postmortem analysis, users can use the `-trace` option to permanently save the LTTng traces for one or more specific ranks. We have validated this approach on a production system and successfully scaled to a 512-node run.

4 Case Studies

In this section, we present examples demonstrating the effectiveness of THAPI. These case studies highlight the unique capabilities of THAPI and its applicability to various use cases.

4.1   Debugging OpenMP Runtime

We utilized trace analysis to diagnose a performance issue within the OpenMP runtime, specifically related to its use of the Copy Engine in the Level-Zero backend. Since the Intel OpenMP runtime is closed-source, direct inspection was not possible. However, by tracing Level-Zero API calls, we were able to analyze its behavior.

Our analysis revealed that the runtime did not leverage Level-Zero's capability to use a dedicated Copy Engine for data transfers. Instead, it consistently relied on the general compute engine, with all command lists bound to it. After identifying this inefficiency, we reported the issue, leading to its resolution. This case demonstrates that even in the absence of source code, access to API call traces provides sufficient context for runtime developers to analyze proprietary runtimes and report performance-related issues.

4.2   Mitigating Undefined Behavior in Level-Zero

In Level-Zero, certain API properties must be explicitly set to NULL. For example, the pNext pointer in `zeDeviceGetProperties` must be initialized correctly. Failing to do so results in undefined behavior. In C, it's easy to overlook this requirement:

```
ze_device_properties_t device_properties;
ret = zeDeviceGetProperties(global_ze_devices_handle[d], &device_properties);
```

Here, `device_properties.pNext` may contain an uninitialized value, leading to unpredictable behavior. The correct approach is to either:

```
ze_device_properties_t device_properties = {0}; or device_properties.pNext = NULL;
```

Bugs of this nature have been observed in real-world applications, reported, and subsequently fixed. To mitigate common low-level API mistakes—including missing NULL assignments, unhandled release events, and non-reset of command lists, we developed a post-mortem validation plugin.

4.3   Analysis of HIPLZ Implementation on Aurora

HIPLZ is a compiler and runtime system that enables HIP implementations to run on Intel GPU architectures via the Level-Zero backend. Although this enhances portability, it also introduces additional complexity, making it essential to understand the interactions between different programming models.

```
BACKEND_HIP,BACKEND_ZE | 1 Hostnames | 1 Processes | 1 Threads |
```

Name	Time	Time(%)	Calls	Average	Min	Max
hipDeviceSynchronize	4.73s	37.39%	16	295.89ms	678ns	867.22ms
zeEventHostSynchronize	4.68s	36.99%	9927772	471.80ns	390ns	3.56ms
hipMemcpy	1.77s	13.98%	7	252.79ms	202.40ms	291.56ms
__hipUnregisterFatBinary	500.91ms	3.96%	1	500.91ms	500.91ms	500.91ms
zeCommandListAppendMemoryCopy	394.50ms	3.12%	7	56.36ms	48.86ms	69.42ms

```
hipLaunchKernel | 262.70ms |   2.07% |   32 |   8.21ms |   9.71us | 261.35ms |
 zeModuleCreate | 256.09ms |   2.02% |    1 | 256.09ms | 256.09ms | 256.09ms |
```

....//...

The table above is a partial snapshot of the summary of the THAPI trace for the mini-app Local Response Normalization (LRN), which is written in HIP and executed on the Aurora (Intel's architecture) using HIPLZ. This evaluation provides insights into performance characteristics of the implementation and the overhead caused by the layering. For example, we can analyze how hipDeviceSynchronize implemented on top of zeEventHostSynchronize spin lock and its impact on performance. Figure 9 shows a timeline visualization of the experiment. The first row, representing host API calls, depicts the overlap between HIP and Level-Zero layers. The second row illustrates device API calls. The remaining rows display device telemetry data, offering deeper insights into runtime behavior.

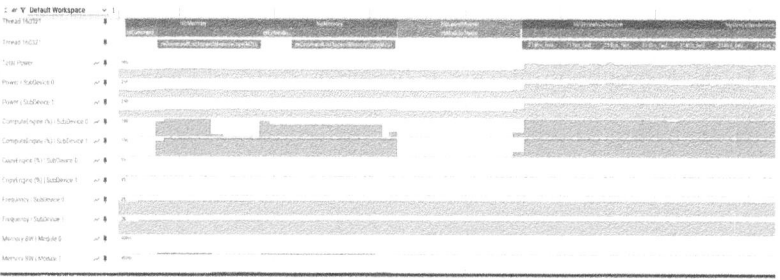

Fig. 9. Timeline for HIP implementation of LRN benchmark on Aurora

5   Evaluation

This section outlines the hardware configuration utilized in our experiments and details the benchmarks employed. Furthermore, we present the results of our experiments.

5.1   Experimental Setup

We validated THAPI on two HPC systems at the Argonne Leadership Computing Facility: Aurora and Polaris. Aurora, built on the HPE Cray-Ex platform, consists of 10,624 nodes, while Polaris, an HPE Apollo 6500 Gen 10+ system, features 560 nodes. The node configurations for both systems are detailed in Table 1.

Table 1. System Configurations

Component	Aurora	Polaris
CPU per Node	Intel Xeon CPU Max 9470C	AMD EPYC Milan 7543P
Cores/Threads per CPU	52/104	32/64
GPU	Intel Data Center Max 1550	NVIDIA A100
GPUs per Node	6	4
No. of Nodes	10,624	560
Programming Model Backend	Level-Zero	CUDA

Benchmarks. We used HeCBench [13] and SPEChpc 2021 [15] benchmark suites for the experiments. The HeCBench, Heterogeneous Computing Benchmark Suite, is an assemblage of various samples, benchmarks, and mini-applications derived from numerous open-source projects. Given that the device telemetry sampling interval is set at 50ms, we opted for benchmarks that run for a minimum of five seconds. Consequently, we selected a total of 70 benchmarks from the suite. In addition to HeCBench, we also tested THAPI using the MPI+OMP target offload version of the SPEChpc 2021 benchmark suite on both Aurora and Polaris.

5.2   Experiment and Results

We executed the benchmarks with THAPI across various tracing modes: minimal, default, and full, each distinguished by the quantity of events THAPI tracks providing trade-off between space requirement and detail. Below is a concise definition of each tracing mode:

- Minimal: Captures kernel execution events, including timings, names, and device commands.
- Default: Captures all events except non-spawned APIs (e.g., cuQueryEvent, mpiEventReady) invoked in spin-lock scenarios.
- Full: Captures all events without exclusions, intended exclusively for debugging purposes.

For each setting, we performed the experiments both with and without device sampling (telemetry), documenting the performance overhead for each of the six configurations relative to the baseline run of the benchmark. We call the three benchmark runs without sampling as `T-min`, `T-default` , `T-full` and the other three runs with sampling as `TS-min`, `TS-default`, `TS-full`.

Tracing Overhead Analysis. The illustration of the runtime overhead incurred by tracing API calls within the programming model across various tracing modes of THAPI, both with and without device sampling, is presented Fig. 10a. The `T-default` demonstrates an average overhead of 5.36% with the median at 1.99%. This suggests that THAPI can capture essential information for reconstructing application state with minimal performance impact. Although in `T-minimal` tracing mode THAPI monitors fewer events than `T-default`, it experiences a slightly higher overhead due to filtering cost. However, the volume of data gathered and the time required for its processing are substantially reduced. Adding device sampling introduces an approximate average additional runtime cost of one percent compared to running THAPI without sampling.

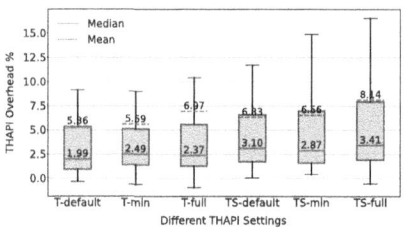
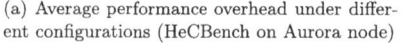

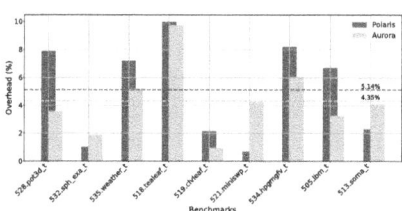

(a) Average performance overhead under different configurations (HeCBench on Aurora node)

(b) Percentage of runtime overhead of THAPI on Polaris vs Aurora

Fig. 10. Performance evaluation of THAPI

We also performed experiments using `SPEChpc 2021-tiny` benchmark suite – the MPI + OMP target offload version – utilizing all the available six GPUs on Aurora node and the four GPUs on Polaris. As we can see from 10b, the mean tracing overheads (default-mode) for the whole benchmark suite on Aurora is 4.35%. The maximum overhead by a benchmark does not exceed 10%.

On the other hand, the experiments on Polaris demonstrated a mean tracing overhead of 5.14% as shown in Fig. 10b. We also witnessed performance variation among benchmarks when they run on Aurora and Polaris. Some applications, such as `532.sph_exa, 521.miniswp` achieved better time to completion on Polaris while others, `505.lbm, 519.clvleaf`, performed better on Aurora.

Space Requirement Assessment. We also analyzed the space requirements for the traces. As shown in Fig. 11a, the minimal tracing modes (`T-min` and `TS-min`) consistently exhibit the lowest space usage across all SPEChpc 2021 benchmarks on an Aurora node. In contrast, the full tracing modes (`T-full` and `TS-full`) require significantly more space, with sampling (in the case of `TS-full`) further increasing the demand. Benchmarks such as `534.hpgmgfv_t` and `521.miniswp_t` show the largest differences between minimal and full tracing modes, both with and without sampling.

As mentioned earlier, the `T-full` tracing mode is intended solely for debugging purposes. The `T-default` mode captures all essential information required to reconstruct the context of an application run. We also analyzed the relative space requirements across tracing modes in Fig. 11b. On average, the default and minimal modes require less than 20% and 17% of the space used by the full mode, respectively. Users also have the option to save only a summary of the trace, without permanently storing the full trace, if a high-level overview meets their needs.

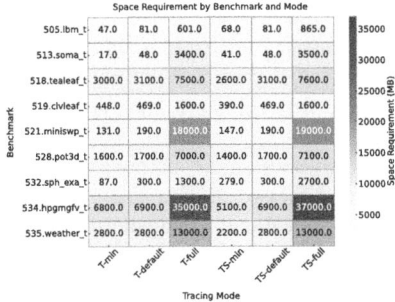

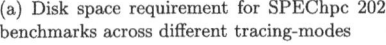

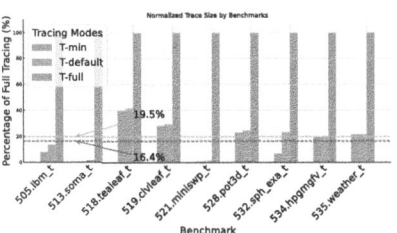

(a) Disk space requirement for SPEChpc 2021 benchmarks across different tracing-modes

(b) Normalized space requirement per tracing-modes

Fig. 11. Disk space requirement of the SPEChpc 2021 traces

6   Conclusion

In recent years, high-performance computing systems, powered by heterogeneous compute components, crossed the exascale performance barrier. Applications running on these systems navigate through different programming models to acquire their performance. However, understanding application performance across diverse programming models has also became more complex requiring innovative approaches. We proposed THAPI, a comprehensive, programming model-centric tracing tool for heterogeneous HPC systems. THAPI uses LTTng, a very efficient Linux tracer, to collect events. In our experiments, we validated the effectiveness of the framework through multiple case studies, and also demonstrated minimal performance overhead – 1.99% for HeCBench applications and 4.11% for SPEChpc 2021 applications – showing its efficiency. As a future prospect, we plan to integrate machine learning technique into THAPI for advanced trace analysis and hidden pattern discovery. Additionally, we are also working on online trace analysis, where tracing and analysis can be performed concurrently to enable adaptive optimizations during application runtime.

Acknowledgment. This research used resources of the Argonne Leadership Computing Facility, a U.S. Department of Energy (DOE) Office of Science user facility at Argonne National Laboratory and is based on research supported by the U.S. DOE Office of Science-Advanced Scientific Computing Research Program, under Contract No. DE-AC02-06CH11357.

Disclosure of Interests. The authors have no competing interests to declare that are relevant to the content of this article

References

1. AMD OmniTrace. https://rocm.docs.amd.com/projects/omnitrace/en/latest/doxygen/html/index.html. Accessed Mar 2025
2. Babeltrace2. https://babeltrace.org/docs/v2.0/man1/babeltrace2.1/. Accessed 20 Jul 2024
3. Intel VTune Profiler. https://www.intel.com/content/www/us/en/docs/vtune-profiler/installation-guide/2025-0/overview.html
4. AMD: ROC Profiler. https://rocm.docs.amd.com/projects/rocprofiler/en/docs-5.5.1/rocprof.html. Accessed 20 Jul 2024
5. AMD: Hip programming guide (2025). https://rocm.docs.amd.com/projects/HIP/en/latest/understand/programming_model.html. Accessed 20 Feb 2025
6. Babej, M., et al.: HIPCL: Tool for porting cuda applications to advanced openCL platforms through HIP. In: IWOCL 2020. ACM, New York, NY, USA (2020). https://doi.org/10.1145/3388333.3388641
7. Boehme, D., et al.: Caliper: Performance introspection for HPC software stacks. In: SC'16, pp. 550–560 (2016). https://doi.org/10.1109/SC.2016.46
8. Couturier, D., Dagenais, M.R.: Lttng CLUST: A system-wide unified CPU and GPU tracing tool for openCL applications. Adv. Softw. Eng. **2015**(1), 940628 (2015). https://doi.org/10.1155/2015/940628
9. Desnoyers, M., Dagenais, M.R.: The LTTng Tracer: A low impact performance and behavior monitor for GNU/Linux. In: Proceedings of the Ottawa Linux Symposium (2006). https://api.semanticscholar.org/CorpusID:11300732
10. Fournier, P.M., de Montréal, É.P., Desnoyers, M., Dagenais, M.R.: Combined tracing of the kernel and applications with LTTng (2010). https://api.semanticscholar.org/CorpusID:215820229
11. Google: Perfetto: Performance instrumentation and tracing. https://perfetto.dev (2024)
12. Intel: Profiling tools interfaces for GPU. https://github.com/intel/pti-gpu. Accessed Mar 2025
13. Jin, Z., Vetter, J.S.: A benchmark suite for improving performance portability of the sycl programming model. In: ISPASS 2023, pp. 325–327 (2023). https://doi.org/10.1109/ISPASS57527.2023.00041
14. Knüpfer, A., Rössel, et al, C.: Score-p: A joint performance measurement run-time infrastructure for periscope,scalasca, tau, and vampir. In: Tools for High Performance Computing 2011, pp. 79–91. Springer Berlin Heidelberg, Berlin, Heidelberg (2012)
15. Li, e.a.: Spechpc 2021 benchmark suites for modern HPC systems, pp. 15–16. ICPE '22, ACM, New York, NY, USA (2022). https://doi.org/10.1145/3491204.3527498
16. Margheritta, P., Dagenais, M.R.: LTTng-HSA: Bringing LTTng tracing to HSA-based GPU runtimes. Concurrency Comput. Prac. Experience **31**(17), e5231 (2019). https://doi.org/10.1002/cpe.5231
17. Nickolls, J., Buck, I., Garland, M., Skadron, K.: Scalable parallel programming with cuda. ACM Queue **6**(2), 40–53 (2008). http://dblp.uni-trier.de/db/journals/queue/queue6.html
18. NVIDIA: Nsight Compute. https://developer.nvidia.com/nsight-compute. Accessed 20 Jul 2024
19. Reyes, R.e.a.: Sycl 2020: More than meets the eye. In: Proceedings of the International Workshop on OpenCL. IWOCL '20, ACM, New York, NY, USA (2020). https://doi.org/10.1145/3388333.3388649

20. Shende, S.S., Malony, A.D.: The tau parallel performance system. Int. J. High Perform. Comput. Appl. **20**(2), 287–311 (2006). https://doi.org/10.1177/1094342006064482

21. Tallent, N., Mellor-Crummey, J., Adhianto, L., Fagan, M., Krentel, M.: HPCToolkit: performance tools for scientific computing. J. Phys. Conf. Ser. **125**(1), 012088 (2008). https://doi.org/10.1088/1742-6596/125/1/012088

22. The TOP500 project : Top500 lists. https://top500.org/lists/top500/2024/06/

23. Trott, C.R., Lebrun-Grandié, D., et al.: Kokkos 3: Programming model extensions for the exascale era. IEEE Trans. Parallel Distrib. Syst. **33**(4), 805–817 (2022). https://doi.org/10.1109/TPDS.2021.3097283

24. Zhao, J., Bertoni, C., Young, J., Harms, K., Sarkar, V., Videau, B.: HIPLZ: Enabling performance portability for exascale systems. Concurrency Comput. Prac. Experience **35**(25), e7866 (2023). https://doi.org/10.1002/cpe.7866

Making MPI Collective Operations Visible: Understanding Their Utility and Algorithmic Insights

Anna-Lena Roth[1]([✉]) [iD], David James[1] [iD], Michael Kuhn[2] [iD], and Dustin Frisch[1] [iD]

[1] Hochschule Fulda, University of Applied Sciences, Fulda, Germany
`{anna-lena.roth,david.james,dustin.frisch}@cs.hs-fulda.de`
[2] Otto von Guericke University Magdeburg, Magdeburg, Germany
`michael.kuhn@ovgu.de`

Abstract. In-depth understanding of collective MPI communication is a major challenge for both beginners and experienced developers. It is challenging to grasp the operations of collective algorithms, as many performance analysis tools cannot break down collective operations into their underlying point-to-point communication. However, collective communication is a key factor in optimizing the performance of parallel programs. EduMPI is a novel tool for parallel programming education, providing near-real-time visualization of collective MPI algorithms. It displays per-process data exchange and highlights performance issues like Late Sender and Late Receiver. This paper introduces the visualization of collective communication in EduMPI, demonstrates how this representation aids in understanding the concept of collective communication and its relevance for performance optimization, and evaluates its effectiveness in an educational context. EduMPI bridges the gap in understanding complex collective MPI operations by providing a transparent view of the underlying processes, enabling students to visualize and better understand the communication flow.

Keywords: Parallel Programming · MPI · Collective Algorithms · Performance Analysis · Education

1 Introduction

Parallel programming using the Message Passing Interface (MPI) [14] is a fundamental part of many computer science curricula. Beyond the basic principles of parallel computing, students must also acquire practical skills in utilizing high-performance computing (HPC) systems and in conducting performance analysis. However, working with HPC clusters is particularly challenging, as it requires familiarity with SSH, Linux commands, and workload management

ⓒ The Author(s), under exclusive license to Springer Nature Switzerland AG 2026
W. E. Nagel et al. (Eds.): Euro-Par 2025, LNCS 15900, pp. 71–84, 2026.
https://doi.org/10.1007/978-3-031-99854-6_5

systems such as SLURM [22]. Additionally, writing a functionally correct parallel program is not sufficient. Students are required to engage deeply with runtime optimization, efficient memory usage, and error minimization. One particularly challenging topic in MPI education, and in MPI performance optimization in general, is *collective communication*. MPI collective operations are generally built upon internal algorithms that rely on standardized point-to-point (P2P) communication. The performance of collective operations strongly depends on the underlying system architecture, especially network structures and topologies. The internal selection of MPI collective algorithms is typically opaque to users, making MPI collective operations a *black box*. In most cases, especially for non-expert developers and beginners, the default MPI settings are used without further consideration. Those seeking deeper insights into the behavior of collective operations typically need to analyze source code and scientific literature. Even the use of performance analysis tools cannot provide a solution here, as commonly used profiling and tracing tools (e.g., mpiP [21], Score-P [10]) do not expose details of internal collective communications. They provide valuable insights into overall communication behavior but lack access to MPI's internal mechanisms. Previous research suggests that most users do not concern themselves with the internal mechanisms of collective operations [3]. However, this lack of understanding means that many MPI users, especially those who do not have in-depth knowledge of HPC architectures, are unaware that collective operations underlie various algorithms. As a result, they cannot recognize existing potential for collective tuning, leading to suboptimal performance. For MPI beginners, the lack of understanding sometimes leads to questioning the fundamental necessity of collective communication, as they seem to be replicable through P2P communication. Moreover, common errors arise, such as incorrectly combining collective and P2P operations, e.g., when rank 0 sends a message using MPI_Bcast while other ranks attempt to receive it with MPI_Recv. Such misunderstandings highlight the need for improved pedagogical tools that make collective operations more transparent. To address these challenges, we developed EduMPI, a learning support and performance analysis tool for parallel programming education, which has been used in our courses for three semesters and continues to be employed. EduMPI is based on Open MPI [4] and adds an intuitive, near-real-time visualization of MPI communication patterns and collective operations, offering immediate insights into their internal processes. This feature benefits both learners and experienced developers or scientists without requiring code instrumentation or manual performance measurement. Performance data is automatically visualized within a Graphical User Interface (GUI) at runtime.

2   Background Collective Operations in Open MPI

Open MPI is a widely used, open-source implementation of MPI. It provides a modular framework with various components for collective operations, which have been continuously refined and extended. The *base* component is the foundation, which implements several algorithms for the various collective operations using send and receive operations. *libNBC* is the equivalent for non-blocking collective operations [5]. Building on the base component, the *tuned* component was presented in 2007 and subsequently integrated into Open MPI [3]. It offers a tuning architecture that selects collective algorithms based either on user-defined (dynamic) decisions or on predefined heuristics (fixed mode). By default, the fixed decision mode is utilized, where a decision tree determines the optimal algorithm based on factors such as message size and communicator size. In Open MPI version 5.x, the default collective communication framework is the Hierarchical AutotuNed Collective Communication Framework (*HAN*) [13]. This framework utilizes homogeneous collectives, as defined in the base component, and applies them in a task-oriented manner. HAN organizes processes according to their physical location and divides them into an intra-node and an inter-node communication level. Existing collective components, such as tuned, are employed within the levels to identify the most efficient algorithm for each scenario. New approaches (e.g., within the *ucc* component [20]) also attempt to break with the common practice of executing collective operations purely based on P2P operations and to support hardware collectives (e.g., InfiniBand Multicast) instead. The optimization of collective operations in MPI remains an active field of research. Over the years, various offline, online, and machine-learning-based tuning mechanisms have been proposed to automatically select the most efficient algorithm for specific hardware architectures, network topologies, and message sizes [6,7,16]. Particularly in the context of exascale computing, efficient collective operations are crucial for performance [1]. Bernholdt et al. have shown that the HAN framework, despite being the current default, sometimes selects suboptimal algorithms for shared-memory communicators due to limited available information [1]. In response, researchers are exploring extensions to the tuned component, further refining its algorithm selection based on base component principles. In addition, the HAN component for collectives in Open MPI only works if the processes are distributed evenly (balanced) across the available nodes. Overall, the continuous development and optimization of collective operations demonstrate that this area is far from fully resolved. Numerous opportunities for improvement remain, underlining the importance of understanding collective communication principles. Even non-specialists and MPI beginners benefit from a deeper comprehension of these mechanisms, as this knowledge enables them to make informed decisions when tuning collective operations for specific applications.

3   Related Work

Most existing performance analysis tools do not capture communication details that can only be obtained from within MPI, such as the decomposition of collective operations into P2P messages. This limitation arises because widely used monitoring and profiling tools operate outside the MPI implementation and lack direct access to internal communication processes. Score-P [10] was developed as a unified instrumentation framework that generates standardized performance data, which can be analyzed using tools such as TAU [19], Vampir [9], and Cube combined with Scalasca [18]. It is based on MPI wrappers and call-path profilers, which retrieve data externally rather than from within the MPI implementation. The PMPI profiling interface, which has been part of the MPI standard for a long time, allows monitoring by intercepting MPI API calls and aggregating related performance data. Well-known profiling tools such as mpiP [21] rely on this mechanism. However, as PMPI operates at the API level, it cannot track internal metrics, including those of collective operations. To enable deeper access to such internal behavior, PERUSE [8] and the MPI Tool Information Interface (MPI_T) were introduced. PERUSE, a callback-based interface for monitoring inside the MPI library, was never part of the official MPI standard. MPI_T, introduced in MPI 3.x [14], provides standardized access to internal MPI metrics but is only partially supported by many profiling tools. Designed for aggregated data collection, MPI_T makes it difficult to attribute metrics to specific operations. Intuitive monitoring of internal MPI data without in-depth MPI_T knowledge remains largely unsupported by commonly used tools, leaving internal performance visualization a non-standardized challenge.

Several efforts have been made to provide the visualization of MPI collective operations. Netterville et al. developed an interactive, web-based system to compare different MPI all-to-all algorithms [15]. Their approach targets beginners by explaining algorithmic behavior but does not rely on runtime traces or monitoring of actual MPI programs. Brown et al. extended PERUSE within Open MPI to visualize collectives over InfiniBand networks using BoxFish [2]. Kunkel et al. introduced PIOViz, a mechanism for tracing MPI-IO, which also maps internal MPI communication within collective operations [12]. Using Jumpshot for post-mortem analysis, PIOViz visualizes underlying P2P operations within collectives, marking each process and function with arrows representing communication steps. However, this approach is specific to MPICH2 and is not easily adaptable to other MPI implementations, such as Open MPI. INAM [11] has utilized MPI_T to provide near-real-time performance insights for MPI applications. It focuses on visualizing the interaction between HPC applications, the MPI library, and the communication fabric, providing aggregated information on collective operations. However, unlike PIOViz, INAM does not enable the identification of P2P exchanges within collectives. Instead, its primary goal is to diagnose network issues, bottlenecks, and throttling problems, making it particularly useful for experienced HPC developers and system administrators. In contrast to these approaches, our system is explicitly designed for parallel programming beginners. It prioritizes ease of use and eliminates unnecessary complexity, ensuring that understanding MPI communication behavior does not pose an additional learning barrier.

4   EduMPI

EduMPI consists of three main components: a measurement system, a time series database, and a GUI. A detailed description of the architecture has been presented in [17]. Our work focuses on developing a learning support tool that simplifies student access to HPC clusters while enabling near-real-time visualization of program execution. This visualization aims to foster an intuitive understanding of MPI behavior, providing clarity without compromising the detail needed for precise analysis of various MPI operations.

4.1   EduMPI's Measurement System

Due to the lack of lightweight standard tools for fine-grained MPI data analysis, we opted early in development to integrate a custom measurement method directly into an Open MPI fork. This approach enabled efficient prototype development and immediate application in teaching, facilitating an iterative evaluation process. At the same time, users no longer have to perform time-consuming manual instrumentation of their code. The automatic measurement is started seamlessly as soon as a program is executed on a cluster via the EduMPI GUI. Students thus benefit directly from detailed runtime information without dealing with the technical challenges of instrumentation. The implementation is based on using a data structure to store communication and performance data for each MPI function called. This struct is passed on throughout the entire implementation so that the recorded data is transmitted to the respective sub-functions. In each MPI process, the collected data is initially stored temporarily in a ring buffer as soon as an MPI function is completed. To enable efficient storage at a central location and implement near-real-time visualization, a separate thread runs in parallel with each MPI process. This extracts the data from the ring buffer at fixed intervals and persists it to a time series database using a particularly efficient binary transport format. Due to the deep integration into the Modular Component Architecture (MCA) of Open MPI, it is possible to capture metrics at different levels of the Open MPI implementation. In particular, this facilitates the detailed analysis of collective communication operations. Since our initial approach is highly specific and not very flexible, we are working on generalizing the measurement method by using and extending PMPI and MPI_T. This will allow a broader applicability and at the same time eliminate the need for direct modifications to the MPI implementation.

4.2   Time Series Database

We use TimescaleDB, a PostgreSQL-based time series database, to store and manage the recorded runtime data. The central database was installed in the same network as our HPC cluster to minimize latency. This enables fast read operations and continuous aggregation of data at defined intervals. Incoming data is aggregated once per second in subdivided materialized views. This ensures that high-performance queries remain possible even with concurrent use by multiple students, without the simultaneous storage of measurement data impairing response time. A major advantage of our approach is that the main table with all the raw data is retained. This contains complete information on each individual MPI function call, including the captured metrics and timestamps. This allows for the visualization of both aggregated data for quick analysis and detailed raw data for more in-depth investigations. Additionally, the database enables long-term storage of previous program executions for historical comparison. This not only facilitates direct comparisons between different runs but also makes past executions available for teaching purposes. For example, teachers can provide program runs to illustrate specific scenarios or support error analysis.

4.3 EduMPI GUI

EduMPI GUI is available as an AppImage for Linux and an .exe file for Windows, both requiring no installation. After a one-time setup of passwordless SSH access, the GUI allows seamless connection to the HPC cluster. Users can directly select programs or directories with all required files. After specifying the desired number of MPI processes to be used, the program is executed on the cluster, with the SSH connection, data transfer, and the generation and execution of the SLURM script being handled automatically in the background. A status monitor provides information on the current state of the job, such as whether it is still pending in the SLURM queue or already running. Visualization of the performance data begins automatically after the program has been started. An interactive timeline at the bottom of the screen shows the time of program execution to which the displayed metrics relate (see Fig. 1). The visualization can be paused or continued at any time, and targeted analyses of specific points in time or intervals are also possible. By default, the display has a granularity of one second. Alternatively, an aggregated *total data* view is available, summarizing all data accumulated up to a specific point in time. Collective communication is broken down in detail by an automatic display of the underlying algorithm. A hover over an MPI function provides further statistics, including the number of calls as well as the minimum, maximum, and average execution times of an operation on the processes.

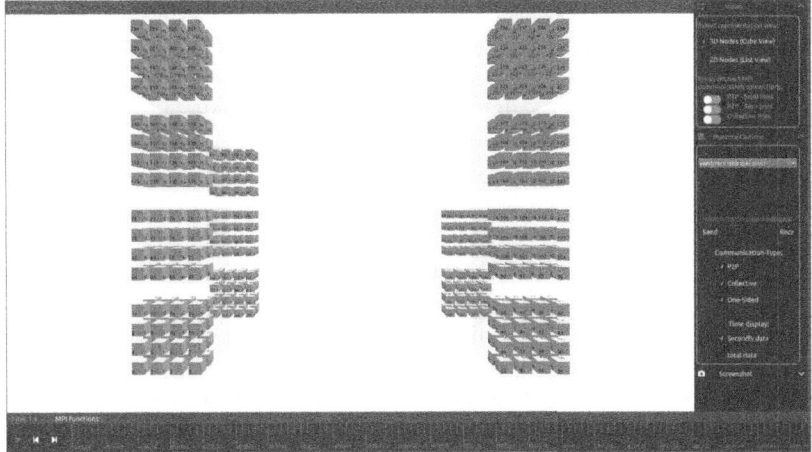

Fig. 1. EduMPI GUI overview

Users can filter on P2P communication, collective operations, one-sided communication, or a combination. The visualization provides two modes of operation: a two-dimensional (2D) and a three-dimensional (3D) representation. In both variants, the physical nodes of the cluster and the processes executed on them are depicted, whereby processes are explicitly assigned to physical cores to enable intuitive interpretation. In the 3D view, nodes are displayed as large cubes, containing the associated processes as smaller, numbered cubes. They are arranged along three axes (left-right, bottom-top, front-back), and the entire structure can be rotated and zoomed as required. Individual nodes can be enlarged with a click to analyze it in detail.

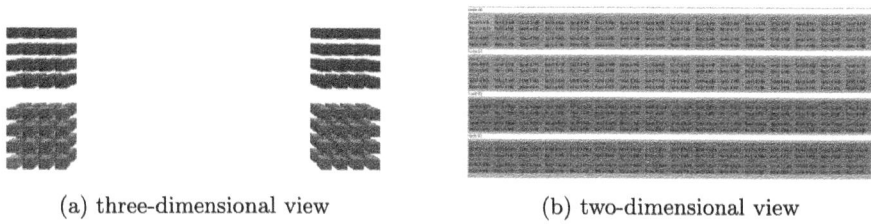

(a) three-dimensional view   (b) two-dimensional view

Fig. 2. MPI_Bcast function (binary tree algorithm), using 4 nodes, 32 cores each

The 2D view represents nodes as rectangles with process elements arranged in a grid structure. The number of columns can be adjusted dynamically to make communication patterns more visible. Process-specific metrics such as transferred bytes or the number of send/receive calls can also be displayed. Collective operations are automatically broken down into their underlying P2P components so that communication algorithms are explicitly visible. The coloring of the processes changes dynamically at runtime according to their communication activity: red for receiving operations, green for sending operations. By default, the ratio between sent and received data per process is calculated and color-coded accordingly (see Fig. 2). Pure senders appear green, pure receivers red, and mixed communication results in a graduated color scale, with balanced processes shown in ochre/brown. Alternatively, a relative scaling can be used that colors processes based on the maximum volume of data sent or received across all processes. In this case, the process with the highest send volume is displayed completely green and the process with the highest receive volume is shown completely red. All other processes are given a color according to their relative share, with processes with low communication volumes appearing increasingly white. This visualization enables an intuitive recording of data distribution and highlights hotspots in communication behavior. A special mode visualizes *wait for Late Sender* and *wait for Late Receiver* metrics by color-coding waiting times due to Late Senders or Receivers (see Fig. 3). This data is based on measurements at internal locations in the MPI implementation similar to PERUSE, enabling identification of communication inefficiencies, even in collective operations. High waiting times appear in blue, low waiting times in white. In addition, the 3D view offers a communication line display: P2P send and receive lines explicitly visualize the exchange of messages between processes. A separate representation of collective communication highlights only the send connections used within a collective algorithm, making the underlying communication pattern visible.

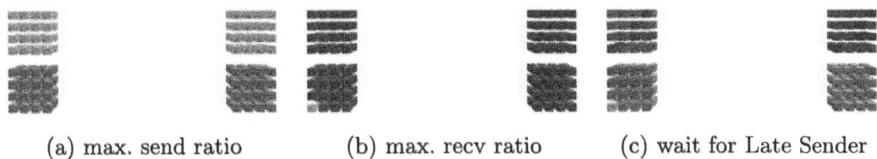

(a) max. send ratio   (b) max. recv ratio   (c) wait for Late Sender

Fig. 3. Display modes in EduMPI, MPI_Bcast function (binary tree algorithm)

4.4 Visualization of Collective Communication

EduMPI provides automatic near-real-time visualization of program behavior during the execution of MPI programs on a cluster. The visualization is designed for intuitive interpretation, allowing MPI beginners to gain a deeper understanding of processes and communication structures. A unique feature of EduMPI is the clear and easy-to-understand presentation of collective operations and the communication algorithms on which they are based. In principle, EduMPI can visualize details of every collective operation in Open MPI. To simplify the representation in this paper, we will use the broadcast function MPI_Bcast as a guide. Figure 2 and Fig. 3 illustrate the execution of an MPI_Bcast, in which an integer array with 1,000,000 elements is distributed across all ranks within the communicator MPI_COMM_WORLD. The MPI implementation uses a binary tree algorithm to distribute the data efficiently. In this scenario, rank 0 serves as the root and initiates the data distribution within the binary tree. Since it only sends data and does not receive any, it is displayed entirely in green in Fig. 2. Figure 3b shows that all other ranks receive the same amount of data (indicated by complete red), while rank 0 is shown in white, signifying that it does not receive any incoming data. The tree structure of the binary tree algorithm is clearly visible in Fig. 2. The leaf nodes, which do not forward data, are fully red. The inner nodes first receive data and then forward it to two subsequent processes, causing the broadcast communication to propagate in stages. An exception is one process (63), which only sends data to a single other process, resulting in a balanced send/receive ratio. In addition to the color coding of collective operations, communication lines can be activated in the three-dimensional view to visualize the actual message exchange along the tree structure (see Fig. 4e). This makes the underlying algorithm visible and allows the intuitive analysis of the communication pattern. Figure 4a-i shows various algorithms implemented in the base component of Open MPI for the broadcast operation. An algorithm is selected via the tuned component, either automatically based on parameters such as message and communicator size or by an explicit user specification. This representation offers significant advantages for both learners and experienced MPI developers. In teaching scenarios, it allows

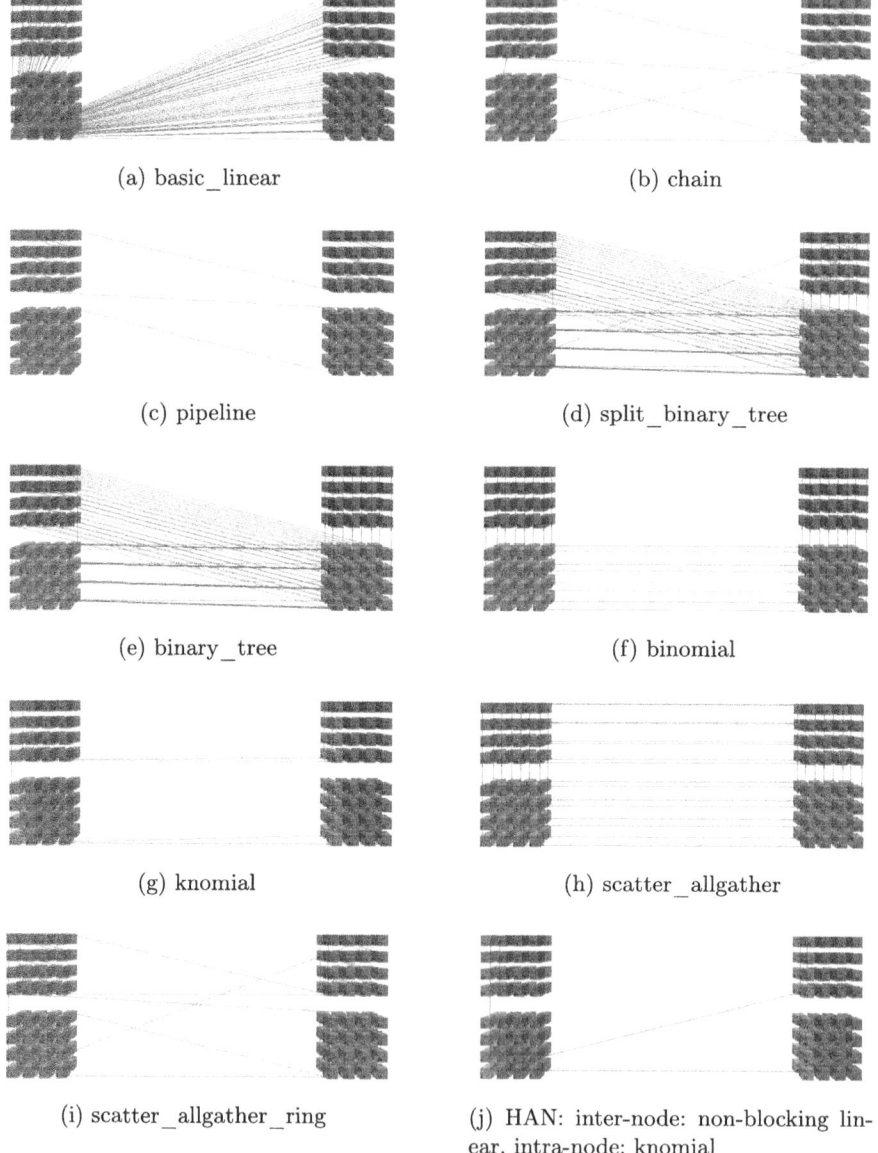

(a) basic_linear

(b) chain

(c) pipeline

(d) split_binary_tree

(e) binary_tree

(f) binomial

(g) knomial

(h) scatter_allgather

(i) scatter_allgather_ring

(j) HAN: inter-node: non-blocking linear, intra-node: knomial

Fig. 4. EduMPI - Visualization of an MPI_Bcast function according to different algorithms, cluster with 4 nodes, 32 processes each (128 processes in total)

for a precise, hardware-related explanation of collective communication mechanisms thus demonstrating why collective operations are often more efficient than custom distribution strategies based on P2P operations. Learners benefit from an intuitive, immediate visualization of the complex processes of collective algorithms, making the underlying concepts easier to understand. Experienced MPI developers can use the visualization to gain deeper insights into the selection mechanisms of the MPI library. Especially in scenarios where the tuned component decides automatically the algorithm to be used, the visualization enables direct identification of the communication pattern currently used. At the same time, the minimum and maximum execution time of the respective operation is made visible across all processes, allowing optimization potential to be identified at an early stage. In addition, the visualization allows a clear distinction to be made between inter-node and intra-node communication. Since communication within a node typically occurs via shared memory, it is usually much faster than inter-node communication, which relies on network-based transmission. The differences between the algorithms can be seen directly in the visualization. For example, the binary tree algorithm (Fig. 4e) generates a high volume of communication between the nodes for a broadcast, which makes it less efficient for the underlying hardware with four nodes. The basic_linear algorithm (Fig. 4a), on the other hand, reveals a bottleneck due to process 0 performing all the send operations, while all other processes are only receiving. The pipeline algorithm (Fig. 4c) reveals a serialization of the broadcast, as each process must first receive the complete message from rank 0 before forwarding it to its immediate neighbor. However, a particularly efficient algorithm is the knomial algorithm (Fig. 4g), where minimal inter-node communication occurs initially, followed by parallel distribution within individual nodes via intra-node communication. This near-real-time visualization makes complex communication patterns immediately comprehensible. Through this, learners can gain a deeper understanding of how different algorithms function and their efficiency. Meanwhile, experienced developers can leverage these detailed insights to choose the most suitable algorithm for their specific application, thereby optimizing communication performance. In addition to analyzing the algorithms from the base component, EduMPI also enables a detailed examination of more advanced mechanisms, such as the HAN component in Open MPI (see Fig. 4j). The example shown includes 128 processes evenly distributed across four physical nodes, allowing the HAN component to be utilized. This task-based strategy combines specialized algorithms for inter-node and intra-node communication using the sub-modules libNBC and tuned for execution. First, a broadcast of rank 0 is made to one representative process within each node, using the non-blocking linear algorithm. This is followed by the actual distribution within the nodes using the knomial algorithm, which was determined to be optimal by the tuned component. This detailed, interactive analysis provides significant added value for both education and the optimization of parallel applications. Students gain a deeper understanding of collective communication mechanisms, while experienced developers are equipped to make informed decisions when selecting the most efficient algorithms, enabling them to optimize application performance more effectively.

5   Evaluation in the Field of Education

To analyze the extent to which EduMPI promotes understanding of the advantages and benefits of collective communication in the educational context, a user test was conducted with master's students. The focus was particularly on differentiating between collective and P2P communication. The test took place during the third MPI session of our parallel programming course and was conducted immediately after the introduction of collective communication. The participants were given two MPI programs with identical functionality: an integer array of size 1,000,000 is created by rank 0, filled, and distributed to all other ranks in the MPI_COMM_WORLD communicator. The first program (p2p_bcast.c) implements a custom broadcast logic using iterative, blocking MPI_Send calls from rank 0. In contrast, the second program (coll_bcast.c) employs the collective MPI_Bcast operation, utilizing the default Open MPI algorithm (knomial broadcast) without explicit user specification. Both programs were executed under the same conditions with 400 processes on a cluster. The students had previously worked with EduMPI without any detailed introduction or tutorials. When conducting the user test, EduMPI had the features described in this paper but did not yet explicitly display the names of the collective algorithms used. The user test included online instructions, free-text questions, multiple-choice tasks, and Likert scale evaluations. Assistance from the teacher, peers, or internet research was permitted. A total of 30 students took part, 80% of whom had attended previous lectures (in part or in full), while 20% had no previous participation. 29 out of 30 students recognized that MPI_Bcast is more efficient than the iterative P2P broadcast. The reasons for this assessment differed in their precision and depth. 19 students cited shorter runtime as the main argument. Three students additionally recognized the scaling issues of P2P broadcasting as the number of ranks increased, signaling a more advanced understanding of communication complexity. Ten described a sequentialization of communication caused by the blocking nature of the loop-based implementation using MPI_Send operations. The explicit mention of communication overhead by four students and the recognition of a Late Sender problem by two others shows that some participants were already able to gain deeper insights into the underlying mechanisms. Remarkably, 14 students voluntarily used screenshots to support their arguments, an indication that the visual representation in EduMPI was perceived as helpful for communicating concepts. A clear correlation exists between answering the questions independently and attending the lecture. Of the 30 students, 23 answered without help, while seven sought assistance, five from peers, and two from the teacher. Those requiring help were predominantly from the group that did not attend the lectures, highlighting the importance of formal instruction for independent problem-solving. The next question tested the understanding of bottlenecks: 28 out of 30 students correctly identified that process 0 in the p2p_bcast.c program is the primary bottleneck. All answers included screenshots, suggesting that students used the visualizations to support their arguments. Additionally, 19 students were able to identify the bottleneck independently. This indicates that the visual representation facilitated this task. Another instruction assessed students' ability to apply theory to observation. The students ran coll_bcast.c with 128 processes and varied the array size (100,000, 1,000, 5,000). Open MPI chose different algorithms depending on the size: the knomial algorithm (100,000), the binary-tree algorithm (1,000), and the basic-linear algorithm (5,000). Ten students explicitly recognized that the underlying algorithms change depending on the message size, and four also concluded that MPI automatically chooses an efficient strategy. Eight other students correctly described differences in the representation without attributing them to algorithms. The final Likert scale question was designed to measure the extent to which students understood the difference between P2P and collective operations through the test and visualizations. In response, 13 participants stated that they fully understood the difference, twelve agreed, four only partially, and one person indicated that they had not gained any knowledge. The results show that EduMPI significantly facilitates the intuitive understanding of program behavior, scalability, and communication bottlenecks. Particularly remarkable is the strong visual support, which enabled students to recognize central concepts independently and to support their reasoning specifically with screenshots. The high rate of independently solved tasks proves that EduMPI promotes the ability to analyze problems independently and reduces the need for teacher explanation.

6   Conclusion and Future Work

We presented EduMPI, a learning support tool offering new features for analyzing collective operations. Using MPI_Bcast, we visualized the various underlying algorithms in Open MPI and showed how they can be analyzed. This offers valuable advantages for both learners and experienced developers. For future development, we plan to make data collection more flexible by using PMPI and MPI_T. However, in the current Open MPI version, PMPI and MPI_T do not provide all the necessary data required for our purposes. Specifically, it is currently not possible to infer which collective algorithms are being used, and MPI_T performance variables typically expose only aggregated data, complicating the association with individual function calls. Therefore, we need to develop solutions to extend their capabilities. Another goal is to allow users to swap collective algorithms at runtime. A challenge here is that MPI_T control variables in Open MPI are read-only during execution. Additionally, we aim to enhance the visualization to distinguish between different communicators. Currently, collective operations using different communicators are displayed together, and this differentiation would greatly improve clarity.

Disclosure of Interests. The authors have no competing interests to declare that are relevant to the content of this article.

References

1. Bernholdt, D.E.: Taking the MPI standard and the open MPI library to exascale. Int. J. High Perform. Comput. Appl. **38**(5), 491–507 (2024). https://doi.org/10.1177/10943420241265936

2. Brown, K.A., Domke, J., Matsuoka, S.: Tracing data movements within MPI collectives. In: Dongarra, J.J., Ishikawa, Y., Hori, A. (eds.) 21st European MPI Users' Group Meeting, EuroMPI/ASIA '14, Kyoto, Japan - September 09 - 12, 2014, p. 117. ACM (2014). https://doi.org/10.1145/2642769.2642789

3. Fagg, G.E., Bosilca, G., Pješivac-Grbović, J., Angskun, T., Dongarra, J.J.: Tuned: an open MPI collective communications component. In: Kacsuk, P., Fahringer, T., Németh, Z. (eds.) Distributed and Parallel Systems, pp. 65–72. Springer US, Boston, MA (2007). https://doi.org/10.1007/978-0-387-69858-8_7

4. Gabriel, E., et al.: Open MPI: goals, concept, and design of a next generation MPI implementation. In: Kranzlmüller, D., Kacsuk, P., Dongarra, J. (eds.) EuroPVM/MPI 2004. LNCS, vol. 3241, pp. 97–104. Springer, Heidelberg (2004). https://doi.org/10.1007/978-3-540-30218-6_19

5. Hoefler, T., Lumsdaine, A.: Design, Implementation, and Usage of LibNBC. Open Systems Lab, Indiana University, Tech. rep. (2006)

6. Hunold, S., Steiner, S.: OMPICollTune: autotuning MPI collectives by incremental online learning. In: IEEE/ACM International Workshop on Performance Modeling, Benchmarking and Simulation of High Performance Computer Systems, PMBS@SC 2022, Dallas, TX, USA, November 13-18, 2022, pp. 123–128. IEEE (2022). https://doi.org/10.1109/PMBS56514.2022.00016

7. Jeannot, E., Lemarinier, P., Mercier, G., Robert-Hayek, S., Sartori, R.: Application-agnostic auto-tuning of open MPI collectives using Bayesian optimization. In: IEEE International Parallel and Distributed Processing Symposium, IPDPS 2024 - Workshop, San Francisco, CA, USA, May 27-31, 2024, pp. 771–781. IEEE (2024). https://doi.org/10.1109/IPDPSW63119.2024.00141

8. Keller, R., Bosilca, G., Fagg, G., Resch, M., Dongarra, J.J.: Implementation and usage of the PERUSE-interface in open MPI. In: Mohr, B., Träff, J.L., Worringen, J., Dongarra, J. (eds.) EuroPVM/MPI 2006. LNCS, vol. 4192, pp. 347–355. Springer, Heidelberg (2006). https://doi.org/10.1007/11846802_48

9. Knüpfer, A., et al.: The Vampir performance analysis tool-set. In: Resch, M.M., Keller, R., Himmler, V., Krammer, B., Schulz, A. (eds.) Tools for High Performance Computing - Proceedings of the 2nd International Workshop on Parallel Tools for High Performance Computing, July 2008, HLRS, Stuttgart, pp. 139–155. Springer (2008). https://doi.org/10.1007/978-3-540-68564-7_9

10. Knüpfer, A., et al.: Score-P: A joint performance measurement run-time infrastructure for periscope, scalasca, TAU, and vampir. In: Brunst, H., Müller, M.S., Nagel, W.E., Resch, M.M. (eds.) Tools for High Performance Computing 2011, pp. 79–91. Springer, Berlin, Heidelberg (2012). https://doi.org/10.1007/978-3-642-31476-6_7

11. Kousha, P., et al.: INAM: cross-stack profiling and analysis of communication in MPI-based applications. In: Paris, J., Milhans, J., Hillery, B., Geva, S.B., Schmitz, P., Sinkovits, R.S. (eds.) PEARC '21: Practice and Experience in Advanced Research Computing, Boston, MA, USA, July 18-22, 2021, pp. 14:1–14:11. ACM (2021). https://doi.org/10.1145/3437359.3465582

12. Kunkel, J.M., Tsujita, Y., Mordvinova, O., Ludwig, T.: Tracing internal communication in MPI and MPI-I/O. In: 2009 International Conference on Parallel and

Distributed Computing, Applications and Technologies, PDCAT 2009, Higashi Hiroshima, Japan, 8-11 December 2009, pp. 280–286. IEEE Computer Society (2009). https://doi.org/10.1109/PDCAT.2009.9

13. Luo, X., et al.: HAN: a hierarchical autotuned collective communication framework. In: IEEE International Conference on Cluster Computing, CLUSTER 2020, Kobe, Japan, September 14-17, 2020, pp. 23–34. IEEE (2020). https://doi.org/10.1109/CLUSTER49012.2020.00013

14. MPI Forum: MPI: A Message-Passing Interface Standard. http://www.mpi-forum.org/. Accessed 27 May 2025

15. Netterville, N., Fan, K., Kumar, S., Gilray, T.: A visual guide to MPI all-to-all. In: 29th IEEE International Conference on High Performance Computing, Data and Analytics Workshop, HiPCW 2022, Bengaluru, India, December 18-21, 2022, pp. 20–27. IEEE (2022). https://doi.org/10.1109/HIPCW57629.2022.00008

16. Nuriyev, E., Rico-Gallego, J., Lastovetsky, A.L.: Model-based selection of optimal MPI broadcast algorithms for multi-core clusters. J. Parallel Distributed Comput. **165**, 1–16 (2022). https://doi.org/10.1016/J.JPDC.2022.03.012

17. Roth, A.L., James, D., Kuhn, M.: Edumpi - simplifying the use of high-performance clusters and focusing performance analysis in parallel programming education. PARS-Mitteilungen **37** (2025)

18. Saviankou, P., Knobloch, M., Visser, A., Mohr, B.: Cube v4: from performance report explorer to performance analysis tool. Procedia Comput. Sci. **51**, 1343–1352 (2015). https://doi.org/10.1016/j.procs.2015.05.320

19. Shende, S., Malony, A.D.: The tau parallel performance system. Int. J. High Perform. Comput. Appl. **20**(2), 287–311 (2006). https://doi.org/10.1177/1094342006064482

20. Venkata, M.G., et al.: Unified collective communication (UCC): An unified library for cpu, gpu, and dpu collectives. In: IEEE Symposium on High-Performance Interconnects, HOTI 2024, Albuquerque, NM, USA, August 21-23, 2024, pp. 37–46. IEEE (2024). https://doi.org/10.1109/HOTI63208.2024.00018

21. Vetter, J., Chambreau, C.: MPIP: Lightweight, scalable MPI profiling (2005). url-http://www.llnl.gov/CASC/mpiP

22. Yoo, A.B., Jette, M.A., Grondona, M.: SLURM: simple Linux utility for resource management. In: Feitelson, D., Rudolph, L., Schwiegelshohn, U. (eds.) JSSPP 2003. LNCS, vol. 2862, pp. 44–60. Springer, Heidelberg (2003). https://doi.org/10.1007/10968987_3

TSim4CXL: Trace-Driven Simulation Framework for CXL-Based High-Performance Computing Systems

Jaewoo Son⊕, Youngchul Yoon⊕, and Soonhoi Ha[✉]⊕

Department of Computer Science and Engineering, Seoul National University,
Seoul, South Korea
{troyson,yyc704,sha}@snu.ac.kr

Abstract. Compute Express Link (CXL) is recognized as a revolutionary technology in high-performance computing (HPC) system design, driven by the growing demand for efficient and scalable memory solutions tailored to memory-centric workloads. However, despite its potential, evaluating CXL performance in real-world scenarios is challenging due to the lack of CXL hardware and the high costs of building a large-scale distributed system. To address this, we propose TSim4CXL, a novel trace-driven simulation framework for CXL-based HPC systems that provides accurate timing simulations within a practical timeframe. TSim4CXL separates computing resources from the CXL memory system, generating traces and simulating the memory system using SystemC's discrete-event modeling. By modeling the CXL interconnect at the protocol level with various configuration parameters, TSim4CXL allows us to explore the design space of HPC architecture. The accuracy of our CXL simulation model is validated using CXL hardware provided by Samsung Electronics. First, we compare load latencies using a custom microbenchmark on CXL hardware with simulation results and adjust the CXL parameters in our simulator accordingly. Second, we assess communication latency by running LAMMPS applications, ensuring the simulation results align with real-world performance. In addition, we perform design space exploration with two memory-centric applications, up to 25 CPU nodes for LAMMPS and 4 GPU nodes for LLM training. Furthermore, we compare the performance of target applications by executing multiple DRAM simulators, demonstrating how the memory bandwidth affects simulated time. These experiments prove the viability of the proposed simulation framework.

Keywords: Compute Express Link(CXL) · High-Performance Computing (HPC) · Trace-driven Simulation

1 Introduction

Compute Express Link (CXL) is a revolutionary technology for high-performance computing (HPC) systems, driven by the growing demand for efficient and scalable memory solutions in memory-centric workloads such as machine learning,

© The Author(s), under exclusive license to Springer Nature Switzerland AG 2026
W. E. Nagel et al. (Eds.): Euro-Par 2025, LNCS 15900, pp. 85–99, 2026.
https://doi.org/10.1007/978-3-031-99854-6_6

big data analysis, and scientific simulations. CXL provides low-latency, high-bandwidth memory expansion and sharing, making it a key technology for next-generation HPC architectures [5,13,16]. However, the lack of real CXL hardware poses challenges for large-scale performance evaluation [14]. Deploying CXL-enabled HPC systems is costly, requiring simulation frameworks to explore architectural trade-offs before implementation.

We propose TSim4CXL, a novel trace-based simulation framework for CXL-based HPC systems. As long as traces contain the necessary information, TSim4CXL supports diverse workloads and trace generation methods, making it adaptable for various applications. Cycle-accurate simulators like gem5 provide high precision but suffer from long runtimes, while high-level simulations often lack architectural details. TSim4CXL balances accuracy and simulation speed by decoupling component simulations from the simulation backplane. It consists of two main components: trace generation and a SystemC-based simulation backplane that performs timing simulation by modeling memory access latency and communication delays.

We validate TSim4CXL using real CXL hardware from Samsung Electronics. First, we measure load latency using an in-house load command microbenchmark validated by the Intel Memory Latency Checker (MLC). Latency comparison between the MLC and our microbenchmark shows negligible error, and we fine-tuned the simulator parameters by increasing the load data sizes. Further validation is conducted with LAMMPS applications, where simulated communication time closely matches CXL hardware measurements, confirming the accuracy of our model.

TSim4CXL enables design space exploration for CXL memory architecture, considering memory bandwidth, interconnect latency, and host scaling across different configurations. The source code is available at https://github.com/cap-lab/TSim4CXL.

In summary, we make the following contributions.

- We introduce TSim4CXL, a novel trace-based simulation framework for CXL-based HPC systems. It balances simulation accuracy and speed by decoupling component simulations from the central simulation backplane.
- We propose a simulation model for the CXL-based memory systems, utilizing memory-sharing features to enable comprehensive performance evaluations across various CXL configurations.
- We validate our CXL simulation model through a two-step process using real CXL hardware provided by Samsung Electronics. First, the simulator parameters are calibrated based on load latency measurements obtained with an in-house microbenchmark. Second, the performance is assessed using the LAMMPS application.
- We conduct design space exploration for memory-centric applications, focusing on LAMMPS and LLM (Large Language Model) workloads. By leveraging trace generation from real hardware, our framework demonstrates its scalability and flexibility by supporting configurations with up to 25 CPU nodes for LAMMPS and 4 GPU nodes for LLM.

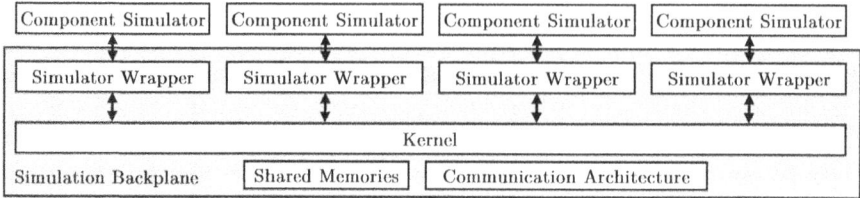

Fig. 1. Structure of HSIM

2 Background

2.1 CXL Interconnect

CXL is an industry-standard interconnect that enables coherent memory sharing between computing devices via three protocols: CXL.io, CXL.cache, and CXL.mem [4]. Our work explicitly focuses on CXL Type-3 devices (CXL.io, CXL.mem), which enable shared memory expansion without requiring cache coherence management. This study does not consider Type-1 and Type-2 devices, which involve coherence protocols and inter-cache synchronization. Incorporating Type-1 and Type-2 support would necessitate additional coherence traffic modeling, significantly increasing simulation complexity and runtime overhead. This remains an open challenge and is planned as future work. TSim4CXL is based on CXL 3.0, which introduces memory-sharing features and flit-based data transmission (68B or 256B). We implement flit-packing and pipelining optimizations to replicate the real hardware behavior closely.

2.2 HSIM Simulation Framework

TSim4CXL is based on the HSIM framework [20], developed for design space exploration of embedded systems. HSIM enables parallel simulation, where each local clock operates independently while the backplane handles the global clock. As shown in Fig. 1, each component simulator communicates with a wrapper, translating local time to global time when accessing shared resources. We adopt this idea of separating the role of component simulators and the backplane for HPC system modeling. Using traces extracted from hardware nodes, TSim4CXL simulates CXL-based memory systems in the backplane by incorporating a custom flit-level CXL interconnect simulator to connect hosts and CXL devices.

3 Related Work

The most straightforward way to evaluate the performance of systems that incorporate CXL memory is through real hardware. Many studies use FPGA-based CXL models [6,11,15,17], while others rely on vendor-provided ASICs and CXL-enabled Intel processors [17] for performance estimation. However,

Table 1. Comparison of the CXL performance models

Architecture	DSE	CXL			Workload
		Latency Model	S.M[†]	H.V [‡]	
OMB-CXL [19]	✗	N/A	✓	✗	OSU Micro-Benchmark
SDM [7]	✓	Analytical	✓	✗	PARSEC, Intel GAP
DRackSim [12]	✓	Detailed	✗	✗	Rodinia Bench, Ligra, NPB
TSim4CXL	✓	**Detailed**	✓	✓	**LAMMPS, LLM Training**

[†] Shared Memory [‡] Hardware Validation

FPGA solutions offer lower performance than ASICs, and real CXL hardware is often unavailable. Some researchers approximate CXL latency using NUMA-based architecture [2], but this approach has faced criticism by [17].

Without hardware support, many studies have focused on software-based simulations to provide reliable performance models. SDM [7] used an analytical model for cache-coherent, multi-node disaggregated memory systems, aiming to highlight the superiority of their approach over a naive method. Their evaluation focused on showing the comparative advantages rather than the accuracy. They used the Intel PIN tool to model cache-coherent memory access to inject user-level load/store instructions from the compute node. However, its CXL memory access latency model is simplified to only two parameters: network interconnection latency and memory node latency.

OMB-CXL [19] utilizes the Flight simulator [10] to demonstrate the advantages of CXL over traditional network operations. Integrated into a QEMU environment, the Flight simulator supports functional simulation with memory sharing between computing nodes but lacks timing simulation. Although OMB-CXL observed that the ratio between network-based and CXL memory latencies in the emulated system closely matched the theoretical estimates, its limited scalability and lack of a clear model make it unsuitable for our work.

DRackSim [12] provides a detailed CXL performance model but lacks support for the shared memory property of CXL Type-3 devices, making it unsuitable for optimizing large-scale systems that distribute a single large application across multiple nodes. Like SDM [7], it uses the Intel PIN tool to inject instructions for coherent memory access between modules. It suffers from long simulation times, making it impractical for the scalability requirements of our study.

Table 1 compares various CXL performance modeling approaches. Our approach stands out by integrating a detailed CXL latency model with a broader set of CXL parameters, enabling fine-grained performance analysis and comprehensive design space exploration. Additionally, TSim4CXL supports cycle-level performance estimation and is the only software-based model validated against real CXL hardware. This validation enhances the accuracy and reliability of our performance predictions. Unlike prior works that rely on analytical or theoretical models, TSim4CXL's scalability allows large-scale application simulations, making it more robust for real-world HPC environments.

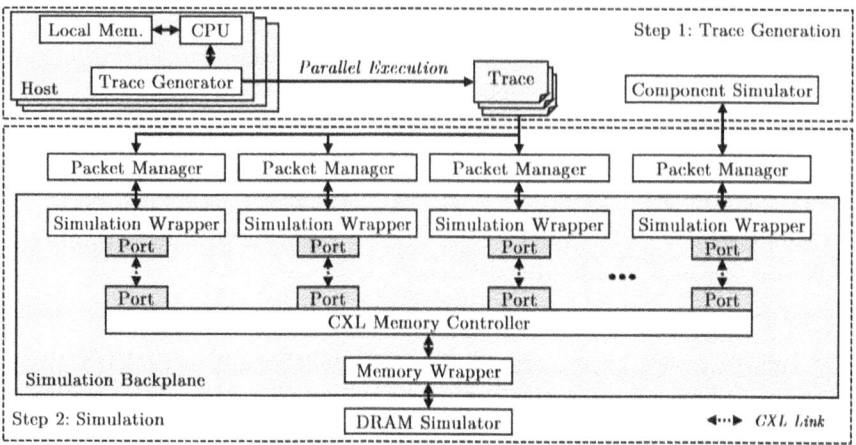

Fig. 2. Structure of TSim4CXL

4   Proposed Simulation Framework

4.1   Overview

Figure 2 illustrates the structure of the TSim4CXL, which extends the baseline simulator in Fig. 1 in two key ways.

- **Trace generation:** TSim4CXL supports various trace generation methods, including real hardware traces, simulation traces, or a hybrid approach. Hardware-based traces improve the simulation speed, while a hybrid approach provides flexibility when hardware resources are unavailable.
- **Simulation of a CXL-based memory system:** The simulation backplane models CXL components to evaluate their impact on memory-centric workloads. The *Packet Manager* reads traces from each processing element and forwards them to the corresponding *Simulation Wrapper*, which initiates the event-driven simulation in the backplane.

Trace generation captures CXL memory access requests during application execution on real hardware. Each host operates independently in a distributed environment, sharing CXL memory for inter-node communication. The *Trace Generator* hooks specific communication functions to record transactions and store them as trace files. Instead of capturing all memory accesses within a node, traces are generated only when shared CXL memory is accessed. The trace format includes: **Type** (Read/Write), **Address** (shared memory location and sync ID), **Data**, **Data size**, and **Delta time** (Δ), which denotes the interval between consecutive memory accesses, including computation time. Since it is measured on actual hardware, it varies depending on hardware configuration.

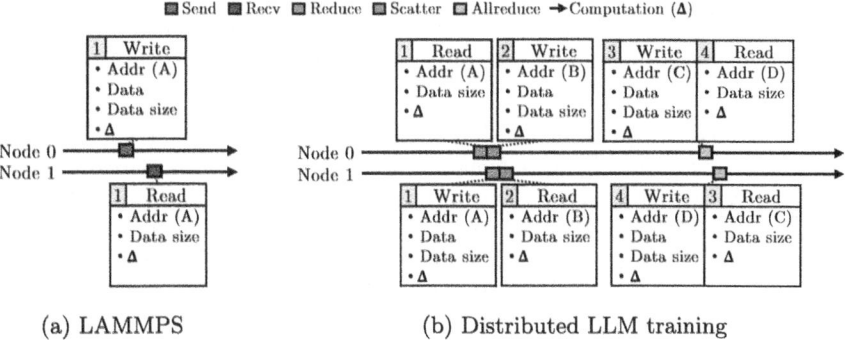

Fig. 3. Trace generation points focusing on inter-node communication events

4.2 Trace Generation

LAMMPS. LAMMPS (Large-scale Atomic/Molecular Massively Parallel Simulator) [18] is an open-source molecular dynamics simulator that leverages MPI and OpenMP. Each MPI rank represents a CPU node with multiple CPU cores responsible for processing local atoms and synchronizing with neighbor ranks. Traces are generated by hooking MPI functions to log target rank, data, and size while addresses are sequentially allocated. Delta time is measured between consecutive trace points to capture computation intervals. Figure 3(a) illustrates a two-node example, where *MPI_Send* is labeled as *"Send"*, and the combination of *MPI_IRecv* and *MPI_Wait* as *"Recv"*. Dependencies in the upper left corner show Node 1's Read depending on Node 0's Write.

Distributed Training for LLM Applications. LLM training utilizes multiple GPUs, each processing a data batch while synchronizing gradients via collective communication (*Broadcast, Reduce, Scatter,* and *Allreduce*). Each node corresponds to a GPU, and inter-GPU communication ensures model synchronization. Traces are generated by hooking collective communication operations, capturing data, size, and delta time. Figure 3(b) illustrates a two-node example. A Write trace is generated in Node 1's *Reduce*, with a corresponding Read trace in Node 0's *Reduce*. In case of *Allreduce*, both Read and Write traces are generated as gradients are aggregated across nodes.

4.3 Simulation of a CXL-Based Memory System

This section describes the simulator modules and their interactions within the simulation backplane. The modules are implemented using the SystemC library [1], providing high-level abstraction and component reusability. Interactions between the modules are managed through Transaction-level Modeling (TLM 2.0) [3], an integral feature of the SystemC library that facilitates efficient communication and synchronization.

Packet Manager. This module reads and parses per-host traces and converts them into simulation packets. It then forwards these to the *Simulation Wrapper*, bridging trace generation and backplane simulation, shown in Fig. 2.

Simulation Wrapper. This module orchestrates requests and responses within TSim4CXL. It receives packets from the *Packet Manager*, generates TLM payloads for CXL memory access, and forwards them to the *CXL Port*. Responses are converted into packets and sent to the corresponding host, enabling bidirectional communication. The backplane' clock cycle is set to the fastest host for precise timing accuracy. Synchronization between the hosts is achieved by blocking the read until the corresponding write is completed, by checking the address. Each *Simulation Wrapper* manages its own clock, which is synchronized with the global clock, to accurately simulate the timing of its associated host or component simulator. It supports various host processors and configuration (e.g., CPU frequency and cache lookup latency) for flexible simulation.

CXL Port. This module serves as an interface to facilitate communication with CXL devices. It models flit-packing and data transmission delays. When simulating a CXL host, the *CXL Port* is connected to the *Simulation Wrapper*. In the case of CXL memory, the *CXL Port* is added to the *CXL Memory Controller*.

CXL Memory Controller. This module manages requests via the *CXL Port* and coordinates data transfers between the host and the memory subsystem. It supports scalable bandwidth by configuring the attached DRAM devices and routes flits to the corresponding *Memory Wrapper*. FIFO scheduling resolves contention when multiple requests or responses arrive simultaneously.

Memory Wrapper. This module connects the *Simulation Wrapper* to the *DRAM Simulator*, ensuring that operations are synchronized with the user-defined DRAM clock frequency. It forwards memory requests to the *DRAM Simulator* and returns responses to the *Simulation Wrapper* via the CXL link.

DRAM Simulator. This module simulates memory operations, allowing for the evaluation of access latency and bandwidth. Although other DRAM simulators can be used, the current implementation uses Ramulator2 [9], which supports DDR5, the latest DRAM standard. Multiple instances of Ramulator2 run concurrently, interacting with the backplane through the *Memory Wrapper*.

5   CXL Latency Model

TSim4CXL models CXL system latency using configurable parameters, as listed in Table 2, allowing customization for specific hardware setups. Figure 4 illustrates the simulator components involved in the CXL latency computation, detailed as follows:

Table 2. Simulation parameters of the TSim4CXL

Simulator Parameters		
Parameter	**Description**	**Value**
Host Number	Number of simulated host processors	1
Host Frequency	Clock frequency of each host CPU	2.1 (GHz)
Cache Lookup Latency	Time required to search data in cache	45 (ns)
Packet Size	Packet size for host-to-backplane communication	1024 (B)
DRAM Number	Number of DRAM simulators used	1
DRAM Configuration	DRAM type	DDR5-4800
DRAM Frequency	Clock frequency of DRAM module	2.4 (GHz)
CXL Parameters		
Flit Mode	CXL interconnect flit size	68 (B)
Port Latency	Delay introduced by CXL port processing	42 (ns)
Device IC Latency	CXL memory controller to DRAM latency	20 (ns)
Link Efficiency	Link utilization ratio	0.924
PCIe Bandwidth	Maximum theoretical bandwidth of PCIe	35 (GB/s)

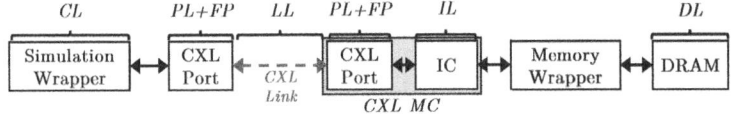

Fig. 4. Simulator components for the CXL latency model

Cache Lookup Latency (CL). CL accounts for the time required to confirm an LLC miss and initiate a CXL memory request. Instead of modeling detailed cache behavior, this is derived from LLC hit time measurements using Intel MLC on a CXL-enabled server in our experiments.

CXL Flit Packing (FP). FP enhances bandwidth efficiency by bundling multiple flits before transmission across the CXL link. TSim4CXL models this process based on the CXL specification, using TLM payloads as transmission units. Each flit carries one or more payloads, depending on size, data arrangement, and packing rules. Payload transmission is synchronized with flit transmission, ensuring that each payload is sent only when its corresponding flit is ready.

CXL Port Latency (PL). PL represents the time required to prepare and initiate the transfer of flits between CXL hosts and devices.

CXL Link Latency (LL). LL represents the flit traversal time between ports over the CXL link. Link bandwidth is computed as the product of CXL link efficiency and PCIe raw bandwidth, considering sync header overhead, skip ordered sets, and flit overhead. Using Intel-provided link efficiency values of 0.924 or 0.939 [14], LL is calculated by dividing the flit size by the link bandwidth.

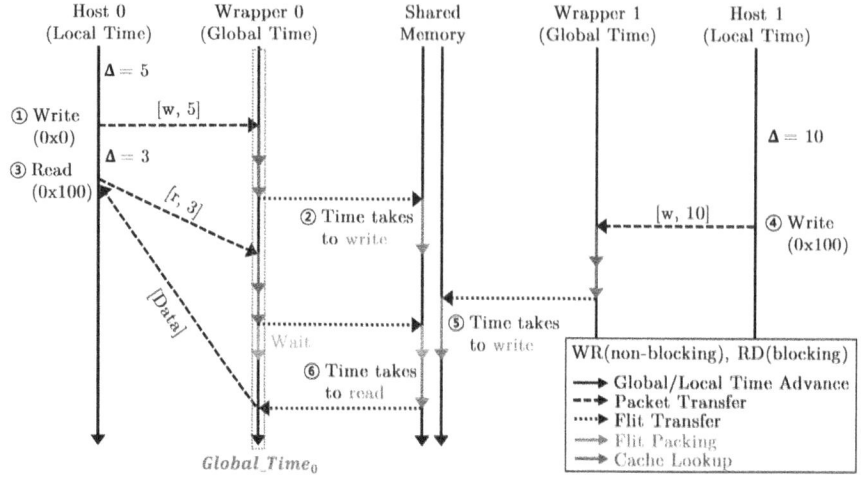

Fig. 5. Execution scenario of the simulation process

CXL Device Interconnector Latency (IL). A decision-making process is needed in a CXL device equipped with multiple DRAMs to identify the target DRAM for a memory address. This latency includes the time to determine the target DRAM and for the memory request to traverse the interconnect. The total latency for the *CXL Memory Controller* is modeled as the sum of the CXL device interconnect latency and the CXL port latency, as depicted in Fig. 4.

DRAM Latency (DL). DL denotes the time taken by the DRAM simulator, with configurable DRAM clock speed for customized simulations.

6   Simulated Time Calculation

Figure 5 illustrates the trace-driven simulation process with two hosts sharing memory. Each host measures time intervals (Δ) between communication events in its traces, which are sent to the backplane. While each *Simulation Wrapper* maintains its own clock, it synchronizes with global time.

The process begins with Host 0 sending a shared memory access request ① to *Simulation Wrapper 0*, which updates its clock, applies cache lookup latency, and performs flit-packing. Non-blocking write proceeds immediately, while a blocking read request ③ waits until the corresponding write ④ completes. The backplane processes the read request and responds after the write finishes at ⑤, updating the global time.

In TSim4CXL, the global simulated time is determined by Δ, read latency (RL), wait latency (WL), flit-packing latency (FP), and cache lookup latency (CL). RL represents read delays, while WL includes time for write completion. CL and FP are added before flit transmission via the *CXL Port*. Additional

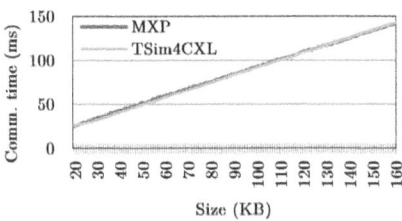
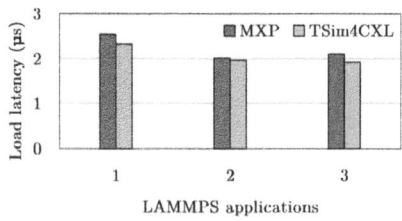

(a) Load latency comparison after tuning   (b) Communication time comparison

Fig. 6. CXL latency validation with Samsung MXP

latencies, including CXL port, CXL link, CXL device interconnector, and DRAM latency affect the time between wrappers and shared memory, contributing to WL. Each *Simulation Wrapper* operates independently, updating its global time by integrating these latencies. The overall simulated time is determined by the maximum global time across wrappers, ensuring synchronized memory access completion across all hosts. Since computation and communication may overlap in some cases, this overlap must be explicitly considered during trace generation.

7   Experiments

We validate TSim4CXL using the Samsung CXL Memory Expander 1.1 (MXP) server, which consists of a CPU-DRAM node and a CXL memory node. Due to confidentiality, CXL parameters remain undisclosed. Validation begins by comparing simulation and hardware CXL memory access latencies with a custom microbenchmark, NUMA Latency Checker, using the NUMA and x86 libraries. We flush cache lines (_mm_clflush), enforce memory ordering (mfence), and measure latency (_rdtsc). We sum the total CPU cycles taken for each trial and compute the average cycle count across all trials. We validated our results using the Intel Memory Latency Checker (MLC). A comparison of the single-line (64-byte) idle load latency measured by MLC and our NUMA Latency Checker revealed negligible discrepancies. While MLC measures latency by executing a chain of loads and calculating the average time per load, it is less suitable for measuring the CXL memory load times for bulk data transfers.

We assess TSim4CXL with two applications: LAMMPS (*DIFFUSE* [18]) and LLM training (*Google T5-small* with *DeepSpeed*). The simulator takes traces from the real hardware, capturing memory access patterns and timing. As Samsung MXP lacks GPUs, LLM validation is left for future work. Experiments generate functional and timing results, including simulated cycles and memory statistics, under various configurations to explore design trade-offs.

7.1   CXL Latency Validation

Load Latency Validation. Figure 6(a) shows the load latencies of MXP and TSim4CXL for data sizes from 20KB to 170KB after fine-tuning the CXL port latency (PL) and device interconnect latency (IL). To match real hardware performance, we incorporate hardware parameters, including PCIe bandwidth, DRAM configuration, DRAM frequency, and host CPU frequency. CXL link efficiency is sourced from Intel, and cache lookup latency is set to the LLC hit time measured via Intel MLC on MXP. We generate single-read requests matching the microbenchmark data sizes and use them as simulation inputs. Table 2 presents the parameter values, with PL and IL fine-tuned to 42 ns and 20 ns, respectively. Prior works [8,14] report PL of 25 ns and IL of 15 ns, but these vary by hardware configuration and may differ across platforms or hardware generations.

Application Validation. Using the CXL parameters from the load latency validation, we compared the latencies observed on the MXP server with our simulated LAMMPS results. On MXP, we redirected the atom buffer allocation for neighbor list computations to CXL memory and used OpenMP for multi-core processing. Traces from this buffer were collected and simulated in a single-host configuration. Figure 6(b) compares the communication time of three LAMMPS applications: *DIFFUSE_1*, *DIFFUSE_2*, and *VISCOSITY* [18], labeled as 1, 2, and 3 on the x-axis. We exclude the computation time (Δ) from the total simulated time to highlight the CXL interconnect latency. The results show that simulation latencies are within 8% of MXP experiments, with minor discrepancies likely due to profiling overheads and operational details not fully captured in the simulation. This validation verifies the accuracy of our CXL simulation model using real hardware, establishing a solid foundation for further analysis.

7.2   Design Space Exploration

We evaluate the impact of scaling the number of hosts and memory bandwidth on performance. While other parameters in Table 2 can be modified, they are primarily hardware-specific. TSim4CXL enables architectural exploration of CXL memory controllers, with further investigation planned for future work.

Varying the Number of Hosts. We evaluate performance variations by increasing the number of hosts using the CXL parameters derived from our latency experiment. As the number of hosts increases, per-host computation workload decreases, leading to reduced simulated time (Fig. 7). For LAMMPS, we test square subdomains of sizes, specifically $2 \times 2, 3 \times 3, 4 \times 4$, and 5×5, while LLM training is limited to 4 GPUs due to hardware constraints. Despite the decreases in simulated time, the actual simulation runtime increases almost linearly. This is because the SystemC simulation speed scales roughly with the number of modules. This demonstrates the scalability of TSim4CXL for multi-host simulations.

Varying Memory Bandwidth. This experiment evaluates the impact of increased memory bandwidth by running multiple DRAM simulators concurrently. Figure 8(a) shows that more memory units reduce communication time and alleviates bottlenecks. However, beyond four DRAM units, the benefit diminishes as bandwidth becomes sufficient. For LLM applications (Fig. 8(b)),

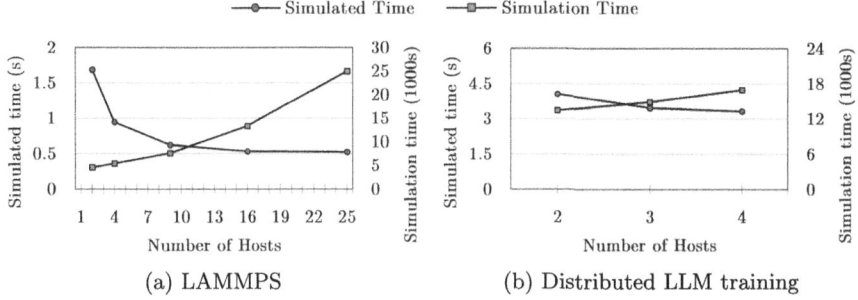

Fig. 7. Impact of the number of hosts on application performance

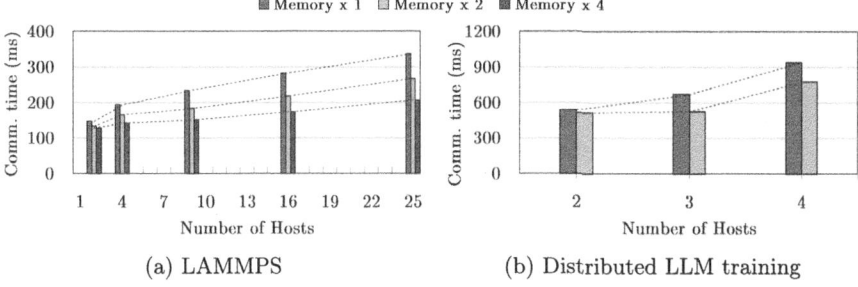

Fig. 8. Impact of the memory bandwidth on application performance

bandwidth improvements are less pronounced than in LAMMPS due to different communication patterns. Read and write operations are often concentrated on a single node, limiting the benefits of additional bandwidth. In a two-host scenario, sequential read/write operations prevent full utilization of increased bandwidth, leading to minimal improvements. This experiment shows that while higher memory bandwidth reduces latency, its impact diminishes beyond a certain point. This helps identify the optimal memory bandwidth for different configurations and highlights TSim4CXL's effectiveness in CXL memory system design exploration.

7.3 CXL Latency Model Comparison

We compare our CXL latency model with DRackSim [12], which simulates CXL at the 64-byte packet level but lacks low-level details. To evaluate the impact, we implement two additional backplane models: *Baseline*, replicating DRackSim, and *Baseline-P*, with latency pipelining. TSim4CXL models both flit-packing overhead and latency pipelining. For this experiment, we tune PL and IL through load latency validation (Sect. 7.1), yielding calibrated values(PL, IL) of (30ns, 20ns) for *Baseline* and (26ns, 15ns) for *Baseline-P*. Using these parameters, we evaluate LAMMPS with varying host counts. Figure 9(a) compares the total

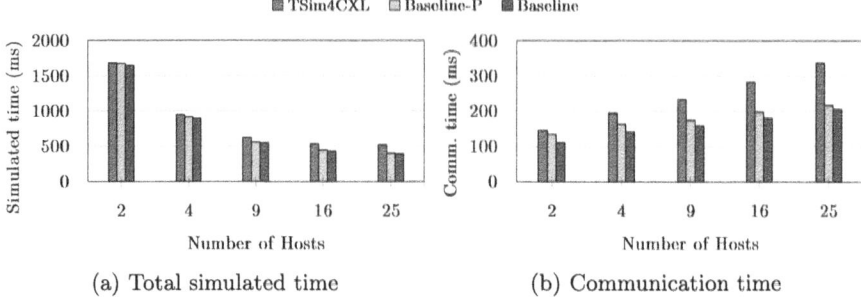

Fig. 9. Performance comparison of CXL simulation models on LAMMPS

simulated time, while Fig. 9(b) isolates communication latency by subtracting delta time. Compared to TSim4CXL, the *Baseline* exhibits a communication time difference of 23%–38%, while *Baseline-P* reduces to 7%–35%. As the number of hosts increases, the effects of latency pipelining become more pronounced, emphasizing the importance of detailed interconnect modeling. These results confirm that flit-packing and pipelining significantly impact communication time, demonstrating TSim4CXL's superiority in accurately simulating CXL interconnect behavior.

8 Conclusion

In this paper, we introduce TSim4CXL, a novel trace-driven simulation framework for evaluating the performance of CXL-based memory systems in HPC environments. The framework operates in two steps: trace generation, supporting application-independent methods, and discrete-event simulations on a SystemC-based backplane. TSim4CXL provides a detailed CXL latency model with flit-based transmission and latency pipelining. We validate TSim4CXL on Samsung CXL hardware by fine-tuning CXL parameters with a custom microbenchmark and evaluating LAMMPS communication time. The framework supports large-scale simulations on up to 25 CPU nodes (LAMMPS) and 4 GPU nodes (LLM), while its scalability extends beyond these configurations. We also assess the impact of increased memory bandwidth using up to 4 DRAM simulators.

Future work includes: (1) Supporting cache coherence to support Type-1 and 2 CXL devices. (2) Enhancing dynamic execution modeling to capture out-of-order execution. These extensions will enable a more comprehensive simulation of CXL-enabled heterogeneous computing environments.

Acknowledgements. This work was supported by Samsung Advanced Institute of Technology, Samsung Electronics Co., Ltd. The research facilities were provided by the ICT at Seoul National University.

Disclosure of Interests. The authors have no competing interests to declare that are relevant to the content of this article.

References

1. IEEE standard for standard systemc® language reference manual. IEEE Std 1666-2023, pp. 1–618 (2023). https://doi.org/10.1109/IEEESTD.2023.10246125
2. Arif, M., Assogba, K., Rafique, M.M., Vazhkudai, S.: Exploiting cxl-based memory for distributed deep learning. In: Proceedings of the 51st International Conference on Parallel Processing (2023). https://doi.org/10.1145/3545008.3545054
3. Cai, L., Gajski, D.: Transaction level modeling. In: IEEE/ACM/IFIP HW/SW Codesign and Systems Synthesis (2003). https://doi.org/10.1109/CODESS.2003.1275250
4. Compute express link consortium: CXL specification 3.0, v1.0 (2022)
5. Gouk, D., Lee, S., Kwon, M., Jung, M.: Direct access, high-performance memory disaggregation with DirectCXL. In: USENIX ATC, pp. 287–294 (2022)
6. Jang, J., Choi, H., Bae, H., Lee, S., Kwon, M., Jung, M.: Bridging software-hardware for cxl memory disaggregation in billion-scale nearest neighbor search. ACM Trans. Storage (2024). https://doi.org/10.1145/3639471
7. Lee, H., Choi, K., Lee, H., Sim, J.: SDM: Sharing-enabled disaggregated memory system with cache coherent compute express link. In: 2023 32nd International Conference on Parallel Architectures and Compilation Techniques (PACT) (2023). https://doi.org/10.1109/PACT58117.2023.00016
8. Li, H., et al.: Pond: CXL-based memory pooling systems for cloud platforms. In: Proceedings of the 28th ACM International Conference on Architectural Support for Programming Languages and Operating Systems, Volume 2 (2023). https://doi.org/10.1145/3575693.3578835
9. Luo, H., et al.: Ramulator 2.0: Dram simulator (2023)
10. MemVerge: CXL flight simulator (2023). https://memverge.com/cxl-qemuemulating-cxl-shared-memory-devices-in-qemu/
11. Park, S.S., et al.: An LPDDR-based CXL-PNM platform for TCO-efficient inference of transformer-based large language models. In: Proceedings 2024 IEEE International Symposium on High-Performance Computer Architecture (HPCA) (2024). https://doi.org/10.1109/HPCA57654.2024.00078
12. Puri, A., Bellamkonda, K., Narreddy, K., Jose, J., Tamarapalli, V., Narayanan, V.: Dracksim: Simulating cxl-enabled large-scale disaggregated memory systems, pp. 3–14. SIGSIM-PADS '24, NY, USA (2024). https://doi.org/10.1145/3615979.3656059
13. Samsung electronics: Scalable memory development kit v1.3 (2023). https://github.com/OpenMPDK/SMDK
14. Sharma, D.D.: Compute express link®: An open industry-standard interconnect enabling heterogeneous data-centric computing. In: IEEE Symposium on High-Performance Interconnects, pp. 5–12 (2022). https://doi.org/10.1109/HOTI55740.2022.00017
15. Sim, J., et al.: Computational cxl-memory solution for accelerating memory-intensive applications. IEEE Comput. Archit. Lett. **22**(1), 5–8 (2023). https://doi.org/10.1109/LCA.2022.3226482
16. SK hynix: HMSDK (2023). https://github.com/skhynix/hmsdk
17. Sun, Y., et al.: Demystifying cxl memory with genuine cxl-ready systems and devices. In: IEEE/ACM International Symposium on Microarchitecture (MICRO) (2023). https://doi.org/10.1145/3613424.3614256
18. Thompson, A.P., et al.: LAMMPS - a flexible simulation tool for particle-based materials modeling. Comp. Phys. Comm. (2022). https://doi.org/10.1016/j.cpc.2021.108171

19. Tran, T., et al.: OMB-cxl: A micro-benchmark suite for evaluating MPI communication utilizing compute express link memory devices. PEARC '24 (2024). https://doi.org/10.1145/3626203.3670533
20. Yun, D., Kim, S., Ha, S.: Relaxed synchronization technique for speeding-up the parallel simulation of multiprocessor systems. In: Asia and South Pacific Design Automation Conference (2012). https://doi.org/10.1109/ASPDAC.2012.6164990

Polymorphic Higher-Order GPU Kernels

André Rauber Du Bois$^{(\boxtimes)}$ ⓘ and Gerson Cavalheiro ⓘ

PPGC - Universidade Federal de Pelotas, Pelotas, RS, Brazil
{dubois,gerson.cavalheiro}@inf.ufpel.edu.br

Abstract. Graphics Processing Units (GPUs) are now widely used in computing systems, not only for graphics processing but also for general-purpose computing. Programming GPUs is challenging, as it is primarily done using low-level languages such as CUDA and OpenCL. Many approaches to simplifying GPU programming rely on algorithmic skeletons, i.e., higher-order functions that encapsulate common patterns of parallel computing. In these frameworks, programmers are provided with a set of skeletons, which must be combined to solve problems using the GPU. However, new skeletons can only be implemented if they can be expressed as a combination of the available skeletons. Otherwise, extending skeleton libraries may require good knowledge of the underlying compiler/runtime system that supports them. This paper presents PolyHok, a low-level imperative domain-specific language (DSL) for GPU computing embedded in the Elixir functional language. PolyHok enables the implementation of polymorphic higher-order GPU kernels, i.e., GPU kernels that can accept device functions, including anonymous functions, as arguments and that are dynamically typed, based on the arguments they receive, and JIT compiled at runtime. With such kernels, programmers can implement high-level abstractions typically associated with higher-order functions, such as algorithmic skeletons and array comprehensions. This paper details the design and current implementation of PolyHok and compares its performance with pure CUDA through experiments with six benchmarks.

Keywords: Parallel Programming · GPU · DSL · Skeletons

1 Introduction

Many language extensions designed to simplify GPU programming are based on the concept of *algorithmic skeletons*, i.e., higher-order functions that encapsulate common patterns of GPU computations, e.g., [3,7,8,16,20]. In such language extensions, programmers are provided with a set of skeletons that must be used to solve the problem in question. New skeletons can only be implemented if they can be expressed as a combination of the available ones, as this simplifies compilation and reduces runtime overhead by relying on pre-optimized building

This study was financed in part by CAPES - Finance Code 001, and by FAPERGS - 24/2551-0001372-5.

blocks. Otherwise, implementing entirely new skeletons requires good knowledge of the underlying compiler/runtime system supporting skeletons.

For a GPU language to support the implementation of algorithmic skeletons, the language must allow the implementation of Higher-Order GPU kernels, i.e., kernels that can take device functions, including anonymous functions, as arguments when they are launched. Furthermore, programmers must be able to reference device functions at host code, as well as anonymous device functions, so that kernels can be configured. Such kernels and device functions ideally should be polymorphic, i.e., they should be able to operate on different data types.

Such abstractions are not directly available in low-level CUDA code. Higher-order kernels can be implemented using a trick with device pointers: if we want to pass a function as an argument to a kernel, we create a device pointer pointing to it and, at run time, we copy the value of this pointer from the device to the host and use it as an argument at kernel launch. Although a certain degree of polymorphism can be obtained by using C++ templates, when compiling a kernel launch, types must be statically known.

This paper presents the PolyHok DSL, a dynamically typed GPU language, embedded in the Elixir functional programming language[1], that allows the definition of low-level Higher-Order GPU kernels. Such low-level kernels can be used to implement high-level abstractions that are usually associated with high-order functions, e.g., composable algorithmic skeletons and array comprehensions. The contributions of this paper are as follows:

- We present PolyHok, a DSL for GPU computing embedded in the Elixir functional programming language. PolyHok is a low-level imperative language for programming GPU kernels. The innovative aspect of PolyHok is that GPU kernels can be higher-order, i.e., they can take device functions and anonymous device functions as arguments when they are launched. Also, kernels written in PolyHok are dynamically typed, and the same kernel can be configured with arguments of different types. Type inference and type checking, performed at runtime, guarantee that for each configuration of a kernel launch, the correct code will be JIT compiled and executed.
- We describe how PolyHok can be used to implement *high-level* abstractions for GPU programming such as *composable algorithmic skeletons* and *array comprehensions*.
- The current implementation of PolyHok, which relies on type inference and JIT compilation of kernels at runtime, is described.
- We present experiments comparing PolyHok and pure CUDA using six benchmarks that show that JIT compiling PolyHok kernels adds a small overhead, especially in programs with large inputs and computationally expensive kernels.

The PolyHok language and the programs used in the experiments can be downloaded from our GitHub repository.[2]

---

[1] https://elixir-lang.org/.
[2] https://github.com/ardubois/poly_hok.

This paper is organized as follows: First, the PolyHok DSL is presented (Sect. 2), and then its use to implement high-level abstractions is described (Sect. 2.3). Next, we report on the current implementation of the DSL (Sect. 3). In the following Section, we present experiments comparing PolyHok and CUDA using six benchmarks. Finally, related work (Sect. 5), conclusions, and future work are presented (Sect. 6).

2   PolyHok: Polymorphic Higher-Order GPU Kernels in Elixir

This section introduces PolyHok, an extension of the Elixir functional language that enables programmers to implement polymorphic higher-order GPU kernels. First, we describe the GNx library that can be used to create arrays on the GPU (Sect. 2.1). Then, we describe the PolyHok DSL by implementing a map skeleton that executes on the GPU (Sect. 2.2). Finally, Sect. 2.3 discusses how PolyHok can be used to implement high-level abstractions.

2.1   GNx: GPU Arrays

In a typical GPU program, one or more arrays that are allocated in the host memory are moved to the GPU memory so that they can be processed by GPU kernels. Once the computation is finished, these arrays must be moved back to the host memory. PolyHok provides compatibility with the Nx library[3], which is a multi-dimensional tensor library for the Elixir language, similar to NumPy. Nx allows the creation of numerical tensors of different types and provides a collection of functions that implement typical tensor operations.

PolyHok provides the GNx abstraction, which represents an Nx tensor that resides on the GPU memory, as can ben seen in the example:

```
1  {h_float,key} = Nx.Random.uniform(Nx.Random.key(1),shape: {1,100000})
2  {h_int,_key} = Nx.Random.randint(key, 1, 1000, shape: {1000,1000})
3
4  d_arr_float = PolyHok.new_gnx(h_float)
5  d_arr_int = PolyHok.new_gnx(h_int)
6  d_arr_double = PolyHok.new_gnx({1,1000}, type: {:f,64})
```

In the example, first two Nx tensors are created: an array of 100,000 random floats (line 1) and a 2D (1,000x1,000) array of integers. Next, these two tensors are transformed into GNx arrays (lines 4 and 5), i.e., arrays that are located in the GPU memory. Also, it is possible to create a new empty GPU array by providing its shape and type (line 6). The current implementation of PolyHok, described in Sect. 3, accepts 1D, 2D and 3D tensors, of types integer ({:s,32}), float ({f:,32}), and double ({:f, 64}), but other types, including structured data, could be supported.

---

[3] https://hexdocs.pm/nx/Nx.html.

The `new_gnx` function accepts up to 3D arrays as an input, but the resulting GNx in the GPU memory is a 1D array in row-major format. When the GNx is transferred back into the CPU, it becomes again an Nx tensor with its initial dimensions. A column major representation of a GNx can be obtained with the `Nx.transpose/1` function from the Nx library.

A GNx is just a reference to an array that resides in the GPU memory and is of no use in regular Elixir programs. A GNx can only be operated inside kernels that are implemented using the PolyHok DSL (Sect. 2.2). A GNx can be transformed back into an Nx tensor using the `get_gnx` function:

```
1  host_nx_tensor = PolyHok.get_gnx(d_arr_float)
```

The `get_gnx` function takes a GNx and transfers it into the host memory, returning a Nx tensor that can be used in a regular Elixir program through the operations of the Nx library.

2.2   The PolyHok DSL

```
1   require PolyHok
2
3   PolyHok.defmodule PMap do
4     defk map_ker(a1,a2,size,f) do
5       ind = blockIdx.x * blockDim.x
6             + threadIdx.x
7       str = blockDim.x * gridDim.x
8
9       for i in range(ind,size,str) do
10          a2[i] = f(a1[i])
11      end
12    end
13    defd inc(x) do
14      x+1
15    end
16  end
```

```
1   def map(input, f) do
2     shape = PolyHok.get_shape(input)
3     type = PolyHok.get_type(input)
4     result_gpu =PolyHok.new_gnx(shape,type)
5     size = Tuple.product(shape)
6     threadsPerBlock = 128;
7     numberOfBlocks = div(size +
8                          threadsPerBlock - 1,
9                          threadsPerBlock)
10
11    PolyHok.spawn(&PMap.map_ker/4,
12          {numberOfBlocks,1,1},
13          {threadsPerBlock,1,1},
14          [input,result_gpu,size, f])
15    result_gpu
16  end
```

(a) A GPU kernel for a map skeleton   (b) Pure Elixir map skeleton

Fig. 1. GPU kernel and Elixir implementation for a map skeleton

GPU kernels are written using the PolyHok DSL, a dynamically typed, imperative language supporting loops, CUDA grid and block constants, and in-place update of arrays. The PolyHok language is similar to the GPotion language (see Sect. 5), the difference being that it supports the implementation of Higher-Order kernels, and is untyped, as can be seen in the example of Fig. 1a, where a kernel for a simple parallel map is presented. In the Figure, we see the definition of a `PolyHok` module (line 3). A `PolyHok` module is just like a regular Elixir module, but it also allows the definition of kernels, using the `defk` keyword (line 4), and device functions, using the `defd` keyword (line 13). Kernels are implemented using the `PolyHok` DSL (lines 4 to 12). The `map_ker` kernel showcases the main characteristics of the DSL: it is imperative, providing loops (line 9) and in-place update (line 10), it gives access to CUDA grid and block constants (lines 5–7), it is higher-order, i.e., function f is an argument to the kernel (line 4) and is applied to all positions of the array argument a1 (line 10), and it is dynamically typed, i.e., the programmer does not type variables and types are inferred at runtime.

The PolyHok DSL can be seen as a low-level language that programmers can use to construct high-level Elixir abstractions. For example, the pure Elixir function defined in Fig. 1b, implements a parallel map using the map_ske kernel. The map skeleton takes as an input a GNx array (input) and a device function (f). It first creates a GNx array to hold the result of the map computation, with the same size and type as the input array (line 4). Then, after computing the number of threads and blocks to be used, the map_ske kernel is launched with the spawn primitive (line 11). PolyHok's spawn takes as arguments a kernel to be launched, two tuples configuring the GPU's grid, and a list of arguments to be passed to the kernel. Finally, once the kernel has been executed, the map skeleton returns the GNx array containing the map's result (line 15).

The reader should notice that in-place updates are limited to PolyHok kernels, and the purely functional part of Elixir cannot offload a GNx from the GPU memory while it is being modified by kernels, since a call to get_gnx is blocked while the GNx is in use on the GPU. A PolyHok kernel can be seen as an isolated Elixir process that does not communicate. However, a kernel can still be executed by a regular Elixir process that communicates and runs PolyHok kernels as needed.

We can use the map skeleton and the inc device function from Fig. 1, on different array types, as can be seen in the script of Fig. 2. First, three host arrays of different types (integer, float, and double) are created using the Nx library (lines 3 to 4). In the example, we employ Elixir's composition operator (|>), which uses the expression on its left as the first argument of the expression on its right. In the first two compositions (lines 6 to 9 and lines 11 to 14), both map and inc are applied to arrays of different types (i.e., integer and float). On the third composition (lines 16 to 19), we perform the same computation on an array of doubles, but instead of using the inc function, a device anonymous function is used. Device anonymous functions are defined using PolyHok.phok primitive. As with device functions, PolyHok anonymous functions can be written using a subset of Elixir or PolyHok. As Elixir values are not valid in the GPU, we do not support variable capture. Also, pure Elixir functions can not be invoked on device anonymous functions, only PolyHok or CUDA functions can be called.

2.3   High-Level Abstractions in PolyHok

Algorithmic Skeletons [3,7,8,20] are higher-order functions that encapsulate common patterns of parallel computing. Skeletons hide from programmers the complexities of task creation, distribution, and synchronization, providing a simple abstraction for parallel computing where programmers only focus on the

```
1   n = 10000000
2   arr1 = Nx.tensor([Enum.to_list(1..n)],type: {:s, 32})
3   arr2 = Nx.tensor([Enum.to_list(1..n)],type: {:f, 32})
4   arr3 = Nx.tensor([Enum.to_list(1..n)],type: {:f, 64})
5
6   host_res1 = arr1
7       |> PolyHok.new_gnx
8       |> PMap.map(&PMap.inc/1)
9       |> PolyHok.get_gnx
10
11  host_res2 = arr2
12      |> PolyHok.new_gnx
13      |> PMap.map(&PMap.inc/1)
14      |> PolyHok.get_gnx
15
16  host_res3 = arr3
17      |> PolyHok.new_gnx
18      |> PMap.map(PolyHok.phok fn x -> x + 1 end)
19      |> PolyHok.get_gnx
```

Fig. 2. Using the map skeleton with arguments of different types

sequential part of the problem being solved. One classic example of an algorithmic skeleton is the map function presented in the previous Section. The reader should notice that our map receives and returns GNx arrays. This allows skeletons to be *composable*, as can be seen in the following implementation of a dot product:

```
1   def dot_product(arr1,arr2) do
2     arr1
3     |> PolyHok.new_gnx
4     |> Ske.map2(PolyHok.new_gnx(arr2),PolyHok.phok fn (a,b)-> a*b end)
5     |> Ske.reduce(0, PolyHok.phok fn (a,b) -> a + b end)
6     |> PolyHok.get_gnx
7   end
```

The dot_product function takes two host Nx tensors as input, and computes their dot product on the GPU by composing a map2 (map that takes two arrays as input) and a reduce skeleton, which were implemented in a similar way to the map from previous section.

Another abstraction that has its implementation based on higher-order functions are *List Comprehensions*, which is an abstraction, usually available in functional languages, where programmers can describe new lists based on existing lists, with a notation similar to set theory. Using macros, it is possible to implement simple array comprehensions, which are translated to calls to skeletons configured with anonymous functions. For example, the following array comprehension:

```
1  host_array =  Nx.tensor(...)
2  host_resp = PolyHok.gpu_for n <- host_array,  do: n * n
```

which returns the squared elements of an input array, can be translated by
the macro on Fig. 3, to the following code:

```
1  PolyHok.new_gnx(host_array)
2    |> PMap.map(PolyHok.phok(fn n -> n * n end))
3    |> PolyHok.get_gnx
```

As PolyHok does not provide variable capture, we can pass free variables as
extra arguments to the comprehension, that will add them as extra arguments
to the anonymous function and map, as in this implementation of *saxpy*:

```
1  host_resp = PolyHok.gpu_for i <- 0..99999, a, b, do:  2 * a[i] + b[i]
```

Map and reduce skeletons are frequently discussed in the literature with many
variations [3,7,9,10,17]. These variations include the type of argument functions
(unary, binary, ternary, etc.), the structure of the input (1D, 2D, etc.), and the
number of input arrays taken as arguments. We have developed several map and
reduce skeletons and utilized them to implement array comprehensions, along
with a set of benchmarks, which are detailed in Sect. 4.

```
1  defmacro gpu_for({:<-, _ ,[var,tensor]},do: b)  do
2    quote do:
3      PolyHok.new_gnx(unquote(tensor))
4      |> PMap.map(PolyHok.phok(fn (unquote(var))->(unquote b) end))
5      |> PolyHok.get_gnx
6    end
```

Fig. 3. Macro for compiling a simple Array Comprehension

3   Implementation

This Section presents the implementation of PolyHok's core features, including
memory management for GPU arrays and JIT compilation of higher-order kernels and anonymous functions. We also discuss how the system leverages Elixir's
meta-programming capabilities to embed GPU programming in Elixir.

3.1   GNx Arrays

Internally, an Nx tensor is represented as a continuous memory space, and such
a representation can be straightforwardly cast into a CUDA array and copied
to/from the device using standard CUDA operations. In order to do a just-in-
time compilation of kernels (see next Section), all calls to CUDA operations

need to use the CUDA Driver API.[4] For example, when a new GNx is created from an existing Nx tensor using `new_gnx`, we first allocate memory in the GPU using `cuMemAlloc`. The Nx tensor is then transferred into the GPU memory using `cuMemcpyHtoD`. Similarly, the `get_gnx` primitive first allocates memory in the host for the new Nx tensor and then copies the existing GNx, using `cuMemcpyDtoH`, from the device memory back into the host memory.

All GNx arrays allocated in a program are automatically garbage collected by the Beam VM, the virtual machine (VM) in which Elixir programs are executed. A GNx is represented internally as a new resource in the VM, and once a resource is not referenced anymore, a destructor is automatically called for it. In the case of a GNx, this destructor uses `cuMemFree` to free the memory allocated for it.

3.2   Higher-Order Kernels

The process of embedding the PolyHok DSL in the Elixir language is heavily based on Elixir's meta-programming features. In Elixir, meta-programming is performed through *macros*, which are special functions only executed at compilation time and that are used to process Elixir's Abstract Syntax Tree (AST). When Elixir's compiler generates the AST of a module, its macros are called and can modify the AST, possibly generating a new one. The `PolyHok.defmodule` primitive is implemented as a macro that, at compilation time, collects the ASTs of kernels and device functions. For each device function and kernel defined in a module, the macro computes its call tree (the tree of function calls for that kernel) and sends this information together with the ASTs to an Elixir process, the AST process, that maintains a dictionary with information about kernels and device functions. The `PolyHok.defmodule` also generates a new version of the module where all regular Elixir functions are maintained, while Kernels and device functions are substituted with functions with the same prototype, but that raise an exception when called, advising the user that such functions can only be used by kernels. A module containing PolyHok code must be imported through Elixir's `use` keyword, which besides importing regular Elixir functions, forces the execution of a macro, generated by the PolyHok compiler, that will populate the AST server with the kernels and device functions of that module.

The following steps are taken by `spawn` to compile a PolyHok kernel:

1. *Type inference/Type checking*: First, it checks the types of the actual parameters passed to the kernel and sends this information to the type inference algorithm, together with the ASTs that are obtained from the AST server. Type inference departs from types that it already knows, e.g., actual parameters, CUDA block and grid constants, indexing expressions, etc., and uses control-flow analysis to detect the types of all variables used in the program. The type inference algorithm used in PolyHok is an extension of the algorithm presented in [5], which used the same technique but only accepted arrays of floats, which allowed the system to statically know types at compilation time

---

[4] https://docs.nvidia.com/cuda/cuda-driver-api/index.html.

instead of at runtime (See Sect. 5). The algorithm was adapted to accept different array types and to use runtime information of actual parameters in the type inference process. Departing from known types in the code, the algorithm spreads this type information to surrounding expressions until all variables are inferred. Type information collected on the kernel is then used to infer the types of function arguments and functions that are contained in the kernel's call dependency tree.

2. *CUDA back-end*: The kernel and its type information are then passed to the CUDA back-end that, besides generating CUDA code for the kernel, substitutes calls to function arguments by direct calls to those functions. Hence, function arguments are omitted from the generated code. The same process is also repeated for function arguments and for the call dependency tree of the kernel. The back-end generates a single CUDA C module containing the kernel and its functions.

3. *JIT-compilation*: In order to JIT compile the CUDA C module generated by the previous step, the NVRTC library is used.[5] NVRTC is a runtime compilation library for CUDA that is used to convert CUDA modules into PTX intermediate code, that can then be loaded and executed by using the CUDA Driver API.[6]

When the `PolyHok.phok` macro receives an anonymous function at compilation time, it transforms it into a structure that contains a randomly generated name and the function's AST. When a kernel receives such a structure as an argument, `spawn` will include it in the call tree of the kernel so that it is also included in the generated CUDA module.

4 Experiments

The objective of the experiments presented in this Section is to give some insight into how the current implementation of PolyHok, described in Sect. 3, behaves in relation to pure CUDA. We have implemented six benchmarks in PolyHok: matrix-multiplication (MM), two image processing applications, a *Ray Tracer* (RT) and *Julia* (JL), which generates images based on the Julia set, both ported from [19], *nBodies* (NB), that simulates how physical forces influence a dynamic system of particles (taken from [18]), Dot Product (DP), taken from Sect. 2.3, and Nearest Neighbor ported from the Rodinia Benchmark Suite [4]. The source code for the benchmarks can be found in our GitHub repository.[7] The CUDA versions of the programs execute the exact same kernel and functions as the PolyHok versions, and the CUDA Runtime API is used to move data to/from the GPU and launch kernels. The times presented for the execution of each instance of an application are the average of 30 executions. The times for PolyHok and CUDA include the time to transfer data to/from the device. The experiments

---

[5] https://docs.nvidia.com/cuda/nvrtc/.

[6] https://docs.nvidia.com/cuda/cuda-driver-api/index.html.

[7] https://github.com/ardubois/poly_hok/tree/main/benchmarks.

were executed on a machine with a 12th Gen Intel(R) Core(TM) i7-12700K CPU @ 3.60GHz with 16 GB of RAM, NVIDIA GeForce RTX 3060 with 8GB, Ubuntu 22.04.3 LTS, Elixir 1.16.1, Erlang OTP 26, and nvcc 12.3.107. Table 1 summarizes the results of the experiments. The following comparative analyses rely on the Mann-Whitney U test (two-tailed) with a significance level of 0.05.

Table 1. Experiment results

	PolyHok (ms)	CUDA (ms)	Difference (%)
MM 5k × 5k	321.1	253.4	26.7%
MM 7k × 7k	713.4	665.6	7.2%
MM 9k × 9k	1501.3	1489.9	0.8%
JL 7168 × 7168	518.9	500.9	3.6%
JL 9216 × 9216	842.0	826.2	1.9%
JL 11264 × 11264	1245.3	1233.2	1.0%
RT 7168 × 7168	289.2	230.7	25.3%
RT 9216 × 9216	435.4	379.5	14.7%
RT 11264 × 11264	615.1	564.8	8.9%
NB 100k	2124.7	2046.0	3.8%
NB 200k	8273.8	8186.1	1.1%
NB 400k	32889.9	32838.2	0.2%
NN 100M	532.7	435.4	22.3%
NN 200M	944.2	849.3	11.2%
NN 300M	1381.4	1267.9	9.0%
DP 400M	603.1	514.5	17.2%
DP 500M	730.3	638.6	14.4%
DP 600M	854.3	764.6	11.7%

Matrix Multiplication (MM), which multiplies matrices of floats, was implemented using an array comprehension, which is translated into a `map` of a function that computes individual values of the resulting matrix. PolyHok and CUDA have similar performance, as can be seen in Fig. 4, but the difference between them, as in other programs of this Section, is more apparent in small instances of problems. While the difference between CUDA and PolyHok is 26.7% in the 5k x 5k instance, it goes to as low as 0.8% in the 9k x 9k instance.

Julia(JL) and Raytracer(RT) are two image processing applications where images are represented as arrays of integers. They are both implemented as a `map` of a function that computes 1 pixel of the resulting image. Julia presents less overhead than Raytracer, when compared to CUDA, due to the higher computational cost on the GPU for iterating over points to determine whether they belong to the Julia set.

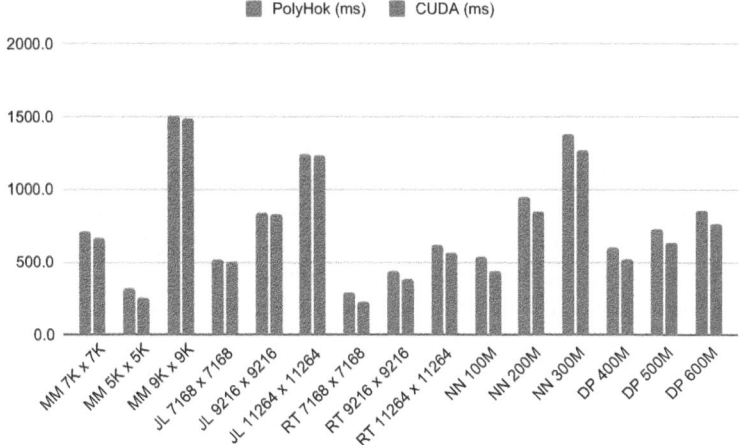

Fig. 4. PolyHok vs. CUDA, runtime (ms): MM, JL, RT, NN and DP

The NBodies problem is implemented as a composition of 2 maps (i.e., two PolyHok kernels). The first one calculates the gravitational impact of all bodies in the system. The second adjusts the bodies to their new position relative to the force impact. Each body has six attributes, represented as doubles, so the kernels work with an array that is 6 times the size of the problem. The first function mapped is very computationally intensive, as each body has to visit all other bodies to compute the force impact. For this reason, this program presented the largest runtime, making up for the overhead of JIT compiling kernels in PolyHok. Hence, NBodies presented the smallest overhead in comparison to CUDA.

Dot Product (DT), presented in Sect. 2.3, and Nearest Neighbor ported from the Rodinia Benchmark Suite [4], are both implemented with a composition of a map and a reduce, i.e., two PolyHok kernels. In DP, the dot product of an array of floats is computed. In Nearest Neighbor, the map calculates the Euclidean distance from each record to a target position in a randomly generated data set composed of doubles. The reduce is used to find the shortest distance. In both programs, the computation performed by the function arguments given to map and reduce is very fast, and although both programs use large data sets consuming most of the resources of the GPU, they presented the largest overheads in comparison to CUDA when using large data sets, 9% in NN, and 11.7% in DP.

In general, it is possible to observe that in small instances of problems that run in around 500ms or less, the overhead of using PolyHok is more apparent. This overhead diminishes as the size of the instance increases. Also, in fast kernels, the overhead of JIT compiling programs will be more noticeable, e.g., DP and NN. In contrast, in more computationally demanding kernels, the overhead is less visible, e.g., MM, NB, and JL.

5   Related Work

The work presented in this paper extends the work done in the GPotion [5] and Hok [6] systems. GPotion was the first version of the PolyHok language, but it did not support higher-order kernels. Furthermore, GPotion kernels only accepted arrays of floats, and hence it was possible to infer types at compilation time, instead of at runtime. Hok [6] was our first attempt at supporting Higher-Order Kernels. It was an extension of GPotion, hence kernels could only accept arrays of floats, which allowed Hok to statically infer types at compilation time as well, and use function pointers to implement higher-order kernels. PolyHok is a major remodeling of the system as now types are inferred at runtime, based on arguments that the kernel receives, which allows the system to accept arrays with elements of different types. Furthermore, in PolyHok kernels are JIT compiled at runtime, and it does not use function pointers, as calls to function arguments are substituted to direct calls to those functions, which is faster than using pointers.

Several studies have examined skeletons across various parallel architectures, including GPUs, e.g., [7–10,20]. A prominent example is the SkePU C++ framework, introduced in 2010 [7] and continuously updated, as seen in [7,9,10]. The SkePU framework offers a set of skeletons designed for different parallel architectures, GPUs included. In the initial version of SkePU, user-defined functions had to be created using specific C++ macros, which were later expanded to work on various architectures. This approach limited users, as function signatures had to match one of the predefined macros. In SkePU 2 [10] and SkePU 3 [9], the macros were replaced by a source-to-source translator (precompiler), leveraging libraries from the Clang project. The goal of this paper is not to develop an efficient skeleton library but to showcase how skeleton programming can be implemented using the abstractions provided by PolyHok.

The Haskell functional programming language was the testbed for the design of many DSLs for GPU programming, e.g., [3,15]. For example, Nikola [15] and Accelerate [3] are DSLs designed for array processing in Haskell. Accelerate allows programmers to use higher-order functions for array manipulation, and the array computations are then compiled into calls to skeletons implemented in CUDA. In addition to Haskell, other functional programming languages, as for example Futhark [12] and Julia [2], also offer higher-order functions targeting the GPU. In general, in the systems providing skeleton programming in functional languages, programmers can only implement new skeletons if they are based on existing ones, e.g., a MapReduce skeleton based on the composition of `map` and `reduce`.

Numba [14] is a Python back-end that allows the JIT compilation of GPU kernels. Triton [21] is similar to Numba but optimized for machine learning workloads. Although Numba also uses runtime type inference for JIT compiling kernels, both Triton and Numba do not support higher-order kernels nor anonymous device functions. Python also provides libraries for GPU programming, e.g., [22], and special purpose libraries that offload computations to the GPU, e.g., TensorFlow [1].

GPU programming within the Actors model has been explored in earlier research, such as [11,13]. In [13], an extension of the C++ Actor Framework (CAF) is presented where low-level OpenCL kernels are expressed within Actors. The Ensemble Actors language [11], also allows OpenCL like calls inside Actors, but as Ensemble is an entirely new language, it requires its own compiler.

6   Conclusions and Future Work

This paper presented PolyHok, a DSL for writing Higher-Order GPU kernels in the Elixir functional language. PolyHok kernels are dynamically typed and JIT compiled at runtime, which allows the same kernel to be applied to arguments of different types. We have demonstrated that PolyHok can be used to implement high-level abstractions for GPU computing like algorithm skeletons and array comprehensions. Experiments comparing PolyHok with pure CUDA demonstrate that the overhead of using PolyHok is acceptable, specially in large problems with computationally expensive kernels. Although the PolyHok system is heavily based on Elixirn's features like meta-programming and processes, we believe that the ideas presented here for supporting Higher-Order GPU kernels could also be applied to other languages that support meta-programming.

As future work, we would like to extend our current prototype to support other types of arrays, including structured data like tuples. Also, we would like implement a more comprehensive skeleton library and to port to Poly-Hok/skeletons larger programs (from [4], for example). PolyHok is a low-level GPU language, which means that programmers have to write optimized code through CUDA primitives. Optimizations could be explored at a higher-level using Metaprogramming to generate optimized PolyHok code. For example, kernel compositions could be processed at compilation time to perform kernel/skeleton fusion, e.g., [12].

Disclosure of Interests. The authors have no competing interests to declare.

References

1. Abadi, M., et al.: Tensorflow: a system for large-scale machine learning. In: Proceedings of OSDI 2016, pp. 265–283. USENIX Association (2016)
2. Besard, T., Foket, C., De Sutter, B.: Effective extensible programming: unleashing Julia on GPUs. IEEE TPDS **30**(4), 827–841 (2019)
3. Chakravarty, M.M., Keller, G., Lee, S., McDonell, T.L., Grover, V.: Accelerating haskell array codes with multicore GPUs. In: Proceedings DAMP 2011, pp. 3–14. ACM, New York (2011)
4. Che, S., et al.: Rodinia: a benchmark suite for heterogeneous computing. In: 2009 IEEE International Symposium on Workload Characterization (IISWC), pp. 44–54 (2009)
5. Du Bois, A.R., Cavalheiro, G.G.H.: GPotion: Embedding GPU programming in Elixir. J. Comput. Lang. **83**, 101323 (2025)

6. Du Bois, A.R., Perlin, T., Antunes, F., Cavalheiro, G.: HoK: higher-order GPU kernels in Elixir. In: Proceedings of SBLP, pp. 71–80. SBC (2024). https://sol.sbc.org.br/index.php/sblp/article/view/30259

7. Enmyren, J., Kessler, C.W.: SkePU: a multi-backend skeleton programming library for multi-GPU systems. In: Proceedings of the Fourth International Workshop on High-Level Parallel Programming and Applications, pp. 5–14 (2010)

8. Ernsting, S., Kuchen, H.: Algorithmic skeletons for multi-core, multi-GPU systems and clusters. Int. J. High Perform. Comput. Networking **7**(2), 129–138 (2012)

9. Ernstsson, A., Ahlqvist, J., Zouzoula, S., Kessler, C.: SkePU 3: portable high-level programming of heterogeneous systems and HPC clusters. Int. J. Parallel Program. **49**(6), 846–866 (2021)

10. Ernstsson, A., Li, L., Kessler, C.: SkePU 2: flexible and type-safe skeleton programming for heterogeneous parallel systems. Int. J. Parallel Prog. **46**, 62–80 (2018)

11. Harvey, P., Hentschel, K., Sventek, J.: Parallel programming in actor-based applications via OpenCL. In: Proceedings of the 16th Annual Middleware Conference, Middleware 2015, pp. 162–172. ACM, New York (2015)

12. Henriksen, T., Serup, N.G.W., Elsman, M., Henglein, F., Oancea, C.E.: Futhark: purely functional GPU-programming with nested parallelism and in-place array updates. SIGPLAN Not. **52**(6), 556–571 (2017)

13. Hiesgen, R., Charousset, D., Schmidt, T.C.: Manyfold actors: extending the C++ actor framework to heterogeneous many-core machines using OpenCL. In: Proceedings of the 5th International Workshop on Programming Based on Actors, Agents, and Decentralized Control, AGERE! 2015, pp. 45–56. ACM, New York (2015)

14. Lam, S.K., Pitrou, A., Seibert, S.: Numba: a LLVM-based python JIT compiler. In: Proceedings of the Second Workshop on the LLVM Compiler Infrastructure in HPC, LLVM 2015. ACM, New York (2015)

15. Mainland, G., Morrisett, G.: Nikola: embedding compiled GPU functions in Haskell. In: Proceedings of Haskell 2010, pp. 67–78. ACM, New York (2010)

16. Marques, R., Paulino, H., Alexandre, F., Medeiros, P.D.: Algorithmic skeleton framework for the orchestration of GPU computations. In: Wolf, F., Mohr, B., an Mey, D. (eds.) Euro-Par 2013. LNCS, vol. 8097, pp. 874–885. Springer, Heidelberg (2013). https://doi.org/10.1007/978-3-642-40047-6_86

17. McDonell, T.L., Chakravarty, M.M., Keller, G., Lippmeier, B.: Optimising purely functional GPU programs. SIGPLAN Not. **48**(9), 49–60 (2013)

18. NVIDIA: Fundamentals of Accelerated Computing with CUDA C/C++. Online Course NVIDIA Deep Learning Institute (2023)

19. Sanders, J., Kandrot, E.: CUDA by Example: An Introduction to General-Purpose GPU Programming. Addison-Wesley Professional (2010)

20. Steuwer, M., Kegel, P., Gorlatch, S.: Skelcl-a portable skeleton library for high-level GPU programming. In: 2011 IEEE International Symposium on Parallel and Distributed Processing Workshops and Phd Forum, pp. 1176–1182. IEEE (2011)

21. Tillet, P., Kung, H.T., Cox, D.: Triton: an intermediate language and compiler for tiled neural network computations. In: Proceedings of MAPL 2019, pp. 10–19. ACM (2019)

22. Yan, Y., Grossman, M., Sarkar, V.: JCUDA: a programmer-friendly interface for accelerating java programs with CUDA. In: Sips, H., Epema, D., Lin, H.-X. (eds.) Euro-Par 2009. LNCS, vol. 5704, pp. 887–899. Springer, Heidelberg (2009). https://doi.org/10.1007/978-3-642-03869-3_82

CoSF: A *Co*-Optimization Framework for Operator *S*plitting and *F*usion

Wei Li, Ao Ren$^{(\boxtimes)}$, Qingqiu Lan, Haining Fang, Zhenyu Wang, Yujuan Tan, Kan Zhong, and Duo Liu

Chongqing University, Chongqing, China
li.wei@stu.cqu.edu.cn,
{ren.ao,lanqingqiu,haining.fang,zhenyuwang,kzhong,liuduo}@cqu.edu.cn

Abstract. Compound operators, such as Log_softmax and RMSNorm, have been widely studied to enhance performance in deep neural networks (DNNs). Nonetheless, these operators often suffer from high hardware adaptation costs and limited optimization effects. AI compilers optimize them through operator splitting and successive operator fusion strategies. However, prior studies indiscriminately split all compound operators and failed to fully explore the fusion search space, incurring inefficient fusion schemes. To overcome these limitations, we propose a Co-Optimization Framework for Operator Splitting and Fusion (CoSF). In the operator splitting phase, we analyze memory reuse levels among operators and classify the compound operators into three types, according to their data locality. Then, we propose a fusion-aware splitting strategy. For each type of compound operator, it evaluates the successive fusion benefits after splitting the compound operator and automatically generates operator splitting strategies. In the operator fusion phase, to reduce the massive computation graph resulting from operator splitting, we propose a dominator tree-based graph partitioning algorithm to efficiently partition the computation graph. We then employ dynamic programming for each partitioned subgraph to generate an optimized fusion strategy. Finally, we propose a hardware-agnostic evaluation model to select the most effective fusion solution from multiple candidates. Experimental results demonstrate that CoSF achieves a 1.3–3.4× speedup on GPU and a 1.59–3.93× speedup on CPU compared to TVM, Pytorch, and TF-XLA.

Keywords: Compiler Optimization · Operation Split · Operation Fusion · Inference Acceleration · Deep Neural Network

1 Introduction

Deep neural networks (DNNs) have recently made significant advances in image recognition [13], machine translation [18], and video analysis. However, rapid growth in model scale and complexity has imposed higher demands on execution efficiency. To adapt to various deployment scenarios, deep learning compilers, such as TVM [3] and XLA [15], have been developed to convert DNN

© The Author(s), under exclusive license to Springer Nature Switzerland AG 2026
W. E. Nagel et al. (Eds.): Euro-Par 2025, LNCS 15900, pp. 114–128, 2026.
https://doi.org/10.1007/978-3-031-99854-6_8

models into highly optimized code for various hardware architectures, effectively decoupling software from hardware. However, as DNN models become increasingly complex, optimization challenges related to compound operators, such as Log_softmax, Sinkhorn, RMSNorm, and other complex custom operators, have become increasingly prominent. Deep learning frameworks and compilers typically rely on high-performance operator libraries supplied by hardware vendors(such as cuBLAS [12]). This approach requires the reimplementation of all operators for each new hardware platform, resulting in prolonged development cycles and high maintenance costs. Besides, current vendor operator libraries typically use generic implementations that are not tailored to specific deep-learning computation graphs or target hardware. This lack of targeted optimization prevents operators from fully leveraging hardware capabilities in parallel execution, memory access, and data transfer, thereby limiting model optimization in speed, energy efficiency, and accuracy.

Operator splitting [20] method significantly enhances the optimizability of computation graphs by splitting compound operators into primitive operators, such as scalar multiplication and vector addition. However, operator splitting incurs a surge in the number of primitive operators and the memory overhead associated with intermediate tensors. Operator fusion [5,16], one of the key techniques in deep learning compilers, reorganizes adjacent operators in the computation graph into a single operator, effectively eliminating the memory overhead of intermediate results and redundant computations, thereby mitigating the execution inefficiency caused by operator splitting.

Conventionally, operation splitting and operator fusion are performed sequentially. In the operator splitting phase, MindSpore [1] directly decomposes compound operators. Paddle [11] relies on manually predefined rules to perform operator splitting. Apollo [20] focuses on the splitting of activation operators. In the operator fusion phase, MindSpore achieves fusion through operator aggregation and reconstruction of the computation graph. Paddle generates fusion schemes by manually identifying frequent operator combinations, and Apollo constructs the fusion rules to explore potential schemes. The TVM and DNNFusion [3,14] employ a rule-based greedy strategy for fusion. MetaFlow [9] designs a backtracking algorithm to conduct a global search for fusion schemes. However, this separate strategy of operator splitting and fusion adopted by the mainstream compilers incurs undesired model execution efficiency. First, all compound operators are indiscriminately split without assessing the potential benefits of subsequent fusion, causing an excessively large fusion search space. Second, the excessively large fusion search space further causes suboptimal fusion solutions, as the manual-based and greedy-based fusion methods fail to efficiently process the large computation graph.

To address these issues, we propose a Co-Optimization Framework for Operator Splitting and Fusion (CoSF). In the operator splitting phase, we analyze memory reuse among operators and classify compound operators into three types based on their data locality. For each type, a splitting strategy is designed. Based on the classification and splitting strategy, we propose a fusion-aware operator splitting method that splits the compound operators and performs a local fusion among the primitive operators by evaluating the potential fusion benefits. This strategy can effectively reduce the number of operators for the successive fusion phase. In the fusion phase, the split operators form a computation graph. To reduce the fusion search space, we propose a dominator tree-based dynamic search algorithm that partitions the computation graph into multiple non-overlapping subgraphs and generates candidate fusion schemes by dynamic programming within each subgraph. In our method, both the splitting and fusion phases require the evaluation of the fusion benefits. Therefore, we propose a hardware-agnostic operator fusion evaluation model that addresses both the computation cost and memory access cost. It quantitatively evaluates the potential benefits of the fusion schemes and the one with the highest score as the final operator fusion strategy. The main contributions of this work are as follows:

- **Fusion-Aware Operator Splitting Method:** It classifies the compound operators according to their memory reuse, and for each type, it performs automatic splitting and preliminary fusion based on the fusion benefits. This approach can effectively reduce the computation graph size caused by splitting and facilitates subsequent operator fusion.
- **Dominator tree-based dynamic search Algorithm:** It partitions the large-scale graph into multiple non-overlapping subgraphs according to dominator relationships, effectively compressing the search space. Subsequently, a dynamic programming-based method is designed to efficiently generate multiple candidate fusion schemes within the reduced search space.
- **Hardware-Agnostic Operator Fusion Evaluation Model:** It quantitatively evaluates the fusion benefits by assessing the reduction of the memory cost and enhancement of the computation intensity. This evaluation model eliminates the time-consuming on-device testing and can be applied to various hardware architectures.
- **Experimental Validation:** Compared to TVM, Pytorch, and TF-XLA, our framework achieves a speedup of 1.3–3.4× on mainstream models on GPU and 1.59–3.93× on CPU.

2   Related Work

Operator splitting [1,11,20] techniques enhance computational graph optimizability by decomposing compound operators into primitive operations. However, this approach introduces new challenges, including exponential growth in primitive operator count and excessive intermediate tensor storage overhead. Operator fusion alleviates these issues by merging adjacent operators into monolithic computation kernels. This effectively eliminates redundant intermediate storage and computation. Existing frameworks adopt independent strategies in operator splitting and fusion: MindSpore [1] performs composite operator decomposition directly during the splitting phase, and PaddlePaddle [11] relies on manually predefined splitting rules. Apollo [20] focuses specifically on activation function decomposition. In the fusion stage, MindSpore achieves fusion through operator aggregation and graph reconstruction, whereas PaddlePaddle manually identifies hot operator combinations. Apollo constructs structured fusion rule libraries for heuristic exploration. Mainstream AI compilers like TVM [3], DNNFusion [14] and Astitch [21] employ rule-based greedy algorithms for fusion. MetaFlow [9] introduces backtracking algorithms for global fusion optimization. However, these approaches still face limitations: Rule-based methods often miss optimal fusion opportunities due to greedy heuristics. Manual strategies (e.g., predefined rules) lack scalability for emerging hardware architectures. Existing frameworks fail to exploit hardware-specific parallelism patterns effectively. Recent studies have begun exploring hardware-aware fusion strategies [10]. These efforts aim to bridge the gap between operator decomposition and hardware acceleration while maintaining computational efficiency.

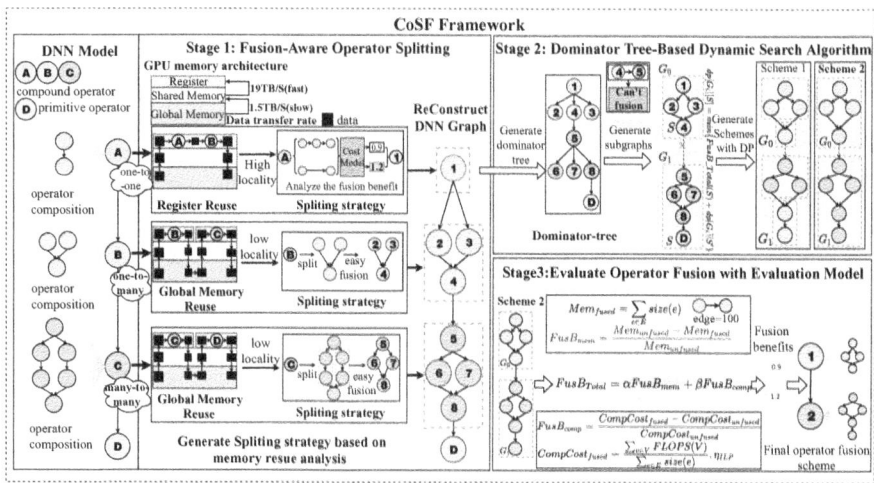

Fig. 1. The Overview of CoSF

3 Methodology

In this work, we propose CoSF, a Co-Optimization framework for operator splitting and fusion. The overall framework architecture is illustrated in Fig. 1. During the operator splitting phase, we propose a fusion-aware splitting method (Sect. 3.1). First, we classify compound operators A, B, and C based on their memory reuse level and design specific splitting strategies for different types. By quantitatively evaluating the impact of splitting strategies on the subsequent fusion phase, we automatically generate an efficient splitting strategy: splitting operators B and C into several primitive operators while retaining operator A without splitting, followed by reconstructing the computation graph. In the operator fusion phase, we propose a dominator tree-based dynamic search algorithm for fusion schemes (Sect. 3.2). Specifically, we first construct a dominator tree to partition the computation graph into multiple non-overlapping subgraphs. Then, within each subgraph, we propose a fusion strategy search algorithm based on dynamic programming to generate multiple fusion strategies within an efficient search space. By integrating a hardware-agnostic evaluation model, we quantitatively assess the potential benefit of each strategy from the perspectives of memory access cost and computation cost. Finally, we select the fusion strategy with the highest score as the final operator fusion strategy.

3.1   Fusion-Aware Operator Splitting Method

Traditional operator splitting methods split all compound operators without considering the fusion benefits, resulting in an overly large search space and suboptimal fusion schemes that hinder runtime efficiency. To address this, we propose a fusion-aware operator splitting method that analyzes fusion benefits during splitting and automatically generates strategies to minimize the number of resulting primitive operators. We first classify the compound operators according to their fusion possibilities and for which different splitting strategies are applied. Existing approaches, such as DNNFusion [14], rely on changes in tensor shapes when analyzing the fusion possibility, neglecting the complex memory reuse level and fusion results caused by multi-level data dependencies within compound operators. To more accurately reflect the fusion possibility of compound operators, we design a classification method based on memory reuse level(as shown in Table 1), which classifies compound operators into three types:

One-to-One Mapping Operators: These operators have strict data correspondence. In the GPU architecture (as shown in Fig. 1), the output data of operator A can be buffered in registers, allowing the following operators to access this data from the registers. This mapping mode maintains thread-level data locality, reduces the frequency of global memory accesses, and yields significant fusion possibilities.

Many-to-Many Mapping Operators: These operators involve complex non-linear data dependencies. As shown in Fig. 1, in the GPU architecture, the output data of operator C is typically confined to global memory storage, preventing the following operators from efficiently caching data using registers or shared memory. This mapping mode results in significantly increased memory access latency and very limited fusion possibility.

One-to-Many Mapping Operators: These operators have variable memory reuse characteristics, The degree of reuse depends on the access patterns of the following operators. When the following operators have a one-to-one type, the intermediate data can be stored in shared memory, achieving thread block-level data locality. Conversely, when following operators have a many-to-many type, the intermediate data must be returned to global memory, thereby reducing data locality and limiting the performance improvements that fusion can deliver.

Table 1. Operator classification based on memory reuse analysis.

Mapping type	Operators		Memory Reuse Level
One-to-One	**Primitive**	Add,Sin,Div,Concat,ReLU	Register
	Compound	NReLU,LeakyReLU,Sigmoid	
One-to-Many	**Primitive**	Transpose,Resize,Upsample	Shared/Global Memory
	Compound	DepthToSpace,SpaceToDepth	
Many-to-Many	**Primitive**	Gemm,Conv,Reduce	Global Memory
	Compound	BatchNorm,RMSNorm Log_Softmax,MaxPool,	

Based on the operator classification, We apply a quantitative analysis of the fusion benefits for different types of compound operators as presented in Table 1, thereby automatically generating efficient splitting strategies. (1) For many-to-many mapping operators (e.g., LayerNorm), their complex data dependencies result in only global memory reuse, making direct fusion inefficient. To increase the fusion exploration space, reduce memory access, and improve performance, these operators must first be split. To avoid the excessive generation of primitive operators caused by traditional indiscriminate splitting, we traverse the sequence of split operators and apply a local fusion to adjacent operators. This reduces the number of primitive operators generated. For example, in traditional methods [11], the LayerNorm operator is split into six primitive operators (such as mean, add, pow, etc.), whereas our approach reduces this to just two, significantly simplifying the computation graph. (2) For compound operators that support cache reuse (e.g., via registers or shared memory), we design two candidate fusion sub-networks: (i) directly fusing the compound operator with adjacent operators and (ii) first performing splitting and a local fusion on the compound operator, followed by fusion with adjacent operators. We then employ a post-order reverse traversal strategy (from leaf nodes to root nodes) to dynamically generate fusion strategies for both sub-networks. These strategies are then sent into the evaluation model (as detailed in Sect. 3.2) to quantify the benefits of fusion. The strategy that yields the highest benefit is selected as the final splitting plan for the given compound operator. In the case of the Sigmoid operator, the traditional method [11] would split it into four primitive operators. However, after quantitative evaluation, our method determines that no splitting is necessary, effectively reducing the number of operators. This automated splitting strategy not only enhances memory access efficiency but also simplifies the computation graph after splitting.

3.2 Dominator-Tree-Based Dynamic Search for Fusion Schemes

Towards efficiently generating fusion strategies from the expanded search space after splitting, we propose a dominator tree-based dynamic search algorithm. Specifically, we first propose a hardware-agnostic fusion evaluation model that predicts the benefits of operator fusion based on memory access cost and computation cost. Then, to address the challenge of searching the large-scale computation graph resulting from operator splitting, we propose a dominator tree-based hierarchical graph partitioning method to partition the computation graph into multiple non-overlapping subgraphs, thereby effectively decoupling the optimization tasks among these subgraphs. Finally, we propose a fusion strategy search method based on dynamic programming to efficiently search for the final fusion strategy.

Hardware-Agnostic Fusion Evaluation Model. Traditional fusion evaluation methods [2,9] rely on runtime tests, requiring repeated tuning and debugging across hardware platforms, which is time-consuming. To improve cross-architecture adaptability, we analyzed the impact of operator fusion on performance. By merging primitive operators into a compound operator, fusion leverages register and cache to reduce memory access and data transfers, lowering both memory and computation costs and improving resource utilization. Building on this insight, we design a hardware-agnostic evaluation model that calculates memory access and computation costs for each operator, providing an effective metric for assessing fusion benefits.

To evaluate the memory access cost, we construct a tensor lifecycle model that quantifies the data dependency relationships between operators as edge weights in the computation graph. The weight of each edge, denoted as $size(e)$, represents the amount of data transferred between adjacent operators, reflecting the cost of storing and accessing that data in memory. For the original computation graph, all data transfers between operators must occur via memory, and thus, the total global memory access cost can be expressed as the sum of the weights of all edges, i.e.,

$$MemCost = \sum_{e \in E} size(e) \tag{1}$$

where E denotes the set of all edges in the computation graph.

After operator fusion, some intermediate tensors can be directly transferred via registers or shared memory, thereby reducing global memory accesses. In this case, we only need to consider tensor transfers across fusion groups, with the corresponding memory access cost $MemCost_{fused}$ being the cumulative sum of the edge weights that span these subgraphs.

To quantify the improvement in memory access benefit due to the fusion strategy, a post-fusion memory benefit metric is defined as follows:

$$FusB_{mem} = \frac{MemCost_{unfused} - MemCost_{fused}}{MemCost_{unfused}} \tag{2}$$

If the fusion eliminates redundant memory transfers (i.e., $MemCost_{fused}$ approaches 0), then $FusB_{mem}$ approaches 1, indicating excellent memory optimization. Conversely, if the fusion yields no memory optimization ($MemCost_{fused} = MemCost_{unfused}$), then $FusB_{mem} = 0$. By normalizing in this manner, the metric can be directly compared across different subgraph partitions and hardware platforms, reflecting the potential of operator fusion for optimizing memory usage.

Traditionally, computational performance is often measured by the number of floating-point operations (FLOPS). However, actual performance depends not only on the computation workload but is also significantly influenced by data transfer patterns (i.e., memory access cost). To better capture real-world performance, we adopt the concept of the Roof-line model [19] by comprehensively evaluating both computation and memory transfers to derive a more realistic Operational intensity metric. We define the computation cost as follows:

$$CompCost = \frac{\sum_{v \in V} FLOPS(V)}{\sum_{e \in E} size(e)} \cdot \eta_{ILP} \tag{3}$$

where $\sum_{v \in V} FLOPS(v)$ represents the total number of floating-point operations across all operators in the computation graph; $\sum_{e \in E} size(e)$ denotes the total data transfer volume corresponding to all edges in the graph, summarizing the memory access cost; and $\eta_{ILP} \in [0, 1]$ is the instruction-level parallelism (ILP) factor, obtained via static program analysis, which indicates the degree to which the processor can exploit ILP. A higher η_{ILP} means that more operations can be executed in parallel, thereby enhancing computational efficiency.

We further define an improvement metric for the computation benefit after fusion:

$$FusB_{comp} = \frac{CompCost_{fused} - CompCost_{unfused}}{CompCost_{unfused}} \tag{4}$$

where $CompCost_{unfused}$ represents the computation cost in the unfused state (i.e., the amount of computation per unit of data transfer in the original computation graph), and $CompCost_{fused}$ represents the computation cost after fusion optimization. The latter is enhanced due to reduced redundant memory accesses and improved data locality, which increases the operational intensity. The value of this metric reflects the relative benefit of the fusion strategy in improving computational efficiency: a higher value indicates a more significant improvement resulting from fusion.

Combining the two dimensions of memory access and computation cost, we construct a comprehensive evaluation model as follows:

$$FusB_{Total} = \alpha FusB_{mem} + \beta FusB_{comp} \tag{5}$$

where α and β are normalization factors that adjust the relative weights of memory access and computation cost.

Fusion Strategy Search Algorithm. To address the challenge posed by the large-scale computation graph resulting from operator splitting, which makes direct search for fusion schemes difficult, we design a dominator tree-based hierarchical graph partitioning method. The core is an analysis of the control dependencies and data flow characteristics among operators in the computation graph to construct a dominator tree. The selection of a dominator tree as the partitioning basis is primarily based on two properties: first, the dominator tree can explicitly represent the strict topological order of the computation flow via the dominator relationships among nodes; second, its inherent hierarchical structure naturally accommodates the need for decoupling between subgraphs.

Algorithm 1. Dominator Tree-Based Dynamic Search For Fusion Schemes

---

Require: Initial computation graph G
Require: Evaluation model FusB_Total($\cdot$)
Ensure: Optimized computation graph G'
 1: **function** GRAPH_SPLIT(G)
 2:    **if** $|G| \leq$ threshold **then**
 3:       **return** G
 4:    **else**
 5:       $dominance\_tree \leftarrow$ BUILD_DOMINANCE_TREE(G)
 6:       $C \leftarrow$ FIND_DOMINATOR_NODES($dominance\_tree$)
 7:       $G_1 \leftarrow \{o_i \in G \mid o_i$ is reachable from $C\}$
 8:       $G_2 \leftarrow G \setminus G_1$
 9:       **return** $\{$GRAPH_SPLIT(G_1), GRAPH_SPLIT(G_2)$\}$
10:    **end if**
11: **end function**
12: subgraphs $\leftarrow$ GRAPH_SPLIT(G)   ▷ Apply graph splitting algorithm
13: **for** each subgraph G_i in subgraphs **do**
14:    dp $\leftarrow \{\}$ ▷ Storage for best fusion costs
15:    best_fusion_plan $\leftarrow \emptyset$
16:    **for** each possible fusion of operators in G_i **do**
17:       fusion_plan $\leftarrow$ APPLY_FUSION(G_i, fusion)
18:       cost $\leftarrow$ FusCost_Total(fusion_plan)   ▷ Evaluate cost
19:       **if** cost $<$ dp[best_fusion_plan] **then**
20:          dp[fusion_plan] $\leftarrow$ cost
21:          best_fusion_plan $\leftarrow$ fusion_plan
22:       **end if**
23:    **end for**
24:    best_fusion$_{G_i}$ $\leftarrow$ best_fusion_plan   ▷ Store optimal plan
25: **end for**
26: final_graph $\leftarrow$ COMBINE_SUBGRAPHS(subgraphs, best_fusion$_{G_i}$)
27: **return** final_graph

In Algorithm 1, we first perform a depth-first search to traverse the computation graph and construct a dominator tree structure. In this process, we define a set of dominator relationships: $D = \{d_i | d_i = (v_j, v_k)\}$, where v_j is the immediate dominator of v_k, that is the last common node that every path from the entry node must pass through. This dominator relationship is established through memory data flow analysis, ensuring that each operator is constrained only by the control flow imposed by its dominator node. Subsequently, the algorithm adopts a post-order reverse traversal strategy on the dominator tree, dynamically aggregating subgraphs in a leaf-to-root order. Specifically, when a node in the dominator tree is visited, the corresponding computation graph operator is evaluated for potential fusion with all its dominated successor nodes. If fusion is possible, the eligible successor nodes are merged with the current node to form the largest contiguous fusible subgraph.

This process partitions the computation graph using two key mechanisms: (1) dominator boundaries and unique fusion feasibility ensure non-overlapping subgraphs, and (2) strict topological ordering preserves execution order and data dependencies. As a result, the graph is divided into independent subgraph units, transforming the global search problem into parallel subgraph-level optimization tasks.

For fusion optimization within each subgraph, we design a dynamic programming-based method to explore fusion schemes. In this method, the state space is defined as the current set of fusible operators, and state transitions correspond to the selection of different fusion strategies. Specifically, as shown in Algorithm 1, for each subgraph G_i, a dynamic programming table dp is initialized to store the minimum cost of each possible operator fusion scheme. The state transition equation is given by:

$$dp[i][fus\_plan] = min(FusB(fusion\_plan), dp[i][best\_fus\_plan]) \qquad (6)$$

where $dp[i][fus\_plan]$ represents the minimum fusion cost for the set of fusible operators S in subgraph G_i. Here, $FusB(fus\_plan)$ denotes the fusion benefit of the current fusion scheme for the operator set. During dynamic fusion exploration, we employ a hardware-agnostic evaluation model to quantify each candidate scheme's benefits. The highest-scoring fusion schemes from all subgraphs are then merged to form a globally optimized computation graph. This approach enhances execution efficiency and memory utilization by maximizing resource usage while minimizing computation and memory access costs.

4 Experiments

4.1 Experimental Setup

Experimental Platform: Our experiments were conducted on the Ubuntu 20.04 LTS operating system and executed on typical CPU and GPU hardware platforms. The GPU used is the NVIDIA A100(80GB memory) with the CUDA Toolkit 11.8, while the CPU is an Intel Xeon Gold 6226R CPU (2.6GHz, 64 cores).

Benchmark Models: to comprehensively evaluate the optimization effects, we selected five representative types of deep neural networks: MobileNet-v1 [8], ResNet50 [7], LSTM [6], Seq2Seq [17], Bert-base [4], including convolutional neural networks (CNNs), recurrent neural networks (RNNs), and attention-based models, ensuring broad representativeness of the evaluation results.

Baseline frameworks: Our framework is implemented on the TVM, constructing a complete optimization system from operator splitting to fusion execution. For baseline comparisons, we selected three mainstream frameworks:(1) PyTorch 2.2.0, (2)TVM 0.9.0, (3)TF-XLA 2.8.0.

Table 2. End-to-end runtime and speedup for five DNN models on the NVIDIA A100.

Network	Runtime(ms)				Speed up		
	Pytorch	TVM	TF-XLA	**CoSF**	Pytorch	TVM	TF-XLA
ResNet50	58.31	7.34	22.57	**5.66**	10.3x	1.3x	3.9x
MobileNet-v1	92	52.23	58.67	**40.12**	2.3x	1.3x	1.45x
Seq2Seq	63.26	19.31	8.40	**5.67**	11.15x	3.4x	1.20x
LSTM	172.0	54.18	32.21	**19.76**	8.70x	2.74x	1.63x
Bert-base	6.59	5.95	4.03	**3.18**	2.07	1.87	1.26

4.2 Execution Latency

We compared inference times on CPU and GPU platforms. Table 2 shows the performance results on GPU at a batch size of 1. Compared to PyTorch, CoSF achieved up to an 11.15× speedup on Seq2Seq and 2.07× on Bert-base, with a geometric mean speedup of 8.58×. Against AI compilers, CoSF delivered a 2.74× acceleration on Seq2Seq and 1.3× on ResNet50, averaging 2.10× over TVM and 1.89× over TF-XLA.

Table 3. End-to-end runtime and speedup for five DNN models on the CPU.

Network	Runtime(ms)				Speed up		
	Pytorch	TVM	TF-XLA	**CoSF**	Pytorch	TVM	TF-XLA
ResNet50	72.15	10.45	11.28	**6.59**	11.0x	1.59x	1.71x
MobileNet-v1	110.14	74.23	87.92	**40.32**	2.70x	1.84x	2.18x
Seq2Seq	97.67	23.15	13.56	**5.88**	14.15x	3.93x	2.30x
LSTM	192.0	45.18	30.25	**15.26**	12.51x	2.96x	1.98x
Bert-base	9.2	6.7	5.46	**3.56**	2.58x	1.88x	1.54x

Table 3 shows the detailed experimental results on the CPU. The CoSF framework achieves average performance improvements of 8.54×, 1.94×, and 2.45× over the baseline frameworks, further verifying the adaptability of our proposed operator splitting and fusion co-optimization framework across different architectures.

4.3 Fusion Rate

To further quantify the effectiveness of the fusion schemes, we conducted experiments focusing on two aspects: memory access and kernel count.

The size of memory access reflects the changes in memory accesses before and after operator fusion, serving as a macro-level indicator of optimization

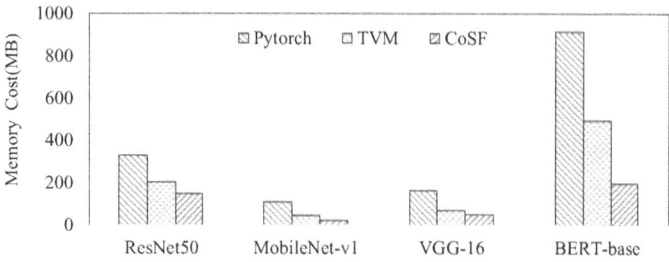

Fig. 2. Memory Access Cost Comparison

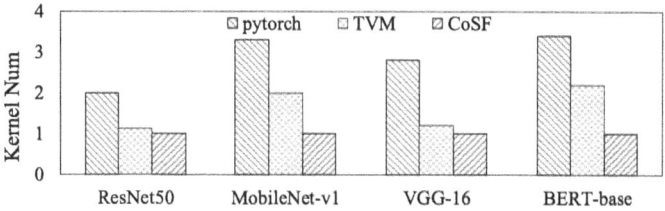

Fig. 3. Kernel num Comparison

efficiency. As shown in Fig. 2, CoSF improves memory access by 28%, 53%, 28%, and 60% for ResNet50, MobileNet-V1, VGG-16, and BERT-base, respectively, compared to TVM. This improvement is achieved by reducing the generation of intermediate results, which enhances cache hit rates and lowers overall memory consumption.

The number of kernels reflects the optimization efficiency from the perspective of computation. Figure 3 illustrates that, for ResNet50, MobileNet-V1, VGG-16, and BERT-base, CoSF reduces kernel counts by 41%, 52%, 19%, and 70% respectively compared to TVM. This reduction decreases context switching frequency, enhancing overall efficiency.

4.4 Ablation Study

To evaluate the impact of fusion-aware operator splitting and dominator tree-based dynamic fusion search, we conducted ablation experiments on benchmark models. The configurations are: (1) Baseline: TVM default with indiscriminate splitting and greedy fusion; (2) MyOS: fusion-aware splitting with greedy fusion; (3) MyOF: indiscriminate splitting with dynamic search; and (4) CoSF: co-optimization with both techniques.

As shown in Table 4, the MyOS degrades performance—ResNet50 and LSTM slow by 1.45× and 1.24× respectively, due to increased operator count and memory access cost. MyOF generally boosts performance but offers limited gains for some models (e.g., ResNet50, MobileNet-V1). In contrast, CoSF consistently enhances performance across all models, reducing ResNet50 runtime from 7.34ms to 5.66ms (1.30× speedup) and Seq2Seq from 19.31ms to 5.67ms (3.4× speedup). These result from refining the optimization space via splitting and mitigating overhead through fusion, demonstrating CoSF's overall effectiveness and generality.

Table 4. The ablation study regarding the fusion-aware splitting method and dynamic search method.

Network	MyOS	MyOF	Runtime(ms)
ResNet50			7.34
	✓		10.66(−1.45x)
		✓	6.45(1.13x)
	✓	✓	**5.66(1.30x)**
MobileNet-v1			52.23
	✓		50.18(1.04x)
		✓	48.06(1.08x)
	✓	✓	**40.12(1.30x)**
Seq2Seq			19.31
	✓		19.31(1.00x)
		✓	16.23(1.19x)
	✓	✓	**5.67(3.4x)**
LSTM			54.18
	✓		50.67(1.96x)
		✓	35.78(1.51x)
	✓	✓	**19.76(2.72x)**
Bert-base			5.95
	✓		12.18(−2.04x)
		✓	4.76(1.25x)
	✓	✓	**3.18(1.80x)**

5   Conclusion

This work presents CoSF, a co-optimization framework for operator splitting and fusion. CoSF performed fusion-aware splitting by analyzing memory reuse to classify compound operators and automatically derives splitting strategies based on fusion benefits. To address graph expansion, it uses a dominator-tree-based approach to partition the graph and applies dynamic programming to generate fusion candidates. A hardware-agnostic evaluation model selects the optimal strategy. Experiments show that CoSF achieves 1.3×–3.4× speedup on GPUs and 1.59×–3.93× on CPUs, outperforming mainstream AI compilers.

Acknowledgements. This work is supported by the National Natural Science Foundation of China (Nos. 62472058 and 62402070) and the research funding from central universities (Nos. 2024CDJGF-032 and 2024CDJGF-019).

Disclosure of Interest. The authors have no competing interests to declare that are relevant to the content of this artticle

References

1. Huawei mindspore. https://www.mindspore.cn/ens
2. Cai, X., Wang, Y.: Optimus: an operator fusion framework for deep neural networks. ACM Trans. Embed. Comput. Syst. **22**(1), 1–26 (2022)
3. Chen, T., Moreau, T., Jiang, Z., Zheng, L., et al.: TVM: an automated end-to-end optimizing compiler for deep learning. In: 13th USENIX Symposium on Operating Systems Design and Implementation (OSDI 2018), pp. 578–594 (2018)
4. Devlin, J., Chang, M.W., et al.: BERT: pre-training of deep bidirectional transformers for language understanding. In: Proceedings of the 2019 Conference of the North American chapter of the Association for Computational Linguistics: Human Language Technologies, volume 1 (Long and Short Papers), pp. 4171–4186 (2019)
5. Fang, J., Shen, Y., Wang, Y.: Optimizing DNN computation graph using graph substitutions. Proc. VLDB Endowment **13**(12), 2734–2746 (2020)
6. Graves, A., Graves, A.: Long short-term memory. In: Supervised Sequence Labelling with Recurrent Neural Networks, pp. 37–45 (2012)
7. He, K., et al.: Deep residual learning for image recognition. In: Proceedings of the IEEE Conference on Computer Vision and Pattern Recognition, pp. 770–778 (2016)
8. Howard, A.G., Zhu, M., et al.: Mobilenets: efficient convolutional neural networks for mobile vision applications. arXiv preprint arXiv:1704.04861 (2017)
9. Jia, Z., Thomas, J., Warszawski, T., Gao, M., Zaharia, M., Aiken, A.: Optimizing DNN computation with relaxed graph substitutions. Proc. Mach. Learn. Syst. **1**, 27–39 (2019)
10. Li, Y., et al.: Sirius: harvesting whole-program optimization opportunities for DNNs. Proc. Mach. Learn. Syst. **5**, 186–202 (2023)
11. Ma, Y., Yu, D., et al.: Paddlepaddle: an open-source deep learning platform from industrial practice. Front. Data Domputing **1**(1), 105–115 (2019)
12. Markidis, S., et al.: Nvidia tensor core programmability, performance & precision. In: 2018 IEEE International Parallel and Distributed Processing Symposium Workshops (IPDPSW), pp. 522–531. IEEE (2018)
13. Meng, L., Li, H., Chen, B.C., et al.: AdaViT: adaptive vision transformers for efficient image recognition. In: Proceedings of the IEEE/CVF Conference on Computer Vision and Pattern Recognition, pp. 12309–12318 (2022)
14. Niu, W., Guan, J., Wang, Y., et al.: DNNFusion: accelerating deep neural networks execution with advanced operator fusion. In: Proceedings of the 42nd ACM SIGPLAN International Conference on Programming Language Design and Implementation, pp. 883–898 (2021)
15. Sabne, A.: Xla : Compiling machine learning for peak performance (2020)
16. Shi, Y., Yang, Z., Xue, J., et al.: Welder: scheduling deep learning memory access via tile-graph. In: 17th USENIX Symposium on Operating Systems Design and Implementation (OSDI 2023), pp. 701–718 (2023)

17. Sutskever, I., Vinyals, O., Le, Q.V.: Sequence to sequence learning with neural networks. In: Advances in Neural Information Processing Systems, vol. 27 (2014)
18. Vaswani, A., Shazeer, N., Parmar, N., et al.: Attention is all you need. In: Advances in Neural Information Processing Systems, vol. 30 (2017)
19. Williams, S., Waterman, A., Patterson, D.: Roofline: an insightful visual performance model for multicore architectures. Commun. ACM **52**(4), 65–76 (2009)
20. Zhao, J., et al.: Apollo: automatic partition-based operator fusion through layer by layer optimization. Proc. Mach. Learn. Syst. **4**, 1–19 (2022)
21. Zheng, Z., et al.: AStitch: enabling a new multi-dimensional optimization space for memory-intensive ml training and inference on modern SIMT architectures. In: Proceedings of the 27th ACM International Conference on Architectural Support for Programming Languages and Operating Systems, pp. 359–373 (2022)

Scheduling, Resource Management, Cloud, Edge Computing, and Workflows

Approximation Bounds for SLACK on Identical Parallel Machines

Louis-Claude Canon, Anthony Dugois$^{(\boxtimes)}$, Pierre-Cyrille Héam, and Ismaël Jecker

Univ. Marie et Louis Pasteur, CNRS, institut FEMTO-ST, 25000 Besançon, France
{louis-claude.canon,anthony.dugois,pierre-cyrille.heam,
ismael.jecker}@univ-fcomte.fr

Abstract. We examine the problem of scheduling tasks on identical parallel machines using the SLACK heuristic. This method sorts tasks in non-increasing order of processing times, partitions them into sets of size m (corresponding to the number of machines), and subsequently schedules them in non-increasing order of slack with a list-based heuristic. Similar to LPT, SLACK has a time complexity of $O(n \log n)$, where n denotes the number of tasks, and exhibits strong empirical performance in some scenarios. However, no formal approximation guarantee has been established for this heuristic. In this work, we provide a 4/3-approximation ratio, which, while slightly worse than with LPT, is tight. Moreover, we derive improved bounds under the constraint that processing times do not exceed a fraction of the optimal makespan. Specifically, we show that SLACK is a $\left(1 + \frac{m-1}{m(k+1)}\right)$-approximation algorithm when the processing time of any task is at most OPT/k for $k \geq 2$.

Keywords: Scheduling · Approximation ratio · Makespan · SLACK

1 Introduction

Despite the extensive literature on scheduling algorithms, parallel scheduling often relies on low-cost heuristics, excluding more computationally expensive approaches such as PTAS [5]. Among these heuristics, LPT [4] has long been a widely used and effective method for scheduling independent tasks to identical machines. In 2020, an alternative heuristic called SLACK was introduced, offering the same computational complexity as LPT while demonstrating strong empirical performance in experimental studies [2]. However, unlike LPT, whose worst-case performance is well established with a $\left(\frac{4}{3} - \frac{1}{3m}\right)$-approximation ratio, no theoretical performance guarantee has been provided for SLACK.

This paper addresses this gap by proving that SLACK is a 4/3-approximation algorithm, a result that, while slightly weaker than LPT's bound, remains comparable and is tight (Sect. 3). Building on the approach of [7], we further refine this analysis by imposing constraints on processing times. This restriction leads to improved approximation ratios for SLACK, aligning closely with those of LPT (Sect. 4). Lastly, we present a class of instances that nearly, but not exactly, match the derived approximation bounds.

© The Author(s), under exclusive license to Springer Nature Switzerland AG 2026
W. E. Nagel et al. (Eds.): Euro-Par 2025, LNCS 15900, pp. 131–144, 2026.
https://doi.org/10.1007/978-3-031-99854-6_9

Related Work. The $P||C_{\max}$ problem is one of the simplest scheduling problems to formulate. It is known to be strongly NP-complete [3]. Several Operational Research approaches have been proposed to solve it, such as integer linear programming [8,9] or Tabu search [12]. In a recent work [10], authors have proposed to improve scheduling results by applying several transformations. It is also possible to tackle $P||C_{\max}$ using Polynomial Time Approximation Schemes [6]. Among efficient approximation algorithms, one can mention approaches based on Bin Packing [11] or list heuristics [4].

It is well-known that any list heuristic provides a $\left(2 - \frac{1}{m}\right)$-approximation [4]. Sorting tasks in non-increasing order of processing times leads to the Longest-Processing-Time-first (LPT) heuristic, which is a $\left(\frac{4}{3} - \frac{1}{3m}\right)$-approximation [4] and has been extensively analyzed in the literature. In a recent work, authors investigate several subclasses of LPT instances, where the processing time of each task is smaller than a fraction $1/k$ of the optimal makespan [7]. They show that LPT is a $\left(1 + \frac{k-1}{k(k+1)}\right)$-approximation when the number of machines lies between k and $\frac{k(k+1)}{2}$. The SLACK heuristic has been introduced recently [2] and proved to be asymptotically efficient for randomly distributed processing times following either a uniform or exponential distribution [1].

2   Model

An *instance* I of the scheduling problem $P||C_{\max}$ is composed of a set of *machines* $M = \{1, 2, \ldots, m\}$ and a set of *tasks* $T = \{1, 2, \ldots, n\}$, each task j having a *processing time* $p_j \in \mathbb{Q}_{\geq 0}$. A *schedule* is a function $\sigma : T \to M$ mapping each task to a machine. The *load* of a machine $i \in M$ according to σ is the sum $C(i) = \sum_{j:\sigma(j)=i} p_j$ of the processing times of all the tasks assigned to i. The *makespan* of σ is the maximal load $C_{\max} = \max_{i \in M} \{C(i)\}$. We note $\mathrm{OPT}(I)$ the minimal makespan on all the schedules of an instance I.

In this paper, we focus on a specific schedule, called SLACK, defined as follows. Consider a scheduling instance I given by a set of machines M and a set of tasks T ordered in non-increasing order of processing times $p_1 \geq p_2 \geq \cdots \geq p_n$. First, the set of tasks is partitioned into $P = \lceil \frac{n}{m} \rceil$ packs of m tasks: the i-th pack contains the tasks $\{(i-1)m+1, (i-1)m+2, \ldots, im\}$. If the number n of tasks is not a multiple of m, the last pack is completed with tasks of size 0. The *slack* β_i of the i-th pack is defined as the difference between the processing times of its longest and smallest tasks. SLACK then schedules packs in non-increasing order of slack (following a *list scheduling* policy). Let π describe this ordering: $\pi(t)$ gives the index of the pack scheduled at step t, that is, the pack with the t-th highest slack.

Starting from pack $\pi(1)$, SLACK considers all the tasks in non-increasing order of processing times, and assigns each of them to one of the machines having the lowest load so far. This process is repeated for pack $\pi(2)$, then pack $\pi(3)$, and so on, until all packs have been scheduled. We denote by $c_t(i)$ the load of machine i when t packs have been scheduled, and we define $\delta_t = \max_{i,i' \in M} |c_t(i) - c_t(i')|$,

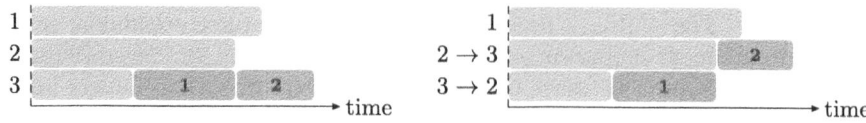

Fig. 1. A tie appears on machines 2 and 3 after task 1 has been scheduled. SLACK can schedule the problematic task 2 either on machine 2 (as shown on the right) or machine 3 (as shown on the left). The two resulting schedules are clearly equivalent, as it suffices to swap machines 2 and 3 to obtain identical load profiles on the machines.

which represents the *maximum imbalance* on machines at the end of step t. Obviously, $c_0(i) = 0$ for each i. We also denote by SLACK(I) the makespan of SLACK on instance I. The *approximation ratio* of SLACK is the maximum ratio r between the makespan of SLACK and the optimal makespan, i.e., $r = \max_I \left\{ \frac{\text{SLACK}(I)}{\text{OPT}(I)} \right\}$. We summarize the notations in Table 1.

Breaking Ties. Observe that there may exist several equivalent SLACK schedules for a given instance if there is a choice to be made for a given task; this situation happens when there is a tie on machines. Obviously, all the possible SLACK schedules for a given instance have the same makespan, because after scheduling the problematic task, it suffices to renumber the machines before pursuing the schedule (see Fig. 1). In the following, we assume that the considered SLACK schedule is the one which, *when possible*, never puts two tasks coming from the same pack on the same machine. Any guarantee on the makespan of this schedule will also apply to the other equivalent SLACK schedules.

Auxiliary Lemmas. Our proofs rely on previously known results. We begin with two lemmas coming from the literature: the first one states an upper bound on the makespan of any list schedule, depending on the maximum imbalance; the second one states that this imbalance is bounded by the highest slack in a SLACK schedule. We then derive another upper bound on the maximum imbalance.

Lemma 1 (Graham's bound [4]). *For any instance I, in any list schedule, we have $C_{\max} \leq OPT(I) + \left(1 - \frac{1}{m}\right)\delta$, where δ is the maximum imbalance at the end of the schedule.*

Table 1. Notations used in this paper.

$M = \{1, 2, \ldots, m\}$	The set of machines
$T = \{1, 2, \ldots, n\}$	The set of tasks
p_j	The processing time of task j
P	The number of packs
β_i	The slack of the i-th pack
$\pi(t)$	The index of the pack scheduled at step t
$c_t(i)$	The load of machine i after t packs have been scheduled
δ_t	The maximum imbalance after t packs have been scheduled

Lemma 2 (Lemma 3 in [1]). *For any instance I, in any SLACK schedule, we have $\delta_t \leq \max\left(\delta_{t-1}, \beta_{\pi(t)}\right)$ for all $1 \leq t \leq P$.*

Observe that, as a corollary of Lemma 2, the maximum imbalance δ_P at the end of SLACK is smaller than or equal to the slack $\beta_{\pi(1)}$ of the first scheduled pack.

Lemma 3. *For any instance I, in any SLACK schedule, we have $\delta_t \leq p_{\ell_t}$ for all t, where ℓ_t is the last task to complete after t packs have been scheduled.*

Proof. Let ℓ_t be the last task to complete after t packs have been scheduled by SLACK, and let i be the machine on which it has been put. As SLACK is a list schedule, the completion times of all machines but i were necessarily higher than the completion time of i when ℓ_t has been scheduled. Thus, $c_t(i') \geq c_t(i) - p_{\ell_t}$ for all $i' \neq i$, which concludes the proof. □

3   Approximation Ratio in the General Setting

We prove our main result establishing the approximation ratio of SLACK.

Theorem 1. *The approximation ratio of SLACK is $\frac{4}{3}$.*

To prove Theorem 1, we introduce DISPATCH, an auxiliary scheduling procedure that modifies how SLACK schedules its last pack. Using DISPATCH, we show an upper bound of $\frac{4}{3}$ on the approximation ratio of SLACK (Lemma 6). Then, to show that this approximation ratio is tight, we build a family of instances whose approximation ratio asymptotically approaches $\frac{4}{3}$ (Lemma 7).

3.1   DISPATCH Procedure

Recall that, at each step t, SLACK processes the tasks of pack $\pi(t)$ in non-increasing order of processing time and greedily assigns each one to the least-loaded machine. We introduce an alternative procedure, DISPATCH_t, that differs from SLACK only at step t. In this policy, the pack $\pi(t)$ is scheduled by putting the k-th largest task on the k-th least loaded machine after the first $t-1$ packs have been scheduled by SLACK. Notably, both SLACK and DISPATCH_t always assign the largest task of pack $\pi(t)$ to the least loaded machine at the end of step $t-1$. However, the procedures may diverge beyond this point: whereas DISPATCH_t distributes tasks evenly, placing one per machine, SLACK may assign several tasks to the same machine if it remains least loaded, as illustrated by Fig. 2.

We prove that DISPATCH_P never performs better than SLACK.

Lemma 4. *All instances I with P packs satisfy $SLACK(I) \leq DISPATCH_P(I)$.*

Proof. We begin by presenting the intuition behind the proof. Observe that both SLACK and DISPATCH_P treat the tasks from pack $\pi(P)$ in non-increasing order of processing time, and SLACK behaves differently from DISPATCH_P only when one of the machines still has the lowest load after assigning a task of $\pi(P)$. This

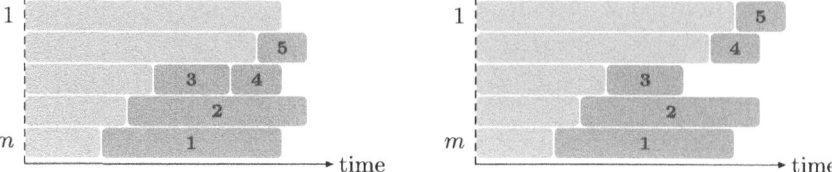

Fig. 2. An example of SLACK schedule at step t (on the left) and the corresponding DISPATCH$_t$ schedule (on the right). The gray area represents the tasks scheduled at steps $1, \ldots, t-1$, and the red area represents the tasks scheduled at step t (Color figure online).

ensures that the makespan of SLACK is at most that of DISPATCH$_P$ so far, and that the machines where DISPATCH$_P$ has yet to assign tasks remain untouched, preserving the option to achieve a similar or better assignment in the future.

To formalize this idea, we begin by introducing some notation. We renumber the machines in non-decreasing order of load after the first $P - 1$ packs have been scheduled, denoting their loads by $c_{P-1}(1) \le c_{P-1}(2) \le \cdots \le c_{P-1}(m)$. Moreover, let μ be the machine with the largest load in the (final) SLACK schedule. If the last task assigned to μ by SLACK does not belong to $\pi(P)$, then SLACK$(I) \le$ DISPATCH$_P(I)$ follows immediately, as both schedules coincide before step P.

Now, suppose that the last task assigned to μ by SLACK is in pack $\pi(P)$. Let ℓ denote this task, and assume this is the k-th scheduled task of $\pi(P)$. Let $c'_{P-1}(1), c'_{P-1}(2), \ldots, c'_{P-1}(m)$ denote the loads of the machines just before SLACK assigns ℓ to the machine μ. Observe that, by definition, DISPATCH$_P$ assigns the k-th task of $\pi(P)$, i.e., the task ℓ, to the k-th machine. Thus, we only need to show that the load $c_{P-1}(k) + p_\ell$ of machine k at the end of DISPATCH$_P$ is greater than or equal to SLACK$(I) = c'_{P-1}(\mu) + p_\ell$, i.e., we need to show that $c'_{P-1}(\mu) \le c_{P-1}(k)$.

First, remark that, since SLACK schedules tasks on the machine with lowest load, $c'_{P-1}(\mu) \le c'_{P-1}(i)$ for every $1 \le i \le m$. Then, as SLACK assigned only $k-1$ tasks of pack $\pi(P)$ before scheduling task ℓ, there exists a machine $1 \le i \le k$ whose load hasn't changed so far, that is, $c'_{P-1}(i) = c_{P-1}(i)$. Finally, $i \le k$ implies that $c_{P-1}(i) \le c_{P-1}(k)$, and combining the three inequalities yields $c'_{P-1}(\mu) \le c'_{P-1}(i) = c_{P-1}(i) \le c_{P-1}(k)$. □

Now we show that, when considering $2m$ tasks on m machines, DISPATCH$_2$ produces a schedule whose makespan is within a factor $\frac{4}{3}$ of the optimal solution. Lemma 7 provides an example of an instance where this exact ratio is achieved.

Lemma 5. *All instances I with two packs satisfy* DISPATCH$_2(I) \le \frac{4}{3}OPT(I)$.

Proof. Let I be an instance with $2m$ tasks and processing times $p_1 \ge p_2 \ge \cdots \ge p_{2m}$ on m machines. To prove the lemma, we show that for every machine $k \in \{1, 2, \ldots, m\}$, the load $p_k + p_{2m-k+1}$ assigned to machine k by DISPATCH$_2$ is smaller than or equal to $\frac{4}{3}OPT(I)$.

Let $\sigma^* : \{1, 2, \ldots, 2m\} \rightarrow \{1, 2, \ldots, m\}$ be an optimal scheduling function. We define the sets $T_1 = \{1, 2, \ldots, k\}$ and $T_2 = \{1, 2, \ldots, 2m - k + 1\}$ containing the tasks larger than or equal to p_k and p_{2m-k+1}, respectively. We now study how σ^* groups the tasks in T_1 and T_2. Notice that either:

1. σ^* assigns a task $t_1 \in T_1$ and a distinct task $t_2 \in T_2$ to the same machine at least once, or
2. σ^* assigns the tasks of T_1 to $|T_1| = k$ distinct machines and distributes the $|T_2| - |T_1| = 2(m - k) + 1$ remaining tasks of T_2 to the $m - k$ leftover machines, thus necessarily assigning three distinct tasks $s_1, s_2, s_3 \in T_2$ to the same machine.

In the former case we get that $p_{t_1} + p_{t_2} \leq \mathrm{OPT}(I)$ holds, thus:

$$p_k + p_{2\,m-k+1} \leq p_{t_1} + p_{t_2} < \frac{4}{3}\mathrm{OPT}(I).$$

Moreover, in the latter case we get that $p_{s_1} + p_{s_2} + p_{s_3} \leq \mathrm{OPT}(I)$ holds, thus:

$$p_k + p_{2\,m-k+1} = p_k + \frac{3 \cdot p_{2\,m-k+1}}{3} \leq \mathrm{OPT}(I) + \frac{p_{s_1} + p_{s_2} + p_{s_3}}{3} \leq \frac{4}{3}\mathrm{OPT}(I).$$

$\square$

3.2   Upper Bound

Now we can show that the ratio between SLACK and OPT is at most $\frac{4}{3}$. Our proof follows a case-based approach. The Lemmas from Sect. 2 handle cases where the slack of the first scheduled pack or the processing time of the last assigned task is sufficiently small, and we show that the DISPATCH scheduling satisfies the desired bound for the remaining cases.

Lemma 6. *The approximation ratio of SLACK is at most $\frac{4}{3}$.*

Proof. Let us fix an instance I of the scheduling problem. If I consists of a single pack, then SLACK is optimal (one task per machine). Thus, in the following we assume there are at least two packs in the instance. Let ℓ_N be the last task to complete in the SLACK schedule, with N denoting the step at which the pack it belongs to has been scheduled. Note that we can safely consider the alternative instance where all tasks belonging to packs scheduled *after* this pack have been removed, as it does not change the makespan for SLACK and can only decrease the optimal makespan, which results in an equal or worse ratio. Hence, we assume in the following that $\pi(N)$ is the last pack to be scheduled.

To bound $\mathrm{SLACK}(I)$, we begin with the result of Lemma 1:

$$\mathrm{SLACK}(I) \leq \mathrm{OPT}(I) + \left(1 - \frac{1}{m}\right)\delta_N. \tag{1}$$

We know that δ_N is at most the slack $\beta_{\pi(1)}$ of the first scheduled pack by Lemma 2. Similarly, δ_N is at most the processing time p_{ℓ_N} of the last scheduled task by Lemma 3. Therefore, if either $\beta_{\pi(1)} \leq \frac{\mathrm{OPT}(I)}{3}$ or $p_{\ell_N} \leq \frac{\mathrm{OPT}(I)}{3}$, Eq. (1) immediately gives $\mathrm{SLACK}(I) \leq \frac{4}{3}\mathrm{OPT}(I)$.

Fig. 3. An example of DISPATCH$_N$ schedule with renumbering applied on machines. The gray/black area represents tasks assigned at steps 1 to $N-1$, and the red area represents tasks assigned at step N (Color figure online).

Assume now that $\beta_{\pi(1)} > \frac{\mathrm{OPT}(I)}{3}$ and $p_{\ell_N} > \frac{\mathrm{OPT}(I)}{3}$. We show that this hypothesis implies that the packs scheduled at steps 1 and N are necessarily packs 1 and 2, i.e., either $\pi(1) = 1$ and $\pi(N) = 2$, or $\pi(1) = 2$ and $\pi(N) = 1$. Remark that every task j belonging to the third pack or more necessarily satisfies $p_j \leq \frac{\mathrm{OPT}(I)}{3}$, otherwise there would be $2m + 1$ tasks satisfying $p_j > \frac{\mathrm{OPT}(I)}{3}$, which is impossible to schedule in time $\mathrm{OPT}(I)$ on m machines. Therefore, $p_{\ell_N} > \frac{\mathrm{OPT}(I)}{3}$ immediately yields $\pi(N) \in \{1,2\}$. Moreover, we get that $\beta_k \leq \frac{\mathrm{OPT}(I)}{3}$ for $k \geq 3$, thus $\beta_{\pi(1)} > \frac{\mathrm{OPT}(I)}{3}$ yields $\pi(1) \in \{1,2\}$.

Now, let us analyze the DISPATCH$_N$ schedule on instance I. To complete the proof, it is sufficient to show that DISPATCH$_N(I) \leq \frac{4}{3}\mathrm{OPT}(I)$, as Lemma 4 then directly implies the desired result, that is, SLACK$(I) \leq$ DISPATCH$_N(I) \leq \frac{4}{3}\mathrm{OPT}(I)$. Recall that the DISPATCH$_N$ schedule is identical to the SLACK schedule up to the $(N-1)$-th scheduled pack, and only differs on task assignment of the pack scheduled at step N. We renumber the machines in non-increasing order of their completion times after step $N - 1$, giving $c_{N-1}(1) \geq c_{N-1}(2) \geq \cdots \geq c_{N-1}(m)$.

Let ℓ'_N be the last task to complete in the DISPATCH$_N$ schedule, and let ν be the machine on which it is assigned. Let μ be the first machine (when taken in-order) on which at least 2 tasks were scheduled before step N. We partition the set of machines into 2 subsets $U = \{1, \ldots, \mu - 1\}$ and $V = \{\mu, \ldots, m\}$. Note that U is empty if $\mu = 1$ and $U = M$ if there is no such machine μ. Moreover, we denote by ℓ_{N-1} the last task to complete on μ at the end of step $N - 1$. An example illustrating this partition is shown in Fig. 3. We have two cases:

- **Case 1**: Suppose that $\nu \in U$. In the DISPATCH$_N$ schedule, each machine of U contains exactly one task from the pack $\pi(1)$ and one task from the pack $\pi(N)$, the k-th longest task of $\pi(1)$ being put with the k-th shortest task of $\pi(N)$ for all $1 \leq k < \mu$. In other words, if we let I' denote the scheduling instance that contains only the tasks from packs $\pi(1)$ and $\pi(N)$, the DISPATCH$_N$ scheduling of I and the DISPATCH$_2$ scheduling of I' assign the same tasks to each machine of U. Therefore, since the machine ν that has the largest load at the end of DISPATCH$_N$ is in U, we get that $\text{DISPATCH}_N(I) \leq \text{DISPATCH}_2(I')$. In turn, Lemma 5 yields $\text{DISPATCH}_2(I') \leq \frac{4}{3}\text{OPT}(I')$. Finally, as $\text{OPT}(I') \leq \text{OPT}(I)$, we conclude that $\text{DISPATCH}_N(I) \leq \frac{4}{3}\text{OPT}(I)$.

– **Case 2**: Suppose that $\nu \in V$. Observe that, in this case, there exists a machine μ (the first machine in V) on which at least two tasks were scheduled before step N, which means that there are at least 3 packs in the instance I, i.e., $N \geq 3$. We show in the following that every machine $i \in \{1, 2, \ldots, m\}$ satisfies $c_N(\nu) \leq c_N(i) + \frac{\text{OPT}(I)}{3}$. Since $\min_i\{c_N(i)\}$ is smaller than or equal to the optimal solution $\text{OPT}(I)$, this yields the required bound:

$$\text{DISPATCH}_N(I) = c_N(\nu) \leq \min_i\{c_N(i)\} + \frac{\text{OPT}(I)}{3} \leq \frac{4}{3}\text{OPT}(I).$$

Let us fix a machine $i \in \{1, 2, \ldots, m\}$, and let $p(i)$ denote the processing time of the task that has been put on machine i during step N.

• **Case 2a**: Suppose that $i < \nu$. We have $c_{N-1}(\nu) \leq c_{N-1}(i)$ as machines are ordered according to their load at step $N-1$, and $p(\nu) \leq p(i) + \beta_{\pi(N)}$ as both tasks belong to the pack $\pi(N)$. Combining both inequalities gives us $c_N(\nu) = c_{N-1}(\nu) + p(\nu) \leq c_{N-1}(i) + p(i) + \beta_{\pi(N)} \leq c_N(i) + \beta_{\pi(N)}$. By definition of DISPATCH_N, we have that $\beta_{\pi(N)} \leq \beta_{\pi(2)}$. Moreover, as $\pi(1), \pi(N) \in \{1, 2\}$, we get that $\pi(2) \geq 3$, thus $\beta_{\pi(2)} \leq \frac{\text{OPT}(I)}{3}$ (because we remarked above that all tasks belonging to the third pack or more necessarily have a processing time smaller than or equal to $\frac{\text{OPT}(I)}{3}$). We conclude that $c_N(\nu) \leq c_N(i) + \frac{\text{OPT}(I)}{3}$.

• **Case 2b**: Suppose that $i > \nu$. Then $p(\nu) \leq p(i)$ and $c_{N-1}(\nu) \leq c_{N-1}(\mu)$ as machines are ordered according to their load at step $N-1$. Moreover, $c_{N-1}(\mu) - p_{\ell_{N-1}} \leq c_{N-1}(i)$ as otherwise ℓ_{N-1} would not be assigned to machine μ, because DISPATCH_N is a list schedule on the first $N-1$ packs. Combining these inequalities yields $c_N(\nu) = c_{N-1}(\nu) + p(\nu) \leq c_{N-1}(\mu) + p(i) \leq c_N(i) + p_{\ell_{N-1}}$. Finally, ℓ_{N-1} necessarily belongs to the third pack or more since $\pi(1), \pi(N) \in \{1, 2\}$, thus $p_{\ell_{N-1}} \leq \frac{\text{OPT}(I)}{3}$. We conclude that $c_N(\nu) \leq c_N(i) + \frac{\text{OPT}(I)}{3}$.   □

3.3   Lower Bound

We show that the bound $\frac{4}{3}$ on the approximation ratio is tight by building a family of instances that reaches it asymptotically. The key idea behind our construction is that, since SLACK schedules its packs sequentially, it fails to match optimal schedules that require placing all the tasks of the pack with the largest slack on a single machine.

Lemma 7. *The approximation ratio of SLACK is at least $\frac{4}{3}$.*

Proof. Let $M > 1$ be a constant. Consider five machines with the following tasks:

– Two *large* tasks with a processing time of $6M - 1$;

- Four *medium* tasks with a processing time of $3M$;
- Three *small* tasks with a processing time of $2M$.

The optimal solution schedules the two large tasks on separate machines, the four medium tasks on two additional machines, and the three small tasks on the last machine, achieving a makespan of $6M$. Now, consider the schedule produced by SLACK. The tasks are divided into two packs of five tasks each:

- Pack 1 contains large tasks and three medium tasks, with slack of $3M - 1$.
- Pack 2 contains the last medium task, the three small tasks, and a task with duration 0 added to match the number of machines, with slack of $3M$.

Since SLACK starts with the pack that has the largest slack, the second pack is scheduled before the first. This results in a makespan of $8M - 1$. Therefore, the ratio between the SLACK makespan and the optimal makespan is $\frac{8M-1}{6M}$, which approaches $\frac{4}{3}$ as M tends to infinity.   □

4   Approximation Ratio in the Bounded Tasks Setting

We now consider that tasks cannot be arbitrarily large, in a similar way than previous authors for LPT [7]. More specifically, we fix an integer $k \geq 2$ and we focus on instances I for which all the tasks have a processing time smaller than $\frac{\mathrm{OPT}(I)}{k}$. We show the following theorems.

Theorem 2. *For all $k \geq 2$, the approximation ratio r_k of SLACK restricted to instances I on m machines containing tasks j such that $p_j \leq \frac{OPT(I)}{k}$ satisfies*

$$r_k \leq 1 + \frac{m-1}{m \cdot (k+1)}.$$

Theorem 3. *For all $k \geq 2$, the approximation ratio r_k of SLACK restricted to instances I on m machines (with $m \geq k$) containing tasks j such that $p_j \leq \frac{OPT(I)}{k}$ satisfies*

$$r_k \geq 1 + \frac{k-1}{k \cdot (k+1)}.$$

Observe that in the specific case $m = k$ our upper and lower bounds match. However, for $m > k$ there is a gap between both, and for $m < k$ we do not have a lower bound. The remaining of this section is devoted to the proof of both theorems: we prove Theorem 2 in Subsect. 4.1, and Theorem 3 in Subsect. 4.2.

4.1   Upper Bound

We prove our upper bound (Theorem 2) with a case-based approach. Let $\mathcal{I}_k$ denote the set of instances I for which all the tasks j satisfy $p_j \leq \frac{\mathrm{OPT}(I)}{k}$, and let $\mathcal{I}_k^h$ denote the subset of $\mathcal{I}_k$ containing all the instances I that satisfy

$$\beta_{\pi(1)} > \frac{\mathrm{OPT}(I)}{k+1} \quad \text{and} \quad \delta_P > \frac{\mathrm{OPT}(I)}{k+1}$$

when scheduled by SLACK.

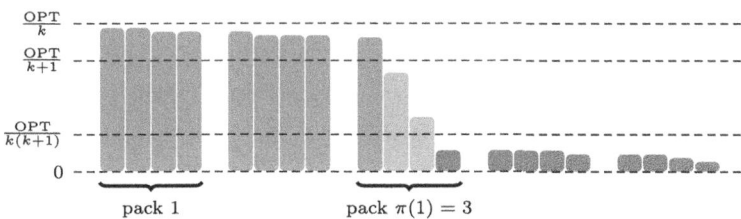

Fig. 4. Profile of an instance $I \in \mathcal{I}_k^h$. Red tasks are strictly greater than $\frac{\text{OPT}(I)}{k+1}$ and blue tasks are strictly smaller than $\frac{\text{OPT}(I)}{k(k+1)}$ because $\beta_{\pi(1)} > \frac{\text{OPT}(I)}{k+1}$.

To prove Theorem 2, we need to show $\frac{\text{SLACK}(I)}{\text{OPT}(I)} \le 1 + \frac{m-1}{m(k+1)}$ for every instance $I \in \mathcal{I}_k$ on m machines. We consider two cases: either I belongs to $\mathcal{I}_k^h$, or it does not. We immediately solve the latter case by using the lemmas of Sect. 2 (Proposition 1), and then we focus on the former case, where we will show that SLACK is actually optimal (Proposition 2).

Proposition 1. *Every instance $I \in \mathcal{I}_k \setminus \mathcal{I}_k^h$ satisfies $\frac{SLACK(I)}{OPT(I)} \le 1 + \frac{m-1}{m(k+1)}$.*

Proof. Let us start with the result of Lemma 1, that is, $\text{SLACK}(I) \le \text{OPT}(I) + \left(\frac{m-1}{m}\right)\delta_P$ for any list schedule. Since $I \notin \mathcal{I}_k^h$ by supposition, either $\beta_{\pi(1)} \le \frac{\text{OPT}(I)}{k+1}$ or $\delta_P \le \frac{\text{OPT}(I)}{k+1}$. The latter case immediately implies the statement. Moreover, as the final imbalance δ_P is at most the slack $\beta_{\pi(1)}$ of the first scheduled pack (by Lemma 2), the former case also implies the statement. $\square$

We now focus on the instances in $\mathcal{I}_k^h$. Observe that these instances have a very specific shape, illustrated in Fig. 4. As $\beta_{\pi(1)} > \frac{\text{OPT}(I)}{k+1}$ and $p_j \le \frac{\text{OPT}(I)}{k}$ for all tasks j, the tasks of packs $1, \ldots, \pi(1)-1$ are strictly greater than $\frac{\text{OPT}(I)}{k+1}$, and the tasks of packs $\pi(1)+1, \ldots, P$ are strictly smaller than $\frac{\text{OPT}(I)}{k} - \frac{\text{OPT}(I)}{k+1} = \frac{\text{OPT}(I)}{k(k+1)}$. In the following, the former are called *large tasks* (the red tasks in Fig. 4), and the latter are called *tiny tasks* (the blue tasks in Fig. 4). Moreover, for any schedule, we call the machines finishing last the *critical* machines.

To show that SLACK is optimal on the instances in $\mathcal{I}_k^h$, we prove that: there are at mot $k-1$ packs with large tasks (Lemma 8); two large tasks coming from the same pack are never put on the same machine (Lemma 10); and there are no tiny tasks on critical machines (Lemma 11).

Lemma 8. *Every instance $I \in \mathcal{I}_k^h$ has at most $k-1$ packs with only large tasks.*

Proof. If this is not the case, we have at least $mk+1$ large tasks (because the pack $\pi(1)$ necessarily contains at least one large task), which cannot fit within $\text{OPT}(I)$; this is a contradiction. $\square$

Lemma 9. *Every instance $I \in \mathcal{I}_k^h$ satisfies $\delta_t > \frac{OPT(I)}{k+1}$ at each step t.*

Proof. We begin by proving that δ is a non-increasing function, i.e., $\delta_t \leq \delta_{t-1}$ for all $t > 1$. We know by Lemma 2 that $\delta_t \leq \max\left(\delta_{t-1}, \beta_{\pi(t)}\right)$ and that $\beta_{\pi(t)} < \frac{\mathrm{OPT}(I)}{k(k+1)}$ for all $t > 1$, since $\pi(t)$ contains either only large tasks or only tiny tasks. Thus, if there exists a step t such that $\delta_t \leq \beta_{\pi(t)}$, then we have $\delta_{t'} < \frac{\mathrm{OPT}(I)}{k(k+1)}$ for all $t' > t$, which contradicts the fact that $\delta_P > \frac{\mathrm{OPT}(I)}{k+1}$ for instances $I \in \mathcal{I}_k^h$. This proves that $\delta_t \leq \delta_{t-1}$ for all $t > 1$.

Therefore, as δ is non-increasing and as $\delta_P > \frac{\mathrm{OPT}(I)}{k+1}$, we necessarily have $\delta_t \geq \delta_P > \frac{\mathrm{OPT}(I)}{k+1}$ for all t. □

Lemma 10. *For every $I \in \mathcal{I}_k^h$, SLACK never puts two large tasks coming from the same pack on the same machine.*

Proof. In the first step, SLACK puts one task per machine. Now suppose that we are at the beginning of step $t > 1$, i.e., SLACK has already scheduled $t - 1$ packs and starts to schedule pack $\pi(t)$. By definition, we know that pack $\pi(t)$ either contains m large tasks, or m tiny tasks. Suppose it contains large tasks.

We know that $\delta_{t-1} \leq \beta_{\pi(1)}$ (by corollary of Lemma 2), and that every large task is greater than or equal to $\beta_{\pi(1)}$ by definition of SLACK. In other words, δ_{t-1} is smaller than or equal to the minimal large task. By contradiction, suppose that at the end of step t, SLACK has put two large tasks j and j' (in this order) of pack $\pi(t)$ on the same machine μ. This means that the machine which was the most-loaded at the beginning of step t did not receive any task during step t. We denote this machine as ν and we note its finishing time $c_{\max}$. Moreover, when j' has been scheduled, μ was one of the least-loaded machines, and we denote their common finishing time at this exact moment by $c_{\min}$. We consider three possibilities, and show that each of them results in a contradiction:

1. If $c_{\min} > c_{\max}$, SLACK would not have put j' on machine μ.
2. If $c_{\min} < c_{\max}$, we get that δ_{t-1} is strictly greater than p_j, since at the start of step t the load of μ is $c_{\min} - p_j$ and the load of ν is $c_{\max}$. This contradicts the fact that δ_{t-1} is smaller than or equal to the minimal large task.
3. If $c_{\min} = c_{\max}$, we get a contradiction with the tie-breaking strategy of SLACK as described in Sect. 2: ν should have received the task j', because it did not receive any task during step t and μ had already received j.   □

Lemma 11. *For every $I \in \mathcal{I}_k^h$, SLACK puts no tiny tasks on critical machines.*

Proof. By contradiction, suppose there is a critical machine μ that receives a tiny task j in the SLACK schedule; we assume that j is the last tiny task on μ. Let t_0 be the step at which SLACK schedules j, thus j belongs to pack $\pi(t_0)$, and let ν be the machine finishing last at step t_0. We derive a contradiction by studying how the imbalance $c_t(\nu) - c_t(\mu)$ between machine ν and μ evolves: we prove that this difference is so large at step t_0 that machine μ cannot catch up by the end of the last step, contradicting the fact that machine μ is critical.

Formally, we prove by induction that for every $t_0 \leq t \leq P$ we have

$$c_t(\nu) - c_t(\mu) > \frac{(k - 1 - x_t)\mathrm{OPT}(I)}{k(k+1)}, \tag{2}$$

where x_t is the number of packs containing only large tasks scheduled between t_0 and t (included). Equation (2) then implies that the final imbalance $c_P(\nu) - c_P(\mu)$ is strictly positive as there are at most $k - 1$ such packs in total by Lemma 8. This contradicts the fact that machine μ is critical, concluding the proof.

Base Case $(t = t_0)$. Observe that the load on machine μ when assigning task j is smaller than or equal to the finishing time of all machines at the end of step t_0, including the least-loaded one, otherwise SLACK would not assign j to μ. Hence, applying Lemma 9 and the fact that j is a tiny task, we get

$$c_{t_0}(\nu) - c_{t_0}(\mu) \geq \delta_{t_0} - p_j > \frac{\mathrm{OPT}(I)}{k+1} - \frac{\mathrm{OPT}(I)}{k(k+1)} = \frac{(k-1)\mathrm{OPT}(I)}{k(k+1)}.$$

Induction Step $(t > t_0)$. Suppose that Eq. 2 holds for $t - 1$.

If the pack $\pi(t)$ scheduled at step t contains only tiny tasks, no new task is assigned to μ during step t as j is the last tiny task scheduled on μ: $c_t(\mu) = c_{t-1}(\mu)$. Therefore, $c_t(\nu) - c_t(\mu) \geq c_{t-1}(\nu) - c_{t-1}(\mu)$, and since $x_t = x_{t-1}$ Eq. (2) still holds.

On the other hand, if the pack $\pi(t)$ scheduled at step t contains only large tasks, we know that μ and ν both receive exactly one large task at this step, as SLACK never puts two large tasks coming from the same pack on the same machine (Lemma 10). Then $c_t(\mu) \leq c_{t-1}(\mu) + \frac{\mathrm{OPT}(I)}{k}$ and $c_t(\nu) > c_{t-1}(\nu) + \frac{\mathrm{OPT}(I)}{k+1}$, because of the known bounds on the size of large tasks. Thus, if we let x_t denote the number of packs containing only large tasks scheduled between t_0 and t (thus $x_t = x_{t-1} + 1$), we get via the induction hypothesis:

$$c_t(\nu) - c_t(\mu) > c_{t-1}(\nu) + \frac{\mathrm{OPT}(I)}{k+1} - c_{t-1}(\mu) - \frac{\mathrm{OPT}(I)}{k}$$
$$> \frac{(k-1-x_{t-1})\mathrm{OPT}(I)}{k(k+1)} - \frac{\mathrm{OPT}(I)}{k(k+1)} = \frac{(k-1-x_t)\mathrm{OPT}(I)}{k(k+1)}.$$

This concludes the proof.   □

We can finally prove that SLACK is optimal for the instances in $\mathcal{I}_k^h$.

Proposition 2. *Every instance* $I \in \mathcal{I}_k^h$ *satisfies* $SLACK(I) = OPT(I)$.

Proof. Let $I \in \mathcal{I}_k^h$, and let us consider a critical machine μ in the SLACK schedule. Observe that machine μ was assigned:

- One task from the first pack scheduled $\pi(1)$;
- One task from each pack containing only large tasks (Lemma 10), and there are at most $k - 1$ such packs (Lemma 8);
- No task coming from the remaining packs that contain only tiny tasks (Lemma 11).

In other words, the critical machine μ contains at most k tasks, and as all the tasks are smaller than or equal to $\frac{\mathrm{OPT}(I)}{k}$ the SLACK schedule is optimal.   □

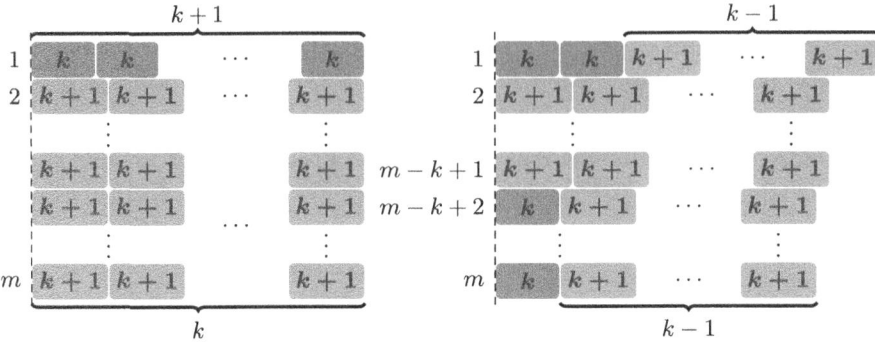

Fig. 5. A comparison of an optimal schedule of tasks that have a processing time smaller than $\frac{\text{OPT}}{k}$ (left), and the corresponding SLACK schedule (right).

4.2 Lower Bound

To prove Theorem 3, for every $m, k \in \mathbb{N}$ such that $m \geq k$ we construct an instance I of the scheduling problem such that every task j of I satisfies $p_j \leq \frac{\text{OPT}(I)}{k}$ and $\frac{\text{SLACK}(I)}{\text{OPT}(I)} = 1 + \frac{k-1}{k \cdot (k+1)}$. We rely once more on the fact that SLACK fails to match optimal schedules that group all small tasks on a single machine.

Proof (Theorem 3). Let us fix an integer k, and let $m \geq k$. We consider the instance I that has m machines with the following tasks:

- $(m-1) \cdot k$ *large* tasks, with processing time $k + 1$;
- $k + 1$ *small* tasks, with processing time k.

On this instance, the optimal scheduling, represented on the left-hand side of Fig. 5, positions the $k + 1$ small tasks on a single machine and k large tasks on each other machine. This results in a load of $k \cdot (k+1)$ on each machine. Remark that this implies that $p_j \leq \frac{\text{OPT}(I)}{k}$ for every task j.

The scheduling resulting from SLACK is represented on the right-hand side of Fig. 5. The first pack, with a slack of k, contains a single small task, that is positioned on the first machine. The second pack, with a slack of 1, contains the k remaining small tasks, along with $m - k$ large tasks: one of the small tasks is added to the first machine, and the others are spread amongst the other machines. Finally, the $k - 1$ remaining packs, with a slack of 0, each contain m large tasks that are spread evenly on all machines. This results in a makespan of $2k + (k-1)(k+1) = k^2 + 2k - 1$, witnessed by machine 1. Therefore, we get:

$$\frac{\text{SLACK}(I)}{\text{OPT}(I)} = \frac{k^2 + 2k - 1}{k \cdot (k+1)} = \frac{k \cdot (k+1) + k - 1}{k \cdot (k+1)} = 1 + \frac{k-1}{k \cdot (k+1)}.$$

This proves the theorem. $\square$

5 Conclusion

The SLACK heuristic was recently introduced to address the problem of scheduling n jobs on m identical machines, without constraints, with the objective of minimizing the total execution time. While empirical results have demonstrated its high efficiency, its approximation remained unknown. In this paper, we theoretically prove that it yields a solution at most $4/3$ of the optimum, a ratio very close to that of the LPT heuristic. Furthermore, we achieve improved approximation ratios by limiting the processing times.

Examples reveal that SLACK can outperform LPT in certain cases and vice versa. This naturally raises the question of whether a hybrid heuristic, which selects the superior scheduling outcome between SLACK and LPT, could offer further improvements. Looking ahead, we aim to narrow the gap between the upper and lower bounds established in Theorems 2 and 3.

Disclosure of Interests. The authors have no competing interests to declare that are relevant to the content of this article.

References

1. Benoit, A., Canon, L., Elghazi, R., Héam, P.: Asymptotic performance and energy consumption of SLACK. In: Euro-Par 2023. Lecture Notes in Computer Science, vol. 14100, pp. 81–95 (2023)
2. Della Croce, F., Scatamacchia, R.: The longest processing time rule for identical parallel machines revisited. J. Sched. **23**(2), 163–176 (2020)
3. Garey, M.R., Johnson, D.S.: "Strong" NP-completeness results: motivation, examples, and implications. J. ACM **25**(3), 499–508 (1978)
4. Graham, R.L.: Bounds on multiprocessing timing anomalies. J. SIAM Appl. Math. **17**(2), 416–429 (1969)
5. Hochbaum, D.S., Shmoys, D.B.: Using dual approximation algorithms for scheduling problems theoretical and practical results. J. ACM (JACM) **34**(1), 144–162 (1987)
6. Jansen, K., Klein, K., Verschae, J.: Closing the gap for makespan scheduling via sparsification techniques. Math. Oper. Res. **45**(4), 1371–1392 (2020)
7. Lee, M., Lee, K., Pinedo, M.: Tight approximation bounds for the LPT rule applied to identical parallel machines with small jobs. J. Sched. **25**(6), 721–740 (2022)
8. Mokotoff, E.: An exact algorithm for the identical parallel machine scheduling problem. Eur. J. Oper. Res. **152**(3), 758–769 (2004)
9. Mrad, M., Souayah, N.: An arc-flow model for the makespan minimization problem on identical parallel machines. IEEE Access **6**, 5300–5307 (2018)
10. Ostojic, D., Davidovic, T., Krüger, T.J., Ramljak, D.: Comparative analysis of heuristic approaches to P||Cmax. In: ICORES 2022, pp. 259–266 (2022)
11. Paletta, G., Ruiz-Torres, A.J.: Partial solutions and multifit algorithm for multiprocessor scheduling. J. Math. Model. Algorithms Oper. Res. **14**(2), 125–143 (2015)
12. Thesen, A.: Design and evaluation of tabu search algorithms for multiprocessor scheduling. J. Heuristics **4**(2), 141–160 (1998)

Leveraging Expert Usage to Speed up LLM Inference with Expert Parallelism

Olivier Beaumont[1], Raphaël Bourgouin[1], Maxime Darrin[2,3],
Loris Marchal[2,3(✉)], and Pablo Piantanida[2,3]

[1] Inria Centre at the University of Bordeaux, Bordeaux, France
{olivier.beaumont,raphael.bourgouin}@inria.fr
[2] International Laboratory on Learning Systems, Montreal, Canada
maxime.darrin@centralesupelec.fr,
{loris.marchal,pablo.piantanida}@cnrs.fr
[3] CNRS, Centrale-Supélec, Université Paris-Saclay and MILA - Québec AI Institute,
Gif-sur-Yvette, France

Abstract. Large language models have become essential for text-processing applications, yet their inference remains time-consuming, as tokens must be generated sequentially. While model sparsification techniques, such as Mixture of Experts (MoE) models, help mitigate computational costs, they introduce new challenges. In MoE models, only a subset of experts is activated at each layer. Note that not all expert subsets (typically pairs) are selected with equal probability. When experts are mapped across multiple GPUs, load imbalances can arise if frequently co-activated experts are assigned to the same GPU, leading to load unbalance and inefficient execution. This paper proposes a strategy that leverages the non-uniform selection of expert subsets to optimize their mapping across GPUs. By ensuring that frequently co-activated experts are placed on separate GPUs, we improve parallel processing and reduce inference time. Despite the NP-completeness of this mapping problem, we introduce simple yet effective greedy strategies that significantly minimize sequential expert processing. Our proof-of-concept experiments on the Mixtral model demonstrate the effectiveness of our approach for reducing inference time.

Keywords: Large Language Models · Mixture-of-Experts · Memory Mapping · Inference Optimization

1 Introduction

Large Language Models (LLMs) have become crucial in tasks such as machine translation and natural language understanding [16], enabling applications such as conversational agents and code generation tools with improved text production fluency and accuracy. However, their efficiency is closely tied to their size, often reaching billions or trillions of parameters [17], leading to substantial computational demands.

W. E. Nagel et al. (Eds.): Euro-Par 2025, LNCS 15900, pp. 145–158, 2026.
https://doi.org/10.1007/978-3-031-99854-6_10

For inference tasks, fast text generation requires optimized computational strategies. One key approach is model compression, including quantization and sparsity, which reduce model size at the price of a (minimal) accuracy loss.

A particularly promising sparsification approach is the Mixture of Experts (MoE) architecture [6,14], which employs conditional computations for efficiency. MoE models are based on transformer-based architectures [19], where each block includes an attention layer and a gating function to dynamically activate experts depending on the input. This structure retains a large number of parameters while ensuring that only a small subset of experts is active per inference, thus reducing computational costs. This process can further accelerated when combined to parallel computing strategies to distribute memory requirements across multiple computational nodes and allow parallel execution of selected experts.

Optimizing inference requires leveraging multi-GPU computational power efficiently. While transformer attention layer distribution has been extensively studied [19], expert layer parallelism has received less attention. Two primary strategies address this: tensor parallelism and expert parallelism. Tensor parallelism distributes computations across devices at each layer but is less effective for expert-specific tasks. Expert parallelism, in contrast, assigns experts to specific devices based on memory availability, enhancing efficiency.

Training ensures relatively balanced expert popularity through penalization mechanisms [2]. The gating function typically selects n experts per transformer block, typically $n = 2$ to $n = 8$. If all selected experts are spread across different GPUs, inference fully benefits from parallel execution. Nevertheless, although individual expert selection is balanced, the selection of specific expert groups is not, thus allowing for optimized expert placement to maximize GPU utilization and minimize inference time as proposed in present paper.

The remainder of this paper is structured as follows. Section 2 reviews related work on MoE models and parallelization strategies. Section 3 presents the model; Sect. 4 formalizes the optimization problem, proves its NP-completeness while Sect. 5 presents a greedy heuristic. Section 6 evaluates these methods using Mixtral expert co-location statistics. Finally, Sect. 7 provides concluding remarks and future directions.

2   Related Work

Mixture of Experts models have gained significant attention [6,14,17]. They maintain strong accuracy in text generation due to their large number of parameters while reducing inference time compared to dense models, as only a subset of experts is selected at each layer. Research continues on optimizing model size, expert count, and selection strategy [17]. Various models follow the same principle but differ significantly, as highlighted in recent surveys [2].

For instance, Mixtral [14] selects 2 out of 8 experts per transformer block, DRBX [5] selects 4 out of 8, Qwen1.5-MoE [18] and DeepSeekMoE [3] select 8 out of 64. Some models, like Switch Transformers [8], use even larger expert counts, ranging from 128 per layer (Switch-Large, 26B parameters) to 2048 per layer (Switch-C, 1571B parameters).

To enhance parallelism and reduce inference time while respecting GPU memory constraints, it is crucial to develop efficient expert allocation strategies. Typically, each GPU stores only a subset of experts, meaning there is no guarantee that selected experts will map to different GPUs. Expert parallelism aims to maximize the likelihood of this mapping.

Many systems [10,15] rely on static expert allocation, while others, like Tutel [13], adapt parallelism dynamically based on previous iterations. Unlike these approaches, we propose leveraging statistical data on expert selection probabilities to maximize the expected matching size between experts and GPUs.

Another class of solutions [7,12] improves expert-GPU distribution through prediction techniques. By analyzing activations in earlier layers, future expert selections can be anticipated, enabling prefetching into GPU memory. This predictive approach can complement static placement, minimizing expert movement during execution and improving overall efficiency.

3   Problem Modeling

In this section, we describe the general MoE architecture in detail. We experimentally study the distribution of expert pairs in the Mixtral model and show that it is highly heterogeneous, which motivates the present study. We formalize the optimization problem to be solved for each layer to minimize inference time and maximize parallelism. We also show that this problem is NP-complete even in the special case where each expert can only be stored in the memory of a single GPU.

3.1   Mixture-of-Experts Architecture

We consider a large language model with L transformer layers, each containing an attention layer, a gating function selecting experts based on the attention output, and an expert mixing module (see Fig. 1). Each module is defined by the total number N of potential experts and the number n of experts activated per layer. As seen in Sect. 2, different MoE models use various (N, n) configurations [2]. The selected experts compute outputs, which are then combined via a weighted sum determined by the gating function.

We focus on the inference phase, which has limited parallelism and poses a greater optimization challenge. Generating each token requires sequential traversal of the L layers, with the output of the last layer for token i serving as the input for token $i + 1$.

During training, penalization techniques ensure that each expert's activation probability is approximately constant and close to $\frac{n}{N}$ [2]. MoE models rely on experts being specialized for different contexts and sharing workload accordingly. This guarantees high-quality results despite using fewer experts per layer than dense models. Since expert selection depends on context, the probabilities of certain expert combinations appearing together are not uniform, as experts for similar contexts are activated more frequently together.

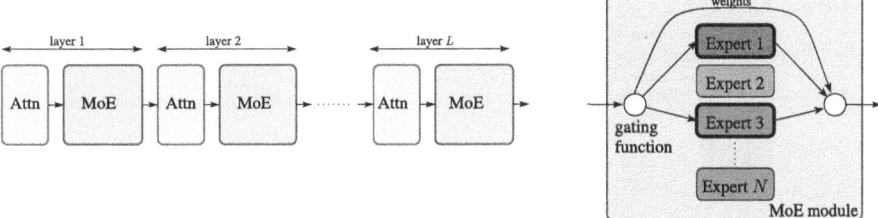

Fig. 1. General Mixter-of-Expert architecture and detail on one MoE module

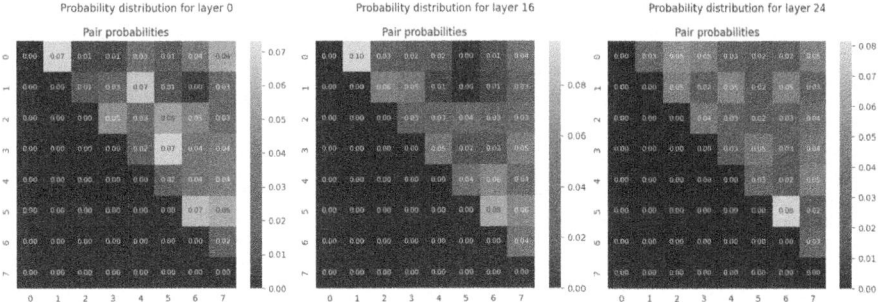

Fig. 2. Probability of simultaneous selection in the Mixtral model, for various layers. Bright colors correspond to highly popular expert pairs. Only pairs (i, j) with $i < j$ are considered.

To test this assumption, we measured the probabilities of simultaneous selection in a Mixtral model with $n = 2$ and $N = 8$ on a representative text corpus. The results for several layers are shown in Fig. 2. We observe (only values above the diagonal make sense) that the popularity of expert pairs is highly variable, even though the probability of each expert is uniform. For example, in layer 16, expert 0 appears very often with expert 1, but seldom with expert 5. This observation suggests that if two GPUs are available and each expert is present on only one, it is more appropriate to allocate experts 0 and 1 on two different GPUs to maximize parallelism, while experts 0 and 5 can be located on the same GPU.

3.2 Platform Model and Objective

The computational platform consists of a node equipped with k identical GPUs, each of which has its own dedicated memory. This memory is used to store model weights and activations. Since we perform inference for a single prompt of limited size, we assume that the memory footprint of activations is negligible compared to model weights. The GPUs are connected to the main memory of the system via a PCIe bus with limited bandwidth (see Fig. 3a). The weights for the tokenizer, the attention mechanisms for each layer, and those for the final stage are distributed equally among all GPUs. The remaining memory M_r on the

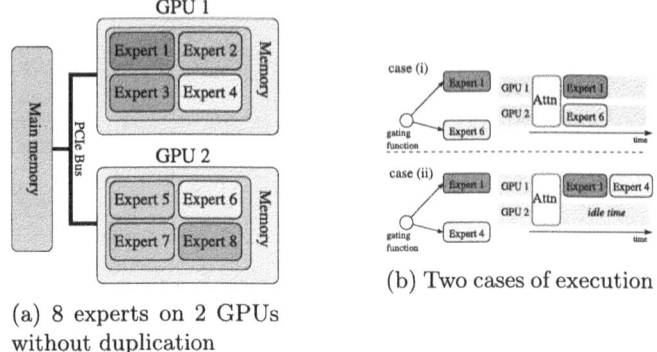

(a) 8 experts on 2 GPUs
without duplication

(b) Two cases of execution

Fig. 3. An example of the distribution of experts without replication and resulting processing time, depending on the co-location of selected experts

GPUs is used to store the weights of the experts, where each expert has a weight M_e, so that each GPU can store $M = \frac{M_r}{LM_e}$ experts for each layer. For the k available GPUs, each expert can therefore be replicated $R_e = \frac{kM_r}{LM_e}$ times.

3.3 Allocating of Experts onto GPUs

We now focus on a specific transformer layer in the LLM. For an expert to run on a GPU, its weights must already be in memory. If not, they must be fetched from main memory or another GPU, causing delays. Since multiple GPUs hold different expert weights, the required weights are often already stored on one of them. In many cases, multiple copies exist across GPUs, making them viable candidates for processing the corresponding expert. Inference for a given layer involves solving both a dynamic and a static problem.

The dynamic problem involves selecting, at runtime, which GPUs should process the activated experts, given a fixed expert placement. This can be approached using matching-based algorithms. Since runtime decisions must be made quickly, pre-computing solutions is a viable strategy. The number of possible expert selection configurations is around N^n, which is manageable for certain models (e.g., $N \leq 32$, $n \leq 4$). We examine this problem in Sect. 4.2.

The static problem determines how to distribute the R_e replicas of the N experts across k GPUs before the computation, in order to minimize the expected maximum load on any GPU, given the dynamic allocation strategy. The complexity of this problem is analyzed in Sect. 4.3.

The different challenges in expert placement for MoE models are illustrated in Figs. 3 and 4. In Fig. 3, a constrained scenario is considered where each expert is assigned to a single GPU without replication. Figure 3a presents the static placement of experts, while Fig. 3b shows two possible execution cases: when Experts 1 and 6 are selected, both GPUs operate in parallel (total expert execution time of 1), but when Experts 1 and 4 are selected, execution must be

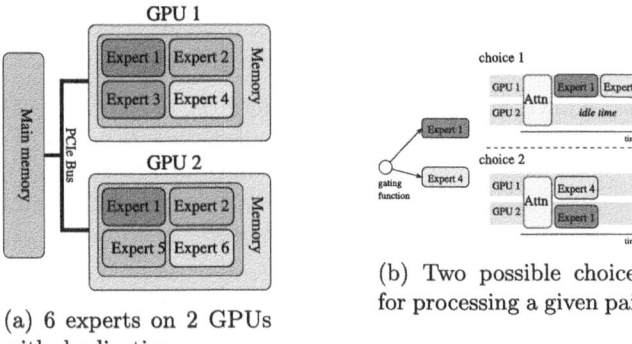

(a) 6 experts on 2 GPUs with duplication

(b) Two possible choices for processing a given pair

Fig. 4. An example of the distribution of experts with replication. The choice of which expert copy is used for a given pair impacts the processing time.

sequential (total time of 2). If only pairs (1,4) and (1,6) were possible, placing Expert 1 on GPU 1 and Experts 4 and 6 on GPU 2 would optimize parallelism. Since each expert is present only once, the dynamic scheduling problem is trivial, but the static allocation problem remains NP-complete, as shown in Sect. 4.3.

Figure 4 extends this to a more flexible setting with 6 experts and 4 memory slots per GPU, allowing expert replication. Figure 4a illustrates this static placement, where Experts 1 and 2 are stored on both GPUs. The dynamic problem arises when Experts 1 and 4 are selected, leading to two possible execution schedules (Fig. 4b), only one of which ensures efficient parallelism. The quality of static allocation depends on dynamic scheduling, making it crucial to solve both problems jointly.

4   Analysis of Static and Dynamic Allocation Problems

4.1   Definitions

In this section, we establish the complexity of the dynamic (ALLOCDYNAMIC) and static (ALLOCSTATIC) allocation problems,

Definition 1 (ALLOCDYNAMIC). *Let a platform consist of k GPUs, let $A(i) \subset \{1, \ldots, k\}$ be the subset of GPUs holding expert i and let $i_1, \ldots, i_n$ be the n experts activated by the gating function. We are looking for an expert replica selection s such that $S(i)$ is the GPU chosen to process expert i, so that*

(a) $\forall i \in \{i_1, \ldots, i_n\}$, $S(i) \in A(i)$ *(validity),*
(b) $T(i_1, \ldots, i_n) = \max_u |\{i \in \{i_1, \ldots, i_n\}, S(i) = u\}|$ *is minimal (parallel efficiency) where $T(i_1, \ldots, i_n)$ denotes the time to process all experts in parallel on the GPUs given the expert allocation.*

We prove in Sect. 4.2 that ALLOCDYNAMIC can be solved in polynomial time using matching algorithms, so that $T(i_1, \ldots, i_n)$ is the optimal parallel time for a given subset of experts and a given static allocation a of experts onto GPU.

We can now define the static allocation problem ALLOCSTATIC, which consists in deciding how to store all experts on the different GPUs.

Definition 2 (ALLOCSTATIC). *Given a platform consisting of k GPUs, let $p(i_1, \ldots, i_n)$ be the probability for the gating function to select the n-uple of experts $(i_1, \ldots, i_n)$. Let M the maximum number of experts a GPU can host depending on the available memory. Let us denote by $A(i)$ is the subset of GPUs holding expert i. We are looking for a static allocation a of the experts on GPUs such that (a) for each GPU g $|\{i, A(i) = g\}| \leq M$ (memory constraint) and (b) the expected time to process activated expert for this layer given by $\sum_{(i_1, \ldots, i_n)} p(i_1, \ldots, i_n) \, T(i_1, \ldots, i_n)$ is minimal.*

We prove in Sect. 4.3 that the decision problem associated with ALLOCSTATIC is NP-Complete, even when each expert is present on only one GPU.

4.2 Optimal Solution for ALLOCDYNAMIC

Let us assume we are given a solution to the ALLOCSTATIC problem, which defines the allocation of experts to GPUs. We show how to solve the ALLOC-DYNAMIC problem, i.e., given the allocation of experts and the result of the activation function, how to determine which GPUs will perform which activated experts to minimize parallel processing time.

Let us denote by $A(i)$ the subset of GPUs that hold expert i and let $i_1, \ldots, i_n$ be the n experts activated by the gating function. Our objective is to determine, for each expert i, which GPU $S(i) \in A(i)$ will process that expert, so as to minimize the maximum number of activated experts to be processed on each GPU.

Algorithm 1 summarizes how to compute S and the cost T that corresponds to the parallel time necessary to process all experts given S. The algorithm tries all possible values of T, from 1 to n. For $T = 1$, we start by building a bipartite graph whose vertices are the activated experts on the one hand, and the GPUs on the other. We connect an activated expert vertex to a GPU vertex if the GPU holds the corresponding expert. We look for a graph matching of cardinality n, i.e. one that covers all the experts in the subset. This can be done, for example, by using the Hopcroft-Karp [11] algorithm to compute a maximum bipartite matching.

If there exists a matching of cardinality n, this means we can select a separate GPU for each expert. Otherwise, it means that $T > 1$ and we proceed to the test for $T = 2$. We create a copy of all GPU nodes: for a GPU g, node $(g, 1)$ corresponds to the first time slot on GPU 1, while node $(g, 2)$ corresponds to its second time slot. Similarly, we search for a matching of size n, which would correspond to a solution with $T = 2$. If such a matching of size n does not exist, we continue to increase T and make additional copies of the GPUs corresponding to the different time slots until we find a solution, what necessarily occurs at least for $T = n$, since $T = n$ corresponds to the case where all activated experts can be processed on the same GPU.

Algorithm 1. Selecting experts for a given mapping

    Inputs: mapping A, subset of experts $(i_1, \ldots, i_n)$
    Output: expert selection S with its cost T
1: $T \leftarrow 0$
2: **repeat**
3:     $T \leftarrow T + 1$
4:     Let $V_1 = \{i_1, \ldots, i_n\}$ and $V_2 = \{(g,j)\}$ for $g \in \{1, \ldots, k\}$ and $j \in \{1, \ldots, T\}$
5:     Let $E = \{(i,(g,j))$ such that $g \in A(i)\}$ for $i \in \{i_1, \ldots, i_n\}$ and $j \in \{1, \ldots, T\}$
6:     Create the bipartite graph $G = (V_1 \cup V_2, E)$
7:     Find a matching $\mathcal{M}$ with maximum cardinality in G
8: **until** $|\mathcal{M}| = n$
9: **for** $i \in \{i_1, \ldots i_n\}$ **do**
10:    $S(i) \leftarrow g$ such that $(i,(g,j)) \in \mathcal{M}$ for some j
11: **Return** S, T

4.3   NP-Completeness of ALLOCSTATIC

To establish the NP-completeness of ALLOCSTATIC, we assume that the memory available on the GPUs is sufficient to store exactly one copy of each expert so that ALLOCDYNAMIC is trivially solvable since there is no choice to be made at runtime. We consider a restricted version of the problem, with $k = 2$ GPUs and $N = 2M_r$ experts and $n = 2$, where M_r is the memory available on each GPU. The memory of each GPU can therefore contain a maximum of $N/2$ experts, and ALLOCSTATIC is equivalent to partitioning the experts into two subsets. When a token is produced, a pair of experts is selected (since $n = 2$). If a pair of experts residing on the same GPU is required, the processing of both experts will be sequentialized. Let us denote by $p_{i,j}$ the probability that experts i and j (with $i < j$) are simultaneously activated by the gating function, and by $A(i) \in \{1,2\}$ the index of the GPU holding expert i. Given the allocation A and the probability distribution p, the expected processing time of the experts is given by $E(a,p) = \sum\limits_{i<j, A(i)\neq A(j)} 1 \times p_{i,j} + \sum\limits_{i<j, A(i)=A(j)} 2 \times p_{i,j}$ and

$$E(a,p) = 1 + \sum_{i<j, A(i)=A(j)} p_{i,j} = 2 - \sum_{i<j, A(i)\neq A(j)} p_{i,j}, \text{ given that } \sum_{i<j} p_{i,j} = 1.$$

The objective is thus to find an allocation A that maximize $\sum_{i<j, A(i)\neq A(j)} p_{i,j}$.

Theorem 1. *The problem* ALLOCSTATIC *of finding a static allocation with minimum expected computation time of the experts on two GPUs with* $M_r = N/2$ *is NP-hard.*

Proof. Given an allocation, computing the expected expert computation time with the previous formula is obviously polynomial so that ALLOCSTATIC $\in NP$. To prove the hardness, let us consider the minimization of $\sum_{i<j, A(i)\neq A(j)} p_{i,j}$ (see the previous formula) and let us consider the decision version of the problem, which consists in finding an allocation with $\sum_{i<j, A(i)\neq A(j)} p_{i,j} \geq B$. We

now perform a reduction from the MAXIMUMBISECTION problem, which is NP-complete [1,9]. Given an edge-weighted graph (with even number of vertices), this problem consists in partitioning the vertices in two subsets of same size such that the total weight of edges going from one part to the other (i.e., the cut-weight) is smaller than K. Consider an instance I_{bisect} of the bisection problem. We build an following instance I_{alloc} of the bisection problem, where each vertex i is associated to an expert i and the probability of using pair i, j is set to $p_{i,j} = (W - w_{i,j})/P$ where $w_{i,j}$ is the weight of edge (i, j) in G (or 0 if there is no such edge), $W = \max_{i,j} w_{i,j}$ and P is a scaling factor so that all probabilities sum to 1 ($P = N^2W/4 - \sum_{i<j} w_{i,j}$). We set the bound to $B = (N^2W/4 - K)/P$.

Assume that I_{alloc} has a valid solution A. We then build a bisection of the graph such that S_1 corresponds to the set of experts mapped on the first GPU, and S_2 corresponds to the set of experts mapped on the second GPU ($S_1 = A^{-1}(1)$ and $S_1 = A^{-1}(2)$). The cut-weight is then given by

$$\sum_{\substack{(i,j) \\ A(i)=1, \\ A(j)=2}} w_{i,j} = \sum_{\substack{i<j \\ A(i)\neq A(j)}} w_{i,j} = \sum_{\substack{i<j \\ A(i)\neq A(j)}} W - Pp_{i,j} = \left(\frac{N}{2}\right)^2 W - P \sum_{\substack{i<j \\ A(i)\neq A(j)}} p_{i,j}$$

as there are exactly $(N/2)^2$ edges from one part to another (each part is of size $N/2$). As $\sum_{i<j,A(i)\neq A(j)} p_{i,j} \geq B$, we get that the cut-weight is at most K, so that (S_1, S_2) is a solution of I_{bisec}.

Conversely, let us assume that I_{bisec} has a solution (S_1, S_2). From this solution, we build an optimal allocation for I_{alloc} by allocating experts corresponding to S_1 to the first GPU, and the others to the second GPU, i.e. $A(i) = 1$ if $i \in S_1$ and 2 if $i \in S_2$. As previously, we can relate the cut-weight to the objective of I_{alloc}:

$$\sum_{\substack{(i,j) \\ A(i)=1 \text{ and } A(j)=2}} w_{i,j} = \left(\frac{N}{2}\right)^2 W - P \sum_{\substack{i<j \\ A(i)\neq A(j)}} p_{i,j}$$

Since we know that the cut-weight is smaller than K, $\sum_{i<j,A(i)\neq A(j)} p_{i,j}$ is at least B, which proves that A is a valid solution for I_{alloc}.

In the companion research report [4], we propose an Integer Linear Programming (ILP) formulation that solves the most general version of the problem, where the memory constraint on each GPU allows the same expert to be allocated to multiple GPUs, as illustrated in Fig. 4. Due to lack of of space, we refer the interested reader to [4] to find the complete formulation. In practice, due to high number of variables, experiments with state-of-the-art LP solvers show that when $N > 2$ or when the memory is large enough to allow a large replication of experts ($M > 4N/k$), the linear program does not help find an optimal solution and the solvers fail to find a solution within a few minutes.

5   Heuristic Algorithms

As mentioned in Sect. 4, the large number of variables in the previous linear program makes it impractical as soon as the number n of simultaneously activated experts is large or, even for a moderate number of experts, when replication allows a large number of different configurations (corresponding to a large value of M). Therefore, there is a strong need for a low-cost solution, i.e., an algorithm capable of finding a good allocation of experts on the GPU with limited complexity. In this section, we propose a greedy heuristic algorithm for solving the ALLOCSTATIC problem, based on the algorithm for the ALLOCDYNAMIC problem proposed earlier in Sect. 4.2.

Algorithm 2. Greedy allocation of experts

Inputs: usage probabilities of expert subsets p
Output: expert allocation $A(i)$ for each expert i
   for $i = 1, \ldots N$ **do** $A(i) \leftarrow \emptyset$
   for $g = 1, \ldots k$ **do** $load(g) \leftarrow 0$
   while $load(g) < M$ for some g **do**
      for each GPU g such that $load(g) < M$ **do**
         for each expert i such that $g \notin A(i)$ **do**
            $a' \leftarrow a,\ a'(i) \leftarrow A(i) \cup \{g\}$
            $gain(i, g) \leftarrow cost(a) - cost(a')$
      Select (i, g) with highest $gain(i, g)$
      $A(i) \leftarrow A(i) \cup \{g\}$
      $load(g) \leftarrow load(g) + 1$
   return A

Algorithm 3. Randomized round-robin allocation of experts

Inputs: usage probabilities p
Output: expert allocation $A(i)$ for each expert i
   for $i = 1, \ldots N$ **do** $A(i) \leftarrow \emptyset$
   $next \leftarrow 0$
   for $it = 1, \ldots M$ **do**
      $L \leftarrow$ list of all GPUs in randomized order
      for each GPU g in L **do**
         $A(next) \leftarrow A(next) \cup \{g\}$
         $next \leftarrow next + 1$
   return A

The proposed algorithm, detailed in Algorithm 2, starts with an empty allocation (no expert assigned to GPUs) and iteratively computes the (expert, GPU) pair maximizing the gain in a cost function. To do this, we define the cost of using an expert that is not yet assigned to any GPU; we set this cost to a high value (fixed at 10 times the time needed to compute an expert in our experiments). We then define the cost of an allocation as the expected parallel computation time of the experts, given the probability distribution for expert subsets. The overall cost of an allocation is computed using Algorithm 1.

To assess the performance of Algorithm 2, we also consider a Randomized Round Robin allocation allocation of experts (Algorithm 3). Figure 5 (left) shows the respective allocation costs of greedy Algorithm 2 (in red) and Randomized algorithm 3, for increasing memory size. For the random mapping, we plot the average and standard deviation for 10 trials. These results are obtained in the particular case of the 16th layer of the DRBX model [5], with $k = 4$ GPUs and $n = 4$ experts activated by the gating function out of $N = 16$ possible experts, on a text corpus representative of the training base[1]. These results show that when the memory is limited and does not allow for a full replication of all experts to GPUs, there is a high incentive to choose the allocation of experts based on their respective usage, as done by our algorithm. For example, as soon as only 2 copies of all experts can be allocated on the whole platform (which corresponds to a memory per GPU of 8), the greedy heuristic can reach an almost parallel computation of experts for all possible subsets (expected cost very close to 1), whereas the random allocation has a cost 30% larger on average, and can reach a parallel processing of experts only for full replication (memory of 16).

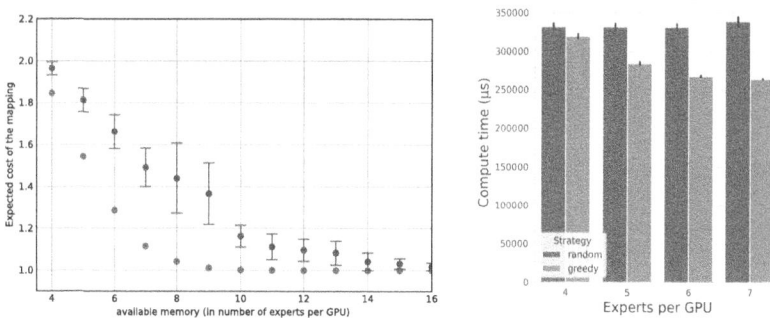

Fig. 5. Expected cost of mappings (left) and runtime on Mixtral (right)

6   Experimental Evaluation

To assess the performance of our proposed expert allocation, we rely on a simplified version of the Mixtral model [14] and measure the time it requires for inference for various expert mapping strategies. We instantiate a two layers model

---

[1] We obtained very similar results on the other DRBX layers and on the Mixtral [14] model, with $n = 2$ and $N = 8$.

with 8 large experts (hidden size of 4096 and intermediary size of 140000). We use the PyTorch tracer to record the time spent on each expert computation and the time spent on the communication between the GPUs. We perform experiments on the inference time using allocations produced by both Algorithm 2 (greedy) and Algorithm 3 (randomized round-robin). We compare the inference time of the two strategies with different expert frequencies and replication factors. We measure the inference time for 150 tokens, and run each experiment 3 times.

6.1   Experimental Setting

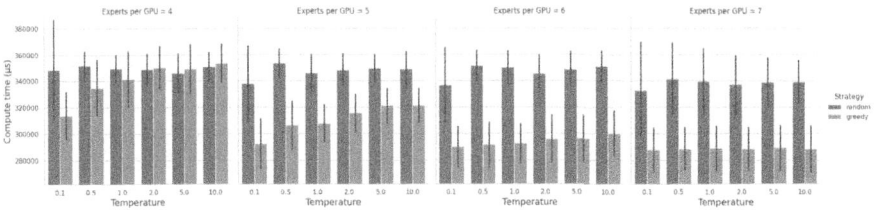

Fig. 6. Impact of the peakiness of the expert pair distribution on the inference time for the synthetic distributions. Low temperature corresponds to very peak distributions, high temperature to quasi-homogeneous distributions.

We run two types of experiments relying either on synthetic distributions, which allows us to test our allocation algorithms on a wide range of parameters, or on real distributions measured from an actual inference on an existing dataset. In both cases, based on the Mixtral model, the gating function activates $n = 2$ experts among the $N = 8$ available ones.

Synthetic Distribution of Pairs. To assess the performance of Algorithm 2 and Algorithm 3 on distributions with a large range of variance, we first randomly generate a probability distribution of the usage of the pairs and rescaled it, using a temperature parameter to control the entropy of the distribution. This setting allows us to arbitrarily tune the entropy of the distribution and to evaluate the impact of this parameter on the performance gains with Algorithm 2. The initial sampled distribution is the same for a given experiment and is simply rescaled differently to ensure fair comparison between the two strategies.

Mixtral-like Distribution. We perform inference with 1000 prompts from VMWare Open Instruct dataset[2] on the Mixtral model and compute the frequency of each pair of experts for all layers over 10^5 tokens. This gives us 32 distributions (one per layer), which we also used as input for our experiments.

---

[2] https://huggingface.co/datasets/VMware/open-instruct.

6.2   Results

Synthetic Experiments. Figure 6 illustrates how the expert pair distribution temperature affects Mixtral inference time. Lower temperatures create "peaky distributions" with dominant expert pairs, while higher temperatures lead to near-uniform distributions. The greedy algorithm consistently outperforms random allocation by leveraging expert distribution and replication, achieving gains even with nearly uniform distributions. Random allocation matches greedy performance only in fully homogeneous cases, which rarely occur in practice.

Simulations with Real Distributions. Figure 5 (right) shows the effect of expert replication on Mixtral inference time across all 32 layers. We report the average computation time and standard deviation. Again, the greedy algorithm effectively exploits expert usage distribution and reduce execution time. Despite improved expert allocation and parallelism, the overall inference performance gain remains limited. This is because the targeted optimization affects only a fraction of the pipeline, while other costly operations (e.g., Attention computations, routing) dominate execution time. Our measurements show that expert computations, even with parallelism, represent just 14% of total inference time. Optimizing these operations is beyond this study's scope, as existing solutions are either proprietary or complex. However, we expect our method's impact to be more significant in optimized frameworks. This work serves as a proof-of-concept for smarter expert allocation, encouraging its integration into high-performance inference systems.

7   Conclusion and Perspectives

We optimize inference for Mixture of Experts models, where expert selection occurs dynamically based on prior attention layers and a gating function. Despite penalization mechanisms enforcing uniform expert selection during training, we show this uniformity does not hold for n-tuples of experts ($n = 2$, 4, up to 256 in some MoE models). This opens the door to optimized allocations, both in expert storage on GPUs and runtime expert selection. We demonstrate that dynamic allocation can be solved in polynomial time using maximal matchings, while the static problem is NP-complete. Two allocation algorithms are proposed and evaluated on the Mixtral model by HuggingFace, showing that leveraging n-tuple distributions enhances expert parallelism during inference. Future work includes learning expert usage distribution dynamically for adaptive reallocation, optimizing memory allocation per layer based on variance in expert selection, and exploring theoretical combinatorial questions on distributing N experts over k GPUs to maximize diversity in n-expert groupings.

Disclosure of Interests. The authors have no competing interests to declare that are relevant to the content of this article.

References

1. Bui, T.N., Jones, C.: Finding good approximate vertex and edge partitions is np-hard. Inf. Process. Lett. **42**(3), 153–159 (1992)
2. Cai, W., Jiang, J., Wang, F., Tang, J., Kim, S., Huang, J.: A survey on mixture of experts (2024). arXiv preprint arXiv:2407.06204
3. Dai, D., et al.: Deepseekmoe: towards ultimate expert specialization in mixture-of-experts language models (2024). arXiv preprint arXiv:2401.06066
4. Darrin, M., Beaumont, O., Bourgouin, R., Marchal, L., Piantanida, P.: Leveraging expert usage to speed up LLM inference with expert parallelism – extended version (2025). https://hal.science/hal-04994839
5. Introducing DBRX: A new state-of-the-art open LLM (2024). https://www.databricks.com/blog/introducing-dbrx-new-state-art-open-llm
6. Du, N., et al.: Glam: efficient scaling of language models with mixture-of-experts. In: ICML 2022 (2022)
7. Eliseev, A., Mazur, D.: Fast inference of mixture-of-experts language models with offloading (2023). https://arxiv.org/abs/2312.17238
8. Fedus, W., Zoph, B., Shazeer, N.: Switch transformers: scaling to trillion parameter models with simple and efficient sparsity. J. Mach. Learn. Res. **23** (2022)
9. Garey, M.R., Johnson, D.S.: Computers and Intractability, a Guide to the Theory of NP-Completeness. W. H, Freeman and Company (1979)
10. He, J., et al.: Fastermoe: modeling and optimizing training of large-scale dynamic pre-trained models. In: Proceedings of the 27th ACM SIGPLAN Symposium on PPOPP, pp. 120–134 (2022)
11. Hopcroft, J.E., Karp, R.M.: An n^5/2 algorithm for maximum matchings in bipartite graphs. SIAM J. Comput. **2**(4), 225–231 (1973)
12. Huang, H., et al.: Towards moe deployment: mitigating inefficiencies in mixture-of-expert (moe) inference (2023). https://arxiv.org/abs/2303.06182
13. Hwang, C., et al.: Tutel: adaptive mixture-of-experts at scale. Proc. Mach. Learn. Syst. **5**, 269–287 (2023)
14. Jiang, A.Q., et al.: Mixtral of experts (2024). arXiv preprint arXiv:2401.04088
15. Lepikhin, D., et al.: Gshard: scaling giant models with conditional computation and automatic sharding (2020). arXiv preprint arXiv:2006.16668
16. Min, B., et al.: Recent advances in natural language processing via large pre-trained language models: a survey. ACM Comput. Surv. **56**(2), 1–40 (2023)
17. Minaee, S., et al.: Large language models: a survey (2024). arXiv preprint arXiv:2402.06196
18. Team, Q.: Qwen1.5-moe: matching 7b model performance with 1/3 activated parameters (2024). https://qwenlm.github.io/blog/qwen-moe/
19. Vaswani, A.: attention is all you need. Adv. Neural Inf. Process. Syst. (2017)

HAS-GPU: Efficient Hybrid Auto-scaling with Fine-Grained GPU Allocation for SLO-Aware Serverless Inferences

Jianfeng Gu[1(✉)], Puxuan Wang[1], Isaac David Núñez Araya[1], Kai Huang[2], and Michael Gerndt[1]

[1] Technical University of Munich,
Munich, Germany
{jianfeng.gu,puxuan.wang,
isaac.nunez}@tum.de,
gerndt@in.tum.de
[2] Sun Yat-sen University, Guangzhou, China
huangk36@mail.sysu.edu.cn

Abstract. Serverless Computing (FaaS) has become a popular paradigm for deep learning inference due to the ease of deployment and pay-per-use benefits. However, current serverless inference platforms encounter the coarse-grained and static GPU resource allocation problems during scaling, which leads to high costs and Service Level Objective (SLO) violations in fluctuating workloads. Meanwhile, current platforms only support horizontal scaling for GPU inferences, thus the cold start problem further exacerbates the problems. In this paper, we propose **HAS-GPU**, an efficient **H**ybrid **A**uto-scaling **S**erverless architecture with fine-grained **GPU** allocation for deep learning inferences. HAS-GPU proposes an agile scheduler capable of allocating GPU Streaming Multiprocessor (SM) partitions and time quotas with arbitrary granularity and enables significant vertical quota scalability at runtime. To resolve performance uncertainty introduced by massive fine-grained resource configuration spaces, we propose the Resource-aware Performance Predictor (RaPP). Furthermore, we present an adaptive hybrid auto-scaling algorithm with both horizontal and vertical scaling to ensure inference SLOs and minimize GPU costs. The experiments demonstrated that compared to the mainstream serverless inference platform, HAS-GPU reduces function costs by an average of **10.8x** with better SLO guarantees. Compared to state-of-the-art spatio-temporal GPU sharing serverless framework, HAS-GPU reduces function SLO violation by **4.8x** and cost by 1.72x on average.

Keywords: Serverless computing · GPU allocation · Auto-scaling

1 Introduction

Serverless computing, also referred to as Function-as-a-Service (FaaS), is emerging as a prominent paradigm for next-generation cloud-native computing due to the ease of deployment, high scalability, and cost-effective pay-per-use benefits.

W. E. Nagel et al. (Eds.): Euro-Par 2025, LNCS 15900, pp. 159–174, 2026.
https://doi.org/10.1007/978-3-031-99854-6_11

It shifts the burden of complex resource allocation and runtime maintenance from users to cloud providers, while its built-in agile scaling and event-driven policies enable applications to dynamically adapt to fluctuating workloads on demand, thereby reducing resource usage and the cost per request. Traditional FaaS platforms primarily support CPU functions, such as AWS Lambda [3] and Google Run Function [5]. However, with the growing prevalence of deep learning (DL) applications, a rising number of inference tasks are being deployed on GPU-enabled serverless computing platforms, such as Azure Functions [6], Alibaba Cloud Function [1], KServe [7], and RunPod [10].

Nevertheless, current serverless inference platforms commonly encounter problems with coarse GPU allocation and limited scalability. First, with advanced GPU manufacturing, modern GPUs integrate more compute units and memory resources in a single board, such as NVIDIA V100 (80 SM (Streaming Multiprocessor) units, 5120 CUDA cores) and H100 (144 SMs, 18432 CUDA cores). The rise of large language models (LLMs) has further driven rapid deployment of high-end, expensive GPUs in modern data centers. Unlike LLM inference, which requires exclusive access to multiple GPUs and customized systems, serverless inference platforms typically run smaller deep learning models [4,12,28] in multi-tenant environments. However, current GPU-based serverless platforms [6,7,10] simply allocate an entire GPU to a single function instance, even though most inference tasks fall far short of fully using the GPU resources. This coarse GPU resource allocation leads to low GPU utilization and increased function costs.

Second, some approaches attempt to enable multiple function instances to share a GPU, but simultaneously undergo the problems of significant scalability limitations and potentially frequent Service Level Objectives (SLOs) violations. Current spatial GPU sharing approaches, such as NVIDIA's Multi-Instance GPU (MIG) support in Kubernetes [8], Alibaba Cloud's cGPU [11], and the MPS-based method GSlice [17], enable the allocation of partial GPU compute units to applications. Meanwhile, other approaches [16,19] introduce spatial and temporal resource allocations. However, these approaches can only statically allocate fixed-size GPU resources to inference tasks. When dealing with highly fluctuant serverless workloads, they can only rely on horizontal scaling, which incurs significant cold start overhead due to the creation of new instances, particularly for deep learning models that require massive model data loading. Unlike serverless CPU functions, which can flexibly scale vertically by adjusting CPU cores/quota and memory via cgroups system, there is currently a lack of system for achieving fine-grained vertical scaling on GPUs. The limitation in vertical scalability prevents GPU functions from effectively ensuring function SLOs.

In this paper, we proposed **HAS-GPU**, an efficient **H**ybrid **A**uto-scaling **S**erverless architecture with both vertical and horizontal scaling and fine-grained **GPU** allocation for deep learning inferences. HAS-GPU incorporates an agile scheduler capable of allocating GPU SM partitions and time quotas with arbitrary granularity and enables dynamic GPU quota reallocation at runtime. The flexible GPU temporal resource reallocation provides significant support for function vertical scaling. HAS-GPU can quickly respond to burst workloads by increasing the time quota and provide a time buffer for horizontal scaling. Meanwhile, it can optimize time quota allocation during low request periods and sustains a keep-alive state with minimal resource consumption, eliminating cold start overhead from scale-to-zero and significantly reducing function costs.

Furthermore, since finer-grained GPU resource allocation also implies a significantly larger search space, we propose an accurate **R**esource-aware **P**erformance **P**rediction (**RaPP**) model to facilitate spatio-temporal GPU resource allocation. The model addresses the inference performance uncertainty introduced by massive resource configuration spaces. RaPP integrates and learns static and runtime features of deep learning operators and computing graphs under resource constraints, enabling accurate latency prediction for different batch sizes and models across any spatio-temporal GPU resource configurations. This eliminates the need for large-scale pre-profiling required in previous work [16,19,28].

Meanwhile, to handle highly fluctuating serverless workloads, we propose an adaptive hybrid auto-scaling algorithm. The algorithm introduces the co-design of fine-grained GPU resource allocation and function scheduling. By efficiently coordinating vertical and horizontal scaling, it enables functions to dynamically and flexibly adjust GPU resources with a fine granularity at runtime to meet their SLOs. Meanwhile, the high elasticity minimizes unnecessary resource consumption, effectively reducing function costs. Moreover, the algorithm introduces SM partition alignment-based GPU resource allocation, effectively addressing resource fragmentation problem in fine-grained allocation.

In a nutshell, the contributions are summarized as follows:

- We propose **HAS-GPU**, an efficient hybrid auto-scaling architecture with fine-grained GPU allocation for serverless inferences to effectively ensure function SLOs and reduce function cost. To our best knowledge, HAS-GPU is the first work providing GPU vertical scaling for serverless computing.
- We propose **RaPP**, an accurate resource-aware performance prediction model, addressing the problem of massive pre-profiling requirement and inference performance uncertainty introduced by massive resource configuration spaces.
- We propose the **hybrid auto-scaling algorithm** to facilitate agile vertical and horizontal scaling, which effectively ensures function SLOs, reduces function cost, and avoids resource fragmentation.
- We implement the HAS-GPU architecture from low-level GPU device management to high-level serverless function scheduling. Experiments on the MLPerf-based benchmark [25] and Azure Trace workload [30] demonstrate that, compared to mainstream serverless inference platforms, HAS-GPU reduces function costs by 10.8x on average with better SLO guarantees. Compared to the state-of-the-art spatio-temporal GPU sharing framework, HAS-GPU reduces function SLO violation by 4.8x and cost by 1.72x on average.

2   Related Work

2.1   Serverless Inference

With the widespread adoption of deep learning (DL) applications, serverless computing, commonly known as Function-as-a-Service (FaaS) [21], has become a popular choice for deploying DL inference applications [4,13]. FaaS platforms offer seamless scalability while abstracting away complex resource management. Additionally, their event-driven, pay-per-use pricing model helps reduce costs. Major cloud providers, including AWS SageMaker [2], Azure Functions [6], and Alibaba Cloud [1], have introduced serverless inference platforms. Meanwhile, various research efforts have introduced optimizations for serverless inference architectures, such as tensor sharing [22] and request batching [12]. However, most of these approaches perform inference on CPU-based functions, while GPU-based architectures [6,7,10] typically allocate an entire GPU to a single inference function instance even though the function cannot fully utilize it. As expensive high-end GPUs are increasingly deployed in cloud and data centers, the cost of function inference continues to rise. Therefore, achieving finer-grained GPU resource allocation for inference functions is critical to reducing inference costs.

2.2   Fine-Grained GPU Allocation

With advancements in GPU manufacturing, modern GPUs integrate more SMs, CUDA cores, and memory on a single board, such as the V100 (80 SMs, 5120 CUDA cores) and H100 (144 SMs, 18,432 CUDA cores). Therefore, research has increasingly focused on finer-grained GPU allocation and sharing to minimize resource waste. To enable GPU sharing, NVIDIA introduced MIG [8] for hardware-based partitioning and MPS [9] for software-based isolation, while Alibaba Cloud implemented cGPU [11] for GPU partitioning in the Linux kernel. Building on these, studies [15,17] have proposed spatial resource allocation and optimization strategies to meet application SLOs. Additionally, some approaches [16,19,20] explore spatio-temporal GPU resource allocation, leveraging workload-based resource management to reduce applications' mutual interference, enhance application throughput, and improve GPU utilization. However, these approaches can only statically allocate fixed-size GPU resources to inference tasks.

2.3   Performance Prediction for Deep Learning Inferences

Inference performance prediction is a crucial technique for reducing the need for extensive pre-profiling. Previous work nn-Meter [29] predicts DL model latency at the kernel level by detecting kernels and summing the latency predictions from per-kernel predictors. But the model is limited to edge devices. DIPPM [24] and NNLQP [23] utilize static model computation graphs and operator features with graph neural network learning to predict the latency, memory, or energy consumption. However, these methods cannot predict performance under different runtimes and fine-grained GPU resource configurations. Currently, there are no methods for predicting model performance across a wide range of different fine-grained GPU resource allocations.

2.4   Horizontal and Vertical Auto-scaling

The CPU-based horizontal and vertical scaling has been widely studied in serverless computing [26]. However, GPU function is primarily limited to horizontal scaling, and almost all cloud providers [1,6,10] only offer horizontal scaling for GPU function. This is mainly because CPU and memory resources can be quickly expanded using the cgroups system, whereas no system currently exists to achieve fine-grained vertical scaling on GPUs. Choi et.al [16] and FaST-GShare [19] proposed to select and scale inference functions with the most efficient spatio-temporal GPU resource configuration to meet a workload. INF-less [28] introduced a horizontal non-uniform scaling policy with heterogeneous CPU/GPU resource allocation to maximize resource efficiency. GSLICE [17] horizontally replaced functions with different spatial GPU resource allocations using the shadow functions. When dealing with highly fluctuating serverless workloads, these methods essentially only rely on horizontal scaling, in which the creation of new instances suffers from significant cold start overhead. Therefore, introducing vertical scaling for GPU functions is essential to further ensure function SLOs.

3   System Design

The design and workflow of HAS-GPU is shown in Fig. 1. The architecture follows the fundamental structure of Kubernetes to support more FaaS platforms and mainly consists of five core components: the Hybrid Auto-Scaler and performance prediction modules (RaPP) on the control plane, as well as the GPU Re-configurator, HAS-GPU-Scheduler, and *libhas* modules on the worker nodes.

In the control plane, when a developer submits a DL inference model, **RaPP** automatically extracts the model and runtime features for performance analysis. By predicting latency and corresponding throughput capability under different batch sizes and fine-grained resource allocations, RaPP provides precise function performance information for the Hybrid Auto-Scaler. The **Hybrid Auto-Scaler** maintains at least one instance with minimal resources for each DL function and continuously retrieves request metrics from the Gateway. When significant fluctuations in user requests occur, the auto-scaler evaluates current pod instances of the function and GPU resource usage in the cluster. Based on the hybrid auto-scaling algorithm, the auto-scaler decides to apply either horizontal or vertical scaling and perform resource allocation and pod scheduling for the function. Meanwhile, the load balancer is updated with request distribution information according to the throughput capability of different function pods.

In GPU worker nodes, **HAS-node-daemon** manages the resource allocation and scheduling of all GPUs within a node and runs on each node. Inside HAS-node-Daemon, **HAS-GPU-Scheduler** abstracts each physical GPU device into

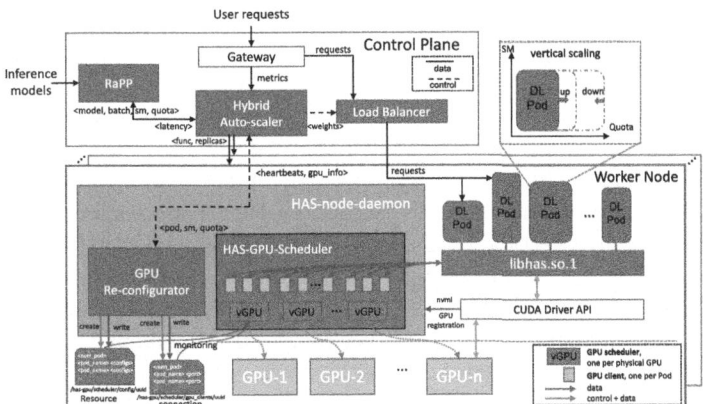

Fig. 1. The architecture of HAS-GPU.

a vGPU and creates a GPU client for each assigned pod to manage its GPU resource usage. Each vGPU coordinates and controls the GPU usage of its assigned GPU clients at runtime and is associated with two resource configuration device files in the host system. The **GPU Re-configurator** dynamically monitors the status of all GPUs within the node and provides real-time GPU information to the Hybrid Auto-Scaler. Meanwhile, it receives fine-grained GPU resource allocation instructions from the auto-scaler for pods and writes this information to the device files. The *libhas* serves as the unified interface for resource control of pods in HAS-GPU. At runtime, pods utilize this library to request and obtain GPU resources from the corresponding GPU client for execution.

3.1   Fine-Grained GPU Resource Allocation and Reallocation

HAS-GPU enables fine-grained allocation of GPU resources through spatio-temporal resource isolation and sharing. This is achieved by leveraging CUDA Driver API interception and MPS-based [9] Streaming Multiprocessor (SM) partitioning techniques. Currently, the proprietary ecosystem of GPU software stacks like CUDA makes it difficult for the system to control the execution prioritization and scheduling of DL tasks when multiple tasks are running together.

However, all deep learning inference tasks ultimately invoke the underlying unified CUDA Driver APIs, such as allocating GPU memory through *cuMemAlloc()*, transferring data from host memory to device memory via *cuMemcpyHtoD()*, and launching kernels using the *cuLaunchKernel()* function. Therefore, HAS-GPU introduces new custom unified APIs and leverages the function interposition technique to load the new shared library *libhas*. The library overrides functions in the standard CUDA library, seamlessly and effectively intercepting the CUDA function calls at runtime. Within the intercepting APIs, we design our resource allocation and scheduling mechanisms. We leverage the intercepted functions related to GPU memory allocation and release to enforce limits on the available GPU memory within a pod. As shown in Fig. 1, the communication between the pod and its GPU client in the HAS-GPU-Scheduler is established through the intercepted *cuLaunchKernel()* function. A pod must request a time token from the vGPU via the GPU client to execute CUDA kernels. By specifying the proportion of time tokens allocated within the time window of a vGPU, HAS-GPU achieves any fine-grained temporal GPU resource allocation for pods. When a pod requires vertical scaling, the HAS-GPU-Scheduler can dynamically modify the time token within the time window to achieve GPU resource reallocation with minimal overhead, as shown in Fig. 2. Meanwhile, the time window can be flexibly adjusted, similar to the CPU subsystem in cgroups, to accommodate varying temporal granularity requirements.

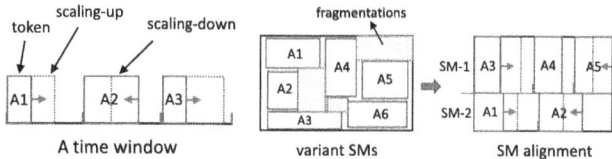

Fig. 2. Flexible vertical scaling and SM alignments to avoid fragmentations.

For spatial resource allocation, NVIDIA offers the Multi-Process Service (MPS) [9] interface, enabling systems to allocate arbitrary proportions of Streaming Multiprocessors (SMs) to certain applications. However, the allocated SMs are deeply tied to the CUDA context and must be specified when the context is initially created, preventing dynamic reallocation of SM resources at runtime. But dynamic SM allocation can easily lead to severe resource fragmentation, as shown in Fig. 2. Therefore, HAS-GPU achieves vertical scaling for a pod by leveraging flexible temporal resource reallocation under a stable SM allocation and by performance prediction across varying configurations. Meanwhile, a pod can be initially assigned any SM partitions if the GPU has no prior allocation.

Traditional serverless inference platforms [7] manage GPU resources through the Kubernetes device plugin. However, the plugin only allows allocating GPUs at the instance level and cannot specify particular GPUs, thus hindering fine-grained GPU resource allocation. As illustrated in Fig. 1, GPU Re-configurator bypasses the device plugin by directly managing GPU topology via NVML and uniquely identifying GPUs through their UUIDs. This enables the auto-scaler to accurately schedule pods to specific nodes and GPUs, and to update the pod connection and resource reconfiguration information to the specific device files.

3.2 Resource-Aware Performance Prediction (RaPP)

HAS-GPU supports resource allocation with any granularity but also introduces massive configuration spaces and performance uncertainty. For example, a deep learning model with 4 batch sizes, 10 quotas, and 10 SM partition configurations brings 400 distinct configuration possibilities and performance outcomes. Relying on traditional pre-profiling methods would incur significant resource and cost consumption. Therefore, HAS-GPU introduces the Resource-aware Performance Prediction (RaPP) model to predict latency for arbitrary batch sizes under any spatio-temporal GPU resource configurations. As shown in Fig. 3, RaPP comprises two main components: feature extraction and the GNN-based predictor. Traditional static feature-based methods [23,24] are not suitable for resource-aware latency prediction, as different SMs and time quotas can significantly affect the execution time of operators and the overall computational graph at runtime. RaPP integrates both static and runtime characteristics at the operator and graph levels to provide a more accurate feature representation.

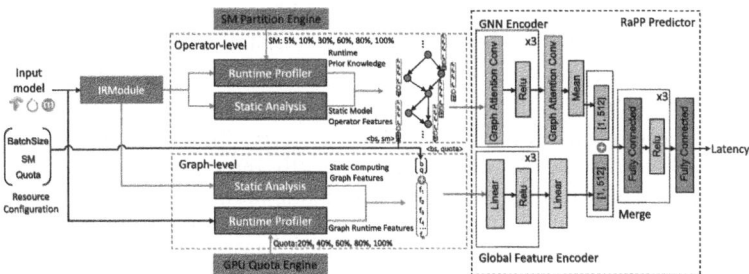

Fig. 3. The Resource-aware Performance Prediction Model.

For operator-level feature extraction, RaPP first transforms the model into TVM's Relay IRModule [14]. Relay IRModule serves as a unified intermediate representation for computational graphs and operators, offering compatibility across various DL frameworks. RaPP introduces an operator-level Runtime Profiler based on TVM's *debug_executor* and enables the collection of runtime statistics for each individual operator under various SM partition configurations. The Runtime Profiler perform operator profiling under a full time quota and six distinct SM configurations. This profiling data is subsequently incorporated as runtime prior knowledge into the operator feature representation graph. We adopt a full time quota since time-window-based quota allocation affects only the latency of the overall computational graph, without impacting the performance of individual operators. The SM configuration is not limited to six types and can be adjusted based on the complexity of the model operators. The execution time of operators also directly integrates performance information related to different GPU architectures and their SM characteristics. Meanwhile, similar to prior studies [23,24], we further incorporate static operator features to the feature graph, such as operator type, kernel size, channel, stride, and so forth.

For graph-level feature extraction, RaPP also incorporates static analysis and a runtime profiler. Specifically, RaPP leverages IRModule to collect static graph features, such as the number of floating-point operations, multiply-accumulate operations, and counts of key operators like *nn.conv* and *nn.dense*, since these features reflect data transfer overhead between GPU and host and the total computational load. Meanwhile, the runtime profiler evaluates the model under a full SM configuration and five distinct quota configurations to obtain the distribution of quota impacts on model computation.

RaPP integrates the input of batch size, quota, and SM partition configuration into operator and graph features for learning. Inside the RaPP Predictor, we utilize multiple Graph Attention Convolution (GAT) [27] blocks to encode the operator feature graph. The attention mechanism in GAT helps to capture potential kernel fusion information among neighboring operators. Meanwhile, the predictor utilizes an MLP to encode the global features. By merging and learning from two types of features, the predictor estimates model inference latency.

3.3 Hybrid Auto-scaling

This section presents the hybrid auto-scaling algorithm which utilizes the cooperation of vertical and horizontal scaling to ensure function SLOs under fluctuating workload. The algorithm introduces the co-design of fine-grained GPU resource allocation, function scheduling, and GPU cluster resource management.

Traditional auto-scaling methods [26] typically integrate workload prediction within the algorithm design. However, workloads across various scenarios often exhibit distinct distribution, making it difficult to develop a universal prediction model. To address this challenge, the HAS autoscaler decouples the request prediction model from the auto-scaling algorithm, enabling integration with alternative prediction models. For fluctuating serverless workloads, HAS-GPU proposes a Kalman filter-based short-term estimation approach that predicts the next request workload R by the current measured request load R_t. The R_t' and P_t' represent the predicted workload and covariance based on the previous prediction. The K is the Kalman gain, balancing the weights of the predicted and observed request workload in the final estimate. By integrating predictions with observations, the request predictor can efficiently adapt to fluctuating workloads.

$$R_t' = AR_{t-1}, \quad P_t' = AR_{t-1}A^T + Q$$

$$K = \frac{P_t'H}{HP_t'H^T + D}, \quad R = R_t' + K(R_t - HR_t'), \quad P = (1 - KH)P_t'$$

As shown in Algorithm 1, once obtaining the predicted RPS (requests per second) R of a function f, the hybrid auto-scaling algorithm starts to perform auto-scaling based on the function's existing pods and their GPU resource usage P_f, as well as current GPUs' occupancy $\{G_j\}$ across the cluster G. The auto-scaler determines the total processing capability of the function's currently running pods at first (Line 1). When the predicted RPS reaches the processing capability threshold α, it triggers scaling up. This threshold helps prevent frequent scaling operations. Additionally, users can adjust it based on their desired sensitivity to scaling up and the required redundancy. To fill the RPS gap ΔR, the auto-scaler tries vertical scaling by adding more quotas to pods at first (Lines 3 – 9). Pods with larger SM partitions are prioritized, as a smaller quota increase can provide a greater boost in throughput capability. For a scaling pod, the system first determines its maximum expandable quota based on its located

GPU and SM partition type, then incrementally increases the quota by step size ΔI_q to match the required RPS gap. Pods within a GPU are managed using SM alignment to prevent resource fragmentation, as shown in Fig. 2. New pods must either follow existing SM configurations or introduce new SM types without exceeding this limit. If the RPS gap remains unmet after vertical scaling, the system selects the least utilized GPU among the used GPUs for horizontal scaling (Lines 10 – 17). We define a new metric, HAS GPU Occupancy (HGO), to evaluate GPU utilization. If no GPU has sufficient resources to meet the RPS gap, the pod is deployed on a new GPU (Lines 18 – 19).

Algorithm 1: Hybrid Vertical and Horizontal Auto-Scaling.

Input: f: Inference function; $\boldsymbol{P_f} = \{P_i\}$: pod instances P_i of function f; $\boldsymbol{R}$: Predicted RPS of the function; $\boldsymbol{G} = \{G_j\}$: The GPU G_j in the cluster G;

Output: $\boldsymbol{S_f} = \{\boldsymbol{S_i}\}$: Scaling actions S_i for function f; $S_i = (f, P_i', \text{type})$;

1   $C_f = \sum C_{P_i}, P_i \in P_f$, where $C_{P_i} = \text{RaPP}(f, b_i, s_i, q_i)$; // current processing capability.

    // Scaling Up.

2   **if** $R > C_f * \alpha$ **then**

3      $\Delta R = R - C_f * \alpha$; $P_f' = \text{sort}_{\downarrow s_i}(\{P_i\}), P_i \in P_f$;   // Pods with more SMs first.

      // Try vertical scaling-up first by adding more quota to pods.

4   **foreach** $P_i \in P_f'$ and $\Delta R > 0$ **do**

5        $A_q = \text{RetrieveMaxAvailQuotaForPod}(P_i, G_j)$, P_i runs in G_j; $\Delta C' = 0$; $n = 1$;

6   **while** $q_i + \Delta I_q \times n \le A_q$ and $\Delta R - \Delta C' > 0$ **do**

7          $C_{P_i}' = \text{RaPP}(f, b_i, s_i, q_i + \Delta I_q \times n)$; $\Delta C' = C_{P_i}' - C_{P_i}$; $n = n + 1$;

8        $P_i' \leftarrow (b_i, s_i, q_i + \Delta I_q \times n)$; $S_i = (f, P_i', \rightarrow)$;   // vertical scale-up.

9        $S = S \cap S_i$; $\Delta R = \Delta R - \Delta C'$;

     // Horizontal scaling-up if vertical scaling is insufficient.

10   **if** $\Delta R > 0$ **then**

      // Horizontal scaling to the used GPU with lowest HGO first.

11       $G_i = \arg\min_{G_j}\{H_{G_j}\}$, where $H_{G_j} = \sum_{P_i} s_i \times q_i, \forall P_i$ run in G_j;

12       $(s_{max}, q_{max}) = \text{RetrieveMaxAvailQuotaAndSM}(G_i)$;

13       $C_{max} = \text{RaPP}(f, s_{max}, q_{max})$

14   **if** $C_{max} > \Delta R$ **then**

15   **while** $\Delta I_q \times n \le q_{max}$ and $\Delta R - C_P' > 0$ **do**

16          $C_P' = \text{RaPP}(f, b_i, s_i, \Delta I_q \times n)$; $n = n + 1$;

17         $P' \leftarrow (b_i, s_i, \Delta I_q \times n)$; $S_i = (f, P', \uparrow)$;   // new pod instance.

     // Horizontal scale-up to a new GPU G' if used ones fall short.

18   **if** $\Delta R > 0$ **then**

19       $(b', s', q') = \text{RaPPbyThroughput}(f, \Delta R)$; // Most efficient for ΔR.

       $P' \leftarrow (b', s', q', G')$; $G = G \cap G'$; $S_i = (f, P', \uparrow)$;   // new pod;

   // Scaling Down.

20 **if** $(R < C_f \times \beta)$ and $(R > R_{min})$ and $(t > T_{cooldonw})$ **then**

21    $\Delta R = C_f - R$; $P_f' = \text{sort}_{\uparrow s_i}(\{P_i\}), P_i \in P_f$;   // fewer SMs first.

22   Reduce the quota progressively in the same stepwise manner until $\Delta R \le 0$;

     $P_i' \leftarrow (b_i, s_i, q_i - \Delta I_q \times n)$; $S_i = (f, P_i', \leftarrow)$;   // vertical scale-down.

23   **if** $q_i - \Delta I_q \le 0$ **then**

24      $S_i = (f, P_i', \downarrow)$; // horizontal scale-down.

25    $S = S \cap S_i$;   **if** $\emptyset$ run in G_j **then**

26      $G = G \setminus G_j$;

When the predicted RPS falls below a certain threshold β of the pods' processing capacity, the auto-scaler triggers the scaling-down (Lines 20 – 26). To prevent frequent scaling, a minimum interval $T_{cooldown}$ is enforced between consecutive scale-down operations, and at least one pod should be retained to guarantee a minimum request capacity R_{min} and avoid the cold start. Pods with smaller SM partitions are prioritized to vertical scaling-down to guarantee potential processing capability. The auto-scaler follows the same stepwise vertical scaling-down and horizontal scaling-down as scaling-up.

4   Experiment and Evaluation

We implemented HAS-GPU based on the Kubernetes and OpenFaaS platform. A new custom resource definition (CRD) and operator, *HASFunc*, was designed and implemented to manage serverless inference functions. We deployed the HAS-GPU system on a GPU cluster with 10 GPUs and nodes on LRZ Compute Cloud. Each node features an NVIDIA Tesla V100 GPU with 16GB device memory and an Intel(R) Xeon(R) Gold CPU @ 2.40GHz with 20 cores and 368GB RAM.

We constructed our serverless inference function benchmark using deep learning applications from the standard MLPerf benchmark [25], and employed real-world application workloads from the Microsoft Azure Trace [30] for evaluation.

For the RaPP training and evaluation, we constructed an inference latency dataset based on all official deep learning models on PyTorch running under various batch sizes, SM partitions, and time quota configurations. The dataset contains 53400 data samples. We randomly selected 42720 samples as the training set, 5340 samples as the validation set, and 5340 samples as the test set.

4.1   Model Performance with Fine-Grained Resource Allocation

Figure 4 illustrates the inference latency of ResNet-152 under different batch sizes, SM partitions, and quota allocations. The results validate the effectiveness of HAS-GPU's fine-grained spatio-temporal resource allocation. With sufficient SM allocation, increasing the quota reduces inference latency and enhances throughput, demonstrating the effectiveness of quota reallocation-based vertical scaling. Since function throughput capability is defined as $\frac{Batch}{Latency}$, even minor latency reductions significantly boost throughput in low latency. Meanwhile, when the batch size is large and the SMs allocated to a function are insufficient, increasing the time quota does not reduce the latency. Conversely, for smaller batch sizes, allocating additional SMs also does not improve performance. These observations highlight the importance of performance prediction in fine-grained resource allocation.

4.2   Resource-Aware Performance Prediction Analysis

Figure 5 presents RaPP's latency predictions for the ConvNeXt model and the overall Mean Absolute Percentage Error (MAPE) of RaPP, compared against

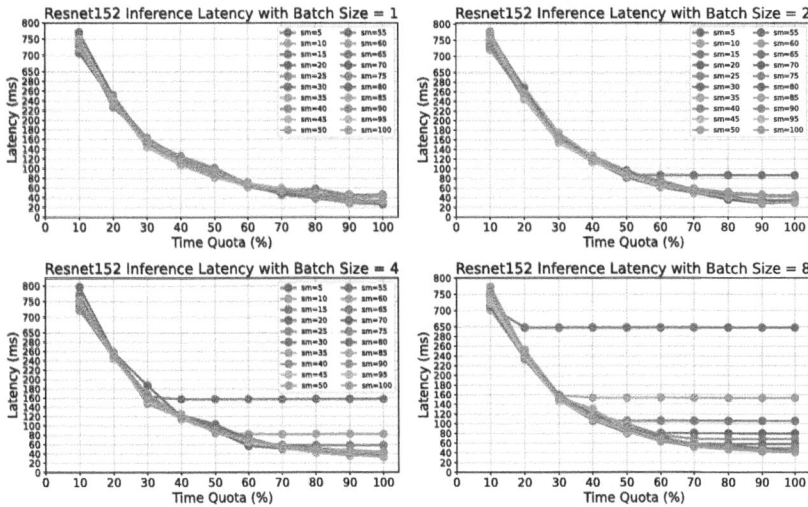

Fig. 4. Inference latencies of Resnet152 under different configurations.

DIPPM [24], a method solely based on static model features. DIPPM does not support fine-grained resource configurations as input. For comparison, we incorporated this information into its static features same as RaPP and retrained the model. The result demonstrates that RaPP consistently aligns closely with the ground truth under various SM and quota resource allocations. RaPP maintains high prediction accuracy even for predicting small latency, whereas DIPPM shows significantly larger deviations. As for MAPE, RaPP maintains a latency prediction error of around 5%, meaning a 20 ms latency prediction deviates by less than 1ms. It consistently outperforms DIPPM on both the validation and test sets, particularly for unseen configurations and models. While DIPPM's error rate rises from 10.14% to 17.7%, RaPP sustains a low error rate. This highlights the importance of extracting operator and graph runtime features, which enables RaPP to robustly adapt to fine-grained resource allocations.

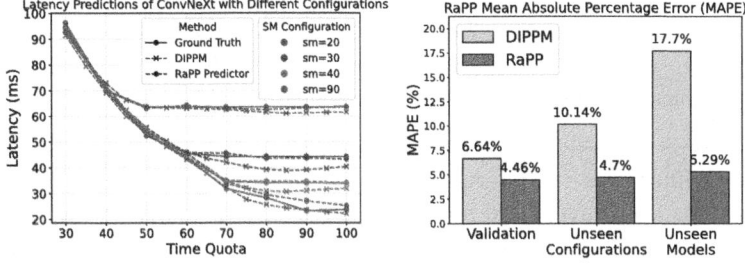

Fig. 5. The latency prediction of the ConvNeXt and the accuracy of RaPP.

4.3   SLO Violation and Function Cost Analysis

To comprehensively reflect the function violations, we use the theoretical short-est inference time of a DL model running in a pure container as the baseline. With a step size of 0.25, we analyze the variation in function violation rate under baseline multipliers ranging from 1 to 10. Figure 6 shows the result of ResNet50 and relative violation rates of all benchmark functions with HAS-GPU's viola-tion rate as the baseline. We compared the HAS-GPU system with the main-stream GPU serverless inference platform KServe [7] and the state-of-the-art spatio-temporal GPU Sharing FaaS framework FaST-GShare [19]. Results from ResNet50 indicate that both HAS-GPU and KServe effectively reduce violation rates under smaller SLOs, while FaST-GShare maintains a higher violation rate. This is because HAS-GPU can quickly adapt to dynamic serverless workloads through vertical scaling, and KServe, with exclusive GPU allocation, benefits from higher concurrent processing capacity. In contrast, FaST-GShare relies on fixed fine-grained resource allocation and can only meet workload changes through horizontal scaling, where cold start delays contribute to its persistently high violation rate. We further analyze the performance of each method on P90, P95, and P99 metrics. HAS-GPU maintains low latency across all metrics, while KServe experiences significant delays at P95 and P99. This is due to KServe's GPU instance-based horizontal scaling, which incurs high latency from GPU device and system initialization, leading to pronounced tail latency effects. In contrast, HAS-GPU's vertical scaling provides buffer time for horizontal scaling, demonstrating the high reliability of hybrid auto-scaling. For all functions, HAS-GPU achieves lower SLO violations than the other two methods under tighter SLOs (baseline multipliers, 1.5x, 2.0x, 2.5x). Compared to FaST-GShare, HAS-GPU reduces SLO violations by an average of 4.8x.

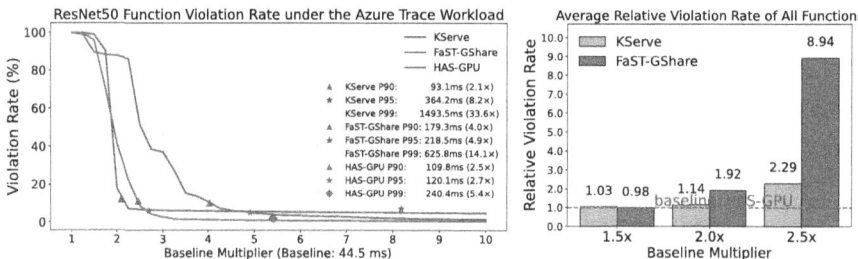

Fig. 6. Function violation rates of ResNet50 and relative rates of all functions.

Figure 7 illustrates the inference costs of each platform under standard and stress workloads. We calculate function costs based on the Google Cloud V100 GPU price ($2.48/hour). For fine-grained GPU allocation, costs are measured using the actual GPU resources and time consumed per function. Since KServe exclusively occupies a GPU during scaling and frequently scales to handle fluctu-ating workloads, it incurs extremely higher costs per 1K requests. FaST-GShare, with its fixed resource allocation, lacks elasticity, making it more expensive than HAS-GPU. In contrast, HAS-GPU's adaptive vertical scaling efficiently adjusts to workload variations, providing a significant cost advantage, especially under stress workloads. Under standard workloads, HAS-GPU reduces costs by up to 10.8x compared to KServe and 1.72x compared to FaST-GShare on average.

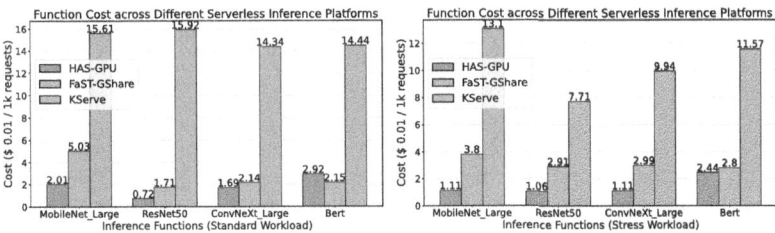

Fig. 7. Function costs of different models under standard and stress workloads.

5   Conclusion

In this paper, we propose HAS-GPU, an efficient Hybrid Auto-scaling Serverless architecture with fine-grained GPU allocation for deep learning inferences. HAS-GPU proposes an agile scheduler capable of allocating SM partitions and time quotas with arbitrary granularity and enables significant vertical quota scalability at runtime. We propose the Resource-aware Performance Prediction model to address performance uncertainty introduced by massive configuration spaces. We present an adaptive hybrid auto-scaling algorithm to ensure inference SLOs and minimize GPU costs. The experiments demonstrated that, HAS-GPU reduces function costs by 10.8x on average compared to the mainstream serverless inference platform, and function SLO violations by 4.8x and cost by 1.72x compared to the state-of-the-art spatio-temporal GPU sharing FaaS framework.

Artifact Availability. The artifact is available in the Zenodo repository [18].

Disclosure of Interests. The authors have no competing interests to declare that are relevant to the content of this article.

References

1. Alibaba Cloud Serverless GPUs (2025). https://tinyurl.com/3pjcz5my
2. Amazon SageMaker (2025). https://aws.amazon.com/sagemaker
3. Aws Lambda (2025). https://aws.amazon.com/lambda/
4. Best practices for AI (2025). https://tinyurl.com/ye27apwt
5. Cloud Run Function (2025). https://cloud.google.com/functions

6. GPU-enabled Pytorch Azure Function (2025). https://github.com/puthurr/python-azure-function-gpu
7. KServe (2025). https://kserve.github.io/website/latest/
8. MIG Support in Kubernetes (2025). http://docs.nvidia.com/datacenter/cloud-native/kubernetes/latest/index.html
9. Multi-process service (2025). https://docs.nvidia.com/deploy/mps/index.html
10. Runpod (2025). https://www.runpod.io/serverless-gpu
11. What is cGPU? (2025). https://www.alibabacloud.com/help/en/egs/what-is-cgpu
12. Ali, A., Pinciroli, R., Yan, F., Smirni, E.: Optimizing inference serving on serverless platforms. Proc. VLDB Endowment **15**(10) (2022)
13. Aslani, A., Ghobaei-Arani, M., et al.: Machine learning inference serving models in serverless computing: a survey. Computing **107**(1), 47 (2025)
14. Chen, T., Moreau, T., Jiang, Z., Zheng, L., et al.: {TVM}: An automated {End-to-End} optimizing compiler for deep learning. In: 13th USENIX Symposium on Operating Systems Design and Implementation (OSDI 18), pp. 578–594 (2018)
15. Cho, J., et al.: Sla-driven ml inference framework for clouds with heterogeneous accelerators. Proc. Mach. Learn. Syst. **4**, 20–32 (2022)
16. Choi, S., Lee, S., Kim, Y., Park, J., Kwon, Y.: Serving heterogeneous machine learning models on {Multi-GPU} servers with {Spatio-Temporal} sharing. In: 2022 USENIX Annual Technical Conference (USENIX ATC 22), pp. 199–216 (2022)
17. Dhakal, A., Kulkarni, S.G., Ramakrishnan, K.: Gslice: controlled spatial sharing of gpus for a scalable inference platform. In: Proceedings of the 11th ACM Symposium on Cloud Computing, pp. 492–506 (2020)
18. Gu, J., Wang, P., Núñez Araya, I.D., Huang, K., Gerndt, M.: Artifact of the paper: HAS-GPU: efficient hybrid auto-scaling with fine-grained GPU allocation for SLO-aware serverless inferences.(2025). https://doi.org/10.5281/zenodo.15596511
19. Gu, J., Zhu, Y., et al.: FaST-GShare: enabling efficient Spatio-temporal GPU sharing in serverless computing for deep learning inference. In: Proceedings of the 52nd International Conference on Parallel Processing (ICPP 23), pp. 635–644 (2023)
20. Han, Z., Zhou, R., Xu, C., Zeng, Y., Zhang, R.: Inss: an intelligent scheduling orchestrator for multi-GPU inference with Spatio-temporal sharing. IEEE Trans. Parallel Distrib. Syst. (2024)
21. Jonas, E., Schleier-Smith, J., et al.: Cloud programming simplified: a berkeley view on serverless computing (2019). arXiv preprint arXiv:1902.03383
22. Li, J., Zhao, L., et al.: Tetris: memory-efficient serverless inference through tensor sharing. In: 2022 USENIX Annual Technical Conference (USENIX ATC 22) (2022)
23. Liu, L., Shen, M., Gong, R., Yu, F.: Nnlqp: a multi-platform neural network latency query and prediction system with an evolving database. In: Proceedings of the 51st International Conference on Parallel Processing, pp. 1–14 (2022)
24. Panner Selvam, K., Brorsson, M.: Dippm: a deep learning inference performance predictive model using graph neural networks. In: European Conference on Parallel Processing, pp. 3–16. Springer (2023)
25. Reddi, V.J., Cheng, C., Kanter, D., Mattson, P., Schmuelling, G., et al.: Mlperf inference benchmark. In: 2020 ACM/IEEE 47th Annual International Symposium on Computer Architecture (ISCA), pp. 446–459. IEEE (2020)
26. Tari, M., Ghobaei-Arani, M., Pouramini, J.: Auto-scaling mechanisms in serverless computing: a comprehensive review. Comput. Sci. Rev. **53**, 100650 (2024)
27. Veličković, P., Cucurull, G., Casanova, A., et al.: Graph attention networks. In: International Conference on Learning Representations (2018)

28. Yang, Y., Zhao, L., Li, Y., Zhang, H., Li, J., Zhao, M., Chen, X., Li, K.: Infless: a native serverless system for low-latency, high-throughput inference. In: Proceedings of the 27th ACM International Conference on Architectural Support for Programming Languages and Operating Systems (ASPLOS '22), pp. 768–781 (2022)
29. Zhang, L.L., et al.: Nn-meter: towards accurate latency prediction of deep-learning model inference on diverse edge devices. In: Proceedings of the Annual International Conference on Mobile Systems, Applications, and Services, pp. 81–93 (2021)
30. Zhang, Y., Goiri, Í., Chaudhry, G.I.: Faster and cheaper serverless computing on harvested resources. In: Proceedings of the ACM SIGOPS 28th Symposium on Operating Systems Principles (SOSP '21), pp. 724–739 (2021)

$ARC\text{-}V$: Vertical Resource Adaptivity for HPC Workloads in Containerized Environments

Daniel Medeiros$^{(\boxtimes)}$, Jeremy J. Williams, Jacob Wahlgren, Leonardo Saud Maia Leite, and Ivy Peng

Department of Computer Science, KTH Royal Institute of Technology, Stockholm, Sweden
{dadm,jjwil,jacobwah,lsml,bopeng}@kth.se

Abstract. Existing state-of-the-art vertical autoscalers for container-ized environments are traditionally built for cloud applications, which might behave differently than HPC workloads with their dynamic resource consumption. In these environments, autoscalers may create an inefficient resource allocation. This work analyzes nine representa-tive HPC applications with different memory consumption patterns. Our results identify the limitations and inefficiencies of the Kubernetes Ver-tical Pod Autoscaler (VPA) for enabling memory elastic execution of HPC applications. We propose, implement, and evaluate ARC-V. This policy leverages both in-flight resource updates of pods in Kubernetes and the knowledge of memory consumption patterns of HPC applications for achieving elastic memory resource provisioning at the node level. Our results show that ARC-V can effectively save memory while eliminating out-of-memory errors compared to the standard Kubernetes VPA.

Keywords: Vertical scaling · HPC workloads · Cloud Computing · Resource Adaptivity · Memory Resource Provisioning

1 Introduction

One of the distinctive features of traditional HPC systems is how infrastruc-ture and computing resources are provisioned. It is common to provision entire bare-metal nodes within the local, on-premise system. One consequence of this approach is that the entire set of resources will be reserved for the user, even if not fully utilized, leading to potential resource waste, as complex HPC work-loads often exhibit varying phases and different resource utilization patterns [1]. Meanwhile, in cloud-first environments, where containerized workloads are exe-cuted, it is usual to define the resources allocated to a specific workload in a finer granularity. This policy potentially allows multi-tenancy of workloads within the same node, while allowing the use of spare resources for scaling or running back-ground processes (Fig. 1).

The execution of HPC workloads in containerized environments requires adopting new strategies to fully leverage the benefits commonly associated with cloud workloads. A key distinction lies in application coupling: while cloud

W. E. Nagel et al. (Eds.): Euro-Par 2025, LNCS 15900, pp. 175–189, 2026.
https://doi.org/10.1007/978-3-031-99854-6_12

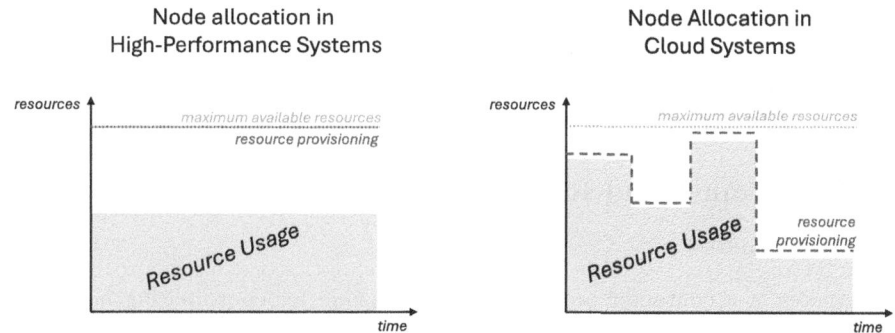

Fig. 1. A high-level overview of how resource allocation for tasks in high-performance systems (HPC) and cloud systems generally works. In the former, allocations are static even if the resources are not fully used, while the latter displays a degree of flexibility for changing the allocations on execution time.

applications tend to be loosely coupled, HPC workloads are often tightly coupled. This tight coupling makes HPC applications highly sensitive to out-of-memory (OOM) errors, as the default behavior of MPI-based applications means that a failure in a single node may cause the entire application to fail. Furthermore, until recently, changing allocated resources in a container during its execution meant that a container would have to be restarted, which creates a major problem for HPC workloads. Although checkpointing measures may mitigate such failures in certain cases [2,3], these measures are not a universal solution and may lead to performance degradation in the workload.

A potential method for optimizing resource utilization for workloads in containerized environments is through the usage of a vertical autoscaler to manage the application's needs without reserving the entire node for it. However, many state-of-the-art autoscalers that were originally built for cloud workloads are not suitable for HPC workloads as different inputs may significantly alter the memory pattern, or they might not properly adapt to these workloads as HPC workloads might run for a shorter time than user-facing cloud services.

Therefore, this paper explores the feasibility of vertical resource adaptivity for the memory of containerized HPC workloads with dynamic memory consumption in a containerized environment. Our key contributions are:

- We discuss how HPC workloads may benefit from elastic memory scaling in cloud environments, and examine several patterns of memory consumption across nine HPC applications and benchmarks;
- We identify the limitations of the state-of-the-art Kubernetes Vertical Pod Autoscaler in HPC workloads, and build a simulator for its scaling policy;
- We propose, implement and evaluate the **A**daptive **R**esource **C**ontroller - **V**ertical (*ARC-V*) to achieve the resource adaptivity in memory through

a reactive vertical autoscaler that does not need *a priori* knowledge of the application, reducing the performance impact on HPC workloads in containerized environments in comparison to the Vertical Pod Autoscaler available in Kubernetes.

2   Background and Related Work

2.1   Kubernetes

Kubernetes is a container orchestrator, responsible for coordinating how containerized workloads are distributed across the available nodes. Containers are encapsulated in an abstraction model called "pod," the smallest deployable unit within Kubernetes. A pod contains at least one container image and the resources (CPU, memory) that are allocated to it, and a pod may contain more than one container. Pods are designed with long-running workloads in mind and if they fail, Kubernetes, by default, attempts to recover them by restarting.

Within a Kubernetes cluster, there are two types of nodes: the control plane and the worker nodes, with the former being mostly responsible for the administrative functions of the cluster. The latter contains a kubelet agent process responsible for interacting with the control plane. The kubelet ensures that pods are running, enforces resource requirements, and monitors resource usage (e.g. containers' health and performance in terms of CPU, memory, I/O and networking), using cAdvisor, which also makes this data available for scraping for third-party application such as Prometheus. Many metrics are exposed by Kubernetes as a whole that might be scrapped by third-party applications, including ones not directly concerning containers (e.g., nodes, storage, etc.). The relevant metrics for this work are the ones that concern respectively the usage of memory, the usage of RSS (resident set size), and the memory swap by the container (`container_memory_usage_bytes`, `container_memory_rss`, and `container_memory_swap`).

2.2   Class of Service

Within a Kubernetes object definition file, CPU and Memory resources may be specified there both in terms of requests and also their allowed usage limits. The former establishes the minimum necessary for executing the object, thus the Kubernetes' scheduler searches for a suitable node for scheduling that has at least the requested resources available. When the pod starts to execute, the limits play a major role by hard enforcing the specified values, therefore the pod can use resources up until the limit values are available. The values of requests and limits play a role in which Quality of Service (QoS) class the pod will be assigned to: `Guaranteed`, `Burstable` or `Best Effort`. In practice, these classes define the priority of resource allocation and execution for the pod. Under pressure, the first tasks to be evicted are the ones in `BestEffort`, then `Burstable`, and then `Guaranteed`. Similarly, `BestEffort` pods may not use the resources that are available for the Guaranteed pods.

In cloud-first environments, especially in systems that deal with multi-tenancy, several research papers [4,5] commonly distinguish between two types of workloads: the latency-critical (LC) and the best-effort (BE) ones. The former is often related to user-facing workloads that have a deadline to reply as a slower response time might affect the users' perception of it. Computing workloads, such as high-performance ones, are usually classified as BE because they attempt to make use of all the resources available in the system.

Setting Limits in the Object Specification. In certain environments, multiple workloads often run concurrently on the same virtualized hardware. When all pods are burstable (i.e., they have no CPU or memory limits set) and request the same amount of resources, the Kubernetes scheduler allocates them across nodes up to the maximum capacity (e.g., if a node's capacity is x and each pod requests y, the node can host up to x/y pods). While this may initially appear optimal, it can lead to inefficient resource usage, as actual utilization is often lower than requested, with pods requiring peak resources only during short bursts. By adjusting resource requests to match real usage patterns, the scheduler could accommodate more pods per node. However, without limits, a single misbehaving pod could monopolize system resources, preventing others from bursting as needed and negatively impacting overall application performance. Therefore, imposing resource limits on pods helps prevent such scenarios.

Resource Adaptivity. Kubernetes plays a key role in managing HPC resources in the cloud. Greneche et al. [6] explored HPC workload scaling, while Pupykina and Agosta [7] surveyed memory management techniques. Autoscalers for cloud workloads are typically proactive or reactive. Proactive scaling anticipates changes in consumption, while reactive scaling responds during or after the event. Many approaches use application-level metrics, such as meeting quality-of-service deadlines, and hardware counters to assess scaling needs. Representative works include Petrucci et al. [8] and Chen et al. [4].

2.3 Vertical Pod Autoscaler

The Vertical Pod Autoscaler (VPA) is the default vertical scaling solution in Kubernetes, designed to automate resource configuration and optimize cluster utilization, and dynamically adjust pod resource requests based on usage while maintaining predefined request-limit ratios. By default, VPA is not enabled in standard Kubernetes installations and requires manual activation.

The VPA scales pods by increasing or decreasing resource requests according to historical usage. Its architecture comprises three components: the Recommender, Updater, and Admission Plugin. The Recommender analyzes historical pod usage to model optimal resource allocations. The Updater enforces these recommendations by evicting and restarting non-compliant pods. The Admission Plugin modifies new pod configurations to align with the Recommender's recommendations.

Memory recommendations in VPA maintain a predefined probability threshold for exceeding requests within a specified time window (e.g., 1% in 24h, per official documentation). Historical execution data is stored for up to 8 days and informs future recommendations. In out-of-memory scenarios, where the requested memory is higher than the available memory, the application restarts with a memory limit equal to its previous request plus a predefined margin (default: 20%).

Additionally, updated pods may be rescheduled to different nodes, potentially disrupting multi-node HPC applications and causing failures or undefined states. Furthermore, Fig. 2 illustrates VPA recommendations for various applications with updating disabled. As it will be discussed later, several workloads exhibit slow VPA adaptation, leading to repeated OOM errors if the recommended updates were enforced. This issue arises because VPA relies on historical patterns, which are inconsistent in HPC workloads due to varying input characteristics.

Due to frequent OOM errors and potential restarts under standard VPA policies for HPC applications, we propose a model that estimates execution time and total memory footprint for HPC workloads. Further details of this approach are provided in Sect. 4.1.

3   Methodology

In this work, we analyze nine different applications and their respective workloads. These applications are representative of several scientific domains and exhibit distinct consumption patterns, both in terms of quantity and variation. For each listed application, we built a containerized version of them. The typical memory usage patterns of these applications are shown in Fig. 2, and a numerical summary of their execution times and memory footprint is presented in Table 1.

As the first step of the work, we propose classifying our analyzed applications into two distinct memory consumption patterns: Growth and Dynamic. We define the Growth (G) pattern as a non-decreasing monotonic function, which also serves when the behaviour of memory consumption is stable. However, a caveat of this definition is that, in real measurements, there may exist slightly deviations due to the existing noise in the measurements. Therefore, we still believe that this definition is still valid if the deviation is a value between $[-2\%, +2\%]$ of the previous one.

For all other functions that do not satisfy the previous definition, we label them as "Dynamic" (D) as their behaviour might either follow an apparently periodic pattern or be inherently stochastic, therefore we are not able to establish a general model for them. These functions are normally characterised by having a decrease in memory consumption at some point during their execution time.

3.1   Applications

AMR. The Adaptive Mesh Refinement is a technique used in several scientific domains, such as fluid dynamics, to dynamically enhance the solution in certain regions of the simulation. In this work, we used the available MiniAMR proxy application by Mantevo [9]. We adapted the available two moving spheres problem to 10 OpenMP threads and one MPI rank.

BFS. Breadth First Search is an algorithm available on the Ligra framework [10], a graph processing framework for shared memory, and we use OpenMP for parallel processing on 10 threads. The algorithm itself explores all the vertices in a graph at the current depth before moving to the next one. We use a tool bundled within the Ligra framework (rMatGen) to pre-generate a graph with 100 million vertices that will serve as input that consists of 9.6 GB in terms of file size.

CM1. The Cloud Model 1 [11] is a numerical model designed for idealized studies of atmospheric phenomena, such as thunderstorms. We use the default input file that is bundled with the application as well as one MPI rank and 10 OpenMP threads.

GROMACS. A molecular dynamics application [12] that is able to simulate proteins, lipids and nucleic acids. In this paper, the used benchmark for GROMACS is the "benchRIB" provided by the Max Planck Institute for Multidisciplinary Sciences (MPINAT). It consists of a simulation with 2 million atoms (ribosome in water), and the benchmark is executed in both MPI and OpenMP (1 thread per MPI rank, 10 ranks).

Kripke. An application [13] designed to be a proxy for an discrete-ordinates transport code, with the focus of studying the performance characteristics of data layouts, programming models, and sweep algorithms. In this work, we use all the default inputs for the application with the exception of the number of groups (640) and the number of iterations (30), 10 OpenMP threads.

LAMMPS. The Large-scale Atomic/Molecular Massively Parallel Simulator is a molecular dynamics code with a focus on materials modeling. There are several example applications that LAMMPS has bundled, and in this work we make use of the HEAT problem that carries simulations of thermal gradients for a Lennard-Jones fluid, with 10 OpenMP threads.

LULESH. The Livermore Unstructured Lagrangian Explicit Shock Hydrodynamics [14] is a proxy application designed to study a simple Sedov blast problem with analytic answers. In this work, we use the OpenMP version of LULESH with a size of 90^3 as input parameter. Classified in this work as having a dynamic memory consumption pattern, LULESH displays a seemingly chaotic memory consumption pattern including many bursts during short period followed by steep decreases.

MiniFE. The Finite Element proxy application [9] (MiniFE) is described by its authors as being the "best approximation to an unstructured implicit finite element or finite volume application, but in 8000 lines or fewer". We use the default input with the size (1000, 1000, 1000) in terms of the dimensions (NX, NY, NZ). MiniFE appears to have a growing pattern up until the end of its execution, where there is a steep decrease followed by a steep increase in consumption.

sputniPIC. This is an application used for space plasma simulations that uses the particle-in-cell method [15]. We built a container image for it using MPI, and used the bundled two-dimensional Geospace Environmental Modeling Challenge (GEM2D) as input problem, adapting it for the usage of 10 MPI ranks.

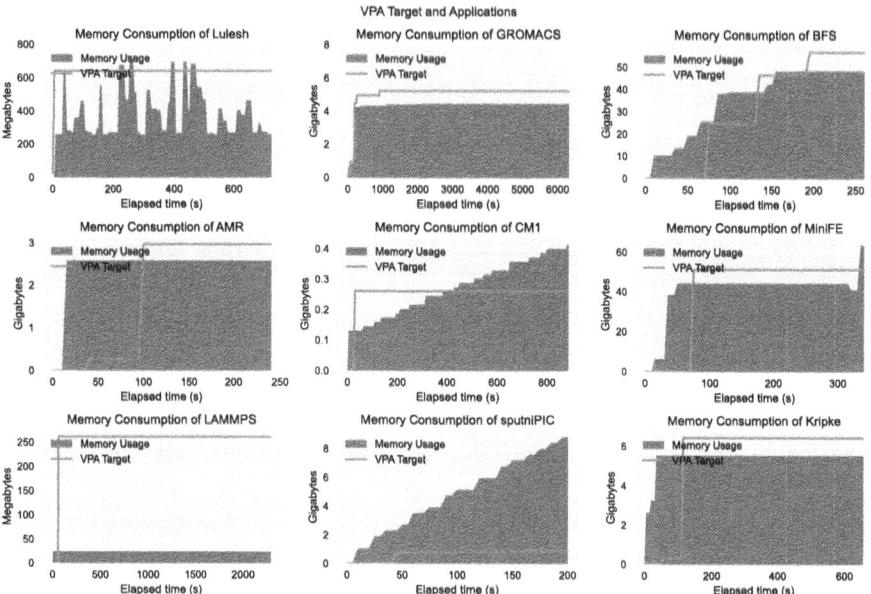

Fig. 2. Memory consumption pattern of all applications listed in Sect. 3.1. The recommendation given by the Vertical Pod Autoscaler is also shown. The data has a sampling time of 5 s.

3.2 In-Flight Pod Updates and Swap

By default, Kubernetes does not allow updating a pod's requests or limits during execution. To modify these settings, the pod must be restarted, which interrupts the workload. However, an alpha feature named "`InPlacePodVerticalScaling`" was recently introduced. By submitting a patch to the pod, the user is able to replace the information regarding the requests and limits of that object. Users may also explicitly specify what should happen when the pod is updated (i.e., not restart the pod or restart it). One of the caveats of this feature is that it is not possible to change the QoS class (as described in Sect. 2) of the pod. In practice, this means that a pod in the Best Effort class can be freely resized but will still keep its QoS class as Best Effort even if it satisfies the requirements to be in other classes.

Another relevant point to mention is that these patches do not necessarily take effect immediately when they are issued. Rather, our empirical evidence suggests that the nominal changes to pod limits are written instantly into the Kubelet; however, there might be a delay of several seconds before these changes synchronize

Table 1. Features of the application workloads in Sect. 3.1. Patterns refers to the memory consumption, i.e., Growth (G) or Dynamic (D). The memory footprint was calculated based on the area of the consumption function from Fig. 2 (in blue).

Application	Pattern	Execution Time	Max. Memory	Memory Footprint
AMR	G	253s	2.6GB	0.62 TB
BFS	D	287s	48.4GB	9.4 TB
CM1	G	913s	415MB	0.24 TB
GROMACS	G	6420s	4.5GB	27.18 TB
Kripke	G	650s	5.5GB	3.5 TB
LAMMPS	G	2321s	23.7MB	0.054 TB
LULESH	D	750s	696MB	0.27 TB
MiniFE	D	352s	63.7GB	13.8 TB
sputniPIC	G	210s	8.8GB	1.0 TB

with the actual container and become *de facto* effective. Additionally, we observe that when a patch is issued for a memory limit lower than the current memory usage, the synchronization process is significantly prolonged. Even if swap usage is enabled within Kubernetes, this synchronization stage may not be able to conclude for the entire duration of the application's execution.

Swap. The usage of swap memory is a new feature in Kubernetes that is leveraged in this work to avoid sudden out-of-memory errors in our applications. The current behaviour of Kubernetes is to fail to start if swap is enabled on the node, hence the feature needs to be manually enabled within Kubernetes and, in the eventual scenario of memory scarcity of a pod, the container will automatically attempt to use the available swap device that is set on the Linux kernel.

Nonetheless, as expected, swap performance strongly depends on the system's storage infrastructure, as this determines the maximum speed for read/write operations (e.g., SSDs are faster than HDDs). A current limitation is the inability to control a per-pod swap limit, meaning the underlying storage infrastructure can easily become bottlenecked if many workloads use swap simultaneously.

3.3   ARC-V

To establish a vertical autoscaling policy that gives suitable recommendations for HPC workloads on containerized environments, we design the Adaptive Resource Controller - Vertical (ARC-V). This policy, together with its implementation, is established as a state machine that requires specific signals (named "memory alerts") to move between its different states whereas a depiction may be seen in Fig. 3. There are two major guiding remarks when designing ARC-V:

HPC Workloads Generally have an Initialization Phase. Many applications spend several seconds increasing their memory usage until reaching a degree of stability in consumption (e.g., GROMACS, Kripke, MiniFE).

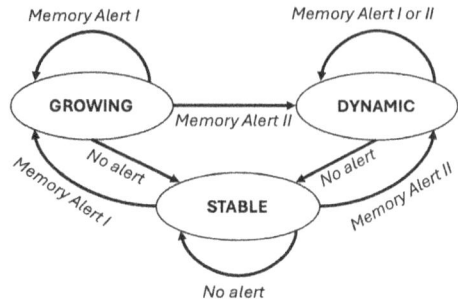

Fig. 3. A depiction of the high-level design of the ARC-V autoscaler.

HPC Workloads Might have Different Phases During its Execution.
Despite we classify the applications in two broad categories, these categories
might also apply through certain stages of the application: an application classified as "Dynamic" might, during certain time, have a "Growth" component in
its execution pattern, and vice versa.

With these guiding remarks in mind, we defined three states in which the
application may be located during its execution, primarily because there is no
prior knowledge about its consumption pattern. The states were named "Growing", "Dynamic", and "Stable", each with its own scaling policy. Therefore, it
is expected that an application will be in one of these states for the majority of
its execution.

As its name implies, the "Stable" state means that memory consumption
within that particular window remains constant for a long period, or with very
little fluctuation, indicating that it is likely possible to reduce memory allocation.
Meanwhile, the "Growing" state is defined when the application displays an
increase in memory consumption. The "Dynamic" state is directly associated
with a decrease in consumption.

The change between these states happens through signals that are sent every
predefined timesteps. The collected data is separately analyzed for trends of
increase, decrease, or stability in consumption (memory signals I, II, and no
signal, respectively). The signal is therefore analyzed by the implementation,
and, depending on the current state of the application, different actions are
performed. If the application is in the "Growing" or "Stable" state, a single signal
is enough to move the application to the "Dynamic" state. However, moving from
"Dynamic" to "Stable" requires the absence of signals for an extended period of
time, and there is no possible direct transition from the "Dynamic" to "Growing"
states..

The scaling policies for each state are defined as follows:

– **Growing**: After a memory signal I, if the difference between the consumption
  and the actual recommendation is lower than certain threshold, a forecast of
  the consumption for the next 60 s is done and the recommendation is adjusted,

else the provided recommendation stays stable. A single signal II moves the application to the "Dynamic" state, and several absence of signals in a row moves the application to the "Stable" state.

- **Dynamic**: As one application enters in this state, there is the need to be very conservative regarding the memory limits as there can be steep spikes. While in this state, the memory decrease is limited to the global maximum that has been achieved by the application,
- **Stable**: A single signal (either I or II) moves it to either the "Dynamic" or "Growing" states. In case the application persists in the state for several timesteps, the memory allocation decreases in 10% each time, up to a limit of 102% of the actual memory usage. This extra 2% was arbitrarily chosen (Sect. 4) to account for very small variations during the measurements, in which we consider the application still persists in the same state.

Finally, we also take swap usage in consideration. Whenever the application makes use of swap due to sudden steep spikes in memory usage in comparison to the current established limit (e.g., the last few seconds of MiniFE), ARC-V also takes into the account the amount of swap used when calculating the new limit, providing enough memory for eventual pages in disk to be transferred to the main memory.

4   Implementation

4.1   VPA Simulator

The major comparison metrics utilized in this paper are the ones derived from the Vertical Pod Autoscaler: runtime and the memory footprint. We define the memory footprint of the VPA as the total area below the provided recommendation during certain application execution time (i.e., the green line in Fig. 2). However, the initial values of the VPA recommendation policy, as displayed by Fig. 2, are not a good parameter for comparison because it uses a bottom-up approach, thus the applications would not even be able to start its execution while the values are lower than the memory usage. Therefore, we established a set of procedures based on the documentation of the VPA to simulate its behaviour.

- The first recommendation of the VPA is zero as it does not have any data regarding of the application. In our algorithm, this is replaced for the first recommendation given instead.
- We consider that all recommendations are static and do not change over time unless there is an out-of-memory error in the application. This is the usual pattern seen in our results when the memory usage has been lower than the recommendation.
- When the recommendation is lower than the memory usage of the application, we consider that there has been an OOM error issue and the application is restarted with the new recommendation being 20% higher in comparison to what was requested by the application immediately before it was restarted. This is in agreement with the design documentation and default values of the VPA.

4.2   ARC-V

The proof-of-concept implementation of our framework is done in Python using the Kubernetes Python API, with the data being retrieved directly from an Kubernetes end point.

Parameters. There are several parameters that were defined and would potentially affect the execution. In particular, we define the "stability factor" as 2%, meaning that the window of collected values may fluctuate between [-2%, 2%]. The change in the value may affect for how long one application might be considered within the "Stable" state, therefore affecting the overall increase/decrease of the provided recommendation from ARC-V. The number of collected metrics as part of the measurement window is also a factor. Finally, as it might take some time for the changes in memory limits to be enforced, we set up a timeout of 60 s before issuing a new decision regarding the changes of states.

Signals. Earlier implementations of the signals relied on linear regressions to see whether there is any trend in the window of measurements, however empirical results found this technique not reliable when dealing with small windows of data and/or abrupt changes of values. Our current implementation relies on the sorting of the elements: a non-sorted order (signal II) means that there might have been a decrease in the window, while a sorted order may possibly mean an increase (signal I) or stability (if all elements are equal, no signal). However, the forecasting for Growing mode, when the difference between the memory consumption and the recommendation policy is small, is performed through linear regression.

Initialization Assumption and Automatic Classification. For the implementation, we assume that the pod has more than enough memory to execute through the initialization phase, which is parametrized to 60 s. This time is necessary for ARC-V to start analyzing the application and defining which state it should place it, based on how the collect data for consumption behaves. Furthermore, while the application will not suffer from out-of-memory error, as swap memory usage is enabled in the cluster, it is very likely that the application would suffer a strong performance degradation through its execution from the beginning, thus the requirement for memory. For the experiments in this work, the initial memory requests/limits were set as 20% of the maximum used in the node (i.e., Table 1 for reference) but could be set to any value as long as the condition discussed above is satisfied. ARC-V would eventually adjust if set too high, and decrease if too low.

5   Evaluation

Infrastructure. We use three nodes from the CloudLab infrastructure [16] for running our experiments. A single node consists of a dual Intel E5-2660 10-core

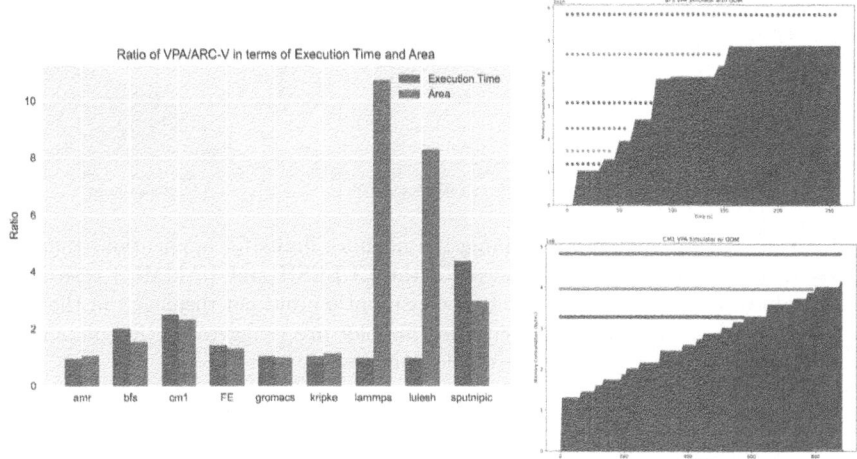

Fig. 4. On left, the ratios between the values of memory footprint and execution time of VPA and the ARC-V policy. On right, a depiction of how the VPA simulator works: every time the recommendation is lower than the actual usage, the application needs to restart with 20% more memory.

CPUs, 256 GB DDR4 RAM, 2x 1TB mechanical disks running at 7200 RPM. Each node executes Ubuntu 22.04, while Kubernetes, with swap usage enabled, is installed within all nodes using the K3s distribution v1.29.6, with one control plane and two working nodes, where VPA v1.29.3 is deployed.

ARC-V vs VPA. Figure 4 displays all the results obtained with ARC-V compared to the simulated VPA policy that is established for Kubernetes and cloud applications. For MiniFE, that uses swap memory just at the end of its execution, we do not count the swap as provisioned memory in ARC-V since the resource being used in this case is disk.

Overhead. Our implementation executes in another node than the one that executes the container. It runs on user space level, requiring only Kubernetes access permissions, and is not containerized. Furthermore, the time steps for scrapping the data from the running node's kubelet is large (5 s), decreasing the chance of possible performance impact in any shared resources. With the exception of MiniFE (which uses swap in order to avoid OOM during certain phases), we observe that the difference of the execution times are usually below 3%.

Memory Provisioning. In all cases, there are major resource savings in terms of consumption, with they being expressive in applications that spend most of the time in "Growing" state, such as CM1 and sputniPIC. We display three example decisions of ARC-V in Fig. 5 for applications that are dominated mostly by a certain state.

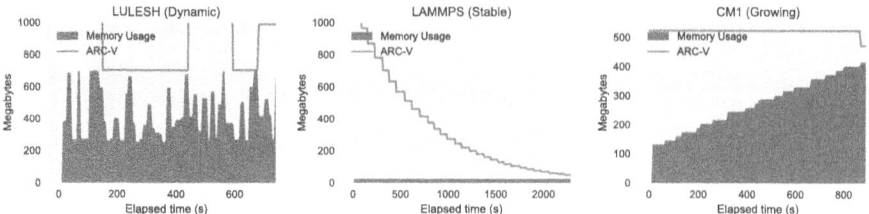

Fig. 5. Example cases of ARC-V defining the memory limits for applications that are dominated mostly by a certain pattern. In the LULESH and LAMMPS cases, the starting values are higher than the actual consumption and not displayed in the plot for scaling purposes. The starting values in this plot are exaggerated (in comparison to the experiments done in Fig. 4) for display purposes.

In the particular case of LAMMPS, the difference of over 10 times is because the VPA allocates automatically too much memory and do not resize its recommendation through the execution time of the application, while ARC-V quickly detects the stable pattern and starts to get closer to the actual usage. The great difference is mostly because LAMMPS makes a small usage of memory. In contrast, AMR displays a stable pattern as well but the ratio between VPA/ARC-V is about 1.06 as AMR makes a large use of memory.

Execution Time. The enforcement of the VPA policy under the assumption of no checkpointing leads to a major increase in its execution time as the application needs to restart several times due to OOM errors as the VPA recommendation falls below the requested memory by the application (i.e., the right part of Fig. 4), while ARC-V avoids OOM by using a top-down approach, and in the case of MiniFE, swap. This effect is strongly seen in applications that are dominated by the Growing state, such as BFS, CM1, and sputniPIC.

Use Cases. The memory savings are important for certain applications, such as Kripke. The recommended value quickly decreases from 6.6GB (20% of maximum memory, initial request) to 5.6GB (around 16%) at around 1/3 of its execution. Such savings would enable one to run concurrently other applications with the same workloads in this work such as CM1, Lulesh or LAMMPS. However, discussing potential effects of resource sharing is out of scope of this paper.

6   Conclusions

In this work, we have identified that the current VPA is inadequate for HPC workloads that exhibit dynamic memory usage, potentially generating resource waste and out-of-memory errors. To address these limitations, we proposed *ARC-V* to improve elastic memory scaling in HPC applications when running on cloud environments. *ARC-V* addresses bursty memory usage in HPC workloads by auto-classifying the memory consumption in three different modes, monitors performance metrics, and proposes a recommendation policy in a top-down approach, while also leveraging swap memory accordingly at runtime when necessary. We evaluated *ARC-V* in nine HPC applications and the results show that *ARC-V* can effectively reduce memory waste and improve performance compared to the standard Kubernetes VPA.

Acknowledgments. This research is supported by the European Commission under the Horizon project OpenCUBE (GA-101092984) and SESSI, SeRC Efficient Simulation Software Initiative for HPC Malleability

Disclosure of Interests. The authors have no competing interests to declare that are relevant to the content of this article.

References

1. Peng, I., et al.: "A holistic view of memory utilization on HPC systems: current and future trends," In: Proceedings of the Intllegience Symposium on Memory Systems (2021)
2. Egwutuoha, I.P., et al.: "A proactive fault tolerance approach to HPC in the cloud," In: 2012 2nd Intllegience Conference on Cloud and Green Computing. IEEE
3. Jin, H., "Checkpointing orchestration: Toward a scalable HPC fault-tolerant environment", In: 12th IEEE/ACM International Symposium on Cluster, Cloud and Grid Computing (ccgrid 2012). IEEE **2012**, 276–283 (2012)
4. Chen, S., et al.: "Parties: Qos-aware resource partitioning for multiple interactive services", In: Proceedings of the 24th International Conference on Architectural Support for Programming Languages and Operating Systems, ser. ASPLOS '19. ACM
5. Aksar, B., et al.: "Prodigy: towards unsupervised anomaly detection in production HPC systems", In: Proceedings of the International Conference for High Performance Computing, Networking, Storage and Analysis, ser. SC '23. ACM, (2023)
6. Greneche, N., Cerin, C.: "Autoscaling of containerized HPC clusters in the cloud", In: 2022 Intelleigence Workshop on Interoperability of Supercomputing and Cloud Tech
7. Pupykina, A., Agosta, G.: "Survey of memory management techniques for HPC and cloud computing", IEEE Access, vol. 7, pp. 167 351–167 373 (2019)
8. Petrucci, V., et al.: "Octopus-man: Qos-driven task management for heterogeneous multicores in warehouse-scale computers", In: 2015 IEEE 21st International Symposium on High Performance Computer Architecture (HPCA). IEEE (2015)
9. Heroux, M.A., Doerfler, D.W., et al.: "Improving Performance via Mini-applications", Sandia National Laboratories, Technical Report SAND2009-5574 (2009)
10. Shun, J., Blelloch, G.E.: "Ligra: a lightweight graph processing framework for shared memory," In: Proceedings of the 18th ACM SIGPLAN symposium on Principles and practice of parallel programming, 2013, pp. 135–146
11. Bryan, G.H., Fritsch, J.M.: A benchmark simulation for moist nonhydrostatic numerical models. Mon. Weather Rev. **130**(12), 2917–2928 (2002)
12. Abraham, M., et al.: "GROMACS: High performance molecular simulations through multi-level parallelism from laptops to supercomputers," SoftwareX '15', vol. 1

13. Kunen, A.J., et al.: "Kripke-a massively parallel transport mini-app," Lawrence Livermore National Lab.(LLNL), Livermore, CA (United States), Technical Report (2015)
14. "Hydrodynamics Challenge Problem, LLNL," Technical Report LLNL-TR-490254
15. Chien, S.W.D., et al.: "sputniPIC: an implicit Particle-in-Cell code for multi-GPU systems," In: 2020 IEEE 32nd International Symposium on Computer Architecture and High Performance Computing (SBAC-PAD), 2020, pp. 149–156
16. Duplyakin, D., et al.: "The design and operation of CloudLab", In: Proceedings of the USENIX Annual Technical Conference (ATC), pp. 1–14 (2019)

MPLS: Stacking Diverse Layers Into One Model for Decentralized Federated Learning

Yang Xu[1,2], Zhiwei Yao[1,2], Hongli Xu[1,2(✉)], Yunming Liao[1,2], and Zuan Xie[1,2]

[1] School of Computer Science and Technology, University of Science and Technology of China, Hefei, China
{xuyangcs,xuhongli}@ustc.edu.cn,
{zhiweiyao,ymliao98,xz1314}@mail.ustc.edu.cn
[2] Suzhou Institute for Advanced Research, University of Science and Technology of China, Suzhou, China

Abstract. Traditional Federated Learning (FL) enables collaborative training of deep neural networks (DNNs) across massive edge devices while preserving data privacy. However, its reliance on a centralized parameter server (PS) introduces communication bottlenecks and security risks. To address these issues, Decentralized Federated Learning (DFL) has emerged, which adopts peer-to-peer (P2P) communication to eliminate the PS. Despite its advantages, DFL faces critical challenges: limited bandwidth resources, dynamic network conditions, and heterogeneous data properties. To conquer these challenges, we design and implement a *communication-efficient DFL framework with peer and layer selection (MPLS)*, which has the following advantages. 1) Different from exchanging an entire model between two workers in previous works, each worker just collects multiple sub-models (*i.e.*, some critical layers) from the chosen peers and stacks them into one model for aggregation. 2) MPLS adopts asynchronous training among workers without any coordinator and enables each worker to develop the peer and layer selection strategy adaptively via the proposed list scheduling algorithm. We implement MPLS on a physical platform, and extensive experiments on real-world DNNs and datasets demonstrate that MPLS achieves 2.1–4.2× speedup compared to the baselines.

Keywords: Decentralized Federated Learning · Edge Network · Device Heterogeneity

1 Introduction

Recently, Federated Learning (FL) has emerged as a promising paradigm for distributed model training among workers (*e.g.*, end devices or edge nodes). Traditional FL relies on a central parameter server (PS) to periodically aggregate and distribute models from/to the local workers. However, this centralized approach can lead to network congestion, making the PS a bottleneck, and pose security risks if the PS is compromised [1]. To conquer this, Decentralized Federated Learning (DFL) [1] has been proposed, allowing workers to collaboratively train models by exchanging model parameters directly. By eliminating the PS, DFL avoids single point of failure and reduces network congestion, thereby accelerating the training process.

W. E. Nagel et al. (Eds.): Euro-Par 2025, LNCS 15900, pp. 190–204, 2026.
https://doi.org/10.1007/978-3-031-99854-6_13

Table 1. Comparison of different DFL systems with different aggregation schemes.

Aggregation Schemes	DFL Systems	Heterogeneity Awareness	Resource Cost		Convergence Performance
			Time	Traffic	
Synchronous	[9]	No	Long	Massive	Good
	[10]	No	Long	Average	Good
	[11, 12]	Yes	Long	Average	Good
Asynchronous	[2]	No	Average	Massive	Good
	[3,4]	Yes	Average	Massive	Good
	[8]	No	Average	Low	Poor
	[7]	Yes	Low	Low	Poor
	MPLS	Yes	Low	Low	Good

DFL systems can operate in synchronous or asynchronous manners. Existing studies mainly focus on improving the training efficiency of the synchronous DFL. Synchronous DFL requires all workers to synchronize their updates, which creates a synchronization barrier. This barrier forces faster workers to wait for slower ones, leading to decreased training efficiency and poor fault tolerance, as a single failed node can disrupt the entire system. To conquer these issues, asynchronous DFL [2–4] has been introduced, allowing workers to train DNNs at their own pace without waiting for others. Since the synchronization barrier among workers can be alleviated, asynchronous DFL is more effective than the synchronous one for handling system heterogeneity [5].

Existing asynchronous DFL systems can be categorized into two types. The first type involves workers collecting *entire* models from multiple or all peers for aggregation [2–4]. While this type can achieve effective convergence, it faces two major challenges: 1) *Huge Bandwidth Pressure*. Transmitting large DNN models consumes substantial bandwidth resources, leading to network congestion. 2) *Long Training Time*. In edge network, workers typically communicate with peers over wireless links with limited bandwidth [6]. Moreover, the communication delay in each epoch always depends on the slowest link, as model aggregation only proceeds once all models from selected peers are received. This results in prolonged training time and slow convergence rate [7]. The second type allows each worker to pull an *entire* model from only one peer, either randomly [8] or based on the highest-speed link [7]. While this reduces communication overhead, it introduces two key limitations: 1) *Inefficient Bandwidth Utilization*. Since each worker aggregates the model only from one peer, the bandwidth resource of other peers remains underutilized. 2) *Poor Convergence Performance*. Since the local data held by different workers are not independent and identically distributed (Non-IID), the data distribution at an individual worker may not represent the overall population distribution. Such data heterogeneity will inevitably deteriorate training convergence [2]. In addition, many asynchronous DFL systems [2,7] rely on a coordinator to determine system parameters, which can become a bottleneck and reduce fault tolerance. A detailed comparison is shown in Table 1.

To this end, we propose MPLS, a communication-efficient decentralized federated learning system. Unlike existing approaches [7,8] that exchange entire models between two workers, MPLS enables each worker to pull multiple sub-models (*i.e.*, some critical layers) from selected peers in parallel for aggregation. In this way, the bandwidth resource of the entire system can be effectively utilized, and the bandwidth pressure on each worker is significantly alleviated. Moreover, MPLS supports fully asynchronous and independent training and aggregation without any coordinator, ensuring high scalability and fault tolerance. However, implementing MPLS is non-trivial due to system and data heterogeneity and network dynamics. Intuitively, peers with higher bandwidth should be selected with larger probability, but selecting too many layers from them can cause unbalanced communication delay among peers and slow down the training speed. Besides, frequent layer collection from fixed peers may hinder model generalization and convergence. Moreover, the development of the aggregation strategy should also vary over training epochs to adapt to network dynamics for improving training performance. The main contributions of this paper are as follows:

- We propose MPLS, a decentralized federated learning system that enables workers to collect multiple sub-models from selected peers for aggregation.
- To accelerate training in heterogeneous and dynamic edge network, MPLS employs a dynamic peer and layer selection strategy using a novel list scheduling algorithm.
- Extensive experiments on a physical platform demonstrate that MPLS can provide 2.1–4.2× speedup over the state-of-the-art DFL systems.

2   Background and Motivation

2.1   Decentralized Federated Learning

DNN Model. A specific DNN model is composed of a sequence of multiple layers with different types (*e.g.*, convolutional layers and fully-connected layers). Let L be the number of layers of a DNN model $w = \{w(1), \cdots, w(L)\}$ and M_l be the size of $w(l), \forall l \in \{1, 2, ..., L\}$. Thus, the size of whole model can be denoted as $\sum_{l=1}^{L} M_l$.

Network Model. DFL uses a set of N workers to collaboratively train models with its local data by peer-to-peer communication, *i.e.*, each worker exchanges model parameters with its connected peers in a network topology. We denote the network topology as a symmetric adjacency matrix $A = \{A_{i,j} \in \{0,1\}, 1 \le i, j \le N\}$, where $A_{i,j} = 1$ denotes a connection link between worker i and j.

Training Procedure. DFL generally consists of two iterative steps. *1) Local training.* Each worker i maintains a local model w_i and a dataset D_i of size $|D_i|$, with the local loss function defined as $f_i(w_i) = \frac{1}{|D_i|} \sum_{\xi \in D_i} F_i(w_i; \xi)$, where ξ is a batch of data samples in D_i and $F_i(w_i; \xi)$ is the loss over ξ. To minimize $f_i(w_i)$, worker i updates its model using stochastic gradient descent (SGD), *i.e.*, $\overline{w}_i = w_i - \eta \nabla f_i(w_i)$, where $\overline{w}_i$ is the local model of worker i after local training, η is the learning rate and $\nabla f_i(w_i)$ is the gradient of the loss with respect to the current model. *2) Model aggregation.* Worker i collects models from connected (or selected) peers and aggregates them to generate a new model for the next epoch. The model aggregation step may vary significantly across different systems. For example, in some systems, each worker i communicates with all its peers and updates its local model asynchronously [4], *i.e.*, $w_i = (\sum_{j=1}^{N} A_{i,j} w_j + \overline{w}_i)/(1 + \sum_{j=1}^{N} A_{i,j})$. In contrast, in [7], each worker i just collects a model from one connected worker j, and sets $w_i = \frac{1}{2}(\overline{w}_i + w_j)$. These two steps are performed iteratively until the predefined termination conditions (*e.g.*, time constraints or target accuracy) are satisfied. Notably, in an asynchronous DFL system [7], local training and model aggregation can overlap, as workers begins to pull models from peers during local training.

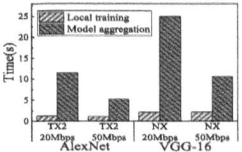

Fig. 1. Per-epoch time consumption.

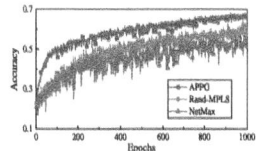

Fig. 2. Training process of DFL systems.

2.2 Why is Communication a Bottleneck?

In DFL, communication costs during model aggregation are a critical bottleneck, especially in edge networks. The rapid growth in DNN size has significantly increased the network burden and delays. While computing performance of edge devices has improved 10–100× compared to CPUs due to hardware accelerators (*e.g.*, NVIDIA TX2/NX), network bandwidth improvements (typically 5-25Mbps for WANs) have lagged. To further analyze the overhead of local training (computing) and model aggregation (communication), we measure delays on NVIDIA TX2 and NX devices (see Table 2) under various network conditions while training AlexNet and VGG-16 over STL-10. Figure 1 shows that communication time dominates training time, often exceeding local training delay by up to 10×. Although the local training time can be increased by performing more iterations of SGD in each epoch, it will deteriorate the training performance and trap the model of each worker in local optima. Therefore, a proper aggregation strategy will result in a significant reduction of training time.

2.3 Observation and Motivation

For asynchronous DFL, different model aggregation strategies greatly impact communication costs and training efficiency. We evaluate three systems: 1) *APPG* [4] lets each worker collect models from all connected peers for aggregation, and achieves the best performance (see Fig. 2). 2) *NetMax* [7] enables each worker to pull models from the peers with the highest bandwidth. 3) *Rand-MPLS* lets each worker pull each layer of a DNN from a randomly selected peer. Compared to APPG, each worker in NetMax and Rand-MPLS only collects one entire model (from only one or many peers) for aggregation. By pulling multiple sub-models to rebuild a complete DNN for aggregation, each worker in Rand-MPLS can learn model information from different peers, and the generalization of the combined model can be improved. NetMax, however, exhibits unstable training performance with significant fluctuations in its training curve. These results verify the potential of MPLS for performance improvement. Unlike Rand-MPLS's random strategy, we will further incorporate dynamic and heterogeneous network conditions and data heterogeneity to develop an efficient aggregation strategy.

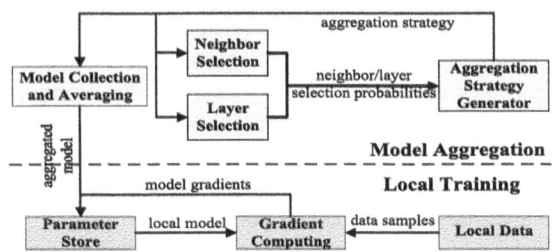

Fig. 3. Key modules and workflow on each worker in MPLS.

3   MPLS Design

3.1   System Overview

Figure 3 presents the key modules of MPLS on each worker with respect to two training processes, *i.e.*, local training and model aggregation. Specifically, three modules (*i.e.*, *gradient computing*, *local data* and *parameter store*) cooperate to perform the local training. Besides, the model aggregation process, which is the focus of MPLS design, consists of four modules, *e.g.*, *aggregation strategy generator*, *peer selection*, *etc.*. The detailed workflow among these modules is as follows: ① In the local training step, the *gradient computing* module pulls the stored local model and a batch of data samples from *parameter store* and *local data*, respectively, and returns the computed model gradients to *parameter store* for model updating. ② In the model aggregation step, the *model collection and averaging* module collects layers from the chosen peers based on the developed aggregation strategy, rebuilds a combined DNN, and averages it with the local model. The aggregated model will be returned to *parameter store*. ③ To accommodate the network dynamics in edge network during model aggregation and improve the model convergence performance, the *peer selection* determines the selection probability for each peer, and the *layer selection* derives the layer selection probabilities guided by historical aggregation strategies. ④ By jointly considering the peer and layer selection probability distribution, the *aggregation strategy generator* is able to determine which layers of a DNN should be collected from each peer for model aggregation.

3.2   Design of Key Components

We now focus on the model aggregation step of an arbitrary worker i and describe its individual modules in Fig. 3. Let K be the total number of local iterations of worker i.

The total number of training epochs T in MPLS is the sum of local iterations among all workers, as all workers perform training asynchronously.

Model Collection and Averaging. This module is responsible for collecting layers from the peers for model aggregation. Take Fig. 4 as an example, where there are 5 workers and a DNN consists of four layers (*i.e.*, $\{P_1, P_2, P_3, P_4\}$). Figure 4 plots the aggregation steps of two consecutive local iterations of worker #3. Firstly, worker #3 pulls $\{P_1, P_4\}$, $\{P_2\}$ and $\{P_3\}$ from the parameter stores of workers #1, #2 and #4 respectively at local iteration k, and averages them with the local model after local training $\overline{w}_3^k$. The aggregated model w_3^{k+1} is used for local training of iteration $k + 1$. Secondly, to adapt to network dynamics and enhance performance, different aggregation strategies may be adopted across iterations. For example, if the link between workers #3 and #4 is broken in iteration $k + 1$, worker #3 will only pull sub-models from workers #1 and #2. Besides, worker #3 pulls $\{P_2\}$ and $\{P_1, P_3, P_4\}$ from workers #1 and #2 respectively, which is different from that of local iteration k. This is because aggregating the same layer from different peers across epochs is conducive to the model generalization.

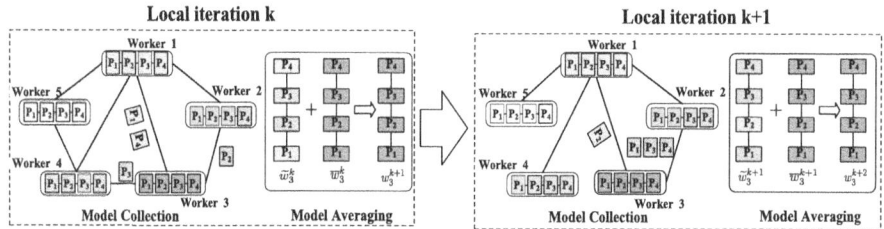

Fig. 4. The procedure of model collection and averaging of worker #3 in MPLS.

Generally, assume that worker i has S peers and performs model collection and averaging at local iteration k, and we adopt $y_s^k(l)$ to represent the layer selection strategy of peer s, *e.g.*, $y_s^k(l) = 1$ means that worker i pulls layer l from peer s at iteration k. The approach of model averaging for worker i as follows

$$w_i^{k+1}(l) = \frac{\sum_{s=1}^{S} y_s^k(l) w_s^k(l) + w_i^k(l)}{\sum_{s=1}^{S} y_s^k(l) + 1} \tag{1}$$

The new model w_i^{k+1} for further local training is a combination of each updated layer, *i.e.*, $w_i^{k+1} = \{w_i^{k+1}(1), ..., w_i^{k+1}(L)\}$. This aggregated model will be sent to parameter store for local training at iteration $k + 1$. Though each worker only collects sub-models from the chosen peers for training, MPLS can still guarantee training convergence. With connected network topology, our theoretical analysis shows that the convergence bound is mainly related to the number of workers N and the total training epochs T, *i.e.*, $\frac{1}{T} \sum_{t=0}^{T-1} \mathbb{E} \|\nabla f(w^t)\|^2 = \mathcal{O}(\frac{N}{T})$, where $w^t = \frac{1}{N} \sum_{i=1}^{N} w_i^t$. We present the detailed proof in https://github.com/Jollydos/MPLS_Euro_Par.

Peer Selection. Since training data on each worker always depends on its local environment and usage pattern, the distribution of the local datasets often varies across workers [13], negatively impacting model convergence. To address this, we focus on the model aggregation process, enabling each worker to incorporate model information trained on datasets with diverse data distributions. Specifically, assume the local data distribution of worker i is $P_i = \{p_i^1, p_i^2, ..., p_i^C\}$, where $C = |P_i|$ is the total number of classes and p_i^c represents the proportion of the local data samples in D_i with label $c \in \{1, 2, ..., C\}$. Thus, the distribution divergence over classes between the local datasets of device i and its peer s is denoted as

$$DD_s = \sum_{c=1}^{C} ||p_i^c - p_s^c||. \tag{2}$$

Intuitively, by aggregating the local model from the peer s with higher DD_s more frequently, the local model of worker i can learn more model information within different data distributions, and then be a good representative of the global model [13].

However, since the bandwidth of workers in edge network may vary with time, such factor should also be considered during peer selection. Specifically, we denote the link speed between worker i and its peer s at iteration k as B_s^k. Jointly considering the heterogeneous network conditions among peers and Non-IID data, we design a two-step peer selection rule: Firstly, we standardize the network status and data distribution divergence of all peers. For each peer s at local iteration k, we have

$$\overline{B}_s^k = \frac{B_s^k}{\sum_{s'=1}^{S} B_{s'}^k}, \qquad \overline{DD}_s = \frac{DD_s}{\sum_{s'=1}^{S} DD_{s'}} \tag{3}$$

Secondly, we introduce two variables τ_1 and τ_2 to control the weight of each factor, where $\tau_1 + \tau_2 = 1$. As the result, we update the communication probability p_s^k for worker i to aggregate layers from peer s at local iteration k as

$$p_s^k = \frac{\tau_1 \overline{B}_s^k + \tau_2 \overline{DD}_s}{\sum_{s'=1}^{S} (\tau_1 \overline{B}_{s'}^k + \tau_2 \overline{DD}_{s'})} \tag{4}$$

A larger τ_1 denotes that device prefers to aggregate layers from the peer with better network conditions, while a larger τ_2 favors peers with greater distribution divergence. The impact of τ_1 and τ_2 on the training performance will be explored in the experiment.

Layer Selection. Each worker i iteratively performs the training process to make its local model w_i^t gradually approach to the global optima w^*. We use $g_i^t(l)$ to represent the distance between $w_i^t(l)$ and $w^*(l)$ for layer l, i.e., $g_i^t(l) = ||w_i^t(l) - w^*(l)||^2$. Intuitively, each worker i can aggregate each layer l from the peer s with a minimum $g_s^t(l)$ to accelerate its training process. However, since w^* is unavailable until model converges, we cannot obtain $g_s^t(l)$ to guide layer selection. Instead, we estimate the training efficiency of each peer s based on its gradient variation and define $g_s^{t,t'}(l)$ as its training performance from epochs t' to t on layer l, i.e.,

$$g_s^{t',t}(l) = ||w_s^t(l) - w_s^{t'}(l)||^2 \tag{5}$$

The peer with stronger training capacity can perform local training and model aggregation more frequently and achieve a higher convergence rate, resulting in a greater $g_s^{t,t'}(l)$. Based on this, we further denote $q_s^k(l)$ as the probability that worker i pulls layer l from peer s at iteration k (epoch t). Assume worker i performs two consecutive model aggregations at epoch t' and t, respectively. For each layer l, we have $\sum_{s=1}^{S} q_s^k(l) = 1$, where $q_s^k(l)$ is derived by

$$q_s^k(l) = \frac{g_s^{t',t}(l)}{\sum_{s'=1}^{S} g_{s'}^{t',t}(l)} \tag{6}$$

The better the training performance of peer s on layer l from epoch t' to t, the higher the probability worker i will pull this layer from it. Notably, worker i only receives $g_s^{t',t}(l)$ values from each peer s for layer selection, incurring minimal communication cost.

Aggregation Strategy Generator. In MPLS, the peer selection and layer selection in MPLS are not independent, and the aggregation strategy generator will jointly optimize them to develop an aggregation strategy for accelerating the training procedure in each iteration k. For a given strategy, the communication cost λ_s^k for collecting several layers from the peer s can be expressed as

$$\lambda_s^k = \sum_{l=1}^{L} \frac{y_s^k(l) M_l}{B_s^k} \tag{7}$$

As a result, for worker i, the total delay λ^k for model aggregation in the local iteration k is determined by the last received layers, i.e., $\lambda^k = \max_s \lambda_s^k$. We target to minimize the total communication delay (i.e., $\min \lambda^k$) at any local iteration k while ensuring the convergence performance. Specifically, we let each worker i pull layer l from a peer s with a probability $p_s^k q_s^k(l)$ (i.e., the product of peer and layer selection probabilities) greater than a lower bound $\theta(l)$ at local iteration k, i.e., $p_s^k q_s^k(l) > \theta(l)$. Intuitively, to ensure that each layer can be aggregated by worker i, we set $\theta(l) = \frac{1}{S} \sum_{s=1}^{S} p_s^k q_s^k(l)$.

By solving this problem, the generator will output the aggregation strategy to the model collection and averaging module. When only considering layer selection, this problem simplifies to the generalized assignment problem [14], i.e., assigning each layer l to a selected peer s for minimizing the delay (an NP-hard problem). Due to its complexity, we propose a list scheduling [15] based algorithm in the next section.

4 Aggregation Strategy Development

We formally present the proposed list scheduling based algorithm for model aggregation strategy development in MPLS, which consists of four phases.

Initialization. In each local iteration k, worker i initializes two $S \times L$ matrixes μ_1 and μ_2. Using the link speed measured by network monitor, the worker can compute the time $\mu_1(s, l)$ for pulling each layer l from each peer s, i.e., $\mu_1(s, l) = M_l / B_s^k$. Besides, $\mu_2(s, l)$ in matrix μ_2 is the probability for aggregating layer l from peer s, i.e., $p_s^k q_s^k(l)$.

Problem Transformation. The development of aggregation strategy can be modeled by an assignment function $\pi : \{1, ..., L\} \rightarrow \{1, ..., S\}$. $\pi(l) = s$ means the layer l will be pulled from peer s. The communication delay of the assignment π is denoted as

$$\lambda(\pi) = \max_{s\in\{1,...,S\}} \sum_{l|\pi(l)=s} \mu_1(s,l) \tag{8}$$

To meet the constraint $p_s^k q_s^k(l) > \theta(l)$, we modify the matrix μ_1 using μ_2. Specifically, for each layer l and peer s, if $\mu_2(s,l) < \theta(l)$, we adjust μ_1 by setting $\mu_1(s,l) = \infty$, which indicates that layer l will not be assigned to peer s.

List Scheduling. To generate an assignment π by list scheduling, we first define the start time ϕ and the finish time ψ for each layer l. Specifically, if worker i pulls layer l from peer s at time $\tilde{t}$, we have $\phi(l) \leq \tilde{t} \leq \psi(l)$, where $\psi(l) = \phi(l) + \mu_1(s,l)$. Then, the total communication delay of model collection is equal to the maximum finish time among all layers, i.e., $\lambda(\pi) = \max_l \psi(l)$. The matrix μ_1 associates S possible transmission time with each layer l, and we define the shortest one as $\varphi(l) = \min_s \mu_1(s,l)$. Furthermore, we obtain the efficiency of pulling layer l from peer s by the shortest transmission time $\varphi(l)$, denoted as $E(s,l)$, i.e.,

$$E(s,l) = \frac{\varphi(l)}{\mu_1(s,l)} \tag{9}$$

where $E(s,l) \in [0,1]$. The larger $E(s,l)$ represents a shorter transmission delay. For each peer s, we sort all layers in a list by descending order of $E(s,l)$. We denote the total efficiency of each peer s on the entire DNN as $rank(s) = \sum_{l=1}^{L} E(s,l)$. Then, we sort all peers in descending order. Each worker likely pulls layers from the peer s with a higher $rank(s)$ for reducing the time consumption.

Algorithm 1. Aggregation Strategy Development in MPLS

1: Initialize μ_1, μ_2 and $sum(s) = 0, \forall s$;
2: Initialize the set of unassigned layers $Q_1 = \{1, 2, ..., L\}$;
3: Initialize the set of available peers $Q_2 = \{1, 2, ..., S\}$;
4: Sort all layers in descending order by $E(s,l), \forall l$ for each peer s;
5: Sort all neighbors in descending order by $rank(s), \forall s$;
6: **while** $Q_1 \neq \emptyset$ **do**
7:     Select a neighbor $k \in Q_2$ such that $sum(s) < sum(s')$ or $rank(s) \geq rank(s')$ when $sum(s) = sum(s'), \forall s'$;
8:     Select a layer $l \in Q_1$ with highest $E(s,l)$ from s's list;
9:     **if** $E(s,l) \leq 1/\sqrt{S}$ **then**
10:         Update $Q_2 \leftarrow Q_2 - \{s\}$;
11:     **else**
12:         Update $Q_1 \leftarrow Q_1 - \{l\}$, and set $\pi(l) = s$;
13:         Update $sum(s) \leftarrow sum(s) + \mu_1(s,l)$;
14:         Update $rank(s) \leftarrow rank(s) - E(s,l)$;
15: Compute $MAX = \max_s sum(s)$;
16: **for** $s \in \{1, 2, ..., S\}$ **do**
17:     **while** peer s's list is not empty **do**
18:         Select a layer l with highest $E(s,l)$ from s's list;
19:         **if** $\pi(l) \neq s$ and $sum(s) + \mu_1(s,l) \leq MAX$ **then**
20:             Aggregate layer l from peer s;
21:             $sum(s) \leftarrow sum(s) + \mu_1(s,l)$;
22:         Remove layer l from s's list;
23: **Return** The final aggregation strategy, i.e., assignment π;

Assignment Generation. The lines 1–5 show the operations in the former three phases. Based on this, each worker is able to develop the preliminary model aggregation strategy by using the proposed list scheduling approach (lines 6–14). Specifically, we adopt $sum(s)=\sum_{l|\pi(l)=s}\mu_1(s,l)$ to record the current transmission delay of each peer s during the process of layer assignment, and create two sets (Q_1 and Q_2) to record the unassigned layers and available peers, respectively. Based on these parameters, worker i firstly chooses the peer s with the minimum $sum(s)$. Worker i then searches for the layer l that has not been assigned (i.e., $l \in Q_1$) and is with the highest $E(s,l)$ in the list of the selected peer s (lines 7–8), and determines whether to pull this layer from it (lines 9–14). If the efficiency $E(s,l)$ of this selected layer is smaller than a predefined lower bound (i.e., $1/\sqrt{S}$ [16]), worker i will remove the peer s from the set Q_2 (lines 9–10) to prevent to pull any other layers from this peer (i.e., leading to long transmission time). Otherwise, worker i will pull layer l from peer k and the parameters, e.g., $sum(s)$, will be updated accordingly (lines 12–14).

Once the preliminary assignment π is obtained (lines 6–14), we compute the maximum delay (i.e., MAX) incurred by any single peer under this assignment (line 15). Then, we search for the layers that should be further aggregated from each peer (lines 16–22). Specifically, for each peer s, we sequentially judge whether each layer l can be aggregated from it or not. If layer l is not assigned to peer s in current assignment π and aggregating this layer will not increase the maximum delay (line 19), worker i will pull this layer l from peer s and update $sum(s)$ (lines 20–21).

Table 2. Different computing modes of TX2/NX devices.

	Mode	Denver2	ARMA57	ARMv8.2	GPU	Numbers	Location
TX2	1	2.0 GHz×2	2.0 GHz×4	–	1.3 GHz	1–5	A
	2	1.4 GHz×2	1.4 GHz×4	–	1.12 GHz	6–10	B
	3	0.0 GHz	1.2 GHz×4	–	0.85 GHz	11–15	C
NX	1	–	–	1.4 GHz×6	1.1 GHz	16–20	A
	2	–	–	1.2 GHz×4	0.8 GHz	21–25	B
	3	–	–	1.5 GHz×2	0.8 GHz	26–30	C

We analyze the computational complexity of Algorithm 1. When we adopt the quick sort, the complexity of lines 4–5 is $O(SL \log L)$. Since each iteration of the loop (lines 6–14) will remove one element from either Q_1 or Q_2, the worst time complexity of this procedure is $O((S + L) \log S)$, where $O(\log S)$ is the time for selecting the peer s by binary search [17]. Similarly, we remove one layer from each peer's list in each iteration in lines 16–22, the time complexity is $O(SL)$. Thus, the total complexity is $O(SL \log L)$. Considering the system performance, this algorithm only incurs negligible cost on each worker in MPLS while improving the training performance.

5   Performance Evaluation

5.1   Experimental Setup

Experimental Environment. We evaluate the efficiency of MPLS on a physical plat-form using PyTorch. The platform includes 15 NVIDIA Jetson TX2 and 15 NVIDIA Jetson Xavier NX devices, labeled from 1 to 30, configured to represent a heteroge-neous edge network: 1) *Computing heterogeneity.* Both TX2 and NX devices are set to 3 different computing modes, with 5 devices per mode (see Table 2). Specifically, the computing capacity of TX2/NX decreases in order from mode 1 to 3. 2) *Communication heterogeneity.* All the devices are interconnected via a 5 GHz WiFi router, distributed across three rooms (10 devices each). The WiFi router is located in room A.

Models and Datasets. We evaluate three well-known DNNs, *i.e.*, LeNet-5, NIN, ResNet-18, over three real datasets, *i.e.*, MNIST, CIFAR-10, CIFAR-100. These cover a wide range of small to large models and datasets for edge network. Models are trained with a batch size of 64 and a learning rate of 0.01 [7]. Datasets are randomly and uni-formly distributed across devices.

Baselines and Metrics. We adopt four baselines, *i.e.*, *NetMax* [7], *APPG* [4], *MPLS-Peer* and *MPLS-Layer*. Here, *MPLS-Peer* and *MPLS-Layer* are variants of MPLS with only peer or layer selection capabilities. The performance is evaluated using the metrics: 1) *Classification accuracy* is used to validate whether an FL algorithm can efficiently guarantee convergence. 2) *Completion time* is used to assess training speed. We adopt the average results of 3 independent experiments to avoid accidents.

Network Topology. For a fair comparison, we evaluate three common network topolo-gies, *i.e.*, ring, randomly-generated graph and fully-connected graph. Specifically, 1) In the ring topology, workers are connected sequentially in the order $1 \to 2 \to \cdots \to 30 \to 1$. 2) In a randomly-generated graph, each pair of workers is connected with a probability of 50%. 3) In the fully-connected graph, each worker is directly connected with all other workers. By default, we adopt the randomly-generated graph.

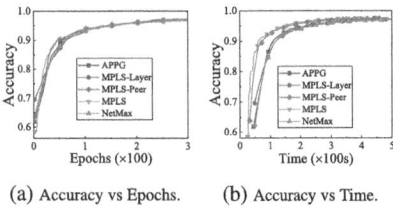

(a) Accuracy vs Epochs.   (b) Accuracy vs Time.

Fig. 5. Training performance for LeNet-5 over MNIST.

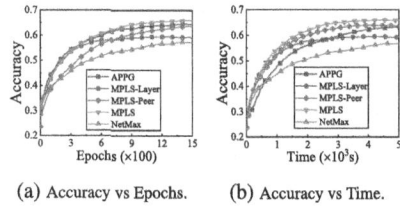

(a) Accuracy vs Epochs.   (b) Accuracy vs Time.

Fig. 6. Training performance for NIN over CIFAR-10.

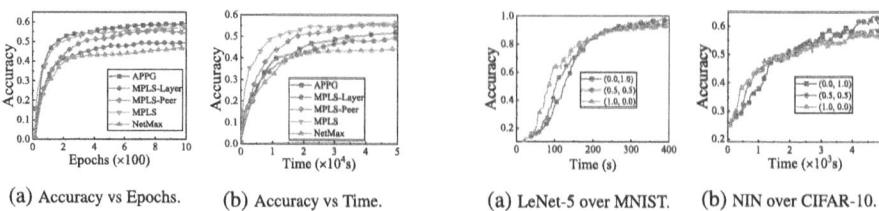

(a) Accuracy vs Epochs.   (b) Accuracy vs Time.

Fig. 7. Training performance for ResNet-18 over CIFAR-100.

(a) LeNet-5 over MNIST.   (b) NIN over CIFAR-10.

Fig. 8. Accuracy vs. Time for LeNet-5 and NIN with different values of τ_1 and τ_2.

5.2 Overall Performance

Convergence Performance. Figures 5, 6 and 7 show the training performance of LeNet-5 over MNIST, NIN over CIFAR-10, and ResNet-18 over CIFAR-100, respectively. For the smallest model (*i.e.*, LeNet-5), Fig. 5a indicates that all systems performed similarly. However, for deeper models, performance gaps between different systems occur in Figs. 6a and 7a. We note that MPLS achieves a higher convergence accuracy, compared with MPLS-Peer, MPLS-Layer and NetMax. That is because MPLS ensures each worker learns more information from its chosen peers than the other three systems in each local iteration without incurring extra time. Specifically, the final accuracy of APPG, NetMax, MPLS-Peer, MPLS and MPLS-Layer is 64.42%, 58.64%, 63.87%, 66.01%, and 57.22% for NIN over CIFAR-10 after 1,500 epochs, respectively. For ResNet-18, the accuracy is 59.12%, 49.71%, 54.27%, 57.43%, and 46.91%, correspondingly. Similarly, for the larger ResNet-18, APPG obtains better convergence performance than MPLS given the same number of epochs due to its strategy of collecting all peers' models for aggregation, at the expense of more resources (*e.g.*, time and traffic) consumption.

Resource Consumption. Figs. 5, 6 and 7 show the comparison of accuracy versus training time. We observe that MPLS-Peer and MPLS converge faster and achieve a higher accuracy given the same time budget. For NIN, MPLS achieves 2.1×, 3.4× and 4.2× speedup compared with APPG, NetMax and MPLS-Layer. Since all systems operate under the same computing environment, MPLS improves training efficiency by significantly reducing communication delays. With the efficient model aggregation strategy, MPLS and MPLS-Peer can maximize bandwidth utilization across all workers. As a result, our systems outperform NetMax, which mainly utilizes high-speed links.

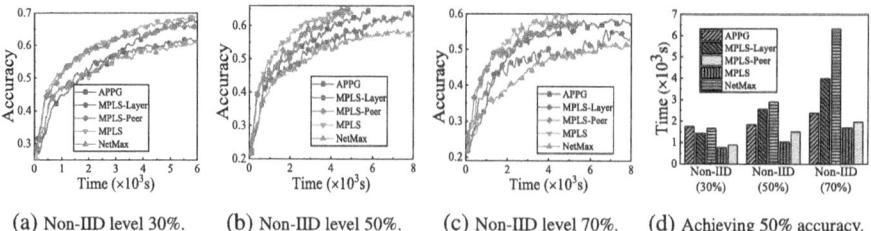

(a) Non-IID level 30%.   (b) Non-IID level 50%.   (c) Non-IID level 70%.   (d) Achieving 50% accuracy.

Fig. 9. Accuracy vs. Time for NIN over CIFAR-10 under different data distribution.

5.3 Hyper-Parameter Evaluation

To evaluate MPLS' sensitivity to the hyperparameters, we adopt different values of (τ_1, τ_2), including $(1.0, 0.0)$, $(0.5, 0.5)$ and $(0.0, 1.0)$. The results for LeNet-5 over MNIST and NIN over CIFAR-10 with Non-IID level 70% are shown in Fig. 8. As the value of τ_1 increases (τ_2 decreases), we observe that models converge faster initially but with a little sacrifice of the final accuracy. A larger τ_1 means that each worker will collect layers from the peers with high link speed and thus guarantees a faster convergence at the early stage. However, due to Non-IID data, the worker may miss diverse class information, leading to slightly lower accuracy. On the contrary, when a larger τ_2 is adopted, each worker more frequently aggregates layers from peers with different data distributions. However, it inevitably increases the time required for model aggregation, resulting in a slower training speed. Achieving an optimal balance between time consumption and convergence performance by tuning τ_1 and τ_2 remains to be studied.

5.4 Effect of Data Distribution

We study the effect of Non-IID data on training efficiency by varying Non-IID levels χ (e.g., 30%, 50%, and 70%) as in [13]. Specifically, for each worker, χ indicates the proportion of local data samples sharing the same label while the remaining $1-\chi$ belong to other labels. The results for NIN over CIFAR-10 are shown in Fig. 9. We make two observations as follows. Firstly, we observe that MPLS outperform baselines across all Non-IID levels. For instance, at $\chi = 30\%$, MPLS achieves 68.89% accuracy, surpassing APPG (68.37%), NetMax (61.68%), MPLS-Layer (61.21%) and MPLS-Peer (66.42%). This highlights the effectiveness of combining peer and layer selection in dealing with Non-IID issues. Secondly, as χ increases, all systems require more time to achieve the same accuracy. However, Fig. 9d shows that our systems achieve greater robustness with minimal time increase compared with NetMax, MPLS-Peer and MPLS-Layer. For example, MPLS completes training in 758.4 s ($\chi = 30\%$), 1025.9 s ($\chi = 50\%$) and 1700.2 s ($\chi = 70\%$), while NetMax takes 1437.6 s, 2551.2 s, and 3982.8 s, respectively. This efficiency stems from MPLS's shorter per-epoch completion time, enabling more iterations and better performance with the same time budget.

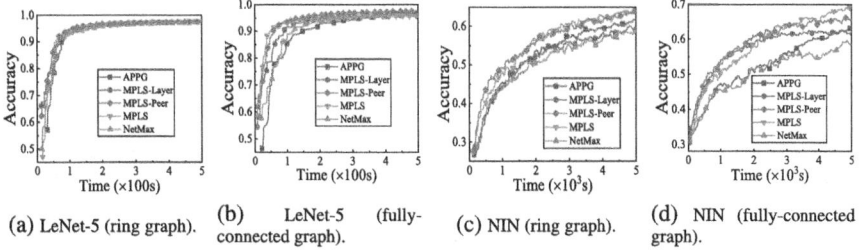

(a) LeNet-5 (ring graph).   (b)   LeNet-5   (fully-connected graph).   (c) NIN (ring graph).   (d) NIN (fully-connected graph).

Fig. 10. Accuracy vs. Time for LeNet-5 over MNIST and NIN over CIFAR-10 with different network topologies.

5.5   Effect of Network Topology

We further investigate the effect of network topology on the training efficiency. The results are shown in Fig. 10. Firstly, for the ring graph, in which each node only has two peers, our systems achieve slightly better performance compared with baselines. Since each worker can only access limited information from its two peers, the performance divergence among different systems will not be significantly widened. Secondly, for the fully-connected graph, training accuracy improves for most systems, as each worker can aggregate models from any other workers. For example, MPLS's accuracy for NIN over CIFAR-10 increases from 63.91% to 65.94% at 5,000 s. In addition, we observe that communication costs rise in systems such as APPG and Rand-MPLS due to increased peer interactions. However, systems like MPLS, Adv-MPLS, and NetMax, which optimize for link speed when performing model aggregation, converge faster on the fully-connected graph compared to the ring graph. As a result, the performance gap between systems widens significantly in the fully-connected graph. For example, for LeNet-5 over MNIST with the fully-connected graph, MPLS achieve 90% accuracy in 57.96 s, achieving a speedup of $2.5\times$, $1.6\times$ and $2.1\times$ over APPG (147.48 s), NetMax (91.6 s), and Rand-MPLS (121.36 s), respectively.

6   Conclusion

In this paper, we have designed MPLS, a communication-efficient and fully decentralized federated learning system to accelerate the DNN training over the heterogeneous and dynamic edge network. We further introduce adaptive algorithms so that each worker can develop the model collection and aggregation strategy independently and adaptively to minimize the completion time while ensuring convergence performance. Experimental results demonstrate that MPLS significantly outperforms baselines.

Acknowledgments. The corresponding author is Hongli Xu. This article is supported by the National Science Foundation of China (NSFC) under Grants 62472401, 62132019, and 624B2136.

Disclosure of Interests. The authors have no competing interests to declare that are relevant to the content of this article.

References

1. Zhang, H., Bosch, J., Olsson, H.H.: Federated learning systems: architecture alternatives. In: 2020 27th Asia-Pacific Software Engineering Conference (APSEC), pp. 385–394. IEEE (2020)
2. Luo, Q., He, J., Zhuo, Y., Qian, X.: Prague: high-performance heterogeneity-aware asynchronous decentralized training. In: Proceedings of the Twenty-Fifth International Conference on Architectural Support for Programming Languages and Operating Systems, pp. 401–416 (2020)
3. Zhao, L., Song, W.-Z., Ye, X., Yujie, G.: Asynchronous broadcast-based decentralized learning in sensor networks. Int. J. Parallel Emergent Distrib. Syst. **33**(6), 589–607 (2018)

4. Zhang, J., You, K.: Asynchronous decentralized optimization in directed networks. arXiv preprint arXiv:1901.08215 (2019)

5. Zhang, H., Hsieh, C.J., Akella, V.: Hogwild++: a new mechanism for decentralized asynchronous stochastic gradient descent. In: 2016 IEEE 16th International Conference on Data Mining (ICDM), pp. 629–638. IEEE (2016)

6. Hu, C., Bao, W., Wang, D., Liu, F.: Dynamic adaptive dnn surgery for inference acceleration on the edge. In: IEEE INFOCOM 2019-IEEE Conference on Computer Communications, pp. 1423–1431. IEEE (2019)

7. Zhou, P., et al.: Communication-efficient decentralized machine learning over heterogeneous networks. In: 2021 IEEE 37th International Conference on Data Engineering (ICDE), pp. 384–395. IEEE (2021)

8. Lian, X., Zhang, W., Zhang, C., Liu, J.: Asynchronous decentralized parallel stochastic gradient descent. In: International Conference on Machine Learning, pp. 3043–3052. PMLR (2018)

9. Lian, X., Zhang, C., Zhang, H., Hsieh, C.J., Zhang, W., Liu, J.: Can decentralized algorithms outperform centralized algorithms? A case study for decentralized parallel stochastic gradient descent. arXiv preprint arXiv:1705.09056 (2017)

10. Koloskova, A., Stich, S., Jaggi, M.: Decentralized stochastic optimization and gossip algorithms with compressed communication. In: International Conference on Machine Learning, pp. 3478–3487. PMLR (2019)

11. Jiang, J., Liang, H., Chenghao, H., Liu, J., Wang, Z.: Bacombo–bandwidth-aware decentralized federated learning. Electronics 9(3), 440 (2020)

12. Hu, C., Jiang, J., Wang, Z.: Decentralized federated learning: a segmented gossip approach. arXiv preprint arXiv:1908.07782 (2019)

13. Wang, H., Kaplan, Z., Niu, D., Li, B.: Optimizing federated learning on non-iid data with reinforcement learning. In: IEEE INFOCOM 2020-IEEE Conference on Computer Communications, pp. 1698–1707. IEEE (2020)

14. Cattrysse, D.G., Van Wassenhove, L.N.: A survey of algorithms for the generalized assignment problem. Eur. J. Oper. Res. 60(3), 260–272 (1992)

15. Arabnejad, H., Barbosa, J.G.: List scheduling algorithm for heterogeneous systems by an optimistic cost table. IEEE Trans. Parallel Distrib. Syst. 25(3), 682–694 (2013)

16. Davis, E., Jaffe, J.M.: Algorithms for scheduling tasks on unrelated processors. J. ACM (JACM) 28(4), 721–736 (1981)

17. Bentley, J.L.: Multidimensional binary search trees used for associative searching. Commun. ACM 18(9), 509–517 (1975)

An Autonomy Loop for Dynamic HPC Job Time Limit Adjustment

Thomas Jakobsche[1], Osman Seckin Simsek[1], Jim Brandt[2,3], Ann Gentile[2,3], and Florina M. Ciorba[1(✉)]

[1] University of Basel, Basel, Switzerland
{thomas.jakobsche,osman.simsek,
florina.ciorba}@unibas.ch
[2] Sandia National Laboratories,
Livermore, CA, USA
{brandt,gentile}@sandia.gov
[3] Sandia National Laboratories, Albuquerque, NM, USA

Abstract. High Performance Computing (HPC) systems currently rely on fixed user-provided estimates of job execution times. These estimates are often inaccurate, resulting in inefficient resource use and the loss of unsaved work if a job times out shortly before reaching its next checkpoint. This work proposes a novel *feedback-driven autonomy loop* that dynamically adjusts the HPC job time limits based on the checkpointing progress reported by the applications. Our approach monitors checkpointing intervals of currently running jobs and the estimated start times of queued jobs, enabling informed decisions to either early cancel a job after its last completed checkpoint or extend the time limit sufficiently to accommodate the next checkpoint. The objective is to minimize *tail waste*, that is, the computation that occurs between the last checkpoint and the termination of a job, which is not saved and hence wasted. Through experiments conducted on a subset of a production workload trace, we show a 95% reduction of *tail waste*, which equates to saving approximately 1.3% of the total CPU time (cores × sec) that would otherwise be wasted. We propose various policies that combine early cancellation and time limit extension, achieving *tail waste* reduction while improving scheduling metrics such as weighted average job wait time. The proposed autonomy loop improves scheduling in HPC environments, where system job schedulers and applications collaborate to significantly reduce resource waste and improve scheduling performance.

Keywords: HPC · Observability · Resource Management · Job Scheduling · Checkpointing · Autonomy Loops

1 Introduction

HPC systems *monitoring* is a well-explored research topic, where large volumes of data are generated. Monitoring typically involves a systematic collection

W. E. Nagel et al. (Eds.): Euro-Par 2025, LNCS 15900, pp. 205–218, 2026.
https://doi.org/10.1007/978-3-031-99854-6_14

of metrics and the generation of alerts when thresholds are exceeded. *Operational Data Analytics* has traditionally relied on postmortem analysis or manual decisions, which is becoming increasingly unfeasible given the growing scale of systems [11]. The move towards *Observability* in HPC indicates that simply logging counters is insufficient due to complex and dynamic applications and system behavior. Application-specific insights are needed while jobs are still running, to enable dynamic diagnosis, proactive understanding of application behavior, and actionable feedback [26]. Autonomy loops in the form of feedback-driven mechanisms that combine monitoring, data analytics, and automated response have recently been proposed to streamline HPC operations [8]. One such approach is to adjust the time limits of running jobs, aiming to reduce wasted compute time due to misaligned timeouts of jobs that use fixed time interval checkpointing.

HPC systems often rely on fixed user-estimated job time limits that are known to be notoriously inaccurate and represent a persistent challenge in HPC [5, 21, 22]. Traditional job schedulers, such as Slurm, terminate a job if it exceeds the requested time provided by the user. This leads to wasted resources if the jobs time out before completion or just before their next checkpoint. In this work, we specifically focus on reducing *tail waste* (i.e., the unsaved computations made between the last completed checkpoint and the time limit).

Mechanisms like Slurm's `OverTimeLimit` offer a grace time interval that extends beyond the time limit [27], but are applied as a *blanket* approach to all jobs, without leveraging insights into the checkpoint progress of currently running applications; this could also mean giving extra time to applications that are 'stuck' and make no progress. While dynamic time interval checkpointing could potentially align checkpoint schedules to time limits (instead of aligning time limits to checkpoint schedules), it is not widely adopted by users [14]. These shortcomings result in wasted compute time, suboptimal resource usage, and an increased risk of partially lost work when jobs are terminated shortly before the next checkpoint.

We propose a novel mechanism for dynamically adjusting job time limits, implemented as an autonomy loop. By monitoring queued jobs and checkpoint intervals reported from executing applications, this mechanism either cancels jobs immediately after their last completed checkpoint or extends their time limit to accommodate the next checkpoint. This reduces resource waste while allowing jobs to align time limits with their checkpoints, thus completing more gracefully than otherwise. As a result, we achieve approximately 95% reduction of *tail waste* (i.e., the unsaved computations made between the last completed checkpoint and the time limit), saving approximately 1.3% of total CPU time (cores × sec) that would otherwise be wasted. We introduce policies for three different scenarios: `Early Cancellation`, which cancels a job after its last completed checkpoint that still fits into the initial time limit, `Time Limit Extension`, which always extends the time limit to allow the next checkpoint, and a `Hybrid` approach, which extends the time limit *only if* it does not delay other jobs, otherwise canceling the job early.

We evaluated the proposed solution on a subset of a production workload trace from `CINECA`'s Marconi supercomputer [9]. The extracted job configurations (approximately 800 jobs) were executed as synthetic jobs on a University research cluster with 20 computing nodes. We compare our proposed approach with the `Baseline` (the current state of the practice of no time limit adjustments), and quantify the impact of early cancellations, time limit extensions, and their hybrid combination. This work makes the following contributions.

1. **An autonomy loop for dynamic time limit adjustment**, which is a feedback-driven mechanism designed to continuously monitor the execution of jobs by checking their checkpointing progress, and the queued jobs to dynamically adjust the job time limits to reduce *tail waste*.
2. **Integrated the proposed solution with existing schedulers** (e.g. Slurm) through standard commands, reducing the *barrier to its adoption* in production HPC environments.
3. **Established and assessed various policies**: `Early cancellation`, `Time limit extension`, and a `Hybrid` approach, to effectively address the diverse scheduling priorities set by system operators.
4. **Empirically validated** the effectiveness of our methodology by deploying jobs from a production trace on a research HPC system, showing quantifiable improvements in minimizing wasted computing time.

The remainder of this paper is structured as follows. Section 2 offers background and positions our work. Section 3 presents the methodology. Section 4 contains the evaluation. The results are provided in Sect. 5 and discussed in Sect. 6. Section 7 reviews the related work, while Sect. 8 concludes the work.

2 Background

Fixed time interval checkpointing is often based on rule-of-thumb intervals or mathematical formulas for optimal checkpoint periods like Young-Daly [12,28]. Dynamic time interval checkpointing approaches adjust checkpointing in real-time and include *outside* approaches, such as distributed multithreaded checkpointing (DMTCP), which works without changes to system or applications [2]. The vast majority of HPC applications do not use dynamic checkpointing approaches due to perceived complexity by HPC users [6,14]. In our context, it is important that the real cost of checkpointing is not just the checkpoint I/O time but also (and often more importantly) the time to re-execute the work lost after a job interruption.

Recently, a number of datasets from Tier-0 supercomputers have been made public. M100 [9] and the PM100 subset [4,10] (which includes job configurations) from `CINECA`'s Marconi, F-DATA [3] from `RIKEN`'s Fugaku, and the data [13] from `NREL`'s Eagle supercomputer. In our experiments, we use job traces from the PM100 dataset; our method can easily be expanded to other datasets.

Slurm employs two schedulers for job execution: the main scheduler (`SchedMain`) which prioritizes the launch of higher priority jobs and the backfill scheduler (`SchedBackfill`) which evaluates all jobs (regardless of priority) and attempts to schedule those that do not delay the start of a higher priority job.

A foundational theoretical framework for self-managing systems was introduced in a seminal work on autonomic computing [19], which forms the basis of our use of feedback loops and dynamic adjustment mechanisms.

Our approach is positioned in relation to the concepts of *malleability* and *dynamism* in HPC as follows: Malleability refers to modifying the number of resources allocated to a job during execution, such as adding or removing compute nodes. In contrast, *dynamically adjusting job time limits* falls under the broader notion of dynamism rather than malleability [23].

3   Methodology

We describe next the proposed methodology, the time limit adjustment policies, and define *tail waste* and the scheduling metrics considered in this work.

Dynamic time limit adjustment is the novel idea of this work, for jobs that are already running. The concept is presented in Fig. 1. A misalignment of the user-provided time limit and the checkpoint schedule of an application leads to *tail waste*. By canceling a job early or extending its time limit, we can align the timeout to the checkpoint schedule and minimize *tail waste*. For this purpose, we define different policies for dynamic time limit adjustments: `Early Cancellation` which cancels jobs after the last completed checkpoint (the last checkpoint that fits successfully during the initial time limit). `Time Limit Extension` that always extends jobs to reach one more checkpoint regardless of other jobs in the queue (potentially delaying them). `Hybrid Approach` which makes best effort decisions between `Early Cancellation` and `Time Limit Extension` without delaying subsequent jobs.

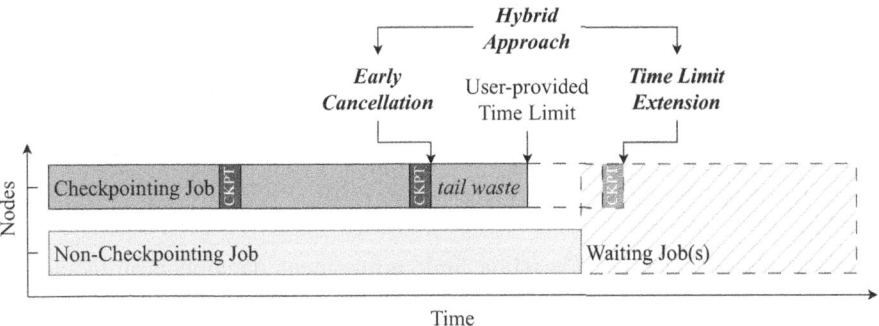

Fig. 1. The key mechanism at the core of the autonomy loop. For the checkpointing job, a misalignment of its user-provided time limit and checkpointing schedule leads to *tail waste*. The non-checkpointing job does not report checkpoint progress and is not further considered by the daemon. *Tail waste* is avoided by adjusting the time limit to align with the checkpoint schedule through different policies: The `Early cancellation` policy which cancels the job early after the last successful checkpoint, the `Time limit extension` policy which extends the time limit to the next checkpoint, even if this delays other jobs, and the `Hybrid approach` policy which either extends the job time limit if this does not delay other jobs or cancels the job early without delays.

We consider several **scheduling metrics** and **characteristics** in our analysis. These include job states (`COMPLETED` or `TIMEOUT`), makespan (the total time to complete a set of jobs), backfill statistics (either `SchedMain` or `SchedBackfill` reported by Slurm), and checkpoint counts (as reported by applications). We also use total CPU time, quantify *tail waste* reduction, and assess job scheduling through both *average job wait time* and *weighted average job wait time*, which are defined below.

CPU time is measured as the product of a job's execution time and the number of cores allocated to it. To accurately measure the efficiency of checkpointing, we introduce the concept of **tail waste**, defined as the CPU time spent on computation that is lost after the last checkpoint, when a job is terminated due to timeout. Thus, *tail waste* directly quantifies the unsaved computation. Jobs completed immediately after a checkpoint have zero *tail waste*. For a given workload, the total *tail waste* is the sum of the *tail waste* across all checkpointing jobs. In our context, non-checkpointing jobs are considered to have zero *tail waste* even if they timeout.

Finally, we examine scheduling efficiency through two distinct metrics: **average job wait time** and **weighted average job wait time**. While *average job wait time* is often used to evaluate scheduling policies, recent studies [7,17] have shown that it disproportionately favors smaller jobs, potentially causing longer delays for larger resource-intensive jobs common in HPC systems. To address this imbalance, we adopt the *weighted average job wait time*, where each job's wait time is weighted proportionally to its allocated resources (measured as *nodes × time*) to ensure fairness toward larger jobs.

4   Experimental Setup and Evaluation

We evaluated the proposed time limit adjustment method by implementing it within an autonomy loop and conducting experiments on a test system. In the following, we detail the experimental platform for conducting the experiments, the experimental setup, and the workload used to evaluate the effectiveness of our approach.

Daemon Architecture. The time limit adjustment daemon is implemented in `Python` (v. 3.9.6), runs on the login node, and interacts with Slurm commands to adjust job time limits. As shown in Fig. 2, checkpointing applications report checkpointing progress by writing timestamps to a temporary file. The daemon estimates the time of the next checkpoint based on the average interval between checkpoints reported by the application. Non-checkpointing jobs remain unchanged since they provide no progress information. The daemon polls the job queue (`squeue`) every 20 s to avoid overloading Slurm, tracks predicted start times and planned node allocations, and decides whether to use `Early Cancellation` or a `Time Limit Extension` via `scontrol`. This forms an autonomy loop among the application (reporting checkpoints), the daemon (calculating time-limit updates) and the Slurm central management daemon (`slurmctld`) (applying new limits). Checkpointing applications must include some mechanism for progress reporting; currently, we rely on writing a timestamp to a temporary file to mark each checkpoint.

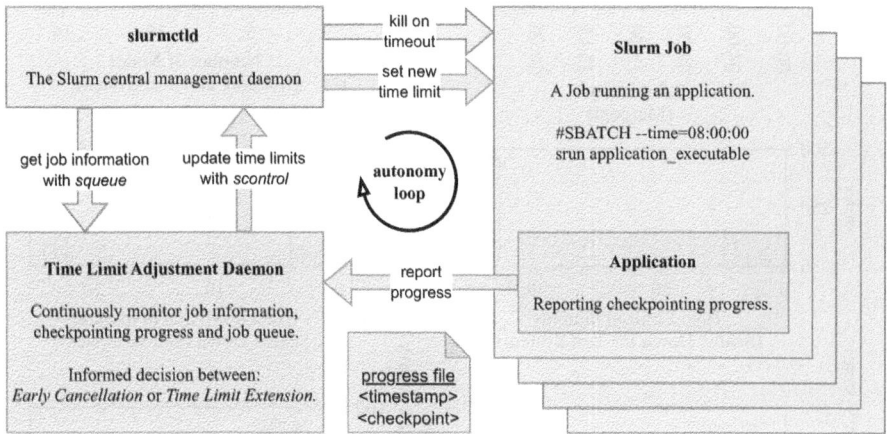

Fig. 2. Autonomy loop architecture and interactions of the time limit adjustment daemon, the applications and the Slurm central management daemon `slurmctld`. A Slurm job executing an application reports its checkpointing progress through a temporary text file to the daemon; the daemon estimates the job's checkpointing interval, predicts the time of the next checkpoint, retrieves job queue information with `squeue`, decides whether early cancellation or time limit extension is appropriate, and issues update commands to `slurmctld` through `scontrol`. Slurm then sets the new time limits for the job as issued by the daemon.

Experimental Setup. Adjusting the time limits of executing jobs requires administrator access to Slurm (in particular for `scontrol`). This prerequisite limits our ability to conduct extensive testing in a production environment, since enabling a daemon to autonomously modify job configurations on a large-scale system is potentially disruptive. However, existing Slurm simulators do not support this type of *dynamic* adjustment to individual job configurations. Consequently, we conducted experiments on a smaller research cluster, where we could implement and evaluate our approach without disturbing production users. This involved applying filters to extract a smaller set of jobs from the available Marconi workload trace, scaling down the jobs in time, and adapting them (as synthetic dummy jobs) to match the available resources of our test environment.

System Specifications. Experiments were conducted on a University research cluster running `Slurm` (v.23.11) with a default scheduling configuration and using 20 `Intel Xeon E5-2640` nodes along with a login node and a storage node. Two networks support system operations: a 100 Gbit/s `Omni-Path` network for communication among compute nodes, and a 10 Gbit/s `Ethernet` network for user and administrator access. A two-level fat tree topology forms the basis of the `Omni-Path` interconnect.

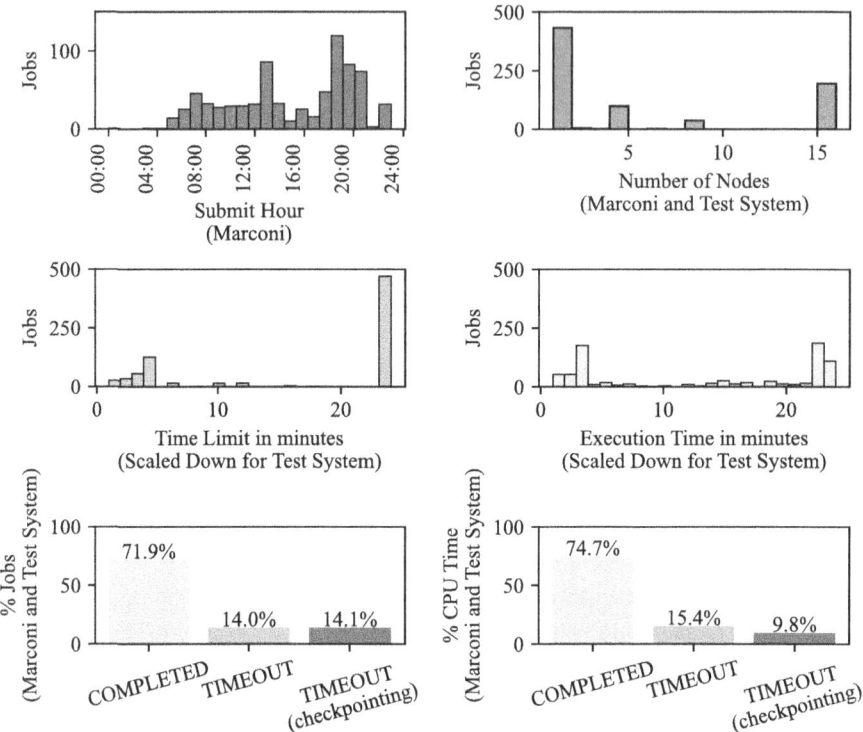

Fig. 3. Overview of the 773 jobs selected and scaled down in time (reducing 1 h to 1 min) from the PM100 dataset. Shown are: the original submission time on Marconi, the original number of requested nodes, the scaled down user provided time limits, the scaled down execution time, the percentage of jobs by state, and the percentage of CPU time by state.

Workload Construction. We derive our workload from the Marconi PM100 dataset of 1,074,576 jobs submitted between May and October 2020 [4,10]. We focused on the partition, queue, and month with most jobs (`Partition=1`, `Queue=1`, and `Month=May`). We filtered for jobs that were executed exclusively on their assigned nodes, with `COMPLETED` or `TIMEOUT` states, and ran for at least one hour, resulting in 773 jobs, shown in Fig. 3.

We adapted the Marconi jobs as synthetic sleep jobs with the same configurations; jobs that timeout at the maximum time limit of 24 h (109 jobs) are adapted as checkpointing jobs that periodically report checkpoints at fixed time intervals. To preserve the structure and dynamics of jobs while allowing the opportunity to study the impact of time limit adjustment on our smaller test system, we scaled job durations by a factor of 60 (one hour becomes one minute) and release all jobs at $t = 0$. Jobs that were executed for less than an hour on Marconi were previously filtered out because after scaling down in time, they would only run for a few seconds, which is too short for meaningful experiments.

The `checkpointing jobs` in our workload report successful checkpoints every 7 min to mimic a fixed time interval checkpoint schedule that is misaligned with the job timeouts, though this interval can be adjusted to other values.

5   Results

We present experimental results comparing the proposed job time limit adjustment against a baseline scenario (no time limit adjustments). The main findings are summarized in Table 1, while the key differences between the policies evaluated are illustrated in Fig. 4. These results are further analyzed and discussed in Sect. 6.

Table 1. Comparison of scheduling scenarios under different daemon policies.

Metric (unit of measure)	Baseline	Early Cancellation	Time Limit Extension	Hybrid Approach
TIMEOUT (jobs)	217	108	108	108
Early canceled (jobs)	–	**109**	–	**62**
Extended time limit (jobs)	–	–	**109**	**47**
COMPLETED (jobs)	556	556	556	556
Total Jobs (jobs)	773	773	773	773
Slurm SchedMain (operations)	203	189	202	201
Slurm SchedBackfill (operations)	570	584	571	572
Total Checkpoints (count)	**327**	**327**	**436**	**374**
Average Wait Time (sec)	35,727	38,513	36,850	39,541
Weighted Avg Wait Time (nodes × sec)	42,349	41,666	43,001	41,923
Tail Waste CPU Time (cores × sec)	**875,520**	**43,120**	**45,020**	**44,000**
Total CPU Time (cores × sec)	58,816,100	58,073,280	59,804,280	58,795,320
Workload Makespan (sec)	90,948	89,424	92,420	89,901

Job Outcomes and Checkpointing. Each policy in Table 1 runs the same 773 jobs: 556 always COMPLETED and 217 TIMEOUT under the *Baseline*. Of these 217, 109 are assumed to use checkpointing (they timeout at the maximum time limit on Marconi), while 108 are assumed to be non-checkpointing and remain TIMEOUT under all new policies. Early Cancellation immediately cancels those 109 checkpointing jobs after their last completed checkpoint; Time Limit Extension extends them to the next checkpoint; and Hybrid cancels 62 and extends 47 jobs. Consequently, *Baseline* and *Early Cancellation* both achieve 327 successful checkpoints, while *Hybrid* yields 374, and *Time Limit Extension* reaches 436.

Tail Waste Reduction. In our experiments (Table 1, Fig. 4), the baseline scenario incurred 875,520 (*cores × seconds*) of tail waste. In comparison: Early Cancellation cut tail waste to 43,120 (*cores × seconds*), a reduction of 95.07%, also saving approximately 1.3% of total CPU time by canceling jobs immediately after their last completed checkpoint before the timeout. Time Limit

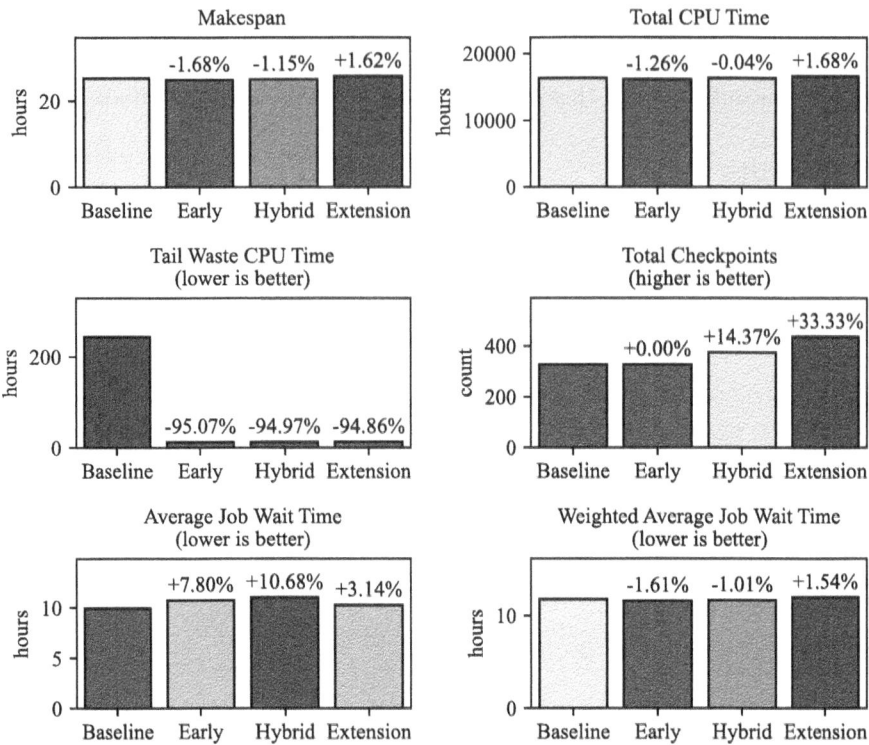

Fig. 4. Comparison of scheduling metrics for the different time limit adjustment policies (Early Cancellation, Time Limit Extension, and Hybrid approach) against the Baseline (no time limit adjustment).

Extension achieved a 94.86% reduction, replacing what would have been wasted CPU time with additional *useful* work through an additional checkpoint. Hybrid reduced tail waste by 94.97% by combining early cancellation with selective time limit extensions (only extending if it does not delay subsequent jobs). All three policies cut tail waste by approximately 95%. However, only Early Cancellation explicitly shows the approximately 1.3% CPU time saving; Time Limit Extension and Hybrid also save the same wasted time but use it for extra checkpoints, which in the case of Time Limit Extension even increases the total CPU time in the results.

Makespan and CPU Time. Compared to the baseline, Early Cancellation reduces the makespan by 1.68%, while Hybrid approach reduces it by 1.15%, shown in Fig. 4. Since Time Limit Extension always extends all jobs to complete another checkpoint, it increases the makespan by 1.62% (of useful work because it was saved through a checkpoint). Early Cancellation reduces total CPU time by approximately 1.3% (total CPU time saved by reducing *tail waste*). Hybrid approach remains close to the baseline, and Time Limit Extension increases CPU time by 1.68%.

Job Wait Times and Backfilling. The *average job wait time* increases by 7.8% for `Early Cancellation`, 10.68% for `Hybrid` approach, and 3.14% for `Time Limit Extension`. However, the *weighted average job wait time* decreases by −1.61% for `Early Cancellation` and −1.01% for `Hybrid` approach, and increases by +1.54% for `Time Limit Extension`, as shown in Fig. 4. The only notable difference in the backfill statistics is in the `Early Cancellation` policy, showing a slight increase of 10 jobs started by Slurm's backfill scheduler `SchedBackfill` instead of the priority scheduler `SchedMain`, as shown in Table 1.

6   Discussion

The `Early Cancellation`, `Time Limit Extension`, and `Hybrid` policies achieve the goal of reducing *tail waste*, by approximately 95%, saving approximately 1.3% of CPU time that would be wasted. Compared to the `Baseline`, with misaligned timeouts, `Early Cancellation` achieves the highest reduction in total CPU time and makespan by proactively freeing resources earlier, while keeping the same number of checkpoints. `Time Limit Extension` achieves more checkpoints, but does so at the cost of increasing total CPU time and makespan because it extends jobs to accommodate an additional checkpoint; it is suited for environments that prioritize additional *useful* work even if others jobs are delayed. The `Hybrid` approach combines both strategies, freeing resources early when another checkpoint does not fit within the original time limit and extending time limits only if it does not delay other jobs.

Benefits and Trade-Offs. The proposed policies significantly reduce wasted computing time. These benefits scale with the proportion of jobs that use checkpoints, more checkpointing jobs translate into more potentially saved *tail waste*. However, policies for extending jobs must be carefully calibrated to avoid delaying other queued jobs. For large-scale HPC centers, `Early Cancellation` and `Hybrid` are more attractive because they reduce *tail waste* and preserve or improve scheduling performance without delaying other jobs. `Time Limit Extension` is preferred where every possible checkpoint is important and the increase of total CPU time and makespan is acceptable.

It is important to note that the higher total CPU time under `Time Limit Extension` reflects additional *useful* work via successful checkpoints rather than wasted resources. Although *average job wait time* rises for all policies, largely because this metric is skewed by many small jobs, *weighted average job wait time* decreases with `Early Cancellation` and `Hybrid`, denoting a more efficient use of resources and job *scheduling*, achieved by freeing resources earlier and only extending the time limits of running jobs if they do not delay other jobs. In contrast, `Time Limit Extension` increases *weighted average job wait time* because it extends the running jobs and potentially delays other queued jobs.

Impact on Scheduling with Backfilling. Only `Early Cancellation` has a significant impact on whether a job was started by the `SchedMain` or `Schedbackfill` scheduler, by slightly increasing the number of backfilled jobs by 10. This is explained by the increased *free resource windows* created by `Early Cancellation` (which frees resources earlier than expected at the start of the job), allowing other jobs to be started sooner by the backfill scheduler. No such impact is observable with the other policies. This is also explained by the fact that `Hybrid` approach and `Time Limit Extension` do not always cancel jobs early, but also extend their time limits, possibly extending an already running job into an empty resource window that would otherwise be used for backfilling.

Limitations. A limitation of our approach is the reliance on accurate checkpointing progress reporting by applications. If jobs delay or misreport their checkpointing events, or if checkpointing intervals vary significantly, the daemon's prediction of the next checkpointing time may become unreliable. Additionally, excessive use of the `Time Limit Extension` policy could adversely impact overall scheduling efficiency by delaying the start of subsequent jobs. Adoption also poses a challenge, as it remains uncertain whether users and application developers will consistently report checkpointing progress. However, implementing basic checkpoint reporting, such as writing a timestamp to a temporary file after a checkpoint, is significantly simpler than adopting dynamic checkpointing mechanisms, which often require code restructuring. This relative simplicity may encourage adoption, especially since HPC users tend to favor practical, low-effort solutions for checkpointing [6,14].

7   Related Work

Changing the job scheduler has been the focus of recent work, which proposed adapting scheduling decisions based on real-time monitoring of I/O usage [16] to avoid file system bottlenecks. This approach integrates `LDMS` (Lightweight Distributed Metric Service) [1] and Slurm to capture real-time `Lustre` throughput and job-level I/O usage. Another related approach is to leverage deep reinforcement learning (DRL) for the prediction of the remaining execution time [25]. Using a neural network to estimate the remaining execution time of each job by analyzing intermediate logs, it employs a DRL policy to decide which jobs to schedule, preempt, or kill. Other work focused on predicting failures and triggering early termination [29], leveraging a neural network trained on system metrics and job history to predict job evolution and states. The use of reinforcement learning to dynamically schedule jobs has also recently been proposed [30]. The approach relies only on minimal manual interventions or expert knowledge; it can continuously learn and improve scheduling decisions and policies over time and uses a kernel-based neural network. Our proposed approach differs from the above approaches in that we do not directly change the configuration or decision making of the job scheduler. Rather, we indirectly change the scheduling of jobs by adjusting the time limits of jobs that are *already* running.

Another line of research involves predicting job time limits to provide better accuracy for backfilling. A hierarchical classification scheme has been proposed to improve the user-provided estimates [20]. This approach avoids underestimation by making a prediction that is higher than a specified percentage of the observed job execution times. Another approach focused on the prediction of time limits [24] separated the kill time from the time limit prediction to avoid jobs being killed because system predictions were wrong. The predictions were achieved by averaging the execution times of the last two jobs by the same user. In contrast to these efforts, which predict job execution times, we focus on the novel perspective of adjusting the time limits of *already* running jobs. Our approach exploits knowledge about the progress of the application and the workload in the job queue, which becomes available only at execution time. We do not change configurations of jobs waiting in the queue, but directly incorporate progress information and change time limits of jobs that are already executing.

There are also recent solutions such as the Maestro-based emergency backup (MEB), enabling users to mark arrays inside the application which will be dumped to persistent storage in case of unexpected interruptions [15]. This emergency backup is a similar effort to save *tail waste* and highlights the importance of this topic.

8   Conclusion and Future Work

This work proposed a mechanism to implement an autonomy loop that dynamically adjusts HPC job time limits based on observed checkpointing progress. By analyzing checkpointing intervals of executing jobs and monitoring queued jobs, a time limit adjustment daemon decides whether to extend a job's time limit or terminate it gracefully, thereby minimizing wasted computation. Experimental results show that our adaptive policy significantly reduces resource waste from timeouts, cutting *tail waste* (i.e., the unsaved computation occurring after the last checkpoint before the timeout) by approximately 95%. This translates into savings of approximately 1.3% in total CPU time that would otherwise be wasted. These results highlight the potential of incorporating real-time, application-specific signals into autonomous control loops to improve resource efficiency and scheduling decisions in HPC environments.

Future work could incorporate real-time I/O load to better account for checkpointing slowdowns due to system noise; enhance checkpoint prediction using historical or application-specific data; and scale up experiments using real workloads in production environments. As HPC workloads and system complexity continue to grow, fully automated feedback-driven mechanisms, such as the dynamic time limit adjustment and its future extensions, will become increasingly vital for effective resource management and scheduling optimization.

Acknowledgements and Artifact Availability. Sandia National Laboratories is a multimission laboratory managed and operated by National Technology & Engineering Solutions of Sandia, LLC, a wholly owned subsidiary of Honeywell International Inc., for the U.S. Department of Energy's National Nuclear Security Administration under contract DE-NA0003525.

This paper describes objective technical results and analysis. Any subjective views or opinions that might be expressed in the paper do not necessarily represent the views of the U.S. Department of Energy or the United States Government.

The artifact is available in the Zenodo repository [18].

Disclosure of Interests. The authors have no competing interests to declare that are relevant to the content of this article.

References

1. Agelastos, A., et al.: The lightweight distributed metric service: a scalable infrastructure for continuous monitoring of large scale computing systems and applications. In: SC 2014: Proceedings of the International Conference for High Performance Computing, Networking, Storage and Analysis, pp. 154–165. IEEE (2014)
2. Ansel, J., Arya, K., Cooperman, G.: DMTCP: transparent checkpointing for cluster computations and the desktop. In: 2009 IEEE International Symposium on Parallel & Distributed Processing, pp. 1–12. IEEE (2009)
3. Antici, F., Bartolini, A., Domke, J., Kiziltan, Z., Yamamoto, K.: F-DATA: A Fugaku Workload Dataset for Job-Centric Predictive Modelling in HPC Systems (2024)
4. Antici, F., Seyedkazemi Ardebili, M., Bartolini, A., Kiziltan, Z.: PM100: a job power consumption dataset of a large-scale production HPC system. In: Proceedings of the SC 2023 Workshops of the International Conference on High Performance Computing, Network, Storage, and Analysis, pp. 1812–1819 (2023)
5. Bailey Lee, C., Schwartzman, Y., Hardy, J., Snavely, A.: Are user runtime estimates inherently inaccurate? In: Feitelson, D.G., Rudolph, L., Schwiegelshohn, U. (eds.) JSSPP 2004. LNCS, vol. 3277, pp. 253–263. Springer, Heidelberg (2005). https://doi.org/10.1007/11407522_14
6. Bautista-Gomez, L., Benoit, A., Di, S., Herault, T., Robert, Y., Sun, H.: A Survey on Checkpointing Strategies: Should We Always Checkpoint à la Young/Daly? Future Generation Computer Systems (2024)
7. Boëzennec, R., Dufossé, F., Pallez, G.: Qualitatively analyzing optimization objectives in the design of HPC resource manager. ACM Trans. Model. Perform. Eval. Comput. Syst. **9**(4), 1–28 (2024)
8. Boito, F., et al.: Autonomy loops for monitoring, operational data analytics, feedback, and response in HPC operations. In: 2023 IEEE International Conference on Cluster Computing Workshops (CLUSTER Workshops), pp. 37–43. IEEE (2023)
9. Borghesi, A., et al.: M100 ExaData: a Data Collection Campaign on the CINECA's Marconi100 Tier-0 Supercomputer (2023)
10. Borghesi, A., et al.: M100 Dataset 1: from 20-03 to 20-12 (2023)
11. Brandt, J., Ciorba, F., Gentile, A., Ott, M., Wilde, T.: Driving HPC Operations With Holistic Monitoring and Operational Data Analytics (Dagstuhl Seminar 23171). Dagstuhl Reports (2023)
12. Daly, J.T.: A higher order estimate of the optimum checkpoint interval for restart dumps. Futur. Gener. Comput. Syst. **22**(3), 303–312 (2006)
13. Duplyakin, Dmitry, Menear, Kevin: NREL Eagle Supercomputer Jobs (2023)
14. El-Sayed, N., Schroeder, B.: Understanding practical tradeoffs in HPC checkpoint-scheduling policies. IEEE Trans. Dependable Secure Comput. **15**(2), 336–350 (2016)
15. Esposito, A., Haine, C., Mohammed, A.: Emergency backup for scientific applications. In: 2022 IEEE/ACM Third International Symposium on Checkpointing for Supercomputing (SuperCheck), pp. 1–8. IEEE (2022)

16. Goponenko, A.V., Izadpanah, R., Brandt, J.M., Dechev, D.: Towards workload-adaptive scheduling for HPC clusters. In: 2020 IEEE International Conference on Cluster Computing (CLUSTER), pp. 449–453. IEEE (2020)

17. Goponenko, A.V., Lamar, K., Peterson, C., Allan, B.A., Brandt, J.M., Dechev, D.: Metrics for packing efficiency and fairness of HPC cluster batch job scheduling. In: 2022 IEEE 34th International Symposium on Computer Architecture and High Performance Computing (SBAC-PAD), pp. 241–252. IEEE (2022)

18. Jakobsche, T., Simsek, O.S., Brandt, J., Gentile, A., Ciorba, F.M.: Artifact of the Paper: An Autonomy Loop for Dynamic HPC Job Time Limit Adjustment (2025). https://doi.org/10.5281/zenodo.15585217

19. Kephart, J.O., Chess, D.M.: The vision of autonomic computing. Computer **36**(1), 41–50 (2003)

20. Lamar, K., Goponenko, A., Peterson, C., Allan, B.A., Brandt, J.M., Dechev, D.: Backfilling HPC jobs with a multimodal-aware predictor. In: 2021 IEEE International Conference on Cluster Computing (CLUSTER), pp. 618–622. IEEE (2021)

21. Patel, T., Liu, Z., Kettimuthu, R., Rich, P., Allcock, W., Tiwari, D.: Job characteristics on large-scale systems: long-term analysis, quantification, and implications. In: SC20: International Conference for High Performance Computing, Networking, Storage and Analysis, pp. 1–17. IEEE (2020)

22. Soysal, M., Berghoff, M., Klusáček, D., Streit, A.: On the quality of wall time estimates for resource allocation prediction. In: Workshop Proceedings of the 48th International Conference on Parallel Processing, pp. 1–8 (2019)

23. Tarraf, A., et al.: Malleability in modern HPC systems: current experiences, challenges, and future opportunities. IEEE Trans. Parallel Distrib. Syst. (2024)

24. Tsafrir, D., Etsion, Y., Feitelson, D.G.: Backfilling using system-generated predictions rather than user runtime estimates. IEEE Trans. Parallel Distrib. Syst. **18**(6), 789–803 (2007)

25. Wang, Q., Zhang, H., Qu, C., Shen, Y., Liu, X., Li, J.: Rlschert: an HPC job scheduler using deep reinforcement learning and remaining time prediction. Appl. Sci. **11**(20), 9448 (2021)

26. Yokelson, D., et al.: SOMA: observability, monitoring, and in situ analytics for exascale applications. Concurr. Comput. Pract. Exp. **36**(19), e8141 (2024)

27. Yoo, A.B., Jette, M.A., Grondona, M.: SLURM: simple Linux utility for resource management. In: Feitelson, D., Rudolph, L., Schwiegelshohn, U. (eds.) JSSPP 2003. LNCS, vol. 2862, pp. 44–60. Springer, Heidelberg (2003). https://doi.org/10.1007/10968987_3

28. Young, J.W.: A first order approximation to the optimum checkpoint interval. Commun. ACM **17**(9), 530–531 (1974)

29. Zasadziński, M., Muntés-Mulero, V., Solé, M., Carrera, D., Ludwig, T.: Early termination of failed HPC jobs through machine and deep learning. In: Aldinucci, M., Padovani, L., Torquati, M. (eds.) Euro-Par 2018. LNCS, vol. 11014, pp. 163–177. Springer, Cham (2018). https://doi.org/10.1007/978-3-319-96983-1_12

30. Zhang, D., Dai, D., He, Y., Bao, F.S., Xie, B.: RLScheduler: an automated HPC batch job scheduler using reinforcement learning. In: SC20: International Conference for High Performance Computing, Networking, Storage and Analysis, pp. 1–15. IEEE (2020)

PRIORITY-BF: A Task Manager for Priority-Based Scheduling

Ana Gainaru[1] , Scott Klasky[1] , and Guillaume Pallez[2]([⊠])

[1] Oak Ridge National Laboratory, Oak Ridge, TN, USA
{gainarua,klasky}@ornl.gov
[2] Inria Rennes, Rennes, France
guillaume.pallez@inria.fr

Abstract. The increasing demand for computational resources, particularly in High-Performance Computing environments, necessitates to rethink how we handle job scheduling strategies. This work addresses the challenge of managing concurrent jobs with differing priorities on overloaded parallel systems, where strict QoS constraints are often difficult for users to define. Our solution relies on a qualitative description of priorities and pulls from two key approaches: the EASY-BF algorithm and the CONSERVATIVE Backfilling algorithms. This solution improves the response time for high-priority jobs by 50% without affecting the overall system utilization. We show its applicability in several critical scenarios such as High-Performance Computing (HPC) resource management and in-situ computing.

Keywords: Scheduling · HPC · Priority execution · Backfilling algorithm

1 Introduction

HPC centers consistently operate at near-peak utilization, often exceeding 95%. This high utilization, while seemingly efficient, translates to substantial wait times for users, particularly for large-scale jobs [16]. Figure 1 shows the evolution of the median wait time for different types of jobs in two HPC systems in Argonne National Laboratory: Mira and Polaris (more details on these machines are provided in Sect. 3.1). Yet, HPC systems need to be overloaded, indeed it is a well-known fact that users overestimate their real machine occupation, and hence if the system is to be used fully, by design the queue has to be theoretically much more loaded than what the system can manage [8].

Faced with resource limitations, it is critical to efficiently decide how to allocate finite computational resources among competing demands. Several computing domains are prompting the exploration of prioritization mechanisms. In "Urgent Computing" Beckman et al. [1] discuss the idea of having "tokens" to grant certain jobs preferential access to resources, allowing them to bypass queues and execute with minimal delay. This approach acknowledges that some

W. E. Nagel et al. (Eds.): Euro-Par 2025, LNCS 15900, pp. 219–232, 2026.
https://doi.org/10.1007/978-3-031-99854-6_15

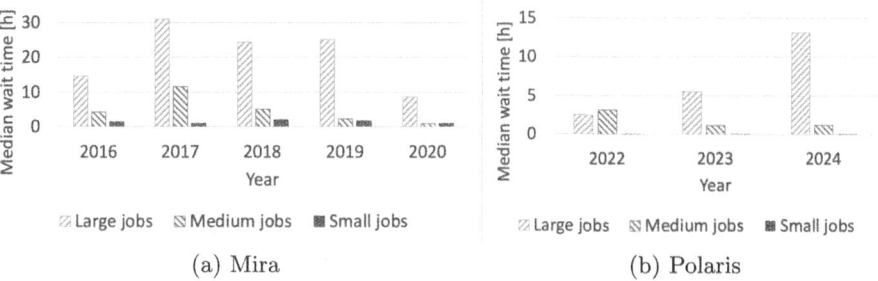

Fig. 1. Jobs submitted to Mira and Polaris, two HPC systems, are exhibiting increasing median wait times of hours, with large jobs being more affected.

computations are time-sensitive and critical, demanding immediate attention. This is also true when periodic generation of data triggers a lot of various analysis function, particularly when the runtime of these analysis functions are extremely input-dependent [7]. Example include data generated by large experimental instruments such as the Square Kilometer Array (SKA). The SKA will generate vast quantities of data that must be processed by several massive workflows within a limited timeframe before new data arrives [13]. Similarly, in in-situ computing, iterative simulations generate data that triggers a large variety of analytical functions [12]. With limited computational resources compared to the number of desired analyses, a priority-driven approach is crucial. Users may want to prioritize analyses based on the simulation's current state, past results, or the last execution time of specific functions [12].

In this work, we study the general question of how to deal with concurrent jobs submitted on a parallel systems, when those jobs do not have the same importance to the users/admins, and when there may or may not be time to execute all the jobs. Through discussions with HPC users, we realized that users often struggle to articulate precise Quality of Service (QoS) requirements. Specifying exact response times for different job types proves difficult, especially as workload patterns fluctuate. Users often prefer qualitative constraints over rigid quantitative metrics. This necessitates a scheduling solution that can adapt to varying workloads and accommodate imprecise user preferences.

Motivating Example: The main algorithms used for resource management in HPC centers are EASY-BF [11] and CONSERVATIVE [14], two backfilling-based algorithms that protect against starvation. In EASY-BF, at each event (end of a job, arrival of a new job), a schedule is recomputed with the constraint that the non-running job with the largest priority cannot be delayed by scheduling a later job prior to this job. In CONSERVATIVE, a job with lower priority cannot delay any job with higher priority. In these algorithms, jobs priority are often based on First Come First Served (FCFS) order, i.e. *release time*, but there exist other implementations of priorities in EASY-BF[1], with different cost functions.

---

[1] https://slurm.schedmd.com/priority_multifactor.html, Accessed January 2025.

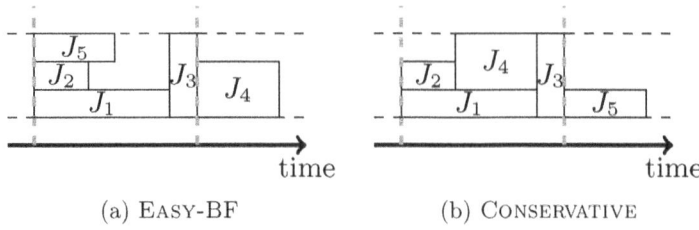

(a) Easy-BF   (b) Conservative

Fig. 2. In a scenario where we have only a limited time to perform as many jobs as possible, and if J_4 has a larger priority than J_5, we would like an algorithm that behaves like Conservative in this case.

While HPC centers tend to favor Easy-BF because it usually provides better performance than Conservative it has limitation when jobs have different priorities and there exist QOS-like constraints.

Consider a set of jobs $\{J_1 = (1, 5, 1), J_2 = (1, 2, 1), J_3 = (3, 1, 1), J_4 = (2, 3, 1), J_5 = (1, 2, 2)\}$, where $J = (n, t, p)$ means that job J uses n nodes, during a time t and has priority p. Consider a deadline of 6. The Gantt chart of both Easy-BF and Conservative is plotted in Fig. 2. In this scenario, Conservative allows to execute more jobs of priority 1.

The core idea of the solution that we propose in the rest of the document is quite simple and uses idea from both Easy-BF and Conservative. When there are multiple priority levels, we propose to use Easy-BF within a priority level, and Conservative when backfilling may impact jobs with a higher priority.

Contributions: Our design philosophy is guided by two core principles: simplicity and robustness. Simplicity ensures that users and system administrators understand the rationale behind scheduling decisions, fostering trust and accountability. This requires an interpretable algorithm that clearly communicates its logic. Robustness allow the system to accommodate diverse workloads. Our algorithm needs to be robust to real scenarios where users do not know exactly their requirements. Hence we rely on qualitative constraints rather than rigid specifications.

To address these challenges, we propose an extension of existing backfilling algorithms: Easy-BF and Conservative. They are well-established scheduling algorithms known for their simplicity and efficiency. Our extension introduces a mechanism for incorporating job importance, allowing users to assign priority levels at the granularity of the job. When all jobs share the same priority, our algorithm seamlessly reverts to the standard Easy-BF behavior. This ensures backward compatibility and maintains the algorithm's proven performance. The paper makes the following contributions:

- A novel priority-based job scheduling algorithm, based on the Easy-BF framework, designed to minimize response times for high-priority jobs while maintaining overall system utilization.

- Simulation evaluation of our algorithm when used for scheduling parallel jobs in an High-Performance Computing (HPC) clusters compared to classical state of the art approaches.
- Deep dive into using the algorithm for scheduling in-situ and in-transit tasks for time sensitive analysis of instrument or simulation data.

In Sect. 2 we discuss our new scheduling strategy. We then present two use-cases to motivate it: scheduling of large jobs in HPC in Sect. 3, then overloaded in-situ/in-transit computing in Sect. 4. We present some related work on priority/Quality of Service (QoS) based scheduling in Sect. 5 before providing concluding remarks in Sect. 6.

2   PRIORITY-BF: A Hierarchical Scheduler Design

PRIORITY-BF was designed with a will to be unfair in scheduling mechanisms. Specifically in scenarios where the scheduler will not be able to execute all jobs, and when some should be treated as first or second-class citizens. We measure the efficiency of this scheduler through a lexicographic order: for a given objective (response time, work done in a limited time frame), we first want to optimize for the jobs with the highest priority, then for those with lower priorities.

In addition to the obvious efficiency objectives, our scheduler design was led by several fundamental principles:

1. **Robustness**: it is well known that the information that one can collect is often inaccurate. The algorithm that we design has to be robust to inaccurate information.
2. **Simplicity**: the scheduler needs to be simple in terms of implementation, but also in terms of usage. Indeed, with the democratization of parallel computing, asking too much information from a user can be counter-productive. Instead we wanted simple qualitative information ("high/low" priority) when qualifying job priorities instead of quantitative information ("response time below X min").

High-level Algorithm Presentation. Rather than reinventing the wheel, we chose to rely on existing and proven solutions: EASY-BF and CONSERVATIVE.

The main idea of the algorithm is to keep several queues, each queue corresponding to job priorities (by decreasing order). The global algorithm satisfies the following properties, reading from the queue by increasing index:

- Within a queue, jobs are scheduled with an EASY-BF strategy
- Between queues, jobs are scheduled conservatively: jobs from a queue with a higher index cannot delay jobs from a queue with a lower index.

Contrarily to the original EASY-BF and CONSERVATIVE (that use FCFS as priority strategy), this algorithm does not guarantee a *no-starvation* strategy. On the contrary, some jobs from the queue with the lowest index could very well never be executed. In its extreme configurations, this scheduling strategy simplifies to the EASY-BF algorithm when all jobs share a single priority level, and to the CONSERVATIVE algorithm when every job possesses a unique priority.

Implementation. Our algorithm employs multiple priority queues, with each submitted job assigned a numerical priority value in ascending order, where 0 denotes the highest priority. Within each priority queue, jobs are initially considered for scheduling in the order given by EASY-BF. The first job is rigidly scheduled (meaning its start time cannot be delayed) into the earliest available time slot that accommodates its resource requirements. When considering backfilling, the algorithm prioritizes scheduling jobs that can start early within the same priority queue. Critically, however, a lower-priority job will never be allowed to delay the potential backfilling of a higher-priority job, even if the higher-priority job could only start at a later time slot.

3   Use Case: Application to Parallel Job Scheduling

In this first use-case we consider the general HPC job scheduling problem. Jobs submitted on HPC machines have very high wait times that continue to increase especially for large jobs (Fig. 1). The consequence is that *Users are now submitting medium-sized jobs because the wait times for larger sizes tend to be longer* [16]. The question that we aim to solve is the following: can we propose a job scheduler which solves the problem of re-balancing large jobs response time without manually tuning and without trading-off on system utilization?

While EASY-BF treats all jobs in a similar manner, we use the PRIORITY-BF algorithm to standardize response times across jobs of varying sizes.

3.1   Evaluation Scenarios

To be able to evaluate the possible impact of our scheduling strategy, we use execution logs[2] from three clusters at Argonne National Laboratory: 1) Mira is a 10-petaflops IBM Blue Gene/Q supercomputer with more than 5 billion computing hours allocated each year, in production between 2012 and 2019; 2) Polaris is a 34-petaflops 560 nodes system operating since 2022; and 3) Theta is an 11.7-petaflops system operating since 2017 consisting of two separate architectures: 24 racks of Intel CPU (Theta KLN) and 7 raks of Nvidia GPUs (Theta GPU). We tag jobs with three different categories for PRIORITY-BF: large jobs have the highest priority, medium sized jobs have medium priority, and smallest jobs have low priority. We define large, medium, and small jobs similar to the study in [16]. For the Mira supercomputer the three classes are represented by jobs with more than $n_1 = 8K$ nodes, jobs with a number of nodes between $2K$ and $8K$ and jobs with less than $n_2 = 2K$ nodes respectively. For the other platforms we choose n_1 and n_2 so that, jobs requesting a number N of nodes s.t. $N > n_1$ (resp. $N \leq n_2$) corresponds to 10% largest (resp. 80% smallest) jobs. Table 1 presents statistics of the four logs we analyzed and the n_1, n_2 values for each system.

Figure 3 shows the percentage of core hours spent running jobs of different size. Even though the large jobs represent a small percentage of the total jobs,

---

[2] https://reports.alcf.anl.gov/data, Accessed January 2025.

Table 1. Log characteristics for 4 systems at ANL that was used to analyze the performance of our scheduler compared with current solutions in HPC.

System	#Nodes	#Cores/Node	Start Date	End Date	#Jobs	n_1 nodes	n_2 nodes
Mira	49,152	16	2016-01-01	2020-12-31	224,003	2k	8k
Polaris	560	64	2022-08-09	2024-12-31	519,296	32	128
Theta-KNL	4,392	64	2017-07-01	2023-12-31	540,623	256	1024
Theta-GPU	24	1	2020-09-22	2023-12-31	147,658	3	8

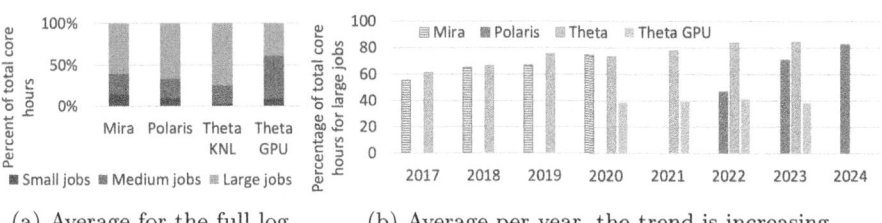

(a) Average for the full log   (b) Average per year, the trend is increasing

Fig. 3. Large jobs represent the majority of node hours on an HPC center.

they represent the majority of the core hours spent on the systems with the exception of Theta-GPU. Moreover, the yearly trend shows a slight increase in the percentage of core hours consumed by large jobs. Theta-GPU has been designed for AI training codes and has a different profile than the other systems so we expect the results to be slightly different. We study, in the next sections, the impact of PRIORITY-BF on the utilization of the system, and on response time, compared to the standard EASY-BF strategy used in HPC centers, namely:

- EASY-BF with no priority, the default scheduler in most HPC centers that uses a FCFS strategy with backfilling choosing jobs that can start the earliest (called EASY-BF).
- an EASY-BF version that was configured to consider different priorities for the backfilling algorithm (called LJF, for Largest Job First).

3.2 Evaluation Methodology

To evaluate our proposed priority-based scheduling algorithm, we employed ScheduleFlow[3], a lightweight simulator we developed for studying the performance of scheduling algorithms. ScheduleFlow inherently supports fundamental scheduling policies such as FCFS, Shortest Job First (SJF), and Largest Job First (LJF), coupled with CONSERVATIVE and EASY-BF backfilling strategies. We augmented ScheduleFlow to execute PRIORITY-BF. This simulator focuses on core scheduling logic without incorporating hardware specifics, I/O operations, or network considerations, an intentional design choice as our experiments

---
[3] Code available at https://github.com/ORNL-Inria/PriorityBF.

utilize execution logs containing precise runtimes, negating the need for variability modeling through proxy applications. ScheduleFlow operates by processing HPC workload logs in seven-day intervals, simulating job scheduling and backfilling under various configurations based on the recorded submission times.

Validation: We compared our ScheduleFlow simulations using the standard Easy-BF algorithm against the actual execution of jobs on the real-world HPC system (based on the log). While perfect accuracy is unattainable in any simulation due to unknown factors such as the initial state of waiting queues and unscheduled node downtimes, our results demonstrated a decent correlation. Overall, the simulation exhibited a marginally higher system utilization and maintained a comparable ratio in the response times across all jobs when contrasted with the real scheduler's performance. This initial comparison provides confidence in the fidelity of our simulation environment for further evaluating our priority-based scheduling extensions.

Evaluation: We focus on several metrics: i) The relationship between job size and response time; ii) Overall system utilization, iii) Analysis of performance under varying workload characteristics, specifically considering priority distributions and submission volumes.

To ensure a representative assessment of system behavior under sustained load, utilization and response time are calculated for all jobs submitted between time s, defined as the point when the system reaches a saturation level where immediate scheduling upon submission is no longer possible, and time e, the timestamp of the last job submission. This approach effectively excludes the initial and final periods of the simulation where the system might not be fully utilized, thereby preventing potential distortions in the reported utilization and response time metrics [5]. For completeness we define utilization and response time, similarly to related work [2]: $U(T) = \sum_{i=0}^{N_J} c_i t_i / (P \times T)$ where utilization U for a timeframe T is represented by sum of the volume occupied by each job (processor cores used c_i multiplied by execution time t_i) to the total volume of the timeframe (namely total processors P multiplied by total loop time T), with N_J the number of all submitted jobs; and the mean response time $R(T) = median([R(0), R(1), .., R(N_J)])$ with $R(i) = t_{\text{start}_i} - t_{\text{submitted}_i}$.

3.3 Simulation Results

Figure 4 illustrates the average system utilization across all simulated time periods alongside the median response time ratio observed with Priority-BF compared to the one for Easy-BF and LJF for each priority level. The system utilization remains consistent and similar to the utilization levels of the real-world system. Furthermore, the implementation of Priority-BF results in an increase in response times for low and medium-priority jobs, while significantly reducing the average response time for higher-priority jobs by 1.2–1.5x across the simulated systems.

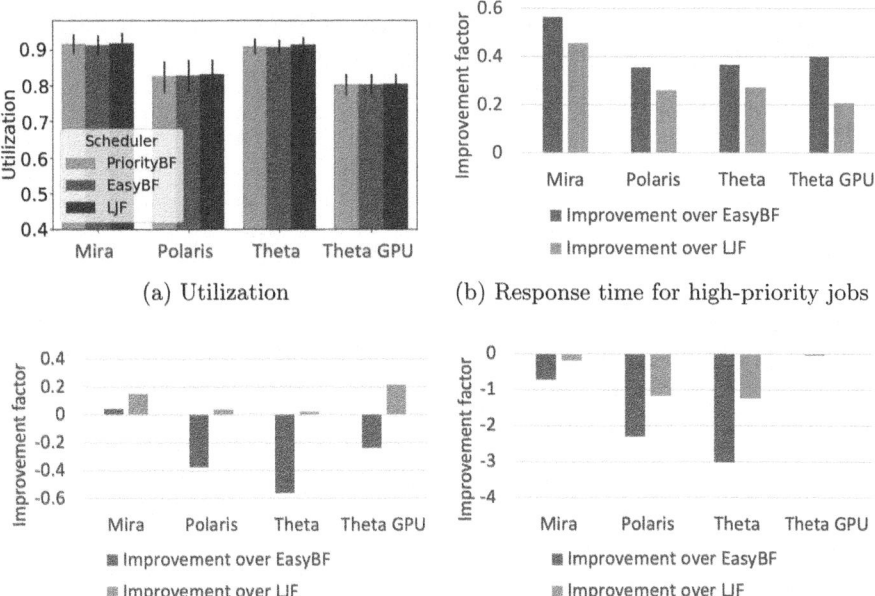

(a) Utilization   (b) Response time for high-priority jobs

(c) Response time for medium-priority jobs   (d) Response time for low-priority jobs

Fig. 4. Average improvement factor of the PRIORITY-BF strategy compared to the other two solutions. PRIORITY-BF improves the response time for high-priority jobs (1.2–1.5x improvement) without impacting the system utilization.

Compared to LJF, our approach still improves the response time for high-priority jobs. This advantage stems from our conservative backfilling algorithm, which prevents higher-priority jobs from being delayed by the execution of lower-priority jobs, even if they can start sooner, something LJF does only for the first largest job of the queue. This last performance really highlights the importance of mixing both CONSERVATIVE and EASY-BF, compared to the solution of including priorities into EASY-BF.

The observed performance variations across the simulated systems can be largely attributed to the fluctuating distribution of high-priority jobs across different time windows. For instance, the Theta-GPU system exhibits a limited number of analyzed timeframes that are predominantly characterized by large jobs. The job priorities are relatively uniformly distributed over time. This consistent submission pattern allows our scheduler to effectively improve the response time of these large, high-priority jobs without significantly impacting smaller jobs, resulting in minimal negative consequences, primarily affecting medium-sized jobs. Conversely, the Theta system demonstrates a highly imbalanced workload, with a large number of high-priority jobs concentrated within specific timeframes. During these peak periods, smaller and medium-sized jobs tend to be greatly delayed, leading to a considerably higher average response time compared to traditional scheduling approaches.

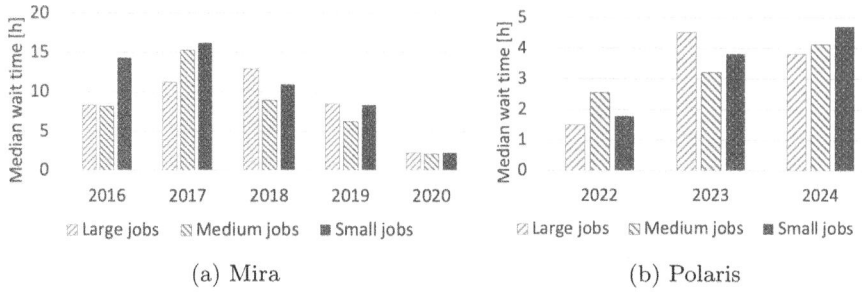

(a) Mira   (b) Polaris

Fig. 5. The wait time across jobs of different size is more uniform when using strategies like PRIORITY-BF that prioritizes large jobs typically in disadvantage compared to smaller jobs when the classic EASY-BF strategy is used.

Comparing in Fig. 5 the results of PRIORITY-BF to our initial observations from Fig. 1 we do not observe the same patterns anymore, the median time wait for large jobs being reduced significantly while the low and medium sized jobs are seeing larger wait times, though keeping a more balanced behavior compared to the original extremely unbalanced performance.

4   Use Case: In-Situ/In-Transit Computing

In this second use case we consider a simulation job or an experiment that iteratively generates data overwriting previous data. At the end of each iteration, several jobs are available to analyze this data on a dedicated cluster/resource. Example include SKA where generated data needs to be compressed and analyzed for discovering patterns, trends and correlations [13]; high fidelity simulations like S3D [10] or E3SM [15] that require extensive analysis tasks in each step to compute derived quantities [9] and identify regions of interest; correctness and fault tolerance tasks needed to check the integrity of the results or the physics correctness [18].

If the size of the analytical cluster is not sufficient to execute all the analytical jobs, a scheduler has to decide which jobs should be executed before the next release of data (i.e. the end of the subsequent iteration). In these cases, users may decide on constraints on those analytical jobs to help with the selection, such as priority levels, or QoS constraints. They can take the form of *Ideally, this job should be executed at least every x units of time* [12].

4.1   Formalization and Methodology

The length of the ith simulation iteration can be represented by a random variable X_i. The simulation jobs are represented via a quadruplet: $J = (n, w, t, p)$, where n is the number of node requested, w is the requested walltime, t is the actual runtime $(t < w)$, and p is the priority function. This priority can be either qualitative (e.g. $[p = 0]$ high priority, $[p = 1]$ medium priority, $[p = 2]$ low priority), or quantitative (e.g. J needs to be executed at least once every p iterations). Other possible descriptions could also include: J needs to be executed p times per iteration with high priority.

Dealing with Quantitative Priorities: To conduct experiments requiring QoS-like behavior, we implemented in the ScheduleFlow simulator a two-tiered priority queue system. Jobs that need execution in the subsequent simulation step are dynamically assigned to the high-priority queue, while all remaining jobs reside in the low-priority queue. This mechanism effectively translates the concept of immediate execution needs into a discrete priority value, allowing our qualitative backfilling algorithm to simulate QoS-driven scheduling decisions.

Analysis Jobs: Given the exploratory and highly stochastic nature of analysis jobs, where execution times vary significantly based on individual studies and high-priority task lists can evolve dynamically based on intermediate results, we opted for a simulation approach grounded in real-world scenarios. Specifically, we modeled analysis tasks after medical simulations triggered by the generation of Magnetic Resonance Imaging (MRI) or Whole Slide Imaging (WSI) data. For this purpose, we selected a diverse set of 20 applications, characterized by the inherent stochasticity observed in prior work [7], to represent the unpredictable nature of these analytical workloads.

We simulate 30 loops of data generation and 20 applications with priority assigned randomly in an uniform fashion (when using two priority levels, around one third will be high-priority jobs). Each time a job is executed we assign an execution time based on the distributions observed in our previous work. Overall we expect the total load of the analysis tasks to exceed the available resources by around 3x. We compare PRIORITY-BF to EASY-BF and CONSERVATIVE in two scenarios:

- *Value-based priorities*: jobs have values associated with their priority (e.g. for two levels, jobs will be either high, value 0, or low, value 1, priority)
- *QoS or frequency-based priorities*: each job has a step requirement associated, e.g. users would require a job to be executed at least every X step

In this last quantitative scenario, job priorities are determined by direct user input rather than inherent job characteristics, rendering EASY-BF incapable of incorporating these preferences. Consequently, our comparative analysis in this section focuses on contrasting our priority-aware algorithm with the standard EASY-BF and CONSERVATIVE approaches, neither of which account for job frequencies.

4.2 Simulation Results

In this section we operate under strict time constraints for analysis. Once data is received, the objective is to execute the maximum number of analysis tasks before the subsequent data generation phase. We explore two potential strategies for handling unfinished jobs when the allotted time expires: either terminate all incomplete tasks immediately, or allow them to complete, potentially encroaching upon the time allocated for analyzing the next batch of data.

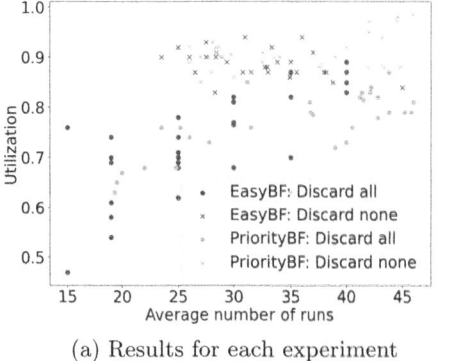 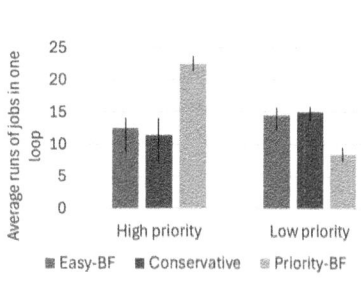

(a) Results for each experiment

(b) Average runs across all experiments

Fig. 6. Utilization and average runs for experiments using value-based priorities and executing in-situ stochastic jobs with time constraints.

Value-Based Priorities. Given the stochastic nature of the jobs, each experiment was repeated multiple times, and the aggregated results are presented in Fig. 6. System utilization is calculated as defined in Sect. 3.2. The "average runs" metric indicates the average number of times a job was executed across all simulation loops, with a maximum possible value equal to the total number of simulation loops (30 in this case). Allowing unfinished jobs to complete beyond the time limit leads to increased overall utilization without negatively impacting the average number of times jobs are executed. Notably, PRIORITY-BF tends to achieve a slightly higher average number of runs when considering all jobs compared to classic EASY-BF. Furthermore, analyzing the combined data from all experiments reveals that PRIORITY-BF executes almost twice as many high-priority jobs compared to both EASY-BF and CONSERVATIVE, with high-priority jobs in average being executed in 90% of the loops.

QoS-Based Priorities. We define the frequency required for the execution of each job so that to create a total volume of execution that would require 3.5x the amount of resources to execute everything successfully. We make several experiments and compute the number of times a job was not executed when it was required (e.g. if a job needs to be executed every 2 steps and it is executed in step 1 and step 5, we record 3 misses). The total number of misses across all jobs in each experiment is reported in Fig. 7a. Overall our solution has fewer misses and a lower standard deviation due to the fact that the EASY-BF strategy is not

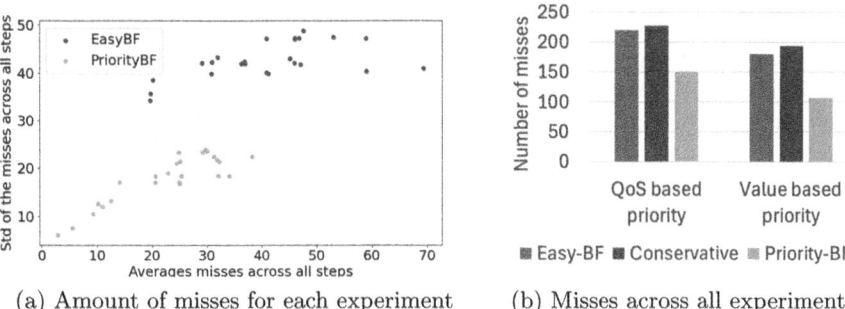

(a) Amount of misses for each experiment   (b) Misses across all experiments

Fig. 7. Average number of misses for QoS based priorities

aware of the QoS restrictions and chooses jobs to better fit the space, running them across multiple steps.

Figure 7b shows the average number of misses across all experiments. In order to monitor the number of misses between our two scenarios, we converted our experiments that use value-based priorities into a QoS problem by making all priority jobs have a requirement of being executed every step and the low priority ones not having any requirement. PRIORITY-BF improves the number of misses by 30–45% in all cases.

5 Related Work

Batch scheduling in HPC has been an ongoing research topic. It requests users to submit an allocation value (how many resources the jobs need) and a time limit/walltime (how long is the run is expected to last). It uses this information to take scheduling decisions often in a greedy way using the EASY-BF algorithm, where jobs are sorted according to a priority function and scheduled while allowing backfilling. Most of the existing work on priority-based scheduling in the HPC batch scheduling literature has been dedicated to improving the quality of a schedule, either by improving utilization, or other objectives such as mean bounded slowdown [2]. For example, Carastan-Santos et al. [3] have discussed replacing the FCFS priority function in EASY-BF by other functions such as Shortest Area First to improve the mean-bounded slowdown. Zrigui et al. [20] have shown that a simple classification (small or large), rather than the estimated runtime, is also enough to improve this objective.

Here, priorities are used to improve machine performance in their globality. An alternative to priority-based scheduling is Quality-Of-Service (QOS). In that case, jobs can have individual requirements (cost [17], deadline [19], energy [4]). This is a topic of particular interest in the Cloud Community where the volume of compute needed is less tight.

In HPC these solutions are presented differently when jobs have different priorities. Fan et al. [6] have discussed "time-critical" jobs: jobs whose demand is known 15–30 min before their release time, but that need to be executed almost instantaneously. To be able to do so, they allow the preemption and reconfiguration of some jobs to leave nodes available to the time-critical jobs. Our approach is different in the sense that we consider jobs with special needs to be no longer the exception. We consider the case of an overloaded system and we accept the fact that the total workload is higher than the capacity of the system. In this case, some jobs can be starved. Our goal is different in the sense that we want to execute all jobs with a high priority, and only execute other jobs if it impacts minimally the higher priority jobs.

6   Conclusions

This work introduced a new priority-aware scheduling algorithm for oversubscribed analysis clusters. Extremely simple in its description and implementation, it combines the benefits of EASY-BF and CONSERVATIVE backfilling. By allowing user-defined priorities, our solution effectively manages diverse job importance, shifting its behavior accordingly. Our results demonstrate the applicability of our solution in different scenarios. In particular this approach significantly improves the response time for high-priority jobs without impacting overall system utilization, offering a more nuanced and equitable resource allocation strategy for urgent computing within HPC environments. Finally, we have shown that this solution is quite expressive and can adapt to more quantitative approaches by updating priorities. Its simplicity makes it reliable and ready for large scale implementation which is going to be our next focus.

Acknowledgments. This material is based upon work supported by the U.S. Department of Energy, Office of Science, Office of Advanced Scientific Computing Research, for Research on Next Generation Data Management under Award Number DE-FOA-00002725. This work has benefited from a national grant managed by the French National Research Agency (Agence Nationale de la Recherche) attributed to the Exa-DoST project of the NumPEx PEPR program, under the reference ANR-22-EXNU-0004. This research uses data that was generated from resources of the Argonne Leadership Computing Facility, which is a DOE Office of Science User Facility supported under Contract DE-AC02-06CH11357. It used resources from Oak Ridge Leadership Computing Facility, which is a DOE Office of Science User Facility supported under Contract DE-AC05-00OR22725.

Disclosure of Interests. The authors have no competing interests to declare that are relevant to the content of this article.

References

1. Beckman, P.H., Beschastnikh, I., Nadella, S., Trebon, N.: Building an infrastructure for urgent computing. In: High Performance Computing Workshop (2006)
2. Boëzennec, R., Dufossé, F., Pallez, G.: Qualitatively analyzing optimization objectives in the design of HPC resource manager. ACM Trans. Modeling Perform. Eval. Comput. Syst. **9**(4), 1–28 (2024)

3. Carastan-Santos, D., De Camargo, R.Y., Trystram, D., Zrigui, S.: One can only gain by replacing EASY backfilling: a simple scheduling policies case study. In: IEEE/ACM CCGrid'19. IEEE (2019)
4. Cordeschi, N., Shojafar, M., Amendola, D., et al.: Energy-efficient adaptive networked datacenters for the QoS support of real-time applications. J. Supercomput. **71**, 448–478 (2015)
5. Du, Y., Marchal, L., Pallez, G., Robert, Y.: Improving batch schedulers with node stealing for failed jobs. CCPE **36**(12), e8043 (2024)
6. Fan, Y., Lan, Z., Rich, P., Allcock, W., et al.: Hybrid workload scheduling on HPC systems. In: IEEE IPDPS'22, pp. 470–480 (2022)
7. Gainaru, A., Goglin, B., Honoré, V., Pallez, G.: Profiles of upcoming HPC applications and their impact on reservation strategies. IEEE TPDS **32**(5), 1178–1190 (2021)
8. Gainaru, A., Pallez (Aupy), G., Sun, H., Raghavan, P.: Speculative scheduling for stochastic HPC applications. In: ICPP'19, pp. 1–10 (2019)
9. Gainaru, A., Podhorszki, N., Dulac, L., Gong, Q., et al.: To derive or not to derive: I/O libraries take charge of derived quantities computation. In: SBAC-PAD'24, pp. 105–115 (2024)
10. Im, H.G., Trouvé, A., Rutland, C.J., Chen, J.H.: Terascale high-fidelity simulations of turbulent combustion with detailed chemistry. Technical report, University of Maryland, College Park MD (2012)
11. Lifka, D.A.: The ANL/IBM SP scheduling system. In: Feitelson, D.G., Rudolph, L. (eds.) JSSPP 1995. LNCS, vol. 949, pp. 295–303. Springer, Heidelberg (1995). https://doi.org/10.1007/3-540-60153-8_35
12. Malakar, P., Vishwanath, V., Munson, T., et al.: Optimal scheduling of in-situ analysis for large-scale scientific simulations. In: SC'15, pp. 1–11 (2015)
13. Marotta, G., et al.: Enhancing ska software testing through data mining strategies. In: Software and Cyberinfrastructure for Astronomy VIII, vol. 13101, pp. 168–181. SPIE (2024)
14. Mu'alem, A.W., Feitelson, D.G.: Utilization, predictability, workloads, and user runtime estimates in scheduling the IBM SP2 with backfilling. IEEE Trans. Parallel Distrib. Syst. **12**(6), 529–543 (2002)
15. Nichol, J.J., Peterson, M.G., Peterson, K.J., et al.: Machine learning feature analysis illuminates disparity between E3SM climate models and observed climate change. J. Comput. Appl. Math. **395**, 113451 (2021)
16. Patel, T., Liu, Z., Kettimuthu, R., Rich, P., et al.: Job characteristics on large-scale systems: long-term analysis, quantification, and implications. In: SC20, pp. 1–17. IEEE (2020)
17. Qavami, H.R., Jamali, S., Akbari, M.K., Javadi, B.: Dynamic resource provisioning in cloud computing: a heuristic Markovian approach. In: Leung, V., Chen, M. (eds.) CloudComp'13. LNICST, vol. 133, pp. 102–111. Springer, Cham (2014). https://doi.org/10.1007/978-3-319-05506-0_10
18. Tan, N., Assogba, K., Ashworth, W.J., Bogale, B., et al.: Towards affordable reproducibility using scalable capture and comparison of intermediate multi-run results. In: Middleware'24, pp. 392–403 (2024)
19. Vecchiola, C., Calheiros, R.N., Karunamoorthy, D., Buyya, R.: Deadline-driven provisioning of resources for scientific applications in hybrid clouds with Aneka. Futur. Gener. Comput. Syst. **28**(1), 58–65 (2012)
20. Zrigui, S., de Camargo, R.Y., Legrand, A., Trystram, D.: Improving the performance of batch schedulers using online job runtime classification. J. Parallel Distrib. Comput. **164**, 83–95 (2022)

WAPA: A Workload-Agnostic CPI-Based Thread-to-Core Allocation Policy

Marta Navarro[1]($\boxtimes$)(ID), Vicent Pallardó-Julià[2](ID), Salvador Petit[1](ID),
María E. Gómez[1](ID), and Julio Sahuquillo[1](ID)

[1] Universitat Politècnica de València, València, Spain
{marnaed,spetit,megomez,jsahuqui}@disca.upv.es
[2] Universitat de València, València, Spain
vicent.pallardo@uv.es

Abstract. Simultaneous multithreading (SMT) processors improve system throughput by sharing core resources among the threads running on the same core. However, intra-core interference can cause co-running applications to degrade each other's performance significantly.

To address this issue, some approaches have focused on balancing contention at the core shared resources (e.g. the shared L1 data cache). A key advantage of these approaches is that they are workload-agnostic. Other approaches improve the previous ones by modeling the inter-application interference across the intra-core shared resources. Unfortunately, these approaches require off-line model training for specific workloads.

This paper presents WAPA, a CPI-based thread-to-core allocation approach that incorporates the best of both worlds. WAPA is a *workload-agnostic* policy that implicitly accounts for *inter-thread interference* across all the shared resources by leveraging the CPI. The proposed approach relies on the optimal transport (OT) theory, a mathematical theory to dynamically select symbiotic pairs of applications.

Experimental results in an Intel Xeon show that WAPA outperforms the default Linux scheduler on average by 8.4% in IPC in workloads dominated by cache and main memory latencies, while performance gains of existing approaches are below 3.2%.

Keywords: SMT Processors · Thread-to-Core Allocation Policies · Job Scheduling · Optimal Transport

1 Introduction

Simultaneous multithreading (SMT) [36] processors improve the processor throughput and resource utilization over single-threaded processors thanks to supporting the execution of multiple threads on the same core. These features have led major industry companies like Intel, IBM, AMD, and ARM to deliver SMT processors.

Unfortunately, most core resources (e.g., the L1 data cache) are shared among the threads (applications), raising inter-application interference. As a result,

© The Author(s), under exclusive license to Springer Nature Switzerland AG 2026
W. E. Nagel et al. (Eds.): Euro-Par 2025, LNCS 15900, pp. 233–247, 2026.
https://doi.org/10.1007/978-3-031-99854-6_16

severe adverse impacts on the execution time of individual applications can appear, which strongly vary depending on the co-runner. To address this issue, thread-to-core (T2C) allocation policies have been proposed [15, 29] aimed at looking for *symbiotic* pairs of applications and allocating them on the same core.

Some works found that the L1 data cache acts as a major performance bottleneck in some commercial processors and propose T2C policies to balance the accesses across the L1 data caches of all the cores [14] or across the shared structures of the cache hierarchy [13]. These approaches fail because they do not properly address workloads mingling frontend-bound and backend-bound applications. To overcome this shortcoming, other approaches [15, 29] model the inter-application interference at the major core shared resources (e.g., instruction cache, arithmetic units, L1 data cache, ...). To this end, a linear regression model (LRM) is built. These models differ in the components used to estimate the interference and the target processor. More precisely, they rely on specific performance counters of the underlying architecture, which prevents them from being used in distinct microarchitectures. For instance, the model developed in [15] for the IBM POWER8 [8] can only be used for IBM processors since the used performance counters are not available in processors of other brands. Another major shortcoming of using linear regression models is that the model's coefficients are obtained offline via training by running a set of workloads. In other words, the model is tied to the workload used to obtain the coefficients, which prevents them from being used in other workloads exhibiting distinct behavior.

This paper proposes WAPA, a novel approach that implicitly considers interference at all the shared resources –incore and offcore– by using the *cycles per instruction* (CPI) as the pivotal metric to pair applications in SMT cores. The proposed approach addresses the two main shortcomings of LRMs; on the one hand, WAPA is workload-agnostic and does not require offline training; on the other hand, it is not microarchitecture dependent since it only uses cycles and instructions, which are universal metrics available in the performance monitoring units (PMU) of any existing processor.

WAPA relies on the optimal transport (OT) theory [26] to estimate the best combination of application pairs. The OT's goal is to determine the most efficient method for reallocating mass from one distribution to another while minimizing an associated cost function, *sum of CPIs in the cores in this work*. This involves finding the combination that minimizes the total transportation cost based on a metric (individual per-application CPI). The OT problem has been extensively studied from a theoretical perspective [10, 19], alongside the development of numerical methods, which has facilitated its application in various contexts. Some examples include telecommunication systems [31, 37], image and signal processing [21, 23] or Machine Learning [22, 27], among others. To the best of our knowledge, this work is pioneering in applying an OT-based approach in computer architecture to mitigate intra-core interference.

Experimental results in an Intel Xeon show that WAPA outperforms the default Linux scheduler on average by 8.4% in IPC in workloads dominated by cache and main memory latencies, while performance gains of existing approaches are below 3.2%.

The main contribution of this paper is the WAPA approach, a T2C allocation policy that meets three main features: CPI-based, workload-agnostic, and microarchitecture-independent. Results show that WAPA outperforms existing T2C policies [14,29] based on LRMs and contention mitigation.

2 Understanding the Problem to Solve: T2C Allocation vs OT Problem Analogy

To illustrate how OT theory can help T2C allocation, this section first introduces the OT problem from an economic perspective –one of its first applications. Let's assume a company aims to transport goods between countries while minimizing transportation costs. This problem can be modeled as a weighted graph: nodes represent countries, arcs represent transport routes, and weights correspond to costs. OT theory then determines the optimal transport strategy.

This idea can be translated to the T2C allocation problem, where applications replace countries, and transportation cost corresponds to the performance metric to minimize –our target metric is the CPI (cycles per instruction). Two applications running in the same core are linked by a weighted arc, where the weight equals the sum of the CPI of both applications. The goal is to pair applications to minimize the total sum of arc weights, analogous to minimizing transportation costs. Each pair will be allocated to a processor core.

For illustrative purposes, let us consider the practical example depicted in Fig. 1. Let us assume four applications (a_1 to a_4) in a two-core processor, and the target metric to be minimized is the total CPI (i.e., the sum of the four CPIs). Since each application can be paired with any other on the same core, we represent this framework as a *weighted complete undirected graph*, where the weight between two applications, a_i and a_j, is denoted by w_{ij} (Fig. 1a). The weight of the arc between two nodes denotes the sum of the CPI of the two linked applications when they run together on the same core. The graph can be represented as a matrix as depicted in Fig. 1b. This matrix is referred to as the *cost matrix* in OT theory.

The scheduler aims to determine the best thread-to-core allocation, that is, the one that minimizes the total CPI. Since there are 4 applications in this example, there are 3 possible sets of pairs or *schedules*: i) $\{(a_1, a_4), (a_2, a_3)\}$, ii) $\{(a_1, a_3), (a_2, a_4)\}$, and iii) $\{(a_1, a_2), (a_3, a_4)\}$. Hereinafter, each *schedule* can be defined with a transport matrix M such that cell $M_{ij} = 1$ if the pair (a_i, a_j) is considered in the schedule and $M_{ij} = 0$ otherwise (Fig. 1c). Using this representation, we define the total CPI for the given schedule as:

$$CPI_M = \left(\sum_{i=1}^{n} \sum_{j=1}^{n} M_{ij} w_{ji} \right) /2, \qquad (1)$$

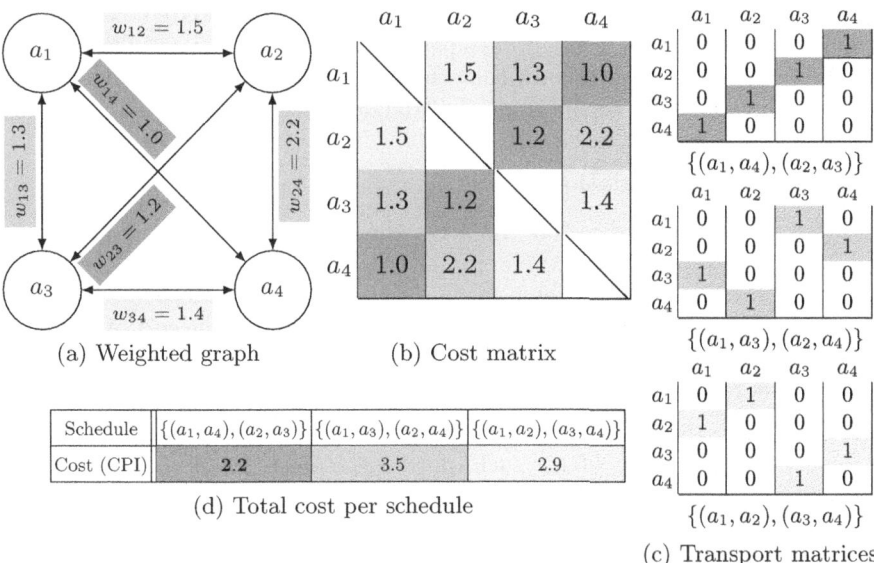

(a) Weighted graph   (b) Cost matrix

Schedule	$\{(a_1,a_4),(a_2,a_3)\}$	$\{(a_1,a_3),(a_2,a_4)\}$	$\{(a_1,a_2),(a_3,a_4)\}$
Cost (CPI)	2.2	3.5	2.9

(d) Total cost per schedule

(c) Transport matrices

Fig. 1. Practical example.

where w denotes the cost matrix, and M is the transport matrix corresponding to a given schedule.

For this simple example, it is straightforward to identify the best schedule, which involves pairing (a_1, a_4) and (a_2, a_3), resulting in the lowest total CPI (2.2 in Fig. 1d). However, the number of possible schedules increases factorially with the number of applications [32], making the problem challenging. More precisely, for $2p$ applications, each schedule is given by p pairs and the number of possible schedules is $(2p)!/(2^p p!)$. For example, for 10 applications, this results in 945 possible schedules. In this work, we leverage the optimal transport theory to address this challenge.

3   Mathematical Formulation

The Optimal Transport (OT) problem can be mathematically formulated as a convex linear programming problem, representing a relaxation of the combinatorial problem of transporting one distribution to another [6,33,35]. In the context of this work, both distributions are discrete and uniform, whose nodes are the set of applications. In this setting, each application is equally represented in both the input and output distributions, and the goal of the OT problem is to transport this distribution onto itself. Broadly speaking, this process defines an optimal redistribution of the mass of each application a_i on the set of applications, subject to certain constraints.

Next, some background is presented to help understand the OT approach implemented in our T2C allocation policy organized into two subsections. First, the problem is formally described and mathematically formulated. Second, the numerical optimization used in this paper to solve the OT problem is discussed. We would like to remark that the presented background simplifies the OT method to adapt it to the context of the devised T2C allocation policy.

3.1   Problem Formulation

Consider a complete undirected graph G, where the set of nodes is denoted by $A = \{a_i\}_{i=1}^n$, where the matrix $w = \{w_{i,j}\}_{i,j=1}^n$ denotes the weight of each arc of G. In Fig. 1a we provided a sketch for $n = 4$ nodes. In the following, we also use a_i to denote applications as well as the weight w_{ij} to denote the cost of matching applications a_i and a_j, for all i, j.

Now, we define the discrete uniform distribution as:

$$\mu(B) = \frac{1}{n}\sum_{i=1}^n \delta_{a_i}(B), \quad \text{such that} \quad \delta_{a_i}(B) = \begin{cases} 1, & \text{iff } a_i \in B, \\ 0, & \text{otherwise.} \end{cases} \tag{2}$$

where $B \subseteq A$, and δ_{a_i} is the Dirac measure on a_i. The measure μ assigns a probabilistic mass of $1/n$ to each node of G. Thus, in our context, this implies that each application a_i has an equal representation in the distribution, establishing an equitable starting point.

In this framework, the OT problem is formulated to minimize the total transportation cost, given by the inner product of matrices, M and w, as:

$$\inf_{M \in \mathcal{S}_1} \langle M, w \rangle = \inf_{M \in \mathcal{S}_1} \sum_{i=1}^n \sum_{j=1}^n M_{ij} w_{ji}, \tag{3}$$

where the expression (1) is tightly recovered. In the above minimization, M is defined on the next feasible set:

$$\mathcal{S}_1 := \left\{ M \in [0,1]^{n \times n} \text{ such that } M\mathbf{1} = M^T\mathbf{1} = \mathbf{1} \right\}. \tag{4}$$

where $\mathbf{1}$ represents the unit vector. Notice that the preservation of the mass of each application is ensured by the definition of $\mathcal{S}_1$. It is direct that a minimizer of (3) is not necessarily a one-to-one map, which means that it does not define a schedule as we expect in Fig. 1. Moreover, if we restrict $\mathcal{S}_1$ to schedule matrices, the problem (3) becomes non-convex, adding complexity to its resolution [17,25].

To address this issue and find a single solution to the problem, we add a quadratic term in (3) as regularizer. Thanks to this adjustment, the optimization gains stability and efficiency in finding a solution, as is shown in large-scale problems (e.g., [3,11,17]).

Then, the quadratically regularization of (3) is defined as:

$$\inf_{M \in \mathcal{S}_1} \mathcal{F}(M, w) = \inf_{M \in \mathcal{S}_1} \langle M, w \rangle + \frac{\alpha}{2} \sum_{i,j} w_{ij} \| M_i - M_j \|_2^2, \tag{5}$$

where $\mathcal{F}(M, w)$ denotes the objective function, $\alpha > 0$, M_i refers to the i-th column of M and $\| \cdot \|_2$ to the Euclidean norm in $\mathbb{R}^2$.

3.2   Numerical Optimization: Frank-Wolfe Method

Distinct numerical optimization methods can be used to solve the OT problem, such as the one proposed by Frank-Wolfe, based on Gauss-Seidel and projective formulation methods [25]. In this work, we use the former, which is the standard method and is efficient in solving the quadratic problem [17].

The Frank-Wolfe method [18] is an iterative first-order optimization algorithm for constrained convex optimization [38], which the efficiency for solving (5) is guaranteed via an interior point technique [30]. This method consists of an algorithm that implements a main two-step loop, which iterates until the transport matrix M converges:

$$1^{st} step: \qquad \tilde{M}^k \in \arg\min_{\tilde{M} \in \mathcal{S}_1} \langle \nabla \mathcal{F}(M^k, w), \tilde{M} \rangle, \qquad (6)$$

$$2^{nd} step: \qquad M^{k+1} \leftarrow (1 - \tau_k)M^k + \tau_k \tilde{M}^k. \qquad (7)$$

The first step obtains an intermediate matrix to define the direction to minimize the objective function $\mathcal{F}$, where k indicates the iteration and $\nabla \mathcal{F}(M^k, w)$ denotes a matrix whose components are defined as:

$$(\nabla \mathcal{F}(M^k, w))_{ij} = w_{ij} + \alpha \sum_{j=1}^{n} w_{ij}(M_{ij}^k - M_{jj}^k). \qquad (8)$$

The second step (see Equation (7)) uses the output of the first step ($\tilde{M}^k$) to obtain a transport matrix M^{k+1} for the next iteration. This is done using the *step size* τ variable corresponding to the k-th iteration (τ_k).

4   WAPA Approach

This section discusses the WAPA implementation organized into four main parts: i) applying the approach, ii) initial matrix filling, iii) proposed OT implementation, and iv) how WAPA deals when a new application reaches the system.

Applying WAPA. This process involves monitoring the `cycles` and `instructions` performance counters, updating the matrix costs, applying OT to identify the best pairs, and assigning these pairs to the cores. In the experiments, the approach executes at the end of each 100ms execution interval. Before applying the WAPA for the first time the cost matrix needs to be filled as discussed below.

Initial Matrix Filling. Since the cost matrix is empty at the beginning of the workload execution, a few quanta are devoted to filling the matrix in a namely *warm-up phase*. For instance, assume that the processor runs 8 (four pairs) applications. Then, the number of cells in the matrix is 64 (8x8), 56 excluding the main diagonal. Since the matrix is symmetric (i.e., the value of cell (i, j) matches the value of cell (j, i)), only 28 different values need to be measured. Therefore, 7 quanta are taken to fill up the matrix since in each interval 4 cells (four running pairs) are filled. In general, for n applications, the number of cells to be filled is given by $\binom{n}{2}$, which, divided by the number of pairs, gives the number of intervals of the warm-up phase. To guarantee that the diagonal cells of the cost matrix (e.g., w_{ij} where $i = j$) are never selected –since an application cannot be paired with itself– these cells are populated with a substantially high value, preventing them from being considered as viable pairing options.

Proposed OT Implementation. The implemented OT consists of two loops composed of the two numerical optimization steps discussed in Sect. 3.2. In the first step, we use the Fast Network Simplex algorithm presented by Bonneel et al. in [9] to compute the intermediate matrix $\tilde{M}^k$, which is then used to define the gradient $\Delta M^k = \tilde{M}^k - M^k$. This gradient is necessary to obtain the direction to minimize the objective function $\mathcal{F}$ and to set up the line search on τ_k in the second step. Regarding the second step, we implemented the Armijo line-search algorithm [7] to determine τ_k. This algorithm finds an optimal τ_k to guarantee efficient progress toward minimizing the objective function. Once τ_k is obtained, it is used to compute the transport matrix for the next iteration, M^{k+1}. These steps repeat until the stabilization criteria are met, which happens when at least one of two conditions is fulfilled. The first condition checks if the absolute difference between M^k and M^{k-1} matrices is small enough (e.g., lower than 10^{-6}) while the second focuses on the relative difference. In particular, we compute if $\frac{|M^{k-1} - M^k|}{|M^k| + 10^{-9}}$ is lower than 10^{-9}. Both absolute and relative limits are set according to the defaults in typical optimization implementations[1].

New Applications Enter the System. Whenever an application reaches the system, the cost matrix must be updated with the information about the incoming application. In this case, only the matrix cells corresponding to the potential pairs involving the new application need to be updated. For this purpose, the application is paired with all other ones in a round-robin manner during the subsequent quanta. Notice that WAPA is workload-agnostic; that is, it works despite the application that enters the system being an *unseen* application. In such a case, this situation would not be handled by an LRM-based approach.

5   Experimental Platform and Methodology

5.1   Platform

We have implemented WAPA in an Intel Xeon Silver 4210R [2] based on the Cascade Lake [1] microarchitecture, with 32 GB DRAM main memory. L1 instruction cache, L1 data cache, L2, and L3 cache capacities are 32KB, 32KB, 10 MB, and 13.8 MB, respectively. The system runs a Linux version 5.4.0–99-generic. The approach was implemented in an *in-house* framework developed for performance evaluation studies. The framework launches the workloads to be executed, utilizes the Perf tool [4] to configure the performance counters with the selected

---

[1] For instance, see https://pythonot.github.io/gen_modules/ot.optim.html#ot.optim. cg.

hardware events to be measured, and gathers the results along the workload execution. The framework reads performance counters at each defined execution interval, where WAPA is applied. The `sched_affinity` system call [5] is used to allocate applications to cores.

5.2   Evaluation Methodology

To evaluate thread-to-core policies, we used multi-program workloads including applications presenting different characteristics from a resource consumption perspective. Notice that if the applications present a homogeneous behavior, no scheduling strategy could provide performance gains.

Workloads' Design. We have used multi-program workloads composed of 8 applications from the SPEC CPU2006 [20] and CPU2017 [24] suites. To design workloads with heterogeneous behavior, we first characterized the static behavior of each application executing alone. Due to the Intel PMU characteristics, this characterization was done at the issue stage. More precisely, at this stage, we computed the fraction of issue slots where instructions were issued and the fraction of slots where no instruction was issued due to stalls caused by critical frontend or backend components. In this regard, we break down stalls due to the backend, such as L1, L2, and L3 caches, as well as main memory and core components. Core refers to stalls caused by structural hazards due to arithmetic operators. Figure 2 presents the results for the 42 applications run alone for 60 s. A wide variety of behaviors can be appreciated across the applications. According to these results, applications can be classified into 3 main groups depending on the particular component that causes a high fraction of the stalls: the L1 (L1) data cache, the Frontend (FE), and the Main Memory (MM). We can see that the values of the MM and FE components present the widest range of variation. For experimental purposes, we assume that an application belongs to the MM,

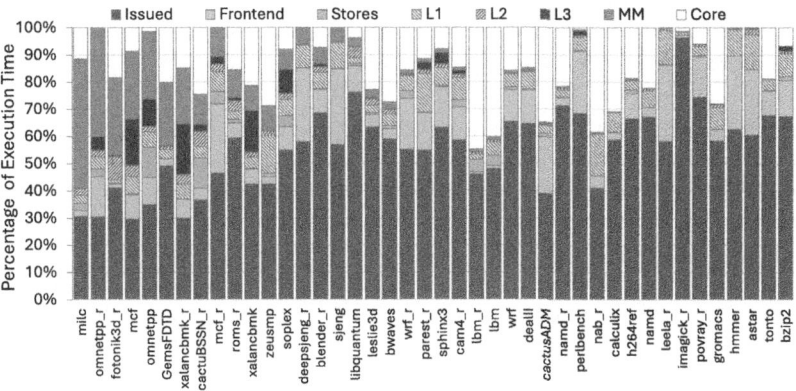

Fig. 2. Characterization of the applications in ST execution.

FE, and L1 group if the fraction of stalls for that component is larger than 22%, 20%, and 5%, respectively.

Workloads of 8 applications were randomly built based on the criterion that each workload should at least contain one application from the FE group, one from the MM group, and three from the L1 group. The reason why the number of applications from the L1 group is three is because of its huge impact on performance. Notice that this cache introduces high intra-core interference despite its relatively small size in individual execution. Applying this criterion results in 5 types of 8-application workloads, denoted by the triplet (xL1, yFE, zMM). The specific triplets are: (3L1, 3FE, 2MM), (3L1, 3FE, 2MM), (3L1, 2FE, 3MM), (4L1, 1FE, 3MM), and (4L1, 2FE, 2MM), which will be referred as workload type [a], [b], [c], [d], and [e], respectively. We build six random workloads for each type, giving a total of 30 workloads.

Workload Measurement Methodology. As mentioned above, for individual characterization, each application was run alone for 60 s. The number of committed instructions is referred to as the target number for each application. When running a workload composed of 8 applications, we read performance counters each 100ms time interval. Due to interference each execution takes a different number of intervals to execute, thus each application runs until the target number is reached. The workload is kept running until the slowest application reaches its target number of instructions; that is, the applications that finish sooner are relaunched to maintain a constant number of running applications.

6   Performance Evaluation

Compared Approaches. This section compares WAPA against SYNPA [29], a recent LRM-based policy, and the Balancing L1D [14] (BaL1D) approach. These policies are summarized next to make the paper self-contained. Farther details can be found in the original papers.

SYNPA, originally designed for ARM-specific performance counters, was adapted for the Intel processor used in this work, resulting in $SYNPA3_{intel}$. The adapted policy accounts for issued instructions and stalls at the issue stage instead of the dispatch stage as done in ARM processors [29]. The gathered values are used to characterize the application behavior. To this end, issue slots are grouped into three main categories depending on whether instructions are issued, no instruction is issued due to a stall caused by the core frontend (e.g., an L1 instruction cache miss), or a stall rises in the core backend (e.g., an L1 data cache miss). This policy builds a linear regression model, based on the three categories, that is used to predict the performance of the distinct pairs and choose the best pairs. Off-line training is required to obtain the model's coefficients.

BaL1D balances accesses among the L1 data caches of all the cores with the aim of minimizing the contention at this resource, which authors show to be critical in most workloads. To this end, the approach pairs applications with the highest and lowest accesses to the L1 data cache, the second highest with the

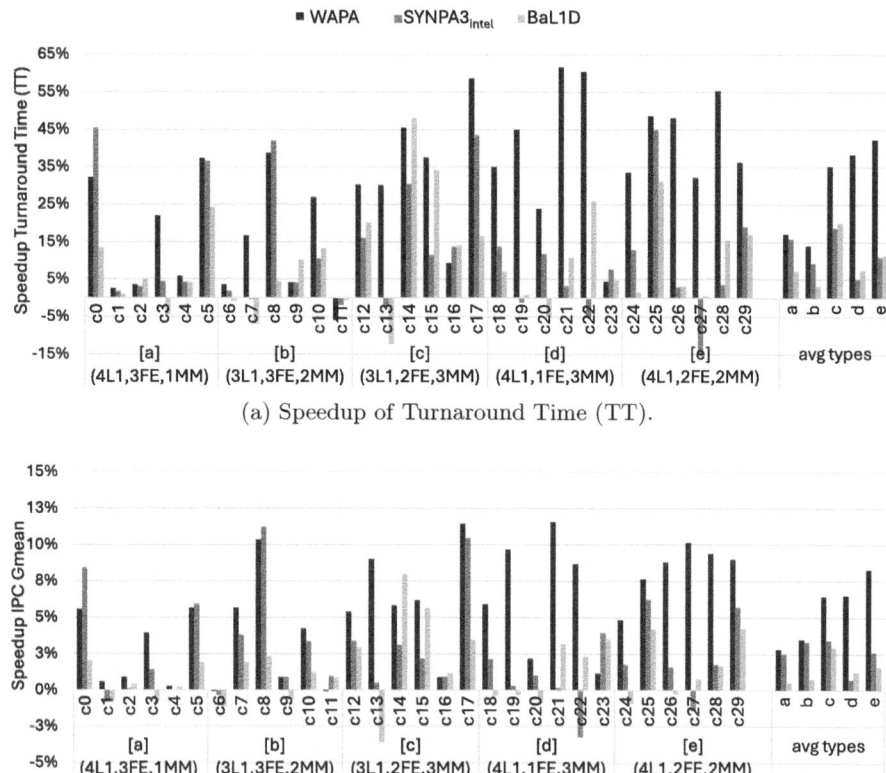

(a) Speedup of Turnaround Time (TT).

(b) Speedup of IPC Gmean.

Fig. 3. Speedups of WAPA, $SYNPA3_{intel}$ and BaL1D over Linux.

second lowest, and so on. In this work, we use counters equivalent to the original approach, as the same counters are no longer available.

Experimental Results. To evaluate WAPA, $SYNPA3_{intel}$, and BaL1D, we compare their performance in terms of Turnaround Time (TT), Instructions Per Cycle (IPC), and overhead. Figure 3 presents the results over the Linux scheduler. Overall, WAPA outperforms $SYNPA3_{intel}$ and BaL1D across all the types of workloads. The three policies similarly perform in workloads with fewer backend applications (i.e., workload types [a] and [b], which include workloads or *combinations* from c0 t0 c11), but differences become more pronounced when the number of backend applications grows.

Notably, $SYNPA3_{intel}$ presents significant performance drops (e.g., by 15% in TT in c27) due to its reliance on pre-trained regression coefficients, limiting its adaptability. BaL1D, which does not need training, depends on workload characteristics, achieving just 7.2% and 3.2% TT improvements in workload types [a] and [b], respectively.

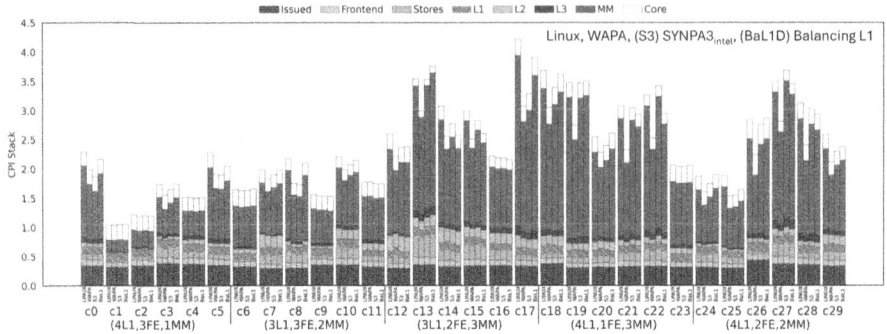

Fig. 4. CPI stack of Linux, WAPA, $SYNPA3_{intel}$ and BaL1D.

Table 1. Comparison of the studied approaches.

Approaches	Performance counters		Overhead			
	NO program.	Program.	Preprocessing	Algorithm	Allocating	Total (in %)
WAPA	2	0	1.19 ms	0.26 ms	0.86 ms	2.31%
$SYNPA3_{intel}$	2	4	2.66 ms	0.88+0.17 ms	0.66 ms	4.37%
BaL1D	0	1	0.20 ms	0.10 ms	0.67 ms	0.97%

In contrast, WAPA dynamically updates scheduling decisions at runtime at each interval, relying just on real-time values. This adaptability makes it particularly more effective for resource-limited workloads (types [c], [d], and [e]). For instance, in workload c21 (type [d]), WAPA achieves a remarkable speedup of around 60% in terms of TT.

CPI Stack. To provide insights on the reasons behind WAPA improves the overall performance, we built a CPI stack to analyze where execution cycles go. The devised stack breaks down the execution cycles according to the categories explained in Sect. 5.2. Figure 4 presents the CPI stack for each workload according to the applied scheduler: Linux, WAPA, $SYNPA3_{intel}$ or BaL1D. As observed, WAPA achieves the best CPI values in almost all the workloads, especially in those exhibiting high CPI values. Notice that these applications present huge off-core interferences (raising the main memory category). Therefore, we can conclude that accurately modeling in-core interference (e.g., frontend, stores, and core bound) can help reduce this interference but not necessarily overall performance. For instance, the store category is improved by $SYNPA3_{intel}$ in workload c17, but WAPA presents better CPI.

Overhead Time Comparison. To evaluate the overhead time, the overall time taken by each policy was broken down into three main components: i) *preprocesing* which consists of reading performance counters and preparing the values for the algorithm (e.g., obtaining categories and normalizing the values) if needed; ii) *algorithm*, that is, applying the *algorithm* itself and storing the results in the corresponding structure (e.g., array or graph); and iii) *allocating*, which consists of reading the structure, select the pairs, and allocate them in cores. Table 1 presents the results for the three studied policies.

An interesting observation is that *preprocesing* is the component that mainly contributes to the overhead time. The main reason is the required processing that $SYNPA3_{intel}$ needs in terms of filling matrices and maps to prepare the structures to apply the algorithm. However, WAPA only requires updating the transport matrix.

Counterintuitively, applying the algorithm itself incurs much less overhead than all the preprocessing. In this regard, WAPA presents by 3× less overhead in the algorithm component (i.e., 0.26ms versus 1.05ms) than $SYNPA3_{intel}$. The reason is twofold: on the one hand, the transport matrix converges in WAPA in just two loop iterations in almost all the intervals; on the other hand, $SYNPA3_{intel}$ requires three main costly actions (applying the inverse model, applying the forward model, and applying the Blossom algorithm). Regarding BaL1D, WAPA incurs twice its overhead, as the former only requires balancing L1 accesses, making it simpler.

7   Related Work

Some previous works [14] identified the L1 data cache as a major contention intra-core resource in current processors. Since this cache acts as a major performance bottleneck, the authors proposed to balance the accesses among the L1 data caches of all the SMT cores. The main advantage of this approach is that it is workload-agnostic, and only two performance counters (L1 accesses and cycles) are required. Linear regression models have been widely applied in the past to reduce the inter-application interference in SMT processors. Moseley et al. [28] apply linear modeling and recursive partitioning to predict speedups when executing two applications simultaneously. Radojkovic et al. [34] present a statistical inference method to optimize task assignment. Eyerman and Eeckhout [12] present an analytical model predicting application slowdowns using performance stacks, although it requires custom hardware events unavailable on commercial processors, limiting its applicability. To address this limitation, Feliu et al. [15,16] use the CPI stack of IBM POWER8 to build a linear regression model to schedule the applications. Similarly, Navarro et al. [29] introduce SYNPA, a thread-to-core allocation policy for SMT ARM processors to minimize intra-core interference and improve the performance of the applications. It uses the Instructions and Stalls Cycles (ISC) stack to model the execution cycle distribution in SMT processors and employs the linear regression model to obtain the prediction of the performance slowdowns, which is used to select the symbiotic pairs. Although the latter models are applicable to real processors, existing approaches are constrained by two major limitations: dependence on specific hardware counters tied to specific processors and effectiveness limited to the workloads used to obtain the model coefficients.

8   Conclusions

Existing T2C allocation policies based on interference estimation to predict the performance of pairs of applications are based on linear regression models. In this paper, we have proposed WAPA, that addresses the main weaknesses of LRM-based approaches: offline model training, workload-dependence, and microarchitecture-dependence. WAPA addresses the former by design, thanks to applying the OT problem to select the schedules. This approach only requires working with matrices whose data are gathered only at execution time and applying two mathematical functions –network simplex simple and Armijo–, which makes WAPA workload-independent. On the other hand, WAPA pursues to minimize the sum of the CPI of the pairs of applications running on each core, only requiring as inputs two universally available performance counters—instructions and cycles—common to all modern processors, which makes WAPA microarchitecture-independent.

Results show that WAPA significantly improves $SYNPA3_{intel}$ and BaL1D. On average, WAPA achieves 4× greater performance improvements over Linux than the studied approaches. Moreover, this is achieved with almost half the overhead than LRM-based approaches. Finally, we would like to emphasize that WAPA's features make it a suitable approach to be implemented in modern Operating Systems deployed on SMT processors.

Acknowledgments. This work has been partially supported by the Spanish Ministerio de Ciencia e Innovación and European ERDF under grants PID2021-123627OB-C51 and TED2021-130233B-C32. Marta Navarro is supported by Subvenciones para la contratación de personal investigador predoctoral by CIACIF/2021/413.

References

1. Cascade Lake - Microarchitectures - Intel. https://en.wikichip.org/wiki/intel/microarchitectures/cascade_lake. Accessed 12 Mar 2025
2. Intel Xeon Silver 4210R. https://en.wikichip.org/wiki/intel/xeon_silver/4210r. Accessed 12 Mar 2025
3. Lightspeed computation of optimal transport (2013)
4. Perf: Linux profiling with performance counters (2023). https://perf.wiki.kernel.org/index.php/Main_Page. Accessed 12 Mar 2025
5. sched_seaffinity(2) - Linux manual page (2023). https://man7.org/linux/man-pages/man2/sched_setaffinity.2.html. Accessed 12 Mar 2025
6. Ambrosio, L., Gigli, N.: Modelling and Optimisation of Flows on Networks, chap. Springer, A User's Guide to Optimal Transport (2013)
7. Armijo, L.: Minimization of functions having lipschitz continuous first partial derivatives. Pacific J. Math. **16**(1), 1–3 (1966)
8. Balaram, B., et al.: IBM POWER8 processor core microarchitecture. IBM J. Res. Dev. **59**(1), 2:1–2:21 (2015)
9. Bonneel, N., et al.: Displacement interpolation using lagrangian mass transport. ACM Trans. Graph. **30**(6), 1–12 (2011)

10. Brenier, Y.: Polar factorization and monotone rearrangement of vector-valued functions. Commun. Pure Appl. Math. **44**(4), 375–417 (1991)
11. Essid, M., Solomon, J.: Quadratically regularized optimal transport on graphs. SIAM J. Sci. Comput. **40**(4), A1961–A1986 (2018)
12. Eyerman, S., Eeckhout, L.: Probabilistic job symbiosis modeling for SMT processor scheduling. In: ASPLOS, pp. 91–102 (2010)
13. Feliu, J., et al.: Understanding cache hierarchy contention in CMPS to improve job scheduling. In: IEEE 26th IPDPS, pp. 508–519 (2012)
14. Feliu, J., et al.: L1-bandwidth aware thread allocation in multicore SMT processors. In: Proceedings of the 22nd International Conference on Parallel Architectures and Compilation Techniques, pp. 123–132 (2013)
15. Feliu, J., et al.: Symbiotic job scheduling on the IBM POWER8. In: HPCA, pp. 669–680 (2016)
16. Feliu, J., et al.: Improving IBM POWER8 performance through symbiotic job scheduling. IEEE TPDS **28**(10), 2838–2851 (2017)
17. Ferradans, S., et al.: Regularized discrete optimal transport. SIAM J. Imaging Sci. **7**(3), 1853–1882 (2014)
18. Frank, M., Wolfe, P.: An algorithm for quadratic programming. Nav. Res. Logist. Q. **3**(1), 95–110 (1956)
19. Gangbo, W., McCann, R.J.: The geometry of optimal transportation. Acta Math. **177**(2), 113–161 (1996)
20. Henning, J.L.: SPEC CPU2006 benchmark descriptions. ACM SIGARCH Comput. Arch. News **34**(4), 1–17 (2006)
21. Kolouri, S., et al.: The radon cumulative distribution transform and its application to image classification. IEEE Trans. Image Process. **25**(2), 920–934 (2016)
22. Kolouri, S., et al.: Optimal mass transport: signal processing and machine-learning applications. IEEE Signal Process. Mag. **34**(4), 43–59 (2017)
23. Li, P., et al.: A novel earth mover's distance methodology for image matching with gaussian mixture models. In: Proceedings of the IEEE International Conference on Computer Vision, pp. 1689–1696 (2013)
24. Limaye, A., et al.: A workload characterization of the spec cpu2017 benchmark suite. In: ISPASS, pp. 149–158 (2018)
25. Lorenz, D.A., et al.: Quadratically regularized optimal transport. Appl. Math. Optim. **33**, 1919–1949 (2021)
26. Monge, G.: Mémoire sur la théorie des déblais et des remblais. Mem. Math. Phys. Acad. Royale Sci. 666–704 (1781)
27. Montesuma, E.F., et al.: Recent advances in optimal transport for machine learning. arXiv preprint arXiv:2306.16156 (2023). https://arxiv.org/abs/2306.16156
28. Moseley, T., et al.: Methods for modeling resource contention on simultaneous multithreading processors. In: International Conference on Computer Design: VLSI in Computers and Processors, pp. 373–380 (2005)
29. Navarro, M., et al.: SYNPA: SMT performance analysis and allocation of threads to cores in ARM processors. In: IPDPS, pp. 705–715 (2024)
30. Nesterov, Y., Nemirovskii, A.: Interior-point polynomial methods in convex programming. SIAM Stud. Appl. Math., vol. 13. SIAM (1994)
31. Oliker, V.I.: Near radially symmetric solutions of an inverse problem in geometric optics. Inverse Prob. **3**, 743–756 (1987)
32. Papadimitriou, C.H., Steiglitz, K.: Combinatorial Optimization, Algorithms and Complexity. Prentice Hall (1982)
33. Peyré, G., Cuturi, M.: Computational optimal transport: with applications to data science. Found. Trends Mach. Learn. **11**(5–6), 355–607 (2019)

34. Radojković, P., et al.: Optimal task assignment in multithreaded processors: a statistical approach. In: International Conference on Architectural Support for Programming Languages and Operating Systems (ASPLOS), pp. 235–248 (2012)
35. Santambrogio, F.: Optimal transport for applied mathematicians, vol. 55. Birkhäuser Cham (2015)
36. Tullsen, D.M., et al.: Simultaneous multithreading: maximizing on-chip parallelism. In: ISCA '95, p. 392–403 (1995)
37. Wang, X.J.: On the design of a reflector antenna. Inverse Prob. **12**, 351–375 (1996)
38. Zaslavskiy, M., et al.: A path following algorithm for the graph matching problem. IEEE Trans. Pattern Anal. Mach. Intell. **31**, 2227–2242 (2009)

Auction-Based Placement of Function Chains in the Fog at Scale

Volodia Parol-Guarino$^{(\boxtimes)}$ and Nikos Parlavantzas

Univ Rennes, Inria, CNRS, IRISA, Rennes, France
volodia.parol-guarino@inria.fr, nikos.parlavantzas@irisa.fr

Abstract. Function-as-a-Service (FaaS) is a programming model in which applications are formed by chaining ephemeral computation units referred to as functions. FaaS is particularly suitable for developing fog-native applications by enabling flexible, on-demand placement of functions across the cloud-to-thing continuum. This continuum encompasses diverse fog nodes ranging from cloud servers to myriads of resource-constrained and geographically-distributed devices. Although many recent studies have focused on efficiently placing functions on fog resources, limited attention has been given to respecting application latency requirements. Moreover, few studies have considered the multiple entities that own fog nodes and explored mechanisms to incentivize fog node owners to share resources within the same fog network to improve quality of service for clients.

This paper addresses the FaaS function placement problem in the fog through a market-based approach. Clients submit function placement requests with expected guarantees over network latency and allocated resources, encapsulated within a Service-Level Agreement (SLA). A marketplace then organizes an auction where fog nodes bid on the SLA to determine the node that will host the function and the revenue of the fog node owner. Our approach is evaluated by emulating networks of fog nodes, utilizing our reproducible and open-source testbed running on the Grid'5000 infrastructure. We evaluate various cooperative baselines on the same testbed and demonstrate that our approach reduces client spending by 70% while maintaining the expected latency across fog networks with up to 663 nodes, under realistic loads from FaaS function chains.

Keywords: fog · cloud-to-thing · continuum · FaaS · function-as-a-service · serverless · auction · SLA · service-level agreement · QoS · quality of service · testbed · Grid'5000

1 Introduction

The rapid growth of Internet of Things (IoT) applications and the resulting data exchange demands have created significant scalability challenges for cloud computing, leading to the emergence of fog computing [22]. Fog computing, sometimes referred to as edge computing, brings computational capabilities closer to

W. E. Nagel et al. (Eds.): Euro-Par 2025, LNCS 15900, pp. 248–263, 2026.
https://doi.org/10.1007/978-3-031-99854-6_17

data sources and consumers, along the cloud-to-thing continuum. Fog computing benefits include enabling low-latency application responses and reducing bandwidth pressure on cloud infrastructures. An effective approach for developing fog applications is the Function-as-a-Service (FaaS) model, the main element of serverless computing [31]. FaaS applications consist of stateless, event-triggered functions, which makes them well-suited for event-driven IoT systems while allowing for flexible deployment across the cloud-to-things continuum. Additionally, the FaaS model enables dynamic, fine-grained provisioning and unprovisioning of resources, promoting efficient utilization of constrained fog infrastructures.

Despite FaaS benefits, deploying FaaS applications in fog environments presents two primary challenges. First, FaaS applications have strict Quality-of-Service (QoS) requirements, particularly low-latency requirements, which are critical for fog deployments. Meeting such QoS requirements is challenging owing to the highly dynamic application workloads and the heterogeneity of fog environments, containing diverse resources and networks. Second, fog infrastructures are owned and managed by various providers, including individuals, companies, communities, and established cloud and edge providers. Offering appropriate incentives for these providers to contribute their computational resources is challenging, especially while also ensuring that applications acquire these resources in a cost-efficient manner.

There is growing research investigating FaaS in fog environments [4,9,21]. However, existing systems do not address the two aforementioned challenges at the same time. Previous work on fog task placement [35] often assumes single-provider scenarios, overlooking the reality of multi-provider infrastructures. Some market-based approaches [26] deal with multi-provider scenarios, but focus mainly on economic aspects, rely on simulations, and lack practical implementations for real-world fog deployments at scale.

This article proposes a market-based approach, called GIRAFF, for FaaS application placement in fog environments that supports QoS requirements as well as provider incentives. Specifically, the approach enables customers to specify latency and resource requirements in Service-Level Agreements (SLAs), satisfied through exclusively reserving resources for functions for specified durations. To incentivize providers to offer resources, the approach applies an auction system in which independently owned fog nodes compete for function hosting and receive payments via a central marketplace. This article makes the following contributions:

(1) We describe a reverse-auction-based approach, GIRAFF, for FaaS application placement in multi-provider fog environments.
(2) We propose a fog-oriented cost model where prices, unlike the fixed rates of cloud nodes, are driven by energy consumption and increase toward the network edge and resource-constrained fog nodes.

(3) We assess the effectiveness of our approach through reproducible experiments on the Grid'5000 testbed[1], comparing it with baseline algorithms at scale of up to 663 autonomous fog nodes. The baselines either deploy functions (i) along the cloud-to-thing path, (ii) the closest possible to the edge, (iii) the furthest possible from the edge, or (iv) using an efficient node selection. The implementation is available as a MIT-licensed public-source repository on GitHub[2].

The rest of this article discusses related work (Sect. 2), followed by a design section (Sect. 3) that presents the system model, our market-based algorithm, four baseline algorithms, and the testbed implementation. Then, the evaluation section (Sect. 4) presents a comparison of the GIRAFF placement algorithm with the baselines using a workload of function chains deployed on the testbed. Finally, Sect. 5 concludes the article and discusses future work directions.

2   Related Work

The current literature describes significant advances in placement strategies for FaaS applications. However, most contributions are focused on fog networks managed by a single administrative entity [33]. Moreover, most contributions fail to consider large-scale applicability, especially with regards to the economic viability of such large-scale fog networks. A lack of large-scale testbeds to validate results in real-world conditions can also be observed. In the following, we discuss placement strategies, distinguishing between cooperative and non-cooperative ones, along with large-scale fog testbeds.

Cooperative Approaches. Cooperative approaches assume fog nodes collaborate [8,33] to offer a unified network to clients. Their economic model is derived from cloud economics [36] with fixed-rate pricing.

Rausch et al. [28] propose a container scheduler for FaaS functions using multi-objective optimization considering network topology, node capabilities, and function data transfer requirements. However, this scheduler focuses on edge clusters rather than fog deployments and overlooks internode latencies. Ascigil et al. [3] propose a tree-shaped fog network model for FaaS resource provisioning that considers both networking and execution latencies but lacks resource guarantees for clients. Yu et al. [41] propose a near-optimal placement framework using online learning to reduce exploration, but neglect latencies in the fog. For their results, the authors leverage a 13-node testbed with 6 functions to generate a load; this is, to our knowledge, the only system among the systems we examine to leverage real functions. Smolka et al. [34] present a decentralized, auction-based approach for edge microservice application placement. The authors show latency improvements (54% reduction compared to a cloud-only

---

[1] grid5000.fr.
[2] github.com/volodiapg/giraff.

or fully decentralized approaches), but their approach offers no guarantees on placement quality. Deng et al. [12] propose a history-based genetic algorithm that aims to predict application response times but cannot guarantee specific response times. Beraldi et al. [7] adapt the *least-loaded-among-d-random-nodes* algorithm [32] for fog computing, approaching the original algorithm's performance. The approach remains best-effort. Yousefpour et al. [40] use live traffic data for dynamic function placement with greedy strategies to minimize latency violations or costs, yet without offering latency guarantees.

Non-cooperative Approaches. Non-cooperative approaches assume nodes act selfishly, driven by economic incentives, as each node seeks to maximize its own utility function.

Xu et al. [39] propose an edge resource allocation model, called *Zenith*, in which service providers establish contracts with edge infrastructure providers based on an auction. These contracts allow service providers to lease micro-datacenter resources for specific time intervals. The service providers then use these resources to schedule applications with latency requirements. The model provides latency guarantees, but the contribution is evaluated through simulations and is limited to micro-datacenter resources rather than using resource-constrained, distributed fog nodes.

Beraldi et al. [8] introduce *CICO*, a credit-based system that aims for cooperative-like outcomes in non-cooperative environments. While reducing costs and latencies [8,12,34] using dynamic pricing managed by fog providers in their simulations, *CICO* treats latencies as soft constraints without client-specific guarantees. Bermbach et al. [9] introduce an auction-based FaaS placement approach, named *AuctionWhisk*, with separate storage and compute bidding. Clients bid for resources proposed by fog nodes. *AuctionWhisk* lacks latency guarantees and adds overhead by processing bids in batches. Our approach avoids this problem by using reverse auctions.

Testbeds at Scale. Little attention has been currently given to testbeds. Usually, fog placement frameworks [5,9,12,23,30,41] include a small testbed to validate their applicability to the real-world. In this cited list, the biggest testbed was 17 fog nodes [30].

Smolka et al.'s [33] survey of 99 fog placement articles revealed that 88% use simulators, while only 18% of the tests on testbeds are done with over 100 fog nodes. Most experiments are conducted on unrealistically small problem instances and lack reliance on real-world infrastructure. Currently, the biggest testbed we are aware of is *Celestial* [25], but is specific to Low Earth Orbit Edge.

A preliminary version of our approach was introduced in [2]. The current paper provides detailed algorithms, supports function chaining, integrates an energy-aware cost model, adds state-of-the-art baselines, and presents a scalable implementation, enabling a large-scale evaluation on up to 663 nodes, establishing, to our knowledge, the largest reproducible fog testbed to date.

3   GIRAFF Design

This section details our system design for function placement in the fog. We describe the SLAs input in the system in Sect. 3.1, followed by our auction-based placement system in Sect. 3.2, comparative baselines in Sect. 3.3, cost model in Sect. 3.4 and the testbed implementation in Sect. 3.5.

3.1   Service-Level Agreement (SLA)

The SLA specifies the constraints that must be met for a single function to run as intended by the client. The SLA constraints are defined as follows:

$SLA_{entrypoint}$ indicates the ideal node to provision the function; it should be the nearest node to the end user or the preceding function in the function chain.

$SLA_{\max\_lat}$ indicates the maximum latency allowed for the function, defined as the delay between the first bytes of a request leaving the $SLA_{entrypoint}$ and the request being fully received by the function (see Sect. 3.5).

$SLA_{duration}$ indicates the duration of the reservation.

SLA_{data_size} indicates the maximum size of the input data.

SLA_{CPU} indicates the CPU constraint, e.g., 0.125 CPU core.

SLA_{mem} indicates the memory constraint, e.g., 256 MiB.

The SLA enables flexible and straightforward function provisioning in fog computing. For applications with multiple functions, we submit separate SLAs for each function.

3.2   GIRAFF System Model

Our system involves the interaction of four key parties: (1) *fog nodes*, owned by providers, offer shared resources; (2) *clients* create and manage stateless function chains, following the FaaS paradigm, and relying on the continuum of fog node resources; (3) *end users* interact with client functions; and (4) *the marketplace* serves as a trusted intermediary between clients and fog nodes, facilitating monetary and placement decisions.

Figure 1 shows the architecture of the GIRAFF system. The control plane, in the upper part of Fig. 1, uses REST APIs to manage interactions between clients (or more accurately, an autonomous agent acting on behalf of the client, referred to as the client's representative in Fig. 2), the marketplace, and fog nodes. The marketplace centralizes payment and client to fog node interaction; and is aware of the fog network topology. The fog node agent (or simply "fog node"; in Fig. 1) implements the protocols to enable communication with the rest of the fog network, including the marketplace and the other neighboring fog nodes. This agent allows fog node providers to integrate their nodes into the broader fog

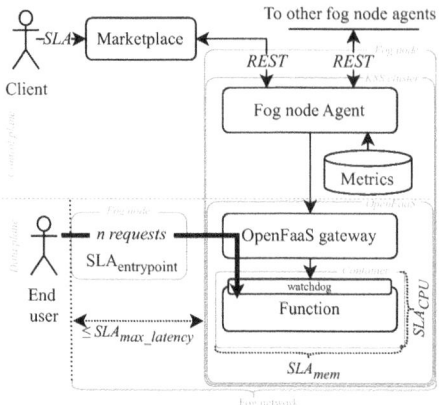

Fig. 1. GIRAFF architecture

Algorithm 1. Fog node bidding

Require: *sla*: Function SLA
 acc_lat: Accumulated latency
 after arriving here (default 0)
Provide: List of bids from all eligible
 nodes
 neighbors ← GETMYNEIGHBORS( )
 bids ← [ ]
 for each *node* in *neighbors* **do**
  acc_lat' ← ACCUMULATE(*acc_lat*,
  node.latency)
  latency ← GETANDESTIMATELA-
  TENCY[3](*node*, *acc_lat'*, *sla*)

  if *latency* < *sla*. max _*lat* **then**
   bids ← *bids*
    + SENDSLA(*sla*, *node*,
    acc_lat')
 if CANIPROVISION[4](*sla*) **then**
  bids ← *bids* + GETMYBID(*sla*) ▷ *The*
  bid is the result of the cost model in
  section 3.4
 return *bids*

---

network. Providers then install a local stack to manage function lifecycles. For instance, we use K3S and OpenFaaS to manage function lifecycle and networking, deploying functions as containers with a watchdog process alongside the client code.

The data plane, illustrated in the lower section of Fig. 1, handles message processing from end users to functions. The fog network begins at the first fog node, typically the $SLA_{entrypoint}$ where the SLA is initially submitted. End users interact with functions by sending multiple messages during their session time, with each message timestamped upon entering the network at the edge. Messages are sent either between the end user and the function or between the functions themselves in a decentralized manner, to circumvent bottlenecks of utilizing a central location.

The **GIRAFF marketplace** facilitates function placement. The marketplace's primary function is to accept client SLAs (step 1 and 2 on Fig. 2), identify the appropriate entry point within the fog network (step 3 on Fig. 2), and initiate a bidding process among fog nodes (step 3 on Fig. 2). This process involves forwarding the SLA to the entry point node, collecting bids from suitable nodes once they passed the SLA between themselves (step 4 on Fig. 2), and conducting a second-price auction [11] to select a winning node (step 5 on Fig. 2). Finally,

---

[3] `getAndEstimateLatency` estimates the latency to transmit a message of size SLA_{data_size} to a neighboring fog node. It is based on the median measured latency in the past 12 min, takes into consideration the uncertainty and accounts for the worst-case scenario by adding a 30% error margin on top of the TCP estimation given by equation (32) of [24] and later found in [18].

[4] `canIProvision` tests if the fog node has enough available resources to maybe provision a function that would use SLA_{CPU} and SLA_{mem} resources.

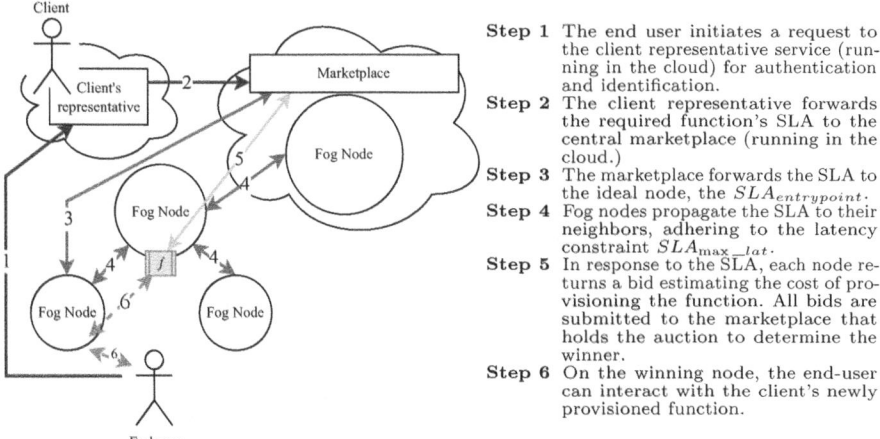

Fig. 2. Provisioning function f step by step

Step 1 The end user initiates a request to the client representative service (running in the cloud) for authentication and identification.

Step 2 The client representative forwards the required function's SLA to the central marketplace (running in the cloud.)

Step 3 The marketplace forwards the SLA to the ideal node, the $SLA_{entrypoint}$.

Step 4 Fog nodes propagate the SLA to their neighbors, adhering to the latency constraint $SLA_{\max\_lat}$.

Step 5 In response to the SLA, each node returns a bid estimating the cost of provisioning the function. All bids are submitted to the marketplace that holds the auction to determine the winner.

Step 6 On the winning node, the end-user can interact with the client's newly provisioned function.

the marketplace validates the provisioning of the function on the chosen node, ensuring the client pays the second-lowest bid. The end user can now interact with the function (step 6 in Fig. 2). This auction mechanism is designed to promote economic efficiency and truthfulness, encouraging fog nodes to bid their actual resource costs (see the cost model in Sect. 3.4, which depends on SLA_{CPU} and SLA_{mem}).

GIRAFF bidding (Algorithm 1) handles the SLA cost evaluation and propagation. Triggered by the SLA reception (step 4 on Fig. 2), it evaluates the function cost, expresses it as a bid, and forwards the SLA to neighbors for further evaluation. While tracking accumulated latency to ensure $SLA_{\max\_lat}$ compliance, it recursively repeats this process until the latency constraint is reached (repeating step 4 on Fig. 2), effectively balancing cost assessment with network-wide propagation.

3.3   Baseline Placement Methods

Here, we introduce baseline placement methods against which we will compare our market-based approach, GIRAFF. These baselines are cooperative algorithms, designed to optimize placement based on various Quality of Service (QoS) metrics, without directly considering provider costs.

We did not use the closest related non-cooperative systems (see Sect. 2), *Zenith* [39] and *AuctionWhisk* [9], as baselines because they operate under a different market structure than GIRAFF. Indeed, *Zenith* and *AuctionWhisk* involve competition among multiple clients (or function requests) for a given fog node; this requires that demand be aggregated into batches periodically, introducing latency. In contrast, GIRAFF involves competition among fog nodes to host functions as soon as they arrive. We did not use *CICO* [8] either because that

Algorithm 3 Power of 2-random mincpu (MinCPU)

Require: *sla*: Function SLA
acc_lat: Accumulated latency after arriving here (default 0)
nb_reqs: Number of candidates to return (initially 2)
Provide: List with at most *nb_reqs* of candidate bids from suitable nodes

bids ← []
if CANIPROVISION(*sla*) **then**
    bids ← *bids* + [GETCPUUSAGE( )]
    nb_reqs ← *nb_reqs* − 1
neighbors ← GETNEIGHBORS( )
neighbors ← RANDOMIZE-ORDER(*neighbors*)
nb_followups ← 1
if *nb_reqs* >= LEN(*neighbors*) **then**
    nb_followups ← ⌈*nb_reqs*/LEN(*neighbors*)⌉
    neighbors ← TAKEUPTONELE-MENTS(*nb_followups*, *neighbors*)
for each *node* in *neighbors* **do**
    acc_lat' ← ACCUMULATE(*acc_lat*, *node.latency*)
    latency ← GETANDESTIMATELA-TENCY(*node*, *acc_lat'*, *sla*)
    if *latency* < *sla.max_lat* **then**
        bids ← *bids* + SENDSLA(*sla*, *node*, *acc_lat'*, *nb_reqs*)
return *bids*

Algorithm 2. Edge-furthest

Require: *sla*: Function SLA
acc_lat: Accumulated latency after arriving here (default 0)
Provide: Single bid from furthest suitable node

sorted_neighbors ← GETNEIGHBORSBY-DESCLATENCY( ) ▷ *Starts the list by the node with greatest latency*
for each *node* in *sorted_neighbors* **do**
    acc_lat' ← ACCUMULATE(*acc_lat*, *node.latency*)
    latency ← GETANDESTIMATELA-TENCY(*node*, *acc_lat'*, *sla*)
    if *latency* < *sla.max_lat* **then**
        bid ← SENDSLA(*sla*, *node*, *acc_lat'*)
        if not ISEMPTY(*bid*) **then**
            return *bid*
if CANIPROVISION(*sla*) **then**
    return GETMYBID(*sla*)
return [ ]

method uses credits to regulate reciprocal cooperation between fog providers without considering individual clients' requirements.

Edge-furthest (Algorithm 2) is a greedy heuristic that accepts the SLA at the furthest possible node within SLA constraints. This approach anticipates future placement demands on the same fog node, preserving node resources as much as possible. Edge-furthest increase acceptance rate of latency-constrained functions.

Edge-first is a greedy heuristic that aims to run functions as close as possible to the $SLA_{entrypoint}$. It accepts the SLA at the first suitable node, exploring neighboring nodes in order of increasing latency. This approach, based on *Zenith* [39], balances minimal risk with latency constraint satisfaction.

Edge-ward allocates functions along a path from the $SLA_{entrypoint}$ to the cloud. It uses a greedy approach, attempting allocation at each layer and stopping at the first successful allocation. First described by Gupta et al. [17], Edge-ward is best-effort and disregards the $SLA_{max\_latency}$ constraint. This algorithm is widely applied in fog computing research [16,22,23,29].

Power-of-2-random-mincpu (Algorithm 3) efficiently provisions functions by selecting the least loaded [20] among two randomly chosen nodes [7]. This approach reduces complexity and delays compared to exhaustive methods, is based on [7][5], and behaves as the original power-of-2-random-choices algorithm, but adapted to the fog and our SLA.

3.4   Cost Model

Our function cost model reflects resource allocation costs at fog nodes for the $SLA_{duration}$. The key principles are: (1) costs decrease closer to the cloud [15], (2) cloud nodes incur fixed costs per unit time, and (3) other nodes incur costs based on energy consumption multiplied by the energy price (p_{elec}).

We express fog node power consumption using a quadratic model [13] as

$$P(u) = au^2 + bu + c$$

where u is resource utilization and a, b, c are sensitivity constants set according to the proximity of the fog node to the cloud. In the following, we set $u_f = \frac{SLA_{CPU}}{available\_CPU}$ for the cost model.

The cost of provisioning function f when the reservation is submitted at t_0 until $t = t_0 + SLA_{duration}$ is then

$$Cost_{f,t_0}(t) = p_{elec} \int_{t_0}^{t} [P(u(y) + u_f) - P(u(y))]dy$$

Here, $u(y)$ is the CPU utilization at time y resulting from previously accepted function reservations.

The cost model calculates the bid value that fog nodes use in the auctions. Fog nodes will only submit a bid if they have sufficient resources and the estimated latency to the target node is within the $SLA_{latency\_max}$.

3.5   Testbed Implementation

Our fog testbed, scales to hundreds of fog nodes thanks to the usage of an eBPF filter and our Nix-based VMs. Each server runs multiple VMs, interconnected in a tree topology [3] with configurable latency and bandwidth via an eBPF filter [6,25]. These VMs execute our bidding software, forming the fog network for FaaS function provisioning. Nix is used to implement our testbed's reproducibility, efficiency, and scalability. It enables the use of custom VM images with K3s, OpenFaaS, and functions, ensuring consistent environments that can be exploited in the exact same conditions across multiple experiments in a timely manner.

4   Evaluation

Our evaluation was conducted on Grid'5000 servers[6]. We deployed fog nodes as VMs with varying resource configurations, ranging from cloud-like nodes (16

---

[5] We set the offloading threshold to 1, effectively using the standard power-of-2-random choices method, at the cost of higher control delays, as the authors indicate.

[6] Servers equipped with Intel Xeon Gold 5220 processors (36 SMT threads, 96 GiB RAM, SSD storage).

vCPUs, 96 GiB RAM) to highly constrained edge nodes (2 vCPUs, 4 GiB RAM). The network topology consisted of a 4-layer fog network with up to 663 virtual nodes distributed across 60 physical servers. The nodes were arranged in a randomly generated tree-shaped structure. As we scaled the network, we maintained a constant depth while horizontally expanding the topology by increasing the number of child nodes per parent. We detail how we ran experiments in Sect. 4.1, the obtained results in Sect. 4.2, followed by a discussion in Sect. 4.3.

4.1   Function Chains

We evaluated GIRAFF against four baseline algorithms using two function chains of three functions each, inspired by *EdgeFaasBench* [27]. For each chain, we defined two variants characterized by different latency constraints: low-latency and high-latency, based upon observable latencies in the web at various degrees of QoE for the end-users. Average latencies between functions are noted as "$low{\downarrow}high$", corresponding to the $SLA_{latency\_max}$ of the low-latency and high-latency configurations. The chain configurations are:

Name	max_lat	CPU	mem	data size	Misc
Object classification in images					
Compress	20 ms ↓ 1 sec	0.1	120 MB	52 KiB	Python
Classify	75 ms ↓ 1 sec	0.7	800 MB	16 KiB	Python + [19]
Echo	200 ms ↓ 1 sec	0.001	40 MB		Rust
Sentiment analysis from speech					
Recognize	20 ms ↓ 1 sec	1	1 GB	32 KiB	Python + [1]
Sentiment	75 ms ↓ 1 sec	0.05	100 MB	4 KiB	Python
Echo	200 ms ↓ 1 sec	0.001	40 MB		Rust

Before the 10-minute experiment, a fog node topology of random size is generated, and multiple $SLA_{entrypoint}$ are selected for multiple function chains to be deployed on the edge nodes at random timestamps, thus emulating the presence of various clients concurrently demanding resources to run their applications. Functions in the chains can be vertically scaled up beforehand depending on the configured load, setting higher resource demands in the SLA. During the 10-minute experiment, the configuration is applied: function placement requests are sent and their load is generated. This way, we achieve various level of stress testing the placement algorithms under the same load.

In a network with N entrypoint nodes, at most $4N$ function chains are deployed concurrently, thus the function chains receive at least $4N$ requests. Some random function chains receive more requests than others. We present the results of 11 different configurations, with different loads, network sizes and topologies in Sect. 4.2. For instance, at 663 nodes, we observe GIRAFF placing 5714 functions in 10 min, processing a total of 8679 requests.

4.2   Results

We classify the obtained results in Fig. 3 in three categories: placement quality, client spending and deployment time.

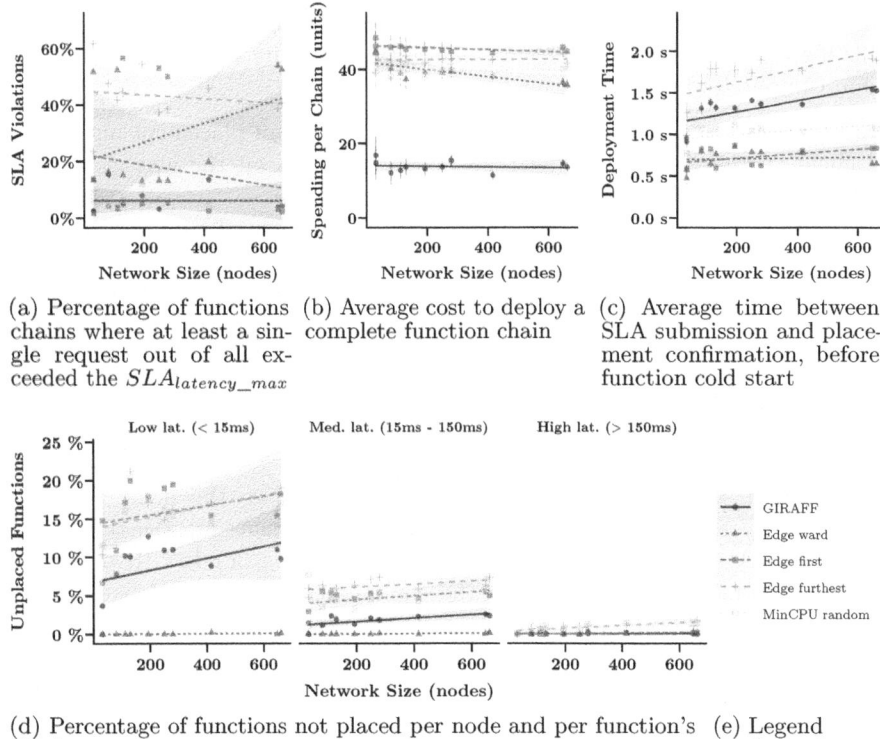

(a) Percentage of functions chains where at least a single request out of all exceeded the $SLA_{latency\_max}$

(b) Average cost to deploy a complete function chain

(c) Average time between SLA submission and placement confirmation, before function cold start

(d) Percentage of functions not placed per node and per function's $SLA_{max\_latency}$ target

(e) Legend for figure 3

Fig. 3. Comparison of GIRAFF against other placement algorithms. Legend is Fig. 3e. Dots represent averages of data points generated by the multiple concurrent requests in a scenario run. Solid lines show a linear fit for illustration purposes only, and shaded regions indicate its 95% confidence interval.

Placement Quality. We evaluate the quality of function placement for the different algorithms across multiple fog network sizes. We focus on two key metrics: (1) *SLA violations*, which represent the percentage of function chains where at least a single request exceeds $SLA_{latency\_max}$ (Fig. 3a), and (2) the percentage of functions not placed (Fig. 3d).

GIRAFF demonstrates a strong performance. It achieves a low average SLA violation rate of $6.1\% \pm 1.3\%$ (Fig. 3a) and successfully places the vast majority of functions, with only $3.5\% \pm 0.8\%$ failing placement (Fig. 3d). This result is comparable to MinCPU (2.9% to 5.7% difference).

Compared to algorithms prioritizing proximity (Edge-first and Edge-ward), GIRAFF exhibits significantly improved SLA adherence, with low variance like the MinCPU random algorithm. Edge-first, for instance, shows a $17.8\% \pm 7.0\%$ SLA violation rate and Edge-ward regularly exceeds 50%, caused by its design (Sect. 3.3).

GIRAFF has the highest compliance rate with client SLAs, respecting SLAs in 93.9% of the cases. GIRAFF also places the most function chains, 96.5% of them, compared to other relevant baselines.

Client Spending. We compare the cost-effectiveness of placement algorithms for clients across various fog network sizes. We focus on the average cost to deploy a complete function chain (Fig. 3b).

GIRAFF reduces client costs by 65% to 70% compared to other baselines. This difference remains stable as networks grow larger (Fig. 3b.)

Stable pricing across network sizes is maintained by all algorithms except Edge-ward which exhibits lower costs in larger networks (Fig. 3b). However, Edge-ward's modest cost savings come at the expense of regularly breaking more than 50% of its SLAs.

GIRAFF demonstrates superior cost-efficiency, consistently reducing clients' costs by 70% compared to all other baselines across all network sizes.

Deployment Time of Function Chains. We compare the delay overhead introduced by the different placement algorithms. We measure the time difference from SLA arrival to complete chain provisioning (Fig. 3c). In GIRAFF, most of this deployment time comes from the communication overhead between fog nodes during the bidding process steps.

GIRAFF deploys chains in $1.3\,\text{s} \pm 0.1\,\text{s}$ on average ($1.54\,\text{s}$ at 663 nodes). It is 54% slower than the fastest algorithm (Edge-ward) but 78% faster than the slowest (Edge-furthest, Fig. 3c.)

Edge-first is faster to deploy functions, but breaks SLAs more often, 17.8% of the time. The fastest comparable baseline is MinCPU with an average of $1\,\text{s}$ to deploy the chain, at similar levels of placement quality, but worse price.

GIRAFF is slower to provision function chains than other baselines; it is 54% slower than Edge-ward, the fastest placement algorithm in the tested baselines. This difference grows with network size because bids are collected in a breadth-first fashion to allow equal participation of fog nodes in the range of $SLA_{latency\_max}$.

4.3   Discussion

GIRAFF proves to be a highly effective function placement approach, achieving good performance while significantly reducing client costs. However, some practical considerations remain.

First, the current GIRAFF implementation does not address provider collusion or Byzantine attacks. Public auction logs and reputation systems [10] could help mitigate collusion, encouraging actors to detect collusive behavior and get a reward [38]. Using multiple marketplaces and SLA entrypoints could mitigate Byzantine attacks against a single marketplace and single fog nodes manipulating bids. Second, GIRAFF does not currently automatically manage SLA violations. Future work will enforce penalties for SLAs violations, and allow fog nodes to factor them into resource allocation and bid calculation decisions [14]. Finally, the current GIRAFF implementation overlooks the costs associated with data transfers as well as downloading function images from container registries and storing them. Future work will extend the SLA and the cost model to consider these factors, enabling more optimized function placement decisions.

5   Conclusion

In this paper, we present GIRAFF, a market-based approach for placing function chains in multi-provider fog infrastructures. The approach organizes reverse auctions where fog nodes bid on function SLAs, optimizing placement costs while meeting described QoS requirements. Using our open-source testbed on Grid'5000, we compared GIRAFF with four baseline methods: Edge-ward [17], Edge-furthest, power-of-2-random-choices MinCPU [7], and Edge-first across networks of up to 663 nodes. Results show that GIRAFF reduces client costs by 70% while maintaining QoS targets with 6.1% SLA violations. The main trade-off is increased deployment time due to communication overhead between neighboring fog nodes.

Our study provides evidence that a market-based approach with independent, competing fog providers can be as effective as carefully crafted cooperative systems. These findings suggest that market-driven strategies can play a crucial role in optimizing fog computing systems, leading to more efficient and cost-effective deployments.

Future research will focus on supporting complex and adaptive function workflows, going beyond function chaining. Furthermore, we intend to enhance the programming model to better support diverse fog use cases, prioritizing abstraction through minimal infrastructure management and ephemeral resource reservation, building on the approach described in this article.

Acknowledgments. The experiments were conducted on the Grid'5000 testbed, supported by a scientific interest group hosted by Inria and including CNRS, RENATER, and several universities and other organizations.

References

1. VOSK speech recognition toolkit. https://github.com/alphacep/vosk-api
2. Parol-Guarino, V., Parlavantzas, N.: GIRAFF: reverse auction-based placement for fog functions. In: Proceedings of the 9th International Workshop on Serverless Computing (2023)
3. Ascigil, O., Tasiopoulos, A.G., Phan, T.K., Sourlas, V., Psaras, I., Pavlou, G.: Resource provisioning and allocation in function-as-a-service edge-clouds. IEEE Trans. Serv. Comput. (2022)
4. Aslanpour, M.S., et al.: Serverless edge computing: vision and challenges. In: Proceedings of the 2021 Australasian Computer Science Week Multiconference (2021)
5. Baresi, L., Hu, D.Y.X., Quattrocchi, G., Terracciano, L.: Neptune: network- and GPU-aware management of serverless functions at the edge. In: Proceedings of the 17th Symposium on Software Engineering for Adaptive and Self-Managing Systems (2022)

6. Becker, S., Pfandzelter, T., Japke, N., Bermbach, D., Kao, O.: Network emulation in large-scale virtual edge testbeds: a note of caution and the way forward. In: Proceedings of the 2nd International Workshop on Testing Distributed Internet of Things Systems (TDIS 2022) (2022)
7. Beraldi, R., Mattia, G.P.: Power of random choices made efficient for fog computing. IEEE Trans. Cloud Comput. (2020)
8. Beraldi, R., Mtibaa, A., Mian, A.N.: CICO: a credit-based incentive mechanism for cooperative fog computing paradigms. In: 2018 IEEE Global Communications Conference (GLOBECOM) (2018)
9. Bermbach, D., Bader, J., Hasenburg, J., Pfandzelter, T., Thamsen, L.: Auction-Whisk: using an auction-inspired approach for function placement in serverless fog platforms. Softw. Pract. Exp. (2022)
10. Bikhchandani, S.: Reputation in repeated second-price auctions. J. Econ. Theory (1988)
11. Choi, P.S., Munoz-Garcia, F.: Second-price auctions. In: Auction Theory: Introductory Exercises with Answer Keys (2021)
12. Deng, Q., Goudarzi, M., Buyya, R.: Fogbus2: a lightweight and distributed container-based framework for integration of IoT-enabled systems with edge and cloud computing. In: Proceedings of the International Workshop on Big Data in Emergent Distributed Environments (2021)
13. Deng, R., Lu, R., Lai, C., Luan, T.H., Liang, H.: Optimal workload allocation in fog-cloud computing toward balanced delay and power consumption. IEEE Internet Things J. (2016)
14. Dib, D., Parlavantzas, N., Morin, C.: SLA-based profit optimization in cloud bursting PAAS. In: 2014 14th IEEE/ACM International Symposium on Cluster, Cloud and Grid Computing, pp. 141–150 (2014)
15. Farzin, P., Azizi, S., Shojafar, M., Rana, O., Singhal, M.: FLEX: a platform for scalable service placement in multi-fog and multi-cloud environments. In: Proceedings of 2022 Australasian Computer Science Week (2022)
16. Goudarzi, M., Palaniswami, M., Buyya, R.: A distributed application placement and migration management techniques for edge and fog computing environments. In: 2021 16th Conference on Computer Science and Intelligence Systems, FedCSIS (2021)
17. Gupta, H., Vahid Dastjerdi, A., Ghosh, S.K., Buyya, R.: iFogSim: a toolkit for modeling and simulation of resource management techniques in the internet of things, edge and fog computing environments. Pract. Exp. Softw. (2017)
18. Hacker, T., Athey, B., Noble, B.: The end-to-end performance effects of parallel TCP sockets on a lossy wide-area network. In: Proceedings 16th International Parallel and Distributed Processing Symposium (2002)
19. Iandola, F.N., Han, S., Moskewicz, M.W., Ashraf, K., Dally, W.J., Keutzer, K.: Squeezenet: alexnet-level accuracy with 50x fewer parameters and <0.5mb model size (2016)
20. Kaffes, K., Yadwadkar, Neeraja, J., Kozyrakis, C.: Hermod: principled and practical scheduling for serverless functions. In: Proceedings of the 13th Symposium on Cloud Computing (2022)
21. Latreche, C., Parlavantzas, N., Duran-Limon, H.A.: FoRLess: a deep reinforcement learning-based approach for FaaS placement in fog. In: 2024 IEEE/ACM 17th International Conference on Utility and Cloud Computing (UCC). IEEE Computer Society (2024)

22. Mahmud, R., Kotagiri, R., Buyya, R.: Fog computing: a taxonomy, survey and future directions. In: Internet of Everything: Algorithms, Methodologies, Technologies and Perspectives (2018)

23. Malekabbasi, M., Pfandzelter, T., Schirmer, T., Bermbach, D.: GeoFaaS: an edge-to-cloud FaaS platform. In: Proceedings of the 12th IEEE International Conference on Cloud Engineering (2024)

24. Padhye, J., Firoiu, V., Towsley, D., Kurose, J.: Modeling TCP throughput: a simple model and its empirical validation. In: ACM SIGCOMM Computer Communication Review (1998)

25. Pfandzelter, T., Bermbach, D.: Celestial: virtual software system testbeds for the LEO edge. In: 23rd ACM/IFIP International Middleware Conference (Middleware 2022) (2022)

26. Qiu, H., Zhu, K., Luong, N.C., Yi, C., Niyato, D., Kim, D.I.: Applications of auction and mechanism design in edge computing: a survey. IEEE Trans. Cogn. Commun. Network. (2022)

27. Rajput, K.R., Kulkarni, C.D., Cho, B., Wang, W., Kim, I.K.: Edgefaasbench: benchmarking edge devices using serverless computing. In: 2022 IEEE International Conference on Edge Computing and Communications (EDGE) (2022)

28. Rausch, T., Rashed, A., Dustdar, S.: Optimized container scheduling for data-intensive serverless edge computing. Future Gener. Comput. Syst. (2021)

29. Russo, G.R., Cardellini, V., Presti, F.L.: Serverless functions in the cloud-edge continuum: challenges and opportunities. In: 2023 31st Euromicro International Conference on Parallel, Distributed and Network-Based Processing (PDP) (2023)

30. Russo, G.R., Mannucci, T., Cardellini, V., Presti, F.L.: Serverledge: decentralized function-as-a-service for the edge-cloud continuum. In: 2023 IEEE International Conference on Pervasive Computing and Communications, PerCom (2023)

31. Schleier-Smith, J., et al.: What serverless computing is and should become: the next phase of cloud computing. Commun. ACM (2021)

32. Richa, A., Mitzenmacher, I., Sitaraman, R.: The power of two random choices: a survey of techniques and results. In: Handbook of Randomized Computing (2001)

33. Smolka, S., Mann, Z.Á.: Evaluation of fog application placement algorithms: a survey. Computing (2022)

34. Smolka, S., Wißenberg, L., Mann, Z.Á.: Edgedecap: an auction-based decentralized algorithm for optimizing application placement in edge computing. J. Parallel Distrib. Comput. (2023)

35. Sonkoly, B., Czentye, J., Szalay, M., Németh, B., Toka, L.: Survey on placement methods in the edge and beyond. IEEE Commun. Surv. Tutor. (2021)

36. Srirama, S.N.: A decade of research in fog computing: relevance, challenges, and future directions. Softw. Pract. Exp. (2024)

37. Tange, O.: GNU parallel 20230622 ('nova kakhovka'), GNU Parallel is a general parallelizer to run multiple serial command line programs in parallel without changing them (2023)

38. Wong, K.S., Kim, M.H.: Toward a fair indictment for sealed-bid auction with self-enforcing privacy. J. Supercomput. (2018)

39. Xu, J., Palanisamy, B., Ludwig, H., Wang, Q.: Zenith: utility-aware resource allocation for edge computing. In: 2017 IEEE International Conference on Edge Computing (EDGE) (2017)

40. Yousefpour, A., et al.: FOGPLAN: a lightweight QOS-aware dynamic fog service provisioning framework. IEEE Internet Things J. (2019)
41. Yu, G., Chen, P., Zheng, Z., Zhang, J., Li, X., He, Z.: Faasdeliver: cost-efficient and QOS-aware function delivery in computing continuum. IEEE Trans. Serv. Comput. (2023)

Federated Learning Within Global Energy Budget over Heterogeneous Edge Accelerators

Roopkatha Banerjee[(⊠)] [iD], Tejus Chandrashekar, Ananth Eswar, and Yogesh Simmhan[iD]

Department of Computational and Data Sciences, Indian Institute of Science, Bangalore, India
{roopkathab,simmhan}@iisc.ac.in

Abstract. Federated Learning (FL) enables collaborative model training across distributed clients while preserving data privacy. However, optimizing both energy efficiency and model accuracy remains a challenge, given device and data heterogeneity. Further, sustainable AI through a global energy budget for FL has not been explored. We propose a novel optimization problem for client selection in FL that maximizes the model accuracy within an overall energy limit and reduces training time. We solve this with a unique bi-level ILP formulation that leverages approximate Shapley values and energy–time prediction models to efficiently solve this. Our FEDJOULE framework achieves superior training accuracies compared to SOTA and simple baselines for diverse energy budgets, non-IID distributions, and realistic experiment configurations, performing 15% and 48% better on accuracy and time, respectively. The results highlight the effectiveness of our method in achieving a viable trade-off between energy usage and performance in FL environments.

1 Introduction

Federated Learning (FL) has transformed distributed Machine Learning (ML) by enabling privacy-preserving model training across decentralized edge devices, without moving data centrally. In FL, clients train local models using their private data and only share model updates with a central server for aggregation into a global model (Fig. 1). This repeats over multiple rounds, using different subsets of clients, till convergence. FL is proving essential, given the pervasive generation of data from diverse and accelerated edge devices and the growing regulatory requirements like GDPR on data privacy.

Context. However, FL poses several challenges due to the *heterogeneity of edge devices and of data* present across them, which affects the training time, energy usage and accuracy achieved. Edge devices ranging from Raspberry Pi to GPU-accelerated NVIDIA Jetsons differ by orders of magnitude in compute performance and peak power load, which affects time to accuracy [6]. Further, Jetsons offer1000 s of *power modes*, which control the active CPU cores and CPU/GPU/memory frequencies, with varying compute–power trade-offs that

W. E. Nagel et al. (Eds.): Euro-Par 2025, LNCS 15900, pp. 264–278, 2026.
https://doi.org/10.1007/978-3-031-99854-6_18

impact the energy footprint for FL [13]. Non-IID data with label and quantity skews across edge devices can cause model drift, increasing training rounds [4].

Time to accuracy (TTA), the time required to achieve a target accuracy, is a critical metric for FL. The push for *sustainable AI* has emphasized energy-efficient FL, as enterprise carbon caps and renewable-powered IoT deployments may enforce collective energy limits on training. Unlike energy constraints imposed on individual devices due to battery limits or power load, *imposing a collective energy constraint for sustainable FL training is a novel problem that has not yet been sufficiently explored.*

Challenges. NVIDIA Jetson accelerated edge devices are well-suited for FL. Besides multi-core Arm CPUs, they have a GPU with 100–1000 s of CUDA cores and 8–32 GB of RAM shared by CPU and GPU (Table 1), allowing them to train non-trivial DNN models with FL. Besides a compact size and a peak power within 60W, they also expose *custom power modes* to change the CPU core count and frequencies of CPU, GPU and memory. E.g., the latest Jetson Orin AGX has 29 CPU frequencies, 13 GPU frequencies, 4 memory frequencies and 12 core-counts to give $\approx 18,000$ power modes, with *MAXN* being the highest power and performance one. Although power modes can help balance compute and energy, their non-linear effects on training time and power load make tuning difficult. Profiling each mode is time-intensive, taking minutes per DNN. Hence, it is challenging to select the right subset of edge accelerated clients and their relevant power modes in each FL round to meet the energy budget and minimize TTA. This is further exacerbated by the non-IID nature of data distribution across clients that affects convergence.

Contributions. We address these challenges through a novel framework, FED-JOULE, and make the following contributions:

1. We formulate a novel *optimization problem* to select clients and their power modes in each FL round from a set of heterogeneous clients with non-IID data distribution such that the model accuracy is maximized while staying within a *global energy budget* and we minimize the training time (Sect. 3).
2. We solve this optimization problem tractably by decomposing it into two parts solved using Integer Linear Programming (ILP)(Sect. 4.1): *(i)ILP-CS:* In each round, we select a subset of clients to maximize improvement in global model accuracy using approximate Kernel-based Shapley values per device while staying within the peak energy budget at MAXN mode (Sect. 4.1), and introduce a *cooldown period* for the selected clients. *(ii) ILP-PM:* We use our prior work, PowerTrain, to build a valuable time–energy Pareto front across power modes (Sect. 4.2) to help pick the best power mode for the FL clients.
3. We evaluate the proposed solution using real-world traces from 4 Jetson device types for three popular DNN models (LSTM, MobileNet, ResNet), and simulate FL training on a heterogeneous cluster of 12 and 48 edge devices (Sect. 5). Our comparison against simple and state-of-the-art (SOTA) baselines, FedAvg [11] and ESCS [10], shows FEDJOULE is 48% faster and reaches a 15% higher accuracy for the given energy budget, enabling sustainable AI.

Besides these, we discuss related work in Sect. 2 and offer our conclusions in Sect. 6.

2   Related Work

Figure 1 shows a typical FL lifecycle. We use FedAvg [11], which is simple and effective under varied conditions compared to more complex strategies. It uses synchronous aggregation, where all clients report their local models before the global model is created from their weighted average. Several variations have been proposed to improve convergence with **data heterogeneity** [7]. However, such methods often lead to biased model updates. Importance sampling is used to prioritize clients with under-represented or sta-

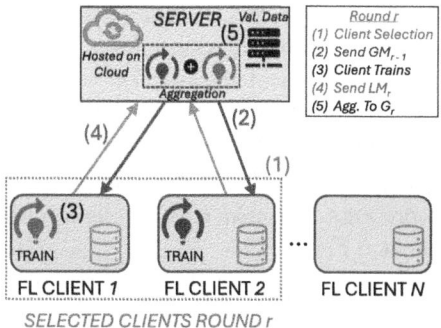

Fig. 1. Typical FL Lifecycle.

tistically significant data to reduce bias in the aggregated model [3]. Also, strategies to mitigate system heterogeneity, such as adaptive client participation, model compression, and asynchronous training. But most FL strategies employ client selection methods that remain inherently biased. In our experiments, FEDJOULE out-performs both an unbiased approach, FedAvg [11], which results in a generalized model but with poor convergence, and a biased one, ESCS [10], which converges faster but generalizes poorly.

Game-theoretic approaches such as **Shapley values** [16] have emerged as a promising method to quantify marginal client contributions in FL. However, exact Shapley computation has exponential time complexity in the number of clients, making it intractable at scale. Some have proposed approximations such as truncated Monte Carlo sampling [5] and gradient-based approximations [18]. We overcome this limitation in three ways: we use historical *surrogate Shapley values* to avoid full client participation [15], we use kernel-based *approximate Shapley* [9] to lower time taken while retaining client fairness, and use *Coreset sampling* of the validation data used in Shapley calculations.

Recent research in **energy-constrained FL** focuses on limiting per-device energy or power load during training. Energy optimization is achieved via client selection strategies [10] and resource optimization [2]. Some [8] reduce energy using hierarchical clustering that avoids redundant compute and communication. However, most methods use an idealized theoretical estimate of energy usage by the devices, and ignore power modes exposed by edge accelerators. Lastly, there is limited research on constraining the total energy across all FL training rounds. Yu et al. [17] propose a global energy-aware device scheduler that optimizes client participation and communication. While most prior works on leveraging Jetson power modes are limited to DNN inferencing, Prashanthi et al. [14] use transfer learning to estimate the latency and power usage of Jetson power modes for training, which we leverage in this paper.

3   Problem Formulation

Preliminaries. We consider a standard FL setting where a single leader coordinates training across a set $\mathcal{C} = \{c_1, c_2, \ldots, c_n\}$ of n *clients*. Each client c_i possesses a local dataset $\mathcal{D}_i = (x_{i,j}, y_{i,j}), j = \{1, \ldots, |\mathcal{D}_i|\}$, where $x_{i,j}$ represents the features and $y_{i,j}$ the corresponding label. The *global objective* in FL is to minimize the empirical loss over all the clients' datasets, $\min_w F(\boldsymbol{w}) = \sum_{i=1}^{n} \frac{|\mathcal{D}_i|}{|\mathcal{D}|} F_i(\boldsymbol{w}, \mathcal{D}_i)$, where $|\mathcal{D}| = \sum_{i=1}^{n} |\mathcal{D}_i|$ is the total number of samples, $\boldsymbol{w}$ represents the *model parameters*, and $F_i(\boldsymbol{w})$ is the *local objective function* for client i: $F_i(\boldsymbol{w}, \mathcal{D}_i) = \frac{1}{|\mathcal{D}_i|} \sum_{(x,y) \in \mathcal{D}_i} \ell(\boldsymbol{w}; x, y)$, with $\ell(\boldsymbol{w}; x, y)$ being the *loss function* for a data point. In each *communication round* r, the leader *selects a subset of clients* $\mathcal{S}^r \subseteq \mathcal{C}$ to participate in the training, limited to a *maximum client count* of γ per round. Each selected client $c_i \in \mathcal{S}^r$ receives the current global model $\boldsymbol{w}^r$ and performs η local epochs of *Stochastic Gradient Descent (SGD)* to obtain an *updated local model* $\boldsymbol{w}_i^{r+1}$, returned to the leader. The leader aggregates all the local models to form the new global model $\boldsymbol{w}^{r+1}$ using a *weighted average*, $\boldsymbol{w}^{r+1} = \sum_{c_i \in \mathcal{S}^r} \frac{|\mathcal{D}_i|}{|\mathcal{D}_{\mathcal{S}^r}|} \boldsymbol{w}_i^{r+1}$, where $|\mathcal{D}_{\mathcal{S}^r}| = \sum_{c_i \in \mathcal{S}^r} |\mathcal{D}_i|$. Let the accuracy of the global model after round r of training be A^r.

Let $\mathcal{P}_i$ be the set of all *power modes* available for client c_i, and for power mode $p_j \in \mathcal{P}_i$, let the corresponding *time to train* one round of the local model be τ_{ij} and ϵ_{ij} be its *energy consumption*. Let Z_{ij}^r be a binary decision variable that is 1 when client $c_i \in \mathcal{S}^r$ selected in round r operates using power mode p_j, and 0 otherwise; only one power mode is selected, $\sum_{p_j \in \mathcal{P}_i} Z_{ij}^r = 1$. Hence, the *local energy* consumed by the client c_i for local model training in a round r will be $E_i^r = \sum_{p_j \in \mathcal{P}_i} Z_{ij}^r \cdot \epsilon_{ij}$ and the *energy for the round* across all selected clients is then $E^r = \sum_{c_i \in \mathcal{S}^r} E_i^r$. We assume the leader's energy usage is negligible, as it remains mostly idle except during client selection and aggregation. Round training time is dictated by the slowest client, as aggregation is typically fast and constant: $T^r = \max_{c_i \in \mathcal{S}^r} Z_{ij}^r \cdot \tau_{ij}$.

Optimization Problem. Given set of clients $\mathcal{C}$, the maximum clients per round γ and an overall energy budget $\widehat{E}$ for the FL training,

Select a set of clients in each round r of FL training, $\mathcal{S}^r \in \mathcal{C}$ and $|\mathcal{S}^r| \le \gamma$, and
Select the set of power modes for the clients, Z_{ij}^r, and
Find the maximum number of training rounds r'
s.t. the *global energy consumed* for FL is within the budget, $\sum_{r \le r'} E^r \le \widehat{E}$, and
we *maximize the accuracy achieved*, $\arg \max A^{r'}$ as a primary goal, and
we *minimize the training time*, $\arg \min \sum_{r \le r'} T^r$ as a secondary goal.

Assumptions. We make certain simplifying and reasonable assumptions. We assume the system is not network-constrained. Although prior work highlights the energy cost of wireless communication in FL, we assume a high-speed LAN where communication energy is $\le 0.2\%$ of computation energy. We leave communication energy modeling for future work. The aggregation server runs in the cloud, where energy is unconstrained and sustainability is prioritized. The framework assumes a trusted environment with pre-deployed models and data, and follows an honest-but-curious threat model. We adopt a synchronous, non-hierarchical FL setup using FedAvg, leaving adversarial scenarios to future work.

4   Methodology

We decompose the optimization into two sub-problems: selecting clients per round (*ILP-CS*) and choosing their power modes (Sect. 4.1) (*ILP-PM*), both solved efficiently using Integer Linear Programming (ILP). To support this, we extend our prior work on PowerTrain (Sect. 4.2) to generate a *energy vs. time Pareto* for local training on each edge device type. During a bootstrap phase, we profile DNN training across tens of power modes per device and build a prediction model that estimates training time (τ_{ij}) and energy consumption (ϵ_{ij}). The resulting Pareto front provides *candidate power modes* for the *ILP-PM* solution.

For each FL round, we *select clients* based on the improvements they offer to the global model quality while staying within overall energy budget. This choice is based on the *Kernel Shapley* values for a client cohort (Sect. 4.1) which address the high computational costs of (exhaustive) Shapley values. We further introduce a *cool-down factor* that avoids selecting the same clients repeatedly. These components are jointly formulated as *ILP-CS* (Eq. 1). For the selected clients, we optimize power mode selection using a Pareto-based ILP formulation (Eq. 2) to minimize round energy use. After each round, we update the remaining global energy budget and proceed to the next round if budget permits. Thus, the number of rounds is determined implicitly.

4.1   Solving Bi-level Optimization Using ILP

We reformulate the problem as a bi-level optimization, significantly reducing the size of the solution space. The solution space decreased from worst case $\mathcal{O}\left((1 + |\mathcal{P}|)^{|\mathcal{C}|}\right)$, choosing γ clients from $|\mathcal{C}| \simeq 100$ each with $|\mathcal{P}| \simeq 10,000$ power modes for the joint optimization problem, to one of $\mathcal{O}(2^{|\mathcal{C}|})$ for client selection alone followed by $\mathcal{O}(|\mathcal{P}'|^{|\mathcal{S}^r|})$ for power mode assignment alone, where $|\mathcal{P}'| \simeq 100$ are power modes on the energy-time Pareto.

We formulate the *ILP-CS problem* to select clients $\mathcal{S}^r$ in round r as:

$$\underset{\mathcal{S}^r}{\arg\min} \; \left(\alpha T^r - (1 - \alpha)A^r\right) \quad \text{s.t.} \quad \dot{E}^r \leq \left(\widehat{E} - \sum_{i<r} E^i\right) \tag{1}$$

Here, E^i for $i < r$, is the energy used in prior rounds. For clients selected in the current round, we assume that they run on MAXN to compute the expected energy, $\dot{E}^r$. This formulation captures the trade-off between *expected accuracy* of the global model, A^r, after the rth aggregation using local models from clients $\mathcal{S}^r$, and the *expected time spent* in the round, T^r, with $\alpha \in [0.0, 1.0]$ being a hyperparameter prioritizing speed over accuracy. Having a faster round time can also indirectly reduce the energy used in the round since it is a product of device time and device power.

We next formulate the *ILP-PM problem* to decide the power modes, Z_{ij}^r, for the $\mathcal{S}^r$ clients selected above so that we reduce the expected energy further, but without increasing the round time.

$$\arg\min_{Z_{ij}^r} \sum_{c_i \in \mathcal{S}^r} \sum_{p_j \in \mathcal{P}_i} (Z_{ij}^r \cdot \epsilon_{ij}) \quad \text{s.t.} \quad \sum_{p_j \in \mathcal{P}_i} Z_{ij}^r \cdot \tau_{ij} \leq T^r, \forall i \in \mathcal{S}^r \quad (2)$$

We assign some clients power modes below MAXN to reduce energy use below $\dot{E}^r$, but avoid modes so low that training exceeds the slowest MAXN client, increasing round time. We note that power mode affects training time, not accuracy. We also introduce a custom *cooldown factor*, defining how many rounds a client skips after selection: $\theta_i = \lceil \rho \cdot A_i^r \rceil$, where A_i^r is the client's local accuracy and ρ is a tunable hyperparameter.

As discussed earlier, our Pareto model (Sect. 4.2) will give the energy and time estimates for a client's power mode. We also need an estimate of A^r, the global model accuracy after a round for the selected clients. We propose to use the cumulative approximate Shapley values for the client cohort to estimate this (Sect. 4.1). Given these, FEDJOULE efficiently solves these two ILP problems at the start of each round using IBM ILOG CPLEX Optimizer to select the clients and their power modes for the round, while remaining within the energy budget.

Exhaustive Shapley Values (ExSH). We conceptualize each training round r as a cooperative game $G(\boldsymbol{w}^r, \mathcal{C}, \mathcal{D}_v, \Psi, \mathcal{A})$, where $\boldsymbol{w}^r$ represents the global model parameters at the start of round r and $\mathcal{C}$ are the set of available clients. The function $\Psi(\boldsymbol{w}^r, \mathcal{S}^r)$ returns the updated model parameters after aggregating contributions from client subset $\mathcal{S}^r$ using the update rule for $\boldsymbol{w}^{r+1}$ in Sect. 3. We define the *utility of a cohort* $\mathcal{S}^r \subseteq \mathcal{C}$ as the performance of the updated global model on validation data, formalized as $A^r = \mathcal{A}(\mathcal{D}_v, \Psi(\boldsymbol{w}^r, S))$, where $\mathcal{A}$ evaluates the model's accuracy on dataset $\mathcal{D}_v$. The *partial federated Shapley value* for client c_i in round r is then defined as:

$$\begin{aligned} \phi_i^r &= \frac{1}{|\mathcal{S}|} \sum_{s \subseteq \mathcal{S} \setminus \{c_i\}} \frac{\mathcal{A}(s \cup \{c_i\}) - \mathcal{A}(s)}{\binom{|\mathcal{S}|-1}{|s|}} \\ &= \sum_{s \subset \mathcal{S} \setminus \{c_i\}} \frac{\mathcal{A}(\mathcal{D}_v, \Psi(\boldsymbol{w}^r, s \cup \{c_i\})) - \mathcal{A}(\mathcal{D}_v, \Psi(\boldsymbol{w}^r, s))}{|\mathcal{S}| \binom{|\mathcal{S}|-1}{|s|}} \end{aligned} \quad (3)$$

This quantifies the marginal contribution of c_i to the model's accuracy across all possible client cohorts in $\mathcal{S}^r$, capturing both data quality and client interaction effects. However, as training progresses, performance gains diminish, leading to uneven partial Shapley value ranges across rounds. To address this, we borrow the *normalization method* from [15] and apply min-max normalization within each round, $\widehat{\phi}_i^r = \frac{\phi_i^r - \min(\phi^r)}{\max(\phi^r) - \min(\phi^r)}$, where $\phi^r = \{\phi_i^r | c_i \in \mathcal{S}^r\}$ is the set of all partial Shapley values in round r, and $\max(\cdot)$ and $\min(\cdot)$ return the maximum and minimum values in the set, respectively. This normalization preserves the relative contributions of clients within each round, which is crucial for fair client selection.

We also maintain the client's historical contribution across rounds through a *surrogate federated Shapley value* [15], as an exponential weighted average of past and current values, $\tilde{\phi}_i^r = \begin{cases} \beta \cdot \tilde{\phi}_i^{r-1} + (1 - \beta) \cdot \bar{\phi}_i^r, & \text{if } c_i \in \mathcal{S}^r \\ \tilde{\phi}_i^{r-1}, & \text{if } c_i \notin \mathcal{S}^r \end{cases}$. Here, $\beta \in$ [0.0, 1.0] controls the update rate of the surrogate value, determining how much weight to place on past contributions by a client versus its recent performance. A smaller β prioritizes recent contributions, allowing the system to adapt quickly to client changes, while a larger β provides stable estimates over time.

Using Shapley values allows us to establish a fair mechanism for client selection. In our energy-aware optimization framework, Shapley values serve as the foundation for identifying high-value clients within the energy constraints of the system, allowing us to effectively select the subset $\mathcal{S}^r$ that maximizes the expected model accuracy A^r while meeting our energy budget.

Kernel-Based Shapley Values for Efficient Computation (KSH). Computing exact Shapley values require evaluating all possible client cohorts in $\mathcal{S}^r$, making it computationally prohibitive for more than a few clients. We use a fast kernel-based Shapley value approximation [9] that does importance sampling of the set of cohorts to be evaluated. We assign weights to a cohort $S \subseteq \mathcal{S}^r$:

$$w(|S|, |\mathcal{S}^r|) = \begin{cases} 1, & \text{if } |S| = |\mathcal{S}^r|, \\ \frac{|\mathcal{S}^r|-1}{\binom{|\mathcal{S}^r|}{|S|} \cdot |S| \cdot (|\mathcal{S}^r|-|S|)}, & \text{otherwise} \end{cases}$$

For our problem, we set the number of cohorts to be sampled as $\min(2^{|\mathcal{S}^r|}, 3 \cdot |\mathcal{S}^r|)$. We use these weights to probabilistically sample $2 \cdot |\mathcal{S}^r|$ unique cohorts to evaluate, which was found to be ideal through an ablation study. Further, we also evaluate each client model individually (singleton cohort), adding up to a total of $3 \cdot |\mathcal{S}^r|$ evaluations every round.

For the set of clients $\mathcal{S}^r$ that have trained in round r, let the set of selected cohorts be $\mathcal{X}^r$ and the evaluation accuracies of a cohort $S \in \mathcal{X}$ be $v_s = \mathcal{A}(\mathcal{D}_v, \Psi(w^r, S))$. Using these values, we then find the approximate Shapley values $\bar{\phi}_i$ for client $c_i \in \mathcal{S}^r$ by solving the weighted least-squares problem, $\min_{\bar{\phi}^r} \sum_{s \in \mathcal{X}^r} w(|s|, |\mathcal{S}^r|) \cdot (v_s - \sum_{c_i \in \mathcal{S}^r} \phi_i^r \mathbf{1}_{c_i \in s})^2$, where $\bar{\phi}^r = \bar{\phi}_i^r$, for $c_i \in \mathbf{S}^r$. We apply the prior equations for normalization and surrogate Shapley to these approximate Shapley values to get the surrogate approximate Shapley values, Φ_i^r for $c_i \in \mathcal{C}$. Hence, the global model accuracy A^r in the optimization problem, Eqn. 1, can be replaced as, $A^r = \sum_{c_i \in \mathcal{S}^r} \Phi_i^{r-1}$, for the candidate client cohorts.

Efficient Cohort Evaluation Using Coreset Sampling. As the number of evaluations in exhaustive Shapley (ExSH) grows exponentially with the number of clients and in Kernel Shapley (KSH) scales linearly, our next objective is to make their evaluations faster. We use a *coreset sampling* methodology based on

Table 1. Specifications of NVIDIA Jetson devices used in our experiments.

	Jetson NX Xavier	Jetson Orin Nano	Jetson AGX Xavier	Jetson Orin AGX
CPU Arch./cores	ARM Carmel/6c	ARM A78AE/6c	ARM Carmel/8c	ARM A78AE/12c
CPU freq.	0.11–1.9 GHz	0.11–1.5 GHz	0.11–2.2 GHz	0.11–2.2 GHz
GPU Arch./cores	Volta/384c	Ampere/1024c	Volta/512c	Ampere/2048c
GPU freq.	0.11–1.1 GHz	0.30–0.62 GHz	0.11–1.3 GHz	0.11–1.3 GHz
Mem./Swap	8 GB/4 GB	8 GB/4 GB	32 GB/16 GB	32 GB/16 GB
Mem freq.	0.20–1.8 GHz	0.20–2.1 GHz	0.20–2.1 GHz	0.20–3.1 GHz

the greedy facility location algorithm, inspired by the coreset construction [12]. Similar to CRAIG [12], we apply a facility location-based strategy to construct a representative subset of test data for efficient cohort evaluation. Given an original test dataset $\mathcal{D}_v$ with $n = |\mathcal{D}_v|$, an optional feature extractor, φ, a subset size ratio $\lambda \in (0.0, 1.0)$, a minimum per-class sample threshold $m_{\min}$, and a cosine distance metric d, the objective is to construct a coreset $\mathcal{D}' \subset \mathcal{D}_v$ with approximately $\lambda \cdot n$ samples while ensuring balanced class representation. The target sample count per class is, $m = \max\left(\left\lfloor \frac{N_{\text{target}}}{k} \right\rfloor, m_{\min}\right)$, where k denotes the number of unique classes and $N_{\text{target}} = \max(\lfloor \lambda \cdot n \rfloor, k \cdot m_{\min})$.

For each class y_j, the subset $\mathcal{D}_{v,j}$ is extracted and processed using the greedy facility location algorithm similar to [12]. It first selects the *medoid*, the point with the minimum sum of distances to all other points, $i_{\text{medoid}} = \arg\min_i \sum_j \Delta_{i,j}$, where $\Delta_{i,j} = d(x_i, x_j)$ represents the pairwise distance matrix. Subsequent points are iteratively selected to maximize the *marginal gain* in feature space coverage, $i_{\text{next}} = \arg\max_{i \notin \mathcal{R}} \sum_j (\mu_j - \min(\mu_j, \Delta_{i,j}))$ where $\mathcal{R}$ is the set of selected samples, $\mu_j = \min_{s \in \mathcal{R}} \Delta_{s,j}$ denotes the minimum distance from x_j to any selected sample $s \in \mathcal{R}$, and $\Delta_{i,j}$ represents the distance between sample x_i and x_j, ensuring that selected points are well-distributed across the feature space. In FEDJOULE, we use coreset sampling for model evaluation during Shapley value computation, with the original dataset serving as the benchmark for final global model assessment. This involves constructing $\mathcal{D}'$ using the coreset sampling algorithm, evaluating cohort models with $\mathcal{D}'$ through ExSH or KSH methods, and then assessing the final aggregated global model on $\mathcal{D}_v$.

4.2   Energy-Time Pareto Estimation

FEDJOULE leverages our prior work [14] on a transfer-learning approach with limited profiling to predict power and time consumption for training a DNN using a given power mode on accelerated Jetson devices. We use *reference Neural Network (NN) models* for power and time predictions, that were earlier trained using exhaustive (one-time) profiling for training ResNet-18 DNN on ImageNet dataset for 4, 368 power modes on a Jetson Orin AGX. We need to generalize these prediction models to the three other edge device types (clients) (Table 1) and two other DNN models we train using FL (Table 2). Instead of performing

Table 2. Models, datasets and key FL hyperparameters.

Model	# params	# layers	Task	Dataset	Classes	Train/Test	Hyperparams
LSTM	0.166M	3	Language detection	Tatoeba	8	71.1k/1.6k	epochs = 3
MobileNetV2	2.3M	53	Image classification	CIFAR-10	10	50k/10k	dropout = 0.2, epochs = 3
ResNet-18	11M	18	Image classification	ImageNet Subset	200	200k/10k	dropout=0.1, epochs=2

Table 3. Non-IID datasets and heterogeneity metrics of clients for FL training.

Model	Dataset	Partitions	#samples per part	Jensen-Shannon divergence
LSTM	Tatoeba	12	$\mu = 5923$, $\sigma = 2819$	0.31
		48	$\mu = 1480$, $\sigma = 1002$	0.34
MobileNetV2	CIFAR10	12	$\mu = 4167$, $\sigma = 1901$	0.44
		48	$\mu = 1042$, $\sigma = 922$	0.43
ResNet-18	ImageNet Subset	12	$\mu = 16,667$, $\sigma = 325$	0.34

costly profiling of 1000 s of power modes for each device–DNN workload combination, we instead profile 90 randomly sampled power modes from each workload to measure their observed minibatch times and power load for one epoch of training. This concise profiling data is used to re-train the reference NN models for power and time predictions [14], and reduces profiling effort by ≈ 96% from an estimated 1,075 hours.

We use these transfer learned models to predict the power and training time for these workloads for *all their power modes*. This is used to estimate the per-round training time and energy usage for each DNN on a device-type workload and shown as a scatter plot of energy vs. time. We identify the set of power modes that lie on the Pareto front of this scatter plot, i.e., the power mode gives the lowest training time for that energy budget. These give the possible set of viable power modes to solve *ILP-PM*. As Fig. 5 shows, we see low prediction errors of ≈ 7% for power and ≈ 9% on time for these power modes.

5   Experiments and Results

We perform extensive experiments to comparatively evaluate FEDJOULE with simple and SOTA FL approaches, for federated learning of three DNN–dataset workloads using two accelerated edge clusters simulated with real-world traces.

5.1   Experimental Setup

Models and Datasets. We run three diverse DNN workloads to comprehensively assess the performance of our proposed FL approach: We use an LSTM for language detection on Tatoeba, MobileNetV2 for CIFAR10, and the larger ResNet-18 for a 200-class ImageNet subset, varying in complexity (0.166–11M parameters) and domain. All models use $lr = 1 \times 10^{-4}$ and $bs = 16$ (Table 2). Each dataset is split non-IID into 12 and 48 client partitions (Table 3). Tatoeba and ImageNet are partitioned by splitting each class into $\lceil \frac{c \times \delta}{l} \rceil$ shards, where c is the number of clients, δ the labels per client, and l the total classes. We use $\delta = 3$ (12 clients) and $\delta = 2$ (48 clients) for Tatoeba, and $\delta = 60$ for ImageNet. CIFAR10 is split using a Dirichlet-based partitioning with concentration parameter $\alpha = 0.05$ for 12 and 48 clients. This is a more challenging non-IID setup with more diverse class distributions across clients.

Simulation Setup. Our FL simulation runs on a GPU workstation with an AMD Ryzen 9 7900X CPU (12-core @5.73GHz), 128GB RAM, and an NVIDIA RTX 4090 GPU (24GB). The 12-device edge cluster includes 2 Jetson Orin AGX, 2 AGX Xavier, 4 Xavier NX, and 4 Orin Nano devices (Table 1). For the 48-device setup, we use 12 of each type to evaluate scalability. While FL training and convergence are simulated, energy and runtime metrics are predicted using PowerTrain for each DNN on the respective Jetson devices.

Baseline Strategies. We evaluate two variants of FEDJOULE, with exhaustive Shapley values (**FedJ-ex**) and Kernel Shapley values (**FedJ-k**) – the former is more accurate but slower while the latter is faster. We also compare with several synchronous FL strategies. As a baseline, we run FedAvg [11] with γ clients randomly chosen in each round (**RND**). We use a simpler Shapley-based strategy with probabilistic sampling (**ExSH**). In the first round, each client is assigned a Shapley value of 1, and thus γ clients are sampled at random. After receiving their local models, the server updates their sampling weights using surrogate Shapley values $\tilde{\phi}_i^r$, and uses these updated weights to select clients in the next round. We also adapt this same strategy but with the Kernel Shapley approximations (**KSH**). These two show the benefits of our Shapley optimizations into FEDJOULE, which go beyond the default Shapley-based FL approaches. Lastly, we compare against a state-of-the-art energy-aware FL strategy, Energy Saving Client Selection (**ESCS**) [10]. This selects clients based on multiple criteria, including battery level, training time capacity, and network quality based on a client utility score. We modified this to use the *system-based utility* and consider only the terms containing loss and the time, and use their deterministic client selection strategy. The training loss for future rounds is obtained by *training all clients* in the first round – a deviation from our problem definition.

5.2   Evaluation of Strategies

We perform a detailed comparative analysis of FL training of the 3 workloads on the two clusters using our **FedJ-k** and **FedJ-ex**, and against **RND**, **ExSH**, **KSH** and **ESCS**. We also vary the *client cohort sizes per round* as 3/12, 6/12, 9/12, 5/48 and 10/48, where m/n means $m = \gamma$ clients are selected from n clients. Since ResNet training is much slower, we only run it on 3/12 and 6/12, which takes 3h and 8h per experiment, respectively. Further, we set the *global energy budget* for each configuration partly based on the DNN model sizes, since

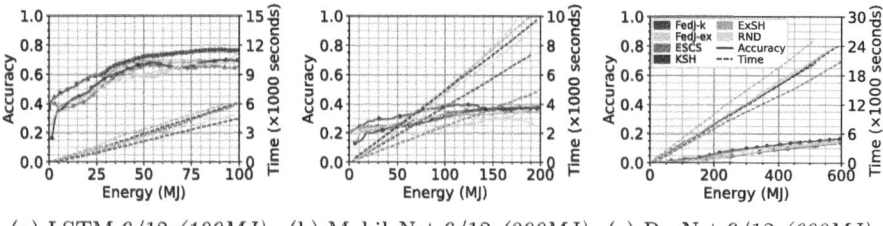

(a) LSTM 6/12 *(100MJ)*   (b) MobileNet 6/12 *(200MJ)*   (c) ResNet 6/12 *(600MJ)*

Fig. 2. Accuracy achieved (left Y axis) and FL training time (right Y axis) as the global energy consumed increase (X axis) as FL rounds progress.

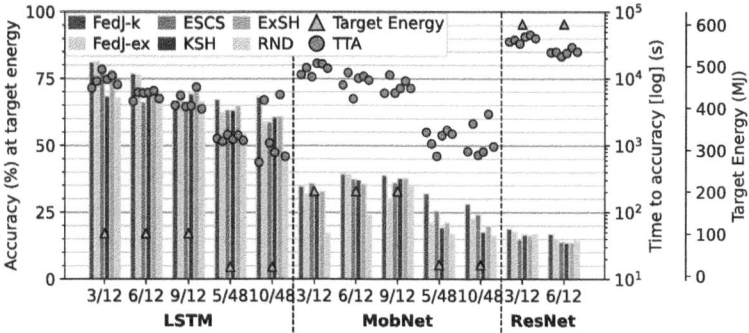

Fig. 3. Accuracy at target energy–100MJ for LSTM-12, 20MJ for LSTM-48, 200MJ for MobNet-12, 15MJ for MobNet-48 and 500MJ for ResNet-18.

larger models take longer to train and consume more energy, as well as minimum aggregate energy required for each model to reach a stable accuracy. These thresholds were thus selected to ensure each model is evaluated at its optimal energy–accuracy tradeoff point, avoiding both under-fitting and wasted energy. For a 12-client cluster, training one round of LSTM consumes $\approx$0.2MJ per client, while ResNet consumes $\approx$2MJ. With more clients, each holds fewer samples, reducing per-client energy use per round. Based on this, we set energy budgets ($\widehat{E}$) for 12/48-client setups as: LSTM – 100MJ/20MJ, MobNet – 200MJ/25MJ, and ResNet – 600MJ/–.

Relaxed Energy Budget. We summarize the *FL training accuracy* based on relaxed energy budgets and *training time* in Fig. 3 for the different setups and strategies. For a subset, 6/12, Fig. 2 shows the increase in global model accuracy (left Y axis) and time taken (right Y axis) over the rounds as the energy budget is used up (X axis). We see that except LSTM-9/12 and MobNet-3/12, **FedJ-k** outperforms all other strategies achieving the highest accuracy. This is because **FedJ-k** usually performs the most number of model updates within the energy budget (e.g., 49% more than **RND** and **ExSH** on average across cohort sizes), which facilitates **FedJ-k**'s lower per-round energy usage compared to the other baselines due to the partial participation of clients. This is even more evident for

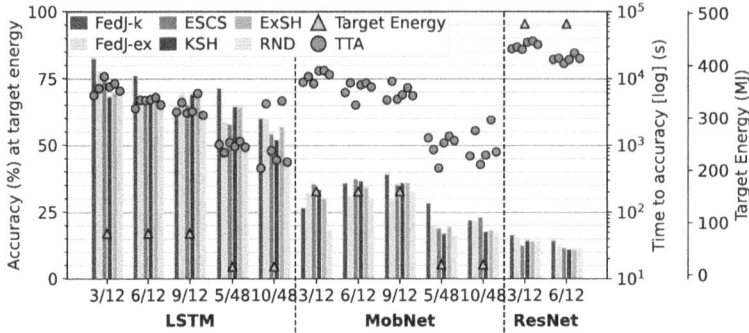

Fig. 4. Accuracy at target energy 80% of original–80MJ for LSTM-12, 16MJ for LSTM-48 , 160MJ for MobNet-12, 20MJ for MobNet-48, 480MJ for Resnet-12

larger cohorts, where **FedJ-k** has a per-round energy usage of 4.65MJ, 2.56MJ and 0.71MJ for MobNet 6/12, 9/12 and 10/48, respectively as compared to **RND**'s 5.4MJ, 8MJ and 2.2MJ. We note from Fig. 2 that despite picking fewer clients per round **FedJ-k** also achieves faster convergence compared to the baseline strategies, thanks to the Shapley value based client contribution measurement. While our approach requires an initial energy investment of 400-8000J for the profiling phase, it forms a very tiny fraction of the energy for the FL session and is significantly offset by energy savings of approximately 50-400MJ per workload. We note that the FL server itself can run on the cloud and will not add to the overall energy cost of the devices.

As participation increases, the energy cost per round also increases. E.g., in ResNet, the average energy consumed per round for **KSH** increases from 8MJ to 17MJ from 3/12 to 6/12, leading to the strategies having an average of ≈50% fewer rounds performed. This trend, however, does not hold for MobileNet, where, due to the extreme skew of the data, the global model benefits from increased participation. As expected, **FedJ-ex** performs on par with **FedJ-k** on smaller cohort sizes, reaching highest or second highest accuracies in two out of the three 3/12 configurations. But we note the decreases in accuracy at target energy as its round-time increases 94% for LSTM and 73% for MobNet for cohort sizes of 5 with respect to 10. This highlights the exponential time complexity of model evaluation for exhaustive Shapley value strategies and the benefits of **FedJ-k**. We also evaluate all strategies in terms of *energy to accuracy* (ETA) and include discussions in the extended version of this paper in [1].

Restricted Energy Budget. Now, we reduce the global energy budget by 20% over the previous and observe the behaviour of these FL strategies for a more sustainable and lower carbon-footprint target. We see the same convergence trends hold in Fig. 4, which show the accuracies and runtimes achieved when 80% of the earlier energy budget was reached for each model-configuration pair. From Figs. 3 and 4, we see that **FedJ-k** and **FedJ-ex** gain the highest increment in accuracy across all strategies in when the energy budget is relaxed by 20%, further highlighting their rapid convergence.

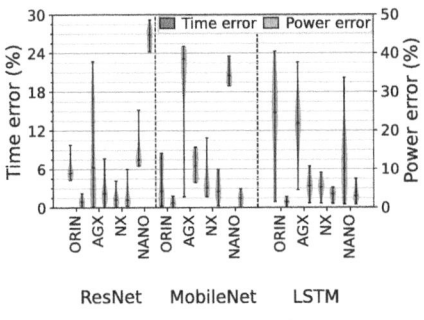

ResNet   MobileNet   LSTM

Fig. 5. Time and power prediction errors for the Energy-Time Pareto points.

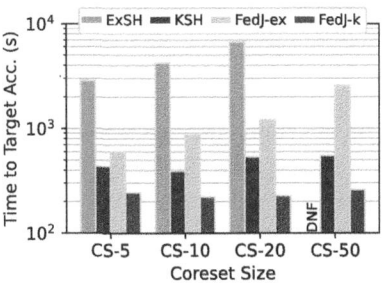

Fig. 6. Time-to-accuracy (16.8%) for **ExSH, KSH, FedJ-ex** and **FedJ-k** for MobNet-10/48 for Coreset sampling 5%, 10%, 20%, and 50%.

Effect of Coreset Sampling Size. The size of the Coreset-sampled evaluation data for strategies based on Shapley values represents a trade-off between lower computation times (smaller datasets will have faster cohort evaluations) and better evaluation of client contributions. Here, we explore this by evaluating the performance of **ExSH, KSH, FedJ-ex** and **FedJ-k** in the MobNet-12/48 setting for four different Coreset sampling percentages: 5% (CS-5), 10% (CS-10), 20% (CS-20) and 50% (CS-50). Figure 6 summarizes the *time-to-target accuracy (TTA)* for CS-5, CS-10, CS-20 and CS-50 for **ExSH, KSH, FedJ-ex** and **FedJ-k**. A strategy's sensitivity to Coreset size stems from the number of model evaluations per round, causing notable performance shifts with varying validation constraints. As expected, **ExSH** and **FedJ-ex** are most impacted by validation set size, performing 1,023 model evaluations per round for MobNet-10/48. For CS-10, **ExSH** takes $4,000$ s to reach the target accuracy, which rises to $6,680$ s for CS-20. **FedJ-ex** requires 859 s for CS-10, increasing to $1,206$ and $2,568$ s for CS-20 and CS-50, respectively. In contrast, **KSH** performs only 30 evaluations per round, with runtimes rising modestly from 436 s (CS-10) to 390 (CS-20) and 535 (CS-50). Similarly, **FedJ-k** consistently achieves the lowest runtimes–240, 220, 225, and 250 s across the four Coreset sizes.

With the smallest Coreset size of CS-5, all strategies see an increase in TTA, as compared to CS-10. This is attributed to the dataset being too small to quantify client contributions, affecting model evaluations. ML literature highlights the critical role of validation set quality and size in model evaluation. A smaller sets introduce noise, hindering reliable assessment of client contributions. Hence, it's important to balance validation size with computational limits.

6   Conclusions

We address the problem of limiting global energy budgets for FL using heterogeneous Jetson edge accelerators over non-IID data. Our unique bi-level ILP formulation leverages approximate Shapley values and energy-time prediction models to efficiently solve this problem. Our FEDJOULE framework achieves superior training accuracies compared to SOTA and baselines for diverse energy budgets and realistic experiment configurations. In future work, we plan to scale experiments on physical edge clusters and extend support to mobile, TPU, and FPGA platforms. We further plan on performing in-depth real-world validation to assess the impact of network conditions, client dropouts, and map energy usage to CO_2 emissions to better assess the environmental impact of our methodology.

Disclosure of Interest. The authors declare that they have no known competing financial interests or personal relationships that could have appeared to influence the work reported in this paper.

References

1. Banerjee, R., Chandrashekar, T., Eswar, A., Simmhan, Y.: Federated learning within global energy budget over heterogeneous edge accelerators. arXiv preprint arXiv:2506.10413 (2025)
2. Chen, R., et al.: EEFL: high-speed wireless communications inspired energy efficient federated learning over mobile devices. In: MobiSys (2023)
3. Cho, Y.J., Wang, J., Joshi, G.: Towards understanding biased client selection in federated learning. In: AISTATS (2022)
4. Hsieh, K., Phanishayee, A., Mutlu, O., Gibbons, P.: The non-IID data quagmire of decentralized machine learning. In: ICML (2020)
5. Jia, R., et al.: Towards efficient data valuation based on the shapley value. In: AISTATS (2019)
6. Kim, G., et al.: Heteroswitch: characterizing and taming system-induced data heterogeneity in federated learning. In: MLSys (2024)
7. Li, T., et al.: Federated optimization in heterogeneous networks. MLSys (2020)
8. Liu, J., et al.: Green federated learning: a sustainable framework for energy-constrained IoT networks. IEEE IoT J. (2023)
9. Lundberg, S.M., Lee, S.I.: A unified approach to interpreting model predictions. In: NeurIPS (2017)
10. Maciel, F., et al.: Federated learning energy saving through client selection. Pervasive Mob. Comput. (2024)
11. McMahan, H.B., et al.: Communication-efficient learning of deep networks from decentralized data. In: AISTATS (2016)
12. Mirzasoleiman, B., Bilmes, J.A., Leskovec, J.: Coresets for data-efficient training of machine learning models. In: ICML (2020)
13. Prashanthi, S., et al.: Characterizing the performance of accelerated Jetson edge devices for training deep learning models. POMACS (2022)
14. Prashanthi, S., et al.: Powertrain: fast, generalizable time and power prediction models to optimize DNN training on accelerated edges. FGCS (2024)

15. Sun, Q., et al.: Shapleyfl: robust federated learning based on shapley value. In: KDD (2023)
16. Wang, H., et al.: Principled weight sharing in federated learning. In: ICLR (2020)
17. Yu, C., Shen, S., Zhang, K., Zhao, H., Shi, Y.: Energy-aware device scheduling for joint federated learning in edge-assisted internet of agriculture things. In: WCNC (2022)
18. Zhang, Z., et al.: GTG-shapley: efficient and accurate participant contribution evaluation in federated learning. In: TPDS (2021)

Bifröst: Peer-to-Peer Load-Balancing for Function Execution in Agentic AI Systems

Giuseppe Coviello[ID], Kunal Rao[✉][ID], Mohammad A. Khojastepour[ID], and Srimat Chakradhar[ID]

NEC Laboratories America, Inc., Princeton, NJ, USA
`{giuseppe.coviello,kunal,amir,chak}@nec-labs.com`

Abstract. Agentic AI systems rely on Large Language Models (LLMs) to execute complex tasks by invoking external functions. The efficiency of these systems depends on how well function execution is managed, especially under heterogeneous and high-variance workloads, where function execution times can range from milliseconds to several seconds. Traditional load-balancing techniques, such as round-robin, least-loaded, and Peak-EWMA (used in Linkerd), struggle in such settings: round-robin ignores load imbalance, least-loaded reacts slowly to rapid workload shifts, and Peak-EWMA relies on latency tracking, which is ineffective for workloads with high execution time variability. In this paper, we introduce Bifröst, a peer-to-peer load-balancing mechanism that distributes function requests based on real-time active request count rather than latency estimates. Instead of relying on centralized load-balancers or client-side decisions, Bifröst enables function-serving pods to dynamically distribute load by comparing queue lengths and offloading requests accordingly. This avoids unnecessary overhead while ensuring better responsiveness under high-variance workloads. Our evaluation on open-vocabulary object detection, multi-modal understanding, and code generation workloads shows that Bifröst improves function completion time by up to 20% when processing 13,700 requests from 137 AI agents on a 32-node Kubernetes cluster, outperforming both OpenFaaS and OpenFaaS with Linkerd. In an AI-driven insurance claims processing workflow, Bifröst achieves up to 25% faster execution.

Keywords: Agentic AI systems · Function as a Service · Distributed systems · Load balancing

1 Introduction

The rise of agentic AI systems [1], powered by Large Language Models (LLMs), has enabled AI agents to autonomously plan and execute complex tasks by invoking external tools and functions. These systems are transforming domains such as finance, healthcare, and transportation, where AI agents orchestrate multiple function calls to complete structured workflows. However, the efficiency of such

W. E. Nagel et al. (Eds.): Euro-Par 2025, LNCS 15900, pp. 279–291, 2026.
https://doi.org/10.1007/978-3-031-99854-6_19

systems critically depends on the underlying function execution infrastructure, as high latency and poor load balancing can degrade responsiveness and overall performance.

A real-world example of such a workflow is automated claims processing in insurance applications. Here, AI agents must first detect vehicles in an accident scene, then identify their make and model, assess damage severity, and finally generate a claims report. Each of these steps involves different AI models, which are best deployed using Function-as-a-Service (FaaS)–allowing developers to define functions while infrastructure management is handled automatically. OpenFaaS [10] is a widely used framework for deploying such functions on Kubernetes, enabling automatic scaling and request routing.

However, existing load-balancing mechanisms in OpenFaaS are inefficient for high-variance workloads. By default, OpenFaaS uses Kubernetes' native "Service" load-balancing, which fails to consider real-time load at each function-serving pod. To improve request distribution, Linkerd [14], a service mesh for Kubernetes, employs Peak Exponential Weighted Moving Average (Peak-EWMA) for load balancing. Peak-EWMA dynamically selects pods with lower latency, but introduces three key challenges. *First*, sub-optimal resource allocation – Peak-EWMA relies on client-side latency tracking, which lacks full visibility into backend pod metrics, leading to misallocations. *Second*, additional overhead – Linkerd requires a sidecar proxy per pod, adding CPU and memory overhead. *Third*, dependency on Kubernetes – Linkerd's tight integration with Kubernetes makes it difficult to deploy in standalone FaaS environments.

To address these challenges, we introduce *Bifröst*, a peer-to-peer load-balancing mechanism. Unlike Linkerd, *Bifröst* does not rely on latency tracking. Instead, it monitors active request queues in a decentralized fashion, allowing function-serving pods to dynamically distribute workload. This approach reduces client-side overhead, and operates independently of Kubernetes, making it more scalable and lightweight.

Our key contributions in this paper are:

- We propose a novel peer-to-peer load-balancing algorithm that dynamically redistributes function requests based on real-time queue lengths, improving execution efficiency in agentic AI systems.
- We develop *Bifröst*, a framework independent from any FaaS middle-ware that transparently integrates with OpenFaaS for function definition while handling load-balancing independently, ensuring efficient execution of high-variance workloads.
- We conduct extensive experiments on three function workloads (object detection, multi-modal understanding, and code generation), as well as a real-world insurance claims application. Our results show that *Bifröst* improves execution time by up to 20% for individual functions and 25% for AI-driven business workflows, outperforming OpenFaaS and OpenFaaS with Linkerd.

The rest of the paper is organized as follows: Sect. 2 discusses related work. Section 3 presents the design and implementation of *Bifröst*, along with details of its load-balancing algorithm. Section 4 reports experimental results for individual functions and the insurance claims application. Finally, Sect. 5 concludes the paper.

2 Related Work

Agentic AI systems leverage Large Language Models (LLMs) to autonomously execute tasks by invoking external tools and functions. Several recent works have explored the architecture and execution strategies of such systems [1,20]. These systems typically integrate third-party APIs and services, making efficient function execution critical for responsiveness. Existing approaches often rely on Function-as-a-Service (FaaS) platforms to manage execution [7,15,18], but they do not address load-balancing inefficiencies that arise in workloads with highly variable function execution times.

FaaS platforms such as OpenFaaS [10], AWS Lambda [17], and Google Cloud Functions [5] provide a serverless execution model where functions are triggered on demand and scaled automatically. While these platforms simplify function deployment, they lack intelligent load-balancing mechanisms, leading to inefficient request distribution under fluctuating workloads. Traditional policies such as round-robin, used in OpenFaaS, distribute requests evenly across available function-serving pods but do not account for real-time load imbalance. Least-loaded algorithm, which assigns requests to the node with the fewest active tasks, reacts slowly to workload bursts, leading to temporary overloads. More sophisticated approaches, such as Peak Exponential Weighted Moving Average (Peak-EWMA) used in Linkerd [4,14], dynamically route requests based on latency. However, Peak-EWMA is most effective in stable, low-variance workloads and struggles when function execution times fluctuate significantly.

Load balancing in distributed computing has been widely studied [6]. Classic techniques such as randomized load balancing [19] and power-of-two-choices [12] improve resource utilization but do not account for real-time queue lengths at execution nodes, which is critical for handling heterogeneous function workloads. More recent research has explored queue-aware load balancing [3], where requests are assigned based on real-time queue states rather than estimated latencies. While these techniques have been successful in distributed systems, they have not been effectively integrated into FaaS-based agentic AI systems.

Our work builds on these prior efforts by introducing *Bifröst*, a peer-to-peer load-balancing mechanism that dynamically redistributes function requests based on real-time queue lengths. Unlike Linkerd, *Bifröst* does not rely on latency tracking, eliminating sidecar proxy overhead and improving adaptability to workload bursts. Furthermore, *Bifröst* operates independently of Kubernetes, making it deployable in a wider range of FaaS environments. Our experimental results demonstrate that *Bifröst* improves execution efficiency by up to 20% for individual functions and 25% for AI-driven business workflows, highlighting its effectiveness in handling high-variance workloads in agentic AI systems.

3   Design and Implementation

In this section, we present the design and implementation of *Bifröst* and describe the algorithm used for making workload load-balancing decisions.

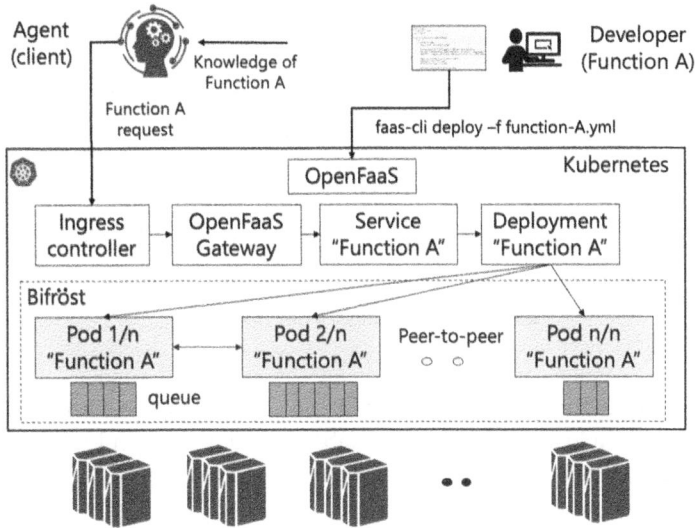

Fig. 1. *Bifröst* system architecture

Table 1. Linkerd vs *Bifröst*

Feature	Linkerd	*Bifröst*
Load metric used	Latency based (Power of two choices: Peak-EWMA)	Active request count (Power of two choices: Least loaded)
Load-balancing decision location	Client-side (Sidecar proxy)	Server-side, Peer-to-peer (Among serving pods)
Overhead on Client	High (Sidecar proxy tracks latency and makes decisions)	Low (No tracking or decision making needed)
Overhead on serving Pod instance	Low (Light traffic measurement through sidecar proxy)	Low (Light processing and 1 extra hop in ∼50 % cases)
Scalability	High (But more client side processing)	High (But may require extra hop at serving pod)
Dependency on Kubernetes	High (Not straight-forward to run standalone)	Low (Easy to run independently)

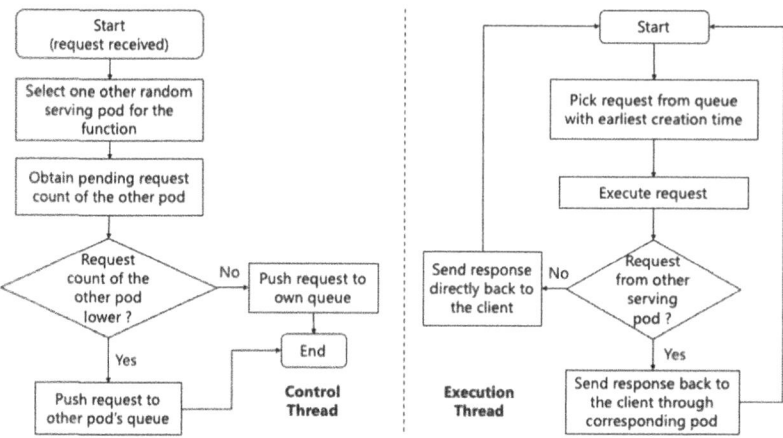

Fig. 2. *Bifröst* algorithm flow chart

The system architecture for *Bifröst* is illustrated in Fig. 1. As described in Sect. 1, *Bifröst* can be used with OpenFaaS to develop and deploy functions. The process begins with the developer (shown on the top right in Fig. 1) implementing the function "handler" with the required business logic. The function is then deployed on OpenFaaS, which runs on a Kubernetes cluster.

When a function is deployed, OpenFaaS automatically creates a corresponding Kubernetes' "Service" object, which allows access to the function's HTTP endpoint (typically on port 8080) within the cluster. Additionally, OpenFaaS generates a "Deployment" object for the function, which manages the life-cycle of its serving instances (Pods). The "replicas" value in the Deployment object specifies the number of active function-serving Pods. This value can be dynamically adjusted to accommodate request load.

After deployment, the function's metadata—including its purpose, input parameters, and expected outputs—is registered with the agentic AI system. Equipped with this knowledge, agents can invoke the function as needed to execute specific tasks in a business workflow. When an agent submits a function request, it is first received by the Kubernetes ingress controller, which forwards it to the OpenFaaS Gateway. The OpenFaaS Gateway then identifies the appropriate "Service" object and routes the request to one of the available function-serving Pods. The selected Pod processes the request and returns the response to the agent.

3.1 Limitations of Existing Approaches

By default, OpenFaaS relies on Kubernetes's naïve "Service" round-robin approach for request distribution, which does not consider the real-time load on serving Pods. To improve upon this, Linkerd can be used as a service mesh solution that enhances request routing. Linkerd operates by deploying sidecar proxies alongside each serving Pod, which monitor request latencies and make decisions based on Peak Exponential Weighted Moving Average (Peak-EWMA) [4].

In this approach, when a new request arrives, Linkerd randomly selects two serving Pods and directs the request to the one with the lower Peak-EWMA latency score. While this improves upon Kubernetes' native load-balancing, it still has inefficiencies. We briefly highlighted these in Sect. 1 and summarize them in Table 1. Specifically, Linkerd's reliance on latency tracking introduces additional overhead and can lead to suboptimal load-balancing under workloads with highly variable execution times.

3.2 *Bifröst* Load-Balancing Algorithm

Figure 2 presents the flow chart of the load-balancing algorithm used by *Bifröst*. The architecture consists of two primary components per serving Pod: a control thread and an execution thread.

When a function request is received by the service object, it is initially assigned to a randomly selected serving Pod. This request is handled by the control thread running on that Pod, which marks a creation timestamp for the request and then selects another randomly chosen serving Pod that is handling the same function. The control thread queries this second Pod to retrieve its current number of pending requests. If the second Pod has a lower queue length than the local Pod, the request is forwarded to it; otherwise, it remains in the current Pod's queue.

The execution thread at each Pod runs continuously in a loop. At each iteration, it picks the function request with the earliest creation time (assigned by the control thread) and processes it. After execution, the thread checks whether the request originated from another Pod or from its own control thread. If the request was forwarded by another serving Pod, the response is relayed back to the original Pod, which then sends it to the client. If the request was locally executed, the response is sent directly to the client.

3.3 Advantages of the *Bifröst* Approach

By separating load-balancing logic into a lightweight control thread and an independent execution thread, *Bifröst* achieves efficient request distribution with minimal overhead. The control thread operates with low computational cost, as it only tracks queue lengths and redirects requests when necessary. Meanwhile, the execution thread ensures that function requests are processed in a priority-driven manner, selecting requests based on their earliest creation timestamp.

Compared to Linkerd, *Bifröst* offers several key advantages:

- More accurate load balancing: Since *Bifröst* considers real-time queue lengths instead of estimated latencies, it adapts better to workloads with high execution time variability.
- Scalability and flexibility: *Bifröst* operates independently of Kubernetes, making it suitable for a broader range of FaaS deployments beyond OpenFaaS.

Ultimately, *Bifröst* provides a low-overhead, queue-aware load-balancing mechanism that improves function execution efficiency in agentic AI systems. By ensuring that function requests are dynamically distributed based on real-time load conditions, *Bifröst* enables faster response times and better resource utilization, making it an effective alternative to existing FaaS load-balancing solutions.

4   Results

To evaluate the effectiveness of the algorithm used by *Bifröst*, we set up a multi-client configuration where multiple AI agents act as clients, concurrently sending function requests. Each agent maintains a stack of function calls and submits a new request as soon as the previous one completes. We measure the total time taken to complete all function requests in the stack for each agent and report the overall end-to-end execution time. Figure 3 illustrates this experimental setup. Incoming requests are assigned to serving pods at random and are processed by *Bifröst* using the load-balancing algorithm described in Sect. 3.

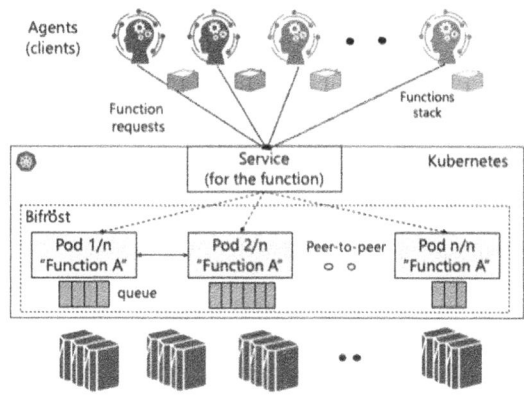

Fig. 3. Multi-client setup

We evaluate *Bifröst* on both individual function workloads and a real-world multi-function application. Each experiment is conducted under three different load scenarios: *low load (17 concurrent clients)*, *medium load (32 concurrent clients)*, and *high load (137 concurrent clients)*. The experiments are performed on a Kubernetes cluster consisting of 32 nodes, where each node is equipped with an AMD Ryzen 7 5800 CPU, an NVIDIA GeForce RTX 3090 GPU, and 48 GB of main memory. This setup ensures a controlled environment to assess the load-balancing efficiency of *Bifröst* under varying levels of request intensity.

The workloads evaluated include the following:

- *Open vocabulary object detection*: We employ Grounded Language-Image Pre-training (GLIP) [11] as the object detection model and evaluate its performance on the LVIS dataset [8]. Each image in the dataset is scaled and cropped to 1080p resolution to standardize processing.

```
1  import base64
2  import io
3  import os
4
5  import requests
6  from PIL import Image
7
8  object_detection_url = "http://object-detection.openfaas-fn:8080/"
9  mm_understanding_url = "http://mm-understanding.openfaas-fn:8080/"
10
11 questions = {
12     "color": "What is the color of the car?",
13     "model": "What is the model of the car?",
14     "is_damaged": "Answer just yes or no. I the car damaged?",
15     "is_overturned": "Answer just yes or no. I the car
       overturned?"
16 }
17
18
19 def submit(url, data):
20     while True:
21         resp = requests.post(url, json=data)
22         if resp.status_code == 200:
23             return resp.json()
24         time.sleep(0.01)
25
26
27 def execute_query(image_filename) -> []:
28     with open(image_filename, "rb") as f:
29         encoded_image = f.read()
30     cars = submit(object_detection_url,
31                   {"image":
    base64.b64encode(encoded_image).decode('utf-8'),
32                   "object_name": "car"})
33     if len(cars) == 0:
34         print("No cars found")
35         return []
36
37     img = Image.open(io.BytesIO(encoded_image)).convert('RGB')
38     report = []
39     for car_id, c in enumerate(cars):
40         car_img = img.crop((c['x'], c['y'], c['x'] + c['width'],
41                             c['y'] + c['height']))
42         b = io.BytesIO()
43         car_img.save(b, "JPEG")
44         img = base64.b64encode(b.getvalue()).decode('utf-8')
45         car_report = {
46             'car_id': car_id,
47             'location': c,
48         }
49         for q in questions:
50             car_report[q] = submit(mm_understanding_url, {
51                 "image": img,
52                 "question": questions[q]
53             })['answer']
54         report.append(car_report)
55
56     return report
```

Fig. 4. Insurance application code generated by DiCE [16]

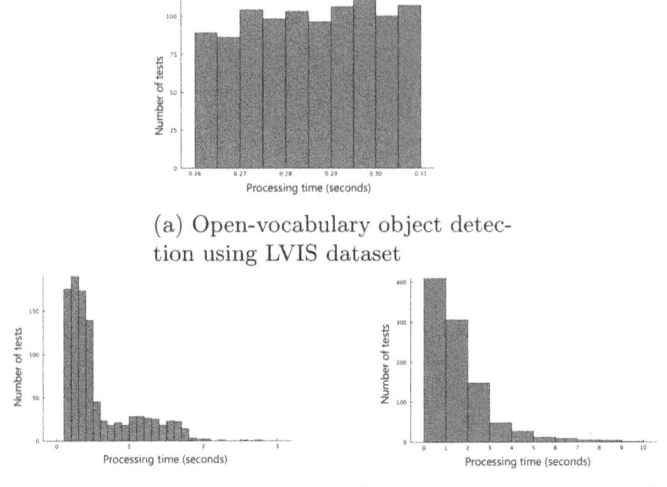

(a) Open-vocabulary object detection using LVIS dataset

(b) Multi-modal understanding using MMBench dataset

(c) Code generation using MBPP dataset

Fig. 5. Profiling of function requests

- *Multi-modal understanding*: We utilize Moondream 2B [13] as our vision-language model and conduct experiments using the MMBench dataset [21]. This workload requires the model to process multi-modal inputs, interpret visual content, and generate responses based on textual queries.
- *Code generation*: We use Qwen2.5-coder-32B [9] as our Code LLM and evaluate its performance on the Mostly Basic Python Problems (MBPP) dataset [2], a widely used benchmark for function-level code generation.
- *Insurance application*: This real-world workload simulates an AI-driven claims processing system, where an agent detects vehicles in an accident scene, identifies their make and model, determines if the vehicle is damaged or overturned, and generates a report. The application combines object detection and multi-modal understanding. Code generated by DiCE [16] is used to analyze images and extract relevant attributes. To optimize resource utilization, we allocate 8 out of 32 nodes for object detection, while the remaining nodes process multi-modal understanding requests. The code used for this application is shown in Fig. 4.

Execution Time Variance Across Workloads. Figure 5a provides a detailed profiling of function execution times for the object detection workload. As seen, object detection workloads exhibit significantly lower variance, with execution times remaining within a narrow range. This lower variance allows latency-based solutions, such as Peak-EWMA in Linkerd, to make effective decisions.

In contrast, Figs. 5b and 5c illustrate the execution time distributions for multi-modal understanding and code generation workloads, respectively. These workloads exhibit *high variance*, with execution times ranging from milliseconds

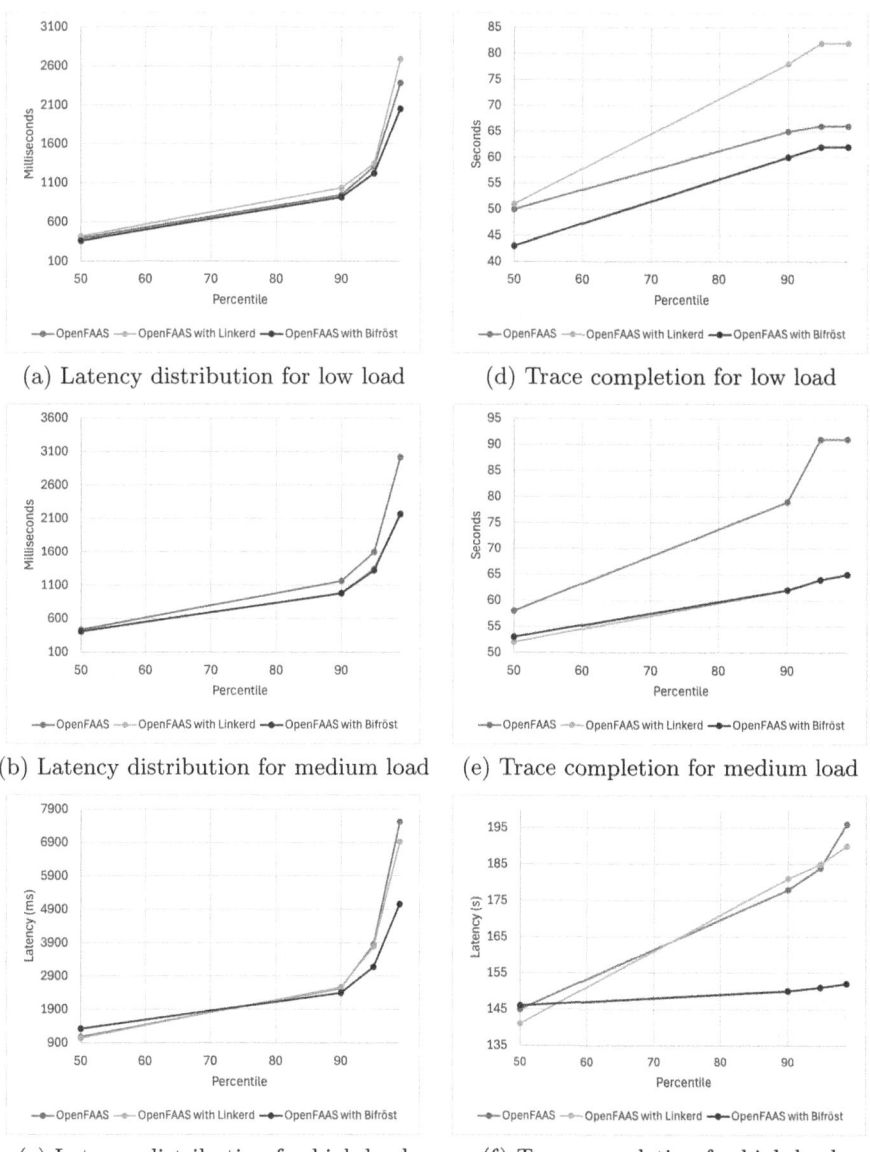

(a) Latency distribution for low load

(d) Trace completion for low load

(b) Latency distribution for medium load

(e) Trace completion for medium load

(c) Latency distribution for high load

(f) Trace completion for high load

Fig. 6. Detailed results for multi-modal understanding function

to multiple seconds. Due to this variability, latency estimates become unreliable, leading to suboptimal request distribution in Linkerd's approach.

Detailed Analysis of Multi-modal Understanding. To further analyze request completion behavior, we focus on the multi-modal understanding workload, illustrated in Fig. 6. This analysis breaks down request latency and trace

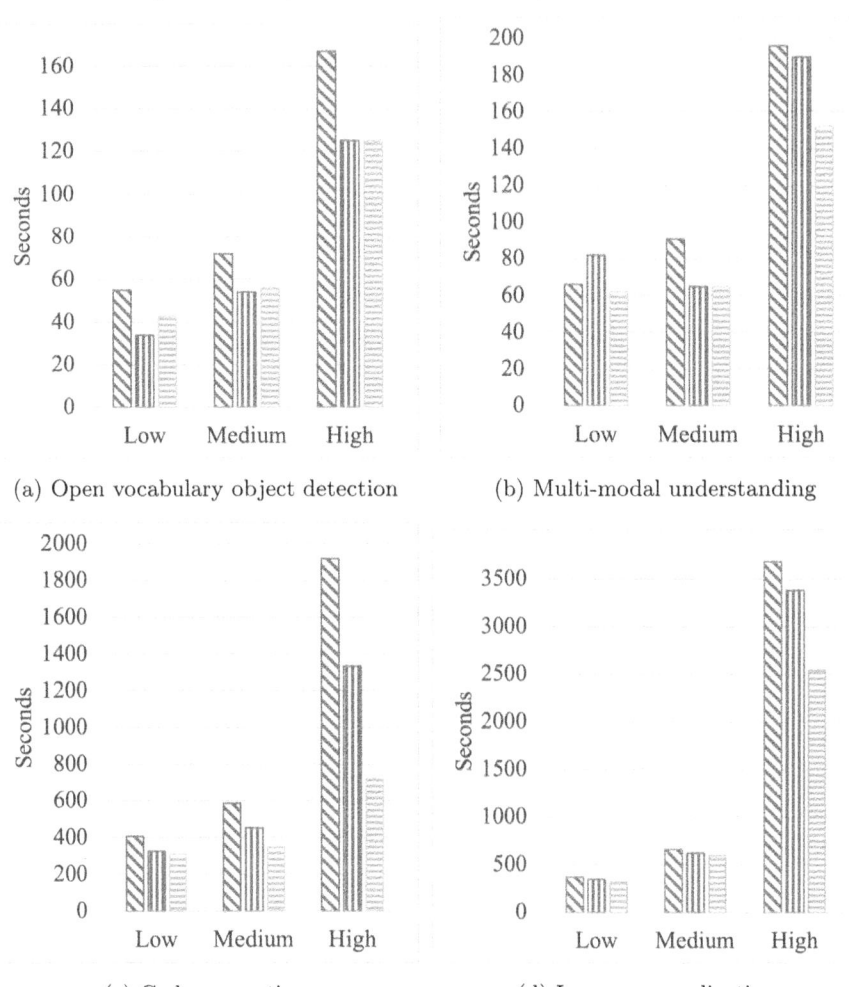

▨ OpenFAAS   ▥ OpenFAAS with Linkerd   ≡ OpenFAAS with Bifröst

(a) Open vocabulary object detection

(b) Multi-modal understanding

(c) Code generation

(d) Insurance application

Fig. 7. Time for processing all the clients' requests

completion across different load scenarios. The results show that *Bifröst* consistently reduces execution time across all load conditions, demonstrating the advantage of queue-aware load-balancing in managing high-variance workloads. Specifically, we observe that at high load, *Bifröst* maintains stable latency distributions while improving overall query throughput.

Performance Comparison. Figure 7 presents the overall execution time for processing all client requests across different workloads. We compare *Bifröst* against two baseline approaches: *vanilla OpenFaaS* (which uses Kubernetes' naïve round-robin solution) and *OpenFaaS with Linkerd* (which employs Peak-

EWMA-based load balancing). Our results indicate that *Bifröst* consistently outperforms vanilla OpenFaaS across all workloads due to its adaptive load-balancing strategy. When compared to OpenFaaS with Linkerd, we observe that *Bifröst* achieves comparable performance in object detection but exhibits significant improvements in other workloads.

For workloads like object detection, where execution times remain relatively stable (few hundred milliseconds per request), Linkerd's latency-aware algorithm remains effective in directing traffic to low-latency pods. However, for computationally intensive workloads such as multi-modal understanding and code generation, where execution times vary widely, latency-based decision making becomes less effective. Linkerd's reliance on Peak-EWMA estimates fails to capture real-time fluctuations in request execution, leading to load imbalance. In contrast, *Bifröst* dynamically adapts to request queue lengths, making load-balancing decisions based on real-time pending request counts rather than estimated latencies. This results in more balanced workload distribution and lower total execution time.

Overall Gains. *Bifröst* reduces the total function execution time by up to 20% for individual function workloads and achieves a 25% reduction in execution time for the AI-driven insurance application. These improvements highlight the effectiveness of *Bifröst*'s peer-to-peer approach in handling workloads with high execution time variability.

5   Conclusion

In this paper, we introduced *Bifröst*, a novel peer-to-peer load-balancing mechanism designed to optimize function execution in agentic AI systems. Unlike existing approaches such as OpenFaaS and OpenFaaS with Linkerd, *Bifröst* dynamically redistributes function requests based on real-time queue lengths, reducing overhead and improving load-balancing. Our experimental results demonstrate that *Bifröst* improves execution performance for individual functions by up to 20%. Additionally, in a real-world insurance claims processing workflow, *Bifröst* reduces execution time by up to 25% compared to traditional load-balancing techniques.

Disclosure of Interests. The authors have no competing interests to declare that are relevant to the content of this article.

References

1. Acharya, D.B., Kuppan, K., Divya, B.: Agentic AI: autonomous intelligence for complex goals a comprehensive survey. IEEE Access **13**, 18912–18936 (2025). https://doi.org/10.1109/ACCESS.2025.3532853
2. Austin, J., et al.: Program synthesis with large language models (2021). https://arxiv.org/abs/2108.07732

3. Bai, W., Zhu, J., Huang, S., Zhang, H.: A queue waiting cost-aware control model for large scale heterogeneous cloud datacenter. IEEE Trans. Cloud Comput. **10**(2), 849–862 (2022). https://doi.org/10.1109/TCC.2020.2990982

4. Beyond round robin: Load balancing for latency. https://linkerd.io/2016/03/16/beyond-round-robin-load-balancing-for-latency/. Accessed 14 Mar 2025

5. Google Cloud: Cloud run functions (2025). https://cloud.google.com/functions. Accessed 16 Mar 2025

6. Darakhshan Syed, S.R., Muhammad, G.: Systematic review: load balancing in cloud computing by using metaheuristic based dynamic algorithms. Intell. Autom. Soft Comput. **39**(3), 437–476 (2024.). https://doi.org/10.32604/iasc.2024.050681. http://www.techscience.com/iasc/v39n3/57288. ISSN 2326-005X

7. Ekwe-Ekwe, N., Amos, L.: The state of FaaS: an analysis of public functions-as-a-service providers. In: 2024 IEEE 17th International Conference on Cloud Computing (CLOUD), pp. 430–438 (2024). https://doi.org/10.1109/CLOUD62652.2024.00055

8. Gupta, A., Dollár, P., Girshick, R.: LVIS: a dataset for large vocabulary instance segmentation (2019). https://arxiv.org/abs/1908.03195

9. Hui, B., et al.: Qwen2.5-coder technical report (2024). https://arxiv.org/abs/2409.12186

10. Le, D.-N., Pal, S., Pattnaik, P.K.: OpenFaaS. In: Cloud Computing Solutions, chap. 17, pp. 287–303. Wiley (2022). https://doi.org/10.1002/9781119682318.ch17.   https://onlinelibrary.wiley.com/doi/abs/10.1002/9781119682318.ch17 doi/abs/10.1002/9781119682318.ch17

11. Li, L.H., et al.: Grounded language-image pre-training. In: CVPR (2022)

12. Mitzenmacher, M.: The power of two choices in randomized load balancing. IEEE Trans. Parallel Distrib. Syst. **12**(10), 1094–1104 (2001). https://doi.org/10.1109/71.963420

13. Moondream AI. Moondream. https://moondream.ai/. Accessed 16 Mar 2025

14. Morgan, J., et al.: Linkerd: Up and Running. O'Reilly Media, Inc. (2024)

15. Palade, A., Kazmi, A., Clarke, S.: An evaluation of open source serverless computing frameworks support at the edge. In: 2019 IEEE World Congress on Services (SERVICES), vol. 2642-939X, pp. 206–211 (2019). https://doi.org/10.1109/SERVICES.2019.00057

16. Rao, K., Coviello, G., Chakradhar, S.: DiCE: distributed code generation and execution. In: 2024 IEEE Conference on Pervasive and Intelligent Computing (PICom), pp. 8–15 (2024). https://doi.org/10.1109/PICom64201.2024.00008

17. Amazon Web Services: AWS lambda: Documentation and best practices (2025). https://docs.aws.amazon.com/lambda. Accessed 16 Mar 2025

18. Shahrad, M., Balkind, J., Wentzlaff, D.: Architectural implications of function-as-a-service computing. In: Proceedings of the 52nd Annual IEEE/ACM International Symposium on Microarchitecture, MICRO 1952, pp. 1063–1075. Association for Computing Machinery, New York (2019). https://doi.org/10.1145/3352460.3358296. ISBN 9781450369381

19. Vöcking, B.: How asymmetry helps load balancing. J. ACM **50**(4), 568–589 (2003). https://doi.org/10.1145/792538.792546. ISSN 0004-5411

20. Wang, L., et al.: A survey on large language model based autonomous agents. Front. Comput. Sci. **18**(6) (2024). https://doi.org/10.1007/s11704-024-40231-1. http://dx.doi.org/10.1007/s11704-024-40231-1. ISSN 2095-2236

21. Liu, Y., et al.: MMbench: Is your multi-modal model an all-around player? arXiv:2307.06281 (2023)

DynoInfer: Adaptive Resource Orchestration for LLM Inference on Resource-Constrained PCs

Yunling Chen[1]📵, Qingyin Lin[1]📵, Zhitao Chen[1]📵, Yang Ou[2(✉)]📵, and Zhiguang Chen[1]📵

[1] School of Computer Science and Engineering, Sun Yat-sen University, Guangzhou, China
{chenyling65,linqy35,chenzht37,chenzhg29}@mail2.sysu.edu.cn
[2] College of Computer Science and Technology, National University of Defense Technology, Changsha, China
ouyang06@nudt.edu.cn

Abstract. As LLMs become popular, there is a growing trend toward deploying LLMs on personal computers (PCs) to save inference costs, reduce network latency, and enhance privacy protection. However, the limited hardware resources of PCs and inefficient resource allocation of existing frameworks slow down the LLM inference. While recent works focus on reducing the resources consumed by LLM inference, they overlook the fact that available resources are changing dynamically due to the multitask nature of PCs. This paper presents DynoInfer, an LLM inference framework that dynamically allocates resources, specifically designed for resource-constrained personal computing environments. Basically, DynoInfer captures and utilizes CPU and memory resources that are not consumed by other running workloads in PCs, to improve overall resource utilization and reduce resource contention. For CPU resources, a locality-aware dynamic thread allocation strategy is adopted to adjust threads allocated for LLM inference. For memory resources, a parameter preloading with dynamic residing strategy is employed to carefully load parameters from storage to memory. Furthermore, DynoInfer capitalizes on idle periods to compress historical conversations, extending the memorized context length under resource-constrained scenarios. Evaluations show that DynoInfer can achieve an inference speedup of $5.76\times$ compared to llama.cpp, while it hardly interferes with other user workloads.

Keywords: AIPC · Large Language Models · Dynamic Resource Allocation

1 Introduction

Large language models (LLMs), such as the GPT series and LLaMA, have catalyzed a significant paradigm shift within the field of artificial intelligence. These models demonstrate exceptional capabilities in natural language understanding,

W. E. Nagel et al. (Eds.): Euro-Par 2025, LNCS 15900, pp. 292–306, 2026.
https://doi.org/10.1007/978-3-031-99854-6_20

text generation, and multimodal processing, highlighting their vast potential for applications across multiple domains. Increasingly, there is a trend toward deploying these models on personal computers (PCs) rather than relying solely on cloud-based solutions. Unlike model training, which incurs a one-time cost, inference remains an ongoing expense that significantly contributes to total cloud expenses. Deploying LLMs on PCs provides a cost-effective solution by enabling local inference, thereby reducing or eliminating the need for cloud-based services. Additionally, it mitigates latency issues often encountered with cloud services, as data does not need to travel to and from remote servers. Perhaps most importantly, deploying LLMs locally helps address privacy concerns by keeping user data on the PC, and reducing the risk of unauthorized access or exposure.

However, deploying LLMs on PCs presents significant challenges. The large size of models and long context required by good user experience demand substantial computational and memory resources, far beyond the capabilities of PCs. For instance, vicuna-13B requires about 24GB of memory for execution and 3GB of memory for storing a context of 4096 tokens, while a consumer-grade device is generally equipped with 16GB or 32GB of DRAM. Moreover, the limited resources of PCs are shared among the operating system, various applications, and background services, leaving only a small portion available for LLM inference.

Previous works have explored various approaches to deploy LLMs on PCs, including model compression and context compression. For model compression, quantization [8, 19] and selective execution [4, 12] are adopted, which reduce computational and memory overhead but harm model accuracy. For context compression, hard prompt methods [7, 10, 11] and soft prompt methods [5, 14, 17] are employed but introduce computational overhead, which interferes with model computation. Although reducing resource consumption of LLM inference, they overlook the special characteristic of PCs. Unlike high-performance clusters where sufficient resources are devoted to LLM inference, personal devices are devoting limited resources for not only LLM inference, but also many other user applications. The resource consumption of user applications changes with user activities. This makes it an opportunity and a challenge for LLM inference on PCs, as the available resources for inference change dynamically. Existing inference frameworks, such as llama.cpp [1], typically allocate fixed amounts of computational and memory resources for inference tasks. Such a static allocation can lead to inefficient utilization of system resources or severe resource contention between inference tasks and other running applications. Consequently, users may experience reduced overall system performance and responsiveness.

To address the above issues, we propose DynoInfer, an innovative LLM inference framework specifically designed for resource-constrained PCs. The main idea behind DynoInfer is dynamically allocating CPU and memory resources for LLM inference according to current user workloads. In this way, DynoInfer improves resource utilization and reduces interference between inference tasks and user workloads, thus improving overall system performance.

DynoInfer comprises three main components: the Thread Allocator, the Model Loader, and the Context Compressor. Each component plays a crucial role in optimizing system performance and resource utilization. The Thread Allocator continuously monitors CPU resource usage and dynamically adjusts thread allocation for inference tasks. To further enhance inference speed, the Thread Allocator employs a locality-aware thread binding mechanism to leverage both the temporal and spatial locality of CPU caches. The Model Loader preloads layers from disks, and further combines with a residing strategy to dynamically adjust layers cached in memory, based on available memory and layer access pattern. Although LLMs demonstrate strong capabilities in instruction comprehension and content generation, they are limited by the restricted context length on PCs, which can significantly impact the user experience. To mitigate this, the Context Compressor selectively compresses historical conversations during system idle periods, extending the context length without compromising performance.

To summarize, this paper makes the following contributions:

- We propose a dynamic thread allocation approach with a locality-aware thread binding strategy to improve overall system performance by dynamically adjusting computational resources allocated for inference.
- We preload model parameters with a dynamic residing strategy to better leverage available memory space and speedup inference, by adaptively deciding the location of parameters.
- We disaggregate conversation compression with inference computation to extend memorized context length without interfering inference, through performing selective compression during idle periods.
- Extensive evaluations show that DynoInfer achieves an inference speedup of up to 5.76× compared to llama.cpp, while it hardly interferes with other user workloads.

2   Background and Related Work

2.1   LLM Inference

Modern LLMs are typically built on autoregressive transformer architectures with multiple stacked layers. Two common inference strategies include fully loading all model parameters into memory before inference or using a pipeline approach, where parameters for subsequent layers are preloaded asynchronously while the current layer is being processed.

The inference process is divided into the prefill stage and the decode stage. In the prefill stage, the model initializes the key-value (KV) cache and generates the first output token. The hidden states of all input tokens are stored in the KV cache, which are reused in the decode phase to improve efficiency. In the decode stage, the model generates tokens autoregressively. At each iteration, the model takes the last generated token and the KV cache entries as inputs. It then updates the KV cache and generates the next token, repeating this process until an end-of-sequence (EOS) token is generated or the maximum allowed generation number is reached. The capacity of the KV cache, determined by the context window size, directly influences the model's ability to retain historical information. This is essential for generating contextually relevant outputs.

2.2 Inference with Limited Resources

Efficient inference with limited resources has emerged as an active research area. Broadly speaking, existing techniques can be classified into two main categories: model compression and selective execution. Model compression methods, such as pruning and quantization, aim to reduce the number of model parameters. For example, STI [8] assembles a quantized model based on the available memory. EdgeMoE [19] assigns each expert a quantization bit-width based on its importance. Wanda [15] evaluates weight importance, removing less important weights. Selective execution techniques dynamically select which portions of the model to compute. Deja Vu [12] uses a learning-based algorithm that predicts a relevant subset of parameters based on the input, while Keivan Alizadeh et al. [4] employ low-rank predictors to selectively load MLP parameters. Pre-gated MoE [9] pre-selects experts to activate for the next MoE block. These strategies sacrifice some model performance in exchange for enhanced inference efficiency.

Memorizing conversation history is crucial for enhancing user experience. However, the resource limitations of PCs restrict the size of the context window that can be supported. Inspired by existing research on prompt compression, we explore techniques to compress conversation histories. Prompt compression aims to expand the context window by distilling prompts into more concise representations while preserving their original intent. Its methods can be grouped into two main categories: (1) Hard Prompt, which reduces the prompt size by removing low-information-value tokens. Selective Context [11] uses a small language model to calculate token perplexities and remove lower-perplexity tokens. LongLLM-Lingua [10] introduces a document reordering strategy aimed at minimizing position bias. Nano-Capsulator [7] encapsulates prompts by using a semantic preservation objective with reward scores. (2) Soft Prompt, which transforms prompts into compact sets of specialized tokens or embeddings. Gist [14] condenses instruction prompts by training a gist token predictor. AutoCompressors [5] divide input prompts into segments, sequentially compressing them into soft prompt fragments. Contrastive contexts [17] train a soft prompt by minimizing the Kullback-Leibler divergence. However, soft prompt techniques often lack generalizability across different models. We focus on applying hard prompt techniques to compress conversation histories.

3 The Design of DynoInfer

3.1 Overview

We introduce DynoInfer, an innovative inference framework specifically designed to optimize the deployment of LLMs on resource-constrained PCs. In DynoInfer, model parameters are stored on the SSD, while only the KV cache and a subset of the weights are kept in DRAM. Figure 1 provides an architectural overview

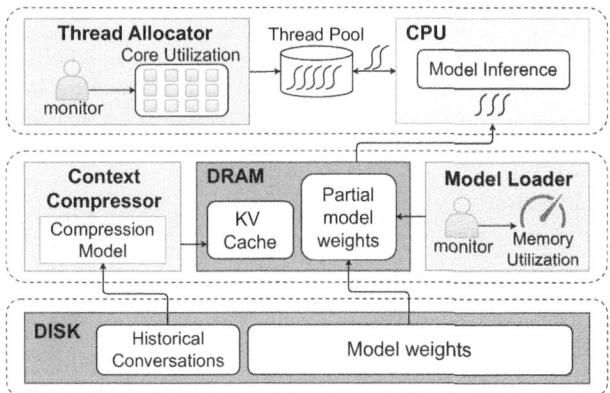

Fig. 1. The overview of DynoInfer.

of DynoInfer, which consists of three main components. The Thread Allocator continuously monitors CPU resource usage, dynamically adjusting thread allocation for inference requests, with a locality-aware thread binding strategy leveraging both temporal and spatial locality of the CPU cache. The Model Loader preloads layers from disks and further combines with a dynamic residing strategy to dynamically adjust layers cached in memory, based on available memory space and layer access pattern. To further enhance the user experience, the Context Compressor selectively compresses historical conversations during system idle periods, effectively extending the context length.

3.2   Locality-Aware Dynamic Thread Allocation

The Thread Allocator dynamically adjusts the number of inference threads based on available idle cores, allowing it to adapt to fluctuations in user workload. These idle cores are to be assigned to worker threads from the thread pool. Firstly, a dedicated monitoring thread continuously tracks the CPU utilization of each core and records the number of idle cores as N_{idle}. Then, when idle cores are detected, the monitor notifies the Thread Allocator to scale up the number of inference threads, thus accelerating the inference process. Notably, the Thread Allocator reserves a portion of idle cores for other user processes, instead of exhausting system resources. Let the number of reserved cores be $N_{reserve}$. The number of cores to be assigned for inference, denoted as N_{assign}, is given by Eq. (1):

$$N_{assign} = \max(N_{idle} - N_{reserve}, 0) \qquad (1)$$

This approach ensures system responsiveness and stability, even during periods of peak resource demand.

To further improve CPU cache utilization when new threads join, the Thread Allocator employs a locality-aware thread binding strategy. For spatial locality, threads are allocated to core groups that share L2 or L3 caches with cores that

Algorithm 1. Locality-Aware Thread Binding

1: $cores[]$ ▷ All cores info: last usage time, idle status, whether it is assigned.
2: $C_{\text{assigned}}[]$ ▷ The set of cores already assigned for inference threads.
3: N_{assign} ▷ Number of cores to be assigned for new inference threads.
4: $C_{\text{cand}}[], C_{\text{idle}}[]$
5: **for** $core \in cores[]$ **do**
6:     **if** $core$ is idle **then**
7:         $C_{\text{idle}} \leftarrow C_{\text{idle}} \cup core$
8:     **end if**
9: **end for**
10: Sort C_{idle} by last usage time (desc)
11: **while** $|C_{\text{cand}}| < N_{\text{assign}}$ **do**
12:     **for** $core \in C_{\text{idle}}$ **do**
13:         **if** $core$ sharing cache with $C_{\text{assigned}}[]$ or $C_{\text{cand}}[]$ **then**
14:             $C_{\text{cand}} \leftarrow C_{\text{cand}} \cup core$
15:             $C_{\text{idle}} \leftarrow C_{\text{idle}} \setminus \{core\}$
16:         **end if**
17:     **end for**
18:     **if** $|C_{\text{cand}}| < N_{\text{assign}}$ **then**
19:         $C_{\text{cand}} \leftarrow C_{\text{cand}} \cup C_{\text{idle}}[0]$
20:         $C_{\text{idle}} \leftarrow C_{\text{idle}} \setminus \{C_{\text{idle}}[0]\}$
21:     **end if**
22: **end while**
23: Bind new threads to $C_{\text{cand}}[0..N_{\text{assign}}]$

---

run inference tasks, reducing cache misses. For temporal locality, threads are assigned to cores that have been recently utilized for inference. The process of the thread binding algorithm is depicted in Algorithm 1. Firstly, current idle cores are picked and arranged as a list according to monitored core information (Line 5–9). Then, these idle cores are sorted by their last usage time in descending order to prioritize the cores that were used most recently (Line 10). After that, this algorithm selects cores from the idle list that share CPU caches with current running cores or future running cores to form a candidate list (Line 12–17). If there are not enough cores that meet the conditions, the most recently used idle core is added to the candidate list (Line 18–21). Finally, the first N_{assign} cores in the candidate list are assigned to the newly joined threads (Line 23).

3.3 Parameter Preloading with Dynamic Residing

Traditional pipeline mechanisms enable the asynchronous preloading of the parameters for the subsequent layer while the current layer is being processed. However, the limited data transfer speed of the SSD lags behind the CPU's inference speed, leadintg to idle cycles within the pipeline. To address this challenge, DynoInfer employs a residing strategy atop the traditional layer-wise preloading mechanism, to hide the long latency of loading parameters from the SSD. Basically, the available memory space is divided into two distinct segments: a preloading window and a residency area. The preloading window, given a fixed small capacity, temporarily holds parameters during inference, releasing them immediately once they have been processed. The residency area, given a dynamic capacity, uses a deferred release strategy, allowing model parameters to be reused across multiple inference turns. This means that the parameters will reside in the residency area once loaded until the eviction condition is triggered. Specifically, a background monitor thread continuously tracks the system's available memory resources. The monitor is responsible for dynamically adjusting the capacity of the residency area according to available memory space. To avoid exhausting the memory space, a specific memory space is preserved, denoted as $M_{\text{preserved}}$. DynoInfer stores the next loaded layer in the residency area if Eq. (2) is satisfied, where M_{avail} is the available memory space and M_{layer} is the size of the layer. Otherwise, the next loaded layer is stored in the preloading window.

$$M_{\text{avail}} - M_{\text{layer}} > M_{\text{preserved}} \tag{2}$$

If available memory falls below the preserved threshold, as depicted in Eq. (3), the model parameters are evicted from the residency area according to their distance to the current running layer, from far to close, until the preserved space is satisfied.

$$M_{\text{avail}} < M_{\text{preserved}} \tag{3}$$

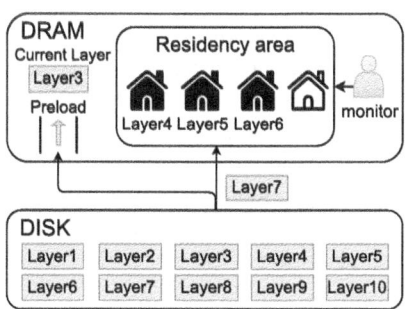

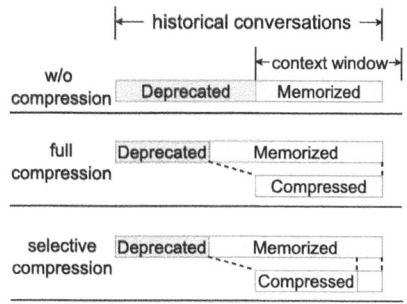

Fig. 2. An illustration of parameter preloading with dynamic residing.

Fig. 3. An illustration of conversations compression.

Figure 2 gives an example of how parameters are preloaded during inference and how the residency area works. The model is currently calculating the third layer, with the residency area holding the parameters of the 4th, 5th, and 6th layers. Consequently, the loading thread must now preload the parameters for the 7th layer. Based on the available memory detected by the monitor thread, it determines whether to store these parameters in the preloading window or retain them in the residency area. If the parameters for the 7th layer are stored in the residency area, they will remain in memory after current iteration, ensuring their availability for subsequent iterations without the need of reloading. Before the computation of a certain layer, DynoInfer firstly searches this layer in the residency area, then in the preloading window.

3.4 Selective Conversation Compression During Idle Periods

Due to the limitation of the model context window, historical conversations can only partially participate in new generations. Therefore, historical conversations can be divided into two parts, one deprecated and one memorized that participates in subsequent generations, as in Fig. 3. Without conversation compression (Top of Fig. 3), the model can only memorize a small part of history. Selective Context [11] leverages full compression (Middle of Fig. 3) for selected historical conversations, thereby extending the memorized length. The Context Compressor of DynoInfer takes a selective compression approach (Bottom of Fig. 3), considering that it is important to retain recent tokens ([3,13,18]). Based on the method proposed by Selective Context [11], DynoInfer defines a recent window where memorized history in the window maintains origin context, while the other part of the memorized history is compressed. In this way, DynoInfer can reduce the information loss caused by compression.

Additionally, to reduce the interference between conversation compression and inference process, the Context Compressor leverages the natural pause between conversations. It records the full conversation text. When the model is waiting for user input, the Compressor evaluates whether the compression conditions are met. Specifically, it checks for sufficient idle CPU cores to avoid triggering compression during peaks in user workload resource usage, as well as available memory for Selective Context compression. The Selective Context compression is implemented by a small language model, such as GPT-2. If the number of idle cores is larger than a predefined threshold and the available memory is large enough to accommodate the GPT-2 model, then the compression is triggered. When triggered, the Context Compressor performs the selective compression, without affecting the inference process.

4 Evaluation

4.1 Experimental Setup

Testbeds. The experiments are conducted on a Linux-based machine equipped with 32 GB of DRAM, a 7 TB NVMe SSD, and a 20-core Intel(R) Xeon(R) Gold 6230N CPU. To emulate the computational resource profile of a typical PC environment, the number of CPU cores used during the experiments is limited to 12 via the cgroups mechanism.

Models and Datasets. We select three open-source models for evaluation, including LLaMA-2-3B [16], Vicuna-7B and Vicuna-13B [6], which require 7.5, 14.6 and 27.4 GB of memory, respectively. Model input data is obtained from ShareGPT [2], with request arrival time following a Poisson distribution.

Workloads. Two types of user workload are used to simulate dynamic resource changes on a PC: a real-world workload collected from user PCs and a simulation workload executing 20 matrix computation tasks. We evaluate the overall performance, the impact of parameter preloading and conversation compression with the real-world workload. We evaluate the effectiveness of dynamic thread allocation with the simulation workload, as it generates more CPU-intensive tasks compared to the collected real-world workload.

Metrics. We evaluate LLM deployment through three aspects: (1) System Impact, assessed through changes in CPU utilization of user workload and extensions in execution time to quantify resource contention, (2) Inference Speed, measured by per-token generation time, (3) Response Quality, evaluated using BLEU, ROUGE, BERTScore, and METEOR to assess semantic relevance and linguistic coherence.

Baseline. We compare DynoInfer with llama.cpp. Note that here we implement a layer-wise pipeline loading mechanism for llama.cpp. Since the real-world workload consumes about 67% of memory, the models cannot be fully loaded into memory with the original llama.cpp. For the number of inference threads, it is set to the number of total system cores by default in llama.cpp.

4.2   Overall Performance

We evaluate the inference speed and the impact on real-world workload for both llama.cpp and DynoInfer.

As shown in Fig. 4, DynoInfer achieves an inference speedup of $5.76\times$, $3.05\times$, and $1.58\times$ compared to llama.cpp for the respective models tested. This improvement comes from DynoInfer's dynamic adjustment of memory and computational resources allocated to inference tasks, based on fluctuations in the real-world workload's resource usage. Figure 5 shows the decode latency over time for llama.cpp and DynoInfer using the LLaMA-2 model. During the first three hours, when available memory is abundant, the fluctuations in decode latency are mainly driven by variations in CPU utilization within the workload. DynoInfer dynamically adjusts the number of inference threads, reducing resource contention and resulting in smaller fluctuations. Between the third and fourth hours, as both the workload's memory usage and CPU utilization increase, decode latency for both llama.cpp and DynoInfer rises. The fluctuations in llama.cpp are mainly due to increased CPU utilization within the workload, while for DynoInfer, higher memory usage by the workload leads to reduced caching of model parameters, which increases the time required for model loading. In the final two hours, as available memory becomes insufficient and fluctuates, DynoInfer's decode latency is primarily influenced by changes in memory availability. In contrast, llama.cpp, which does not utilize memory caching for model parameters, exhibits more stable decode latency.

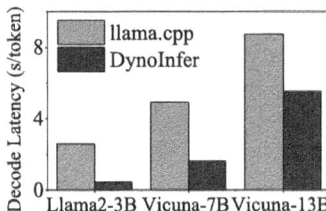
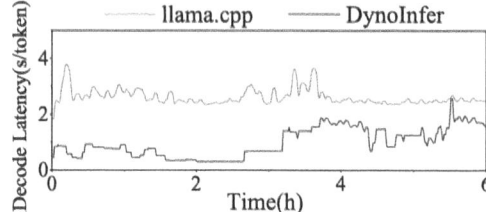

Fig. 4. Average decode latency.   **Fig. 5.** LLaMA-2 decode latency over time.

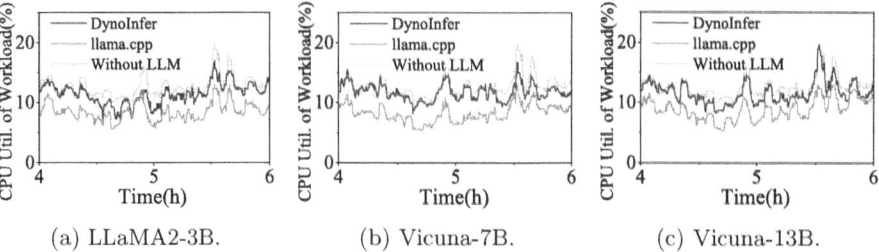

(a) LLaMA2-3B.   (b) Vicuna-7B.   (c) Vicuna-13B.

Fig. 6. Execution efficiency of user workloads during inference of different models.

Figure 6 shows CPU utilization fluctuations of the user workload over two hours, comparing the performance impact of llama.cpp and DynoInfer on the real-world workload. Since DynoInfer dynamically adjusts its inference threads based on the workload's CPU utilization, it reduces resource contention with the user workload. In contrast, llama.cpp depends on the operating system to manage CPU resource allocation for both the user workload and LLM inference, causing significant performance degradation of the user workload.

4.3 Efficiency of Dynamic Thread Allocation

We conduct experiments on the simulation workload using the Vicuna-7B model, ensuring sufficient memory allocation to fully load all model parameters. We compare the impact of using dynamic threads versus fixed threads on both simulation workload performance and inference speed, and evaluate the effectiveness of the thread binding algorithm.

As shown in Fig. 7a and Fig. 7b, the dynamic thread configuration achieves the lowest decode latency and the fastest matrix workload execution. DynoInfer monitors CPU utilization and dynamically adjusts the number of threads for inference, reducing contention during high utilization and maximizing idle resource usage during low utilization. In contrast, using the fixed thread configuration with fewer than six inference threads leads to suboptimal performance due to underutilized core resources. Exceeding eight threads exacerbates resource contention with matrix computations, increasing decode latency. Additionally, more allocated fixed threads increase resource contention and extend workload execution time.

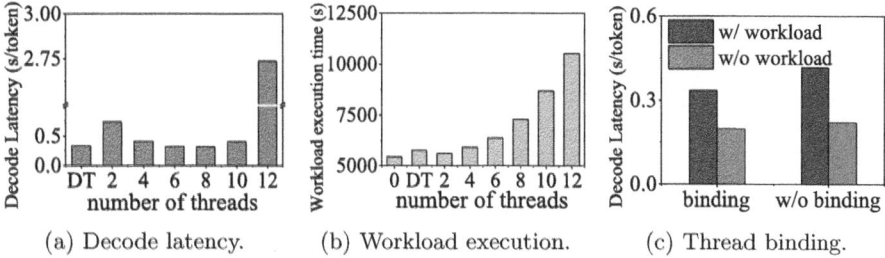

(a) Decode latency.   (b) Workload execution.   (c) Thread binding.

Fig. 7. Impact of inference thread number on decode latency(a) and workload execution time(b). Impact of thread binding on decode latency(c).

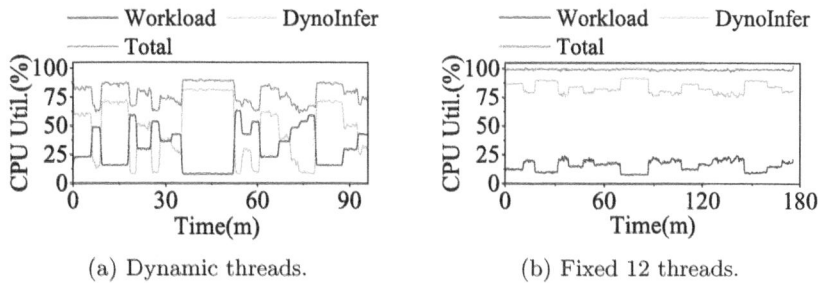

(a) Dynamic threads.   (b) Fixed 12 threads.

Fig. 8. The CPU utilization over time under different thread configuration.

Figure 8a and Fig. 8b illustrate that under the dynamic threads configuration, CPU utilization for LLM inference dynamically adjusts according to the CPU demands of the matrix computations. In contrast, with 12 fixed threads, the inference task seizes most of the CPU resources, leading to low CPU utilization for matrix computation tasks and significantly increasing their execution time.

In Fig. 7c, we evaluate the impact of the locality-aware thread binding algorithm on inference speed. Under simulation workloads, the algorithm improves inference speed by 19.8%, and with no workload, it enhances speed by 10%. This improvement can be attributed to the thread binding algorithm's consideration of spatial and temporal cache locality, as well as core availability.

4.4 Efficiency of Dynamic Residing

We evaluate the efficiency of parameter preloading with dynamic residing (DR) in terms of memory usage and decode latency across three models.

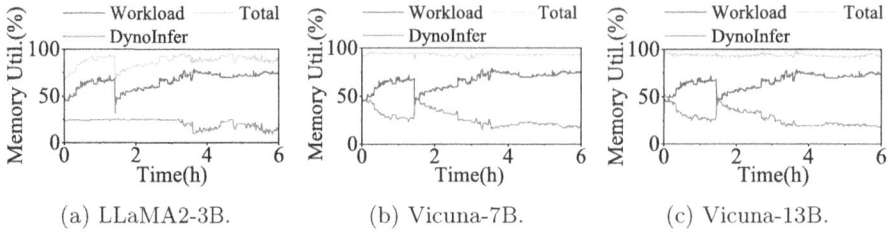

(a) LLaMA2-3B.   (b) Vicuna-7B.   (c) Vicuna-13B.

Fig. 9. Memory utilization over time.

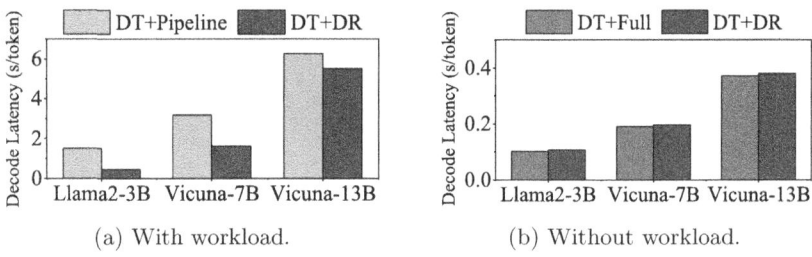

(a) With workload.   (b) Without workload.

Fig. 10. Impact of different parameter loading strategy on decode latency.

For memory usage, the dynamic residing strategy successfully maintains proper memory utilization. As shown in Fig. 9, DynoInfer dynamically adjusts the memory consumption of model inference based on the available memory, maximizing memory utilization while keeping total memory usage within system limits. When the memory consumption of the workload gradually increases, DynoInfer reduces memory usage by evicting certain parameters from the residency area. Note that in Fig. 9a DynoInfer consumes constant memory during the first three hours. This is because the user workload imposes a low memory demand, allowing the entire LLaMA-2 3B model to be fully loaded into memory.

For decode latency, the location of parameters is significant for it decides the access time. Traditional parameter loading methods include two approaches: (1) Pipeline: sequentially loading one layer parameter into memory in a pipelined manner; (2) Full: loading the entire model into memory before inference. To eliminate the impact of dynamic thread allocation on decode latency, we combine the Pipeline and Full strategies with dynamic thread allocation. Note that the Full strategy can only be applied without running the user workload. As shown in Fig. 10a, DR outperforms the Pipeline strategy in inference latency. This improvement is due to leveraging available free memory to cache model parameters, thereby reducing loading time. As shown in Fig. 10b, compared to the Full strategy, DR's inference speed is slightly slower. This is due to the overhead introduced by factors such as conditional checks, locking operations, and synchronization delays. However, the Full strategy consumes a large amount of memory, and when the model is too large or other programs are running on the PC, inference may be interrupted.

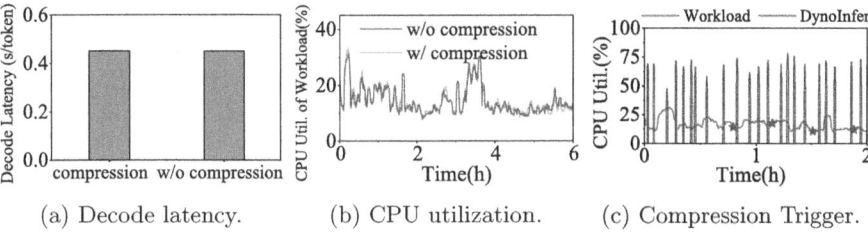

(a) Decode latency.   (b) CPU utilization.   (c) Compression Trigger.

Fig. 11. Impact of Context Compression on decode latency (a) and CPU utilization of user workload (b). In subfigure (c), stars indicate the moments when compression is triggered.

Table 1. Performance comparison with Selective Context.

Method	Ratio	BLEU	METEOR	ROUGE			BERTScore		
				rouge1	rouge2	rougeL	Precision	Recall	F1
sc	1.3	.323	.458	.571	.398	.457	.900	.897	.898
	1.5	.280	.422	.543	.360	.423	.895	.889	.892
	2.0	**.215**	**.368**	**.497**	**.297**	**.365**	**.885**	**.878**	**.881**
ours	**2.0**	**.285**	**.437**	**.538**	**.349**	**.411**	**.890**	**.889**	**.889**

4.5 Efficiency of Selective Conversation Compression

We evaluate the selective conversation compression strategy of DynoInfer in terms of model performance and impacts on both decode speed and workload performance.

For model performance, we compare DynoInfer to the Selective Context strategy, which compresses selected context. In DynoInfer, some recent tokens remain uncompressed to maintain more accurate information. We set the same length of selected context between DynoInfer and Selective Context, and the recent 20% of tokens are preserved in DynoInfer. As shown in Table 1, our strategy outperforms Selective Context in all metrics with the same compression ratio of 2.0. When Selective Context applies a smaller compression ratio such as 1.5, our strategy still achieves comparable model performance.

For decode speed, DynoInfer performs compression during idle periods between conversations (Fig. 11c), introducing negligible overhead in decode latency, as shown in Fig. 11a. As illustrated in Fig. 11b, compression does not interfere with the execution of the user workload because it is triggered only when sufficient idle CPU cores and memory resources are detected, thereby preventing resource contention with user workloads.

5 Conclusion

This paper introduces DynoInfer, an innovative LLM inference framework specifically designed for resource-constrained PCs. DynoInfer dynamically monitors and adjusts computational and memory resource allocation in real time, adapting to the fluctuating availability of resources on PCs. By leveraging idle periods to compress historical conversations, DynoInfer further extends the context length, enhancing user experience. Evaluation results show that DynoInfer achieves an inference speedup of up to 5.76× compared to llama.cpp, while it hardly interferes with other user workloads.

Acknowledgments. This work is Supported by Guangdong S&T Program under Grant NO. 2024B0101040005, the National Natural Science Foundation of China (NSFC) under Grant NO. 62272499, 62332021, the Guangdong Province Special Support Program for Cultivating High-Level Talents under Grant NO. 2021T006X160, and Pazhou Lab under Grant NO. PZL2023KF0001.

Disclosure of Interests. The authors have no competing interests to declare that are relevant to the content of this article.

References

1. llama.cpp. https://github.com/ggml-org/llama.cpp
2. philschmid. https://huggingface.co/datasets/philschmid/sharegpt-raw
3. Adnan, M., et al.: Keyformer: Kv cache reduction through key tokens selection for efficient generative inference. Proc. Mach. Learn. Syst. **6**, 114–127 (2024)
4. Alizadeh, K., et al.: Llm in a flash: efficient large language model inference with limited memory. In: Proceedings of the 62nd Annual Meeting of the Association for Computational Linguistics (Volume 1: Long Papers), pp. 12562–12584 (2024)
5. Chevalier, A., et al.: Adapting language models to compress contexts. arXiv preprint arXiv:2305.14788 (2023)
6. Chiang, W.L., et al.: Vicuna: an open-source chatbot impressing gpt-4 with 90%* chatgpt quality, march 2023. https://lmsys.org/blog/2023-03-30-vicuna **3**(5) (2023)
7. Chuang, Y.N., et al.: Learning to compress prompt in natural language formats. In: Proceedings of the 2024 Conference of the North American Chapter of the Association for Computational Linguistics: Human Language Technologies (Volume 1: Long Papers), pp. 7749–7760 (2024)
8. Guo, L., et al.: Sti: Turbocharge nlp inference at the edge via elastic pipelining. In: Proceedings of the 28th ACM International Conference on Architectural Support for Programming Languages and Operating Systems (2023)
9. Hwang, R., et al.: Pre-gated moe: an algorithm-system co-design for fast and scalable mixture-of-expert inference. In: 2024 ACM/IEEE 51st Annual International Symposium on Computer Architecture (ISCA), pp. 1018–1031. IEEE (2024)
10. Jiang, H., et al.: Longllmlingua: accelerating and enhancing llms in long context scenarios via prompt compression. arXiv preprint arXiv:2310.06839 (2023)
11. Li, Y., et al.: Compressing context to enhance inference efficiency of large language models. arXiv preprint arXiv:2310.06201 (2023)
12. Liu, Z., et al.: Deja vu: contextual sparsity for efficient llms at inference time. In: Proceedings of the 40th International Conference on Machine Learning, pp. 22137–22176 (2023)

13. Liu, Z., et al.: Scissorhands: exploiting the persistence of importance hypothesis for llm kv cache compression at test time. Adv. Neural. Inf. Process. Syst. **36**, 52342–52364 (2023)
14. Mu, J., et al.: Learning to compress prompts with gist tokens. Adv. Neural. Inf. Process. Syst. **36**, 19327–19352 (2023)
15. Sun, M., et al.: A simple and effective pruning approach for large language models. arXiv preprint arXiv:2306.11695 (2023)
16. Touvron, H., et al.: Llama 2: open foundation and fine-tuned chat models. arXiv preprint arXiv:2307.09288 (2023)
17. Wingate, D., et al.: Prompt compression and contrastive conditioning for controllability and toxicity reduction in language models. In: Findings of the Association for Computational Linguistics: EMNLP 2022, pp. 5621–5634 (2022)
18. Xiao, G., et al.: Efficient streaming language models with attention sinks. arXiv preprint arXiv:2309.17453 (2023)
19. Yi, R., et al.: Edgemoe: fast on-device inference of moe-based large language models. arXiv preprint arXiv:2308.14352 (2023)

Enabling Elasticity in Scientific Workflows for High-Performance Computing Systems

Rajat Bhattarai[1]([✉]) [iD], Howard Pritchard[2] [iD], and Sheikh Ghafoor[1] [iD]

[1] Tennessee Tech University, Cookeville, TN 38505, USA
{rbhattara43,sghafoor}@tntech.edu
[2] Los Alamos National Laboratory, Los Alamos, NM 87544, USA
howardp@lanl.gov

Abstract. Modern workflows are increasingly data and event-driven, particularly with the growing integration of AI/ML tasks. Static workflows lack the flexibility to adapt at runtime in response to dynamic, event-driven tasks or fluctuating system demands, leading to suboptimal resource utilization and reduced efficiency. Elastic workflows, which can dynamically adjust resource usage based on system availability and workload demands, can enhance computational efficiency through intelligent resource management strategies. This paper presents the design and implementation of an elastic workflow framework for high-performance computing (HPC), highlighting key challenges and design considerations. Our framework is based on an elastic Parsl workflow manager and a custom elastic resource manager, both leveraging capabilities of an implementation of the Process Management Interface for Exscale (PMIx) API. Through real-world and synthetic workflow case studies, we demonstrate improved resource utilization and reduced execution times, showcasing the benefits of elasticity in HPC workflows.

Keywords: Dynamic Resources · Parsl · PMIx · Scientific Workflows

1 Introduction

Scientific workflows are crucial across disciplines for solving large-scale computing and data analysis problems, requiring substantial computational, storage, and communication resources. These workflows often run on HPC systems, including exascale platforms [11], and make up a significant portion of HPC workloads. Most HPC systems still use static resource allocation, which lacks the flexibility to adapt to evolving workflow and system demands, impacting efficiency, especially for event and data driven modern dynamic workflows. To address this, compute elasticity and dynamic resource adjustment based on workload and system availability is essential.

Emerging AI-converged workflows on HPC systems [6,10] challenge traditional static resource allocation, which fails to accommodate their dynamic

W. E. Nagel et al. (Eds.): Euro-Par 2025, LNCS 15900, pp. 307–321, 2026.
https://doi.org/10.1007/978-3-031-99854-6_21

nature. These event-driven workflows, such as AI-steered simulation ensembles, evolve based on real-time AI inference, spawning or terminating HPC simulations on the fly. This unpredictability demands elastic resource management for optimal performance and efficiency. Beyond the workflows, HPC systems require elasticity to improve resource utilization and efficiency. As we enter the exascale era, enhancing the energy efficiency of supercomputers, optimizing resource allocation, and minimizing operational costs have become increasingly critical. To achieve these goals, HPC software stacks must be capable of dynamically managing resources and efficiently supporting elastic applications [19].

Achieving elasticity in HPC is challenging, requiring changes across the software stack. Key issues include limited elasticity support in workflow managers, the lack of workflow-aware elastic schedulers and resource managers (RMs), no standardized communication between workflow managers (WFMs) and RMs, and a lack of studies on elastic workflow scenarios. This work presents the design and implementation of an elastic workflow ecosystem for HPC, featuring a prototype based on the PMIx-enabled Parsl framework and a custom elastic resource manager. We outline the necessary modifications to the HPC software stack and the communication mechanisms between components. Building on our prior work [4,5], we enhance Parsl to support better manager elasticity for Python-based workflows. Through real science workflows, including AI-driven ones, we demonstrate that dynamic resource management improves performance of both workflow and HPC system.

2   Background

Several key components make up the HPC software stack for scientific workflows: resource managers, workflow management systems, middlewares, and workflow programs themselves, each responsible for ensuring efficient execution.

Scientific workflows are structured programs that orchestrate and execute complex computational and data-intensive tasks. They are typically represented

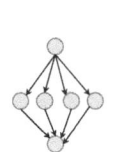 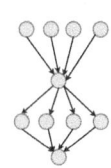 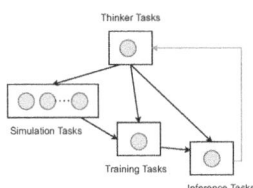 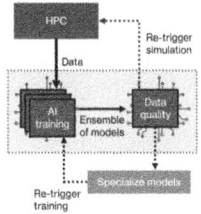

(a) BLAST workflow   (b) Synthetic Workflow II   (c) ExaMol-type Active Learning Workflow   (d) AI-driven HPC workflow: Adaptive training with simulation-generated data [6]

Fig. 1. Workflow DAGs

as Directed Acyclic Graphs (DAGs), where nodes represent workflow tasks and edges define their dependencies like Figs. 1a–1c.

In our work, the BLAST workflow represents a traditional static HPC workflow (Fig. 1a), with pre-defined tasks across three stages: dividing the input, executing multiple BLAST instances concurrently, and merging results. BLAST is used to match protein or DNA sequences against large databases [2]. We also created Synthetic Workflow II, inspired by the Parsl paper [3] (Fig. 1b), which includes four stages with dummy tasks of varying durations: 200 s for first and third stage and 100 s for second and fourth. The varying resource needs across stages highlight the importance of elasticity.

AI-driven HPC workflows are inherently dynamic, meaning tasks are not predefined but adapt based on real-time needs. In this work, we have used the ExaMol [25] workflow as a dynamic AI-driven HPC workflow. ExaMol is a machine learning-driven molecular discovery framework designed to efficiently explore vast chemical spaces based on Colmena [30] that uses Parsl. It integrates active learning with quantum chemistry simulations, iteratively selecting and evaluating promising molecular candidates. The execution motif of such workflows is shown in Fig. 1d. As shown in the Fig. 1c, for Examol, the number of simulation, retraining, and inference tasks is decided on the fly, making DAGs dynamically, necessitating elastic resource management in execution.

Workflow Managers orchestrate the execution of scientific workflows, managing task dependencies, resource allocation, and data flow. In this work, we use Parsl as the WFM. Parsl [3] allows users to define and execute complex workflows, enabling concurrent execution of Python functions with the @python_app decorator and asynchronous shell command execution with the @bash_app decorator. When a Parsl app is invoked, it returns a future object, enabling asynchronous execution on available remote resources.

Parsl's runtime architecture consists of three key components: the DataFlowKernel (DFK), Executor, and Provider (Fig. 2). The DFK manages task graphs (DAGs) and orchestrates workflow execution. Parsl follows a pilot job abstraction for resource management. The Provider (e.g. SlurmProvider) acquires resources from the RM based on user configurations and DFK scaling logic. After resource allocation, the Executor (e.g. HighThroughputExecutor or HTEx) deploys managers (pilot jobs) on the allocated nodes, which create worker pools based on Parsl's Launcher specification. These managers then pull tasks from Parsl's interchange and distribute them to workers.

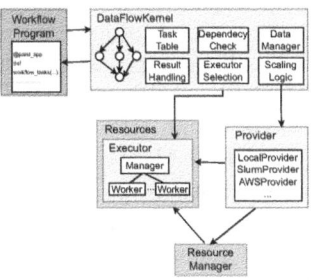
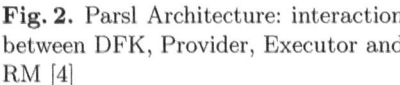

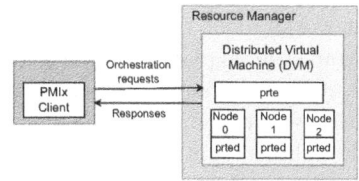

Fig. 2. Parsl Architecture: interaction between DFK, Provider, Executor and RM [4]

Fig. 3. PMIx Client interaction with PRRTE's Distributed Virtual Machine (DVM)

Middleware abstracts hardware complexity and simplifies execution, with components like MPI, Process Management Interfaces, and Parallel File Systems. For elastic computing, we use PMIx as the process manager middleware to dynamically launch and manage processes. PMIx [7] is a standardized API designed for exascale HPC, supporting process management, resource allocation, event notifications, and job control.

The OpenPMIx project [22] provides the PMIx Reference Runtime Environment (PRRTE): a runtime system that includes a PMIx server and a flexible way to explore PMIx capabilities. PRRTE can work with various external resource managers, including Slurm and PBSPro [21], serving as flexible and adaptable solution. PRRTE supports dynamic resource changes through its host file management system. It can be initialized with a host file, launching a daemon (prted) on each node listed in the hostfile to create a Distributed Virtual Machine (DVM), Fig. 3. The PMIx client connects to the DVM and executes applications on DVM's resources. PRRTE allows for the elastic scaling of an existing DVM using –*add-hostfile* option. This functionality forms the foundation of our elastic workflow system, allowing workflows as PMIx clients to dynamically adapt to available resources.

Resource Manager is responsible for the low-level provisioning of resources, including batch scheduling, job management and task placement. Examples of RMs include job scheduling systems like Slurm, PBS, and others.

2.1   Related Work on Elasticity in HPC Systems

Most HPC elasticity research has been theoretical or focused on simulating elasticity, mainly optimizing scheduling for malleable jobs due to limited native support in the HPC software stack [9,18,23]. Few dynamic resource management implementations exist. Aliaga et al. provide a survey on malleable HPC applications [1]. Additionally, research has been conducted on extending MPI-4 Sessions and process sets, along with enhancements to OpenPMIx and PRRTE, for malleable MPI applications [17]. Chadha et al. [8] introduced an adaptive scheduler and resource change process that aligns with our objectives but relies on srun, while we aim for a more flexible scheduler. Their approach is tailored for the iMPI layer, where new nodes replicate the existing iMPI application. These prior works focus exclusively on MPI applications within HPC systems. Prabhakaran et al. explored modifications to PBSPro and the Maui scheduler to facilitate system-driven expansion and shrinkage of applications [24]. Although their solution was tailored for the Charm++, their methodology could be adapted for PMIx-enabled runtime systems and other resource managers.

In the context of workflow elasticity in HPC systems, progress has been limited in both conceptualization and practical implementation. Workflow frameworks like DASK [26], Parsl [3], and PyCOMPSs [14,29] offer elasticity inspired by cloud environments, dynamically scaling workflows through multiple job allocation requests to HPC resource manager. Other approaches, such as Elastic-HPC (E-HPC) [15] and DyFlow [27], use checkpoint-and-restart mechanisms to allow workflows to move across resources. Dorier et al. [12] propose an alternative method, replacing MPI with a more flexible messaging system to facilitate dynamic resource management while maintaining comparable performance on RDMA-capable interconnects. Their work also explores the challenges of elastic in situ analysis and visualization, highlighting the complexity of supporting various forms of elasticity within existing HPC infrastructures [13].

Earlier research agrees that achieving elasticity in HPC requires changes across the entire software stack. Efforts to integrate elasticity into MPI and PMIx standards, such as MPI Sessions, ParaStation MPI, and Dynamic Processes with Process Sets [28] have introduced prototype interfaces, however, a fully integrated, end-to-end solution remains elusive. A recurring theme across these approaches is the structuring of malleability into layers with well-defined tasks and services, leveraging PMIx. Our work builds on these concepts but focuses specifically on workflow-level elasticity.

3   Design and Implementation

As discussed in previous section, our approach aligns with the layered malleability paradigm, aiming to address malleability challenges across multiple levels of the HPC software stack, as illustrated in Fig. 4. We envision a robust model of elasticity where workflows can dynamically expand or contract in response to directives from the RM, WFM, or even the workflow itself, fostering a more adaptive and efficient HPC ecosystem.

3.1   Elastic Resource Manager

An elastic resource manager should dynamically adjust resources to meet changing workflow demands and system requirements. Since existing resource managers lack dynamic allocation and elastic scheduling, we developed a custom manager to address these needs.

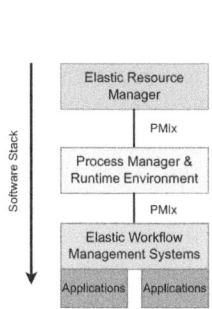

Fig. 4. Elastic HPC Software Stack Based on the Proposed Design: PMIx is employed as the process manager in this work, that helps in dynamic resource and process management.

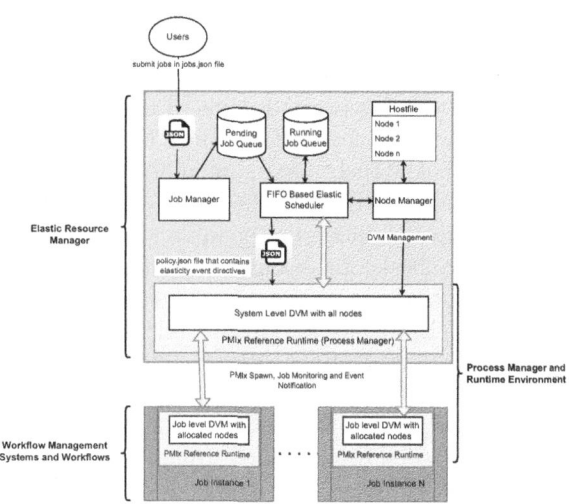

Fig. 5. Elastic Resource Manager Design showing Scheduler, Process Manager with hierarchical DVMs that are capable of elastically changing resources

Our elastic RM model as shown in Fig. 5 consists of three main components: Job Manager, Node Manager, and Scheduler. The Job Manager manages the job queue, reading pending jobs from a JSON file where users submit their jobs. It adds these jobs to the pending queue, to be read by the Scheduler. Each job in the queue has seven key attributes: a unique ID generated by the Job Manager, arrival time, execution time, minimum required resources, maximum scalable resources, the command to launch the job, and job type: either rigid or elastic.

Similarly, the Node Manager tracks the state of nodes and manages their availability. It maintains a hostfile listing the available nodes and, based on scheduler directives, allocates and deallocates resources by updating the hostfile accordingly. The current entries in the hostfile reflect the nodes that are available for use. We employed a hostfile-based approach since the process manager runtime, PRRTE, also heavily relies on this mechanism. Additionally, the Node Manager is responsible for initiating and maintaining the system-level PRRTE's Distributed Virtual Machine (DVM).

The scheduler allocates resources based on a scheduling algorithm and launches jobs on the assigned nodes. In our model, the scheduler conceptually integrates with the Process Manager (PRRTE) for job spawning, monitoring, and event notifications. Since our primary goal is to demonstrate the feasibility of our model, we have implemented a very simple first-in, first-out (FIFO)-based scheduler with two basic elastic scheduling algorithms: (I) Elastic scheduling with pending job priority and (II) Elastic scheduling with running job priority, both primarily focused on reducing resource fragmentation and improving resource utilization.

Elastic scheduling with pending job priority (type I) begins by allocating the minimum required resources to pending jobs. After resource distribution, the scheduler checks for fragmentation, where available resources are insufficient for the next job, leaving nodes idle. If fragmentation is detected, the scheduler scans the running queue and, following a FIFO order, expands the longest-running elastic jobs below their maximum allocation to efficiently utilize available resources.

In contrast, Elastic scheduling with running job priority, (type II), starts by allocating the maximum possible resources to pending jobs. After allocation, it similarly checks for resource fragmentation. If fragmentation occurs, the scheduler identifies elastic jobs in the running queue. Following FIFO, the longest-running elastic jobs are shrunk, releasing just enough resources back to the Node Manager to schedule the next pending job with the minimum required resources. This allows the scheduler to accommodate the next pending job.

In both elastic scheduling scenarios, if additional nodes become available and are not needed by pending or running jobs, the scheduler expands running elastic jobs to optimize resource utilization. Once the elastic schedules are finalized, they are recorded in a JSON policy file, which currently serves as a notification mechanism for running workflow jobs, informing them of their elastic allocations. Eventually, this should be replaced by a more efficient event notification system integrated with the process manager.

3.2 Process Manager and Runtime Environment

In our model, the Process Manager and Runtime Environment serve as middleware, integrated with the Elastic RM and Elastic WFM. It is responsible for launching processes triggered by either the RM to initiate jobs or the WFM to launch executors and tasks. The Process Manager elastically allocates resources and launches additional processes as needed, while also facilitating communication between the RM and the WFM by handling event exchanges.

We use PRRTE as the process manager, leveraging its DVM extension and pruning mechanism for dynamic resource scaling. We also employ a hierarchical DVM setup for running workflow jobs, as illustrated in Fig. 5. The RM initiates a system-level DVM encompassing all available nodes. Subsequently, it launches jobs against this DVM, with each workflow job creating its own job-level DVM. The top-level DVM is utilized by the scheduler to spawn jobs, while lower-level DVMs are used by the WFM to spawn executors and workflow tasks. Thanks to the elasticity of DVMs, each job can be made elastic, provided the running application or workflow can adapt to the elastic DVM structure.

Ideally, the Process Manager should send events from the top-level DVM to each lower-level DVM, a function PMIx could handle. However, since the required APIs are not yet implemented, we currently use a JSON file-based communication approach, allowing the RM to send resource change events to the WFM.

3.3 Elastic Workflow Managers

Elastic workflow managers are responsible for orchestrating the execution of complex workflows that consist of multiple interdependent tasks or jobs elastically. Specifically, we focus on WFMs that follow the pilot job execution model like Parsl. We have identified two key areas where compute elasticity can be applied in pilot-based workflow management systems: (i) Worker Level, and (ii) Manager Level. To enable elasticity in the WFM, the job-level DVM at the workflow level must first be resized. Then, the WFM must implement these changes in the running workflow instance.

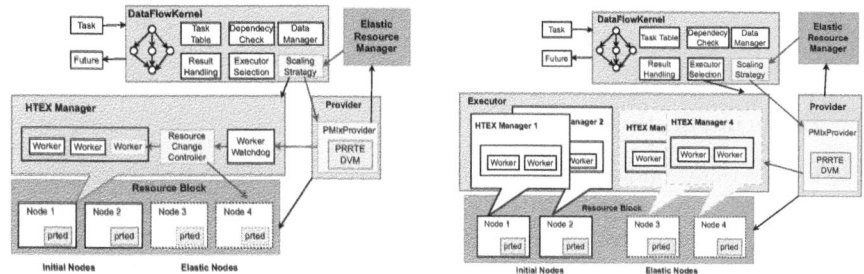

(a) Parsl worker-level elasticity via PMIx   (b) Parsl manager-level elasticity via PMIx

Fig. 6. The Elastic RM generates schedules that the Parsl's scaling strategy uses to dynamically resize the PRRTE DVM via the PMIxProvider and adjust the worker pool through the HTEx manager (worker-level elasticity). For manager-level elasticity, the PMIxProvider spawns or terminates managers as needed.

In worker-level elasticity, we add or remove workers within an existing manager-worker pool, as depicted in Fig. 6a. When resources are added or removed, workers are dynamically spawned or terminated to match the available resources [4]. This ensures that newly added workers can spawn tasks on the newly allocated resources. Conversely, during resource shrinkage, the removal of workers ensures that remaining workers do not compete for tasks in a resource-constrained environment, maintaining a balanced resource-worker distribution. This type of elasticity is particularly well-suited for workflow tasks that workers can spawn, such as MPI tasks in Parsl.

In manager-level elasticity, we add or remove managers with their own worker pool, as shown in Fig. 6b. When resources are added or removed, managers are started or terminated on these resources. Shrinking requires careful handling, Currently, we halt task assignment to the targeted manager and terminate it once all running tasks are completed. This type of elasticity is suitable to workflow tasks which are pure python functions in Parsl.

In terms of implementation, we added a new PMIxProvider, two launchers: SimplePMIxLauncher and PMIxLauncher, and a new scaling strategy to execute required elasticity. The PMIxProvider interacts with our PMIx-based elastic resource manager to obtain resources dynamically. The launchers facilitate the execution of pilot jobs (executors) on allocated nodes. SimplePMIxLauncher is similar to Parsl's SimpleLauncher, designed for workflows containing MPI applications as tasks. It deploys a manager and a worker pool on the head node. Workers then spawn tasks on remote nodes using PRRTE. PMIxLauncher, which is similar to Parsl's SrunLauncher, deploys a manager on each allocated node, each with its own worker pool. It is suitable for workflows executing Python-based tasks. Workers run Python processes capable of executing pickled Python functions. Likewise, the new scaling strategy module handles elasticity by monitoring resource changes or elastic directives in a policy file managed by the elastic resource manager. Based on workflow type and resource status, the workflow manager applies the appropriate elasticity adjustments.

4   Evaluation

4.1   Experimentation

Experiments were conducted on a cluster of 47 Cavium ThunderX2 nodes, each with two 32-core processors (2.0 GHz) and 256 GB of DDR4 memory, running RHEL 8 and managed by Slurm 22.05.10.

For workload, apart from the BLAST, Examol, and Synthetic II mentioned before, we created Synthetic Workflow I and used the CloverLeaf application. Synthetic Workflow I consisted of 200 parallel dummy MPI applications, simulating parallel workflow phases. CloverLeaf [20], a hydrodynamics mini-application solving compressible Euler equations, represented a rigid MPI/OpenMP job. We designed the workload so that all jobs are submitted simultaneously. For the BLAST workflow, we set the minimum resources to 4 nodes and the maximum to 12 nodes, while for other workflows, we set to 4 and 8 nodes. The workload was submitted to the resource manager using the *jobs.json* file, and consisted of the following: Job 1 - BLAST workflow, Job 2 – ExaMol, Job 3 – CloverLeaf application, Job 4 – Synthetic Workflow I, and Job 5 – Synthetic Workflow II.

We ran the workload on rigid mode with static allocation and elastic mode with two types of scheduling algorithm: Elastic scheduling with pending job priority (Type I) and Elastic scheduling with running job priority (Type II). The primary goal of these experiments was to demonstrate the feasibility of our elastic framework and test simple elastic scheduling algorithms. We measured total time to run the workload and resource utilization at different timestamps. We used 15 nodes of the cluster and ran our elastic scheduler on top of them.

4.2   Results

Figure 7a presents the average makespan across five runs of the workload under three different scheduling cases. Rigid scheduling results in the longest execution time. In comparison, Elastic Scheduling Type I reduces the total runtime by 17%, while Elastic Scheduling Type II achieves a 8% improvement.

Additionally, we analyzed node occupation across these three scheduling approaches. For each scheduling type, we selected the run with the highest

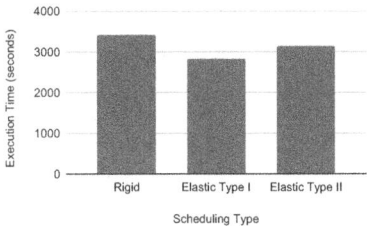

(a) Workload execution time (Total makespan)

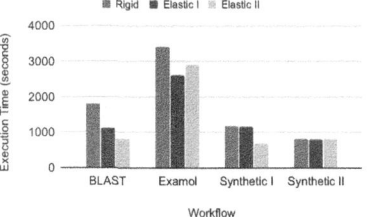

(b) Average makespan of each workflow under different scheduling algorithms

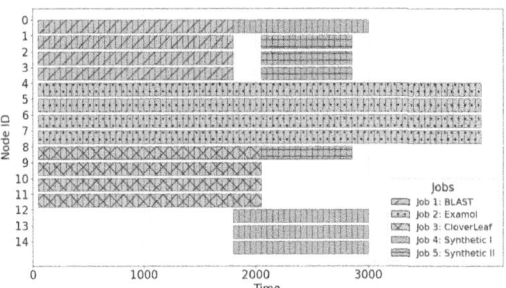

(c) Node occupation in Rigid Scheduling

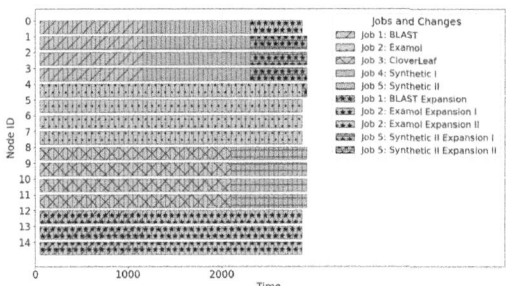

(d) Node occupation in Elastic Scheduling Type I (* = elastic events, Job 3 is rigid)

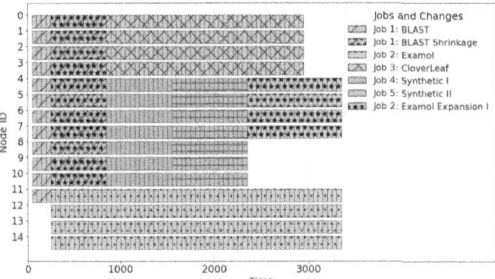

(e) Node occupation in Elastic Scheduling Type II (* = elastic events, Job 3 is rigid)

Fig. 7. Makespans and node occupation under different scheduling algorithms

runtime (worst case) to illustrate node usage shown in the Figs. 7c–7e. These figures depict node occupation, highlighting the expansion and shrinkage phases according to the respective scheduling algorithms.

Figure 7c illustrates node occupation during rigid scheduling, where resource allocation remains static. As shown, resource fragmentation persists for an extended period, leading to significant underutilization. For nearly the entire execution time, only 80% of the total nodes are in use (12), leaving 3 nodes idle. This inefficiency contributes to the longer runtime of individual jobs and an overall higher makespan.

In contrast, Elastic Scheduling Type I achieves the highest resource utilization with no resource fragmentation. As shown in Fig. 7d, each job starts with a minimum allocation and dynamically expands to occupy available fragmented resources whenever possible. This adaptive approach maximizes resource usage, reaching nearly 100% node utilization, while also reducing total runtime.

Similarly, Elastic Scheduling Type II optimizes resource utilization, keeping nearly 100% node utilization. In this approach, jobs begin with maximum allocation and dynamically shrink to free up resources for pending jobs, allowing them to start execution sooner. This strategy minimizes fragmentation and contributes to a lower overall makespan, as illustrated in Fig. 7a.

We also measured the makespan of each workflow and observed that the elasticity led to improvements in the individual runtimes of some workflows, as illustrated in Fig. 7b. Notably, BLAST and ExaMol workflows saw significant reductions in makespan up to 38% and 23%, respectively, in Elastic Scheduling Type I, and 54% and 14% in Elastic Scheduling Type II.

For Synthetic Workflow I and Synthetic Workflow II, we observed little to no change in makespan under Elastic Scheduling Type I. This is because they were not scheduled elastically and, therefore, did not undergo expansion or shrinkage (Fig. 7d). However, under Elastic Scheduling Type II, Synthetic Workflow I experienced a significant 40% reduction in makespan, while Synthetic Workflow II remained unchanged. Even after scaling up to three nodes, the makespan of Synthetic Workflow II was unaffected, likely due to its inherent scalability limitations at that particular node count.

Our results for this workload indicate that Elastic Scheduling Type I is more effective than Type II. In Type I, node utilization is more balanced, enabling more efficient resource allocation. Notably, the longest-running workflow, ExaMol, benefits significantly: it expands to at least 7 nodes shortly after the first third of the execution and reaches 8 nodes during the final quarter. This leads to an earlier completion of ExaMol and a reduction in overall workload execution time. In contrast, under Type II, ExaMol is restricted to a maximum of 4 nodes for most of the runtime, only scaling to 8 nodes in the final quarter, leading to longer execution of both ExaMol and the overall workload. It is important to note that the performance of both scheduling strategies is influenced by the job submission order, as scheduling decisions follow a FIFO policy, even for elastic expansion and contraction. Nonetheless, it is safe to say that elastic scheduling generally improves individual workflow runtimes, contributing to a shorter total workload duration.

4.3 Discussion and Future Work

Design Considerations for an Elastic HPC Workflow Ecosystem. This work demonstrates how targeted modifications across the HPC software stack can enable elasticity in scientific workflows. Existing RMs need new development to dynamically allocate and deallocate resources based on real-time system conditions and workflow fluctuations, incorporating elastic scheduling. Also, pilot-job-based WFMs must dynamically resize manager and worker pools while balancing loads, as demonstrated in our modified Parsl implementation.

While this study focused on system-initiated elasticity, the framework also supports application-initiated elasticity. In our previous work [4], we explored workload-specific elasticity driven by throughput. Going forward, we aim to integrate both system- and application-initiated approaches. To support this, the RM will incorporate a component that evaluates resource requests from workflows and makes allocation decisions using more sophisticated scheduling logic. Currently, scheduling relies on a basic FIFO policy, which may not scale effectively for complex or large-scale workflows. Advanced scheduling strategies are better suited for scenarios involving dynamically evolving workloads, such as AI-coupled HPC workflows that require real-time resource adaptation. Ultimately, this approach will enable the development of a fully elastic HPC system capable of adapting to diverse and changing workload and system demands.

Dynamic Workflows and Elasticity. Dynamic workflows like ExaMol exhibit variability, leading to fluctuating task counts and completion times, even under identical conditions. In this study, we executed ExaMol up to a predefined number of quantum chemistry computations. Despite this constraint, the total number of tasks varied within a certain range from 369–472 (simulation), 12–15 (training), and 120–180 (inference). Execution times also varied but in a range, even with fixed resources. To improve scalability, we configured the Examol Thinker to generate more tasks than available slots, increasing parallelism capability. Our experiments showed that elasticity improves performance in such case, but greater efficiency requires real-time dynamic scaling in normal cases for optimal resource utilization. We aim to implement more sophisticated workflow-initiated elasticity for such dynamic workflows to further enhance performance.

File-Based Communication Between the Scheduler and Workflows. At present, we rely on a policy file to transfer resource change information between the RM and the WFM, due to the limitations of existing RMs, middlewares like PMIx, and WFMs such as Parsl for advanced communication. While this may limit scalability and responsiveness, this study primarily focuses on demonstrating the design and feasibility of an elastic system prototype, rather than developing a comprehensive communication framework. In future, we envision addressing this by developing PMIx APIs built on event notification features, or by integrating other tools such as ZeroMQ [16] for more efficient communication.

5 Conclusion

In this work, we presented the design and implementation of a framework for elastic scientific workflows in HPC. We emphasized the need to modify existing resource and workflow managers to support elastic scaling, allowing workflows to adapt in real time. Building on previous work, we introduced elasticity at the manager level using PMIx, in addition to the worker-level elasticity, which communicates with an elastic resource manager to dynamically scale resources. With two simple algorithms, we demonstrated the feasibility of elastic scheduling. Our experimental results showed the advantages of elasticity by reducing execution time and enhancing resource utilization, also for AI-coupled workflow. This study lays the foundation for the development of fully elastic HPC workflow systems that can autonomously scale in response to the evolving needs of resource managers and scientific workflows. In the future, we aim to refine these scaling mechanisms further and integrate advanced communication protocols to optimize performance in complex, real-time HPC environments.

Acknowledgments. This work was supported by the National Nuclear Security Administration and NASA grant 80NSSC22K1913. Los Alamos National Laboratory is operated by Triad National Security, LLC for the U.S. Department of Energy under contract 89233218CNA000001. LA-UR-25-22993.

Disclosure of Interests. The authors have no competing interests to declare that are relevant to the content of this article.

References

1. Aliaga, J.I., Castillo, M., Iserte, S., et al.: A survey on malleability solutions for high-performance distributed computing. Appl. Sci. **12**(10), 5231 (2022)
2. Altschul, S.F., Gish, W., Miller, W., et al.: Basic local alignment search tool. J. Mol. Biol. **215**(3), 403–410 (1990)
3. Babuji, Y., Woodard, A., Li, Z., Katz, D.S., et al.: Parsl: pervasive parallel programming in python. In: Proceedings of the 28th International Symposium on High-Performance Parallel and Distributed Computing, pp. 25–36 (2019)
4. Bhattarai, R., Pritchard, H., Ghafoor, S.: Dynamic resource management for elastic scientific workflows using pmix. In: 2024 IEEE International Parallel and Distributed Processing Symposium Workshops (IPDPSW), pp. 686–695. IEEE (2024)
5. Bhattarai, R., Pritchard, H., Ghafoor, S.: Evaluation of a dynamic resource management strategy for elastic scientific workflows. In: Euro-Par 2024 International Workshops (2024)
6. Brewer, W., Gainaru, A., Suter, F., et al.: Ai-coupled hpc workflow applications, middleware and performance. arXiv preprint arXiv:2406.14315 (2024)
7. Castain, R.H., Hursey, J., Bouteiller, A., Solt, D.: Pmix: process management for exascale environments. Parallel Comput. **79**, 9–29 (2018)

8. Chadha, M., John, J., Gerndt, M.: Extending slurm for dynamic resource-aware adaptive batch scheduling. 2020 IEEE 27th International Conference on High Performance Computing, Data, and Analytics (HiPC), pp. 223–232 (2020)
9. Comprés, I., Arima, E., Schulz, M., et al.: Probabilistic job history conversion and performance model generation for malleable scheduling simulations. In: High Performance Computing, pp. 82–94. Springer, Cham (2023)
10. Da Silva, R.F., Bard, D., Chard, K., et al.: Workflows community summit 2024: Future trends and challenges in scientific workflows. arXiv preprint arXiv:2410.14943 (2024)
11. Da Silva, R.F., Casanova, H., Chard, K., et al.: A community roadmap for scientific workflows research and development. In: 2021 IEEE Workshop on Workflows in Support of Large-Scale Science (WORKS), pp. 81–90. IEEE (2021)
12. Dorier, M., Wang, Z., Ayachit, U., et al.: Colza: enabling elastic in situ visualization for high-performance computing simulations. In: 2022 IEEE International Parallel and Distributed Processing Symposium (IPDPS), pp. 538–548. IEEE (2022)
13. Dorier, M., Yildiz, O., Peterka, T., Ross, R.: The challenges of elastic in situ analysis and visualization. In: Proceedings of the Workshop on In Situ Infrastructures for Enabling Extreme-Scale Analysis and Visualization, pp. 23–28 (2019)
14. Ejarque, J., Andrio, P., Hospital, A., et al.: The bioexcel methodology for developing dynamic, scalable, reliable and portable computational biomolecular workflows. In: 2022 IEEE 18th International Conference on e-Science (e-Science), pp. 357–366. IEEE (2022)
15. Fox, W., Ghoshal, D., Souza, A., et al.: E-hpc: a library for elastic resource management in hpc environments. In: Proceedings of the 12th Workshop on Workflows in Support of Large-Scale Science, pp. 1–11 (2017)
16. Hintjens, P.: ZeroMQ: messaging for many applications. O'Reilly Media, Inc. (2013)
17. Huber, D., Streubel, M., Comprés, I., Schulz, M., Schreiber, M., Pritchard, H.: Towards dynamic resource management with mpi sessions and pmix. In: Proceedings of the 29th European MPI Users' Group Meeting, pp. 57–67 (2022)
18. Lina, D.H., Ghafoor, S., Hines, T.: Scheduling of elastic message passing applications on hpc systems. In: Workshop on Job Scheduling Strategies for Parallel Processing, pp. 172–191. Springer (2022)
19. Lucas, R., Ang, J., Bergman, K., et al.: Doe advanced scientific computing advisory subcommittee (ascac) report: top ten exascale research challenges. Technical report, USDOE Office of Science (SC)(United States) (2014)
20. Mallinson, A., Beckingsale, D.A., Gaudin, W., et al.: Cloverleaf: preparing hydrodynamics codes for exascale. The Cray User Group **2013** (2013)
21. Nitzberg, B., Schopf, J.M., Jones, J.P.: Pbs pro: grid computing and scheduling attributes. In: Grid Resource Management: State of the Art and Future Trends, pp. 183–190. Springer (2004)
22. OpenPMIx: Openpmix: Reference implementation of the process management interface for exascale (2023). https://openpmix.github.io/. Accessed 01 Aug 2023
23. Özden, T., Beringer, T., Mazaheri, A., et al.: Elastisim: a batch-system simulator for malleable workloads. In: Proceedings of the 51st International Conference on Parallel Processing, pp. 1–11 (2022)
24. Prabhakaran, S., Neumann, M., Rinke, S., et al.: A batch system with efficient adaptive scheduling for malleable and evolving applications. In: 2015 IEEE International Parallel and Distributed Processing Symposium, pp. 429–438. IEEE (2015)
25. Project, E.: Examol: Machine learning for molecular discovery (2023). https://exalearn.github.io/ExaMol/index.html. Accessed 10 Mar 2025

26. Rocklin, M.: Dask: Parallel computation with blocked algorithms and task scheduling. In: SciPy, pp. 126–132 (2015)
27. Singhal, S., Sussman, A., Wolf, M., et al.: Dyflow: a flexible framework for orchestrating scientific workflows on supercomputers. In: 50th International Conference on Parallel Processing Workshop, pp. 1–11 (2021)
28. Tarraf, A., Schreiber, M., Cascajo, A., et al.: Malleability in modern hpc systems: current experiences, challenges, and future opportunities. IEEE Trans. Parallel Distribut. Syst. (2024)
29. Tejedor, E., Becerra, Y., Alomar, G., et al.: Pycompss: parallel computational workflows in python. Int. J. High Performance Comput. Appl. **31**(1), 66–82 (2017)
30. Ward, L., Sivaraman, G., Pauloski, J.G., et al.: Colmena: scalable machine-learning-based steering of ensemble simulations for high performance computing. In: 2021 IEEE/ACM Workshop on Machine Learning in High Performance Computing Environments (MLHPC), pp. 9–20. IEEE (2021)

Container Workload Prediction Using Deep Domain Adaptation in Transfer Learning

Yunlan Wang[1], Yutong Liu[1(✉)], Tianhai Zhao[1], Mingxuan Liu[1], Jianhua Gu[1], Zhengxiong Hou[1], and Chengwen Zhong[2,3(✉)]

[1] School of Computer Science, Northwestern Polytechnical University, Xi'an, Shaanxi, China
`yutongliu0110@gmail.com`
[2] School of Aeronautics, Northwestern Polytechnical University, Xi'an, Shaanxi, China
`zhongcw@nwpu.edu.cn`
[3] National Key Laboratory of Aircraft Configuration Design, Xi'an, Shaanxi, China

Abstract. Containers are the primary deployment method for cloud applications, and accurate workload prediction is essential for resource allocation and energy optimization. Traditional statistical models struggle to capture complex workload variations, while classical neural network models require extensive historical data, which is challenging due to containers' short lifespan. This paper proposes a container workload prediction model based on deep domain adaptation in transfer learning (CWPDDA). The model includes a feature extractor with self-attention and cross-attention mechanisms to extract private and shared features, a domain adversarial adapter to reduce distribution differences, and a workload predictor to directly apply source-target data for prediction, avoiding performance degradation from domain shift. To validate the accuracy of the proposed model, this study utilized the Alibaba cluster-trace-v2017 dataset as the target domain and the Google cluster-usage traces v3 dataset as the source domain. Experimental results showed that the proposed model achieved a substantial improvement in prediction accuracy compared to the Autoregressive Integrated Moving Average (ARIMA), Long Short-Term Memory (LSTM), Autoregressive Recurrent Neural Network (DeepAR), Deep Renewal Processes (DRP), and Multivariate Quantile Function Forecaster (MQF2) models.

Keywords: Docker containers · workload prediction · transfer learning · deep domain adaptation

1 Introduction

With the development of virtualisation technology, containers have been increasingly adopted as the preferred deployment method for cloud applications. As

W. E. Nagel et al. (Eds.): Euro-Par 2025, LNCS 15900, pp. 322–336, 2026.
https://doi.org/10.1007/978-3-031-99854-6_22

more enterprises deploy applications on container cloud platforms, accurate workload prediction [1] becomes increasingly important for efficient resource allocation and management, energy consumption optimization [2], and load balancing in cloud computing environments [3].

Workload prediction methods forecast workload by constructing mathematical models. Existing models include traditional statistical models such as those based on grey theory and ARIMA, as well as machine learning (ML)-based neural network models. Although statistical models can develop simple quantitative models with limited historical data, they often struggle to capture the complex variations in workload. In contrast, neural network models can capture intricate patterns but require sufficient historical data [4,5].

In cloud-based container environments, the rapid startup and shutdown times of containers pose a challenge in collecting sufficient historical workload data. This lack of data hinders the development of accurate workload models, limiting their ability to adapt to changing load patterns [6]. Therefore, existing methods do not provide effective solutions for predicting container loads.

Transfer learning (TL) is a powerful technique that leverages knowledge from one task to improve performance on a related task. In light of the aforementioned challenges, we proposed an approach for container load prediction based on TL in this paper. By training the load prediction model on a large amount of source domain data and a smaller amount of target domain data, the model can effectively predict the workload of target containers by using the acquired knowledge.

Real-world scenarios often involve domain shifts due to distribution differences between the source and target domains [7,8]. To mitigate performance degradation caused by domain shift, we propose a container workload prediction model incorporating deep domain adaptation in TL. The model consists of three components: a feature extractor, a domain adversarial adapter, and a workload predictor.

– The feature extractor incorporates self-attention and cross-attention mechanisms to extract private and shared features from the source and target domains, respectively.
– The domain adversarial adapter introduces domain discrimination for adversarial learning to address the distribution differences between the source and target domains.
– The workload predictor generates load predictions for the target containers. The workload prediction model trained on source-target container data can be directly applied to predict the workload of target containers while avoiding performance degradation due to domain shift.

The rest of this paper is organized as follows. In Sect. 2, related works are discussed. In Sect. 3, the proposed container load prediction model based on deep domain adaptation in TL is presented. In Sect. 4, experimental comparison results are provided. Finally, conclusions and future directions are given in Sect. 5.

2   Related Work

Improving the accuracy of container workload prediction methods is an active area of research. Many studies have discussed this using traditional statistical models, classical neural network models, and TL methods.

2.1   Prediction Methods Based on Traditional Statistical Models

Statistical models can generate simple quantitative models based on a relatively small amount of historical data, such as moving averages (MA), autoregressive (AR), exponential smoothing (ES), autoregressive integrated moving average (ARIMA) models and their variants (e.g., improved multicriteria gray-theoretic algorithms), and combinatorial models (e.g., triple exponential smoothing and ARIMA combined forecasting). For example, Zou [9] designed a real-time load prediction approach using cubic exponential smoothing and ARIMA models. Gupta et al. [10] used an AR time-series prediction model for load prediction. These methods are typically linear, simple, fast, and easy to apply but cannot describe complex patterns of change in the predicted objects.

2.2   Prediction Methods Based on Classical Neural Network Models

Neural network models can accurately describe complex patterns and can handle high-dimensional nonlinear data. However, they require a large amount of historical data. Commonly used models for prediction include convolutional neural network (CNN), recurrent neural network (RNN), long short-term memory network (LSTM), and some integrated neural network prediction models. For example, Zhang [11] proposed an active prediction method for Docker container workloads by using a hybrid model that combines triple exponential smoothing and LSTM. Patel [12] proposed an active prediction method consisting of a one-dimensional CNN and LSTM for predicting CPU utilization on cloud servers at multiple consecutive time steps. Maiyza et al. [13] used generative adversarial network (GAN) to construct predictive cloud workload model. These methods require sufficient historical data to generate predictive models.

2.3   Prediction Methods Based on Transfer Learning

In TL, the model is trained on data in the source domain and then directly applied to the target domain, avoiding the need to train the model from scratch for the target domain. In addition, TL can make full use of the feature representations that have already been learned and can help solve the problems of data scarcity, sample imbalance, and domain change, thus improving the generalization ability and adaptability of the model [14].

There are two main ideas in TL methods: parameter sharing and domain adaptation. Parameter sharing, also known as parameter freezing or fine-tuning, has the characteristics of practicality, simplicity, and feasibility, and is the most widely used TL method [15,16]. First, a similarity calculation is performed to find the source domain object that is most similar to the target domain object. Next, the source domain data is used to pretrain the neural network to obtain the source model. Subsequently, the parameters of most layers in the source model are frozen. Finally, the last layers are fine-tuned with a smaller amount of the target domain data to generate the target network [17]. However, parameter sharing does not effectively produce satisfactory transmission results when there are significant differences in data distributions between the source and target domains.

Domain adaptation (DA) is a specialized TL technique that specifically addresses substantial distributional disparities between the source and target domains [18–20]. Common DA methods include feature transformation, domain adversarial training, and weight adjustment. Deep domain adaptation (DDA) combines the concepts of deep learning (DL) and domain adaptation [21]. In DDA, a deep neural network is generally used as a feature extractor, which can be a pretrained CNN or RNN. This network maps the input data to a high-dimensional feature space, where each feature vector represents some aspect or characteristic of the input [22,23].

In summary, using TL methods for container load prediction shows promise. TL can utilize knowledge from a large amount of historical data in the source container and apply it to the target container, even with limited data, to predict the load of the target domain. This approach effectively addresses the issue of disparate data distributions typically encountered in conventional DL methods during training and testing.

3 Container Workload Prediction Using Deep Domain Adaptation in Transfer Learning

Neural networks require training and test data to follow the same distribution and have sufficient samples for effective training. However, in real-world scenarios, load data distributions often change over time, and the short lifespan of containers limits historical data, hindering model accuracy. Transfer learning (TL) addresses this by transferring knowledge from one task to another [24,25]. Thus, we propose a container workload prediction model based on deep domain adaptation in TL. The model includes three components: a feature extractor, a domain adversarial adaptor, and a workload predictor. Figure 1 illustrates the structure of the prediction model.

3.1 Feature Extractor

The feature extractor utilizes self-attention and cross-attention mechanisms to extract private and shared features from the source and target domains, respectively. This mechanism effectively filters important feature information relevant to container load prediction from a large dataset. The feature extractor $G_f(\cdot)$ can be expressed using Eq. (1):

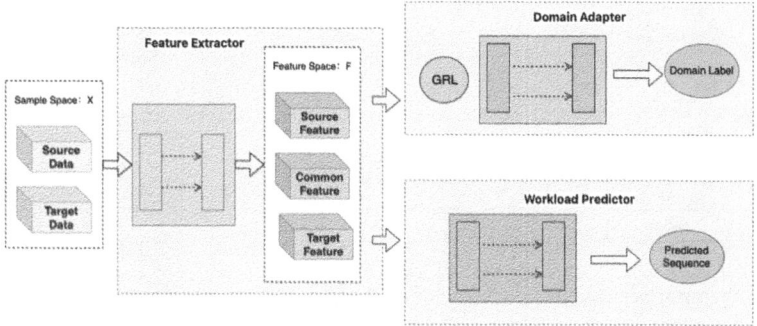

Fig. 1. Architecture of the container workload prediction model based on deep domain adaptation in transfer learning.

$$G_f(\theta_f) = \{SelfAttention(\theta_f), CrossAttention(\theta_f)\}. \tag{1}$$

where θ_f is the feature extractor parameter, which includes the projection parameter matrices for query(Q), key(K), and value(V).

Container load feature information consists of multiple K–V pairs, and Q is used to retrieve the corresponding V. The attention value, representing the importance of the retrieved content, is determined by the similarity between the Q and K. The V then weighted and summed to obtain the attention value.

The feature extractor has three branches with shared attention weights, as shown in Fig. 2: a source branch (left branch), a source-target branch (middle branch), and a target branch (right branch).

Source and target container data are fed into to their respective branches, where the self-attention mechanism generates private features for each domain. The Q, K, and V in the self-attention mechanism indicate that the self-attention mechanism prioritizes the internal relationships within the source/target containers. The similarity between Q and K is determined through dot product computation, followed by scaling to constrain the magnitude of the resulting values. The self-attention mechanism can be mathematically expressed using Eqs. (2), (3), (4), and (5):

$$Q = XW^Q, \quad K = XW^K, \quad V = XW^V. \tag{2}$$

$$Similarity(Q, K_i) = \frac{QK_i^T}{\sqrt{d_k}}. \tag{3}$$

$$Softmax(Similarity_i) = \frac{e^{Similarity_i}}{\sum_{j=1}^{n} e^{Similarity_j}}. \tag{4}$$

$$SelfAttention(Q, K, V) = \sum_{i=1}^{n} Softmax(Similarity(Q, K_i)) \cdot V_i. \tag{5}$$

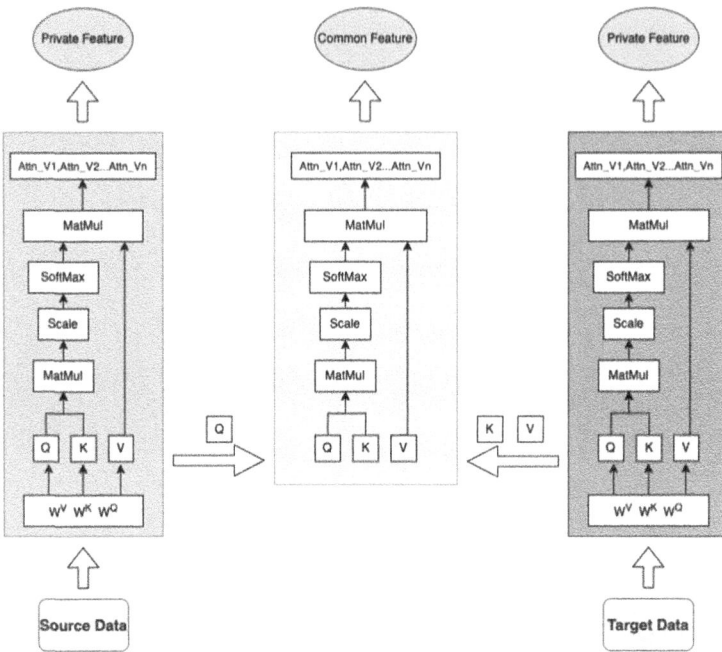

Fig. 2. Structure of the feature extractor.

where X is the input container data sequence; W^Q, W^K, and W^V are the three trainable projection parameter matrices; and d_k is the vector dimensions of Q and K. When calculating the inner product of the vectors of each row of the matrices Q and K, dot product scaling is performed to prevent the inner product from being overly large, therefore, the inner product is divided by the square root of d_k. And the n determines number of sequence elements that need to be considered when computing the attention weights, the SoftMax activation function is employed to normalize the self-attention weights.

The cross-attention mechanism plays a crucial role in the source-target branch because it integrates inputs from the other two branches. Q is sourced from the source branch, while K and V are obtained from the target branch. The primary objective of the source-target branch is to generate features that are relevant to both the source and target domains. The cross-attention mechanism extends the self-attention mechanism, facilitating the handling of relationships between multiple input sequences; it achieves this by computing the similarity between Q and K from different input sequences and then performing a weighted summation of the corresponding V. The computations involved in the cross-attention mechanism are outlined in Eqs. (6), (7), (8), and (9):

$$Q_s = X_s W^{Qs}, \quad K_t = X_t W^{Kt}, \quad V_t = X_t W^{Vt}. \tag{6}$$

$$Similarity\left(Q_s, K_{ti}\right) = \frac{Q_s K_{ti}^T}{\sqrt{d_k}}. \tag{7}$$

$$Softmax\left(Similarity_k\right) = \frac{e^{Similarity_k}}{\sum_{j=1}^{m} e^{Similarity_j}}. \tag{8}$$

$$CrossAttention\left(Q_s, K_t, V_t\right) = \sum_{j=1}^{m} Softmax\left(Similarity\left(Q_s, K_{tj}\right)\right) * V_{tj}. \tag{9}$$

where X_s is the source domain input data sequence; X_t is the target-domain input data sequence; and W^{Qs}, W^{Kt}, and W^{Vt} are the three trainable projection parameter matrices. The d_k is performed to prevent the inner product from being overly large. And the m represents the length of the target sequence, the SoftMax activation function is used to normalize the cross-attention weights.

The loss function of the feature extractor can be defined using Eq. (10):

$$L_f\left(G_f\left(\cdot\right)\right) = \frac{1}{MMD\left(SelfAttention, CrossAttention\right)}. \tag{10}$$

The maximum mean difference (MMD) function is used to calculate the feature distribution distance. When the distance between private and shared features is small, it indicates that there is no clear distinction between private and shared features. Therefore, the loss function should guide the feature extractor to better differentiate between private and shared features.

The feature extractor can simultaneously extract private and shared features from both the source and target. The cross-attention module is robust to noise in the input and focuses more on similar information in the data of source and target domains, effectively avoiding the negative transfer phenomenon.

3.2 Domain Adversarial Adapter

The domain adversarial adapter addresses the problem of distributional differences between source and target domains by achieving Nash equilibrium through adversarial games for domain adaptation. The domain adversarial adapter distinguishes features belonging to the source or target domain, while the feature extractor focuses on similar information in the source and target domains and provides shared features to the load predictor for container load prediction. To achieve these diametrically opposite optimization objectives simultaneously during training, a gradient reversal layer (GRL) is introduced. The GRL keeps depth features unchanged as the forward-propagating network flow passes through the layer and multiplies the gradient of the backward-propagating network flow by a negative constant. The structure of the domain adversarial adapter is shown in Fig. 3.

The domain adversarial adapter takes the output of the feature extractor as input and generates the corresponding domain label by discriminating whether

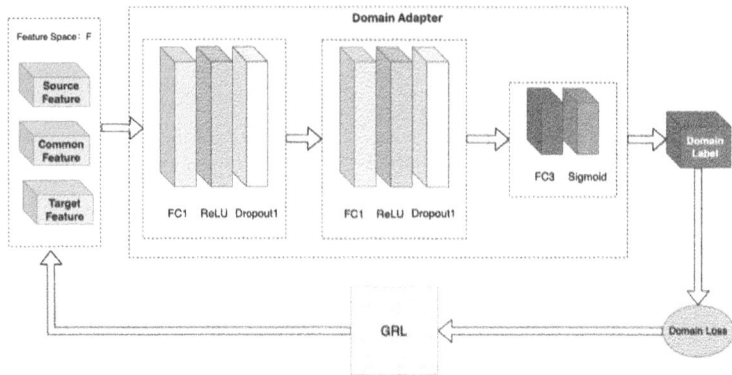

Fig. 3. Structure of the domain adversarial adapter.

the input features originate from the source or target domain. The feature extractor $G_d(\cdot)$ can be expressed using Eq. (11):

$$G_d(\theta_d) = G_d(feature, u, z) = Sigmoid(u^T feature + z)$$
$$with \; Sigmoid(x) = \frac{1}{1 + e^{-x}}. \tag{11}$$

where *feature* is the output of the feature extractor, u and z are trainable parameter matrices, and the Sigmoid activation function is used to normalize the domain label. The range of the domain label outputted by $G_d(\cdot)$ is (0,1), representing the probability that the feature comes from the target domain. A value closer to 1 indicates a higher probability that the feature comes from the target domain, whereas a value closer to 0 indicates a higher probability that the feature comes from the source domain. The loss of $G_d(\cdot)$ is defined using negative log likelihood as the loss function, as shown in Eq. (12):

$$L_d(G_d(\cdot), d_j) = d_j log \frac{1}{G_d(\cdot)} + (1 - d_j) log \frac{1}{1 - G_d(\cdot)}. \tag{12}$$

where d_j is the real domain label of the feature, $d_j = 0$ indicates that the feature comes from the source domain, whereas $d_j = 1$ indicates that the feature comes from the target domain. The smaller the loss function, the higher the accuracy of domain discrimination. After introducing GRL, the optimization objective function can be defined as Eq. (13):

$$E(\theta_d) = max \left\{ \lambda_{GRL} \left[\frac{1}{n} \sum_{i=1}^{n} L_d^i(\theta_d) + \frac{1}{n'} \sum_{i=n+1}^{N} L_d^i(\theta_d) \right] \right\}. \tag{13}$$

where θ_d is the parameter that needs to be optimized using the optimization objective function, λ_{GRL} is the GRL coefficient, $L_d(\cdot)$ is the domain loss function given by Eqs. (11) and (12), n is the number of samples in the source domain, and n' is the number of samples in the target domain.

By utilizing an adversarial game, the domain adversarial adaptor encourages the feature extractor to learn feature representations that are useful for both the source and target domains. This reduces domain differences, thus improving the model's capacity for generalization to the target domain and achieving domain adaptation at the feature level.

3.3 Workload Predictor

The workload predictor generates workload predictions for target containers. By leveraging a domain-adaptive learning framework that incorporates both source and target container data during model training, the prediction model effectively mitigates performance degradation caused by domain shift, thereby maintaining consistent prediction accuracy across different container environments.

The feature extractor and domain adversarial adapter jointly produce a high-dimensional common feature vector, which serves as input to the workload predictor. Utilizing multiple LSTMs and a fully connected layer, the workload predictor produces a sequence of predicted workload values, as shown in Fig. 4.

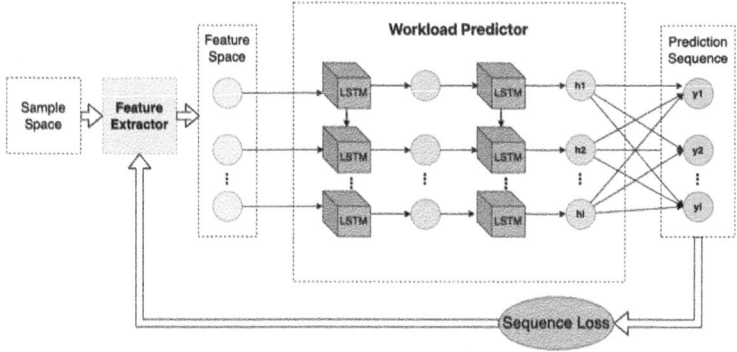

Fig. 4. Structure of the workload predictor.

The workload predictor $G_y (\cdot)$ can be defined using Eq. (14):

$$G_y (\theta_y) = LSTM (G_f (\cdot), W_i, W_f, W_c, W_o). \tag{14}$$

Among them, $G_f (\cdot)$ is the output of the feature extractor, and W_i, W_f, W_c, W_o are the weight matrices for the input gate, forget gate, cell state, and output gate, respectively. The loss function is defined by mean-square error (MSE), as shown in Eq. (15):

$$L_y (G_y (\cdot)) = \frac{1}{N_s} \sum_{i=1}^{N_s} \left(\widehat{y_s^i} - y_s^i \right)^2. \tag{15}$$

Here, $\widehat{y_s^i}$ represents the predicted value, and y_s^i represents the true value. The workload predictor enhances feature-based workload prediction and delivers good prediction performance.

4   Experimental Evaluation

4.1   Experiment Preparation

To validate the prediction accuracy of the proposed model, this study utilized containers in the Alibaba cluster-trace-v2017 [26] dataset that met the small sample condition as the target domain container set, and containers in the Google cluster-usage traces v3 [27] dataset as the source domain container set. Perform data cleaning and normalization on the input sample sets from the source and target domains, then split them into 70% training set, 20% validation set, and 10% test set. The training set is used to minimize training error via gradient descent, the validation set is utilized for hyperparameter tuning and optimization, while the test set serves for final model performance evaluation. Details of the training environment configuration for the prediction model are presented in Table 1.

Table 1. Training environment configuration for the prediction model

Software and Hardware	Configuration
CPU	XEON 6132 $\times$ 4, 56Core
GPU	TESLA V100 32GB -E3 $\times$ 3, 250W $\times$ 3
MEM	DDR4 2666 32G $\times$ 12
OS	CentOS 7.4
Cuda	11.8
Python	3.8
PyTorch	2.0.1

4.2   Analysis of Experimental Results

To illustrate the prediction performance of the proposed model, we selected the statistical model ARIMA and the neural network model LSTM as classical comparison methods. We used the GluonTS [28] prediction toolbox and DeepAR [29], deep renewal processes [30], and multivariate quantile function forecasting (MQF2) [31] as the latest research comparison methods. Experimental parameters for all models are presented in Table 2.

The container CPU workload prediction results of different models are shown in Fig. 5(a)-(f). Among them, 0.5 and 0.8 represent the confidence levels. Due to space limitations, memory load prediction results are not presented.

Table 2. Model parameters

Models	Parameters
ARIMA	P(autoregressive order): 5
	Q(moving average order): 5
	D(difference order, generally values are 0, 1, 2): 1
LSTM	Number of layers: 2
	Number of cells for each layer: 40
	Learning rate: 1e-3
DeepAR	Number of RNN layers: 2
	Number of RNN cells for each layer: 40
	Learning rate: 1e-3
	Type of recurrent cells to use: lstm
DRP	Number of hidden units used in the RNN cell: 16
	Number of layers in the LSTM: 2
	Dropout regularization parameter: 0.1
MQF2	Number of RNN layers: 2
	Hidden state size of RNN: 40
	Learning rate: 1e-3
	Weight decay regularization parameter: 0.1
	Number of samples drawn to approximate the energy score: 50
	Hyperparameter of the energy score: 1.0
CWPDDA	Learning rate: 1e-3
	Dropout regularization parameter: 0.1
	Hyperparameter of learning: $\alpha = 10$, $\beta = 0.75$

To analyze and evaluate the experimental results, we employed three commonly used indicators as evaluation metrics: mean absolute error (MAE), mean absolute percentage error (MAPE), and root mean squared error (RMSE). The smaller the values of MAE, MAPE, and RMSE, the better the prediction performance of the model. The comparison of container workload prediction errors is presented in Table 3 and Table 4.

Compared to other algorithms, the CWPDDA proposed in this paper demonstrates superior performance in predicting CPU load in terms of MAE, MAPE, and RMSE. Specifically, when compared to ARIMA, LSTM, DeepAR, DRP, and MQF2, the MAE of the CWPDDA method is reduced by 60.01%, 51.27%, 33.91%, 53.41%, and 58.27%, respectively. The MAPE is reduced by 56.82%, 47.39%, 31.76%, 50.12%, and 56.62%, respectively. The RMSE is reduced by 60.42%, 47.41%, 33.40%, 51.73%, and 56.38%, respectively. This indicates that the CWPDDA outperforms other approaches in CPU load forecasting accuracy.

Similarly, the CWPDDA outperforms comparative algorithms in predicting container memory load in terms of MAE, MAPE, and RMSE metrics. Specifi-

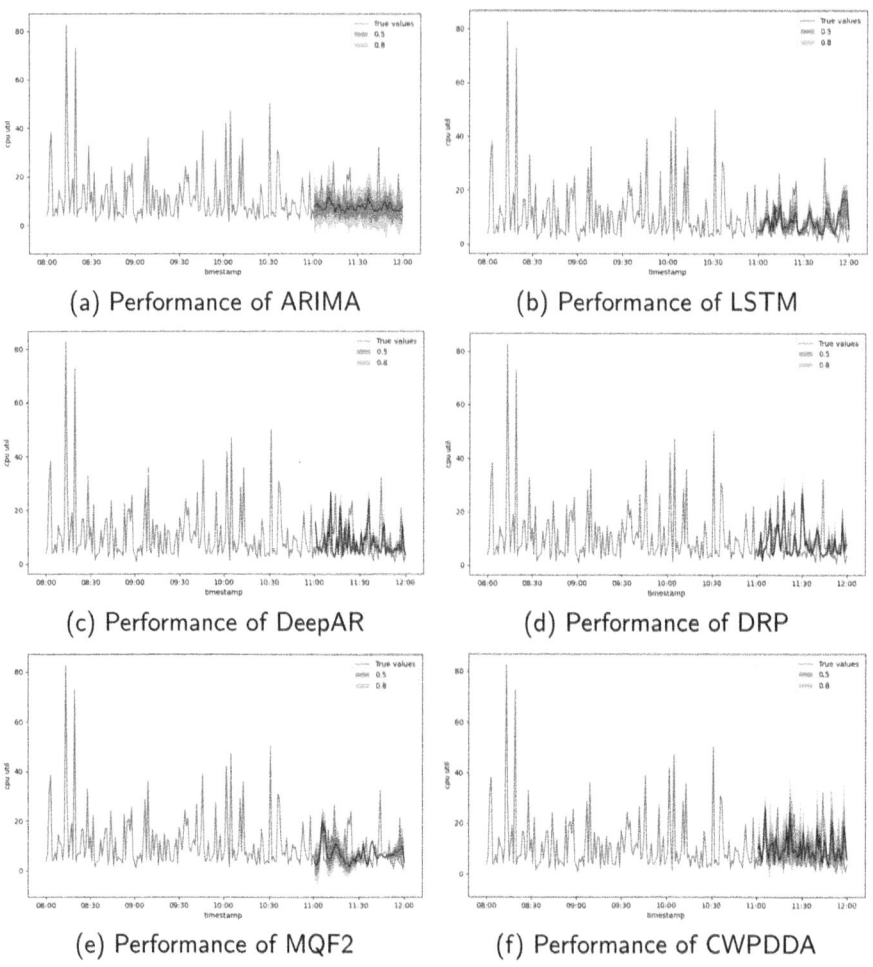

(a) Performance of ARIMA

(b) Performance of LSTM

(c) Performance of DeepAR

(d) Performance of DRP

(e) Performance of MQF2

(f) Performance of CWPDDA

Fig. 5. Container CPU workload prediction results

Table 3. Comparison of CPU load prediction errors

Method	MAE	MAPE (%)	RMSE
ARIMA	6.0486	20.0486	6.5402
LSTM	4.9632	16.4551	4.9173
DeepAR	3.6593	12.6866	3.8828
DRP	5.1916	17.3585	5.3581
MQF2	5.7957	19.9593	5.9283
CWPDDA	2.4183	8.6567	2.5859

Table 4. Comparison of Memory load prediction errors

Method	MAE	MAPE (%)	RMSE
ARIMA	13.702	27.8368	15.3341
LSTM	7.1407	15.5679	8.2574
DeepAR	7.1529	14.9228	7.9565
DRP	8.6762	17.127	9.8311
MQF2	9.4782	19.7971	10.1095
CWPDDA	4.8528	9.1127	5.9989

cally, compared to ARIMA, LSTM, DeepAR, DRP, and MQF2, the MAE of the CWPDDA is reduced by 64.58%, 32.04%, 32.15%, 44.06%, and 48.80%, respectively. The MAPE is reduced by 67.26%, 41.46%, 38.93%, 46.79%, and 53.96%, respectively. The RMSE is reduced by 60.87%, 27.35%, 24.60%, 38.98%, and 40.66%, respectively. This demonstrates that the CWPDDA also exhibits exceptional performance in predicting memory load.

5   Conclusion

This paper proposes a container workload prediction model based on deep domain adaptation in TL to address the limitations of traditional statistical models and classical neural network models, which struggle with complex workload variations and require extensive historical data, respectively. The model comprises a feature extractor, a domain adversarial adapter, and a workload predictor, achieving significant improvements in prediction accuracy. Future research directions include enhancing the model's robustness to domain shifts in diverse operational environments and exploring applications in fine-grained resource allocation strategies, such as QoS-aware autoscaling, to enable more efficient cluster resource utilization.

Acknowledgments. This work is supported by the National Key R&D Program of China, NO. 2022YFB4501701.

Disclosure of Interests. The authors have no competing interests to declare that are relevant to the content of this article.

References

1. Kashyap, S., Singh, A.: Prediction-based scheduling techniques for cloud data center's workload: a systematic review. Clust. Comput. **26**(5), 3209–3235 (2023)
2. Tang, X., Liao, X., Zheng, J., et al.: Energy efficient job scheduling with workload prediction on cloud data center. Clust. Comput. **21**(3), 1581–1593 (2018)
3. Xiao, J., Pan, X., Liu, J., et al.: Load balancing strategy for SDN multi-controller clusters based on load prediction. J. Supercomput. **80**(4), 5136–5162 (2024)

4. Saxena, D., Kumar, J., Singh, A.K., et al.: Performance analysis of machine learning centered workload prediction models for cloud. IEEE Trans. Parallel Distrib. Syst. **34**(4), 1313–1330 (2023)
5. Kashyap, S., Singh, A.: Prediction-based scheduling techniques for cloud data center's workload: a systematic review. Clust. Comput. **26**(5), 3209–3235 (2023)
6. Ding, Z., Feng, B., Jiang, C.: Coin: a container workload prediction model focusing on common and individual changes in workloads. IEEE Trans. Parallel Distrib. Syst. **33**(12), 4738–4751 (2022)
7. Fang, Y., Yap, P.-T., Lin, W., et al.: Source-free unsupervised domain adaptation: a survey. Neural Netw. **174**, 106230 (2024)
8. Fan, M., Cai, Z., Zhang, T., et al.: A survey of deep domain adaptation based on label set classification. Multimed. Tools App. **81**(27), 39545–39576 (2022)
9. Xie, Y., Jin, M., Zou, Z., et al.: Real-time prediction of docker container resource load based on a hybrid model of ARIMA and triple exponential smoothing. IEEE Trans. Cloud Comput. **10**(2), 1386–1401 (2022)
10. Gupta, R.K., Pateriya, R.K.: Balance resource utilization (BRU) approach for the dynamic load balancing in cloud environment by using AR prediction model. J. Organ. End User Comput. (JOEUC) IGI Global **29**(4), 24–50 (2017)
11. Zhang, L., Xie, Y., Jin, M., et al.: A novel hybrid model for docker container workload prediction. IEEE Trans. Netw. Serv. Manage. **20**(3), 2726–2743 (2023)
12. Patel, E., Kushwaha, D.S.: A hybrid CNN-LSTM model for predicting server load in cloud computing. J. Supercomput. **78**(8), 1–30 (2022)
13. Maiyza, A.I., Korany, N.O., Banawan, K., et al.: VTGAN: hybrid generative adversarial networks for cloud workload prediction. J. Cloud Comput. **12**(1), 97 (2023)
14. Day, O., Khoshgoftaar, T.M.: A survey on heterogeneous transfer learning. J. Big Data **4**(1), 29 (2017)
15. Huang, K., Yao, K., Guo, Y., et al.: State of health estimation of lithium-ion batteries based on fine-tuning or rebuilding transfer learning strategies combined with new features mining. Energy **282**, 128739 (2023)
16. Davila, A., Colan, J., Hasegawa, Y.: Comparison of fine-tuning strategies for transfer learning in medical image classification. Image Vis. Comput. **146**, 105012 (2024)
17. Yang, X., Liu, Q., Su, R., et al.: Click-through rate prediction using transfer learning with fine-tuned parameters. Inf. Sci. **612**, 188–200 (2022)
18. Sifan, L., Shengsheng, W., Xin, Z., et al.: Cross-domain feature enhancement for unsupervised domain adaptation. Appl. Intell. **52**(15), 17326–17340 (2022)
19. Jing, M., Zhao, J., Li, J., et al.: Adaptive component embedding for domain adaptation. IEEE Trans. Cybern. **51**(7), 3390–3403 (2021)
20. Wu, K., Wu, M., Chen, Z., et al.: Reinforced adaptation network for partial domain adaptation. IEEE Trans. Circuits Syst. Video Technol. **33**(5), 2370–2380 (2023)
21. Wilson, G., Cook, D.J.: A survey of unsupervised deep domain adaptation. ACM Trans. Intell. Syst. Technol. **11**(5), 51:1-51:46 (2020)
22. Lu, J., Shi, J., Zhu, H., et al.: Depth guidance and intradomain adaptation for semantic segmentation. IEEE Trans. Instrum. Meas. **72**, 1–13 (2023)
23. Wang, M., Deng, W.: Deep visual domain adaptation: a survey. Neurocomputing **312**, 135–153 (2018)
24. Weiss, K., Khoshgoftaar, T.M., Wang, D.: A survey of transfer learning [J]. Journal of Big Data **3**(1), 9 (2016)
25. Hosna, A., Merry, E., Gyalmo, J., et al.: Transfer learning: a friendly introduction. J. Big Data **9**(1), 102 (2022)
26. Alibaba Cluster Data. https://github.com/alibaba/clusterdata/tree/master

27. Google Cluster Data. https://github.com/google/cluster-data
28. Alexandrov, A., Benidis, K., Bohlke-Schneider, M., et al.: GluonTS: probabilistic and neural time series modeling in python. J. Mach. Learn. Res. **21**(116), 1–6 (2020)
29. Salinas, D., Flunkert, V., Gasthaus, J., et al.: DeepAR: probabilistic forecasting with autoregressive recurrent networks. Int. J. Forecast. **36**(3), 1181–1191 (2020)
30. Türkmen, A.C., Januschowski, T., Wang, Y., et al.: Forecasting intermittent and sparse time series: a unified probabilistic framework via deep renewal processes. PLOS ONE, Publ. Libr. Sci. **16**(11), e0259764 (2021)
31. Kan, K., et al.: Multivariate quantile function forecaster. In: International Conference on Artificial Intelligence and Statistics. PMLR (2022)

CGP-Graphless: Towards Efficient Serverless Graph Processing via CPU-GPU Pipelined Collaboration

Yiming Sun[1,2,3], Jiaqi Zhang[1,2,3], Jie Zhang[1], Huawei Cao[1,2,3(✉)],
Xuejun An[1,3], and Xiaochun Ye[1]

[1] SKLP, Institute of Computing Technology, CAS, Beijing, China
[2] School of Computer Science and Technology, UCAS, Beijing, China
[3] Zhongguancun Laboratory, Beijing, China
caohuawei@ict.ac.cn

Abstract. The serverless computing model offers users flexible, pay-as-you-go services. However, existing frameworks face challenges such as resource over-subscription and workload over-scaling when deploying graph processing jobs in serverless environments. To address these limitations, we introduce CGP–Graphless, a CPU–GPU heterogeneous computing framework designed for efficient vertical scaling. This approach divides graph processing into two phases: querying on a core proxy graph and correction on the full graph. GPU containers execute the querying phase, while CPU containers perform the correction. Furthermore, we propose an adaptive pipelined scheduling strategy for these phases, which leverages pressure-aware intra-pipeline scaling to convert excessive horizontal scaling into vertical scaling, enhancing serverless graph computation efficiency. Experiments show that CGP–Graphless improves end-to-end performance by up to 2.00× over FaaSGraph under concurrent stress evaluations, while reducing CPU core allocation by half through GPU container utilization. In short-interval query scenarios, CGP–Graphless further reduces average request latency by 3.30× compared to FaaS-Graph.

Keywords: Serverless Computing · Graph Processing · Heterogeneous computing · Vertical Scaling

1 Introduction

Graph analysis has become crucial for many enterprises due to its ability to naturally model relationships between real-world entities, such as social media, online shopping, and complex relational networks. With the rapid growth in user numbers, scalable graph processing frameworks for CPU and GPU platforms have been extensively studied to meet increasing business demands [12,15]. Real-world

---

Y. Sun and J. Zhang—Contribute equally to this work.

W. E. Nagel et al. (Eds.): Euro-Par 2025, LNCS 15900, pp. 337–350, 2026.
https://doi.org/10.1007/978-3-031-99854-6_23

entity graphs are often irregular and massive, driving enterprises to adopt graph processing frameworks on cloud platforms to reduce hardware infrastructure costs.

Traditional cloud vendors provide Infrastructure-as-a-Service (IaaS), allowing users to rent hardware and virtualization resources. However, limited elasticity of IaaS requires users to estimate peak loads and continuously run graph processing frameworks on cloud platforms [3]. Serverless computing, particularly Function-as-a-Service (FaaS), addresses these limitations by introducing a pay-as-you-go model, where users are charged based on function execution rather than underlying cloud resources. With features such as seamless resource management, automatic scaling, and cost efficiency, serverless computing has been successfully applied to large-scale model inference and web services. This paradigm enables users to focus on core function development while cloud vendors manage resource allocation and cost control. However, achieving high resource utilization and cost-effectiveness in serverless systems remains a challenge. Graph processing has been deployed in FaaS environments, but existing FaaS-based systems face two key issues: **resource over-subscription** and **workload over-scaling**. During graph processing, the number of active edges and vertices varies significantly across iterations. To maintain performance, cloud vendors provision resources based on peak demand, resulting in resource over-subscription. When serverless platforms face sudden workload surges, horizontal scaling is commonly used to manage increased user queries. However, this approach may lead to excessive scaling, causing resource exhaustion and high latency.

With the increasing adoption of GPUs in data centers and advancements in heterogeneous serverless computing, enabling efficient graph processing in such environments has become crucial. This paper presents **CGP-Graphless**, a novel serverless graph processing framework that integrates CPU-GPU collaboration for optimized execution. Leveraging a serverless architecture, CGP-Graphless mitigates resource over-subscription and prevents workload over-scaling. The framework processes graph queries in two phases: GPUs generate approximate results from smaller subgraphs, which are then refined on CPUs using the full graph. These two-phase jobs form a **PipeSet**, a core execution unit that enhances throughput via a two-level pipeline. A PipeSet consists of multiple CPU and GPU containers, each processing a subgraph for efficient graph algorithm execution. Furthermore, CGP-Graphless employs an elastic scalability strategy within PipeSet to prevent workload over-scaling. Experimental evaluations demonstrate its superiority—under concurrent stress conditions, CGP-Graphless improves end-to-end performance by up to **2.00×** compared to the state-of-the-art serverless graph processing framework FaaSGraph [10]. In summary, our key contributions are as follows:

- Identifying the issues of resource over-subscription and workload over-scaling in graph processing on the state-of-the-art serverless cloud platform.
- Proposing a serverless graph processing model that partitions graph processing into decoupled GPU and CPU phases, achieving vertical scaling through heterogeneous pipelining.

– Designing a pressure-aware scaling mechanism for heterogeneous pipelines, reducing the extent of horizontal scaling by duplicating pipeline phases and employing work-stealing.

2   Background and Motivation

2.1   Background

Graph Processing Frameworks. Graph processing frameworks process large-scale graphs through an "iteration-convergence" process, where active vertices are updated and changes propagated until no active vertices remain. Data is partitioned into subgraphs, with each node handling one subgraph and collecting states from others to update vertices. In serverless graph processing, users provide algorithms and datasets while cloud vendors manage resources. FaaSGraph, a state-of-the-art system, assigns a container to each subgraph and consolidates them into a ContainerSet. Vertices update their states during iterations using shared memory within the ContainerSet.

Two-phase Graph Processing. Two-phase graph processing is a novel approach that accelerates graph computation by generating a smaller, lossy abstraction of the full graph. Processing is first applied to the abstract graph, and the results are then transferred to the full graph for faster convergence. A typical graph processing workflow follows three steps: subgraph generation, then two successive computation steps (two-phase processing).

– Reduce full graph G to G': Extract the frequently accessed vertices and edges from the large input graph G and transform it into a smaller subgraph G'.
– Compute results for G': Execute the graph processing on the smaller subgraph G'. The time for computing G' is shorter than that for computing G, and computing G' has a higher efficiency of resource utilization.
– Obtain results for G: The vertex state values computed on the small subgraph G' are transferred to the full graph G, and the incorrectly computed vertex state values are rectified. Graph queries on the full graph can converge at a relatively higher speed.

2.2   Problems and Motivation

We evaluate the performance and resource utilization of the state-of-the-art serverless graph processing framework, FaaSGraph [10], using the same platform and datasets as described in Sect. 4.1.

Resource Over-Subscription. The number of active edges and vertices in graph processing algorithms fluctuates during execution, requiring substantial processing only in specific iterations. To ensure performance, cloud providers allocate resources based on the job's peak demand. Figure 1 shows the CPU utilization for six jobs assigned to a container set. During execution, the Single-Source Shortest Path (SSSP) algorithm for the TW dataset (SSSP-TW) was allocated 16 CPU cores, yet its average CPU utilization remained at only 35%.

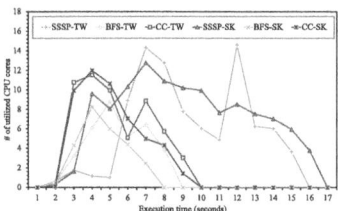
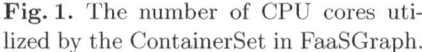

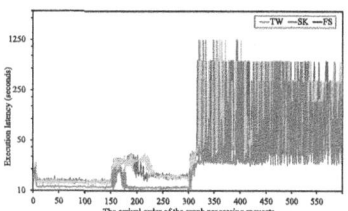

Fig. 1. The number of CPU cores utilized by the ContainerSet in FaaSGraph.

Fig. 2. End-to-end latency for six hundred sequentially submitted requests.

Workload Over-Scaling. User-facing services frequently experience peak workloads during specific times of the day. Serverless platforms address these peaks through horizontal scaling, which creates identical instances to handle growing workloads. As workloads increase, the system generates additional instances to maintain functionality. However, in graph processing, a single instance often underutilizes resources, leading to rapid resource consumption and service limits. To simulate over-scaling caused by request bursts, we increased graph processing request frequency every 150 requests. Figure 2 shows the end-to-end latency across algorithms and datasets, where the x-axis denotes request arrival order and the y-axis represents processing latency. All curves in this figure correspond to executions on the same platform. In FaaSGraph, over-scaling causes long wait times and request timeouts, with delays for requests beyond the 300th reaching up to 600 s.

To address over-subscription and over-scaling, we propose a novel serverless graph processing model that divides graph queries into two phases. By extracting frequently accessed vertices and edges during query handling, the model ensures their active status across multiple iterations, alleviating over-subscription. GPU resources are allocated to frequently accessed subgraphs, while CPU resources process the full graph, with pipelining between the two phases improving throughput. This approach transforms **horizontal scaling** into **vertical scaling**, effectively mitigating over-scaling.

3   CGP-Graphless Design

To tackle over-subscription and over-scaling in serverless graph processing, we propose CGP-Graphless, a heterogeneous system leveraging vertical scaling.

3.1   System Overview

The CGP-Graphless processing flow, illustrated in Fig. 3, starts when users submit graph processing jobs specifying the dataset, algorithm, and configuration. First, the *Optimizer* extracts significant vertices and edges to create a smaller subgraph called the core proxy graph. The full graph is then partitioned into non-overlapping sections. The *Scheduler* allocates the basic unit, *PipeSet*, based on resource utilization across the serverless cluster. The Scheduler either initiates new PipeSets or utilizes idle ones as needed. If a single host's resources are insufficient, PipeSet containers are distributed among hosts. To enable pipelined execution, the core proxy graph container and the full graph container maintain waiting queues. The *Pipeline Manager* manages these queues, while the *Pressure-aware Engine* determines elastic scaling based on queue status. PipeSet enables data sharing across phases and nodes using *Shared Memory*.

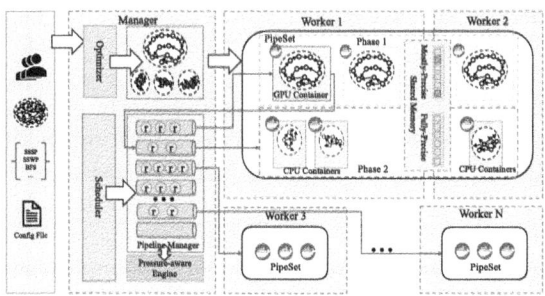

Fig. 3. The overview of CGP-Graphless.

3.2 Generating Core Proxy Graph

The core idea of two-phase serverless graph processing is to extract a smaller core proxy graph from the full graph. This subgraph approximates query results, with vertices and edges remaining active across iterations. As serverless platforms often lack large instance specifications [6], the full graph must be partitioned into containers, each processing a section of the graph. In two-phase processing, CGP-Graphless first performs critical computations on the smaller subgraph, optimizing resource utilization. The second phase involves minimal corrections on the full graph distributed across containers, reducing communication overhead.

When users submit graph data and algorithms, the CGP-Graphless Optimizer constructs a core proxy graph tailored to each algorithm. This proxy graph captures the core structure of the full graph, including the frequently accessed parts of the graph data. Due to the power-law distribution of graph data, only a few high-degree vertices exist, making them more likely to be accessed during processing. Since the first phase requires approximate results, a simplified method is used to build the proxy graph. Inspired by CoreGraph [7], the 20 highest-degree vertices (10 highest in-degrees and 10 highest out-degrees for directed graphs) are identified. Forward and backward traversals from these vertices collect non-zero centrality edges, which are included in the proxy graph. In graph algorithms, we denote propagation by $\oplus$. For an edge $\langle a, b \rangle$, if the state value of a after propagation $a \rightarrow b$ matches the state value of b, the edge is considered to have non-zero centrality:

$$a.StateVal \oplus w(a,b) = b.StateVal \tag{1}$$

3.3   Implementing Two-Phase Pipeline

Two-phase graph processing divides serverless graph processing jobs into two sequential phases with distinct characteristics. Previous studies [7] show that the core proxy graph typically constitutes only 10% of the full graph data size, but achieves precision 94.5% to 99.9% in the values of the vertex state. Phase 1, performed on the smaller core proxy graph, is compute-bound, requiring intensive computation on a small-scale graph. GPUs, commonly used to accelerate graph processing, are well suited for this phase due to their computational characteristics, though their limited memory restricts large-scale graph handling.

As Phase 1 produces precise results for most vertices, Phase 2 only needs to correct a few remaining vertices. This phase requires relatively light computation on a large-scale full graph, making it well-suited for CPU and main memory utilization. Assigning GPUs to Phase 1 and CPUs to Phase 2, CGP-Graphless introduces an innovative approach to serverless graph processing, enabling collaborative computation across heterogeneous resources. A pipeline-based execution strategy between the two phases ensures efficient data dependency management and enhances framework throughput, enabling vertical scaling.

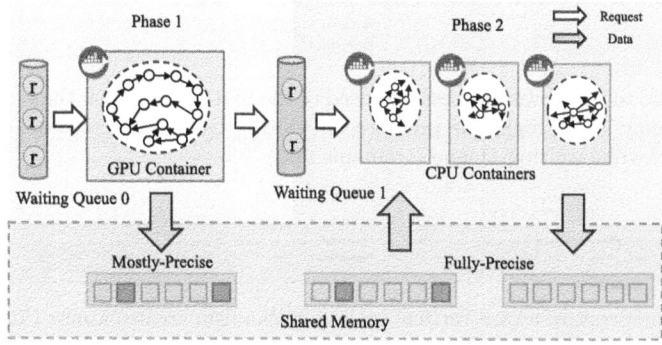

Fig. 4. Two-Phase Pipeline Diagram.

To achieve heterogeneous pipelining in serverless graph processing, CGP-Graphless incorporates a pipeline manager that maintains a waiting queue for each phase. By delegating complex pipeline management to the manager node, worker nodes can focus solely on two-phase computations. Figure 4 illustrates the execution model of the two-phase pipeline: user requests are first dispatched to Queue 0, where Phase 1 processes them on the core proxy graph. Phase 1 then stores the results in shared memory and forwards the requests to Queue 1, enabling it to begin handling the next request immediately. Subsequently, Phase 2 retrieves pending requests from Queue 1, accesses the results of Phase 1 from shared memory, and corrects these results over the full graph. By leveraging shared memory and the pipeline manager, CGP-Graphless effectively decouples the two phases. Ideally, with only minimal additional GPU resources, the pipeline can double the throughput of serverless graph processing systems, alleviating resource over-subscription. Furthermore, the core proxy graph, derived from frequently accessed portions of the graph data, optimizes resource allocation under peak demand conditions.

3.4 Pressure-Aware Vertical Scaling

The core optimization of CGP-Graphless is to convert horizontal scaling across PipeSets into vertical scaling within a PipeSet whenever feasible. To enable pipelining, the Pipeline Manager maintains two-phase waiting queues, dynamically updating the average execution latency $\bar{T}$ and arrival rate R_a for each phase. Since Phase 1 handles more than 90% of the vertex state values, its execution latency is usually longer than Phase 2. Therefore, the Pressure-aware Engine monitors the pressure on waiting Queue 0 and replicates the pipeline phase when pressure is high. Figure 5(a) illustrates this mechanism.

(a) Due to the slower processing speed of the first phase, when the request frequency is too high, the pressure on waiting Queue 0 increases significantly, while waiting Queue 1 remains idle.

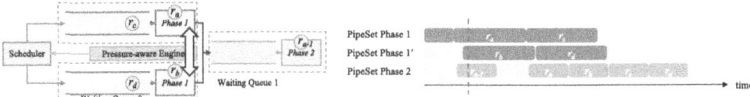

(b) The pressure-aware vertical scaling mechanism creates a new Phase 1 container within a PipeSet and forwards some requests to the new Phase 1 waiting queue.

Fig. 5. Pressure-Aware Vertical Scaling Mechanism and Pipelined Spatiotemporal Diagram.

In Fig. 5(a), waiting Queue 0 receives four requests from the scheduler, with request R_a executed in the Phase 1 container. The pipelined spatiotemporal diagram illustrates request execution, highlighting how Phase 1 dominates total delay due to dependencies between phases, even when Phase 2 remains idle. When the request arrival rate exceeds the consumption rate, system delay increases significantly. Traditional serverless systems address this by horizontally scaling and forwarding requests to a new PipeSet, but this approach introduces issues with over-scaling. To mitigate this, we propose a pressure-aware vertical scaling method, as depicted in Fig. 5(b). Equation 2 computes the pressure value to determine whether vertical scaling within a PipeSet is necessary.

$$Pressure = R_a - \frac{1}{\bar{T}_0} \tag{2}$$

The pressure value represents the difference between arrival and consumption rates. When the pressure is less than or equal to 0, the queue experiences no pressure, and scaling is unnecessary. When the pressure exceeds 0, a new Phase 1 container is created within a PipeSet, and requests, such as R_b and R_d in Fig. 5(b), are forwarded to it. Replicating the pipelined phase increases PipeSet throughput and reduces bubbles (gray areas) in the spatiotemporal diagram. The maximum replication factor is determined by the ratio of the average latency $\bar{T}_0$ in waiting Queue 0 to the average latency $\tilde{T}_1$ in waiting Queue 1. Each PipeSet tracks its current number of replicated pipeline phases and the maximum replication capacity. To further minimize vertical scaling costs, NVIDIA MIG is used to allow multiple GPU containers to share the same GPU. The vertically scaled container resides on the same worker node as the current Phase 1 container. If no MIG resources are available, CPU resources are allocated as a fallback. When all resources are exhausted, the PipeSet is marked as fully replicated.

The Pressure-aware Engine also monitors pressure in waiting Queue 1. If the pressure exceeds 0, work-stealing alleviates it. Since phases 1 and 2 are decoupled, Phase 2 containers in other PipeSets can retrieve active vertices from shared memory and complete Phase 2 computations. The work-stealing process involves the Pipeline Manager identifying a PipeSet with low pressure in waiting Queue 1. Once this PipeSet's requests are completed, it retrieves Phase 1 results from shared memory and performs Phase 2 computations. Pressure-aware vertical scaling boosts the throughput of individual PipeSet, enabling it to handle more user requests and alleviating over-scaling.

3.5   Scheduler

The scheduler manages three key jobs: forwarding user requests to the appropriate waiting queue, determining when to initiate horizontal scaling, and creating new PipeSets on suitable worker nodes.

When assigning requests to waiting queues, the scheduler excludes PipeSets with a pressure value above 0 in waiting Queue 1, as their Phase 2 containers cannot handle additional requests. It then selects the waiting Queue 0 with the lowest pressure value and assigns the request to its PipeSet. If all waiting queues have a pressure value exceeding 0 and all PipeSets have reached the maximum number of pipeline phase replications, the scheduler initiates horizontal scaling by creating a new PipeSet.

In CGP-Graphless, worker nodes periodically report their resource status to the management node, which maintains a global view of resources, including the number of MIG instances per node. To minimize the overhead of spreading PipeSet containers across nodes, the scheduler first ranks worker nodes by available non-GPU resources in descending order. It assigns the PipeSet to the first node with available MIG instances. If resources on that node are insufficient to support all Phase 2 containers (Phase 1 starts with only one container before vertical scaling), the scheduler expands the PipeSet to additional nodes following the descending resource order. When no GPU resources are available, the scheduler assigns a CPU container for Phase 1 to the most resource-rich nodes.

4   Evaluation

This section first evaluates the overall performance of CGP-Graphless and compares it with other state-of-the-art solutions, focusing on its performance advantages under peak load conditions.

4.1   Experiment Setup

Hardware and Software Setups. We implement CGP-Graphless based on the open-source code of FaaSGraph [10], using Docker to create containers for graph processing. To configure the nodes, we utilize two hosts, with the specific hardware and software configurations detailed in Table 1. Network configuration is established by connecting the nodes via a switch, and graph data access across nodes is facilitated through NAS. Each CPU container is allocated 2 CPU cores and 3 GB of memory. This decision is made based on the consensus that serverless platforms rarely offer large instance specifications [6]. To maximize GPU utilization, devices are configured with MIG and MPS enabled by default.

Baseline. We select FaaSGraph [10], a state-of-the-art serverless graph processing framework, as a benchmark to evaluate the advantages of CGP-Graphless.

Graph Datasets and Algorithms. We use three representative graph datasets [1,2,8]: Twitter (TW), sk-2005 (SK), and Friendster (FS). Four common graph algorithms are evaluated: Breadth-First Search (BFS), Single-Source Shortest Path (SSSP), Single-Source Widest Path (SSWP), and Connected Components (CC). Table 2 lists the number of vertices, edges, and the size of each dataset.

4.2   Performance Comparison

Single Job Performance Comparison. The two-phase graph processing approach divides a user's request into core proxy graph queries on the GPU and full graph queries. This section evaluates the performance of the two-phase processing. Figure 6 compares the overall performance of CGP-Graphless and FaaS-Graph, focusing only on graph query time and excluding cold start overhead. The results show that CGP-Graphless achieves speedups ranging from 0.57× to

Table 1. Hardware and software specifications

	Manager (Worker 0)	Worker 1
Hardware	Intel(R) Xeon(R) Gold 5218R	Intel(R) Xeon(R) CPU E5-2683
	CPU @ 2.10GHz 40-cores	v3 @ 2.00GHz 56-cores
	768GB Main Memory	576GB Main Memory
	NVIDIA A800 * 2	NVIDIA V100 * 3
Software	CentOS Linux release 7.9.2009	CentOS Linux release 7.9.2009
	CUDA 12.2	CUDA 11.0
	Linux with kernel 3.10.0	Linux with kernel 3.10.0
	Golang version: 1.21.6	Golang version: 1.21.6
	Docker version: 26.1.1	Docker version: 26.0.1

Table 2. Graph Datasets Properties

Graph	Abbr.	Vertices	Edges	CSR Sizes
Twitter	TW	41,652,230	1,468,364,884	23 Gb
sk-2005	SK	50,636,154	1,949,412,601	31 Gb
Friendster	FS	65,608,366	1,806,067,135	28 Gb

1.55× in single-job scenarios. However, the separation and decoupling of the two-phase pipeline introduce an intermediate result storage step, causing some performance loss. For BFS, its shorter execution time amplifies the relative impact of this storage overhead. For CC, the initially large number of active vertices, equal to the total graph size, leads to nearly universal vertex updates, affecting overall performance. In contrast, CGP-Graphless achieves significant acceleration for SSSP and SSWP, demonstrating its effectiveness. Subsequent experiments reveal that CGP-Graphless effectively mitigates performance limitations in peak-load conditions.

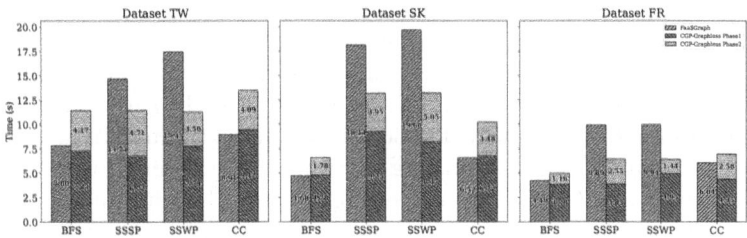

Fig. 6. Comparison of two-phase graph processing and FaaSGraph execution times for a single graph processing job.

Simulate Peak Load Evaluation. To address the issues of over-subscription and over-scaling in FaaSGraph, we design a solution tailored for peak load scenarios and evaluate the ability of CGP-Graphless to mitigate these challenges. We concurrently submit 8 graph processing jobs to CGP-Graphless and FaaSGraph and record the overall latency from submission to completion, as illustrated in Fig. 7. Across all scenarios, CGP-Graphless achieves equal or superior latency relative to FaaSGraph under peak load conditions. By analyzing the completion time of the final request, CGP-Graphless demonstrates a speedup ranging from 0.95× to 2.00×, averaging 1.45× overall. As shown in the figure, CGP-Graphless also exhibits a more concentrated query latency distribution compared to FaaS-Graph, effectively reducing resource waste from over-subscription and minimizing queuing delays caused by over-scaling.

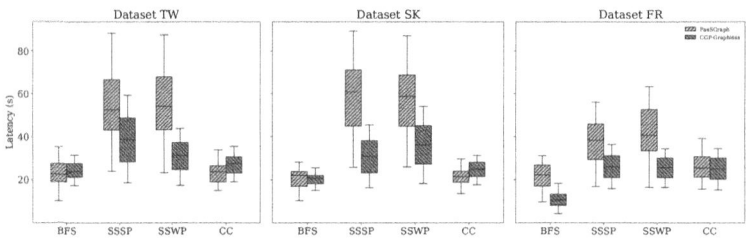

Fig. 7. To simulate high-load scenarios, eight graph processing jobs are concurrently submitted. The query latency distributions of these eight jobs are compared.

Further, we evaluate CGP-Graphless's ability to handle extreme peak loads by varying the number of concurrently submitted jobs to 8, 16, and 32, using SSSP jobs for this analysis, as shown in Fig. 8. As the number of concurrent requests increases, CGP-Graphless maintains robust performance. Even with 32 concurrent jobs, the latency distribution remains relatively concentrated. Notably, with 16 requests, CGP-Graphless utilizes only 40 CPU cores and 4 MIG (or MPS) instances, whereas FaaSGraph scales horizontally to 80 CPU cores for the same workload. Despite this scaling, FaaSGraph exhibits higher latency and greater dispersion.

To assess CGP-Graphless's performance in real-world scenarios, we simulate a realistic business environment by submitting graph processing requests at 10-second intervals. Every 150 requests, we halve the interval to simulate burst peak loads. Figure 9 displays the results of this experiment. In this scenario, FaaS-Graph performance significantly deteriorates beyond 300 requests, with latency increasing substantially. By leveraging vertical scaling through pressure-aware pipeline execution, CGP-Graphless demonstrates a clear advantage in short-interval scenarios. As the request frequency increases, per-request latency rises only marginally. Over 600 requests, CGP-Graphless achieves an average speedup of 3.30× compared to FaaSGraph. Through effective vertical scaling within the pressure-aware PipeSet, CGP-Graphless mitigates high latency issues caused by workload over-scaling. Figure 10 presents the comparison of CPU utilization between CGP-Graphless and FaaSGraph when executing the SSSP algorithm on four datasets. By employing optimized pipeline scheduling, CGP-Graphless resolves inefficiencies caused by resource over-subscription.

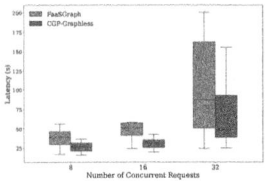   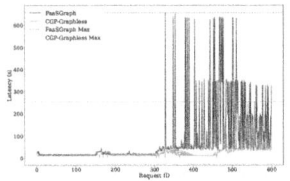   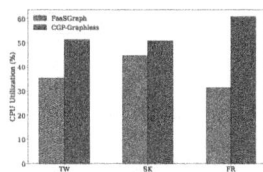

Fig. 8. To simulate peak load scenarios, the number of concurrently submitted jobs is varied from 8 to 32. The figure shows the distribution of job request latencies.

Fig. 9. The end-to-end latency of sequentially submitting 600 graph processing jobs is measured, with the submission interval shortened every 150 requests.

Fig. 10. The comparison of CPU utilization between the two frameworks calculates the average resource utilization over the complete execution cycles of the jobs.

5   Related Work

Graph Processing. Graph processing systems can be categorized based on data scale and hardware storage into in-memory, out-of-core, and distributed systems. In-memory systems handle smaller graphs by storing all data, attributes, and state information in memory. Examples include Ligra [13] and GraphIt [16]. Out-of-core systems process medium-scale graphs that cannot be fully loaded into memory, requiring external storage like hard disks. Examples include Grid-Graph [18], Liberator [9] and Subway [12]. Distributed systems handle large-scale graphs using multiple nodes for distributed storage and computation, dividing data into subgraphs for parallel processing. Examples include Gemini [17] and Graphite [11]. In order to improve resource utilization, some works introduce heterogeneous computing. TOTEM [5] implements large-scale graph processing on a hybrid CPU-GPU system. CGgraph [4] implements a CPU-GPU collaborative processing scheme, optimizing single-query performance on static graphs while overlooking concurrent query efficiency in dynamic graphs.

Serverless Graph Processing. Graphless [14] establishes a serverless graph processing framework using AWS, deploying functions through push or pull operations on predefined worker resources with static and super-step schedulers. However, it suffers from lower performance by simply sending jobs to AWS Lambda. FaaSGraph [10] effectively handles large-scale graphs in a cost-efficient manner by bridging traditional graph processing frameworks and serverless computing. Despite these advancements, serverless graph processing systems still face challenges in efficient resource utilization, managing horizontal scaling overhead, and addressing short-interval user requests. Existing CPU-GPU heterogeneous computing methods cannot be directly applied to serverless graph processing systems. CGP-Graphless introduces a pipeline-based approach to alleviate issues related to over-subscription and over-scaling.

6 Conclusion

This paper presents CGP-Graphless, which aims to efficiently perform serverless graph processing through vertical scaling of heterogeneous resources. The core idea of CGP-Graphless is to convert horizontal scaling into vertical scaling by employing heterogeneous computing and pressure-sensitive pipeline scheduling. This approach mitigates resource waste and reduces the overall latency of requests. Experiments demonstrate that CGP-Graphless achieves efficient and fast graph processing on serverless platforms.

Acknowledgments. This work was supported by National Key Research and Development Program (Grant No. 2023YFB4502305), National Science and Technology Major Project (TC240A9ED-74) and the Beijing Natural Science Foundation (4232036).

Disclosure of Interests. The authors declare that there is no competing interest.

References

1. Boldi, P., Rosa, M., Santini, M., Vigna, S.: Layered label propagation: a multiresolution coordinate-free ordering for compressing social networks. In: Srinivasan, S., Ramamritham, K., Kumar, A., Ravindra, M.P., Bertino, E., Kumar, R. (eds.) Proceedings of the 20th international conference on World Wide Web, pp. 587–596. ACM Press (2011)
2. Boldi, P., Vigna, S.: The WebGraph framework I: compression techniques. In: Proceedings of the Thirteenth International World Wide Web Conference (WWW 2004), pp. 595–601. ACM Press, Manhattan, USA (2004)
3. Chen, R., Weng, X., He, B., Yang, M.: Large graph processing in the cloud. In: Proceedings of the 2010 ACM SIGMOD International Conference on Management of Data. p. 1123–1126. SIGMOD 2010, Association for Computing Machinery, New York, NY, USA (2010). https://doi.org/10.1145/1807167.1807297
4. Cui, P., Liu, H., Tang, B., Yuan, Y.: CGGraph: an ultra-fast graph processing system on modern commodity cpu-gpu co-processor. Proc. VLDB Endow. **17**(6), 1405–1417 (2024). https://doi.org/10.14778/3648160.3648179
5. Gharaibeh, A., Reza, T., Santos-Neto, E., Costa, L.B., Sallinen, S., Ripeanu, M.: Efficient large-scale graph processing on hybrid CPU and GPU systems (2014)
6. Jiang, J., et al.: Towards demystifying serverless machine learning training. In: Proceedings of the 2021 International Conference on Management of Data, pp. 857–871. SIGMOD 2021, Association for Computing Machinery, New York, NY, USA (2021). https://doi.org/10.1145/3448016.3459240

7. Jiang, X., Afarin, M., Zhao, Z., Abu-Ghazaleh, N., Gupta, R.: Core graph: exploiting edge centrality to speedup the evaluation of iterative graph queries. In: Proceedings of the Nineteenth European Conference on Computer Systems, pp. 18–32. EuroSys 2024, Association for Computing Machinery, New York, NY, USA (2024). https://doi.org/10.1145/3627703.3629571

8. Leskovec, J., Krevl, A.: SNAP Datasets: Stanford large network dataset collection, June 2014. http://snap.stanford.edu/data

9. Li, S., et al.: Liberator: a data reuse framework for out-of-memory graph computing on GPUs. IEEE Trans. Parallel Distrib. Syst. **34**(6), 1954–1967 (2023). https://doi.org/10.1109/TPDS.2023.3268662

10. Liu, Y., et al.: FAASGraph: enabling scalable, efficient, and cost-effective graph processing with serverless computing. In: Proceedings of the 29th ACM International Conference on Architectural Support for Programming Languages and Operating Systems, Volume 2, pp. 385–400. ASPLOS 2024, Association for Computing Machinery, New York, NY, USA (2024). https://doi.org/10.1145/3620665.3640361

11. Mofrad, M.H., Melhem, R., Ahmad, Y., Hammoud, M.: Graphite: a NUMA-aware HPC system for graph analytics based on a new MPI * X parallelism model. Proc. VLDB Endow. **13**(6), 783–797 (2020). https://doi.org/10.14778/3380750.3380751

12. Sabet, A.H.N., Zhao, Z., Gupta, R.: Subway: minimizing data transfer during out-of-GPU-memory graph processing. In: Proceedings of the Fifteenth European Conference on Computer Systems. EuroSys 2020, Association for Computing Machinery, New York, NY, USA (2020). https://doi.org/10.1145/3342195.3387537

13. Shun, J., Blelloch, G.E.: Ligra: a lightweight graph processing framework for shared memory. In: Proceedings of the 18th ACM SIGPLAN Symposium on Principles and Practice of Parallel Programming, pp. 135–146 (2013)

14. Toader, L., Uta, A., Musaafir, A., Iosup, A.: Graphless: toward serverless graph processing. In: 2019 18th International Symposium on Parallel and Distributed Computing (ISPDC), pp. 66–73 (2019). https://doi.org/10.1109/ISPDC.2019.00012

15. Wang, H., Geng, L., Lee, R., Hou, K., Zhang, Y., Zhang, X.: SEP-graph: finding shortest execution paths for graph processing under a hybrid framework on GPU. In: Proceedings of the 24th Symposium on Principles and Practice of Parallel Programming, pp. 38–52 (2019)

16. Zhang, Y., Yang, M., Baghdadi, R., Kamil, S., Shun, J., Amarasinghe, S.: Graphit: a high-performance graph DSL. Proc. ACM Program. Lang. **2**, 1–30 (2018). https://doi.org/10.1145/3276491

17. Zhu, X., Chen, W., Zheng, W., Ma, X.: Gemini: a computation-centric distributed graph processing system. In: 12th USENIX Symposium on Operating Systems Design and Implementation (OSDI 2016), pp. 301–316. USENIX Association, Savannah, GA (Nov 2016). https://www.usenix.org/conference/osdi16/technical-sessions/presentation/zhu

18. Zhu, X., Han, W., Chen, W.: {GridGraph}:{Large-Scale} graph processing on a single machine using 2-level hierarchical partitioning. In: 2015 USENIX Annual Technical Conference (USENIX ATC 2015), pp. 375–386 (2015)

KarmaPM: Reward-Driven Power Manager

Sunil Kumar[(✉)] [iD] and Vivek Kumar[(✉)] [iD]

IIIT-Delhi, New Delhi, India
{sunilk,vivekk}@iiitd.ac.in

Abstract. Hardware overprovisioning is a widely used technique to improve the average power utilization of computing systems by capping the processor's power consumption. However, applying a uniform power cap across multiprocessor system sockets can significantly impact co-running applications due to workload variations. This paper introduces *KarmaPM*, a novel power management library for co-running applications on multiprocessor systems, independent of the parallel programming model, based on application power donation phases. KarmaPM dynamically redistributes power bidirectionally across the sockets to improve overall system throughput for co-running applications while maintaining fairness between them. KarmaPM periodically profiles the CPU utilization of each application. When it detects an application underutilizing its CPU resources, it donates the surplus power from this donor application's sockets to the other sockets (receivers), exhibiting high CPU utilization. When the donor application enters a high CPU utilization phase, KarmaPM employs a reward power scheme that rewards the donor application by returning a portion of the power transferred to the receiver sockets. We evaluated KarmaPM across various exascale proxy application mixes and power caps on a four-socket, 72-core Intel Cooper Lake processor. Our results show that KarmaPM improved the system throughput (geometric mean) by 13.2% at a lower power cap and 6.6% at a higher power cap. Additionally, KarmaPM delivered improvements of 12.5% and 4.4% in system throughput (geomean) compared to an existing power manager at these respective power caps.

Keywords: Hardware overprovisioning · mulitprocessor · system throughput · co-running applications

1 Introduction

The number of compute elements, including cores and sockets, is increasing rapidly in modern multiprocessor systems used in cloud infrastructures, data centres, and supercomputers [1]. This advancement enables concurrent execution of multiple applications on multiprocessor systems. However, varying power

W. E. Nagel et al. (Eds.): Euro-Par 2025, LNCS 15900, pp. 351–365, 2026.
https://doi.org/10.1007/978-3-031-99854-6_24

requirements among co-running applications necessitate limiting processor consumption to reduce the carbon footprint. To manage rising power demands, data centres and supercomputers commonly employ hardware overprovisioning for capping power usage at some processors below their Thermal Design Power (TDP) limit [11] while reallocating unused power to support additional computing systems (e.g., GPUs, and nodes in the HPC cluster). Modern processors support hardware overprovisioning through power capping (PCAP), which enforces user-defined limits by throttling frequency at the hardware level. However, operating a processor under a PCAP can significantly degrade the application's performance [15]. Parallel applications often exhibit intermittent phases of low CPU utilization during execution, referred to as slacks. These phases occur when only a subset of the allocated cores actively execute application threads while the remaining cores remain idle. Slacks typically arise during sequential execution, I/O operations, or synchronization barriers, in contrast to parallel regions where CPU resources are fully utilized. A well-studied approach to improving the performance of such applications running under PCAP in an HPC cluster is to use power managers (PMs) that redistribute surplus power from slack-experiencing nodes to busy nodes [4,5,9,10]. However, a common limitation of these solutions is that they do not focus on inter-socket power scheduling within a multiprocessor system. Additionally, they fail to account for fairness in the system by not rewarding the power donor, as power is transferred unidirectionally from processors running under slack to those executing parallel regions.

This paper proposes KarmaPM, a novel reward-based power manager designed to enhance the fairness and throughput of co-running applications in a multi-socket system under a PCAP based on the application's power donation $karmas^1$. KarmaPM operates independently as a lightweight daemon process alongside the co-running applications and requires no prior knowledge of application characteristics. KarmaPM periodically monitors the CPU utilization of applications at each socket. When it identifies an application underutilizing its CPU resources, it reallocates surplus power from this donor application's sockets to other receiver sockets that fully utilize its CPU resources. KarmaPM records the duration the donor application has provided power to the receiver sockets. When the donor application resumes fully utilizing its CPU resources, KarmaPM rewards that application by returning a fraction of the total power previously donated to the receiver sockets. The power transfer between sockets is achieved by reducing the PCAP at the donor socket while increasing the PCAP at the receiver socket by the same amount, ensuring that the overall power consumption remains within the user-set PCAP limits.

In summary, this paper makes the following contributions:

– KarmaPM, a library-based power management solution for multiprocessor systems that enhances fairness and throughput for co-running parallel applications on a power-capped multiprocessor server while adhering to the system power budget.

---

[1] Sanskrit word referring to the sum of somebody's good and bad actions in one of their lives. KarmaPM only pays attention to good karmas.

- A lightweight profiler that monitors CPU utilization across each socket, facilitating the transfer of excess power from underutilized sockets to those fully utilizing their CPU resources.
- A novel power reward mechanism designed to promote fairness and throughput by compensating power-donating sockets with a portion of the donated power as they transition from low to high CPU utilization phases.
- An evaluation of KarmaPM on a quad-socket 72-core Intel Xeon processor using diverse mixes of exascale proxy applications [2] and various PCAPs, demonstrating that KarmaPM can substantially improve the system throughput and application fairness.

2   Related Work

Hardware overprovisioning [11] is widely used to reduce the increasing power consumption cost and carbon footprint of data centres and supercomputers. It has been used extensively both at the cluster and single server levels. Broadly, these solutions can be divided into two categories: one that aims to improve the performance of applications running at cluster level using inter-node power scheduling, and the other that seeks to improve the performance of applications running at server level. Patki *et al.* [11] proposed an approach for cluster-level power budgeting by configuring a fixed power budget at each node. However, applying uniform power allocation at each node impacts the application's performance when its power demand increases at some nodes. Such issues are common in MPI applications where some ranks could experience slack while others are busy (e.g., due to barrier synchronization [5] or manufacturing variability in processors [7]). Several approaches exist for power scheduling across nodes running different MPI applications for improving system throughput [4,9,16] and application level fairness [10]. Improving the system throughput at a multiprocessor server has been explored by configuring processor frequency for a single running application [6,14] or combining it along with tuning the thread count for co-running applications [15].

Cluster-based power managers transfer power unidirectionally, redistributing it from donor to receiver nodes without ensuring fairness through rewarding donors. Existing server-level solutions optimize processor resources to minimize performance loss. However, none of the approaches *transparently* enhances system throughput and fairness for co-running applications on a multiprocessor system using power scheduling. Recently, Costero *et al.* [3] proposed a dynamic power distribution solution for such systems, but it requires modifications to the OpenMP runtime and is limited to co-running applications using OpenMP tasking pragma. KarmaPM bridges this gap with a programming model-oblivious, reward-based inter-socket power scheduling approach that dynamically adjusts power allocation based on an application's instantaneous usage, requiring no prior knowledge of input applications. A power rewarding scheme was recently explored for the Fugaku supercomputer, where applications with low power usage earn tokens to reduce their wait time in the job queue during relaunch [13].

3   Experimental Methodology

We first describe our experimental methodology, followed by a motivating analysis for KarmaPM. We used eight exascale proxy applications for our experimental evaluations [2]. These applications and input parameters are: (1) **SimpleMOC** (n_azimuthal=64, cai=3, fai=3, decomp_assemblies_ax=5), (2) **PathFinder** (input_file=10kx750.adj_list), (3) **CG** (class=C), (4) **MiniFE** (nx=256, ny=300, nz=512, iterations=60), (5) **RSBench** (p=1000000), (6) **Quicksilver** (input_file=Coral2_P1.inp, n=200000), (7) **Pennant** (input_file=leblancbig.pnt, meshparams=120 × 1080, tstop=10.0), (8) **CoMD** (n=40 × 40x40, nSteps=800). We choose different parallel programming models in these applications as discussed in Sect. 6 to demonstrate the parallel runtime obliviousness in KarmaPM. We did not modify the applications otherwise, but we changed the default parameters to control the execution time on our machine. We used GNU compiler version 10.3 with the -O3 optimization to compile the applications. We performed all experimental evaluations on a quad-socket Intel(R) Xeon(R) Gold Cooperlake 5318H processor, which has 18 cores per socket (totalling 72 cores). Hyperthreading was disabled, and turbo boost was enabled. Our machine had 512GB of RAM and Ubuntu 20.04.5 LTS operating system (OS) with Linux Kernel 5.4. To set the socket-level power cap (PCAP), we used the Intel RAPL (Running Average Power Limit) interface by writing to the MSR_PKG_POWER_LIMIT register for each socket. Our experimental evaluations used three different PCAPs: 83 W (55% of TDP), 98 W (65% of TDP), and 112 W (75% of TDP). A PCAP setting of 150 W (the TDP for each socket) indicates that each socket's PCAP is individually set to 150 W, resulting in a total system-level PCAP of 600 W. We preserved the same system and application settings across all PCAPs.

4   Motivating Analysis

This section explains the rationale behind KarmaPM's design by analyzing our selected application's CPU utilization and power consumption patterns during execution. We conducted these experiments by running each application on a single socket of our quad-socket machine. Figure 1(a) presents CPU utilization trends for SimpleMoC, Pathfinder, MiniFE, and CG, demonstrating periods of slack due to sequential execution phases. For CG, slack occurs twice, totalling approximately 25% of the total execution time. The other three applications initially exhibit slack, ranging from 23% to 49% of execution. The remaining four applications, RSBench, Quicksilver, Pennant, and CoMD, do not experience any slack during their execution timeline. Slack also impacts power consumption, as shown in Fig. 1(b), where reductions align with the slacks in Fig. 1(a)

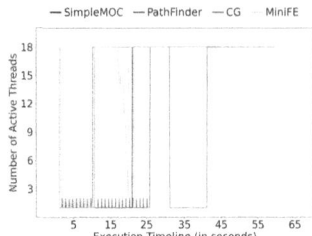

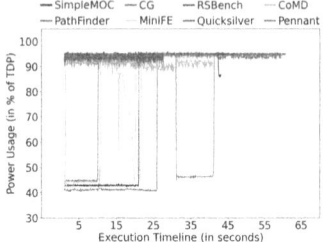

(a) Periods of slack resulting from
sequential phases

(b) Power usage correlates with
the presence of slack

Fig. 1. Execution timeline of applications at TDP

5   Design and Implementation

The previous section highlighted that a parallel application's power consumption is influenced by its instantaneous CPU utilization. These two metrics can be measured dynamically using a lightweight online daemon profiler, eliminating the need for prior application execution data. This daemon facilitates inter-application power scheduling based on the CPU utilization of individual applications within a multiprocessor server. Our approach employs a lightweight daemon process called KarmaPM, which is launched alongside parallel applications and periodically monitors the active core count and power usage of each co-running application. Applications are launched on the server ensuring that sockets are not shared between applications, although a single application may use multiple sockets. Each application exclusively uses local socket resources such as CPU and memory. KarmaPM activates at regular intervals to minimize interference with the application's execution. No changes to applications are needed to use KarmaPM. Our insight is to initially redirect surplus power from an underutilized sockets of one application to the busier sockets of other applications to enhance overall system performance. Subsequently, when the donor application transitions to a busy state, it is rewarded with a portion of the transferred power to maintain fairness in the system.

$$P_{\text{Donated}}(X,Y) = \left(\sum_{i=1}^{k} P_{\text{Donated},i} \cdot n_i \right) \Big/ \left(\sum_{i=1}^{k} n_i \right)$$

- $P_{\text{Donated}}(X,Y)$: Average power donated from App X to App Y over $\sum_{i=1}^{k} n_i$ epochs.
- $P_{\text{Donated},i}$: Power donated from x to y in the i-th epoch group (continuous phase of execution).
- n_i: Number of epochs in the i-th epoch group.
- k: Total number of epoch groups.

Fig. 2. Formula to calculate net average power donated from application X to Y

Algorithm 1: KarmaPM daemon process loop

---

1 **Initialization:**
2 State[$N_{Application}$], P_{Usage}[$N_{Application}$];
3 Set PCAP$_{Default}$ on each socket;
4 sleep(warmup duration);
5 **while** *atleast two applications are running* **do**
6   **for** *application* $= 1$ *to* $N_{Application}$ **do**
7   **if** *application is running* **then**
8   Store application's socket power into P_{Usage}[*application*];
9   **if** *all cores are busy* **then**
10 | State[*application*] $\leftarrow$ CPU_Busy;
11   **else**
12 | State[*application*] $\leftarrow$ CPU_Slack;
13   **end**
14   **else**
15   State[*application*] $\leftarrow$ INACTIVE;
16   Set PCAP$_{Default}$ on application's socket;
17   **end**
18   **end**
19   KarmaPM _Policy(P_{Usage}, State);
20   sleep (T_{epoch});
21 **end**
22 Set PCAP$_{Default}$ on each socket;

5.1 KarmaPM Daemon Loop

Algorithm 1 presents the pseudocode implementation of the KarmaPM daemon process designed for a multicore server with multiple sockets. Initially, it sets the default PCAP for each socket as specified by the user (Line 3). The daemon operates in a loop as long as at least two applications remain active (Line 5). Within each iteration, it iterates over all running applications (Line 6) to measure their power consumption (Line 8) and CPU utilization (Lines 9–13) on the sockets where they are executing. If an application terminates on a socket, the daemon marks that application's state as inactive (Line 15) and resets the PCAP to the default value set by the user (Line 16). An alternative design choice would be distributing the surplus power available at an inactive socket due to its application termination among the busy applications. We did not follow it in KarmaPM implementation to ensure a fair evaluation. Subsequently, the daemon applies the application-level KarmaPM power scheduling policy (Line 19). Finally, it returns to sleep for a fixed epoch of 100ms (Line 20). Due to cold caches at the start of the execution, the KarmaPM daemon loop activates only after a warmup duration of two seconds (Line 4) to allow the system to stabilize. Before concluding its operation, the KarmaPM daemon resets the PCAP on each socket to the user-defined default value (Line 22).

5.2 KarmaPM Power Scheduling Policy

Figure 3 demonstrates the working of KarmaPM power scheduling policy, illustrated through a running example of a multiprocessor server with four sockets labelled $Socket_A$, $Socket_B$, $Socket_C$, and $Socket_D$. A single instance of the KarmaPM daemon process is launched on this server alongside applications $Bench_A$, $Bench_B$, $Bench_C$, and $Bench_D$, which are assigned to sockets $Socket_A$,

Socket$_B$, Socket$_C$, and Socket$_D$, respectively. The KarmaPM process is pinned to the last core in Socket$A$, and the affinity of an application's threads is set to its respective sockets using the *taskset* command (the daemon process shares a core with the last thread of Bench$_A$). To ensure socket-local memory allocation, the `numactl` command line tool is utilized, allowing the memory pages of each application to be allocated in their respective socket-local DRAM.

Distributing Unused Power to Busy Applications. Each of these four sockets is initially assigned the user-set power cap of PCAP$_{Default}$=98W, which is 65% of the Thermal Design Power (TDP), resulting in a total system-level PCAP$_{Default}$=392W (Fig. 3(a)). The KarmaPM policy begins at Epoch 20, as illustrated in Fig. 3(a). The initial two seconds, corresponding to the first twenty Epochs, were excluded as a warmup duration (refer to Sect. 5.1). At Epoch 20, the KarmaPM daemon identified that Bench$_A$ and Bench$_B$ were experiencing slack, while Bench$_C$ and Bench$_D$ were operating under full load. As a result, power usage (P$_{Usage}$) for Socket$_A$ and Socket$_B$ reduced to 78W and 68W, respectively. Hence, KarmaPM reduces the PCAP at Socket$_A$ and Socket$_B$ in Epoch 21 to their current power consumption levels to avoid wastage of power while simultaneously increasing the PCAP of both Socket$_C$ and Socket$_D$ by 25W (Fig. 3(b)). This situation persisted for the following twenty Epochs. After this period, the KarmaPM daemon noted that Bench$_A$ had returned to full CPU utilization, while Bench$_B$ was still displaying slack (Fig. 3(c)). KarmaPM then equally distributed the combined surplus power of 30W from Socket$_C$ and Socket$_D$ among all busy sockets, resulting in a PCAP of 108W for Socket$_A$, Socket$_C$, and Socket$_D$ (Fig. 3(d)).

Rewarding Donor Applications with Surplus Power. A receiver application is required to reward the donor application once the donor enters a busy state to ensure fairness in the system. KarmaPM computes the average total power donated to a application using the equation shown in Fig. 2. The reward power allocated to the donor application is half the average power received by that application and is provided for the same number of total Epochs it donated. Since Bench$_C$ and Bench$_D$ each received 10W from Bench$_A$ over a span of twenty Epochs (from Epoch 22 to 41), KarmaPM subsequently rewarded Bench$_A$ by granting 5W of power from both Socket$_C$ and Socket$_D$ (Fig. 3(e)) during the following twenty Epochs (Fig. 3(f)). By Epoch 65, KarmaPM recognized that Bench$_B$ had returned to full CPU utilization (Fig. 3(f)). With all four applications now busy, KarmaPM will first reset the PCAP at each socket to PCAP$_{Default}$ (Fig. 3(g)) before calculating the reward power to Bench$_B$ from Bench$_A$, Bench$_C$, and Bench$_D$ (see Fig. 2). The average power donated by Socket$_B$ to Socket$_A$ was 10W for 20 Epochs, while it donated 12.5W each to Socket$_C$ and Socket$_D$ for 40 Epochs. Consequently, Socket$_A$, Socket$_C$, and Socket$_D$ will reward Socket$_B$ by providing 5W, 6.25W, and 6.25W of power, respectively, for 20 Epochs (Fig. 3(h)). By Epoch 88, the PCAP at Socket$_A$ is reset to the user-defined default PCAP, while Socket$_C$ and Socket$_D$ continue to

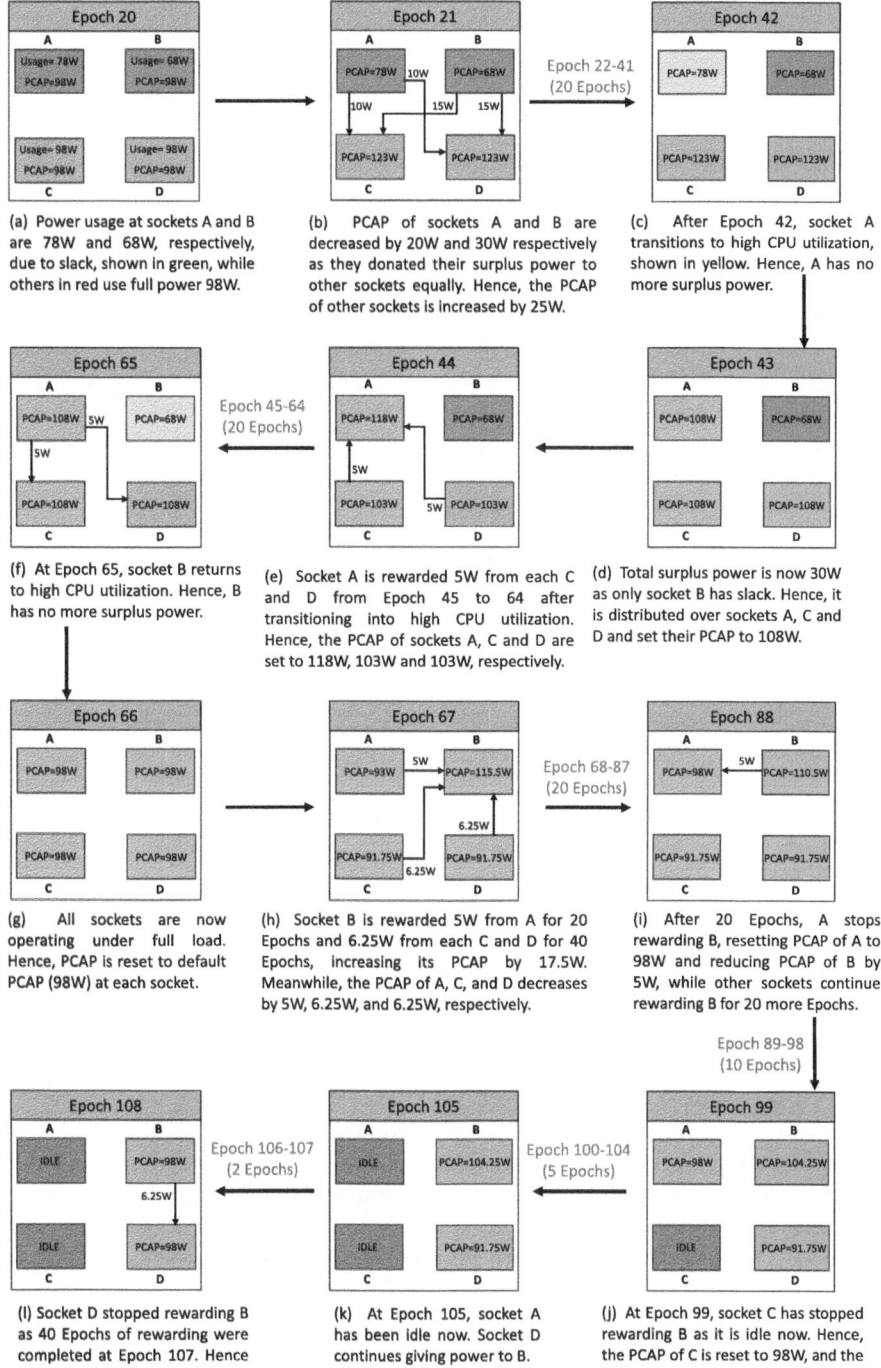

(a) Power usage at sockets A and B are 78W and 68W, respectively, due to slack, shown in green, while others in red use full power 98W.

(b) PCAP of sockets A and B are decreased by 20W and 30W respectively as they donated their surplus power to other sockets equally. Hence, the PCAP of other sockets is increased by 25W.

(c) After Epoch 42, socket A transitions to high CPU utilization, shown in yellow. Hence, A has no more surplus power.

(f) At Epoch 65, socket B returns to high CPU utilization. Hence, B has no more surplus power.

(e) Socket A is rewarded 5W from each C and D from Epoch 45 to 64 after transitioning into high CPU utilization. Hence, the PCAP of sockets A, C and D are set to 118W, 103W and 103W, respectively.

(d) Total surplus power is now 30W as only socket B has slack. Hence, it is distributed over sockets A, C and D and set their PCAP to 108W.

(g) All sockets are now operating under full load. Hence, PCAP is reset to default PCAP (98W) at each socket.

(h) Socket B is rewarded 5W from A for 20 Epochs and 6.25W from each C and D for 40 Epochs, increasing its PCAP by 17.5W. Meanwhile, the PCAP of A, C, and D decreases by 5W, 6.25W, and 6.25W, respectively.

(i) After 20 Epochs, A stops rewarding B, resetting PCAP of A to 98W and reducing PCAP of B by 5W, while other sockets continue rewarding B for 20 more Epochs.

(l) Socket D stopped rewarding B as 40 Epochs of rewarding were completed at Epoch 107. Hence reset PCAP of B and D to 98W.

(k) At Epoch 105, socket A has been idle now. Socket D continues giving power to B.

(j) At Epoch 99, socket C has stopped rewarding B as it is idle now. Hence, the PCAP of C is reset to 98W, and the PCAP of B is decreased by 6.25W.

Fig. 3. KarmaPM power scheduling policy for improving throughput and fairness

$$\text{Speedup}_{\text{Mix}} = \frac{\left(\prod_{i=0}^{n-1} \text{Time}_{\text{Default}_{\text{App}_i}}\right)^{\frac{1}{n}}}{\left(\prod_{i=0}^{n-1} \text{Time}_{\text{PM}_{\text{App}_i}}\right)^{\frac{1}{n}}}$$

Fig. 4. Speedup from using a Power Manager (PM) with a mix of n applications

reward Socket_B by contributing 6.25W each for the next 20 Epochs (Fig. 3(i)). However, after 10 Epochs, the application running at Socket_C terminated. Consequently, the PCAP at Socket_C will be revert to the default user-set PCAP, and Socket_B will now continue receiving the reward power only from Socket_D (Fig. 3(j)). The PCAP will also be reset at Socket_A to the default PCAP at Epoch 105 as its application terminated (Fig. 3(k)). Finally, Socket_B would continue receiving reward power until Epoch 107, after which its PCAP will revert to the default user-set PCAP (Fig. 3(l)).

6 Experimental Evaluation

Table 1. Details of the application mixes used for evaluations

Mixes	Mix1 (OpenMP/Kokkos)	Mix2 (OpenMP/Kokkos)	Mix3 (OpenMP-only)	Mix4 (OpenMP-only)	Mix5 (OpenMP-only)	Mix6
App0	PathFinder	CG	SimpleMOC	CG	CG	SimpleMOC (MPI+OpenMP)
App1	MiniFE (Kokkos)	MiniFE (Kokkos)	PathFinder	SimpleMOC	SimpleMOC	Pennant (MPI-only)
App2	RSBench	CoMD	Pennnant	CoMD	PathFinder	-
App3	Quicksilver	Pennant	Quicksilver	Quicksilver	RSBench	-

This section presents the experimental evaluation of KarmaPM using the co-running mixes shown in Table 1. We created six mixes of co-running applications, as shown in Table 1. The rationale behind these mixes was to create two and four co-running pairs, combine applications that exhibit slack with those that fully utilize CPU resources, and include different parallel programming models (shown in the same Table). The sockets were divided equally among each co-runner in each mix (using the *taskset* command). None of the applications in any mix shared socket-local resources with others in that mix. The SimpleMOC in Mix6 was executed with two MPI ranks, each allocated to a separate socket, and each rank used 18 OpenMP threads with affinity set to the local socket. Pennant in the same Mix6 was executed with 36 MPI ranks spanning across two sockets. We executed each mix ten times and reported the mean value along with a 95% confidence interval. We developed a variant of KarmaPM called SimplePM, which operates similarly to KarmaPM but does not reward the power donor sockets. The work most closely related to SimplePM is PShifter [5], which functions at the cluster level. We ported a single server-level implementation of PShifter to

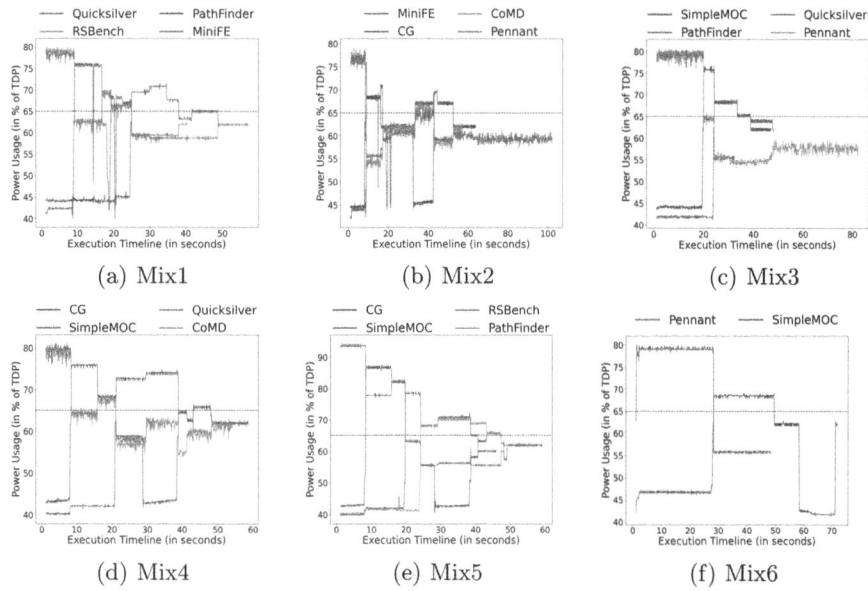

Fig. 5. Timeline of power distribution from KarmaPM across sockets at PCAP=65%

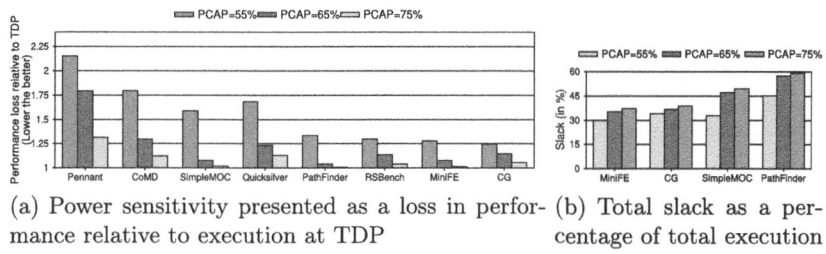

(a) Power sensitivity presented as a loss in performance relative to execution at TDP

(b) Total slack as a percentage of total execution

Fig. 6. Analysis of power sensitivity and slack at each PCAP

facilitate power transfer among sockets. PShifter differs from SimplePM by its power donation strategy, as it distributes surplus power equally among all four sockets. In contrast, SimplePM improves this approach by allocating surplus power exclusively to the sockets, fully utilizing CPU resources. While we evaluated KarmaPM on an Intel Cooperlake processor, it can be adapted for other Intel and AMD processors by updating the specific MSRs accordingly.

Figure 5 shows the timeline of power scheduling from KarmaPM for each mix at 65% PCAP. We can observe that the reduction in power at one socket increases the power of the other socket without overshooting the system power budget. A similar trend holds at the other two PCAPs. We used the formula shown in Fig. 4 to calculate the improvement in throughput over the `Default` execution at each of the three PCAPs by using PShifter, SimplePM, or KarmaPM while executing each of our six mixes [12]. The `Default` run uses

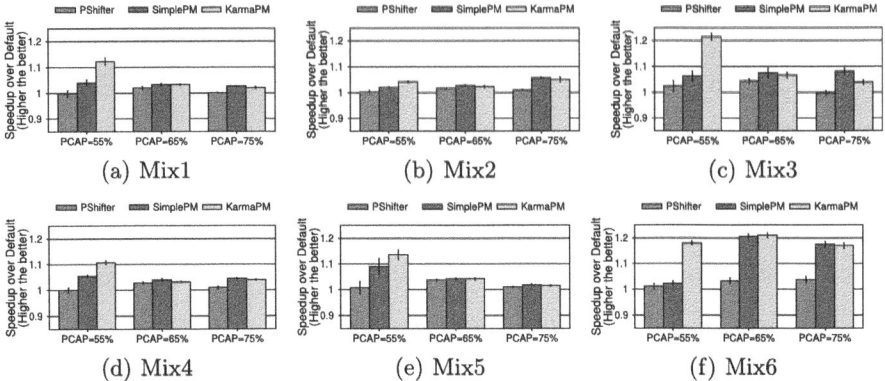

(a) Mix1   (b) Mix2   (c) Mix3

(d) Mix4   (e) Mix5   (f) Mix6

Fig. 7. Improvement in overall system throughput at each PCAP

the same settings as the other three Power Managers (PMs) but does not perform power transfers across sockets. The result of this experiment is shown in Fig. 7. Table 2 compares the speedup for individual applications between SimplePM and KarmaPM at each PCAP. The throughput achieved by any of the three power managers (PMs) is influenced by several factors: Point-1) the user-set PCAP and the power sensitivity of each application at that PCAP, Point-2) the percentage of total slack in power donor applications, Point-3) the number of applications in the mix that possess slack, and Point-4) the number of power receiver applications. Figure 6(a) illustrates each application's power sensitivity as performance loss at various PCAPs relative to the execution time at TDP. Notably, at higher PCAPs (65% and 75%), the performance loss is minimal for CG, MiniFE, RSBench, PathFinder, and SimpleMoC. In contrast, Quicksilver, CoMD, and Pennant demonstrate relatively significant performance losses at these two PCAPs. Figure 6(b) shows the percentage of total execution time during which slack occurred at each PCAP level for low power sensitivity applications (MiniFE and CG) and high power sensitivity applications (SimpleMoC and PathFinder). During slack periods, each application's power consumption remained below the selected PCAPs, resulting in consistent slack durations for each application across PCAP levels. However, non-slack execution time varies based on an application's power sensitivity, decreasing as the PCAP increases. As a result, the slack percentage increases with higher PCAP levels in Simple-MoC and PathFinder (Fig. 6(b)). This rising slack proportion causes these highly power-sensitive applications to appear relatively less sensitive in Fig. 6(a).

Table 2. Speedup by three PMs for individual applications across mixes at each PCAPs

		PCAP=55%				PCAP=65%				PCAP=75%			
Performance improvement relative to `Default` (in %)													
Mixes	Policy	App0	App1	App2	App3	App0	App1	App2	App3	App0	App1	App2	App3
Mix1	PShifter	−0.7	−0.7	0.6	−0.1	0.2	1.2	3.0	3.6	−0.1	0.2	0.3	0.0
	SimplePM	−0.5	3.0	5.4	8.2	0.2	2.0	4.0	7.2	−0.3	0.0	1.3	10.2
	KarmaPM	36.9	8.5	3.8	3.1	3.8	3.1	2.1	4.1	0.5	−0.4	0.1	8.7
Mix2	PShifter	−0.3	0.4	1.2	−0.2	0.8	0.3	3.2	2.2	3.1	1.7	0.5	−0.7
	SimplePM	0.0	0.0	5.5	2.5	0.6	0.5	4.4	5.5	1.9	0.9	5.7	14.5
	KarmaPM	0.5	8.3	4.3	3.8	2.2	1.6	0.1	5.5	0.6	1.4	2.1	16.6
Mix3	PShifter	0.3	7.8	1.5	−0.2	1.2	−0.1	7.6	9.2	1.1	−0.1	−0.8	0.2
	SimplePM	4.7	2.1	3.0	15.2	0.6	−0.1	16.2	14.2	−0.7	−0.3	25.7	10.4
	KarmaPM	43.4	22.6	4.7	17.9	3.9	2.4	11.7	8.9	1.4	0.7	3.4	10.6
Mix4	PShifter	0.4	0.6	1.0	−1.9	−0.5	1.0	4.7	5.9	3.3	1.2	−0.1	−0.5
	SimplePM	0.6	1.1	6.6	13.7	0.2	3.0	6.3	6.2	1.0	0.8	7.4	9.1
	KarmaPM	1.1	32.7	4.0	7.4	1.7	6.7	0.5	3.9	1.7	2.1	5.1	7.3
Mix5	PShifter	0.5	0.3	-2.5	4.8	2.3	3.5	1.0	8.2	2.7	1.3	−0.1	0.2
	SimplePM	2.0	24.7	−0.4	10.9	3.7	2.8	1.0	9.4	1.9	2.7	0.1	2.6
	KarmaPM	2.3	37.3	9.7	8.7	3.0	6.0	3.7	4.1	2.2	2.7	0.6	0.5
Mix6	PShifter	2.7	0.6	-	-	5.4	1.0	-	-	−0.3	8.1	-	-
	SimplePM	1.0	3.1	-	-	−0.8	53.1	-	-	−0.7	49.2	-	-
	KarmaPM	26.3	15.2	-	-	1.6	48.1	-	-	0.6	45.8	-	-

6.1 Speedup at Higher PCAPs (65% and 75%)

Mix6 achieved significantly higher throughput at higher PCAPs with SimplePM
and KarmaPM compared to all other mixes (53% at PCAP=65% and 49%
at PCAP=75%). In this case, a single power-sensitive application (Pennant)
received the donated power, leading to substantial performance gains. As shown
in Fig. 5(f), SimpleMOC donated power from its slack region to Pennant and
briefly received reward power in return. However, since Pennant terminated
shortly thereafter, the throughput remained similar for both SimplePM and
KarmaPM. Despite overall system throughput being the same in this mix, unlike
SimplePM, KarmaPM promoted fairness by improving the speedup of SimpleMOC (see Table 2). Mix3 showed marginally better throughput with SimplePM (7.5% at PCAP=65% and 8.2% at PCAP=75%) and KarmaPM (6.6%
at PCAP=65% and 3.9% at PCAP=75%). It was primarily due to the overlapping slack regions in SimpleMoC and PathFinder. However, at 75% PCAP,
SimplePM achieved comparatively higher throughput than KarmaPM. This difference arises from KarmaPM's reward policy, prioritising fairness by distributing speedup improvements across all applications. As shown in Table 2, SimplePM only enhanced the speedup of Pennant and Quicksilver in Mix3, whereas
KarmaPM promoted fairness by boosting the speedup of other co-runners. Mix2
and Mix4 contain two applications with slack regions (CG and MiniFE in Mix2,

CG and SimpleMoC in Mix4). However, unlike Mix3, their slack periods do not fully overlap, leading to only minor and similar throughput improvements at both PCAPs (up to 5.6%). Although CG experiences slack twice, only the first instance overlaps with another application's slack. Mix1 has a single application sensitive to these two PCAPs (Quicksilver), whereas Mix5 lacks any of the three power-sensitive applications, so these two pairs performed similarly to `Default`. Overall, at each of these two high PCAPs, KarmaPM attained fairness in each mix by enhancing the speedup of each application through its power reward policy (Table 2). Overall, PShifter performed worse than both SimplePM and KarmaPM across all mixes and PCAPs, including PCAP=55%. It was designed for cluster environments with many nodes, where a node's surplus power is evenly distributed among the rest of the nodes in the cluster. In a large cluster, the proportion of nodes experiencing slack (at the same time) is lower than that of sockets experiencing slack in a single multiprocessor server. While effective at the cluster level, this approach is less suitable for a single-server environment.

6.2 Speedup at Lower PCAP (55%)

At lower PCAP, KarmaPM performed better than SimplePM in all mixes. The improvement in throughput in KarmaPM relative to SimplePM were 8% in Mix1, 2.2% in Mix2, 14.3% in Mix3, 5% in Mix4, 4.4% in Mix5, and 15.4% in Mix6 (geomean improvement of 6.6% over SimplePM and 12% over `Default`). At the same time, owing to its novel reward policy, unlike SimplePM, it significantly improved the speedup of the slack-experiencing applications in each mix (Table 2). MiniFE and CG were exceptions. Despite experiencing slack, their insensitivity to power means that even at low PCAP (Fig. 6(a)), receiving reward power results in only marginal performance gains. In contrast, SimpleMoC and PathFinder, despite experiencing slack, showed notable performance improvements when receiving reward power. Among the four applications that do not experience slack, QuickSilver, CoMD, and Pennant exhibited high sensitivity to power transfers at low PCAPs. As a result, their performance was significantly influenced by both receiving and donating power. KarmaPM achieved the highest throughput improvements in Mix3 and Mix6. It was due to the high-power sensitivity applications in both mixes and overlapping slacks in Mix3 (SimpleMOC and PathFinder). The effect of KarmaPM was least visible in Mix2 because MiniFE had a comparatively short slack region (Fig. 6(b)), with some slack instances not overlapping with that in CG (Fig. 1(a)). SimplePM's performance was best in Mix5 due to three applications exhibiting slack (CG, SimpleMoC, and PathFinder).

At present, KarmaPM redistributes unused power from one application to others in equal shares without considering the power sensitivity of the receiver applications. In future work, we intend to improve KarmaPM by making power distribution sensitivity-aware. Similarly, KarmaPM will transfer reward power based on the power sensitivity of the recipient application.

6.3   Energy Usage

Figure 8 shows the geometric mean energy consumption of SimplePM and KarmaPM at each PCAP for all mixes relative to `Default`. Overall, KarmaPM consumed less energy than `Default` across all mixes, with savings ranging from −0.1% to 7.9%. Except for Mix3, KarmaPM's energy use was comparable to or lower than

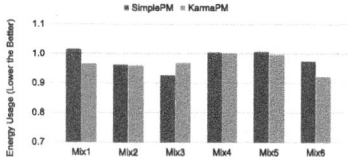

Fig. 8. Geomean energy usage at all PCAPs relative to `Default` for each mix

that of SimplePM. The higher energy usage in Mix3 arises from SimplePM achieving greater system throughput than KarmaPM at higher PCAPs (see Sect. 6.1). In Mix2, Mix4, and Mix5, both KarmaPM and SimplePM showed similar energy usage due to CG, a low power-sensitive application, resulting in comparable performance at higher PCAPs. In Mix1 and Mix6, although both KarmaPM and SimplePM achieved similar throughput, KarmaPM consumed 4.9% and 5.3% less energy, respectively, due to the presence of two highly power-sensitive applications that experienced slack and benefited from KarmaPM's reward mechanism.

7   Conclusion

This paper proposes a programming model oblivious power management solution for multiprocessor servers to improve system throughput and application fairness under a limited power budget for co-running parallel applications. Our approach uses a novel reward-based scheme to boost the performance of a power donor application by rewarding them with additional power usage based on their previous power donation activities to other co-running applications. Our empirical results demonstrate that our reward-driven power management solution can achieve better throughput and energy savings than traditional approaches.

Acknowledgement and Artifact Availability. This research was supported by the Google PhD Fellowship 2022 program. The artifact of this paper is available in the Zenodo repository [8].

References

1. TOP500 (2024). https://top500.org/lists/top500/2024/11/
2. ECP proxy applications (Released). https://proxyapps.exascaleproject.org
3. Costero, L., Igual, F.D., Olcoz, K.: Dynamic power budget redistribution under a power cap on multi-application environments. SUSCOM (2023). https://doi.org/10.1016/j.suscom.2023.100865
4. Ding, J., Hoffmann, H.: DPS: adaptive power management for overprovisioned systems. In: SC (2023). https://doi.org/10.1145/3581784.3607091

5. Gholkar, N., Mueller, F., Rountree, B., Marathe, A.: PShifter: feedback-based dynamic power shifting within HPC jobs for performance. In: HPDC (2018). https://doi.org/10.1145/3208040.3208047

6. Huang, D., Costero, L., Atienza, D.: Is the powersave governor really saving power? In: CCGrid (2024). https://doi.org/10.1109/CCGrid59990.2024.00039

7. Inadomi, Y., et al.: Analyzing and mitigating the impact of manufacturing variability in power-constrained supercomputing. In: SC (2015). https://doi.org/10.1145/2807591.2807638

8. Kumar, S., Kumar, V.: KarmaPM: reward-driven power manager (2025). https://doi.org/10.5281/zenodo.15602982

9. Lee, S., et al.: I/o aware power shifting. In: IPDPS (2016). https://doi.org/10.1109/IPDPS.2016.15

10. Patel, T., Tiwari, D.: PERQ: fair and efficient power management of power-constrained large-scale computing systems. In: HPDC (2019). https://doi.org/10.1145/3307681.3326607

11. Patki, T., Lowenthal, D.K., Rountree, B., Schulz, M., de Supinski, B.R.: Exploring hardware overprovisioning in power-constrained, high performance computing. In: ICS (2013). https://doi.org/10.1145/2464996.2465009

12. Roy, R.B., Patel, T., Tiwari, D.: Satori: efficient and fair resource partitioning by sacrificing short-term benefits for long-term gains. In: ISCA (2021). https://doi.org/10.1109/ISCA52012.2021.00031

13. Solórzano, A.L.V., et al.: Toward sustainable HPC: in-production deployment of incentive-based power efficiency mechanism on the Fugaku supercomputer. In: SC (2024). https://doi.org/10.1109/SC41406.2024.00030

14. Wang, B., Miller, J., Terboven, C., Müller, M.: Operation-aware power capping. In: Malawski, M., Rzadca, K. (eds.) Euro-Par 2020. LNCS, vol. 12247, pp. 68–82. Springer, Cham (2020). https://doi.org/10.1007/978-3-030-57675-2_5

15. Zhang, H., Hoffmann, H.: Maximizing performance under a power cap: a comparison of hardware, software, and hybrid techniques. In: ASPLOS (2016). https://doi.org/10.1145/2872362.2872375

16. Zhang, H., Hoffmann, H.: PoDD: power-capping dependent distributed applications. In: SC (2019). https://doi.org/10.1145/3295500.3356174

A Sparsity Predicting Approach for Large Language Models via Activation Pattern Clustering

Nobel Dhar[ID], Bobin Deng[ID], Md Romyull Islam[ID], Xinyue Zhang[ID],
Kazi Fahim Ahmad Nasif[ID], and Kun Suo[(✉)][ID]

Kennesaw State University, Kennesaw, GA 30144, USA
{ndhar,mislam22,knasif}@students.kennesaw.edu,
{bdeng2,xzhang48,ksuo}@kennesaw.edu

Abstract. Large Language Models (LLMs) exhibit significant activation sparsity, where only a subset of neurons are active for a given input. Although this sparsity presents opportunities to reduce computational cost, efficiently utilizing it requires predicting activation patterns in a scalable manner. However, direct prediction at the neuron level is computationally expensive due to the vast number of neurons in modern LLMs. To enable efficient prediction and utilization of activation sparsity, we propose a clustering-based activation pattern compression framework. Instead of treating each neuron independently, we group similar activation patterns into a small set of representative clusters. Our method achieves up to 79.34% clustering precision, outperforming standard binary clustering approaches while maintaining minimal degradation in perplexity (PPL) scores. With a sufficiently large number of clusters, our approach attains a PPL score as low as 12.49, demonstrating its effectiveness in preserving model quality while reducing computational overhead. By predicting cluster assignments rather than individual neuron states, future models can efficiently infer activation patterns from pre-computed centroids. We detail the clustering algorithm, analyze its effectiveness in capturing meaningful activation structures, and demonstrate its potential to improve sparse computation efficiency. This clustering-based formulation serves as a foundation for future work on activation pattern prediction, paving the way for efficient inference in large-scale language models.

Keywords: LLMs · Optimization · Activation sparsity · Clustering

1 Introduction

The fast-paced evolution in transformer-based AI models, such as Large Language Models (LLMs), Large Vision Models (LVMs), and Large Multimodal Models (LMMs), have quickly expanded the smart capabilities to various real-life applications. These large models typically contain several hundred billion or

© The Author(s), under exclusive license to Springer Nature Switzerland AG 2026
W. E. Nagel et al. (Eds.): Euro-Par 2025, LNCS 15900, pp. 366–379, 2026.
https://doi.org/10.1007/978-3-031-99854-6_25

even trillions of parameters—for instance, GPT-4.5 [2] has approximately 12.8 trillion parameters—and must operate on high-performance computing (HPC) systems or large data centers. Centralized processing systems come with significant limitations. First, AI processing requests depend entirely on a stable network connection, requiring end users to transmit their requests to remote HPC systems and wait for the results. Second, as the number of active users grows and AI models become more complex, centralized data centers must adopt increasingly sophisticated designs to maintain the same level of Quality of Service (QoS). However, this will require us to upgrade the complicated cooling system further, which consumes most of the supply power, even more than the computing task itself. Third, remote server processing introduces higher latency and raises concerns about data privacy due to potential security risks during transmission. Therefore, we are motivated to keep a portion of AI tasks on edge devices instead of submitting them to centralized data centers. This edge AI processing on multiple smaller devices essentially increases the AI parallelism for our real-world applications.

To compress the large AI model and run locally on the resource-constraint edge devices, the leading solutions are quantization [3], pruning [13], and weight sparsification [6]. Another promising approach is the Mixture of Experts (MoE), which has been adopted in many state-of-the-art LLMs [7]. MoE models improve efficiency by activating only a subset of expert networks at each inference step rather than using all model parameters simultaneously. MoE consists of multiple independent feedforward networks that serve as experts, with a gating mechanism dynamically selecting which ones to use. A small neural network, known as a router, dynamically selects the most suitable experts for each input instance [16]. This dynamic selection can lower computational costs by only activating the parameters of the most relevant expert. Besides MoE, directly exploring the activation sparsity of pre-trained LLMs can also improve resource efficiency. Unlike MoE, which is explicitly trained with internal expert selection mechanisms, the activation sparsity approach follows the conventional transformer training paradigm. Recent research [4] demonstrates that enforcing activation output with smaller absolute values to zero can obtain additional activation sparsity with negligible accuracy degradation, even in non-ReLU-based models.

By effectively utilizing sparsity, it is possible to activate only a subset of neurons during inference, significantly reducing resource consumption without modifying the model's original architecture. While MoE models dynamically activate different sets of neurons through a routing mechanism, leveraging activation sparsity in pre-trained models presents a different challenge: identifying which neurons should be active without an explicit selection process. Since these models were not trained with built-in expert selection, determining neuron activations becomes nontrivial. Common approaches attempt to address this by utilizing the similarity of activated channels among semantically related tokens [5], analyzing activations after the gate projection [10], or employing a learnable predictor [12]. The overall effectiveness of these strategies largely depends on the accuracy of predicting active neurons. However, existing methods have not fully explored the possibility of predicting neuron activations solely based on inputs before computation. This omission is largely due to the immense computational and memory costs associated with directly predicting activations across billions of neurons. Without an efficient mechanism to address this scalability issue, the overhead of such predictions could outweigh the benefits, limiting the practicality of activation sparsity in large-scale models. A more scalable alternative is to cluster activation patterns into a small set of representative centroids, allowing for efficient prediction at pattern level rather than at the individual neuron level.

In this work, we explore the activation sparsity in Mistral-7B and propose a clustering-based approach to optimize inference efficiency. Instead of predicting activations at an individual neuron level, we identify recurring activation patterns and use centroids to approximate neuron states, significantly reducing the computational burden. To introduce sparsity, we apply a thresholding mechanism proposed by Dhar et al. [4], which enforces 50% sparsity in the FFN layers of Mistral-7B while maintaining a PPL score of 6.45. This ensures that half of the neurons remain inactive during inference We use the WikiText-2 [14] dataset as the input to the Mistral-7B model to extract activation patterns in the MLP layers for our clustering approach. WikiText-2 is a widely used benchmark dataset that provides a diverse yet relatively clean textual corpus, making it an ideal choice for studying activation behaviors in LLMs.

Figure 1 provides an overview of our clustering method, illustrating how activation patterns that exhibit similarity are grouped together, forming clusters that share common activation characteristics. Each cluster is represented by a centroid, which is calculated to best approximate the activation status of individual neurons within the group. Each centroid captures a unique activation pattern observed across multiple inputs, allowing us to map future activations to their closest centroid rather than processing them independently. In other words, the centroid serves as a compact representation of the most frequently occurring activation states across multiple patterns. This structured clustering serves as the foundation for our key contributions, which are summarized as follows:

– We developed a customized clustering algorithm designed specifically to address activation sparsity in LLMs.
– The proposed algorithm achieves high clustering precision across 10.64 million activation patterns while maintaining minimal perplexity (PPL) degradation, ensuring efficient neuron representation without compromising model performance.
– We proposed a scalable approach to optimizing sparse activation patterns by clustering billions of neurons into representative centroids, fundamentally reducing the overhead of activation prediction.

This work presents a scalable clustering approach to leverage the activation sparsity in LLMs. By grouping similar activation patterns and representing them with centroids, we reduce the computational overhead of activation prediction while preserving the model's accuracy. This method enables efficient inference,

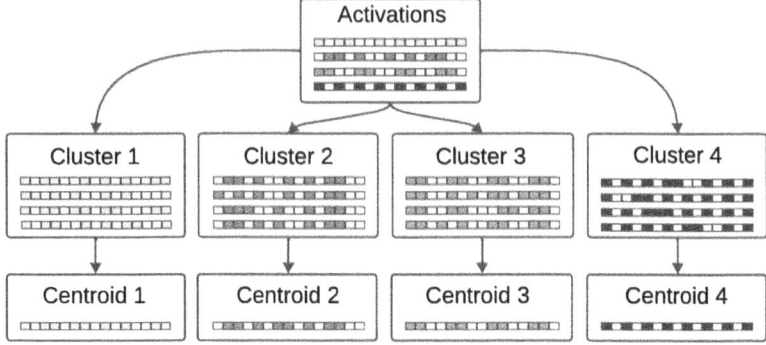

Fig. 1. Clustering Patterns Into Representative Centroids

optimizing resource usage without altering the model architecture, and serves as a foundational step toward sparse activation-based optimization for LLMs.

The remaining of this paper are structured as follows. Section 2 states our motivations and rationale for selecting binary clustering approaches. Section 3 provides an overview of relevant previous research. Section 4 analyzes the performance of standard clustering algorithms and their limitations in activation sparsity. Section 5 presents the development of our customized clustering algorithm, AWC', designed specifically for activation sparsity. Section 6 evaluates effectiveness of AWC in terms of clustering accuracy and computational efficiency, and Sect. 7 concludes the paper with key findings and future directions.

2   Background and Motivation

2.1   The Need for Predicting Neuron Activation Status

LLMs exhibit activation sparsity, where only a small fraction of neurons activate for a given input, making full computation unnecessary. Despite this, standard LLMs still compute all neurons at every layer, leading to inefficiencies. Predicting active neurons before computation could significantly reduce overhead, but direct prediction at the neuron level is impractical due to the massive number of neurons. A scalable approach to activation prediction is essential to leverage sparsity efficiently for real-world deployment.

2.2   Cost-Effectiveness of Clustering-Based Activation Prediction: A Case Study

LLMs exhibit inherent activation sparsity, where only a subset of neurons is active for a given input. However, predicting individual neuron activations across billions of parameters imposes a substantial computational burden. Given an LLM with N total neurons, L layers, T tokens per sequence, and a per-neuron computation cost of C, the total cost of direct neuron-level prediction is:

$$\mathcal{C}_{\text{direct}} = N \times L \times T \times C \tag{1}$$

For a 7 billion parameter model, approximately $\frac{2}{3}$ of the parameters belong to the feed-forward network (FFN) layers:

$$N_{\text{FFN}} \approx \frac{2}{3} \times 7 \times 10^9 = 4.67 \times 10^9 \tag{2}$$

Since FFN layers consist of three separate projection sub-layers—Gate, Up, and Down—predicting each neuron independently is computationally prohibitive. Instead, our Activation-Aware Patterns Clustering (APC) approach groups activation patterns into a small number of representative clusters, significantly reducing prediction complexity. Assuming 2048 clusters per sub-layer, the total number of clusters is:

$$K = 2048 \times 3 = 6144 \tag{3}$$

This clustering reduces the activation prediction cost to:

$$\mathcal{C}_{\text{clustered}} = K \times L \times T \times C \tag{4}$$

The efficiency gain is:

$$\frac{\mathcal{C}_{\text{direct}}}{\mathcal{C}_{\text{clustered}}} = \frac{N_{\text{FFN}}}{K} = \frac{4.67 \times 10^9}{6144} \approx 7.6 \times 10^5 \tag{5}$$

This means our clustering-based activation prediction method reduces computational overhead by a factor of 760,000, making activation sparsity prediction computationally feasible. Unlike direct neuron-level prediction, which incurs prohibitive costs, APC enables structured sparsity exploitation while preserving model accuracy, thereby unlocking significant efficiency gains for practical LLM deployments. The clustering algorithm is executed as a pre-processing step and is not involved during inference. Its computational complexity is primarily influenced by the number of activation vectors, the number of centroids, and the centroid update iterations. For our dataset of approximately 10.6 million activation patterns, clustering with 8192 centroids required 36 h using 8 NVIDIA A100 GPUs. Importantly, this is a one-time offline cost and does not affect runtime inference performance. During inference, no clustering operation is executed. Instead, for each layer of the LLM, one of the precomputed centroids can be predicted based on the input to the LLM. As a result, the cost of clustering itself is completely excluded from the inference runtime. This design significantly reduces the computational load within the MLP layers when compared to dense FFN execution.

3   Clustering with Standard Binary Clustering Algorithms

3.1   Binary Matrix Factorization (BMF)

In this section, we explore a clustering algorithm called Binary Matrix Factorization (BMF) [9] and its performance on the activation values for three projection types—*gate_proj*, *up_proj*, and *down_proj*—across 32 layers. To effectively evaluate the quality of clustering in activation-aware scenarios, we introduce a key metric: clustering precision.

Clustering precision measures how effectively centroids represent the original data points assigned to them. In the context of activation-aware clustering, we focus on the representation of *active neurons* since these are the most significant contributors to computation and the model's performance. Instead of assessing the representation quality over all neurons, our approach evaluates how well the centroids preserve the activation patterns of nonzero neurons.

To quantify clustering precision, we define $\mathbf{A} \in \{0,1\}^{N \times D}$ as the binary matrix representing the activation states of neurons in the dataset, where N is the number of data points and D is the total number of neurons in the model. $A_{ij} = 1$ indicates an active neuron at position (i, j). Similarly, $\mathbf{C} \in \{0,1\}^{N \times D}$ represents the binary state of the assigned centroids.

We compute the clustering precision as the fraction of correctly represented active neurons:

$$\text{Precision} = \frac{\sum_{i=1}^{N} \sum_{j=1}^{D} (A_{ij} \cdot C_{ij})}{\sum_{i=1}^{N} \sum_{j=1}^{D} A_{ij}} \tag{6}$$

where the numerator counts the correctly represented active neurons, and the denominator gives the total number of active neurons in the dataset.

This evaluation ensures that clustering quality is assessed based on the most critical neurons rather than all neurons. By focusing on active neurons, we maintain computational efficiency while preserving the accuracy of activation-aware clustering.

Table 1. Clustering Results for BMF

Projection Type	Total Elements	Clustering Error	Centroid Precision (%)
Gate_proj	939,524,096	275,938,227	70.62%
Up_proj	939,524,096	368,293,446	60.79%
Down_proj	268,435,456	137,573,172	48.74%

The clustering was performed using the same set of clusters for all 32 layers. For *gate_proj* and *up_proj*, the tensors had a shape of $[2048, 14336]$, and for *down_proj*, the tensors had a shape of $[2048, 4096]$. The number of clusters was set to $k = 2048$. Since the features are different among the sub-layers, we used different sets of clusters for the sublayers. The total number of elements processed was 939,524,096 for *gate_proj* and *up_proj*, and 268,435,456 for *down_proj*.

As shown in Table 1, *gate_proj* achieved the highest centroid precision of 70.62% with the lowest error. In contrast, *down_proj* had the lowest centroid precision at 48.74% and the highest error percentage. The *up_proj* demonstrated moderate performance with a centroid precision of 60.79%. These results suggest that the clustering approach is more effective for the *gate_proj* layers.

3.2 Binary-to-Real-and-Back K-Means (BRB-KMeans)

Binary-to-Real-and-Back K-Means (BRB-KMeans) [11] is an innovative clustering algorithm tailored for binary data applications in Binary Product Quantization (BPQ). Traditional methods, such as the k-majority algorithm, rely on Hamming distance and majority voting to cluster binary data. However, these approaches often lead to clustering quality degradation, impacting BPQ performance significantly. BRB-KMeans overcomes these challenges by leveraging the high-quality clustering capabilities of k-means in the real-valued vector space. The process begins by transforming binary data into real-valued vectors, applying k-means clustering, and then converting the centroids back into binary format. This transformation capitalizes on the advantages of Euclidean distance and mean-based centroid updates inherent to k-means, providing a significant improvement in clustering quality and BPQ centroid precision.

Table 2. Clustering Precisions for Same Clusters Across 32 Layers

Projection Type	k = 2048	k = 4096	k = 8192	k = 16384
Gate_proj	69.57%	71.90%	74.43%	77.68%
Up_proj	59.90%	62.57%	65.94%	70.19%
Down_proj	46.74%	50.12%	54.48%	60.86%

Table 2 further explores clustering precision across different layers and projection types—Gate_proj, Up_proj, and Down_proj—for varying cluster sizes (k). The percentage values in this table represent clustering precision for the respective projection types. Gate_proj consistently demonstrates the highest clustering precision, reflecting its ability to effectively capture the structure of the data. For instance, at k = 16384, Gate_proj achieves clustering precision of 77.68%, while Up_proj and Down_proj show lower clustering precision values of 70.19% and 60.86%, respectively. These results highlight variations in data distribution across different projection types. Gate_proj stands out for its higher fidelity in representing data points, even with fewer clusters in some cases. The table also reveals that as increases, clustering precision improves across all projection types, demonstrating the algorithm's adaptability to the complexities of high-dimensional data.

4   Enhancing Clustering Precision: A Customized Approach

The previous section discussed our initial approach, where we experimented with two standard binary clustering algorithms to group active and inactive neurons.

However, both methods performed similarly and failed to produce acceptable results, as they did not effectively capture the structure of activation sparsity in large language models. The primary limitation was their inability to account for the unique distribution and correlation of active neurons, leading to suboptimal centroid assignments. To address these challenges, we customized the clustering process to better fit the sparsity patterns of activation functions. This led to the development of Activation-Aware Clustering (AWC), a tailored clustering approach designed for efficient and accurate activation sparsity modeling.

4.1   Assignment

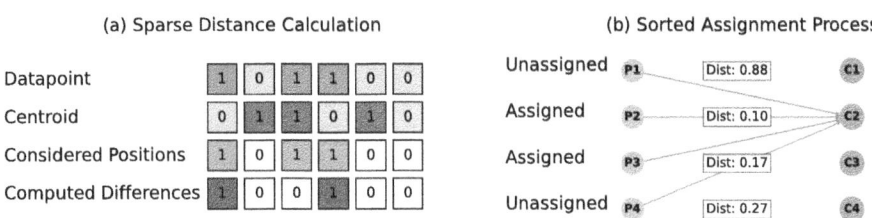

Fig. 2. Distance Calculation and Assignment Process

Figure 2 demonstrates the motivation and methodology behind focusing solely on active neurons (1 s) during the assignment phase of clustering. In LLMs, activation patterns are often sparse, with a significant number of inactive neurons (0 s) in the high-dimensional space. Traditional distance calculations that treat all positions equally dilute the impact of active neurons, leading to less accurate and less meaningful clustering outcomes.

To address this, we developed a sparsity-aware approach that considers only the active neurons when computing distances between datapoints and centroids. This targeted strategy ensures that the assignment process focuses on the most meaningful dimensions, where the activations contribute to the semantics of the data. By excluding inactive neurons, the computational cost of the assignment step is reduced, allowing the method to scale effectively with the large number of dimensions typically present in LLM activations. Additionally, focusing on 1 s aligns the clustering process with the underlying data distribution, as active neurons represent features that are critical for the model's output. This ensures that centroids are updated to better capture the essential patterns of their assigned datapoints, ultimately leading to more accurate and interpretable clustering results. The sparsity-aware assignment, as shown in the figure, is a fundamental step in addressing the unique challenges posed by LLM activations, improving both efficiency and effectiveness.

Figure 2(b) highlights the mechanism for evenly distributing activation patterns across centroids during the assignment phase. A significant challenge in clustering LLM activations is ensuring that no single centroid becomes overloaded with datapoints, which would result in suboptimal representation of the overall data distribution. Without balancing, a centroid might need to represent a disproportionately large subset of activation patterns, degrading the quality of the clustering.

To address this, the approach sorts unassigned datapoints by their distances to centroids, ensuring that the closest datapoints are assigned first. For each centroid, a fixed number of datapoints is selected based on proximity. In the example shown, centroid C2 receives assignments from datapoints P2 and P3, which are closest to it with distances of 0.31 and 0.43, respectively. This process guarantees that the assignments are not only driven by distances but are also constrained to maintain balanced cluster sizes.

4.2   Centroid Update

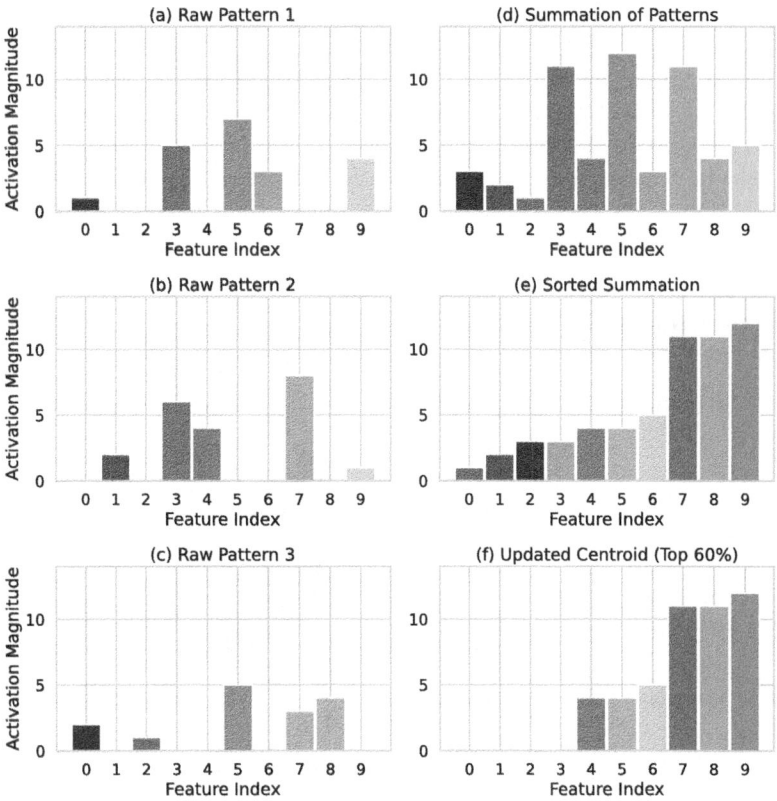

Fig. 3. Evenly Distributed Assignments

The methodology for updating centroids during clustering, as illustrated in Fig. 3, is designed to retain the most significant activations (neurons) while achieving a desired level of sparsity. Each cluster's centroid is calculated by aggregating activation patterns from data points assigned to that cluster. Initially, the raw patterns illustrated in Figs. 4(a), 4(b), and 4(c) represent the activations of individual neurons for different input tokens. These patterns always include both zero and non-zero values, capturing the sparsity and intensity of the activations.

To compute the centroid, the activation values are summed feature-wise across all patterns in the cluster, as shown in Fig. 3(d). This summation aggregates the contributions of individual patterns, creating a single representation that reflects the collective behavior of the activations. Figure 3(e) depicts the next step, where the summed activations are then sorted to identify the most important features. By applying a percentile threshold, the top 60% of features with the highest activation values are selected to form the updated centroid, as demonstrated in Fig. 3(f). This ensures that only the most significant activations are retained while the remaining low-importance features are excluded.

This approach is particularly effective in leveraging the inherent sparsity of LLMs, where only a subset of neurons contributes to any given task. By focusing on the most important activations, the method captures the key information while reducing noise from less relevant features. The percentile-based threshold introduces a consistent level of sparsity across all centroids, ensuring efficiency in both memory usage and computational cost. Moreover, retaining the original activation values for the selected features, rather than binarizing them, helps preserve the intensity information necessary for accurate representation.

5   Experimental Results

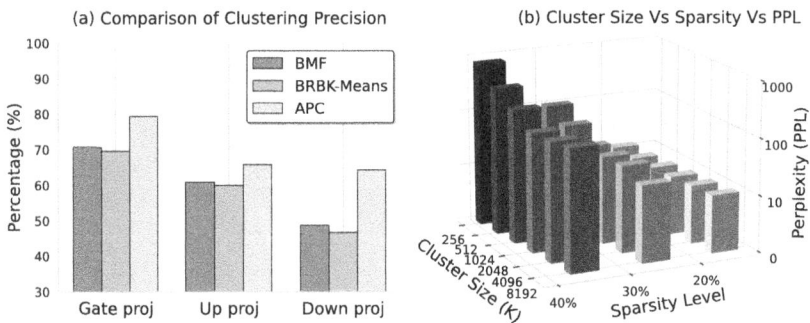

Fig. 4. Results Analysis and Comparison

5.1   Evaluation of Clustering Precision

We applied our customized clustering algorithm to the activation values derived from the input of 163 data points in the WikiText-2 dataset. Each data point consisted of 2048 tokens and went through 32 layers of the LLM. This resulted in a total of $163 \times 32 \times 2048 = 10682368$ activation patterns processed during cluster-ing. The activation values were taken from the *gate_proj*, *up_proj*, and *down_proj* layers separately, with each activation pattern represented by a feature vector of dimensionality 14336. By clustering these high-dimensional activation patterns, the algorithm efficiently compressed and represented the data while maintaining high clustering precision for active features (1's). This experiment validated the effectiveness of our approach in handling large-scale datasets with substantial feature sparsity.

Figure 4(a) illustrates the clustering precision of APC compared to BMF and BRBK-Means across different projection types, highlighting APC's superior abil-ity to capture activation patterns effectively. The Activation-Aware Patterns Clustering (APC) algorithm demonstrates superior performance compared to traditional clustering methods such as BMF and BRBK-Means, particularly in capturing activation patterns across different projection types. APC achieves the highest centroid precision for the Gate proj (79%), significantly outperform-ing BMF (70.62%) and BRBK-Means (69.57%). Similarly, for Up proj, APC maintains a notable edge, reaching 65%, whereas BMF and BRBK-Means lag behind at 60.79% and 59.90%, respectively. The most striking improvement is observed in Down proj, where APC achieves 64%, surpassing both BMF (48.74%) and BRBK-Means (46.74%) by a substantial margin. This improve-ment highlights APC's ability to better represent neuron activation patterns, making it a more effective clustering strategy for activation sparsity-aware opti-mization. The results validate APC's potential to enhance computational effi-ciency while preserving model accuracy.

5.2   Clustering Precision, Centroid Sparsity and Their Impact on LLM Perplexity

To evaluate the impact of our clustering-based approach on model performance, we assigned neuron activations based on the centroid of each cluster. We sim-ulated the prediction process with 100% accuracy in cluster selection, allowing us to assess how using these clusters would affect the model's PPL score. For reference, the 50% sparse Mistral-7B model without clustering achieves a PPL score of 6.45 [4], which serves as a lower bound when comparing the effectiveness of clustered activation representations.

Figure 4(b) presents the final evaluation of our clustering-based activation sparsity approach, demonstrating its impact on model performance across dif-ferent cluster sizes (K) and sparsity levels. The experiments were conducted with six cluster sizes (K = 256 to 8192), each tested under three sparsity levels—40%, 30%, and 20%. The key metrics include the number of active neurons in the Gate, Up, and Down projection layers of the feed-forward network (FFN), along with the corresponding PPL scores.

The key takeaway from this result is that our clustering-based approach maintains low PPL scores even under high sparsity, demonstrating its effective-ness in reducing computational and memory overhead while preserving model performance. Notably, at 40% sparsity, a moderate increase in cluster size (e.g., from K = 256 to K = 2048) significantly improves PPL, reducing it from 933.78 to 58.84. This trend remains consistent across larger cluster sizes, where higher K compensates for increased sparsity, allowing efficient trade-offs between computational cost and model accuracy. At K = 8192, even at 20% sparsity, PPL remains as low as 12.49, indicating that our clustering method enables highly sparse yet effective activation representations.

These results validate the effectiveness of Activation-Aware Clustering (APC) method in preserving model accuracy while reducing computational overhead. By leveraging efficient clustering, our approach ensures that the model retains activation patterns without requiring an excessive number of centroids, thereby striking an optimal balance between performance and computational efficiency. Furthermore, the results suggest higher cluster sizes compensate for increased sparsity, allowing trade-offs between computational cost and model accuracy.

6   Related Works

6.1   Inference Acceleration for LLMs

Despite the impressive performance of LLMs, the continuous increase in their size has led to a significant rise in the computational demands for inference, making their deployment challenging [12]. To address these high computational costs, various methods for model compression have been developed. These include techniques like quantization [8], which reduces the precision of model parameters, pruning [15], which removes less critical elements, and distillation [19], which transfers knowledge to smaller models. In addition, efficient sampling methods have been proposed to speed up the decoding process during inference [20]. Generally, these acceleration strategies do not utilize the inherent mechanisms within LLMs. However, our approach leverages activation sparsity by clustering similar activation patterns, enabling efficient neuron selection without modifying model weights or altering inference dynamics.

6.2   Leveraging Activation Sparsity for Computational Efficiency

Recent research has identified both inherent activation sparsity, which naturally emerges in certain LLMs, and forced sparsity, where activations are deliberately constrained using thresholding mechanisms to enhance efficiency [4,18]. Activation sparsity refers to the presence of numerous zero or near-zero values in the activation outputs, which correspond to specific neurons that have minimal impact on the final output for a given input. These neurons can be skipped during the inference process, thereby reducing computational load. Notably, activation sparsity is complementary to other methods like model compression and efficient sampling and can be combined with these techniques to enhance inference speed. DEJAVU [12] proposed leveraging activation sparsity in both the Attention and MLP blocks of a Transformer layer using a sparsity predictor composed of two fully connected layers. While this approach is claimed to be less computationally expensive than a nearest-neighbor-based predictor, it still introduces significant overhead. Notably, DEJAVU predicts activation status at the individual neuron level, which scales poorly for large LLMs, as it requires running separate predictors for each MLP layer. Another notable approach, SparseInfer [17], focuses on exploiting activation sparsity in Transformer models but is inherently limited to ReLU-based architectures. The method relies on sign-based comparisons between inputs and weights, which only works for ReLU activations since they naturally produce a large number of zeros. However, modern LLMs predominantly use SiLU or GELU activations, which do not exhibit the same natural sparsity. As a result, SparseInfer requires modifying the activation function of the pre-trained LLM, making it incompatible with non-ReLU-based architectures. In contrast, our proposed Activation-Aware Clustering (AWC) approach addresses these limitations by grouping neurons into activation clusters, allowing activation sparsity to be predicted at the cluster level rather than for each individual neuron. This significantly reduces the prediction overhead while maintaining accuracy. Additionally, AWC does not require any modification to the activation functions of pre-trained LLMs, making it applicable to a broader range of architectures, including those that utilize SiLU and GELU activations.

7   Conclusion and Future Directions

In this work, we introduced a clustering-based approach to leverage activation sparsity in LLMs. By grouping similar activation patterns and predicting cluster assignments instead of individual neuron states, we significantly reduced the complexity of activation modeling. Our method efficiently captures the underlying activation structures and enables sparse inference without modifying the original model architecture. The experimental results demonstrated that our approach preserves accuracy while achieving substantial reductions in computational cost and memory usage. Specifically, we showed that selecting an optimal sparsity level (20%) provides the best tradeoff between efficiency and perplexity, making activation sparsity a viable direction for optimizing LLM inference. Additionally, by replacing direct neuron-wise activation prediction with centroid-based cluster assignment, our technique substantially lowers the cost of prediction, making activation sparsity more feasible in large-scale models.

Acknowledgement. We are grateful to the anonymous reviewers for their comments and suggestions on this paper. This work was supported in part by U.S. National Science Foundation (NSF) grants SHF-2210744, IIS-2348417 and CNS-2431597. The code is available in the Github repository [1].

Disclosure of Interests. The authors have no competing interests to declare that are relevant to the content of this article.

References

1. Artifact of activation aware clustering in European conference on parallel processing (euro-par) (2025). https://github.com/nobeldhar/Activation-Aware-Clustering

2. Gpt-4.5 (2025). https://en.wikipedia.org/wiki/GPT-4.5
3. Dettmers, T., Lewis, M., Belkada, Y., Zettlemoyer, L.: Llm.int8(): 8-bit matrix multiplication for transformers at scale (2022). https://arxiv.org/abs/2208.07339
4. Dhar, N., Deng, B., Islam, M.R., Ahmad Nasif, K.F., Zhao, L., Suo, K.: Activation sparsity opportunities for compressing general large language models, pp. 1–9. IEEE Computer Society, Los Alamitos (2024). https://doi.org/10.1109/IPCCC59868.2024.10850382. https://doi.ieeecomputersociety.org/10.1109/IPCCC59868.2024.10850382
5. Dong, H., Chen, B., Chi, Y.: Prompt-prompted adaptive structured pruning for efficient llm generation (2024). https://arxiv.org/abs/2404.01365
6. Frantar, E., Alistarh, D.: Sparsegpt: massive language models can be accurately pruned in one-shot (2023). https://arxiv.org/abs/2301.00774
7. Guo, D., et al.: Deepseek-r1: Incentivizing reasoning capability in llms via reinforcement learning (2025). https://arxiv.org/abs/2501.12948
8. Jacob, B., et al.: Quantization and training of neural networks for efficient integer-arithmetic-only inference (2017). https://arxiv.org/abs/1712.05877
9. Jiang, P., Heath, M.T.: Pattern discovery in high dimensional binary data, pp. 474–481 (2013). https://doi.org/10.1109/ICDMW.2013.154
10. Lee, D., Lee, J.Y., Zhang, G., Tiwari, M., Mirhoseini, A.: Cats: contextually-aware thresholding for sparsity in large language models (2024). https://arxiv.org/abs/2404.08763
11. Lee, S., Choi, S.M.: Brb-kmeans: enhancing binary data clustering for binary product quantization. In: SIGIR '24, pp. 2306–2310. Association for Computing Machinery, New York (2024). https://doi.org/10.1145/3626772.3657898
12. Liu, Z., et al.: Deja vu: Contextual sparsity for efficient LLMs at inference time. In: Proceedings of Machine Learning Research, vol. 202, pp. 22137–22176. PMLR (2023). https://proceedings.mlr.press/v202/liu23am.html
13. Ma, X., Fang, G., Wang, X.: Llm-pruner: on the structural pruning of large language models (2023). https://arxiv.org/abs/2305.11627
14. Merity, S., Xiong, C., Bradbury, J., Socher, R.: Pointer sentinel mixture models (2016)
15. Molchanov, P., Tyree, S., Karras, T., Aila, T., Kautz, J.: Pruning convolutional neural networks for resource efficient inference (2017). https://arxiv.org/abs/1611.06440
16. Rajbhandari, S., Rasley, J., Ruwase, O., He, Y.: Zero: memory optimizations toward training trillion parameter models, pp. 1–16 (2020). https://doi.org/10.1109/SC41405.2020.00024
17. Shin, J., Yang, H., Yi, Y.: Sparseinfer: training-free prediction of activation sparsity for fast llm inference (2025). https://arxiv.org/abs/2411.12692
18. Song, Y., Mi, Z., Xie, H., Chen, H.: Powerinfer: fast large language model serving with a consumer-grade gpu (2023). https://arxiv.org/abs/2312.12456
19. Tang, R., Lu, Y., Liu, L., Mou, L., Vechtomova, O., Lin, J.: Distilling task-specific knowledge from bert into simple neural networks (2019). https://arxiv.org/abs/1903.12136
20. Wang, Y., Chen, K., Tan, H., Guo, K.: Tabi: an efficient multi-level inference system for large language models, pp. 233–248 (2023). https://doi.org/10.1145/3552326.3587438

Green Scheduling on the Edge

Joachim Cendrier[1]() [ID], Rajini Wijayawardana[2] [ID], Anne Benoit[1,3] [ID], Yves Robert[1] [ID], Frédéric Vivien[1] [ID], and Andrew A. Chien[2] [ID]

[1] CNRS, Inria, ENS Lyon, UCBL, LIP UMR 5668, Lyon, France
{joachim.cendrier,anne.benoit,yves.robert,frederic.vivien}@ens-lyon.fr
[2] University of Chicago, Chicago, IL, USA
{rajini,acchien}@uchicago.edu
[3] Institut Universitaire de France and IDEaS, Georgia Tech, Atlant, USA

Abstract. This work aims at designing and evaluating scheduling algorithms that minimize carbon cost on edge platforms. When a job is released to some edge server, difficult scheduling questions arise: should the job be executed on that server? If yes, when? If no, which other edge server should the job be transferred to? Typically, jobs are submitted online, and have a deadline to enforce. Online scheduling problems are already difficult without accounting for different energy sources, so one should not expect any optimal solution. Still, an important research goal is to revisit standard algorithms such as *Earliest Completion Time* (ECT) and *Earliest Deadline First* (EDF) in order to design and evaluate carbon-aware variants. This paper introduces several new algorithms that use sophisticated scheduling policies to efficiently decrease carbon cost; these algorithms maximize the use of green energy both on local and remote edge servers, by re-evaluating previous decisions whenever needed to accommodate newly released jobs. We provide a comprehensive simulation campaign based on actual platform/job data and carbon traces and report an average gain of 42% over standard approaches.

1 Introduction and Related Work

With growing concern about climate change and the corollary desire to make computing "greener" (e.g., reduce its carbon footprint), there is much interest in powering computing resources with renewable energy, and aligning the use of computing resources with when renewable energy is available. The progress in decarbonizing the power grid has reduced the carbon emissions of datacenters [4]; the results have been shown to vary heavily based on location (what renewables are available, weather, etc.) and use (load types, load competition). These variations create opportunities for sophisticated scheduling across time (temporal load shifting) and space (geographic load shifting) to reduce the carbon emissions associated with computing [5,6,10]. The rapid growth in computing is not only happening in the cloud, but also at the edge where the rise of intelligent city, consumer AI services, hierarchical machine-learning models are increasingly deployed [3]. Because of their distributed deployment, varying

W. E. Nagel et al. (Eds.): Euro-Par 2025, LNCS 15900, pp. 380–394, 2026.
https://doi.org/10.1007/978-3-031-99854-6_26

local consumer use, and even varying weather factors, edge resources often have excess computing capacity. From the perspective of "greening" computing use, the situation at the edge is perhaps even more complex and varied. Choice of power supplier, different on site renewables (solar or wind), competing local electrical load, competing compute load, and more, create a landscape in which the carbon-emission content of power locally consumed varies from 0 to 100's grams of CO2e/kWh.

To address this need, this work aims at designing and evaluating scheduling algorithms that minimize carbon cost on edge platforms. We provide in this section a high-level overview of the problem and a brief description of the novel algorithms that we have designed to minimize carbon cost. Edge platforms typically consist of a completely connected set of edge servers, complemented by a powerful but carbon-costly CLOUD resource, as illustrated in Fig. 1. The edge servers are identical but have different carbon profiles. A carbon profile is defined as a continuous set of alternating *green* and *brown* intervals; as the name indicates, computing during a *green* interval has no carbon cost, while computing during a *brown* interval incurs some cost per second of execution[1]. Each job is submitted online to a local edge server, called its *origin*, and has several parameters: length, release time, deadline, and data volume. When a job is submitted, there are three possibilities: the job can be (i) executed locally, (ii) transferred to another edge server, or (iii) delegated to the CLOUD. Each job should meet its deadline, and the schedules must follow rules that are detailed in Sect. 2.

We point out that the addition of the CLOUD is a sine-qua-non to use total carbon cost as a metric. To see why, consider an overloaded system: some jobs will not be able to match their deadline on the edge servers. How do we account for (the carbon cost) of these failed jobs? The addition of the CLOUD nicely

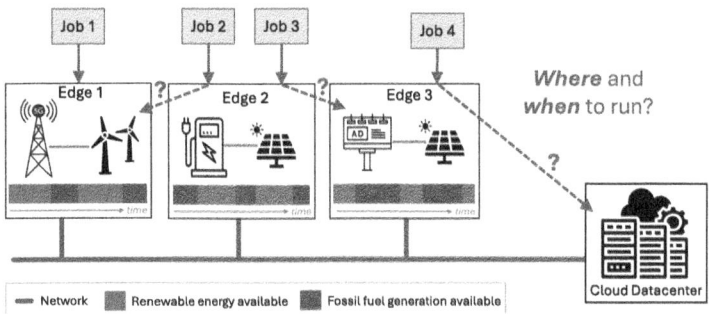

Fig. 1. The edge green scheduling problem: minimizing carbon emissions from computing, while balancing job deadlines, carbon costs of communication, and distributed resources. All in the presence of varying carbon emissions from power. (Color figure online)

---

[1] Having zero carbon cost for *green* is not a restriction: what matters is the cost difference between *green* and *brown*.

answers the question: some jobs will be executed at a very high cost on the CLOUD, but at the end of the day all jobs will have executed successfully, and total carbon cost becomes a fair metric.

Now, for scheduling algorithms, the de-facto greedy standard is *Earliest Completion Time* (ECT): schedule each job when it is released, and assign it the edge server that will allow for the earliest completion time, given already taken decisions. Note that: (i) if the job is not assigned on its *origin*, transfer times are taken into account into the completion time; and (ii) if the job cannot match its deadline, it is executed on the CLOUD. ECT does not account for *green* and *brown* intervals to make decisions, and one can envision several variants to explore. A first heuristic is to give priority to *locality* and assign a job to its *origin* server, but while aiming at using as much *green* periods as possible before the job deadline. A second heuristic is to give priority to carbon cost and to assign the job on the edge that maximizes the green fraction of its execution, while still ensuring that the job deadline is met. In the latter assignment, the carbon cost of transfer must be included in the comparison.

In addition, more sophisticated algorithms like *Earliest Deadline First* (EDF) may revisit previous scheduling decisions: upon release of a new job, the priority of all the jobs that have been scheduled already but have not actually started execution yet, can be re-evaluated, and the priority ordering used by the scheduler to map jobs can be updated. Several combinations can be designed, and we refer to Sect. 3 for a complete description.

Altogether, our first contribution is a realistic yet tractable model for this important scheduling problem, and a complexity analysis (Sect. 2). Our second contribution is the design of an optimal algorithm for the offline version of the problem with a single edge server, which is used as a key building block for the design of novel scheduling algorithms with multiple servers (Sect. 3). We also perform a thorough evaluation of several carbon-aware algorithms on a variety of problem instances arising from experimental traces and report that an important fraction of carbon consumption can be avoided (Sect. 4). This is good news at a time where computing consumes a larger and larger fraction of energy resources! Due to lack of space, extensive discussion of related work, as well as additional results, can be found in the companion research report [2].

2   Framework

Target Platform. The platform consists of a completely connected set of n edge servers e_i, $1 \leq i \leq n$, each with identical speed. W.l.o.g, we assume unit speed for the edge servers. The execution horizon is a (long) interval of T seconds, which is partitioned into *green* and *brown* intervals on each edge. Specifically, edge e_i has u_i intervals: $I_1^{(i)} = [0, \tau_1^{(i)}[, I_2^{(i)} = [\tau_1^{(i)}, \tau_2^{(i)}[, \ldots, I_{u_i}^{(i)} = [\tau_{u_i-1}^{(i)}, \tau_{u_i}^{(i)}[$, where $\tau_{u_i}^{(i)} = T$. Each interval $I_j^{(i)} = [\tau_{j-1}^{(i)}, \tau_j^{(i)}[$ is either *green*, with carbon cost 0, or *brown*, with carbon cost k per second. Like some related work [5], we assume full a priori knowledge of *green* and *brown* intervals, for instance through predictions based on statistical and machine learning techniques. The bandwidth between two edge servers is b_{trans}, while the carbon cost of the transfer is k_{trans} per Mbit. The platform is complemented by a powerful CLOUD server with high processing capacity, which has the capacity to process all the jobs present in the system if needed (which is unlikely).

Jobs, Execution Times and Carbon Cost. Jobs are submitted online, at any time in $[0, T[$, for a total of m jobs during the whole horizon. Job J_j, $1 \leq j \leq m$ is submitted to its *origin* edge server o_j and is characterized by several parameters: release time r_j, deadline d_j, job duration on an edge ℓ_j (in seconds), data/communication input volume f_j^{in} and output volume f_j^{out} (in bits), execution time $t_j^{(cloud)}$ and carbon cost $C_j^{(cloud)}$ when delegated to the cloud. Note that $t_j^{(cloud)}$ and $C_j^{(cloud)}$ are constants that only depend on the job, not on the schedule, since the CLOUD can process all jobs in parallel. Furthermore, we enforce that $t_j^{(cloud)} \leq d_j - r_j$ for all jobs, to ensure that each job can be executed on the CLOUD within its deadline. A job that is executed on an edge server cannot be migrated during execution: once the execution has started on some edge server, it has to finish on that server. However, the execution can be temporarily frozen to benefit from forthcoming *green* intervals. Similarly, once the decision to delegate a job to the CLOUD is taken, it cannot be reversed; but no freezing is needed since the CLOUD is always carbon-costly. Hence, the execution duration and carbon cost on an edge server (the counterparts of $t_j^{(cloud)}$ and $C_j^{(cloud)}$) depend on the intervals used by the job, the time when the job was eventually frozen, and whether the execution is local or remote. A detailed description on how to account for transfer times and carbon costs is available in [2].

There remains to describe how the scheduler decides where to map each incoming job and at which time to start its execution. This is a complicated process that we describe below.

Scheduling Rules. Online scheduling problems are known to be difficult. The release of a new job, called *event*, may lead the scheduler to re-evaluate its decisions. At each event, there are two possible states for the jobs that have been previously submitted and whose execution is not yet complete:

- state *started*: execution has already started: then the scheduler cannot re-assign the job (no migration in our model) but can change the current plan for the remaining of the execution, which includes changing the use of *green* and *brown* intervals, and idling (freezing) the job. The aim of re-evaluating the current plan for a job on a server is to benefit from a larger *green* portion globally for all jobs scheduled on that server. Of course, any change of plan must enforce that the totality of the job is executed before its deadline. Note that at any instant, at most one job can be *started* on each server;
- state *planned*: execution is scheduled but has not started yet: then the scheduler can change the whole assignment. In addition to enforcing that the

totality of the job is executed before its deadline, the scheduler must account for the input communication in case of a transfer to another edge.

Basically, the scheduler takes decisions ALAP (As Late As Possible). For instance, say there was an event at time t_1, namely the release of some job J_j, and that the scheduler plans to execute it at time t_2 on a remote edge $e_i \neq o_j$. Hence, at time t_1, job J_j is *planned*; the current schedule plans the input communication ALAP so that execution starts at t_2. Now, say there is a new event (a new job $J_{j'}$ released) at time t_3 where $t_1 < t_3 < t_2$. At time t_3, the state of job J_j is still *planned*, even if the input communication has been initiated. The scheduler may well re-evaluate its plan and decide to assign job J_j somewhere else, for instance to another edge or to the CLOUD. Note that J_j is still *planned* at time t_3 unless it starts its execution immediately. Also, if the input communication of job J_j from o_j to e_i has started at time t_3, then it will (uselessly) proceed until completion, and the corresponding carbon cost will be paid for. In this scenario, J_j may be re-assigned at time t_3 upon release of job $J_{j'}$, but it is not the only one! The scheduler may re-evaluate its whole plan and re-assign all the jobs that are in state *planned*. As mentioned, it can also update the execution of the jobs that are in state *planned* and scheduled to execute on some edge server to try and benefit from a larger *green* portion globally on that server. A job J_j *planned* to execute on the CLOUD is always started ALAP, i.e., at time $d_j - t_j^{(cloud)}$.

Admittedly, the rules are complicated! But the intuition is simple: take any decision ALAP in order to better be able to react to new job releases, and re-evaluate the schedule at each event, completely for *planned* jobs, and partially for *started* jobs, which are pinned to their resource but whose execution may be shifted if it leads to a lower total cost for all jobs. Now, to design a scheduling algorithm, we only need to detail the scheduling policy: at each event, the scheduler will order the jobs, both *planned* and *started*, according to some priority rule, and will schedule them according to some criterion. We discuss various priority ordering and assignment criteria in Sect. 3.

Objective Function. The objective is to minimize the total carbon cost, with the constraint that all submitted jobs must have been successfully executed before the end of the horizon T. Owing to the addition of the CLOUD, there is always a solution to this problem. In practical scenarios, it is likely that executing on the CLOUD will be faster but more carbon costly. But if the edge platform is overloaded, some jobs will have to be delegated to the CLOUD, and it is crucial to determine which ones.

Complexity. The offline version of the edge scheduling problem resembles the classical scheduling problem of scheduling with limited machine availability [8], whose objective is to minimize makespan instead of carbon cost. We prove that this problem is difficult even with a single edge server: it is NP-complete in the strong sense, and unless P=NP, there is no constant approximation algorithm.

To prove the NP-completeness, the reduction is done from 3-partition, using a set of jobs with tight deadlines that partition the execution horizon. Due to lack of space, the detailed proof can be found in the companion research report [2].

3   Algorithms

This section is devoted to the design of algorithms to solve the EDGESCHED problem. Further details and the pseudo-code of the OFFLINEGREENEST algorithm are available in the companion research report [2].

Throughout this section, for the study of the complexity of the algorithms, we denote by l the average job length, and by a the average elapsed time between the release date and the deadline of a job. Each job spans over an average of pa intervals, where $p = \frac{\sum_{i=1}^{n} u_i}{nT}$ is the inverse of the average interval length.

Greedy Baseline Algorithms.   The five algorithms presented in this section serve as baselines, since they only take basic greedy decisions each time a new job arrives in the system. Depending on its priority, a heuristic decides where to execute the newly released job, without reconsidering decisions that had been taken before. The first three algorithms (ALLCLOUD, LOCAL and ECT) are not aware of *green* intervals and just decide where to execute the job (cloud server, local edge server, or another edge server), while LOCALGREEN and ECTGREEN do account for *green* intervals.

ALLCLOUD: This baseline sends all jobs to the cloud upon their release; hence, there is no execution on edge servers. The complexity is in $O(1)$ per job.

LOCAL: This algorithm favors locality: a newly released job is scheduled on its *origin* edge server, as soon as possible after the last job that is already scheduled on it, if it is possible to finish its execution before its deadline. Otherwise, the job is immediately sent to the cloud server. The complexity is again in $O(1)$ per job.

ECT: This *Earliest Completion Time* algorithm schedules the new job on the edge server on which it will complete first, taking into account the time needed to transfer the job (for a non-local execution). If no server is able to complete the job before its deadline, the job is sent to the cloud server. The complexity is in $O(n)$ per job, since we try all possible n edge servers.

LOCALGREEN: This algorithm aims at a local execution similarly to LOCAL, but it also cares about *green* intervals. Hence, the new job is scheduled on its *origin* edge server, after the last job that is already scheduled on it, but using as much *green* intervals as possible while finishing before its deadline. If not enough *green* intervals are available, it completes the execution with the latest *brown* intervals before its deadline. If the deadline cannot be met locally, the job is sent to the cloud server. For each job, we consider all edge intervals until its deadline; hence, a complexity of $O(pa)$ per job.

ECTGREEN: In this algorithm, the new job is scheduled on an edge server that can execute it before its deadline (similarly to ECT), and among these, the algorithm chooses the edge server that has a *green* interval at the earliest time, taking into account transfer time. If no server can execute the job before its deadline, the job is sent to the cloud. ECTGREEN allocates the job, if possible, only on *green* intervals. Otherwise, it completes the execution with the latest *brown* intervals before its deadline, similarly to LOCALGREEN. The complexity is $O(npa)$ per job, since we now consider all edge intervals until the job's deadline, but on all edges.

OFFLINEGREENEST – **Optimal Carbon Cost for Ordered Jobs in One Edge.** The OFFLINEGREENEST algorithm runs on a single edge server, in offline mode, on an ordered list of m jobs $J_j, 1 \leq j \leq m$. It executes jobs in the given order on that edge server, maximizing the amount of *green* seconds used. Furthermore, if there is a solution for allocating all these jobs, then OFFLINE-GREENEST will find the optimal solution that uses the server as soon as possible for each job. This property becomes especially useful when the algorithm is used in an online setting because, then, when a new job arrives on the system, a good fraction of the load will already have been processed.

During its initialization phase, OFFLINEGREENEST computes *restricted release dates* and *restricted deadlines*. The restricted release date rr_j of a job J_j is its earliest possible starting time, defined as the minimum between its release date and the earliest possible completion time of the preceding job J_{j-1}. Similarly, the restricted deadline rd_j of job J_j is its latest possible completion time, defined as the minimum between its deadline and the latest possible starting time of the succeeding job, J_{j+1}.

OFFLINEGREENEST then works in two passes. It first goes through the intervals from time 0 to T, and reserves as much time on the *green* intervals as possible, given the restricted release dates and deadlines of jobs, without yet deciding which job to execute on which interval. The second pass is done in reverse order, from time T to 0, and it identifies the amount of *brown* intervals that will be used in the final schedule. While the first pass is enough to guarantee the optimality by using as much *green* as possible, the second pass ensures that jobs are completed as early as possible. Please refer to [2] for details. We can then prove the following theorem:

Theorem 1. *Given a set of m ordered jobs $J_j, 1 \leq j \leq m$, if a valid schedule of these jobs exist, OFFLINEGREENEST successfully executes them while optimally minimizing the carbon-cost. Furthermore, among all such executions, it completes each job at the earliest possible time.*

The detailed proof is available in [2]. We first show the optimality of the choices of *green* by induction on the dates considered during the first pass. We then prove that OFFLINEGREENEST builds a valid schedule by showing that the second pass is always successful.

The overall complexity of OFFLINEGREENEST is $O(u + m)$, where u is the total number of *green* and *brown* intervals on the edge server.

Algorithms Building on OFFLINEGREENEST. We designed sophisticated algorithms that rely on three mapping strategies and two job priorities to schedule

jobs; once an ordered list of jobs is specified for each server, the algorithms use
OFFLINEGREENEST to obtain an optimal schedule that, in addition, uses the
server as soon as possible for each job. The three mapping strategies are:

INPLACE: We assign, if possible, jobs on their *origin* server. If there is no feasible
schedule, we resort to the LOWCARB strategy for the current job.

LOWCARB: We assign jobs on servers so that total carbon cost is minimized. If
there is no feasible schedule, we delegate jobs to the cloud.

NOCARBCOMM: This is a strategy similar to LOWCARB, except that the carbon
cost of transfers is ignored when designing the schedule, with the hope of
favoring early starts on remote servers. Of course, the actual total carbon cost,
including transfers, is computed in the end. If there is no feasible schedule,
we delegate jobs to the cloud.

A first approach is to apply these strategies without re-evaluating previous
decisions: upon a job release at time t, we do not update the schedule of planned
jobs on each edge, but instead we insert the incoming job into the schedule of the
edge server chosen by the strategy. To insert job J_j into the schedule of server e_i,
we use OFFLINEGREENEST on each period $[t, d_j[$, where t is the current time,
that can accommodate J_j. Recall that some planned jobs may be frozen and
restarted, so we are looking for all periods of length at least ℓ_j during which
edge e_i is completely idle. We use OFFLINEGREENEST to compute the schedule
for J_j in a given period and keep the schedule with lowest carbon cost; using
OFFLINEGREENEST for a single job is not an overkill, because at most two passes
are needed to find the earliest optimal schedule for J_j.

This first approach leads to greedy heuristics GREEDYINPLACE, GREEDY-
LOWCARB and GREEDYNOCARBCOMM. The INPLACE rule ensures that we
favor a local execution, while LOWCARB aims at minimizing the carbon cost
(which may induce more communications). Finally, by pretending to ignore
transfer costs, ¿aims at starting a job as soon as possible. On each edge, the
complexity is in $O(pa)$; hence, a total complexity for these greedy heuristics in
$O(npa)$, to tentatively schedule the job on each edge server.

Much more ambitiously, a second approach re-evaluates previous scheduling
decisions upon release of each new job. There is some flexibility because *planned*
jobs may be completely re-scheduled, e.g., on other edge servers, and *started*
jobs may have their execution frozen and restarted differently. We consider two
priority functions when re-evaluating scheduling decisions:

LOOSENESS: Jobs are prioritized according to the time remaining before their
deadline, weighted by their size, in non-decreasing order; at time t, the looseness of job J_j is $\frac{d_j - t}{\ell_j}$;

EDF: Jobs are prioritized according to the time remaining before their deadline,
in non-decreasing order (*Earliest Deadline First*).

We combine the three mapping strategies with the two priority rules,
hence, obtaining six algorithms performing reallocation, denoted REALLOCIN-
PLACELOOSENESS, REALLOCINPLACEEDF, REALLOCLOWCARBLOOSENESS,

REALLOCLOWCARBEDF, REALLOCNOCARBCOMMLOOSENESS, and REALL-
OCNOCARBCOMMEDF. At each new job release, these six algorithms recon-
sider all previous decisions for *planned* jobs. They all sort *planned* jobs and the
new job according to the priority function, and schedule them one by one, in this
order. To this purpose, they follow the target strategy. Initially, we keep in the
local list of each edge server only the job that has already started its execution,
if such a job exists, since it will always remain the first job on the ordered list
of the server. As the schedule is being rebuilt, new jobs are assigned to the list
of each server. To assign a new job on a server, we call OFFLINEGREENEST for
all the jobs currently in the list, including the first one (for the remainder of
its execution). Altogether, this second approach is much more costly, because it
computes a new schedule, job after job, potentially considering each edge server,
and each time applying OFFLINEGREENEST. However, we expect dramatic cost
savings!

We conclude with a technical exception to the general rule above: for the
REALLOCINPLACE variants, if a job cannot be executed locally, we do not assign
it to another edge server until all the remaining planned jobs have been assigned.

Table 1. Values of the different parameters for the experiments.

b_{trans}	$\{10, 100, 500, 1000\}$ Mbit/s
k_{trans}	$\{1, 10, 100, 1000\}$ units of carbon/Mbit
k	180 units of carbon/second
Edge servers	10
Solar only	all powered by solar generation with a grid connection
Wind only	all powered by wind generation with a grid connection
Solar and Wind	all powered by solar and wind generation with a grid connection
Mix	30% powered by solar generation, 30% by wind genera-tion, 30% by solar and wind, all with a grid connection
Job duration	Right skewed in [0.4,340] min with mean 60 min
Job data volume	Uniformly distributed in [2, 200] Gbit
Load	$\{0.1, 0.2, 0.3, 0.4, 0.5, 0.6, 0.7, 0.8, 0.9, 1.0\}$
Looseness	$\{2, 4, 6\}$ ±10%
Uniform workload	workload uniformly distributed across all edge servers
Clustered workload	30% of the edge servers receive 90% of the workload
Mall workload	10% of the edge servers receive 80% of the workload
T	30 days
CLOUD speed	10 times edge speed
CLOUD carbon cost	10 times edge carbon cost
CLOUD bandwidth	250 Mbit/s
CLOUD transfer cost	1000 units of carbon/Mbit

Once all jobs that could be assigned locally have been scheduled, we perform a second pass on the jobs that need to be sent to another edge server, following the LowCarb strategy. The complexity of running these algorithms is in $O(pa\overline{m}(\overline{m}+m))$ at each release date, where $\overline{m}$ is the maximum number of overlapping jobs at any time ($\overline{m} = \max_{0 \le t \le T} \{|\{J_j \mid r_j \le t < d_j\}|\}$).

4   Experiments

We briefly describe the simulation settings; all parameters are summarized in Table 1 and a detailed description is available in the companion research report [2]. Simulation results are then discussed.

Modeling Edge Resources. We consider four edge server models: (1) with solar generation, (2) with wind generation, (3) with both solar and wind generation, and (4) with no on-site renewable generation (with only an electric grid connection). Renewable generation produces *green* intervals (carbon intensity = 0). However, renewable generation is only intermittently available, requiring the electric grid for power supply when unavailable. The electric grid is a mix of both renewable (solar, wind) and non-renewable (gas, coal, nuclear) generation sources. Therefore, consuming power from the grid produces *brown* intervals. Figure 2 illustrates *green* and *brown* intervals across the edge server models over a one-week period.

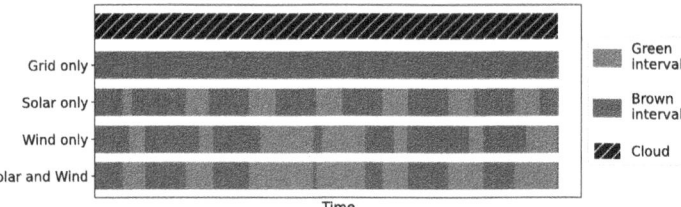

Fig. 2. Green and brown intervals across edge server models over a one-week period. (Color figure online)

We assume an edge location in California, USA, and model the electric grid's carbon intensity based on the CAISO grid [1]. We use data from [9] from August 2023 to August 2024 at 5-minute granularity. The carbon intensity of *brown* intervals is modeled as a constant $k = 180$ units of carbon/second, based on CAISO's average carbon intensity over the considered period. To model on-site solar generation, we use CAISO's grid-wide solar generation, while we consider the LZ_WEST zone in the ERCOT grid (Texas, USA) for wind generation, due to its substantial wind penetration [7]. Model details are in [2]. Four configurations of 10-server platforms are considered, see Table 1 (*Solar only, Wind only, Solar and Wind,* and *Mix*).

Modeling Edge Workloads. We generate synthetic edge workloads based on the properties of realistic edge workloads. Each job is assumed to consume all cores on an edge server, with job durations that are right skewed in $[0.4, 340]$ min, with mean 60 min. The *Load* of the system is the ratio of the total length of jobs $(\sum_{j=1}^{m} \ell_j)$ to the number of edges by the execution horizon $(n\,T)$. The *Looseness* of a job J_j is the ratio of the length of its execution window $(d_j - r_j)$ relative to its length ℓ_j. This essentially models the workload's temporal flexibility. Parameter values are given in Table 1, as well as three different job arrival models (*Uniform*, *Clustered*, and *Mall*). These models account for the fact that some edge servers may receive more requests than others due to geographical factors, such as higher demand in densely populated areas.

We randomly generate 10 workloads for each triplet of parameters (job arrival model; *Load*; *Looseness*) and assign each job an *origin* server edge according to the chosen job model, a deadline according to looseness, and a data/communication volume drawn uniformly between 2 and 200 Gbit. We impose the same communication volume for input and for output ($f_j = f_j^{in} = f_j^{out}$). The number of jobs of a set depends on the *Load* and of the execution horizon ($T = 30$ days).

Metrics. The performance measure is the total carbon cost of the solutions produced by the different scheduling algorithms. In order to fairly compare different schedules on different instances, we use an ORACLE that knows, for each instance, which algorithm is providing the best solution. Then, for each algorithm, we compute its *RatioOracle*, that is, for each instance, the ratio of its carbon cost to the carbon cost found by ORACLE (*RatioOracle* ≥ 1, the smaller the better). We can then build statistics on the *RatioOracle*, like its (geometric) mean. Using an omniscient oracle as baseline enables to determine the apparent overhead of always using the same algorithm to build solutions. We also consider *RatioLocal*, using LOCAL as a baseline. If the average *RatioLocal* of an algorithm is 0.2, it has a geometric average cost equal to 20% of that of LOCAL; in other words, using it rather than LOCAL divides the carbon cost by 5 (on average).

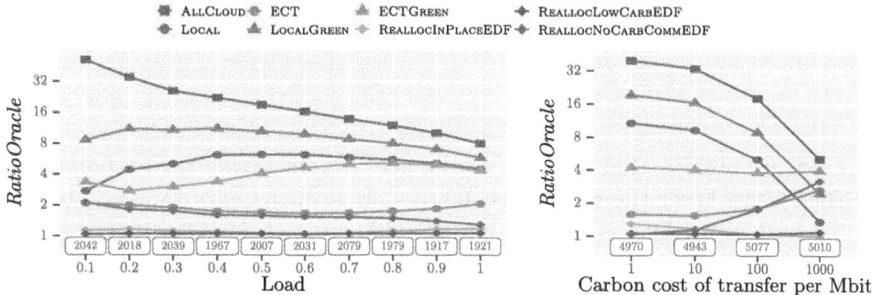

Fig. 3. Impact of the load (on the left) and of the carbon cost of transfer (on the right) on the *RatioOracle* performance of algorithms (with a logarithmic scale). Numbers in purple indicate the number of instances corresponding to each case.

Results. We now report the simulation results. To avoid combining all possible values of all parameters, we generated 20,000 instances by randomly drawing an instance for each of the parameters and models.

• *Statistics on all algorithms.* Table 2 presents statistics on the *RatioOracle* performance of all algorithms. The best algorithm is REALLOCLOWCARBEDF, closely followed by REALLOCINPLACEEDF. All the other heuristics perform at least 50% worse than REALLOCLOWCARBEDF in the average. In addition, REALLOCLOWCARBEDF has a standard deviation close to 1; hence, its performance is very stable. And for half of the instances, REALLOCLOWCARBEDF found the solution with lowest cost, similarly to REALLOCINPLACEEDF also found but achieving a lower mean and standard deviation. Finally, if we allow a carbon overhead of 10% with respect to the performance of the best solution, once again REALLOCLOWCARBEDF achieves the best performance: it achieves a *RatioOracle* no larger than 1.1 in 78% of instances.

Each algorithm with re-evaluation and EDF priority achieves a significantly better performance average than its LOOSENESS counterpart. Therefore, in the remainder of this section, we focus on the algorithms with re-evaluation and EDF priority and on the greedy baseline algorithms.

• *Baselines vs. re-evaluation algorithms with* EDF *priority.* Figure 3 presents the influence of the load (on the left) and of the carbon cost of transfer (per Mbit of data/communication volume of the job, on the right) for the main algorithms for the *RatioOracle* metric, using a logarithmic scale.

Table 2. Statistics on 20,000 random instances. Geometric means (*Mean*) and standard deviations (*SD*) of *RatioOracle*. Percentage of instances for which the algorithm achieves the lowest cost (*Best*), or with a solution whose cost is within 10% of the best solution.

Algorithms	Mean	SD	Best 10%	Algorithms	Mean	SD	Best 10%
AllCloud	18.511	3.602	0	GreedyInPlace	1.895	1.683	8
LocalGreen	9.040	3.166	0	ECT	1.843	1.657	2
Local	5.071	3.291	3	ReallocLowCarbLooseness	1.620	1.496	14
ECTGreen	3.974	2.461	2	ReallocNoCarbCommEDF	1.606	1.956	37
GreedyNoCarbComm	2.665	2.141	5	ReallocInPlaceLooseness	1.590	1.435	9
ReallocNoCarbCommLooseness	2.341	1.981	6	ReallocInPlaceEDF	1.118	1.261	70
GreedyLowCarb	2.014	1.818	10	ReallocLowCarbEDF	1.060	1.090	78

First, we observe that the heavier the load (or the higher the carbon cost of transfers), the lower the cost of ALLCLOUD. Hence, the improvement obtained by the best algorithms is less significant. The curve of ALLCLOUD gives us an idea of the difficulty of the instances or, conversely, the room for improvement. Therefore, regardless of algorithm decisions, the relative gain will be lower when the system is overloaded and/or with a high carbon cost of transfers.

Most conclusions drawn from the comparison of the performance of the greedy algorithms were expected. ECT generally finds better results than

LOCAL (respectively ECTGREEN than LOCALGREEN): because LOCAL and LOCALGREEN do not transfer jobs, they end up using the cloud more often to meet deadlines, which penalizes them (on average, respectively 13% and 37% of jobs are executed on the cloud by LOCAL and LOCALGREEN, compared to 1.8% for ECT and 2.8% for ECTGREEN, see Technical Report [2]. This trend is reversed when the carbon cost of transfers becomes too large. Because ECT and ECTGREEN have no control over transfers, they allow transfers to happen even if this is more expensive than running jobs on the CLOUD. There is one potentially surprising phenomenon: LOCALGREEN, which is aware of *green* intervals, obtain significantly worse results than LOCAL, which is unaware of them. This can be explained: LOCALGREEN sends more jobs to the cloud, because rather than executing jobs immediately it waits for *green* intervals and, thus, wastes time, leaving less room for subsequent jobs which then have to run on the CLOUD. Its lower usage of *brown* intervals does not compensate for its overutilization of the CLOUD. ECTGREEN does not achieve better performance than ECT because it performs more transfers whose costs are not compensated by their benefit: this is exemplified when the carbon cost of transfer is at least 100.

REALLOCNOCARBCOMMEDF achieves better overall performance than ECT, performing slightly more job transfers but using less the CLOUD. REALLOCNOCARBCOMMEDF becomes competitive when the load is very high and very competitive when the carbon cost of transfer is negligible. On the contrary, it is useless when this transfer cost becomes very high, which explains its poor ranking in Table 2. The performance of REALLOCINPLACEEDF is good in general but rather poor when the carbon cost of transfer is small because it does not use this opportunity to transfer jobs. Finally, the performance of REALLOC-LOWCARBEDF is excellent and consistent, as expected from Table 2. It is the best algorithm, except when the carbon cost of transfer becomes negligible, a case in which it is very slightly underperforming.

The parameters other than the load and the carbon cost of transfer have little impact on the relative performance of the different algorithms, see Technical Report [2]. However, when the job *Looseness* increases (see Fig. 4), the performance of REALLOCLOWCARBEDF and REALLOCINPLACEEDF improves with

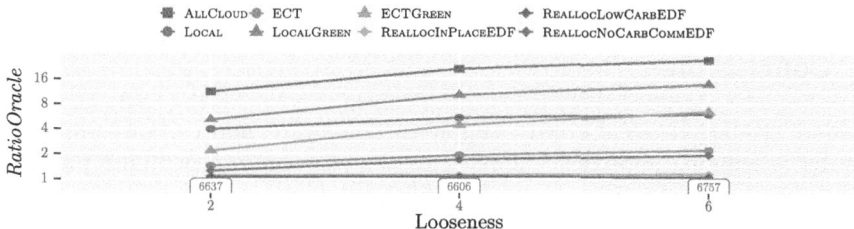

Fig. 4. Impact of looseness on the *RatioOracle* performance of algorithms (logarithmic scale). Numbers in purple indicate the number of instances corresponding to each case.

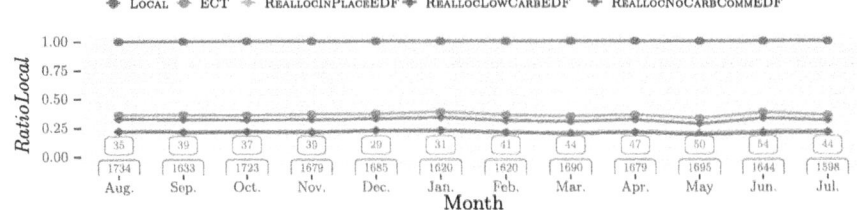

Fig. 5. Impact of the month on the *RatioLocal* metric. Numbers in green indicate the average percentage of *green* for the month. (Color figure online)

respect to the other algorithms: as the looseness increases, there are more opportunities of optimization which these algorithms succeed to benefit from.

- *Comparison of algorithms with re-evaluation to* LOCAL. Here, we compare the performance of ECT and of the three re-evaluation algorithms with EDF priority using the *RatioLocal* metric. Figure 5 presents the influence of months on the performance of algorithms. We obtained this figure by grouping the results obtained from all simulations, especially those using different edge models. Hence, the percentage of green for a given month corresponds to the average percentage of green in the *Solar only*, *Wind only*, and *Solar and Wind* models. We can note that, in June, edge servers are powered 54% of the time by renewable energies, compared with only 29% in December (looking only at the *Solar only* model, the amount of renewable energy is 5% in December but 44% in June). Hence, there is a significant variation in the proportion of renewable energy depending on the month. Therefore, one could have expected that the month of the year would have had an impact on the relative performance of the algorithms. It is immediately apparent that this is not at all the case.

Overall, the carbon cost of ECT is only 36% of the cost of LOCAL. This cost falls to 32% for REALLOCNOCARBCOMMEDF, to 22% for REALLOCIN-PLACEEDF and to 21% REALLOCLOWCARBEDF. When comparing their carbon cost to that of ECT, REALLOCNOCARBCOMMEDF still gets a saving of 13%, REALLOCINPLACEEDF, a saving of 39%, and REALLOCLOWCARBEDF, a saving of 42%.

5   Conclusion

We have studied classical greedy, simple carbon-aware, and carbon-aware with transfer scheduling approaches applied to the edge green scheduling problem. The carbon-aware algorithms consider additional dimensions of carbon variation as well as the cost of job transfer (communication carbon costs). The results show that carbon-aware schedulers can robustly reduce carbon emissions for workload, across a variety of load and communication carbon costs. The best two of the more sophisticated algorithms that consider reallocation consistently outperform these simple carbon-aware schedulers. These results are also robust to seasonal variations in edge site carbon content of power, and workload flexibility (looseness).

Future work will extend OFFLINEGREENEST to a more general case with c different costs for the intervals, with $2(c-1)$ passes likely needed to obtain an optimal solution. We will also investigate scenarios where brown and green intervals are not completely known in advance, which would require the scheduling algorithms to dynamically re-act and reallocate jobs to cope with sudden (unexpected) variations. It would also be interesting to adapt the algorithms to a communication model with contention.

Acknowledgements. We thank the anonymous reviewers for their insightful feedback. This work is supported in part by NSF Grants CNS-1901466, CNS-2325956, the VMware University Research Fund, and the UChicago-CNRS joint PhD Program.

Disclosure of Interests. The authors have no competing interests to declare that are relevant to the content of this article.

References

1. California ISO team. California Independent System Operator (CAISO) (2025). https://www.caiso.com. Accessed 12 Mar 2025
2. Cendrier, J., Wijayawardana, R., Benoit, A., Robert, Y., Vivien, F., Chien, A.A.: Green scheduling on the edge. Research report 9580, INRIA (2025). https://inria.hal.science/hal-04994586
3. European Union. The AI@EDGE H2020 Project (2020). https://aiatedge.eu/
4. Google. Google 2024 Environmental Report (2024). https://sustainability.google/reports/google-2024-environmental-report/
5. Hall, S., Micheli, F., Belgioioso, G., Radovanović, A., Dörfler, F.: Carbon-aware computing for data centers with probabilistic performance guarantees (2024). arXiv preprint arXiv:2410.21510
6. Murillo, J., Hanafy, W.A., Irwin, D., Sitaraman, R., Shenoy, P.: CDN-shifter: leveraging spatial workload shifting to decarbonize content delivery networks. In: Proceedings of the 2024 ACM Symposium on Cloud Computing, SoCC '24, pp. 505–521. Association for Computing Machinery, New York (2024)
7. Potomac Economics. 2023 State of the Market Report for the ERCOT Electricity Markets (2024). https://www.potomaceconomics.com/wp-content/uploads/2024/05/2023-State-of-the-Market-Report_Final.pdf. Accessed 12 Mar 2025
8. Schmidt, G.: Scheduling with limited machine availability. Eur. J. Oper. Res. **121**(1), 1–15 (2000)
9. University of Chicago. Right Place, Right Time (RiPiT) Carbon Emissions Service. http://ripit.uchicago.edu/Part1/ripit-part1.html. Accessed 12 Mar 2025
10. Wu, L., et al.: Carbonedge: leveraging mesoscale spatial carbon-intensity variations for low carbon edge computing. arXiv:2502.14076 (2025)

Design and Operation of Elastic GPU-Pooling on Campus

Kaicheng Guo[1] (ID), Jingyi Chen[1], Yun Wang[1] (ID), Semakin Anton[2],
Tovmachenko Dmitry[2], Jiajie Sheng[3], Jianwen Wei[3], James Lin[3],
Zhengwei Qi[1(✉)] (ID), and Haibing Guan[1]

[1] Shanghai Jiao Tong University, Shanghai, China
{guokaicheng,yunwang94,qizhwei,hbguan}@sjtu.edu.cn
[2] Huawei Technologies Co. Ltd., Shenzhen, China
{semakin.anton,tovmachenko.dmitry}@huawei.com
[3] Center for High Performance Computing, Shanghai Jiao Tong University,
Shanghai, China
{jiajie.sheng,weijianwen,james}@sjtu.edu.cn

Abstract. With the rapid advancement of Artificial Intelligence (AI) and High-Performance Computing (HPC), GPU-centric clusters have become pivotal in driving research across diverse disciplines. Consequently, campus data centers are increasingly aggregating substantial computing resources. However, akin to commercial GPU and AI clusters, campus GPU clusters frequently encounter challenges related to GPU underutilization. While pooling technologies offer a viable solution to this issue, existing GPU pooling approaches fall short in effectively supporting environments where multiple applications coexist within campus data centers. This paper presents gPooling, a novel pooling scheme that leverages device driver hijacking to optimize GPU resource allocation. We designed a benchmark based on real-world traces from a campus data center and deployed gPooling within a GPU cluster environment. Experimental results from both benchmarking and actual deployment demonstrate that gPooling significantly enhances GPU utilization and reduces user waiting times, thereby improving the overall efficiency of campus GPU clusters.

Keyword: GPU Pooling, Resource Management, GPU virtualization

1 Introduction

In recent years, GPUs have become a core computing resource of supercomputing centers due to their excellent acceleration of multiple computational tasks [1,5,16]. GPUs are more costly than other resources, but suffer underutilization in multiple data centers and various application scenarios [8,13,17,20]. On the other hand, GPU-accelerated computing - particularly in AI and HPC technologies - has become foundational to advancing research across multiple scientific disciplines. Consequently, the demand for GPU resources within the

W. E. Nagel et al. (Eds.): Euro-Par 2025, LNCS 15900, pp. 395–409, 2026.
https://doi.org/10.1007/978-3-031-99854-6_27

research community has surged dramatically [1,7,10]. However, academic data centers face more acute GPU shortages compared to commercial counterparts operated by profit-driven organizations [9][1].

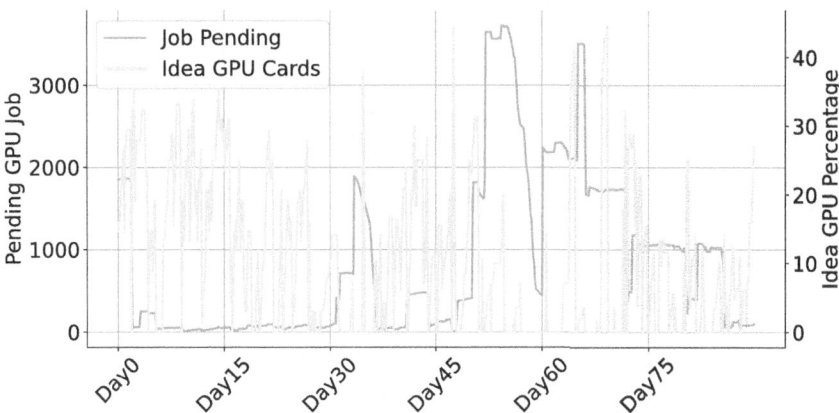

Fig. 1. The GPU utilization and the number of pending jobs trace: GPU underutilization and GPU shortage coexist.

We observe a paradoxical coexistence of chronic GPU underutilization and severe resource scarcity in campus data centers, a phenomenon uniquely shaped by their distinctive workload patterns. Figure 1 illustrates the GPU utilization and the number of pending jobs for 8 nodes in a campus data center over a 12-h period. As shown in Fig. 1, the GPU utilization of the 8 nodes is just below 25%, but at the same time, the number of pending jobs is over 200. Based on the statistics of the number of submitted jobs, the load in this data center is, at the moment, mainly small model machine learning models, large model machine learning, and scientific computing. Most of the tasks do not use the full GPU capacity but monopolize a GPU card. This causes significant resource waste, leading to GPU underutilization and long user queues.

Pooling based on GPU sharing is an effective solution to this problem [13,14, 19]. Various technical approaches have been proposed in recent years to achieve effective and stable GPU sharing. Hardware vendors have proposed solutions including MPS[2], MIG[3], and vGPU. However, the software solutions among them face reliability issues and limited usage scenarios. Hardware solutions can only provide limited elasticity. The academic community's solutions [12,18], on the other hand, generally utilize API intercept forwarding at the CUDA layer or the application layer for optimizations that are deeply coupled with the application.

---

[1] https://www.nature.com/articles/d41586-024-03792-6.
[2] https://docs.nvidia.com/deploy/mps/index.html.
[3] https://docs.nvidia.com/cuda/mig/index.html.

In this paper, we develop gPooling, a kernel-hijacking GPU-pooling system. By intercepting GPU driver APIs, gPooling achieves fine-grained arithmetic, storage control and state management of GPUs. gPooling achieves accurate arithmetic slicing through time-slice control and accurate memory control through interception of memory APIs. Its design is orthogonal to the aforementioned scheme. As such gPooling provides both flexibility and generality at a low-performance overhead.

We have operated gPooling in a real-world GPU cluster. We equip gPooling with GPU nodes in a campus data center. The cluster manages the scheduling of submitted tasks through a Slurm system. We combine gPooling and Slurm by registering vGPUs virtualized through gPooling in Slurm and scheduling them through the Slurm system.

This paper makes the following contributions.

- This paper introduces gPooling, a novel GPU pooling scheme that leverages driver API hijacking to achieve fine-grained resource allocation with low performance overhead.
- gPooling is specifically designed to address the unique challenges of GPU underutilization and long job queues in campus data centers, significantly enhancing GPU utilization and reducing user waiting times.
- gPooling integrates seamlessly with resource management systems like Slurm without modifying their source code or user job scripts, maintaining system stability while enabling efficient vGPU registration and scheduling.
- gPooling employs time-slice multiplexing and real-time utilization feedback to achieve precise computational slicing and performance isolation between vGPUs, ensuring low overhead and dynamic resource adaptation.

2 Background and Motivation

2.1 Characterization of GPU Datacenter on Campus

In this section, we perform a thorough analysis of our job traces. Some prior works [6,8,11,20] analyzed the traditional big data traces from real-world datacenters. In contrast, less work has been done to reveal how campus data centers [15] have been characterized in recent years.

Job Queuing. We analyzed the operational data of a campus data center for a month. This data center employs Slurm for task management and resource allocation across multiple clusters.

We analyzed the job queuing situation within the data center. We examined the number of queued jobs in the clusters. We calculated the ratio of queued jobs to running jobs as an indicator of the severity of queuing issues within the clusters.

Figure 2 illustrates the number of pending and running jobs across different clusters. Figure 3 shows the ratio of pending jobs to running jobs for each cluster.

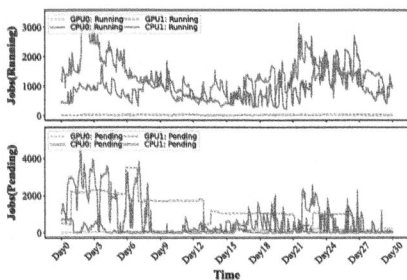

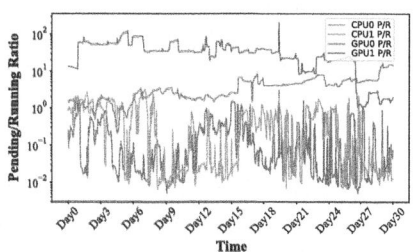

Fig. 2. Ratio of Pending to Running Jobs Across Clusters

Fig. 3. Ratio of Pending to Running Jobs Across Clusters

As observed, the job queuing in GPU clusters is significantly higher than in CPU clusters. The average queue-to-execution ratio for the two CPU clusters is 0.23 and 0.53, while for the two GPU clusters, the ratios are 3.97 and 36.07, respectively.

The severe queuing issue in the GPU clusters is primarily due to the lack of flexibility in the current GPU scheduling system. At present, the GPU clusters use Slurm-based scheduling. Each job submits the number of GPUs it requires to the scheduling system, which allocates resources at the GPU card level. GPU jobs in the cluster typically require multiple GPU cards. As a result, we also observed *resource fragmentation* at the GPU card level. That is, while multiple tasks are waiting, there is still a certain number of GPU cards that remain idle.

Table 1. Workload categorization statistic.

Application	GPU-hours	Categorization	Percent
PyTorch	310885	ML	33.17%
Visual platform	255763	Mixed	27.23%
Python	241909	Mixed	25.73%
AlphaFold [7]	21896	AI for science	2.34%
TensorFlow	18700	ML	2.00%
GPUMD	16309	HPC	1.74%
Amber	5840	HPC	0.62%
RELION	4500	HPC	0.48%
PLUMED	2991	HPC	0.32%
ColabFold	2451	HPC	0.26%
GROMACS	1068	HPC	0.11%

GPU Workload Statistic. Table 1 presents the categorization of workloads in terms of GPU-hours for various applications. The table includes the total GPU hours utilized by each application, as well as the corresponding categorization, which ranges from machine learning to high-performance computing (HPC) and AI for science. The final column shows the percentage of total GPU hours occupied by each application.

From the table, it is evident that *PyTorch*, *Visualization platform*, and *Python* account for the majority of GPU usage, with *PyTorch* alone consuming over 33% of the total GPU hours. Other applications, such as *AlphaFold* and *TensorFlow*, contribute a smaller portion, highlighting the diverse range of workloads in the GPU clusters. The distribution of GPU-hours also reflects the varying demands across different fields, with machine learning applications occupying a significant share of the total GPU resources.

3   gPooling

To address the problems of GPU underutilization and long queuing times for users (Sect. 2), we propose gPooling, a driver-intercept-based GPU virtualization framework that provides low overhead, and highly elastic virtual GPUs (vGPUs) on demand. The core concept behind gPooling is to establish a cooperative and interactive relationship between the application and accelerator to proactively intercept and identify the application's computational power, memory, and management operations on the device and make subsequent optimizations based on this.

3.1   gPooling Architecture

The architecture of gPooling is presented in Fig. 4. The gPooling consists of several modules that operate both in the operating system kernel and user mode. gPooling exposes virtual GPUs to the user and provides the same kernel driver interface to the user. The computation will be performed in the kernel driver module of gPooling by calling the driver API of the physical device.

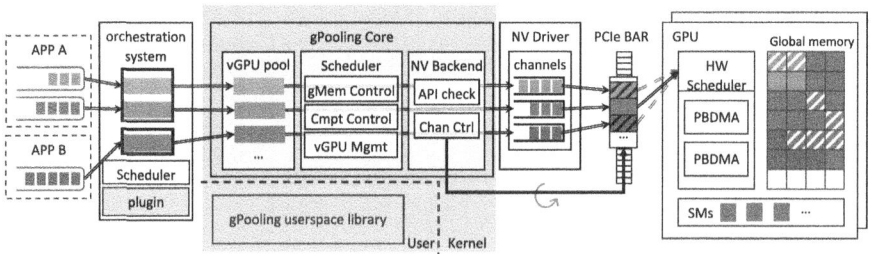

Fig. 4. gPooling architecture

gPooling Components

User Space Library. This module wraps system calls to the gPooling kernel module into library functions called by the container management system. User applications, libraries, and schedule framework invoke functions from this library to manage gPooling virtual devices including but not limited to creating, deleting, and retrieving information. Table 2 lists parts of the API of gPooling's userspace library.

Table 2. gPooling's declarative API

API	Parameters
create_vgpu	p_vgpu_config, p_vgpu_address, vendor_id
delete_vgpu	p_vgpu_address
get_vgpu_status	p_vgpu_address
set_vgpu_config	p_vgpu_address, p_vgpu_config

Kernel Module. The kernel module is the core of the gPooling system. It maintains information about the virtual gPooling device pool and physical device drivers. It contains modules for gPooling scheduler, gPooling device control, and gPooling device management. The kernel module is registered as an operating system kernel module on host and provides a unified call interface to the gPooling userspace library through system calls.

Device Adapter. gPooling enables hardware devices from different vendors to support the unified gPooling core interface through device adapters. The gPooling device adapters implement the functions in the gPooling core module according to the implementation details and driver interfaces of devices from different vendors. For the widely used CUDA ecosystem, we implement the gPooling-NV adapter to intercept CUDA calls. The NV-adapter analyzes all intercepted packet data and examines key packets with specific information, such as memory allocation and deallocation. It also manages the switching tasks that are executed on the GPU. This allows setting limits on memory allocation and GPU computing power utilization and controlling their usage.

Framework Adapter. gPooling has good compatibility with mainstream resource management or job scheduling systems, such as K8S and Slurm. gPooling's user mode library provides APIs for vGPU creation, registration and deletion. With these APIs, we can quickly implement plug-ins adapted to upper-layer frameworks to realize the integration of gPooling and mainstream ecosystems.

gPooling Workflow. During the initialization phase of gPooling, the userspace library creates a pool of vGPU containing multiple vGPUs and registers these vGPUs in the management system (k8s or). During registration, the gPooling user library calls the GPU memory management interface in the gPooling kernel module to bind physical GPUs and allocate memory for each vGPU. In scenarios where the management framework is adapted, the scheduler in the management framework assigns vGPUs to tasks or resource units, on demand. At runtime, gPooling scheduler achieves computational power control and performance isolation between vGPUs by managing time slices (Sect. 3.2).

Timeslicer. gPooling currently implements GPU virtualization through time-slice multiplexing. Therefore the implementation of the time slice mechanism is the core of the virtualization part of gPooling. The low overhead of the time slice component ensures the low-performance loss of gPooling. The granularity of time slices also determines the granularity of GPU arithmetic slicing by gPooling. Previous work [2] has done time-slice rotation at the framework layer, in the user state. However, these solutions cannot meet gPooling's design goals in terms of time slice granularity and overhead. Therefore, gPooling chooses to intercept the device driver calls and decrypt the GPU details based on the field position, and realizes a low overhead and fine-grained time slice rotation mechanism with the help of TSG.

3.2   gPooling Scheduler

As shown in Fig. 4, the gPooling scheduler contains a series of interfaces for arithmetic control and virtual device management, with three main modules: video memory control, arithmetic control, and device management. The scheduler module provides a unified scheduling interface to realize the operation of specific physical devices by corresponding to the accelerator of different vendors. For Nvidia GPUs, gPooling implements these functions based on the interception of the CUDA/Driver API. Specifically, the NV compactor examines memory-related API calls to enable partitioning and control of vGPU graphics memory. For arithmetic control, gPooling realizes accurate arithmetic slicing based on time-division multiplexing by controlling channels in NV Driver.

vGPU Schedule in NV Backend. For Nvidia GPUs, gPooling's **NV backend** implements Scheduler's features based on the interception of the CUDA/Driver API. Specifically, the **API check** in the NV backend checks memory-related API calls to enable partitioning and control of vGPU graphics memory.

For computational power control, based on previous GPU decryption work [3, 4] and Nvidia's open-source GPUs[4,5], we realized accurate computational power

---

[4] git://nv-tegra.nvidia.com/linux-nvgpu.git.
[5] https://github.com/NVIDIA/open-gpu-doc.

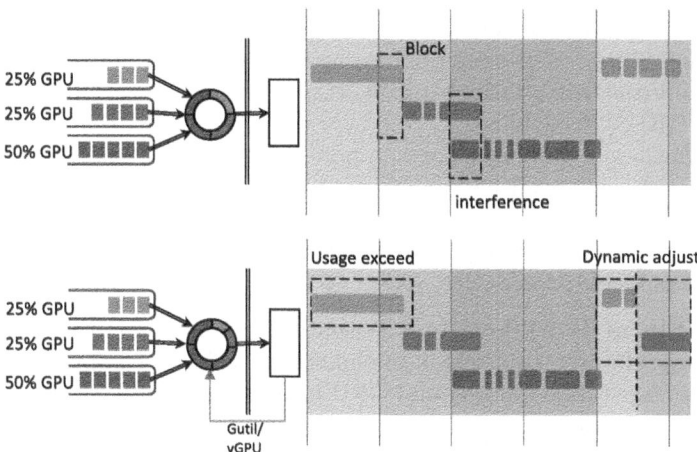

Fig. 5. An example of timeline in gPooling Scheduler

slicing based on time-division multiplexing by controlling the channels in the NV Driver. The NV GPU's hardware scheduler will only pull commands from the PushBuffer of a valid channel [4]. Therefore, gPooling binds a corresponding channel to each vGPU. The channel control module ensures that only one channel, i.e., vGPU, is active at any given time. This design, together with a reasonable time rotation algorithm, realizes the precise control of GPUs.

Computational Control Based on Utilization Feedback Adjustment. Previous work on GPU arithmetic control through a similar mechanism, such as stream APIs at the application layer or in the user state, exists. However, these works can only achieve time-slice-based slicing, and cannot achieve accurate arithmetic control. Figure 5 illustrates an example comparing static slicing and dynamically regulated time-slice control. In this scenario, the GPU is divided into three vGPUs, each with 25%, 25%, and 50% of the arithmetic power.

In even timeslice, for kernels with time granularity larger than time slice granularity, kernel blocks or inter-vGPU kernel executions may interfere with each other. This will lead to the inability to realize the preset GPU arithmetic slicing. On the other hand, gPooling's utilization feedback mechanism reads the GPU utilization in real time. It reduces the length of the next time window after observing that a vGPU exceeds the preset utilization, which realizes accurate arithmetic power slicing.

3.3   Integrating the gPooling into Slurm

Slurm is one of the most widely used workload management systems, especially in various university clusters. Provides users with rich and direct usage interfaces that simultaneously meet the needs of different scenarios. Therefore, to maintain the stability and maintainability of the cluster, when designing the integration of gPooling and Slurm, we need to fulfill: 1. no modification of Slurm's source code, 2. not modify the user's task scripts, 3. vGPU Adaptation for Slurm's Generic Resource (GRES) Scheduling.

To fulfill these requirements, we propose the gPooling-Slurm compute node. Facing the typical control node-compute node architecture of, we only modify the compute node, while using the native control node and login node. The gPooling-service and gPooling-SPANK plugin are integrated on the node loaded with the gPooling virtual device.

gPooling-Slurm Workflow. In initialization, gPooling-service first calls the gPooling user library to register a number of vGPUs equipped with fixed resources (computational power and GPU memory) according to the configuration. After that, gPooling-SPANK plugin registers a Linux namespace for each vGPU to isolate and restrict access to them in the user mode. The gPooling-SPANK compute node is registered with Slurm by starting slurmd. The Slurm Control Node recognizes the vGPUs of the gPooling-Slurm compute node and schedules them together with the physical devices on the general physical node.

4   Implementation

gPooling core is implemented as a kernel module within the system. It introduces a miscellaneous device that facilitates the management of virtual GPUs (vGPUs) through IOCTL (Input/Output Control) commands. The gPooling schedule implements a set of methods for controlling and managing virtual devices. These methods are built upon the foundational methods defined within the gPooling core. In the gPooling core, these foundational methods are declared as virtual functions, enabling different backends to provide their specific implementations. Various backends, such as the NV backend, register themselves with the gPooling core and provide the interface functions.

gPooling user library is a user-mode shared object library that serves as an interface to the gPooling core. It facilitates communication with the gPooling core by implementing IOCTL calls to the gPoolingcore kernel module. Designed to simplify the management of gPooling virtual devices, the library enables management systems and users to interact with GPU pooling functionalities efficiently.

This library encompasses a comprehensive set of functions that allow client applications to execute precise IOCTL operations on the gPoolingcore. These functions are engineered to ensure accurate and reliable invocation of kernel-level commands, incorporating essential validation checks on incoming requests. This modular design not only improves the robustness of GPU resource management but also provides a user-friendly and adaptable interface for diverse application requirements.

NV backend implements the virtual device management methods for Nvidia GPUs. When it receives the request to create a virtual GPU, it creates one char device file corresponding physical GPU (*/dev/nvidia0*) and one control char device file corresponding to the native control char device (*/dev/nvidiactl*). GPU call from user mode will use the vgpu device files instead of original device files.

The NV backend module has UNLOCKED_IOCTL, OPEN, CLOSE, MMAP file operation functions. These functions are set for the created vgpu device files. Commands received by the module from CUDA are processed by the file operation functions in the NV backend and then transmitted to the NVidia driver by calling the original file operation functions. The NV backend creates a scheduling thread for each physical GPU to monitor memory-related APIs and manage GPU utilization.

5   Evaluations

5.1   Environment Setup

Testbed. In this section, we describe the environment setup used for the experiments. The experiments were conducted on a large-scale, high-performance computing cluster designed to support both CPU and GPU-intensive workloads. The cluster hardware platform is built on dual Intel Xeon Platinum 8358 processors, with each processor featuring 32 cores and a base clock speed of 2.6 GHz. In total, the cluster comprises 936 compute nodes, providing ample processing power for large-scale computations.

For GPU-based tasks, the cluster is equipped with NVIDIA HGX A100 systems. Each of these systems features 4 GPUs, delivering state-of-the-art performance for GPU-accelerated workloads such as deep learning, scientific simulations, and high-performance data analytics. The GPU resources are distributed across 23 compute nodes, ensuring balanced and efficient handling of tasks requiring parallel computation.

To facilitate high-speed communication between compute nodes, the cluster employs Mellanox 100 Gbps InfiniBand.

Workloads. Based on the workload characteristics of the data center (Sect. 2), we selected four representative tasks to construct our workloads: (A) GROMACS [1], representing HPC tasks, (B) ResNet-50 [5] training on ImageNet, representing deep learning training tasks, (C) Baichuan-2 [16], representing LLM tasks. During the evaluation, we submitted a certain number of single or mixed tasks to Slurm, which were then allocated to GPUs for execution.

Metrics. In the evaluation, we used the job completion time as the primary performance metric. Additionally, we also examined GPU utilization as a secondary metric.

5.2   System Performance

We evaluated gPooling in single-GPU and three-GPU cluster configurations, testing GPU virtualization into 2, 4, and 7 vGPUs with non-virtualized GPUs as controls. In both environments, we tested three independent task types and one mixed-task workload comprising all three tasks. For independent tasks, we submitted a batch of 21 identical task instances to the Slurm system in a single submission. For the mixed-task scenario, we simultaneously submitted 21 instances of each of the three distinct task types to Slurm. For the Baichuan-7B task, we only evaluated two configurations: non-virtualized physical GPUs (w/o virtualization) and 2 vGPUs per GPU. This limitation occurred because our GPU virtualization strategy evenly partitioned the GPU memory across vGPUs. Under this design, deploying 4 or 7 Baichuan-7B instances on a single physical GPU would trigger out-of-memory (OOM) errors. Similarly, in mixed-task experiments, the 4 vGPU and 7 vGPU tests excluded Baichuan-7B and were only tested with the other two task types.

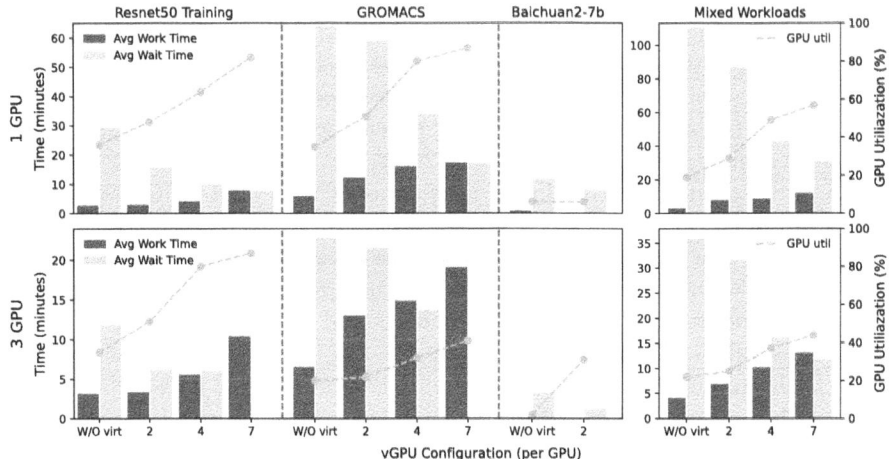

Fig. 6. System Performance

Figure 6 demonstrates the experimental results, comparing the average queuing time, average completion time, and average GPU utilization across different configurations.

Mixed Workloads. Under mixed workloads, compared to the non-virtualized baseline, for single-GPU configurations, the average queuing time decreased by 21.33%, 60.94%, and 71.75% in 2 vGPU, 4 vGPU, and 7 vGPU setups respectively. For 3-GPU clusters, the reductions reached 11.97%, 54.60%, and 66.73% under equivalent vGPU configurations. The performance gains primarily stem from significant improvements in average GPU utilization. Under the 7 vGPU configuration, we observed a twofold increase in GPU utilization for single-GPU tests and an equivalent improvement in the 3-GPU experiments. While transitioning from physical GPUs to vGPUs with constrained compute and memory resources inherently increases per-task execution time, our mixed workload experiments demonstrated a 0.66× to 2.47× rise in average task duration across six test groups. However, when holistically evaluating job completion times (i.e., from submission to finish):

Under single-GPU configurations, the 2 vGPU, 4 vGPU, and 7 vGPU setups reduced average job completion times by 16.68%, 54.22%, and 61.78% respectively. In 3-GPU clusters, equivalent vGPU configurations achieved reductions of 3.72%, 33.66%, and 37.40%. A key observation is that gPooling achieves more pronounced improvements in average job completion time under single-GPU configurations. This disparity stems from the heavier per-GPU task loads in single-node environments, where virtualized GPUs (vGPUs) substantially reduce queuing delays. Notably, while task execution times increase due to resource partitioning, this overhead remains comparable between single-GPU and 3-GPU clusters—the performance divergence primarily originates from queuing efficiency gains under high-load single-GPU scenarios.

Single-Type Workloads. In the single-type workload results, we observe that the average queuing time drops to zero in 3-GPU clusters configured with 7 vGPUs per GPU. This phenomenon occurs because the number of submitted jobs (21) exactly matches the total available vGPUs (3 GPUs × 7 vGPUs = 21), eliminating resource contention and enabling immediate job execution.

Furthermore, when comparing the average task duration between ResNet-50 training and GROMACS under 2 vGPU configurations against physical GPUs, ResNet-50 training exhibits negligible changes in average task duration, whereas GROMACS shows a significant increase. This discrepancy arises because gPooling employs time-slicing-based multiplexing with dynamic adjustments for vGPU compute isolation. Deep learning workloads like ResNet-50 training inherently align with such virtualization due to their fluctuating utilization patterns, which naturally accommodate time-slicing intervals [2]. In contrast, HPC tasks like GROMACS lack natural synchronization points, leading to frequent context-switching overheads and exacerbated performance degradation.

In the Baichuan2-7B evaluation under low token input/output scenarios, we observed reduced GPU utilization and shorter task completion times. Notably, in both single-GPU and 3-GPU configurations, virtual GPUs (vGPUs) allocated 50% memory and 50% compute capacity unexpectedly outperformed physical GPUs. This anomaly originated from memory constraints: the 50% memory limitation compelled the framework to enforce aggressive optimizations, such as kv-cache retention policies and memory reuse strategies, which paradoxically improved performance in low-token workloads.

5.3   Compute Partitioning Efficiency

We then evaluate the compute partitioning capability of gPooling's virtualization component. We use a matrix multiplication from NVIDIA CUDA samples[6], configuring large matrix dimensions to fully saturate the GPU. By observing the GPU utilization of this task under vGPUs with varying compute constraints, we assess whether gPooling can precisely partition compute resources. For this test, we selected a mainstream industry solution[7] as the baseline.

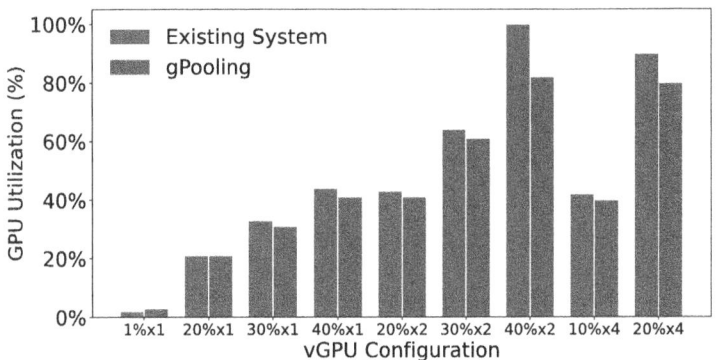

Fig. 7. Compute Partitioning Efficiency: gPooling vs. Exist System

Figure 7 presents the results. We tested multiple vGPU configuration modes (denoted as m%×n, where n slices are created with each allocated m% of the GPU's compute capacity).

Key observations include: gPooling outperforms existing solutions in compute partitioning stability and precision under 1vGPU, 2vGPU, and 4vGPU configurations. Notably, its compute control capability becomes more robust when the total allocated compute exceeds 80%. In extreme scenarios with 1% compute constraints, gPooling achieves comparable performance to existing solutions.

6   Conclusion

In this paper, we introduce gPooling, a versatile GPU pooling framework designed to optimize GPU resource utilization through low-overhead, high-performance time-division multiplexing based on GPU driver hijacking. By analyzing application characteristics from a university data center, we highlight the distinct differences between these environments and commercial data centers, underscoring the unique challenges faced in academic settings. Our real-world deployment and experimental evaluations demonstrate that gPooling significantly enhances GPU utilization and improves the overall user experience within GPU clusters.

---

[6] https://github.com/NVIDIA/cuda-samples.

[7] https://virtaitech.com/.

Acknowledgments. This work was supported in part by the National NSF of China (NO. 62141218, 62232012), and Shanghai Key Laboratory of Scalable Computing and Systems. The experiments in this paper were run on the Siyuan-1 supercomputer supported by the HPC Center at Shanghai Jiao Tong University.

Disclosure of Interests. The authors have no competing interests to declare that are relevant to the content of this article.

References

1. Abraham, M.J., et al.: Gromacs: high performance molecular simulations through multi-level parallelism from laptops to supercomputers. SoftwareX **1–2**, 19–25 (2015). https://doi.org/10.1016/j.softx.2015.06.001
2. Bai, Z., et al.: Pipeswitch: Fast pipelined context switching for deep learning applications. In: 14th USENIX OSDI (2020)
3. Bakita, J., Anderson, J.H.: Hardware compute partitioning on NVIDIA gpus. In: 29th IEEE RTAS (2023). https://doi.org/10.1109/RTAS58335.2023.00012
4. Bakita, J., Anderson, J.H.: Demystifying NVIDIA GPU internals to enable reliable GPU management. In: 30th IEEE RTAS (2024). https://doi.org/10.1109/RTAS61025.2024.00031
5. He, K., Zhang, X., Ren, S., Sun, J.: Deep residual learning for image recognition. In: IEEE CVPR (2016). https://doi.org/10.1109/CVPR.2016.90
6. Hu, Q., et al.: Characterization and prediction of deep learning workloads in large-scale GPU datacenters. In: ACM SC (2021). https://doi.org/10.1145/3458817.3476223
7. Jumper, J., et al.: Highly accurate protein structure prediction with alphafold. Nature (2021). https://www.nature.com/articles/s41586-021-03819-2
8. Jiang, Z., et al.: Megascale: scaling large language model training to more than 10, 000 gpus. In: 21st USENIX NSDI (2024). https://www.usenix.org/conference/nsdi24/presentation/jiang-ziheng
9. Khandelwal, A., et al.: $100k or 100 days: trade-offs when pre-training with academic resources (2024)
10. Park, H., et al.: A generative artificial intelligence framework based on a molecular diffusion model for the design of metal-organic frameworks for carbon capture. Commun. Chem. (2024). https://doi.org/10.1038/s42004-023-01090-2
11. Stojkovic, J., et al.: Dynamollm: designing LLM inference clusters for performance and energy efficiency. In: IEEE HPCA (2025). https://doi.org/10.1109/HPCA61900.2025.00102
12. Strati, F., et al.: Orion: interference-aware, fine-grained GPU sharing for ML applications. In: ACM EuroSys (2024). https://doi.org/10.1145/3627703.3629578
13. Weng, Q., et. al: Beware of fragmentation: scheduling gpu-sharing workloads with fragmentation gradient descent. In: USENIX ATC (2023). https://www.usenix.org/conference/atc23/presentation/weng
14. Xiao, W., et al.: Antman: dynamic scaling on GPU clusters for deep learning. In: 14th USENIX OSDI 2020 (2020). https://www.usenix.org/conference/osdi20/presentation/xiao
15. Xu, K., et al.: Design and operation of shared machine learning clusters on campus. In: 30th ACM ASPLOS (2025). https://doi.org/10.1145/3669940.3707266

16. Yang, A., et al.: Baichuan 2: open large-scale language models. CoRR arxiv:2309.10305 (2023). https://doi.org/10.48550/ARXIV.2309.10305
17. Ye, Z., et al.: Deep learning workload scheduling in GPU datacenters: a survey. ACM Comput. Surv. (2024). https://doi.org/10.1145/3638757
18. Yu, P., Chowdhury, M.: Salus: Fine-grained GPU sharing primitives for deep learning applications. CoRR arxiv:1902.04610 (2019)
19. Zhang, S., et al.: Improving GPU sharing performance through adaptive bubble-less spatial-temporal sharing. In: ACM EuroSys (2025). https://doi.org/10.1145/3689031.3696070
20. Zhang, Y., et al.: Workload consolidation in alibaba clusters: the good, the bad, and the ugly. In: 13th ACM SoCC (2022). https://doi.org/10.1145/3542929.3563465

ServerlessRec: Fast Serverless Inference for Embedding-Based Recommender Systems with Disaggregated Memory

Mingxuan Liu[ID], Jianhua Gu$^{(\boxtimes)}$[ID], and Tianhai Zhao[ID]

School of Computer Science, Northwestern Polytechnical University, Xi'an, China
liumingxuan@mail.nwpu.edu.cn, {gujh,zhaoth}@nwpu.edu.cn

Abstract. Embedding-based recommender systems (RecSys) face critical bottlenecks in storing massive embedding tables (EMTs) and accelerating latency-sensitive lookup operations. While serverless computing and disaggregated memory architectures offer resource efficiency, existing solutions struggle with cold-start penalties, state transfer overheads, and rigid resource scaling for EMT-bound workloads. We present ServerlessRec, a serverless framework that integrates memory disaggregation with kernel-space RDMA-based remote memory mapping (rmap) and remote fork (rfork) to enable elastic EMT lookups. ServerlessRec decouples compute nodes (CNs) from memory nodes (MNs), dynamically autoscaling serverless functions on CNs for bursty lookups while storing EMTs on MNs. ServerlessRec improves latency-bounded throughput by $3.8\times$ over DisaggRec, reduces resource waste by 62% vs. ElasticRec, which demonstrates how kernel-level memory disaggregation unlocks serverless advantages for EMT-bound applications.

Keywords: Serverless · Recommender system · Disaggregated memory · Embedding Table · Autoscaling

1 Introduction

Deep learning recommender model (DLRM) [23] plays a central role in machine learning inference cycles in modern datacenters (75% in Meta [8], 25% in Google [13]). These systems operate under stringent service-level agreements (SLAs) for tail latency, making the optimization of latency-bounded throughput—the number of queries processed per second. As a representative of DLRM, embedding-based recommender systems (RecSys), which have seen popularity in both research [9,20] and industry deployments [19,24]. However, it faces critical bottlenecks in storing massive embedding tables (EMTs) and accelerating latency-sensitive EMT-lookup operations.

Two emerging architectures aim to solve EMT-related bottlenecks: RDMA-based disaggregated systems [15] (Fig. 1(a)) and microservice-oriented elastic designs [3] (Fig. 1(b)). Disaggregated systems decouple compute and memory

© The Author(s), under exclusive license to Springer Nature Switzerland AG 2026
W. E. Nagel et al. (Eds.): Euro-Par 2025, LNCS 15900, pp. 410–423, 2026.
https://doi.org/10.1007/978-3-031-99854-6_28

resources, allowing independent scaling of compute nodes (CNs) optimized for processing and memory nodes (MNs) tailored for high-capacity embedding tables storage [4,26,30]. While this approach improves resource utilization by up to 50% and reduces hardware costs by 7% [26], its reliance on pre-provisioned, long-running EMT-lookup threads leads to compute resource waste. Conversely, microservice-based systems partition monolithic RecSys into fine-grained shards managed by Kubernetes [17], enabling elastic scaling of individual components [5,17]. However, distributing EMT fragments across containers introduces memory fragmentation, negating the benefits of disaggregation.

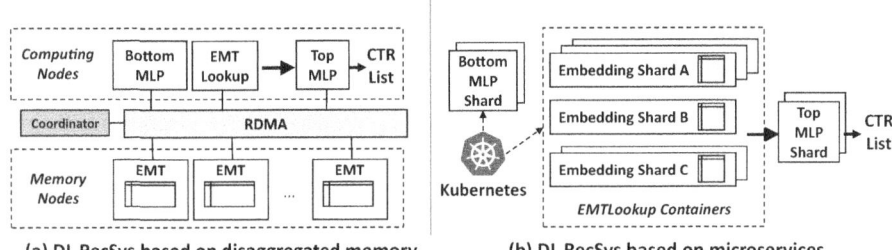

(a) DL RecSys based on disaggregated memory   (b) DL RecSys based on microservices

Fig. 1. Emerging architectures for RecSys: Disaggregated Memory vs. Microservices

Serverless computing [12] offers a promising synthesis of these architectures by combining "pay-as-you-go" elasticity with fine-grained resource provisioning. Yet, existing serverless frameworks remain incompatible with EMT-bound workloads due to unresolved challenges in *cold-start latency* and *state transfer overheads*. For example, Azure Functions exhibit invocation surges of up to 150,000 calls per minute [25], requiring rapid container provisioning across machines—a task hindered by the unpredictable nature of workloads. Commercial platforms like AWS Lambda [2] mitigate this with provisioned concurrency, but such reserved resources violate the serverless's cost-efficiency promise. Worse, state sharing between functions relies on serialization and cloud storage, consuming 95% of execution time [10,16]. While co-locating functions on the same machine reduces local overheads [10], remote coordination remains prohibitively expensive.

To overcome these limitations, we propose *remote memory mapping (rmap)* and *remote container fork (rfork)* as foundational primitives for serverless workflows. Inspired by OS kernel process forking and shared-memory inter-process communication (IPC) [21,32]—we extend this mechanism to distributed environments using kernel-space RDMA [1,6,29,31], which can achieve near-instant container provisioning across machines and transparent state sharing via zero-copy access to pre-materialized EMTs. Unlike user-space RDMA implementations, our kernel-integrated approach fully leverages RDMA's low-latency capabilities.

However, integrating rmap and rfork into Serverless RecSys introduces some challenges despite their apparent benefits. (1) Container autoscaling via rfork must preserve kernel-space RDMA connections, as traditional checkpointing [28] fails to migrate physical NIC-bound queue pairs (QPs). (2) The latency trade-off between remote CN lookups and MN-local computations creates a fundamental tension. Although autoscaled EMT-Lookup containers[1] in CNs handle bursty requests, overusing this mechanism increases tail latency due to network contention, especially when conflicting with MN-local workflows that employ a two-stage RDMA protocol [15]. (3) Determining optimal scaling triggers for ephemeral EMT workloads requires moving beyond static thresholds to avoid SLA violations or resource overprovisioning.

We present ServerlessRec, a serverless framework that integrates memory disaggregation with kernel-space RDMA-based rmap and rfork to enable elastic EMT lookups. ServerlessRec dynamically provisions serverless functions on CNs for bursty lookups while storing EMTs on MNs. ServerlessRec addresses distributed challenges via: (1) virtual queue pair (VQP) binding for seamless RDMA connection migration during autoscaling; (2) a latency-aware scheduler dynamically balancing remote CN lookups and MN-local computations; (3) a proactive scaling algorithm predicting EMT workloads using lightweight performance counters. ServerlessRec improves latency-bounded throughput by 3.8× over DisaggRec, reduces resource waste by 62% vs. microservice-based systems, which demonstrates how kernel-level memory disaggregation unlocks serverless advantages for EMT-bound applications without performance compromises.

2   Related Work

2.1   RecSys Inference

Modern recommender systems (RecSys) increasingly rely on embedding-based deep learning models to capture sparse user-item interactions [3,7–9,13,15]. These models combine dense neural networks (e.g., MLPs) with sparse embedding layers, where embedding tables (EMTs) map categorical features (e.g., user click history) into dense vectors. EMTs dominate system requirements: a single table can span tens of gigabytes due to billions of unique items (e.g., products in e-commerce). Unlike compute-intensive DNN layers, embedding operations involve memory-bound gather-and-pool tasks with low arithmetic intensity. This creates a dual challenge: EMT storage demands strain server memory capacity, while latency-sensitive lookups limit inference throughput.

Current deployments address these challenges using CPU-centric architectures [11,14,22]. Even in hybrid CPU-GPU systems, EMTs reside in CPU memory due to GPU memory constraints [7,27]. While GPUs accelerate DNN layers, embedding operations remain CPU-bound, making CPU memory efficiency critical. For example, fleet-wide query-per-second (QPS) scales inversely with per-server CPU memory requirements. However, monolithic server designs rigidly couple compute and memory, forcing overprovisioning to handle EMT growth. This inefficiency motivates exploration of resource-disaggregated and serverless architectures to decouple memory and compute scaling.

---

[1] We focus on executing serverless functions with containers in this paper.

2.2 Emerging Architectures for RecSys

Disaggregated memory (DM) architectures [4,6,26] separate compute nodes (CNs) and memory nodes (MNs), enabling independent scaling. CNs provide high-performance processors with minimal local memory, while MNs offer scalable DRAM pools. Early DM systems like LegoOS [26] demonstrated improved resource utilization but suffered performance penalties (25%–68%) due to remote memory access overheads. Recent work, such as DisaggRec [15], applies DM to RecSys, reducing total cost of ownership (TCO) by 49.3% through dynamic resource scaling. By decoupling EMT storage on MNs from compute on CNs, DisaggRec mitigates memory overprovisioning and improves reliability. However, it retains static resource allocation for EMT lookups, missing opportunities for fine-grained elasticity. Furthermore, its reliance on user-space RDMA incurs cold-start and state transfer overheads during scaling, limiting latency compliance for bursty workloads. These gaps highlight the need for kernel-level memory disaggregation and serverless coordination to fully exploit DM's potential.

Serverless computing abstracts infrastructure management, allowing developers to deploy functions that autoscale with demand. Microservice-based systems like ElasticRec [3] leverage this elasticity for RecSys, reducing deployment costs by 1.6× via fine-grained resource allocation. However, existing serverless solutions face three key limitations for EMT-bound workloads [25]. First, cold starts delay function initialization, violating strict latency SLAs. Second, state transfer between functions (e.g., intermediate embeddings) introduces serialization and I/O overheads. Third, rigid microservice granularity prevents dynamic scaling of EMT lookups independent of DNN computations.

3 ServerlessRec Design

3.1 Architecture

ServerlessRec employs a disaggregated architecture that decouples compute-intensive operations from memory-bound EMT lookups. The architecture's end-to-end workflow—from sparse feature scattering to CTR list generation—achieves tail latency compliance by jointly optimizing compute elasticity, memory disaggregation, and kernel-space RDMA acceleration.

As illustrated in Fig. 2(a), CNs host five container types: (1) **Bottom MLP containers** process dense features via GPU-accelerated multi-layer perceptrons; (2) **EMT-Lookup containers** execute two-phase EMT retrievals—first fetching remote EMT page mappings' metadata, then performing RDMA READ operations during embedding lookup(Sect. 3.3); (3) **Interaction containers** fuse sparse and dense embeddings for cross-feature computations; (4) **Top MLP containers** generate final click-through rate (CTR) predictions using GPU-based neural networks. Long-running Bottom/Top MLP and Interaction containers occupy dedicated GPU/CPU resources, while EMT-Lookup containers scale elastically via kernel-space remote fork(Sect. 3.3) across CPU cores to handle volatile sparse workloads.

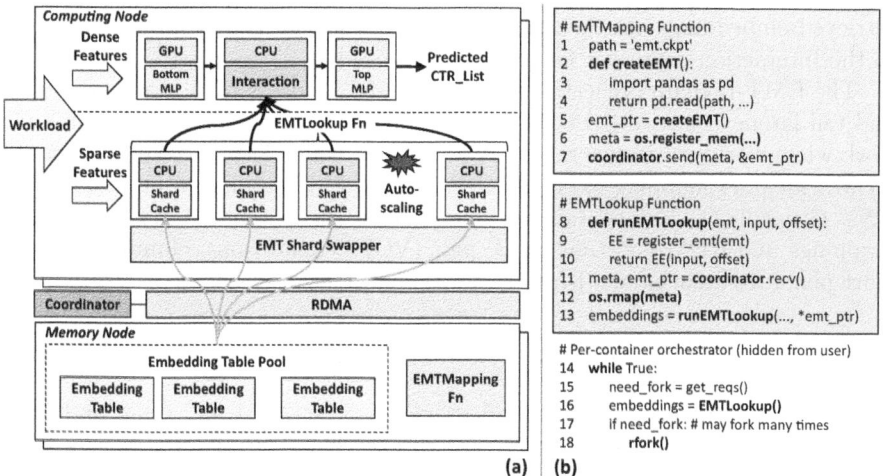

Fig. 2. Overview of ServerlessRec. (a) Disaggregated computing-memory architecture of ServerlessRec. (b) Simplified code of core serverless functions. The Fn in the figure is the abbreviation of Function.

To optimize EMT lookup locality, (5) **EMT Shard Swapper** dynamically migrates frequently accessed shards to CN-local caches using RDMA WRITE operations. During idle cycles, the swapper prefetches hot embeddings identified by lightweight access counters. In addition to storing a large number of EMTs, the MN also has an **EMT Mapping container** that is specifically responsible for assisting the EMT Lookup container on the CN to establish remote page mappings for the EMTs.

3.2   Execution Flow

ServerlessRec's execution flow begins with the MN daemon initializing and registering EMTs. As serverless function codes shown in Fig. 2(b), the EMT Mapping container load EMT shards from checkpoint files (e.g., emt.ckpt) into the global EMT pool (L1-5). Then the container maps these shards into virtual memory regions and propagates metadata (physical addresses, access keys) to CN coordinator(L6-7). The coordinator then sends EMT locations to CNs, enabling EMT-Lookup containers to establish pre-mapped connections via rmap.

When a query arrives, the sparse feature indices are partitioned into shard-aligned batches. Each batch is dispatched to an EMT-Lookup container, which then fetch the target EMT's metadata via the coordinator from the MN (L11). The rmap step resolves remote-to-local address mappings for the requested embeddings (L12). During the subsequent reduction phase, the container performs RDMA READ operations using the pre-mapped emt_ptr (L8-10, L13), directly accessing remote EMT data without intermediate buffering. The retrieved embeddings are then pooled via element-wise addition and forwarded to the Interaction container for feature fusion.

The EMT-Lookup orchestrator continuously monitors request queue depths and tail latency metrics (L14-18). It dynamically triggers horizontal scaling via rfork when workload surges risk SLA violations, which leverages kernel-assisted RDMA memory mapping to clone pre-initialized EMT-Lookup containers across CNs. Crucially, forked containers inherit both the parent's EMT page table mappings and RDMA virtual queue pair (VQP) connections, eliminating cold-start penalties associated with traditional container provisioning.

3.3   Remote Map and Fork

Inspired by Linux's mmap, fork and previous work [21,31,32], rmap and rfork mechanisms enable zero-copy access to disaggregated EMTs and near-instant container scaling. Both distributed primitives are supported by inserting modules into the OS kernel.

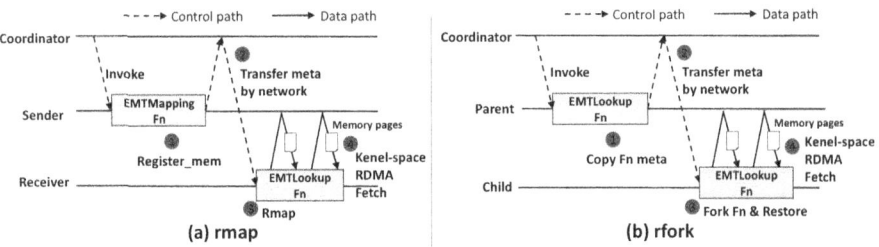

Fig. 3. The illustration of rmap and rfork in ServerlessRec.

rmap, as illustrated in Fig. 3(a), employs a control-data path decoupled architecture for cross-node memory mapping. The control path (dashed lines) begins when the sender invokes the EMT Mapping function in kernel space (step 1), triggering metadata transfer (e.g., page permissions, addresses) via the coordinator to the receiver (step 2). The receiver's kernel registers the memory region, establishing a virtual mapping. Meanwhile, the data path (solid lines) bypasses the kernel: the receiver's user-space EMT Lookup directly initiates an RDMA READ (step 3) to pull memory pages from the sender, leveraging zero-copy RDMA for low-latency data transfer (step 4).

rfork, depicted in Fig. 3(b), atomically replicates function states via paral-lelized control and data paths. The control path (dashed lines) starts when the parent invokes EMT Lookup (step 1), prompting the coordinator to copy func-tion metadata (e.g., pointers, stack traces) to the child (step 2). Concurrently, the data path (solid lines) enables the child to RDMA READ the parent's frozen memory state directly (step 4), followed by a restore operation to reconstruct the execution context (step 3).

3.4   Special Designs

Realizing these insights introduces three fundamental challenges and Serverless-Rec give three special designs.

How to Preserve RDMA Connections During Container Autoscaling?
Autoscaling EMT-Lookup containers via rfork requires replicating both compute state and kernel-space RDMA connections. Traditional checkpoint/restore mechanisms (e.g., CRIU [28]) fail to migrate active RDMA queue pairs (QPs), as they are tightly bound to physical NICs. Disconnected QPs force newly forked containers to reinitialize RDMA connections, incurring 100+ ms cold-start penalties and violating sub-millisecond scaling requirements [32].

  Solution: Virtual Queue Pair (VQP) Binding with Kernel Interception. ServerlessRec introduces virtual queue pairs (VQPs)—logical abstractions of RDMA connections, decoupling RDMA endpoints from physical NICs. When machines in the cluster are started, physical QP connections are pre-established between them, and VQPs are dynamically bound to these physical QPs. During remote forking, the kernel intercepts QP states and binds them to VQPs. Forked containers inherit these VQPs, enabling immediate reuse of pre-established connections without renegotiating MN endpoints.

How to Balance Remote CN Lookups with MN-Local Computations? ServerlessRec's autoscaling mechanism dynamically provisions EMT-Lookup containers on CNs to handle bursty sparse feature requests via RDMA-based remote EMT lookup. However, this introduces a tension with MN-local lookups optimized through two-stage RDMA operations [15]. The input data is first transmitted to MN via RDMA WRITE operations. The MN subsequently executes local EMT lookups and temporarily caches the results. Finally, the CN retrieves the processed embeddings using RDMA READ. Over-reliance on remote CN lookups increases tail latency due to network contention, while prioritizing MN-local computations limits elasticity during workload spikes. The system must balance these two modes to meet strict SLAs while minimizing resource waste.

Solution: Latency-Aware Hybrid Access with EMT Shard Swapper. ServerlessRec integrates a tiered access policy and the EMT Shard Swapper. The swapper monitors EMT lookup patterns, proactively migrating frequently accessed shards to CN-local caches via RDMA READ, while cold shards remain in the MN pool. A latency-aware scheduler prioritizes MN-local lookups for latency-critical queries and routes best-effort requests to autoscaled CN containers. By dynamically adjusting the ratio of remote-to-local lookups based on real-time queue depths and RDMA bandwidth utilization, the system reduces 99th percentile latency.

How to Determining Optimal Elastic Scaling Triggers? ServerlessRec must decide when to scale EMT-Lookup containers to avoid SLA violations without overprovisioning resources. Static thresholds (e.g., CPU utilization) fail to capture the ephemeral nature of EMT-bound workloads, leading to delayed scaling or redundant container deployments.

Solution: Proactive Scaling via Lightweight Performance Counters. A predictive autoscaling algorithm analyzes real-time metrics—request queue depths, RDMA bandwidth utilization, and cache hit rates—using an Exponentially Weighted Moving Average (EWMA) to forecast workload spikes. When predicted latency exceeds SLA thresholds, the orchestrator triggers rfork using pre-reserved idle compute credits. Conversely, underutilized containers are reclaimed via lazy RDMA teardown during troughs. Integrated with the EMT Shard Swapper, the algorithm avoids redundant scaling for cache-resolvable requests.

4   Evaluation

4.1   Experiment Setup

Platform. Our testbed comprises four heterogeneous servers interconnected via 100 Gb/s RDMA (Mellanox EDR Connectx-4 NICs). Three compute nodes (CN) each feature four 14-core Intel Xeon Gold 6132 CPUs, 32 GB constrained DDR4 memory, and NVIDIA K20m GPUs for sustained execution of RecSys GPU components (e.g., Bottom MLP). The memory node (MN) operates with only two active CPU cores to set computational constraints, while retaining full 256 GB memory capacity. All nodes run our customized Linux 4.15 kernel with kernel-bypass RDMA optimizations on Ubuntu 18.04.5.

Baseline. We containerized two state-of-the-art baselines: 1) **DisaggRec**, the state-of-the-art disaggregated memory-based RecSys, and 2) **ElasticRec**, the state-of-the-art microservice-based RecSys. Both implementations strictly adhere to original papers' design parameters, with container resource limits matching our platform constraints (32 GB memory/CN, 2 cores/MN).

Table 1. Recommendation Model Configurations [3,8]

Parameter	RM1	RM2	RM3
Bottom MLP	256-128-32	256-128-32	2560-512-32
Top MLP	256-64-1	512-128-1	512-128-1
Embedding Tables	10	32	10
Embedding Dim	32	32	32
Gathers/Query	128	128	32
Locality (P)	90%	90%	90%

Workload. Table 1 details three real-world recommendation models (RM1-3) adapted from ElasticRec's configurations. These models vary in MLP architectures (Bottom/Top layers), embedding table counts (10–32), and feature gathering operations (32–128 gathers/query), representing diverse production workloads. The 90% locality parameter ensures temporal access pattern alignment with practical RecSys deployments. We evaluate two complementary traffic patterns: 1) Synthetic workload with Poisson arrival rates ($\lambda = 50$–500 req/s) and production-derived request sizes, generated by the model of [9]; 2) Real-world trace replay from Azure Serverless [25], scaled across QPS levels (50–800). Both workloads inject spiky traffic patterns with 3:1 peak-to-trough ratios.

Methodology. Our testing harness replays timestamped request sequences using instrumented *curl* commands that transmit sparse/dense features from our hybrid dataset, which combines randomly generated features with Criteo Kaggle production data [18] containing 20M embeddings across 50 feature categories.

4.2   End-To-End Performance

Through controlled experiments across hybrid and bursty traffic patterns, we analyze two critical aspects of system performance: (1) latency-throughput boundaries under sustained load, and (2) dynamic compliance with strict service-level agreements (SLAs) during traffic spikes. The evaluation leverages our hybrid testbed configured with real-world recommendation models and traces from Azure Serverless applications.

Figure 4(a) quantifies the fundamental trade-off between throughput and tail latency under linearly increasing load. Taking RM1 as example, as QPS escalates from 0 to 800 requests/s, ServerlessRec maintains sub-150 ms 99th percentile latency up to 800 QPS through its hybrid memory orchestration and RDMA-optimized feature gathering. In contrast, DisaggRec exceeds 500 ms latency at 400 QPS due to contention in remote memory accesses, while ElasticRec shows intermediate degradation from redundant computation in its reactive scaling mechanism. The logarithmic latency axis accentuates ServerlessRec's order-of-magnitude advantage in balancing throughput and responsiveness, particularly in the 400–800 QPS range where production systems typically operate.

The temporal SLA compliance analysis in Fig. 4(b) reveals ServerlessRec's resilience to real-world traffic dynamics. Taking RM2 as example, during the 30-min Azure trace replay featuring 3:1 peak-to-trough fluctuations, ServerlessRec sustains >90% SLA adherence, with momentary dips never exceeding 8%. DisaggRec's rigid resource allocation causes severe QoS erosion to 79% during peak demand, while ElasticRec's delayed scaling decisions result in 83–95% compliance due to cold-start penalties. The stacked area visualization highlights ServerlessRec's proactive scaling through our orchestrator, which pre-allocates containers 5–8 s ahead of demand spikes as shown by the anticipatory capacity curves.

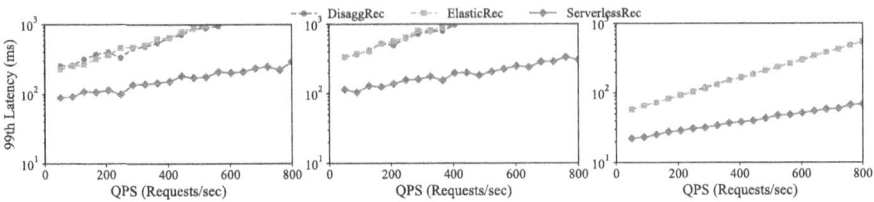

(a) Latency-throughput boundary. Left: RM1, middle: RM2 and right: RM3.

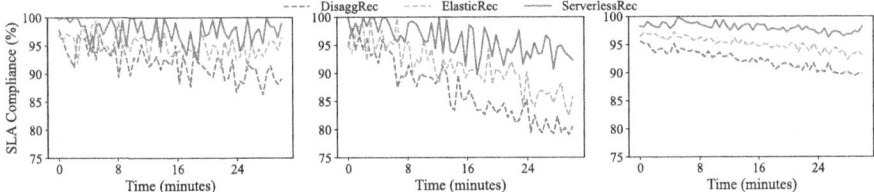

(b) SLA under burst workload. Left: RM1, middle: RM2 and right: RM3.

Fig. 4. End-to-End performance.

4.3   Elastic Scaling Effectiveness

Through systematic benchmarking under production-grade Azure Serverless Trace workloads with the RM2 model (EMT-bound), then we test two spcial designs, latency-aware hybrid access and proactive scaling.

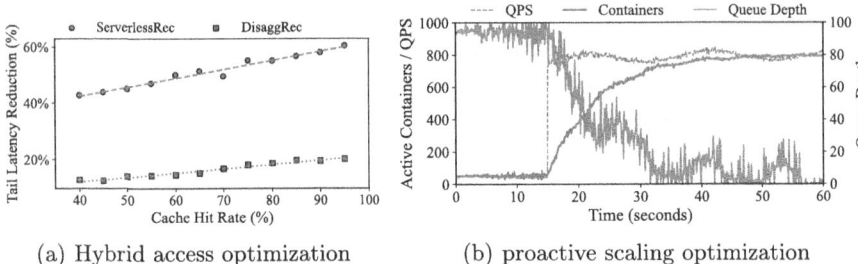

(a) Hybrid access optimization   (b) proactive scaling optimization

Fig. 5. Elastic scaling effectiveness. (Color figure online)

The hybrid memory access method demonstrates significant advantages in mitigating the latency overhead of feature gathering, a critical bottleneck in memory-intensive recommendation workloads. As quantified in Fig. 5(a), the quadratic trend line for ServerlessRec (green dashed curve) reveals that every 10% increase in cache hit rate translates to 5.3–6.8% additional latency reduction, with the dynamic migration strategy contributing 58% maximum latency reduction at 95% hit rate. This nonlinear relationship stems from our proactive data placement mechanism, which prioritizes hot embeddings in near-memory compute nodes while maintaining RDMA-optimized access paths for cold features. In contrast, DisaggRec's linear improvement (blue dashed line) plateaus at 19% latency reduction due to its static partitioning. The widening performance gap at higher hit rates highlights ServerlessRec's ability to leverage temporal access patterns, which reduces remote access latency variance by 73% compared to traditional cache hierarchies. These results validate that hybrid memory orchestration, rather than pure caching or disaggregation, is essential for latency-sensitive recommendation services.

The temporal analysis of ServerlessRec's scaling dynamics validates its ability to maintain service stability under abrupt workload surges while minimizing resource overprovisioning. As illustrated by the 60-s trace in Fig. 5(b), ServerlessRec's orchestrator reacts to the QPS spike from 50 to 800 requests/s within a 1.2-s detection window (15–16.2 s). The orchestrator drives container count growth along an exponential saturation curve, reaching 90% target capacity within 10 s while avoiding overshoot. Three critical rfork operations (marked at 15.8 s, 23.5 s, and 34.2 s) inject additional containers precisely when queue depth approaches 80% of the 100-request safety threshold, maintaining end-to-end latency below the 50 ms SLA despite the 16× workload increase. This temporal behavior contrasts with conventional cold-start approaches that typically exhibit 5–8 s decision lag and 20–30% queue overflow under equivalent load transitions.

4.4   Resource Efficiency

ServerlessRec demonstrates transformative improvements in resource utilization efficiency while maintaining stringent QoS, as evidenced by our analysis of computational resource allocation and infrastructure cost dynamics. Through systematic benchmarking under production-grade Azure Serverless Trace workloads with the RM2 model, we evaluate two critical dimensions.

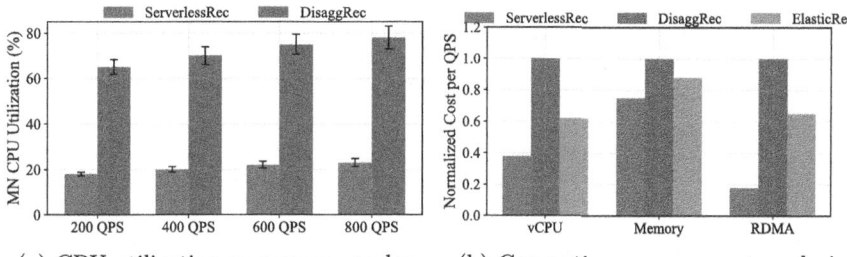

(a) CPU utilization on memory nodes   (b) Computing resource cost analysis

Fig. 6. Resource Efficiency.

Figure 6(a) exposes the fundamental limitation of memory-disaggregated architectures through MN CPU utilization comparisons. At 800 QPS, Serverless-

Rec maintains MN CPU usage at 23% through our RDMA-optimized zero-copy protocol, while DisaggRec's design escalates utilization to 78% due to metadata processing overhead. The normalized cost analysis in Fig. 6(b) further quantifies ServerlessRec's architectural advantages across resource dimensions. Our hybrid approach reduces RDMA bandwidth consumption to $0.18\times$ of DisaggRec's baseline through locality-driven data placement and selective replication. Concurrently, vCPU requirements decrease by 62% via container forking and MLP computation offloading to near-memory units. The cost matrix reveals synergistic benefits: ServerlessRec maintains 38% memory footprint reduction (38.2 GB vs. 42.5 GB) despite handling equivalent workloads, achieved through dynamic embedding table compression and access pattern-guided cache allocation.

5   Conclusion

ServerlessRec demonstrates that kernel-space memory disaggregation, combined with serverless autoscaling, effectively addresses the dual challenges of low-latency EMT lookups and resource efficiency in recommendation systems. By unifying rmap's RDMA-based remote memory mapping with lightweight rfork-driven container scaling, ServerlessRec showcases how serverless computing and disaggregated architectures can coexist without trade-offs for EMT-bound workloads, enabling elastic, high-performance recommendation services.

Acknowledgment. This work is supported by the National Key R&D Program of China, NO.2022YFB4501701.

Disclosure of Interests. The authors have no competing interests to declare that are relevant to the content of this article.

References

1. Amaro, E., et al.: Can far memory improve job throughput? In: Proceedings of the Fifteenth European Conference on Computer Systems, pp. 1–16 (2020)
2. Amazon Web Services: AWS Lambda developer guide (2023). https://docs.aws.amazon.com/lambda/latest/dg/welcome.html, version 4.0. Accessed 2 June 2025
3. Choi, Y., Kim, J., Rhu, M.: Elasticrec: a microservice-based model serving architecture enabling elastic resource scaling for recommendation models. In: 2024 ACM/IEEE 51st Annual International Symposium on Computer Architecture (ISCA), pp. 410–423. IEEE (2024)
4. Dragojević, A., Narayanan, D., Castro, M., Hodson, O.: {FaRM}: fast remote memory. In: 11th USENIX Symposium on Networked Systems Design and Implementation (NSDI 14), pp. 401–414 (2014)
5. Dragoni, N., et al.: Microservices: yesterday, today, and tomorrow. In: Present and Ulterior Software Engineering, pp. 195–216 (2017)
6. Gu, J., Lee, Y., Zhang, Y., Chowdhury, M., Shin, K.G.: Efficient memory disaggregation with infiniswap. In: 14th USENIX Symposium on Networked Systems Design and Implementation (NSDI 17), pp. 649–667 (2017)

7. Gupta, U., et al.: Deeprecsys: a system for optimizing end-to-end at-scale neural recommendation inference. In: 2020 ACM/IEEE 47th Annual International Symposium on Computer Architecture (ISCA), pp. 982–995. IEEE (2020)

8. Gupta, U., et al.: The architectural implications of facebook's dnn-based personalized recommendation. In: 2020 IEEE International Symposium on High Performance Computer Architecture (HPCA), pp. 488–501. IEEE (2020)

9. Han, J., Ma, Y., Mei, Q., Liu, X.: Deeprec: on-device deep learning for privacy-preserving sequential recommendation in mobile commerce. In: Proceedings of the Web Conference 2021, pp. 900–911 (2021)

10. Hellerstein, J.M., et al.: Serverless computing: one step forward, two steps back. arXiv preprint arXiv:1812.03651 (2018)

11. Jain, R., et al.: Optimizing cpu performance for recommendation systems at-scale. In: Proceedings of the 50th Annual International Symposium on Computer Architecture, pp. 1–15 (2023)

12. Jonas, E., et al.: Cloud programming simplified: a berkeley view on serverless computing. arXiv preprint arXiv:1902.03383 (2019)

13. Jouppi, N., et al.: Tpu v4: an optically reconfigurable supercomputer for machine learning with hardware support for embeddings. In: Proceedings of the 50th Annual International Symposium on Computer Architecture, pp. 1–14 (2023)

14. Ke, L., Gupta, U., Hempstead, M., Wu, C.J., Lee, H.H.S., Zhang, X.: Hercules: heterogeneity-aware inference serving for at-scale personalized recommendation. In: 2022 IEEE International Symposium on High-Performance Computer Architecture (HPCA), pp. 141–154. IEEE (2022)

15. Ke, L., Zhang, X., Lee, B., Suh, G.E., Lee, H.H.S.: Disaggrec: architecting disaggregated systems for large-scale personalized recommendation. arXiv preprint arXiv:2212.00939 (2022)

16. Kotni, S., Nayak, A., Ganapathy, V., Basu, A.: Faastlane: accelerating function-as-a-Service workflows. In: 2021 USENIX Annual Technical Conference (USENIX ATC 21), pp. 805–820 (2021)

17. Kubernetes Authors: Kubernetes: Production-grade container orchestration. https://kubernetes.io. Accessed 2 June 2025

18. Labs, C.: Criteo display advertising challenge dataset. Kaggle Dataset. https://www.kaggle.com/c/criteo-display-ad-challenge

19. Lam, M., et al.: Gpu-based private information retrieval for on-device machine learning inference. arXiv preprint arXiv:2301.10904 (2023)

20. Long, J., Chen, T., Nguyen, Q.V.H., Xu, G., Zheng, K., Yin, H.: Model-agnostic decentralized collaborative learning for on-device poi recommendation. In: Proceedings of the 46th International ACM SIGIR Conference on Research and Development in Information Retrieval, pp. 423–432 (2023)

21. Lu, F., Wei, X., Huang, Z., Chen, R., Wu, M., Chen, H.: Serialization/deserialization-free state transfer in serverless workflows. In: Proceedings of the Nineteenth European Conference on Computer Systems, pp. 132–147 (2024)

22. Lui, M., Yetim, Y., Özkan, Ö., Zhao, Z., Tsai, S.Y., Wu, C.J., Hempstead, M.: Understanding capacity-driven scale-out neural recommendation inference. In: 2021 IEEE International Symposium on Performance Analysis of Systems and Software (ISPASS), pp. 162–171. IEEE (2021)

23. Naumov, M., et al.: Deep learning recommendation model for personalization and recommendation systems. arXiv preprint arXiv:1906.00091 (2019)

24. Pansare, N., Katukuri, J., Arora, A., Cipollone, F., Shaik, R., Tokgozoglu, N., Venkataraman, C.: Learning compressed embeddings for on-device inference. Proc. Mach. Learn. Syst. **4**, 382–397 (2022)
25. Shahrad, M., et al.: Serverless in the wild: characterizing and optimizing the serverless workload at a large cloud provider. In: 2020 USENIX Annual Technical Conference (USENIX ATC 20), pp. 205–218 (2020)
26. Shan, Y., Huang, Y., Chen, Y., Zhang, Y.: LegoOS: a disseminated, distributed OS for hardware resource disaggregation. In: 13th USENIX Symposium on Operating Systems Design and Implementation (OSDI 18), pp. 69–87 (2018)
27. Song, X., Zhang, Y., Chen, R., Chen, H.: Ugache: a unified gpu cache for embedding-based deep learning. In: Proceedings of the 29th Symposium on Operating Systems Principles, pp. 627–641 (2023)
28. Team, C.: Criu: Checkpoint/restore in userspace (2011). https://criu.org. Accessed 2 June 2025
29. Tsai, S.Y., Zhang, Y.: Lite kernel rdma support for datacenter applications. In: Proceedings of the 26th Symposium on Operating Systems Principles, pp. 306–324 (2017)
30. Wang, C., et al.: Semeru: a memory-disaggregated managed runtime. In: 14th USENIX Symposium on Operating Systems Design and Implementation (OSDI 20), pp. 261–280 (2020)
31. Wei, X., Lu, F., Chen, R., Chen, H.: KRCORE: a microsecond-scale RDMA control plane for elastic computing. In: 2022 USENIX Annual Technical Conference (USENIX ATC 22), pp. 121–136 (2022)
32. Wei, X., et al.: No provisioned concurrency: fast RDMA-codesigned remote fork for serverless computing. In: 17th USENIX Symposium on Operating Systems Design and Implementation (OSDI 23), pp. 497–517 (2023)

Author Index

© The Editor(s) (if applicable) and The Author(s), under exclusive license
to Springer Nature Switzerland AG 2026
W. E. Nagel et al. (Eds.): Euro-Par 2025, LNCS 15900, pp. 425–429, 2026.
https://doi.org/10.1007/978-3-031-99854-6

The manufacturer's authorised representative in the EU is Springer
Nature Customer Service Centre GmbH, Europaplatz 3, 69115 Heidelberg,
Germany. If you have any concerns regarding our products, please
contact ProductSafety@springernature.com

Printed and bound by CPI Group (UK) Ltd, Croydon, CR0 4YY
28/04/2026
02098518-0009